Early Childhood Special Education–0 to 8 Years

Strategies for Positive Outcomes

Sharon A. Raver
Old Dominion University

Merrill
is an imprint of

Upper Saddle River, New Jersey
Columbus, Ohio

Library of Congress Cataloging in Publication Data
Raver, Sharon A.
  Early childhood special education, 0 to 8 years : strategies for positive outcomes / Sharon A. Raver.
     p. cm.
  Includes index.
  ISBN-13: 978-0-13-174598-8
  ISBN-10: 0-13-174598-0
  1. Children with disabilities—Education (Early childhood)—United States. I. Title.
  LC4019.3.R38 2009
  371.9'0472—dc22   2007052965

Vice President and Executive Publisher:
  Jeffery W. Johnston
Executive Editor: Ann Castel Davis
Editorial Assistant: Penny Burleson
Production Editor: Sheryl Glicker Langner
Production Coordination: Suganya Karuppasamy,
  GGS Book Services/India

Design Coordinator: Diane C. Lorenzo
Photo Coordinator: Valerie Schultz
Cover Designer: Janna Thompson-Chordas
Cover image: Ariel Skelley/Getty Images
Production Manager: Laura Messerly
Director of Marketing: Quinn Perkson
Marketing Coordinator: Brian Mounts

This book was set in Giovanni Book by GGS Book Services. It was printed and bound by R. R. Donnelley & Sons Company. The cover was printed by R. R. Donnelley & Sons Company.

Photo Credits: Carol Ann Harrigan/PH College, p. 14; Anthony Magnacca/Merrill, pp. 20, 51, 65, 113, 272; Adam Crowley/Photodisc/Getty Images, p. 27; David Mager/Pearson Learning Photo Studio, p. 33; Liz Moore/Merrill, p. 37; Scott Cunningham/Merrill, pp. 96, 167, 309; L. Morris Nantz/PH College, p. 121; Todd Yarrington/Merrill, p. 209; Charles Gatewood/PH College, p. 225; Barbara Schwartz/Merrill, p. 279; Katelyn Metzger/Merrill, p. 327

Additional Photo Credits: Photos on pp. 3, 79, 124, 149, 164, 177, 189, 199, 206, 232, 247, 255, 286, 302, and 321 are provided by the author.

Pearson Education Ltd.
Pearson Education Singapore Pte. Ltd.
Pearson Education Canada, Ltd.
Pearson Education—Japan

Pearson Education Australia Pty. Limited
Pearson Education North Asia Ltd.
Pearson Educación de Mexico, S.A. de C.V.
Pearson Education Malaysia Pte. Ltd.

Merrill
is an imprint of

ISBN 13: 978-0-13-174598-8
ISBN 10:   0-13-174598-0

DEDICATION

for Greg and Emmy who give me daily inspiration, love and laughter

Preface

Early Childhood Special Education–0 to 8 Years: Strategies for Positive Outcomes covers the professional knowledge and skill competencies teachers must have to promote optimal development in children with special needs from birth through 8 years of age. This introduction–methods book uses the application of evidence-based strategies, ecological and family-based approaches, effective teaming, and appropriate cultural/linguistic practices as thematic threads. Each chapter presents disability definitions, child characteristics, assessment practices, and practical methods for providing interventions to support the development and learning of infants, toddlers, preschoolers, and primary-aged students in special education and inclusive settings. Using real-life stories to illustrate easy-to-implement procedures, this book describes techniques used in special education, speech-language pathology, occupational/physical therapy, and vision and hearing education so general and special education teachers can develop and implement integrated, comprehensive, and meaningful services for children, and families. Specifically, professional competencies from *DEC Recommended Practices: A Comprehensive Guide for Practical Application in Early Intervention/Early Childhood Special Education* (Sandall, Hemmeter, Smith, & McLean, 2005) and the Council for Exceptional Children (2003) are systematically embedded throughout the book.

This book was designed to meet a specific need. As more school systems rely on early childhood special education teachers to teach children in kindergarten through third grade, an understanding of how to teach developmental skills to children from birth to 5 years of age, as well as how to teach academics and appropriate social skills to primary-aged children with learning and behavior needs, has become essential. This book attempts to provide new professionals with the skills they need to effectively serve young children, and their families, in the many service delivery configurations among which families and professionals have to choose, from self-contained classrooms to consultative support in general education settings.

There are three major parts to this book. Part I examines the legal, philosophical, and instructional foundations of early childhood special education. The historical perspective for early services, working in teams with professionals from diverse disciplines, supporting families, assessing young children, developing individualized programs, and utilizing evidence-based practices and strategies in special education and inclusive settings are discussed. Part II describes easy-to-implement, practical techniques used to maximize communicative, cognitive/literacy, fine and gross motor, adaptive, and social-emotional development in young children. Part III emphasizes procedures for promoting development and learning in children with specific needs. The characteristics and learning needs of children with mild learning and behavior problems; children with moderate/severe or multiple disabilities; children with hearing loss; and children with visual impairment are detailed.

Preservice and in-service early childhood special education (ECSE) teachers, general early childhood education (ECE) teachers, administrators of ECSE/ECE programs, and families will find the content of this book immediately useful.

ACKNOWLEDGMENTS

Appreciation is extended to the families who allowed their stories to be shared in the case studies. Although the information is theirs, in some cases the names have been changed to protect their identities as requested. A heartfelt thanks to the colleagues who contributed to the writing of this book: Deena Bernstein, Liat Seiger-Gardner, Paige C. Pullen, Toby M. Long, M. Janet Thomas, Jamie M. Hall, Tina L. Stanton-Chapman, Silvana M. R. Watson, Jonna Bobzien, Sabra Gear, Eva Horn, Cynthia Chambers, Yumiko Saito, Jan Christian Hafer, and Tanni L. Anthony. I would like to thank my family, who supported me every day in the completion of this project. I would also like to thank my colleagues in the Early Childhood/ Speech-Language Pathology/Special Education Department of Old Dominion University for their personal and professional support. Further, sincere appreciation is extended to the reviewers who guided the completion of this book: Karen Applequist, Northern Arizona University; Sylvia Dietrich, Western Kentucky University; David M. Finn, Samford University; Robin Hasslen, Bethel University; Barbara Lowenthal, Northeastern Illinois University; Melissa Olive, University of Texas at Austin; Amy Sue Reilly, Auburn University; Michael Rettig, Washburn University; Phyllis G. Weisberg, The College of New Jersey; and Yaoying Xu, Virginia Commonwealth University.

A thank-you goes to my copyeditor, Sherry Goldbecker, for her work on the manuscript, and to my editor, Ann Davis, and her editorial assistant, Penny Burleson. However, my most sincere appreciation goes to the young children with special needs, and to their families, who have enriched my life. This book is the product of what they have taught me—and continue to teach me every day.

About the Author

Sharon A. Raver, a professor of special education at Old Dominion University, has worked in the area of early childhood special education (ECSE) for over 35 years. She has worked with infants, toddlers, preschoolers, and school-aged children with special needs and their families. She has administered programs, served as an international ECSE consultant, and published extensively. She has been a Fulbright Scholar four times and received a number of awards for excellence in research and teaching.

She currently lives in Norfolk, Virginia, with her husband, Greg, and daughter, Emmy.

List of Contributors

Cynthia R. Chambers, Ph.D.
University of Kansas
Lawrence, KS

Deena Bernstein, Ph.D.
Lehman College
The City University of New York
Bronx, NY

Eva Horn, Ph.D.
University of Kansas
Lawrence, KS

Jamie M. Hall, PT, DPT
Georgetown University Child
    Development Center
Washington, DC

Jan Christian Hafer, Ed.D.
Gallaudet University
Washington, DC

Jonna Bobzien, M.S.
Old Dominion University
Norfolk, VA

Liat Seiger-Gardner, Ph.D.
Lehman College and the Graduate Center
The City University of New York
Bronx, NY

M. Janet Thomas, MEd.
Division of Occupational Therapy
Georgetown University Child
    Development Center
Washington, DC

Paige C. Pullen, Ph.D.
University of Virginia
Charlottesville, VA

Sabra Gear, M.S.
Old Dominion University
Norfolk, VA

Silvana M. R. Watson, Ph.D.
Old Dominion University
Norfolk, VA

Tanni L. Anthony, Ph.D.
Colorado Department of Education
Denver, CO

Tina L. Stanton-Chapman, Ph.D.
University of Virginia
Charlottesville, VA

Toby M. Long, Ph.D.
Division of Physical Therapy
Georgetown University Child
    Development Center
Washington, DC

Yumiko Saito, MSEd.
National Institute of Special
    Needs Education
Kanagawa, Japan

Jennifer L. Kilgo, Ed.D.
University of Alabama
Birmingham, GA

Brief Contents

Contents

Chapter 6   Promoting Cognitive and Literacy Development   149

Chapter 7   Promoting Fine and Gross Motor and Adaptive Skills Development   177

Chapter 11 Techniques for Teaching Young Children with Hearing Loss 279

NOTE: Every effort has been made to provide accurate and current Internet information in this book. However, the Internet and information posted on it are constantly changing, and it is inevitable that some of the Internet addresses listed in this textbook will change.

PART I

FOUNDATIONS OF EARLY CHILDHOOD SPECIAL EDUCATION

Chapter
1

Introduction to Working with Infants, Toddlers, Preschoolers, and Primary-Aged Children with Special Needs

Sharon A. Raver

Overview

This chapter discusses the foundations of early childhood special education, including

federal legislation affecting early childhood special education services

characteristics of early childhood special education and general early childhood education

characteristics of children receiving early childhood special education services

program objectives and service delivery models for educating young children with special needs

an ecological approach to early childhood special education

professional standards

CASE STUDY: Angela and Danny

Angela, age 25, was referred to an infant-toddler program by the courts when her two older children, ages 7 and 9, were removed from her home and placed in foster care after neglect was determined. Angela was suspected of drug use, but was not charged. Angela's youngest son, Danny, age 2, was kept in the home. A team assessment at the infant-toddler program determined that Danny was delayed in communication and social-emotional development. Angela appeared to have a low-normal intellectual level and expressed difficulty in knowing how to manage her life. During the intake interview, she requested assistance with learning nutrition and child-rearing skills as well as job skills. Since these were the contingencies for having her two other children returned, Angela was eager to begin services immediately.

Danny was enrolled in a community-based daycare program by the infant-toddler program, according to Angela's preference. Initially, Danny had difficulty adjusting to the structure of the daycare program, but gradually he began to participate, and his communication skills improved rapidly. Once-a-month home visits were also provided for the family. When he was 4 years old, Danny transitioned to a community preschool where the staff received consultative services from an early childhood special educator. Angela progressed in her parenting skills to designated levels and had good attendance at her job-training program. Consequently, her two older children were returned. Angela exhibited pride in this accomplishment and expressed enjoyment in Danny's development.

In first grade, Danny displayed difficulty with reading and had poor impulse control, frequently leading to intense tantrums. Based on parent and teacher requests, a multidisciplinary team assessment was conducted. With Angela's consent, Danny began attending a self-contained class for children with learning disabilities. Today, Angela reports that she is grateful to the many agencies and professionals that have helped her cope with being a single parent and manage her unstable employment.

Early childhood specialists agree that the earlier intervention begins with children with special needs, the better the outcome. Intervention can significantly benefit young children with developmental delays and/or disabilities as well as their families. Children with developmental problems do not simply catch up with their peers, as was believed by some in the past. A 20-year follow-up of children identified as having developmental delays when they were 3 years old confirmed that signs of developmental delay in the preschool years were a strong signal of continuing problems into adulthood (Keogh, Bernheimer, & Guthrie, 2004). Providing early services to children can reduce the need for costly residential care for some young children. Considerable money can be saved if children are able to participate in general education as a result of intervention in the first five years of their life. Today, it is commonly accepted that the benefits of early childhood special education (ECSE) outweigh, or at least justify, its costs (Guralnick, 1997). Federal legislation has reflected this growing understanding of the value of early intervention for children with developmental problems.

FEDERAL LEGISLATION AFFECTING EARLY CHILDHOOD SPECIAL EDUCATION SERVICES

The American value of equality for all citizens is reflected in our federal laws. Less than 50 years ago there were no federal policies for serving children with disabilities in the United States. Although families and professionals continue to strive for additional funding, the government's commitment to supporting the development of very young children with special needs has consistently increased over the last four decades.

Early intervention services were initially developed for children considered at risk for school and health problems due to psychosocial disadvantage, a combination of social and environmental deprivations resulting from poor economic conditions. These programs were funded to provide educational, medical, and nutritional supports to young children and were designed to rectify the unequal circumstances of children living in economically disadvantaged environments.

One of these programs, the Abecedarian Project, produced impressive results. The project demonstrated that intensive intervention provided from birth to kindergarten increased IQ in at-risk children in the experimental group and demonstrated that the benefits of services continued to be evidenced by higher reading and mathematics achievement scores through third grade (Martin, Ramey, & Ramey, 1990). This project followed the economically disadvantaged children in the experimental group until they were 21 years old. The researchers reported that children who received "high quality" early education were more likely to score higher on IQ tests and reading and mathematics tests, to be enrolled in or graduated from a four-year college, to delay parenthood, and to be gainfully employed than were those in the control group (Carolina Abecedarian Project, 2006).

Another program, Project Head Start, was the first national attempt to intervene directly with preschool-aged children with the goal of improving their development through a variety of educational, medical, nutritional, and parent-training services. Developed in 1965 to help children from low-income homes realize their potential, Project Head Start attempts to remedy the damaging effects of poverty through early intervention. In the early 1970s, Public Laws 92–924 and 93–644 established the requirement that children with disabilities make up 10% of the enrollment in Head Start programs (U.S. Department of Health and Human Services, 1986). Head Start is now a leading inclusion program in the country.

Federal legislation has been essential in creating our present educational system for young children who are at risk for or who have disabilities as well as for their families. The legislation that has been most significant in shaping the ECSE field is listed chronologically in Table 1.1.

1973—Section 504 of the Rehabilitation Act

This act was passed to promote participation in and ensure equal access to federally funded programs for individuals with disabilities (Yell, 2006). Students who qualify for services under the Individuals with Disabilities Education Improvement Act (IDEIA) of 2004 are automatically protected from discrimination under Section 504. Today, schools use Section 504 to provide accommodations for children with learning difficulties who do not qualify for special education under the IDEA disability categories (Turnbull, Huerta, & Stowe, 2006). These students require only reasonable accommodations to be successful in the general education classroom. For these students, schools may develop a Section 504 Accommodation Plan. The Section 504 Plan is frequently used to provide additional support for students with attention deficit/hyperactivity disorder (AD/HD) and AIDS (Richards, 1999). The plan makes accommodations (e.g., sitting away from distractions such as a window) and curricular/testing modifications (e.g., taking tests after school with additional time offered) legally required.

1990—Individuals with Disabilities Education Act

The Individuals with Disabilities Education Act (IDEA) incorporated such well-known legislation as Public Law 94–142, the Education for All Handicapped Children Act of 1975; Public Law 99–457, the 1986 amendments that outlined provisions for statewide service systems for infants and toddlers; Public Law 101-476, the 1990 amendments that included transition services; and Public Law 105–17, the 1997 amendments that encouraged services in natural environments for young children. The 1997 amendments to the IDEA also provided mandatory preschool services for children with disabilities between 3 and 5 years of age and a voluntary program for services for children from birth through age 2, which is called Part C of the IDEA (U.S. Office of Special Education, 1997). Part C offered financial assistance to states that elected to participate in a comprehensive service system for infants and toddlers at risk for disabilities and for those with disabilities. Today, all states participate in Part C (Yell, 2006).

Since 1975, Congress has enacted five bills reauthorizing and amending the original legislation that came to be referred to as the IDEA. IDEA was based on these six major principles:

❏ Schools must educate all children, irrespective of the nature or severity of their disability.

❏ Schools must use nonbiased methods to determine if a disability exists and if special education is needed.

❏ Schools must provide children with disabilities a free and individualized educational program.

❏ Schools must educate children with disabilities with children without disabilities to the extent possible.

❏ Schools must offer safeguards to protect the rights of children with disabilities and their parents.

❏ Schools must collaborate with students with disabilities and their families in designing programs and services.

1973—Section 504 of the Rehabilitation Act (Public Law 93–112)

- Section 504 was passed to promote participation in and ensure equal access to federally funded programs for individuals with disabilities. It created the impetus to educate students with disabilities that resulted in the Education for the Handicapped Act (EHA), later renamed the Individuals with Disabilities Education Act (IDEA).
- To be eligible for a free appropriate public education (FAPE) under Section 504, a child must have a physical or mental impairment that substantially limits a major life activity.

1975—Education for All Handicapped Children Act (Education for the Handicapped Act or EHA) (Public Law 94–142)

- All children with disabilities must be given an education.
- The education must be provided in the least restrictive environment.
- The education must be individualized, free, and appropriate for the child.
- Procedural protections require due process.

1986—EHA Amendments (Public Law 99–457)

- This law extended special education to children with disabilities who are 3–5 years of age.
- Services to infants and toddlers were provided at states' discretion.

1990—Americans with Disabilities Act (ADA)

- The ADA covers the accessibility of public buildings, transportation, and communication to people with disabilities.
- The ADA does not address obligations to provide educational services to students with disabilities.

1990—Individuals with Disabilities Education Act (IDEA)

- The IDEA expanded the foundations established in Public Laws 94–142 and 99–457.
- It has six principles:
  - No student can be excluded from public education because of a disability.
  - Procedural due process protections ensure student and parent rights.
  - Parents are encouraged to participate in their child's education.
  - Assessment must be fair and unbiased.
  - Students must receive a free and appropriate public education in the least restrictive environment.
  - Confidentiality must be maintained.

1997—Reauthorization of the IDEA (Public Law 108–446)

- The reauthorized IDEA ensured that children with disabilities had greater access to the general education curriculum.
- It also expanded opportunities for family members, teachers, and other professionals to work collaboratively.

(continued)

TABLE 1.1 (continued)

2001—No Child Left Behind (NCLB)

- NCLB is the reauthorization of the Elementary and Secondary Education Act (ESEA) and emphasized the following:
  - *Accountability for results:* NCLB is intended to identify schools and districts in need of improvement and to ensure teacher quality. Standardized test scores from children with disabilities must be included in school performance data.
  - *Emphasis on what works in scientific research:* NCLB is intended to improve teaching and learning by providing better information to teachers and principals and by giving more resources to schools.
  - *Expanded parental options:* NCLB is intended to provide more information to parents about their child's progress and the school's performance.
  - *Expanded local control and flexibility:* NCLB provides flexibility in the use of federal education funds and in the improvement of teacher qualifications, in part, by including alternative certification.

2004—Individuals with Disabilities Education Improvement Act (IDEIA)

- This reauthorization addresses several issues: better aligning the IDEA and NCLB, appropriately identifying students needing special education, providing freedom to exercise reasonable discipline while protecting students with special needs, identifying parameters for "highly qualified teachers," reducing paperwork, and fostering more cooperation in order to reduce litigation.

2001—No Child Left Behind

No Child Left Behind (NCLB), which is the current reauthorization of the Elementary and Secondary Education Act (ESEA), has four principal components. First, NCLB is intended to identify schools and districts that need improvement and to ensure that all schools have quality teachers. It requires students with disabilities to be included in the standardized tests used to determine school performance ratings (ACCESS–Inclusive Classrooms, 2005). Second, NCLB requires schools to use evidence-based methodology and provide better information to principals and teachers. Third, NCLB requires that parents be provided more information about their child's progress and about his or her school's performance. And fourth, NCLB provides more flexibility in how schools use federal education funds and certify teachers to ensure teacher quality (NCLB, 2002). Although NCLB was not written for children with disabilities, it has had an impact on the education of primary-aged students with disabilities.

2004—Individuals with Disabilities Education Improvement Act

The Individuals with Disabilities Education Improvement Act of 2004 (IDEIA), Public Law 108–446, amended the 1997 IDEA. Despite an official name change, the 2004 reauthorization of IDEA continues to be referred to as the IDEA and will be addressed by this acronym throughout this book. This law establishes a new entity, the Institute of Education Sciences (IES), to conduct special education research. Even though many had hoped for and expected it, this reauthorization does not provide full funding of special education from birth through age 21 (New IDEA, 2005).

Highlights of the bill include provisions that (1) increase teacher quality; (2) increase accountability by requiring all children with disabilities to be included in state- and districtwide assessment programs, with appropriate accommodations, and by permitting alternate assessments for students with more severe disabilities; (3) reduce paperwork by eliminating benchmarks/short-term objectives in Individualized Education Programs

(IEPs) except for children who take alternate assessments; (4) allow a response-to-intervention model to determine students with a learning disability; (5) reduce overidentification of minority students as eligible for special education through an enhanced prereferral process; and (6) offer an optional birth–age 6 program that permits parents of children eligible for preschool services to continue early intervention services until their child enters kindergarten (Turnbull et al., 2006).

Each of these bills has changed the landscape of professional preparation, influenced the comprehensiveness of services offered, and modified the language professionals and families use in early childhood special education.

CHARACTERISTICS OF EARLY CHILDHOOD SPECIAL EDUCATION

ECSE involves a network of services for children from birth through 8 years of age and for their families. These services involve a range of educational, developmental, and therapeutic activities. Systems for providing intervention for infants and toddlers exist in every state, and all state departments of education provide special education to preschool children (Odom & Wolery, 2003). **Early intervention** is the term used to describe the system of services for children with developmental needs from birth to age 3 and for their families. **Early childhood special education** is the term used to describe the family-focused services for children with special needs from birth through age 8. ECSE is a specialty area that has a theory of practice and shared values that have their roots in evidence-based practices (Odom & Wolery, 2003). **Evidence-based practice** refers to empirical and published research that documents the relationship between practices and outcomes for children, families, professionals, and systems. ECSE practice is based on the following essential evidence-based and value-based tenets (Odom & Wolery, 2003):

❏ Families and homes are the primary nurturing contexts.

❏ Strengthening relationships is essential.

❏ Children learn through acting on and observing their environment.

❏ Adults mediate children's experiences to promote learning.

❏ Children's access to and participation in more developmentally advanced settings (at times with assistance) is necessary for further successful and independent participation.

❏ Practice is individually and dynamically goal-oriented.

❏ Transitions across programs are enhanced by responsive adults.

❏ Families and programs are influenced by the broader context.

Table 1.2 shows the empirical basis for each of these tenets.

ECSE may involve the use of direct or indirect services. **Direct services** involve an early childhood special educator working with a child, or a member of the child's family, in a one-to-one, small-group, or classroom to address the child's or family's specific needs. **Indirect services** involve an early childhood special educator guiding and supporting another adult who provides services to a child and/or family. This individual could be a parent, a family member, another professional from the special education team, and/or a general early childhood professional. If you review the case study of Angela and Danny, you see that they received both direct services (e.g., home visits were provided) and indirect services (e.g., the ECSE professionals trained the daycare and general education teachers who worked with Danny).

The national organization for ECSE professionals, the Division of Early Childhood (DEC) of the Council for Exceptional Children (CEC), has identified the following three values as guiding the ECSE field: (1) respecting all children and families; (2) offering high quality, comprehensive, coordinated, and family-centered services and supports; and (3) respecting the right of all children to participate actively and meaningfully within their families and communities (Sandall, Hemmeter, Smith, & McLean, 2005).

TABLE 1.2 Fundamental tenets and evidence-based practices in early childhood special education

Family and homes are primary nurturing contexts

- Family-centered practices (Thompson et al., 1997)
- Social support and resource-based models (Trivette et al., 1997)
- Parent-implemented milieu teaching approaches (Kaiser et al., 2000)
- Parent-education programs (Mahoney et al., 1999)

Strengthening relationships is an essential feature of EI/ECSE

- Relationship-based programs (Rauh et al., 1988)
- Parent–infant interaction programs (Girolametto et al., 1994)
- Peer-interaction programs (Odom et al., 1999)
- Professional collaboration programs (Lieber et al., 2001)

Children learn through acting on and observing their environment

- Contingently responsive environments (Landry et al., 2001)
- Participation in natural learning opportunities (Dunst et al., 2001)
- Participation in classrooms employing evidence-based practices (Schwartz et al., 1996)

Adults mediate children's experiences to promote learning

- Embedded learning opportunities (Horn, Lieber, Li, Sandall, & Schwartz, 2000)
- Activity-based intervention (Losardo & Bricker, 1994)
- Routine structuring (Wolery et al., 1998)
- High-probability requests (Davis et al., 1994)
- Prompting and prompt-fading strategies (Venn et al., 1993)

Children's participation in more developmentally advanced settings, at times with assistance, is necessary for successful and independent participation in those settings

- Learning opportunities occurring in community and home contexts (Dunst, Hambry, et al., 2000)
- Participation in inclusive preschool play groups (Guralnick et al., 1996)
- Social integration interventions in inclusive settings (Jenkins et al., 1989)

EI/ECSE practice is individually and dynamically goal oriented

- Goal identification linked with learning strategies (Wolery, 2005)
- Parent input solicited by routines-based interviews (McWilliam, 1992)
- Demands of environments source of goal identification (Thurman & Widerstrom, 1990)

Transitions across programs are enhanced by a developmentally instigative adult

- Assessing the demands of the next setting and teaching needed skills (Ager & Shapiro, 1995)
- Preparing personnel and/or family for transition to next setting (Wyly et al., 1996)
- Interagency agreement to smooth transitions (Rosenkoetter et al., 2001)

Families and programs are influenced by the broader context

- Family-centered planning (McWilliam et al., 1998)
- Resource mapping (Trivette et al., 1997)
- Designing culturally sensitive programs (Catlett et al., 2000)

Early childhood special educators provide services to children with a range of abilities and needs. Services for infants, toddlers, and preschoolers are noncategorical. **Noncategorical** means that services are organized not by disability, but by age or need. Instruction for infants, toddlers, preschoolers, and many kindergarteners is organized around domain areas. **Domains** are separate areas of development. The **fine motor domain** addresses small muscle planning and coordination, such as cutting with scissors. The **gross motor domain** deals with large muscle planning and coordination, such as jumping and walking with balance. The **self-help/adaptive domain** involves the ability to do things for one's self, such as dressing and eating. Chapter 7 discusses fine and gross motor development and adaptive skills. The **communication domain** involves the child's ability to understand and produce language. Chapter 5 discusses communication development. The **cognitive domain** incorporates solving problems and communicating what one knows. Chapter 6 discusses cognitive and literacy development. Interacting effectively with others and understanding and communicating emotions appropriately are aspects of the **social/emotional domain**. Chapter 8 discusses social and emotional development. All these domains are interrelated and interdependent. Attachment, for example, a component of the social/emotional domain, involves the use of cognitive, communicative, and social skills.

Instruction with primary-aged students, those in kindergarten through third grade, is organized around the traditional academic subject areas, such as reading and social studies. Although social skills may not be identified as a separate area of instruction in the general curriculum, intervention in this area is just as critical for primary-aged students with learning and behavioral needs as it is for younger children with the same challenges.

CHARACTERISTICS OF GENERAL EARLY CHILDHOOD EDUCATION

A principal tenet of general early childhood education (ECE) is that of **developmentally appropriate practice (DAP)** (Garguilo & Kilgo, 2000).

General early childhood educators are committed to creating environments that are *developmentally appropriate* for children so that each child's *individual abilities* and interests are supported (Bredekamp & Copple, 1997). This focus on individualization is the cornerstone of ECSE practice as well (Raver, 1999; Sandall et al., 2005). Nonetheless, ECE and ECSE often differ in how they define individualization and DAP. In general, there are four important differences between ECE and ECSE practices.

First, according to ECSE practice, professionals are required to identify and teach *specific* goals and objectives to address *each* child's unique developmental deficits (Pretti-Frontczak & Bricker, 2004; Odom & Wolery, 2003; Sandall et al., 2005). While DAP means educators are concerned with meeting the needs of individual students and differentiating instruction, in practice the concern in ECE continues to be *global* developmental issues, such as improving self-esteem and teaching preacademic and/or academic skills. In essence, ECSE attempts to build programs that "fit" the specific needs of individual children, while ECE helps children "fit" into existing programs.

Second, ECSE professionals are required to use comprehensive, repeated assessments to determine mastery of goals and objectives toward a stated performance criterion (Grisham-Brown & Pretti-Frontczak, 2003; Sandall et al., 2005). They must document each child's progress and the effectiveness of the individualized intervention programs. This often involves gathering daily child performance data and adjusting instruction based on these data. General early childhood educators are not required to use assessment or evaluation tools as frequently or in the same way.

Third, ECSE professionals are required to focus on family-centered services, particularly when working with infants and toddlers. General early childhood educators acknowledge families as critical in supporting children's development and learning, but do not view families as pivotal agents for change or as educational collaborators in the same way as ECSE professionals do (Odom & Wolery, 2003).

Fourth, ECSE professionals have adopted general early childhood teaching approaches and, in addition, use specialized strategies, such as prompting, time delay, and parallel talk, to promote children's development. They use these techniques to teach early developmental skills that are precursors for current and later school success (Odom & Wolery, 2003; Sandall et al., 2005). At a minimum, for children with disabilities to be successful in inclusive programs, professionals need to use individualized instructional strategies in addition to completely individualized planning (Grisham-Brown & Pretti-Frontczak, 2003).

Although there are definitely compatible features in the ECE and ECSE philosophies (Kilgo et al., 1999), the differences seem most apparent in inclusive settings, where they may cause tension in the collaborative relationship (McDonnell, Brownell, & Wolery, 2001).

Least Restrictive Environment

Recommended practice dictates that children with disabilities be educated with children without disabilities as much as is possible and beneficial. This practice is known as educating a child in the **least restrictive environment (LRE)**. For some children, the least restrictive environment means that they will receive all their education in a general education classroom, including their special education services. For others with more significant needs, the least restrictive environment may be a setting with other children with disabilities, with scheduled interactions with children without disabilities.

Infants, Toddlers, and Preschoolers. Often children with delays and impairments are placed in community-based, or inclusive, childcare or preschool programs, although any placement decision must always be based on each child's Individualized Family Service Plan or his or her Individual Education Plan. When a child is placed in an inclusive program, his or her family, ECE staff, and ECSE team members must meet frequently to discuss the type of instructional supports and accommodations necessary for the child to be maintained successfully in that program. Through effective indirect services, such as monitoring and consultation, ECSE professionals provide specialized training regularly to general early childhood staff. Some ECSE professionals have expressed concern about poorly coordinated interventions in inclusive settings and a lack of understanding regarding what ECE professionals can expect from the consultation process (Wesley, Buysse, & Skinner, 2001; Horn & Sandall, 2000).

Primary-Aged Students. Despite years of discussion about inclusive schools and practices, families and educators are still dealing with the distance between typical practices and desired practices. Schools that seem to be the most effective in providing inclusive education tend to have the following characteristics: (1) They possess a shared vision that all children have the right to receive their education in neighborhood schools, (2) they work to develop family partnerships, (3) they encourage high expectations for general/special educators and students, (4) they use collaborative approaches for problem solving, (5) they place value on continuing staff development, and (6) they use research-based strategies (Malarz, 1996). In other words, effective programs take an ecological approach to serving children and families. Children who receive ECSE services have a broad spectrum of characteristics, abilities, and needs.

CHARACTERISTICS OF CHILDREN RECEIVING EARLY CHILDHOOD SPECIAL EDUCATION SERVICES

The term **developmental delay** is used by most states to describe children from birth to their ninth birthday who manifest a significant delay in or an atypical pattern of cognitive, physical, communicative, social, emotional, and/or adaptive development and who as a result are eligible for ECSE services. Infants, toddlers, and preschoolers with established risk conditions are also served. **Established risk conditions** are diagnosed physical or mental conditions that have a high probability of resulting in a developmental delay or developmental problem. Cerebral palsy, hearing and/or visual impairments, and chromosome abnormalities such as Turner's syndrome and Down syndrome are examples. Infant-toddler programs may also choose to serve children who are experiencing **environmental risk conditions.** These may be children who live in extreme poverty, who have been victims of abuse or neglect, who have parent(s) who abuse substances, or who are experiencing other conditions that are associated with a higher than expected probability of developmental delay.

Table 1.3 lists the disabilities served by the IDEA (2004). Most states use these categorical labels to describe children who qualify for special

TABLE 1.3 Categories of exceptionality under the Individuals with Disabilities Education Act (IDEA), 34 C.F.R. § 300.8

Federal Disability Term	Description
• Mental retardation	Significant limitations in cognitive ability and adaptive behavior; occurs in a range of severity; also called intellectual disability or cognitive impairment
• Specific learning disability	A disorder related to the processing of information that leads to difficulties in reading, writing, and/or mathematics
• Emotional disturbance	Significant problems in the social-emotional area to the degree that learning is negatively affected; also called behavior disorder or emotional disability
• Autism	A disorder characterized by extraordinary difficulty in social responsiveness and communication; may be mild to significant; also called autism spectrum disorder (ASD)
• Speech or language impairment	A disorder related to the accurate production of speech or the meaningful use of language to communicate; also called communication disorder (CD)
• Hearing impairment	A partial or complete loss of hearing; also called hard of hearing or deaf
• Visual impairment including blindness	A partial or complete loss of vision
• Orthopedic impairment	A significant physical limitation that impairs the ability to move or to complete motor activities; also called physical disability
• Other health impairment	A disease or health disorder so significant that it negatively affects learning
• Multiple disabilities	The presence of two or more disabilities such that neither can be determined as the primary disability
• Traumatic brain injury	A medical condition involving a serious brain injury from an accident or injury that may affect learning, behavior, social skills, and language

In addition to these categories from the IDEA, the term *developmental delay* is used to describe a nonspecific disability that impacts learning in children from birth to age 5; states may also choose to use this term as an alternative to specific disability labels to identify students between the ages of 6 and 8 who need special education.

education services when they enter first grade. In some states, these disability terms may be used to describe children with special needs beginning in kindergarten. However, according to federal legislation, parents have the prerogative to request that the term *developmental delay* be used to describe their child's needs until the child turns 9.

Characteristics of Infants and Toddlers

The majority of infants and toddlers identified as having a developmental delay display no organic basis for the problem (La Paro, Olsen, & Pianta, 2002). A national survey of infants served under Part C of the IDEA, The Infant and Toddler Program, revealed a varied portrait of children and families when they enter the early intervention system (Scarborough et al., 2004). A large number of infants were found to be from low-income families, to represent ethnic minorities, to be in foster care, and to be male. Nearly one-third were found to have low birth weight, four times the rate in the general population. Children in early intervention were found to be eight times more likely to be rated as having only fair health.

Children described as having developmental delays tended to enroll in programs when they were toddlers, while children who had diagnosed conditions or who were subject to biological or environmental risk factors tended to enter in the first year of life. The diverse medical, social, and educational needs of children receiving infant-toddler services reinforce the requirement of individualized early intervention services. Since many children, and families, have compounding issues that influence their ability to accept services, it is critical that the unique needs of each child be considered within the broader ecological context of the family in order to optimize the child's development.

Characteristics of Preschoolers

As mentioned above, when preschoolers are determined to be manifesting a developmental delay or possess an established risk condition,

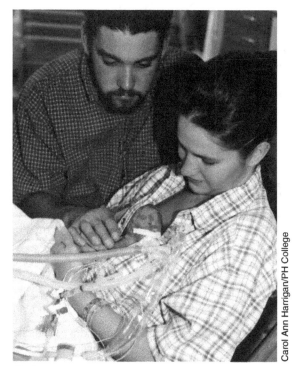

Early childhood special education has a long history of providing beneficial supports to children with special needs and their families.

Carol Ann Harrigan/PH College

they may receive preschool services. At their discretion, states may also use ECSE funds to serve students who are at risk for developmental difficulties. Many children receiving preschool services have participated in infant-toddler programs, and the majority have established risk conditions, such as hearing or visual impairments and delayed and/or disordered communication skills (Heward, 2006).

Characteristics of Primary-Aged Students

First- through third-grade students with special needs may qualify for services under learning disabilities, orthopedic impairments, or any of the other IDEA-defined disabilities. The largest group of school-aged students served is students with learning disabilities, followed by students with speech or language impairments (Wood, 2003). Some students qualify for services under more than one disability category, such as a student with a visual impairment who also has a learning disability.

PROGRAM OBJECTIVES FOR EDUCATING YOUNG CHILDREN WITH SPECIAL NEEDS

Although programs for young children with special needs are committed to supporting children so they may realize their potential, programs for infants, toddlers, preschoolers, and primary-aged children have specific objectives that reflect the needs of children, and their families, at a particular stage of life.

Intervention with Infants and Toddlers

Infant-toddler intervention and **early intervention** are terms used to describe a cluster of services made available to children, and their families, from birth to their third birthday who are at risk for or who have developmental problems. The earlier these services are begun, the better, since a child's age at the start of services has been found to be a significant variable in predicting cognitive progress (Lee & Kahn, 1998). Unfortunely, this does not always occur. For example, a study of infant-toddler services in North Carolina conducted by Buysse, Bernier, and McWilliam (2002) found that the mean age of entry into infant programs was 17 months, still later than desired for most children.

Despite some differences in philosophy, characteristics, and service options, most infant-toddler programs have these three broad program objectives:

❏ to provide information, support, and assistance to families dealing with the needs associated with their child's development;

❏ to build parental confidence as the primary facilitator of their child's development and the principal advocate for their child; and

❏ to promote interactions between family members that encourage feelings of competence and enjoyment.

Studies of parents' perceptions of infant-toddler programs suggest that parents highly value the services provided. Programs that provide technological knowledge and skills and emotional support have been rated as most beneficial by families (Wehman & Gilkerson, 1999).

Intervention with Preschoolers

Preschool intervention is a term used to describe a variety of services provided for children who are 3 to 5 years of age and who manifest developmental delays or have an established risk condition. The majority of preschool programs provide services directly to children at centers. Most preschool programs have these five broad program objectives:

❏ to support and promote a child's development of cognitive, fine and gross motor, adaptive, social/emotional, and communication skills so that child can participate more effectively in the next setting;

❏ to expose a child to preliteracy skills that will increase the child's chances of participating in the general education curriculum;

❏ to build and support social competence;

❏ to promote developmentally appropriate independence so a child may more fully participate in family, school, and community life; and

❏ to prevent or minimize the development of future problems and disabilities.

Intervention with Primary-Aged Students

Intervention with children with special needs in kindergarten through third grade (ages 5 through 8) is called **early childhood intervention**. With the parents' permission, the child is given a multidisciplinary team evaluation to determine if he or she needs special education supports to be successful in school. The child who is deemed eligible for special education services may be served in a general education classroom, a resource room, a self-contained special education classroom, or a combination of these. Most programs for primary-aged students with disabilities in general education classrooms and resource rooms have these two broad program objectives:

❏ to offer appropriate curricular and instructional modifications (e.g., less material, different expectations) and accommodations (e.g., alternative acquisition modes, such as having material read to child) so the child is able to participate in the general education curriculum (Jitendra, Edwards, Choutka, & Treadway, 2002)

❏ to offer team support to the child, the child's family, the general education teacher, and other professionals serving the child.

Programs for primary-aged children with special needs in self-contained classrooms have these three broad program objectives:

❏ to foster the child's potential in the cognitive, fine and gross motor, adaptive, social/ emotional, and communication areas.

❏ to promote the child's independence, self-determination, and self-advocacy skills.

❏ to develop the child's social and academic skills, which encourage his or her inclusion in school and community.

Programs for infants, toddlers, preschoolers, and primary-aged students may have slightly different service models depending on the state, the staffing resources, the child's age, and the school system.

SERVICE DELIVERY MODELS FOR EDUCATING YOUNG CHILDREN WITH SPECIAL NEEDS

Services for infants, toddlers, and preschoolers may be provided in home-based, center-based, or home-center programs. Although these programs must be administered by a state agency, services from other agencies may be contracted to meet the requirement that programs provide a full range of services. Local education agencies may use a variety of service delivery options, and the length of intervention time for infants and toddlers and the length of the school day for preschoolers may vary. Each model has certain advantages and disadvantages for children, and their families.

Home-Based Program Model

In home-based programs, an ECSE professional travels to a family's home to work directly with the child and the child's family. The child and the family are both the focus of intervention (D'Amato & Yoshida, 1991). While in the home, the ECSE professional may work directly with the child (e.g., playing with the child on the floor) or may work indirectly with the child (e.g., guiding a caretaker as he or she plays with the child on the floor). The pace of interactions, teaching, and discussion is dictated by the parents' preferences and needs and by the child's ability to profit from what is being offered. The following are considered recommended practices for home-based programs (Sandall et al., 2005):

❏ Interventions should be embedded into activities of daily living, such as bathing, mealtimes, play, family recreation, and bedtime at home and in natural environments.

❏ Interventions should include all family members who wish to be involved.

❏ The level of intensity and range of services provided should match the level of need identified by the family.

Generally during a home visit, the ECSE professional participates in the following activities: (1) modeling ways to facilitate the child's play and learning for family members present, (2) providing feedback on family members' interactions with the child, (3) observing the child's ability to use a skill in different ways and in different situations, and (4) brainstorming with parents/caretakers about ways to promote the child's skills and learning.

Home visits may be arranged in the family's home or occur at other locations, such as the neighborhood park or the child's daycare center, if the family prefers or requests it. Environments that are typical for the family, such as the family's home, the grocery store, and Sunday dinners at Grandmother's house, are considered **natural environments**. With parents' input, the professional attempts to find ways to logically embed teaching the child skills within family activities. For example, if a child's outcome is to raise his head and hold it up for three seconds while engaged in an activity, it is natural to have the child hold his head up while his shirt is being put on in the morning, while he is playing with Dad on the sofa after work, and while he is reaching for toys in the bathtub. Although intervention in natural environments is based on brainstorming with parents and a good deal of common sense, research has found that experienced practitioners are better able to describe natural environments in terms of their learning opportunities than are less-experienced professionals (Raab & Dunst, 2004). Many families find that embedding the teaching of outcomes into their routines feels comfortable and saves them time. However, a child's entire intervention program need not be embedded into existing family routines unless that is the family's choice (FACETS, 2000).

Interactions during a home visit should be relaxed, structured, supportive, and professional. A professional's presence in the family's home can arouse strong feelings in parents regarding their attitudes toward their child's disability, their living circumstances, and their competence as parents (Peterson, Luze, Eshbaugh, Jeon, & Kantz, 2007). Family members' reactions to home visits can range from feelings of gratitude to feelings of resentfulness. There is no one way to handle the range of emotions family members may express during home visits. Usually by finding a balance between empathy and objectivity, the professional can find a way to address most of the family's

more significant needs. Chapter 2 discusses the dynamics of working with families further.

Home-based programs offer several advantages for children, families, and professionals: (1) continuous contact with the child and his or her family in their own environment, (2) time flexibility, (3) increased contact with all family members, (4) flexibility in the intensity of services, and (5) the relatively low cost of the services. Disadvantages of this model include: (1) inconsistency in training and experience among service providers in infant-toddler programs, (2) limited opportunities to coordinate additional services such as therapies, and (3) limited contact with other children the same age with and without disabilities.

The best home teaching activities are those that are simple and enjoyable to the child and family members (Dunst, Hamby, Trivette, Raab, & Bruder, 2000). Home-based programs are the most common model for providing services to infants and toddlers, and to their families, but they may also be offered to preschoolers.

Center-Based Program Model

Children are brought to a central location to receive services in center-based programs. The services provided will vary depending on the number of staff and the resources of the sponsoring agencies. In some programs, professionals provide the majority of direct services to the children and offer regular conferences to their families. In others, parents come to a center where they are guided through intervention activities with their children while professionals act as facilitators or models. Some programs offer information, training, or social sessions for families that may involve siblings and/or extended family members on a regular schedule. Recommended practices for center-based programs include the following (Sandall et al., 2005):

❑ The physical setting should be safe, clean, barrier-free, and accessible to children to promote independent play and learning.

❏ The ratio of adult staff to children should be such that it maximizes safety, health, and the promotion of goals.

❏ Isolated support services, such as speech-language therapy and physical therapy, should be avoided unless identified child and/or family needs cannot be met within family routines.

❏ Materials and toys provided should be developmentally appropriate.

❏ Activities should stimulate children's initiations, choices, and involvement/engagement with adults, peers, and materials.

❏ Team members should communicate regularly with other staff and families.

The services offered in center-based programs vary based on the child's age, the needs of the child and his or her family, and the resources of the providing agency. For example, infant-toddler center-based programs tend to offer a variable attendance schedule, with few requiring daily attendance. Preschool center-based programs tend to require regular attendance.

Center-based programs provide many advantages for children, families, and professionals: (1) a consistent, prearranged program for both children and families; (2) opportunities for children to interact with other children the same age; and (3) the provision of most services, including therapies and occasionally transportation, at the center. This model also has some disadvantages: (1) the difficulty of accommodating the needs of individual children and their families in groups, (2) the prospect of limited interaction with children without disabilities, and (3) the gap in services during the summer months.

Home–Center Program Model

Some states offer a combination of home- and center-based options to families. For example, family members may choose to have services provided for their preschool-aged child in a preschool or daycare program for children with typical development and to have the child also receive home visits. When home visits are offered in conjunction with center programs, visits usually occur about once a month.

Financial considerations and geographic location often dictate whether center-home programs are available. Due to limited financial resources and restricted access to trained professionals, some localities are limited in the range of service delivery options that can be offered. Despite this, professionals still make every effort to individualize services based on each child's characteristics, abilities, and health as well as his or her family's preference and needs.

Itinerant Teacher Model/Inclusion

In this model, an ECSE teacher serves as an inclusion specialist, supporting infants, toddlers, preschoolers, and primary-aged students. Young children with disabilities who receive instruction in general education settings receive it from itinerant ECSE teachers (Raver, 1980). In fact, nearly 50% of school-aged students with mild disabilities are served with this model (IDEA, 2004). Despite a growing reliance on consultation as a primary support for ECE professionals, there is little agreement in the field on a particular approach or set of procedures to guide the consultation practice (Sadler, 2003).

In general, itinerant services combine direct services (e.g., work with the child in the child's setting) and collaborative-consultative services (e.g., work with another professional in the child's setting to support that professional in better including the child). Many early childhood special educators describe their itinerant teaching activities as involving the following:

❏ providing direct services to children through individualized classroom routines,

❏ coaching/consulting with ECE staff on how to address children's IEP objectives during the remainder of the week,

❏ providing emotional support and encouragement to ECE classroom staff, and

❏ serving as a resource for information and other services for ECE staff and families.

To support general education staff in meeting individual children's goals and objectives, itinerant teachers may help staff develop the organizational strategies needed to systematically build objectives for children with special needs into the curriculum and the schedule (Raver, 2003). Further, environmental adaptations to maximize a child's engagement in all activities in the classroom might need to be discussed and arranged. Commonsense interventions such as permitting toddlers and preschoolers to participate in only one learning center at a time may help them experience more productive interactions with that center, rather than moving from one center to another without an apparent purpose. ECE staff may need guidance in how to improve the social-communicative environment for a child. For example, by requiring a preschooler to use picture cards and words to request center changes, the teacher is structuring a way for that child to increase communication and problem-solving skills. Itinerant teachers demonstrate and reinforce general education staff members' use of specific strategies for teaching developmental skills. By encouraging staff to wait five seconds before offering assistance (called time-delay), for instance, communicative responding in some toddlers and/or preschoolers may increase (Wolery, 2001).

Models for Primary-Aged Students

Commonly in kindergarten and first-grade settings, itinerant teachers have the critical role of helping general education teachers identify appropriate preacademics for children who are not ready to begin systematic academic instruction or who require a different pace of academic instruction. Children with complex and severe needs may not benefit as much from full-group participation, and itinerant teachers can help staff identify ways to create individual or small-group settings in which to provide direct instruction to these children (Sadler, 2003). Chapter 4 discusses this model further.

Many children with disabilities in kindergarten through third grade are educated in three primary placements or variations of these placements (IDEA, 2004). A description of these—the general education classroom, the resource room, and the separate special education classroom—follow.

General Education Classroom. Students who receive the majority of their schooling in the general education classroom and who receive special education and related services, such as speech-language therapy, outside the general education classroom for less than 21% of the school day are said to be educated in the **regular classroom**. These students tend to have mild learning difficulties and display social behaviors that do not pose special discipline problems. They receive the services of a special education teacher and/or paraprofessional within the general education classroom. These professionals provide both direct and indirect, or consultative services, for varying amounts of time each day.

Resource Room. Students who receive special education and related services in a resource room and other settings outside the general education classroom for 21% to 60% of the school day are considered to be educated in the **resource room**. These students tend to have one or more academic need areas. That is, they may have difficulty with reading, mathematics, or both. However, their academic needs are not so significant that they do not benefit from the general education curriculum. These students leave the general education classroom for an established period of time each week (e.g., one hour a day, one hour four times a week, etc.) to receive intensive, individualized instruction from a special educator or other specialist, such as a reading specialist, with the intention of remediating their present difficulties.

Separate Special Education Classroom. Students who are outside the general education classroom 61% to 100% of the school day, receiving special education and related services, are considered to be educated in a **separate classroom**. These students are taught by a special educator and tend to have academic needs that are too great to be managed appropriately in a resource room or a general education classroom. Further, they may have social and/or behavioral issues that are extreme enough to reduce their chances of success in a general education classroom.

AN ECOLOGICAL APPROACH TO EARLY CHILDHOOD SPECIAL EDUCATION

The ecological systems perspective views the many settings that make up the fabric of family, school, and community life as contexts of development-influencing experiences. Experiences in different settings can positively or negatively impact a child's development and learning.

Ecological contexts, or settings, have been described as activity settings (Farver, 1999), microsystems (Bronfenbrenner, 1979), and natural learning environments (Dunst et al., 2000). For any child, learning results from experiences in daily living, child and family routines, family rituals, school activities, and family and community traditions. Learning may be planned, or it may happen serendipitously.

ECSE professionals recognize that factors outside the immediate environment of a child and family exert an influence on development and learning (Odom & Wolery, 2003). Many conditions facing contemporary families, such as single-parent homes and significant financial pressures, may dramatically affect a child's passage through early childhood.

Bronfenbrenner's (1979, 1992) ecological systems model may be useful in identifying factors that can support or interfere with a child's functioning or a family's coping. Many families with a child with special needs face multiple conditions that can negatively or positively impact their ability to provide intervention or support for their child. Awareness of these risk factors allows teams to secure appropriate supports for families. Bronfenbrenner grouped ecological risk

Without appropriate supports and accommodations, it may be difficult for students with learning and/or behavior needs to be successful in general education classrooms.

Anthony Magnacca/Merrill

factors into microsystems, mesosystems, and exosystems, which will be briefly discussed.

Microsystem

A child's microsystem involves the capabilities of his or her parents and the family unit in meeting the child's emotional, physical, and material needs (Bronfenbrenner, 1992). Adolescent mothers of children with disabilities may present a special communication challenge to professionals, since these mothers may perceive themselves as powerless (Lea, 2006). Their sudden and unpredictable intrusive control, harsh physical punishment, lack of play, lack of consolation and comfort of child distress, inconsistent feeding patterns, and generally erratic expressions of emotions are behaviors that may have an unfavorable impact on their child, particularly if the child has developmental problems (Crockenberg & Smith, 2002).

Mesosystem

The mesosystem involves the interaction between two or more settings in which a child is living (Bronfenbrenner, 1992). Clearly, economic, cultural, and health factors often overlap (Park, Turnbull, & Turnbull, 2002). A family with a child who has a disability or developmental delay and who also has severe medical issues will need different support than a family with a healthy child with a disability.

Exosystem

The exosystem involves a family's social conditions (Bronfenbrenner, 1992). Social conditions such as unemployment, poor health care, and unsafe housing can impact a child's development and increase the chances his or her family will experience illness, family stress, and a lack of social support (Zeanah, Boris, & Larrieu, 1997). Poverty may limit a child's learning because his or her family cannot afford to buy stimulating toys, books, and school supplies that are associated with school success (Bradley et al., 1994).

In reviewing the case study of Angela and Danny, it is clear that this family experienced several of the microsystem, mesosystem, and exosystem issues discussed. Several agencies attempted to address these difficulties so Danny and his family could better cope with their situation. At times, ECSE professionals may feel overwhelmed by the magnitude of problems facing some of the families they serve. To rally the commitment required, professionals need to look for value in their everyday interactions with families, find value in families' interactions, and strive for nonjudgmental intervention practices (Glascoe, 1999). The field of ECSE assumes an ecological approach to supporting children and families by attempting to strengthen the child-family relationship (e.g., relationships with parents, siblings), strengthen the family's resources (e.g., access to services and information), and strengthen the family's social supports (e.g., those who assist the family in meeting child-family needs). It is hoped that these actions may reduce some of the deleterious effects of a disability on the young child and enable the family to better support "the whole child" in all contexts.

PROFESSIONAL STANDARDS

The field of ECSE has turned away from *whether* to provide services to *how* to provide services that produce the outcomes that programs and families desire (Wolery & Bailey, 2002). Currently, there is movement toward clarifying professional standards and developing comprehensive guidelines for the types and levels of evidence needed to identify a practice as evidence-based and effective (Buysse, Wesley, Synder, & Winton, 2006; Odom et al., 2005). Historically, ECSE research has been characterized by the following: (1) The lack of methodological consistency has made effectiveness comparisons between studies challenging (Wolery & Bailey, 2002); (2) most research has been conducted with small numbers of subjects (Sandall, Smith, McLean, & Ramsey, 2000); and (3) although research has evaluated treatments, there has been little evidence of the maintenance of treatments (i.e., data showing that treatment effects continue after treatment has been discontinued) and the generalization of treatments (i.e., data showing that children are able to use the learned skills with different materials, people, and situations) (Odom & Strain, 2002).

In 2000, the CEC's DEC published *DEC Recommended Practices: A Comprehensive Guide for Practical Application in Early Intervention/Early Childhood Special Education* (Sandall et al., 2005), which was the product of a national effort to develop a set of evidence-based unifying practices for the field (Smith et al., 2002; McLean, Synder, Smith, & Sandall, 2002). Despite these efforts, the federal special education policy, and the strong empirical base of ECSE procedures and practices, there still exists a gap between what is considered to be recommended practice in ECSE and what actually occurs in the field (Harbin, 2001). In an effort to lessen this gap, DEC-recommended knowledge and skills have been embedded into each chapter of this book, and some are listed in Appendices A and B. Additionally, readers are referred to *What Every Special Educator Must Know: Ethics, Standards, and Guidelines for Special Educators* (Council for Exceptional Children, 2003), which lists national competencies for all special educators, including ECSE teachers.

Standards-Based Education

Learning standards identify the things learners should know at different grade levels and thus establish the curriculum (Salend, 2005). General education reforms based on learning standards emerged from NCLB, which promotes "adequate yearly progress" (AYP) for all children and requires high-stakes assessment for all learners. Although school-aged children, including kindergarteners, have been the focus of these standards, educators of preschoolers have begun to experience a drive toward higher levels of achievement and accountability as well (Rous, Lobianco, Moffett, & Lund, 2005). Over 40 states have developed standards for early childhood programs, including some for

children with special needs (Rous, Kohner-Coogle, & Stewart, 2004). Standards-based education has prompted concern among some professionals working with preschoolers with special needs; they fear that these children will be overloaded with preacademic instruction before their developmental gaps are adequately addressed, which will lead only to more school difficulties later (Rous et al., 2005).

Some states have begun to assess school-aged students with disabilities at the grade level at which they are taught according to their IEPs, rather than giving them the tests given to their age-peers (Parker, 2005). This practice is seen by many as a more appropriate and fair way to assess children with special needs (Ascione, 2005).

CONCLUSION

Although federal legislation has increased the services available to young children with special needs and to their families, ensuring the quality of these services continues to be the responsibility of ECSE professionals (Raver, 2001). As the case study of Angela and Danny demonstrates, ECSE professionals take an ecological, family-focused approach to supporting children and families so that comprehensive and coordinated services are provided. As research clarifies which approaches and strategies work best for which children and families and as collaboration with other professionals in inclusive programs improves, it is hoped that the gap between recommended practice and actual practice in the field is lessened.

SUMMARY

Federal legislation affecting early childhood special education services

- The Individuals with Disabilities Education Improvement Act" (2004) amended earlier versions of the Education for the Handicapped Act (EHA)/Individuals with Disabilities Education Act (IDEA), reducing paperwork, offering another way to identify students with learning disabilities, and attempting to address the overrepresentation of minorities in special education programs.

Characteristics of early childhood special education

- Early childhood special education practice is based on eight evidence-based and value-based tenets: (1) Families and homes are the primary nurturing contexts, (2) strengthening relationships is essential, (3) children learn through acting on and observing their environment, (4) adults mediate children's experiences to promote learning, (5) children's access to and participation in more developmentally advanced settings (at times with assistance) is necessary for further successful and independent participation, (6) practice is individually and dynamically goal-oriented, (7) transitions across programs are enhanced by responsive adults, and (8) families and programs are influenced by the broader context.

Characteristics of general early childhood education

- Although there are similarities in practice and philosophy between ECE and ECSE, there are also differences that may strain collaborative relationships when there is insufficient training.

Characteristics of children receiving ECSE services

- To receive services, infants, toddlers, and preschoolers must show significant delays or atypical patterns in one or more areas of development or have a diagnosed physical or mental condition that has a high probability of resulting in a developmental delay.
- The majority of primary-aged students receiving special education have a learning disability and/or require services for speech or language impairments.

Program objectives for educating young children with special needs

- Most infant-toddler programs (birth to 3 years) have these program objectives: (1) to provide information, support, and assistance to families dealing with the needs associated with their child's development; (2) to build parental confidence as the primary facilitator of their child's development and the principal advocate for their child; and (3) to promote interactions between family members that encourage feelings of competence and enjoyment.

- Most preschool programs (3 to 5 years) have these program objectives: (1) to support and promote a child's development of cognitive, fine and gross motor, adaptive, social/emotional, and communication skills so that a child can participate more effectively in the next setting, (2) to expose a child to pre-literacy skills that will increase the child's chances of participating in the general education curriculum, (3) to build and support social competence, (4) to promote developmentally appropriate independence so a child may more fully participate in family, school, and community life, and (5) to prevent or minimize the development of future problems and disabilities.
- Most programs for primary-aged students (kindergarten–third grade) in general education and resource classrooms have these program objectives: (1) to offer appropriate curricular and instructional modifications (e.g., less material, different expectations) and accommodations (e.g., alternative acquisition modes, such as having material read to child) so a child is able to participate in the general education curriculum and (2) to offer team support to the child, the child's family, the general education teacher, and other professionals serving the child.
- Programs for primary-aged children in separate special education classrooms have these program objectives: (1) to foster a child's potential in the cognitive, fine and gross motor, adaptive, social/emotional, and communication areas; (2) to promote a child's independence, self-determination, and self-advocacy skills; and (3) to develop a child's social and academic skills, which encourage his or her inclusion in school and community.

Service delivery models for educating young children with special needs

- Infants, toddlers, and preschoolers are usually served in home-based, center-based, or home-center programs.
- Primary-aged students with disabilities tend to be served by an itinerant special education teacher/paraprofessional in the general education classroom or to receive services in a resource room or a separate special education classroom.

An ecological approach to ECSE

- The ecological systems perspective views the different settings that make up family, school, and community life as contexts of development-influencing experiences.

Professional standards

- The field of ECSE is shaped by professional standards and the effort to identify sound evidence-based practices.

DISCUSSION QUESTIONS/ACTIVITIES

1. What similarities and/or differences do you note in program objectives as children become older? Explain your answer.

2. Discuss four tasks performed by itinerant ECSE teachers in inclusive settings. Describe the task you might find most challenging, and explain how you plan to overcome this difficulty.

3. Discuss two aspects of the ecological approach that professionals used to support Angela's and Danny's needs as described in the case study.

REFERENCES

ACCESS–Inclusive Classrooms (2005). *Inclusive classrooms: Child development resources.* Retrieved August 10, 2005, from http://www.cdr.org

Ascione, L. (2005, August 25). *NCLB backlash expected to grow.* Retrieved September 6, 2005, from http://www.eschoolnews

Bradley, R., Whiteside, L., Mundfrom, D., Casey, P. H., Kelleher, K., & Pope, S. (1994). Early indications of resilience and their relation to experiences in the home environment of low birthweight, premature children living in poverty. *Child Development, 65*(2), 346–360.

Bredekamp, S., & Copple, C. (Eds) (1997). *Developmentally appropriate practice for early childhood programs.* Washington, DC: National Association for the Education of Young Children.

Bronfenbrenner, U. (1979). *The ecology of human development: Experiments by nature and design.* Cambridge: Harvard University Press.

Bronfenbrenner, U. (1992). Ecological systems theory. In R. Vasta (Ed.), *Six theories of child development: Revised formulations and current issues* (pp. 187–248). Philadelphia: Jessica Kingsley.

Buysse, V., Bernier, K., & McWilliam, R. (2002). A statewide profile of early intervention services using the Part C data system. *Journal of Early Intervention, 25*(1), 15–26.

Buysse, V., Wesley, P., Synder, P., & Winton, P. (2006). Evidence-based practice: What does it really mean for the early childhood field? *Young Exceptional Children, 9,* 2–11.

Carolina Abecedarian Project (2006). *Summary of project outcomes.* Retrieved June 20, 2006, from http://www.fpg.unc.edu

Council for Exceptional Children (2003). *What every special educator must know: Ethics, standards, and guidelines for special educators* (5th ed.). Reston, VA: Council for Exceptional Children.

Crockenberg, S. B., & Smith, P. (2002). Antecedents of mother-infant interaction and infant irritability in the first 3 months of life. *Infant Behavior and Development, 25*(1), 2–15.

D'Amato, E., & Yoshida, R. K. (1991). Parental needs: An educational life cycle perspective. *Journal of Early Intervention, 15*(3), 246–254.

Dunst, C., Hamby, D., Trivette, C., Raab, M., & Bruder, M. (2000). Everyday family and community life and children's naturally occurring learning opportunities. *Journal of Early Intervention, 23*(3), 151–164.

FACETS: Family-Guided Approaches to Collaborative Early-Intervention Training and Services (2000). *Family-guided home visiting.* Retrieved June 1, 2005, from http://www.parsons.lsi.ku.edu/facets

Farver, J. (1999). Activity setting analysis: A model for examining the role of culture in development. In A. Goncu (Ed.), *Children's engagement in the world: Sociocultural perspectives* (pp. 99–127). Cambridge, England: Cambridge University Press.

Garguilo, R., & Kilgo, J. (2000). *Young children with special needs.* Albany, NY: Delmar.

Glascoe, F. (1999). Communicating with parents. *Young Exceptional Children, 2*(4), 17–25.

Grisham-Brown, J., & Pretti-Frontczak, K. (2003). Using planning time to individualize instruction for preschoolers with special needs. *Journal of Early Intervention, 26*(1), 31–46.

Guralnick, M. (1997). *The effectiveness of early intervention.* Baltimore, MD: Brookes.

Harbin, G. (2001). Implementing early intervention policy: Are we making progress? *Journal of Early Intervention, 24*(2), 103–105.

Heward, W. (2006). *Exceptional children: An introduction to special education.* Upper Saddle River, NJ: Merrill/Prentice Hall.

Horn, E., & Sandall, S. (2000). The visiting teacher: A model of inclusive ECSE service delivery. In S. Sandall & M. Ostrosky, *Natural environments and inclusion*

(YEC Monograph No. 2) (pp. 49–58). Longmont, CO: Sopris West.

Individuals with Disabilities Education Improvement Act (2004) Pub. L. No. 108–446.

Jitendra, A., Edwards, L., Choutka, C., & Treadway, P. (2002). A collaborative approach to planning in the content areas for students with learning disabilities: Accessing the general curriculum. *Learning Disabilities Research and Practice, 17,* 252–267.

Keogh, B., Bernheimer, L., & Guthrie, D. (2004). Children with developmental delays twenty years later: Where are they? How are they? *American Journal of Mental Retardation, 109,* 219–230.

Kilgo, J., Johnson, L., LaMontagne, M., Stayton, M., Cook, M., & Cooper, C. (1999). Importance of practices: A national study of general and special early childhood educators. *Journal of Early Intervention, 22*(4), 294–305.

La Paro, K., Olsen, K., & Pianta, R. (2002). Special education eligibility: Developmental precursors over the first three years of life. *Exceptional Children, 69*(1), 55–66.

Lea, D. (2006). "You don't know me like that": Patterns of disconnect between adolescent mothers of children with disabilities and their early interventionists. *Journal of Early Intervention, 28,* 264–282.

Lee, S., & Kahn, J. (1998). Relationships of child progress with selected child, family and program variables in early intervention. *Infant-Toddler Intervention, 8*(1), 85–101.

Malarz, L. (1996). Using staff development to create inclusive schools. *Journal of Staff Development, 17*(3), 15–17.

Martin, S., Ramey, C., & Ramey, S. (1990). The prevention of intellectual impairment in children of impoverished families: Findings in randomized trial of educational daycare. *American Journal of Public Health, 80,* 844–847.

McDonnell, A., Brownell, K., & Wolery, M. (2001). Teachers' views concerning individualized intervention and support roles within developmentally appropriate preschools. *Journal of Early Intervention, 24*(1), 67–83.

McLean, M., Synder, P., Smith, B., & Sandall, S. (2002). The DEC recommended practices in early intervention/early childhood special education: Social validity. *Journal of Early Intervention, 25*(2), 120–128.

Neimeyer, J., & Proctor, R. (l995). Facilitating family-centered competencies in early intervention. *Infant-Toddler Intervention, 5*(4), 315–324.

New IDEA delivers for students with disabilities (2005). *CEC Today, 12*(3), 1–6.

No Child Left Behind Act of 2001, Pub. L. No. 107–110, 115 Stat. 1425 (2002).

Odom, S., Brantlinger, E., Gersten, R., Horner, R., Thompson, B., & Harris, K. (2005). Research in special education: Scientific methods and evidence-based practices. *Exceptional Children, 71,* 137–148.

Odom, S., & Strain, P. (2002). Evidence-based practice in early intervention/early childhood special education: Single-subject design research. *Journal of Early Intervention, 25*(2), 152–160.

Odom, S., & Wolery, M. (2003). A unified theory of practice in early intervention/early childhood special education: Evidence-based practices. *Journal of Special Education, 37*(3), 164–173.

Park, J., Turnbull, A., & Turnbull, H. R. (2002). Impacts of poverty on quality of life in families of children with disabilities. *Exceptional Children, 68*(2), 151–170.

Parker, M. (2005, August 24). Law loosens special-education testing: No Child Left Behind required them to be tested at grade level. *Peoria Journal Star.* Retrieved August 25, 2005, from http://www.pjstar.com/stories

Peterson, C., Luze, G., Eshbaugh, E., Jeon, H., & Kantz, K. (2007). Enhancing parent-child interactions through home visiting: Promising practice or unfulfilled promise? *Journal of Early Intervention, 29,* 119–140.

Pretti-Frontczak, K., & Bricker, D. (2004). *An activity-based approach to early intervention* (3rd ed.). Baltimore, MD: Brookes.

Raab, M., & Dunst, C. (2004). Early intervention practitioner approaches to natural environment interventions. *Journal of Early Intervention, 27*(1), 15–26.

Raver, S. (1980). Ten rules for success in preschool mainstreaming. *Education Unlimited, 2,* 47–52.

Raver, S. (1999). *Intervention strategies for infants and toddlers with special needs: A team approach* (2nd ed.). Upper Saddle River, NJ: Merrill/Prentice Hall.

Raver, S. (2001) India: Training teachers of children with mental retardation. *International Journal of Special Education, 16*(1), 54–66.

Raver, S. (2003). Keeping track: Routine-based instruction and monitoring. *Young Exceptional Children, 6*(3), 12–20.

Richards, D. M. (1999). *Overview of Section 504.* Retrieved August 24, 2005, from http://www.504idea.org/504overview.html

Rous, B., Kohner-Coogle, M., & Stewart, J. (2004). *Links to early childhood standards.* Lexington, KY: University of Kentucky State Preschool Accountability Research Collaborative. Available at www.ihdi.uky.edu/Sparc

Rous, B., Lobianco, T., Moffett, C., & Lund, I. (2005). Building preschool accountability systems: Guidelines resulting from a national study. *Journal of Early Intervention, 28*(1), 50–64.

Sadler, F. H. (2003). The itinerant special education teacher in the early childhood classroom. *TEACHING Exceptional Children, 35*(3), 8–15.

Salend, S. (2005). *Creating inclusive classrooms: Effective and reflective practices for all students* (5th ed.). Upper Saddle River, NJ: Merrill/Prentice-Hall.

Sandall, S., Hemmeter, M. L., Smith, B., & McLean, M. (2005). *DEC recommended practices: A comprehensive guide for practical application in early intervention/early childhood special education.* Longmont, CO: Sopris West.

Sandall, S., Smith, B., McLean, M., & Ramsey, A. (2002). Qualitative research in early intervention/early childhood special education. *Journal of Early Intervention, 25*(2), 129–136.

Scarborough, A., Spiker, D., Mallik, S., Hebbeler, K., Bailey, D., & Simeonsson, R. (2004). A national look at children and families entering early intervention. *Exceptional Children, 70*(4), 469–483.

Smith, B., Strain, P., Synder, P., Sandall, S., McLean, M., Ramsey, A., & Sumi, W. (2002). DEC recommended practices: A review of 9 years of EI/ECSE research literature. *Journal of Early Intervention, 25*(2), 108–119.

Turnbull, R., Huerta, N., & Stowe, M. (2006). *The Individuals with Disabilities Education Act as amended in 2004.* Upper Saddle River, NJ: Merrill/Prentice Hall.

U.S. Department of Education, Office of Special Education and Rehabilitative Services (1997). *Annual report to Congress on the implementation of the Individuals with Disabilities Education Act.* Washington, DC: Author.

U.S. Department of Health and Human Services (1986). *The status of handicapped children in Head Start programs.* Washington, DC: U.S. Government Printing Office.

Wehman, T., & Gilkerson, L. (1999). Parents of young children with special needs speak out: Perceptions of early intervention services. *Infant-Toddler Intervention, 9*(2), 137–167.

Wesley, P., Buysse, V., & Skinner, D. (2001). Early interventionists' perspectives on professional comfort as consultants. *Journal of Early Intervention, 24*(2), 112–128.

Wolery, M. (2001). Embedding time delay procedures in classroom activities. In S. Sandall & M. Ostrosky, *Teaching strategies: What to do to support young children's development* (YEC Monograph No. 3) (pp. 81–90). Longmont, CO: Sopris West.

Wolery, M., & Bailey, D. (2002). Early childhood special education research. *Journal of Early Intervention, 25*(2), 88–99.

Wood, C. (2003). Defining special education. In W. L. Heward, *Exceptional children: An introduction to special education.* (pp. 6–45). Upper Saddle River, NJ: Merrill/Prentice Hall.

Yell, M. L. (2006). *The law and special education* (2nd ed.). Upper Saddle River, NJ: Merrill/Prentice Hall.

Zeanah, C., Boris, N., & Larrieu, J. (1997). Infant development and developmental risk: A review of the past 10 years. *Journal of the American Academy of Child and Adolescent Psychiatry, 36*(2), 165–178.

Chapter

2

Building Partnerships
in Culturally/Linguistically
Diverse Settings

Jennifer L. Kilgo

Sharon A. Raver

Overview

This chapter discusses issues related to creating partnerships with families and building teams with families and other professionals, including

building partnerships with families

communication with parents and professionals

the family systems approach

serving families from culturally/ethnically/linguistically diverse
    backgrounds

parent's personal rights

building effective teams

CASE STUDY: Rachel's Mother Speaks Out

At 32 months of age, Rachel, the ninth of ten children, was referred to a pre-school program for children with developmental delays by the family's pediatrician. An arena assessment revealed that Rachel had significant communicative, cognitive, and fine motor delays. Since Rachel's mother worked days, Rachel attended a full-day preschool intervention program, and once-a-month home visits were scheduled for evenings.

At 5 years old, based on a later team assessment, Rachel's mother agreed with school officials that a separate kindergarten class for children with developmental delays would be the best placement for improving Rachel's continuing communication and learning needs. At the end of kindergarten, Rachel was reassessed and determined to meet the requirements for services for children with moderate mental retardation. Since Rachel's tantrums had grown more severe in kindergarten, a behavior plan focusing on improving self-control and verbal compliance was added to her Individualized Education Program (IEP). Now in third grade, Rachel attends a separate classroom for students with moderate mental retardation. She enjoys music, physical education, and lunch with other children her age. Her program focuses on providing survival academics, expanding her independent living skills, and increasing appropriate social interactions with peers and adults. Today, her mother reports: "I work with Rach the best I can. I want her to learn how to swim . . . it would be good if she could do more with the regular third grade classes too."

Services for young children with special needs have always emphasized the importance of parental involvement. Professionals recognize that their support can benefit families. They also understand that when families are involved, children have an opportunity to receive more intervention because professionals can teach family members how to support the child's development when the professionals are not present. The field of early childhood special education (ECSE) acknowledges that parents can be the best advocates for their children when they are armed with information, encouragement, and optimism (Trivette & Dunst, 2004). The way in which families react to the new circumstances imposed by the diagnosis of a disability or a developmental delay may influence how families utilize services.

BUILDING PARTNERSHIPS WITH FAMILIES

A disability is a culturally and socially constructed phenomenon; thus, each society defines the parameters of what is considered "typical" (Linan-Thompson & Jean, 1997). Parents, siblings, and extended family members often respond to a disability or a developmental delay in different ways.

Impact of a Disability/Developmental Delay on Parents

Parents often do not perceive a disability the same way as professionals do, especially when the diagnosis involves very young children. The literature on this topic suggests that parents vary in their early reactions and that most parents go through a significant period of adjustment. Some have reported that families tend to move through a "grief cycle" of shock, denial, guilt, anger, shame and depression, and acceptance following a diagnosis (Turnbull & Turnbull, 2001). However, the idea of a stage or cycle theory of adjustment is probably an oversimplification of a very complex process that families experience (Gallagher, Fialka,

Rhodes, & Arceneaux, 2003; Raver, 1999). Within the same family, mothers and fathers may experience different emotions and rarely have the same feelings at the same time. The sequence of reactions and the time needed for adjustment are different for each parent—and for each family. Developing a personalized approach to *each child*, and *each family*, is a core tenet of ECSE practices (Bailey et al., 2006; Woods & McCormick, 2002). Professionals should not expect parents to integrate new information about their child in the same manner or within the same time frame as professionals do (Gallagher et al, 2003).

Impact of a Disability/Developmental Delay on Siblings

The way in which siblings adjust is strongly influenced by the responses and dynamics of their family. Parents' attitudes about a disability are potent in shaping a sibling's adjustment. The emotional climate in some families may be so unstable that the adjustment of siblings may be unfavorable even if the child with a disability was not considered. In other families, siblings' needs may be neglected due to disproportionate parental time devoted to the child with special needs. For this reason, professionals must play a role in supporting parents in their efforts to create a *balanced* family life (Kilgo & Raver, 1999). A balanced family is one in which the needs of all members are appropriately and equally addressed.

Encouraging open communication regarding both positive and negative feelings can aid sibling adjustment. Brothers and sisters often have concerns about their sibling's disability or developmental delay, such as (1) uncertainty regarding the cause of the disability/developmental delay and its effect on them, (2) uneasiness over the reactions of their friends, (3) feelings of being left out, and (4) resentment about being required to do more for the child with special needs (Dyson, Edgar, & Crnic, 1989; Summers, Bridge, & Summers, 1991). Siblings need accurate information about a disability/developmental delay to prevent fears that may stem from misunderstandings. It is beneficial for professionals to promote strong sibling relationships in families. When there are strong bonds, children with disabilities or developmental delays tend to develop better social skills, and families seem to enjoy less stress.

Impact of a Disability/Developmental Delay on Extended Family

Extended family is a term used to identify family members outside the immediate family, such as grandparents, aunts, uncles, and cousins (Kilgo et al., 1999). These individuals may experience varying reactions to the diagnosis of a disability or developmental delay. Grandparents, for example, may experience sorrow for their grandchildren and express concerns about their own children's burdens and responsibilities in caring for a child with special needs (Sandler, Warren, & Raver, 1995).

Because of the transactional nature of human relationships, each immediate and each extended family member operates as both an agent for change and a target of influence on others. Extended family members, particularly grandparents, may provide support, comfort, and understanding (Sandler et al., 1995). Or, when there is significant difficulty with adjustment, grandparents may be of limited assistance to parents. In fact, some families may perceive extended family members as additional burdens to their own adjustment.

Not all reactions to the diagnosis of a disability/developmental delay and the subsequent influences on a family can be characterized as negative (Turnbull, Turnbull, Erwin, & Soodak, 2006). Despite the fact that the professional literature tends to minimize the positive influences of a child with a disability/developmental delay on family life, many parents and families make successful adjustments to their situation and report positive effects, such as increased family cohesion and a renewed appreciation for life (Raver, 2005; Turnbull & Turnbull, 2001). Over time, most parents and extended family members rebuild their hopes and dreams and learn to adapt to the new circumstances of their lives, while remaining steadfast in their commitment to their child with a disability (Gallagher et al., 2003). The reactions of parents, siblings, and extended family members are important, since ECSE professionals are committed to working with the entire family, not merely the child. To do this, professionals need a sound understanding of the family-based approach.

A Family-Based Approach

Under a **family-based approach**, professionals view parents as active collaborators in assessing the child and, planning and implementing interventions before the child enters kindergarten and as active collaborators in planning and selecting service options when the child is in first through third grade. Particularly in infant-toddler and preschool programs, increases in the intensity of intervention and the level of participation by children and their families have been linked to more positive outcomes in children (Guralnick, 1997; Ramey & Ramey, 1992).

The literature suggests that the earlier family involvement occurs, the better it is for a child who is developmentally vulnerable (Moeller, 2000). Family-based practices rest on three broad assumptions (Bailey, Buysse, Edmondson, & Smith, 1992; Sandall, Hemmeter, Smith, & McLean, 2005):

❑ Involving and supporting families is a more powerful intervention than one that focuses exclusively on a child.

❑ Encouraging family members to choose their level of involvement in program planning, decision making, and service delivery benefits both the child and the family.

❑ Using family priorities for goals and services benefits the child and the family.

Professionals do not have to ask how to get families more involved in their child's educational needs. Families are *already* involved simply by being a family. The question professionals need to ask is, What amount and type of involvement might be best for a child and his or her family. The family-based approach to providing services requires professionals to develop specific ways of perceiving and interacting with children and families (Turnbull et al., 2007). Figure 2.1 summarizes the philosophy, attitudes, processes, and approaches of family-based practices. Each of these aspects of family-based practices will be discussed.

Philosophy Guiding the Family-Based Approach.

The family-based approach hinges on the belief that the overwhelming majority of parents of children with special needs possess the emotional investment necessary to encourage, motivate, and support their child's development, particularly when professionals give them the appropriate knowledge and skills supports (Trivette & Dunst, 2005). It acknowledges that children, and their families, possess strengths that are as important as their needs. ECSE personnel operate from an assets model of intervention—not from a deficits model—and assume a **strengths-based approach** to conceptualizing child and family supports.

However, in actual practice, this philosophy may be more the ideal than the reality of how programs serve families. For example, staff from 40 Early Head Start programs in six states stated that they believed in the importance of the family-based model of intervention (e.g., family-professional partnerships, a strength-based approach, family decision making), but their actual practices revealed that this model was inconsistently implemented (Zhang & Bennett, 2001b).

A principal objective of family-based practices is to enhance parents' confidence in their ability to parent and encourage their child's progress (Dunst, 2001). Professionals who believe parents are capable of supporting their children communicate this belief. Trivette and Dunst (2004) found that a staff's strong beliefs about parents' abilities to support their child's learning are linked to more positive parental judgments about their parenting competence. That is, when professionals appropriately guide family members in supporting their child's development and communicate their belief that parents are competent supporters of their child's learning, family members tend to be more positive in evaluating their own abilities to promote positive outcomes. Appendix C lists websites that may be useful resources for families and professionals.

Attitudes Guiding the Family-Based Approach.

Family members, not professionals, provide the majority of direct intervention to children with special needs until they enter kindergarten or first grade. Since parents take such a direct role in intervention, professionals attempt to develop educational plans that focus on their child's needs as well as his or her strengths. In the broadest sense, a child's strengths are those aspects of the child's personality or abilities that are received positively by others (Dunst, Herter, & Shields, 2000). Assessment tools are generally effective in identifying a child's needs, but many may not be

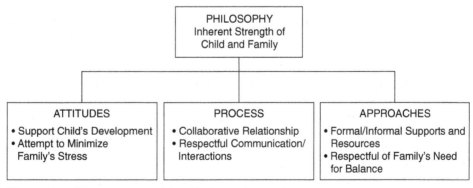

Figure 2.1 Dimensions of family-based practices

as adequate in identifying the full spectrum of the child's strengths.

For example, 4-year-old Nicholas, who has hemiplegic cerebral palsy, resulting in significant weakness on the right side of his body, was assessed by a multidisciplinary team. The team members reported that he had fine motor needs (e.g., difficulty using both hands together with coordination in repetitive tasks, difficulty stabilizing materials with his right hand while he activated them with his left) as well as gross motor needs (e.g., difficulty with motor planning when stooping and recovering, difficulty with balance while running). The team members also made an effort to report many of Nicholas's strengths, some of which were gained through observation, not formal assessments. The team's assessment report stated: "Nicholas has a sunny personality—he laughs easily, is eager to learn, loves computer games and enjoys physical games like tag and soccer. . . ." By using these positive characteristics—that is, his strengths—the team, with the help of his parents, was able to develop intervention activities that used Nicholas's unique abilities and interests. His preschool and home objectives were written this way:

1) While in his preschool class, Nicholas will play computer games with Martin that require both hands to manipulate for at least 15 minutes, 3 times a week and play computer games at home with his sister, Kara, for 30 minutes each day.

2) While in his preschool class, Nicholas will play running games at least 3 times a week, with no more than 3 falls each time, and play soccer with his sister and Dad at least once each weekend with no more than 3 falls each time.

Also guiding the family-based approach is the attitude that ECSE professionals are committed to supporting parents in their efforts to manage family stress. As a group, families of children with disabilities appear to be susceptible to increased stress; report feelings of isolation from friends, neighbors, and their community; and may have smaller supportive networks than families with children without special needs (Kazak & Marvin, 1984). All parents have to cope with stress at one time or another, but parents of children with special needs tend to have additional daily stressors that may impede a child's development (Hooste & Maes, 2003). Unfortunately, even exemplary services may inadvertently introduce stress into a family's life (Wehman & Gilkerson, 1999). Professionals must take special care in the way they manage services so unintended stress is never introduced.

Processes Guiding the Family-Based Approach. Family-based practices advocate that professionals develop collaborative relationships with families. Basic interpersonal skills—such as following through on plans and paying attention during conversations, for example—are courtesies viewed as critical to successful collaboration from parents' point of view (Dinnebeil, Fox, & Rule, 1998). Professionals who display tact and honesty in presenting information in an understandable way tend to be most successful.

To help children realize their potential and to support families, professionals offer formal and informal supports and resources (McWilliam, Tocci, & Harbin, 1998). **Formal supports and resources** are services that promote a child's development and support family life, such as making home visits, providing consultative services, giving assistance with locating information, providing therapies (speech-language/physical/occupational), and making referrals to specialists (Cooper & Allred, 1992) (e.g., a referral to a community health nurse when a child is having difficulty gaining weight). For primary-aged students, formal supports might involve providing regular communication or interaction with families through individual weekly reports, sending "positive" notes commenting on a specific accomplishment, publishing a class newsletter, organizing a parent group meeting, sending home copies of articles from *Exceptional Parent* that may be interesting or useful to families, and organizing a workshop on parent-identified topics (Dardig, 2005).

Informal supports and resources involve making contacts with other families (those with and without children with special needs) and offering information about community programs, such as Family Fun Dates at the public library, as well as providing emotional support. For example, Rachel's mother in the case study noted that contact with other families and their children was one of the most positive aspects of the assistance she received from ECSE services.

Delivery of Supports and Services. All supports should be offered in a *competency-enhancing* manner. A competency-enhancing manner:

1) avoids overwhelming a family with information or services,

2) uses a supportive communication style, and

3) mobilizes resources in ways that do not disrupt family life. (Brinker, Pretti-Frontczak, Johnson, & Straka, 2002)

It is the job of professionals to ensure that families are supported, not overburdened.

Use of Family Routines. A common strategy used with the family-based approach is that of "natural learning opportunities" (Dunst et al., 2000; McWilliam, 2000; Dunst, 2001; Raver, 2004). When working with infants and toddlers particularly, professionals do not remove a family from its natural environment, but rather work with a family to make its environment more responsive to their child's needs.

For example, 7-year-old Michael, who has Down syndrome, spends most Saturdays with his family on the softball field, watching his older brother's games or practices. Michael is a second grader in a general education class. He works with a resource teacher one hour a day, five days a week. Michael's educational team (e.g., resource teacher, general education teacher, parents) decided that softball games offered Michael a good natural learning opportunity in which to practice some of his learning objectives. Therefore, Michael's mother and teachers developed these objectives for games:

1) Michael will write 3 sentences about what is happening with at least 5 words in each sentence.

Parents report that using family routines to teach skills to their children saves time and makes learning more enjoyable for their children.

David Mager/Pearson Learning Photo Studio

2) Michael will match color words and clothing words with the clothing of the spectators and players on the field.

3) Michael will keep track of the number of hits, runs, and fouls and compare them (using subtraction) with the statistics of the previous week's game.

Michael's mother, who is single and working full-time, struggles to meet the needs her two children. In short, this mother, like all parents, must attempt to balance the needs of her whole family, not merely address Michael's needs. Parents need support from professionals in their relentless struggle to ration their limited physical, emotional, and financial resources. To accomplish this, professionals need to develop exemplary communication skills.

COMMUNICATING WITH PARENTS AND PROFESSIONALS

A central component of any positive relationship is effective communication. **Communication** is a process by which information and feelings are sent between and received by individuals. The importance of effective communication in developing respectful interactions with family members cannot be overstated (Whitbread, Bruder, Fleming, & Park, 2007). Respectful interactions stem from professionals' commitment to being nonjudgmental about families' values, beliefs, and lifestyles (Zhang & Bennett, 2001a). Professionals who demonstrate understanding of and empathy for a family's beliefs tend to be more effective in family relationships.

The way in which professionals communicate with families has a direct impact on parent-professional relationships (Banks, Santos, & Roof, 2003). Parents must be given the time they need to brainstorm options and make decisions (Raver & Lambert, 1995). Despite the fact that professionals seem to be always pressed for time, there is a price for not providing families with the time necessary to consider important life decisions. If adequate support is not given, over time parents may experience increased anxiety and stress, develop decreased respect for professionals, and develop increased dissatisfaction with services.

Unfortunately, some professionals are unaware that their communication skills make it difficult for family members to form warm relationships with them. Effective communication skills demand practice and experience. Because communication skills are the platform for all effective intervention, ECSE personnel must commit to developing these skills with the same professional dedication that they devote to developing other skills related to serving children and families. Good communication involves the use of nonverbal and verbal communication techniques.

Nonverbal Communication Skills

Eighty-five percent of all information conveyed is communicated nonverbally. Nonverbal communication uses body language, including gestures, facial expressions, posture, and body movements that convey information. It is important to learn to monitor one's body language, to respond to others' body language, to become familiar with nonverbal

signals, and to note discrepancies in nonverbal and verbal messages (Kilgo et al., 1999). Nonverbal communication requires one to attend to physical surroundings and be a good listener. Table 2.1 provides a list of desirable nonverbal and verbal communication behaviors.

Control Physical Surroundings. Attending to another person, either visually or auditorily, can be difficult when there are distractions. Minor physical barriers to quality communication can often be controlled (Kilgo et al., 1999). For instance, light distractions, such as a television playing during a home visit, can be eliminated by scheduling visits when they do not interfere with favorite programs or asking to have the

TABLE 2.1 Desirable nonverbal and verbal behaviors used in effective communication

Facial Expressions

Comfortable eye contact
Warmth and concern reflected in facial expression
Eyes at same level as communication partner
Appropriately varied and animated facial
    expressions
Mouth relaxed
Occasional smiles, when appropriate

Posture

Arms and hands moderately expressive
Use of appropriate gestures
Body leaning slightly forward (attentive, but
    relaxed)
Arms resting on arm of chair or on table
Absence of repetitive movements (e.g., tapping
    pen, shaking foot)

Voice

Clearly audible, but not loud
Warmth in tone of voice
Natural speech tempo

Physical Proximity

Three to five feet between chairs/speakers

sound turned down during a visit. Sibling interferences during home visits or school conferences can be handled by having special toys for siblings, structuring activities for siblings, or giving siblings some role in the intervention activities.

Be a Good Listener. The importance of listening cannot be overemphasized. A common complaint of parents is that professionals do not listen to them (Montgomery, 2005). Most professionals say they do listen, but in actuality, a good listener is a rare find. Many individuals use the time the other person is speaking to plan their own points and outline their own agenda.

Quality listening is an *active process*, requiring conscious attending skills. An active listener leans slightly forward and maintains more than the usual amount of eye contact during a conversation. A relaxed and alert face-to-face position, within a comfortable distance, and natural gestures demonstrate that the listener is attentive. Quality listening is expressed nonverbally and/or verbally.

Verbal Communication Skills

The techniques of using minimal encouragers, reflecting content and emotions, using appropriate questioning, avoiding jargon, reframing, and structuring are the foundations of effective verbal communication with parents, family members, and other professionals.

Use Minimal Encouragers. These are brief statements or gestures made by an individual, such as "uh-huh," "yes," a slight head nod, or a smile, that indicate to the communication partner that the listener wants him or her to continue talking.

Use Reflecting Content and Emotions. Reflecting **content** is a method used by the listener to determine if he or she correctly understood what the speaker said. The listener paraphrases what was said, such as, "So the doctor left you waiting for an hour and a half?" **Reflecting emotions** refers to the ability of the listener to identify how the speaker really feels, even if the speaker may not

verbally express those feelings (Kilgo et al., 1999). It involves accepting or clarifying the feelings of another in a nonthreatening manner. The process requires one to listen for feeling words (e.g., "hurt," "frustrated"), listen for the emotional content of a message, observe body language, and ask one's self, "What would *I* feel if this were *me*?" The professional then describes the feelings he or she is observing by saying something like "It upset you when the doctor left you waiting for so long?" or "I can see that waiting that long really bothered you." Such statements demonstrate that the professional is listening empathically.

Research has found that in interviews when a family member expresses feelings, most professionals tend to react to the *content* of the statement, not to the expression of *feelings* (Brady, Peters, Gamel-McCormick, & Venuto, 2004). Generally, it is best to acknowledge the feelings first and then move on to supplying information or content. For example, if during a home visit a mother states, "I really want her to walk but she isn't even sitting," a professional should validate the feelings in this statement *first* and then begin to supply information about when this mother might be able to expect her child to walk. To acknowledge the emotion or feeling in that statement, a professional could make a comment like "It can be disappointing that she is developing more slowly than her sister." Whatever phrase or comment is used, it must sound sincere and be integrated naturally into each professional's communication style.

Use Effective Questioning. Johnson, McGonigel, and Kauffman (1989) describe effective questioning as the ability to ask questions in a manner in which desired information will be disclosed. They state there are two types of questions: closed-ended and open-ended. A closed-ended question can usually be answered with "yes," "no," or another brief response (Kilgo et al., 1999). Closed-ended questions request specific information: "Does Maria-Kay have seizures?" "What does Maria-Kay eat for breakfast?" When more information is desired, open-ended questions are used. Open-ended questions elicit more complete responses. Questions such as "Can you tell me about Maria-Kay's seizures?" and "How are mealtimes with Maria-Kay?" allow parents to more completely describe their observations, concerns and perceptions.

Questions that inhibit freedom of response such as "You don't have difficulty feeding Maria-Kay, do you?" should always be avoided. This type of question can make parents feel that their behavior is incorrect or unacceptable.

The use of appropriate questioning can guide parents in generating goals and solutions to their problems. For example, "What would you like to see Maria-Kay doing at mealtimes?" and "How can we help Maria-Kay learn to feed herself?" clearly communicate that intervention involves "shared problem solving." These questions also help professionals avoid offering solutions too quickly, which may block or hinder joint problem solving (Friend & Cook, 2007). For instance, instead of saying "Well, she does that because . . ." and begin to immediately offer an explanation and solution, it is usually better to get information about a parent's perspective on the subject first by asking something such as "Why do you think she is doing that?" In this way, professionals are involving parents in a process of brainstorming that is more likely to result in collaborative solutions.

Control the Use of Jargon.

Communication is effective only when everyone involved understands the message. Professional jargon may interfere with clarity and may serve as a barrier to developing quality relationships with parents as well as other team members. Occasionally, professionals may have to use a term that is unfamiliar to a parent or team member because the term is the most accurate descriptor. When this is the case, the new term must be defined so it becomes a part of professionals' and parents' shared language. A mother of an infant who was recently diagnosed with a malignant brain tumor offered this perspective: "I feel like I need a medical dictionary to just talk to the doctors and intervention people I see. After awhile, I ask them to write things down and I look it up when I get home.

But half the time, I nod and act like I'm not stupid and completely lost. Sometimes, I leave with knots in my stomach."

Use Reframing.

Reframing involves defining a situation in a more positive way to promote coping. Usually, the special strengths or positive qualities of a situation or a child may be emphasized to facilitate assimilation of information. For example, when a mother learned that her 14-month-old son was deaf, she used reframing when she stated: "Well, the fact that Jordan is smart and stubborn will probably help him, even with being deaf." This mother took a difficult situation and framed it in a way that made it more manageable for her. Professionals tend to use reframing frequently in their conversations with families and other professionals.

Use Structuring.

Having a structure for interactions with parents ensures more effective communication. There are five components for structuring productive meetings, interviews, or conferences. First, before the meeting, the purpose of the meeting and the time allotted should be stated—and understood—by everyone involved. Second, at the onset of the meeting, the objectives, activities, or tasks to be accomplished need to be stated. Third, a "cute child story" is a good ice breaker and is usually appreciated by family members before formal business is addressed. This is a brief, specific story that captures the child's unique strengths or characteristics (Raver, 1997). Global comments such as "He is a wonderful little boy" seem less genuine than a specific story that reveals some quality of the child or some recent accomplishment. The purpose of the story is to create a positive emotional connection with parents. For example, a second-grade teacher of a student with a learning disability said this to the child's father during a school conference:

Before we begin, I want to share something that happened last week. Benny earned 15 minutes with the Math Blaster program (computer program) for following classroom rules last Thursday. The computer is usually his choice for a reward, but Thursday he asked if he could share his minutes with Angelo. They had a lot of fun trying to beat one another.

If a child is unfamiliar to a professional, then a general, positive comment about the child and/or family can be made. A professional might say, for example, "We are excited you contacted our program. We already have one set of twins enrolled, and I'm sure your boys will be just as much fun."

Fourth, professionals need to ask many open-ended questions to ensure that a family's priorities and concerns are addressed; for example, they might ask, "What concerns or topics would you like us to discuss today?" The fifth component of structuring is verbally summarizing what was accomplished and agreed to at the end of the conference. Summaries are best when they are handled with a sense of congeniality and a touch of humor.

Use Negotiation. Especially when initially accepting special education services, some parents experience intense feelings of powerlessness as they grieve and attempt to adjust (Stonestreet, Johnston, & Acton, 1991). These feelings may trigger anger or hostility toward a system or an individual that seems unable to "fix" their child.

Whenever hostility or disagreement is expressed, professionals need to resolve it swiftly. It is best to remain calm, soften one's voice, and permit parents to express their point of view with little interruption, except to ask for elaborations or clarifications. The key ingredient to resolving conflict is listening empathetically (e.g., "How would I feel if I were this parent?"), rather than trying to place blame or defend one's actions.

To diffuse a confrontation, professionals must make sincere efforts to come to a mutually acceptable resolution. Although there is never just one way to handle any situation, generally if professionals acknowledge the legitimacy of family members' strong feelings (or colleagues' feelings), negotiation will follow. Professionals build trust when they avoid becoming defensive.

Frequently eliciting and interpreting parents' concerns and priorities ensures that parents have an opportunity to discuss their child's development and behavior frequently with a concerned, invested professional. However, Glascoe (1999) found that when professionals do not repeatedly, and directly, elicit parents' concerns, almost 40% of the families surveyed reported that they did not share their worries with professionals. Regularly "checking in" with families seems to be necessary to laying the foundation for negotiating and building relationships with parents. Practicing communication strategies during supervised role-play situations seems to be an effective way of changing professionals' behavior.

THE FAMILY SYSTEMS APPROACH

The family systems approach considers the roles of different family members, the role of a family in larger social networks, and the impact of family and

Liz Moore/Merrill

To avoid common problems, teams should develop a mission statement, discuss a plan for managing conflicts, and participate in team building activities.

social networks on intervention (Healy, Keesee, & Smith, 1989). Family systems theory is a way of conceptualizing how family characteristics, family interactions, and family functions impact a family's adaptation to critical events. Understanding this model permits ECSE professionals to more effectively support very young children, and their families, through what may feel like a maze of services and regulations.

Family systems theory views family members as interrelated; what happens to one member of a family affects all members in some way. Similarly, it follows that whatever benefits the child will benefit the family. Turnbull and colleagues (Turnbull, Turnbull, Erwin, & Soodak, 2006) compare the family systems perspective to the metaphor of a mobile. They state: "If you put one part of a mobile into action, you will create motion in all of the other parts. This is how it is with families, too: the characteristics of family members, their ways of interacting with each other . . . and how they move through the stages of their lives" (p. 3). Thus, children and parents are changed by the process of living together (Smith, Gartin, Murdick, & Hilton, 2006). Family characteristics, family interactions, and family functions will be discussed.

Family Characteristics

Family characteristics are attributes of a family that a family shares as a unit. For example, a family's size, its cultural background, its socioeconomic status, the characteristics of individual members, and the life management skills of the parents are characteristics that may influence a family's adaptation. Clearly, an unemployed single mother who lives with two children in a dangerous neighborhood has different characteristics and resources than an upper-income, two-parent family. As discussed earlier in the ecological model, the severity of a child's disability, physical appearance, temperament, and behavior can influence a family's adjustment and functioning. It has been found that families whose members display physical and mental well-being,

whether drawn from spiritual or personal belief systems, tend to have more resources to draw on during periods of stress (Skinner, Rodriquez, & Bailey, 1999).

Family Interaction

Family interaction involves the relationships between individual members and subsystems. Relationships within families can be discussed within four subsystems: (1) marital (husband-wife), (2) parental (parent-child), (3) sibling (child-child), and (4) extended family (grandparents, aunts, uncles) (Turnbull et al., 2006).

Family systems theory predicts that subsystems are biased toward preserving stability and established roles. Consequently, a family member may inadvertently or deliberately undermine changes in parenting behavior that are being encouraged by professionals. If significant changes occur in family roles, and in the balance of power among members, roles in a family may be disrupted. Each family member has his or her own needs and abilities, and if these clash, there can be conflict.

When family conditions change, as with the birth of a child with a disability, dramatic changes may occur in the roles of individuals within the family. An illustration of this is revealed in this mother's remarks:

Before our child I was always the one who took care of the details and kept us going as a family. But after we adopted Mark, and then found out he had so many disabilities, I fell to pieces. Since Mark, our responsibilities have switched. . . . Now [my husband] does the big stuff because I just can't seem to get myself organized.

Family Functions

Family functions involve the needs that families are responsible for, such as economic needs, daily care, recreation needs, socialization needs, affection needs, and educational/vocational tasks (Turnbull et al., 2006). A child with special needs may use energy that was previously available for siblings, the marital relationship, and extended family. On occasion, family outcomes on Individualized Family Service Plans (IFSPs) address concerns associated with family functioning. For example, a mother forced to return to work to cover the costs of her child's medical needs now must find reliable child care as well as accommodating changes in how family duties will be distributed. When professionals help this mother meet these needs, all members of the family, including the child, benefit.

Developing Professional–Family Partnerships in Planning

Too often partnerships between families and professionals fall short of recommended practice, particularly with school-aged children (Summers et al., 2005). Although the term *partnership* is now commonly used, there are four misunderstandings professionals tend to exhibit regarding the concept of professional-family partnerships (Fletcher & Deal, 1993). The first is the belief that a partnership is a type of friendship. Although partnerships with families may be cordial and supportive, there is a professional boundary established that is rarely present in friendships.

A second misconception is that there is a 50/50 division of responsibility. In reality, no relationship is a true 50/50 split of effort. Because of training and experience, it is appropriate for professionals to assume more responsibility.

A third fallacy is that ECSE professionals address only the goals and concerns that are indicated as priorities by parents (Sandall et al., 2005). Fortunately, more often than not, professionals and parents agree on areas of concern. However, when differences occur, it is important that professionals avoid forcing their values on families. It is important that professionals demonstrate an understanding of each family's perspective, but they are also obligated to communicate their concerns to parents when they encounter decisions that they fear may negatively impact a child and/or a family.

A final misconception is that it takes too much time to build partnerships. The reality is that the ECSE field is a relationship-oriented discipline. Without a relationship with the child, and the child's family, it is impossible for professionals to make meaningful changes. ESCE professionals tend to develop strong, lasting relationships with families that are undoubtedly strengthened by the amount of time shared (Kilgo et al., 1999).

Time is a fundamental resource for any family (Brotherson & Goldstein, 1992). When time is not available, it can present a significant constraint and become one of the major stresses in families' lives. In the process of offering services, it is essential that professionals understand the importance of the efficient use of time and recognize it as a resource that is painfully limited for many families.

SERVING FAMILIES FROM CULTURALLY/ETHNICALLY/ LINGUISTICALLY DIVERSE BACKGROUNDS

Families receiving services are becoming increasingly culturally, linguistically, and ethnically diverse (Correa & Heward, 2003). In fact, ethnic minorities are one-third of the total population receiving early intervention services (Lynch & Hanson, 2004). However, because most professionals are not minorities, there can be a poor match between the background of professionals and that of the families they serve.

Culture influences a family's attitude about illness and about a child's disability as well as its structure and identity, child-rearing practices, communication style, choice of intervention goals, and view of professionals (Kilgo et al., 1999). An understanding of multicultural views will enable professionals to improve their practice and encourage full participation with families (Hains et al., 2005).

Culture is not a static concept; there is considerable variation within cultural groups, caused by social class, geographic location, and generational status. Families must be viewed by professionals as unique units that are influenced, but not defined, by their culture and ethnicity. *DEC Recommended Practices* (Sandall et al., 2005) indicates that family-professional relationship building should be "accomplished in ways that are responsive to cultural, language, and other family characteristics" (p. 114). Professionals need to avoid the assumption that all individuals within a cultural group react in a predetermined manner. Such assumptions lead to stereotyping, which limits understanding and is difficult to overcome (Matuszny, Banda, & Coleman, 2007). Professionals may find that some families value self-sufficiency and prefer to keep family problems and issues private. Recognizing this value can help professionals use this as a starting point for addressing a child's needs (Banks et al., 2003; Santos & McCollum, 2007).

Having cultural knowledge and being culturally sensitive do not mean professionals know everything about the cultures they serve. Yet at the most fundamental level, cultural sensitivity implies a refusal to assign values—such as better or worse, more or less intelligent, right or wrong—to cultural differences and similarities (Al-Hassan & Gardner, 2002). To serve children and families with diverse cultural, ethnic, or linguistic backgrounds, professionals should

❑ develop a program commitment to honor diversity and find or adapt materials to ensure they respect, reflect, and include the values, beliefs, and customs of intended users (Corso, Santos, & Roof, 2002);

❑ individualize interactions with parents in a way similar to that which they use with children;

❑ take the time necessary to establish the trust needed to fully involve all families;

❑ use bilingual and bicultural staff, mediators, and/or translators;

❑ participate in staff training in multicultural practices and knowledge; and

❑ conduct ongoing discussions with practitioners, parents, policy makers, and members of the cultural/ethnic communities a program serves.

Until these practices are commonplace in all programs, it should come as no surprise that parents of color and other traditionally underrepresented groups are reported as having lower levels of involvement in early education than other groups (Arcia & Gallagher, 1993). Similarly, minority parents of primary-aged children tend to be less involved and less informed than other parents (Linan-Thompson & Jean, 1997). Differences in perspectives between school and home, especially for primary-aged children with learning problems, can be a source of distrust and confusion for parents. Good intentions alone will not produce appropriate services. How responsive programs are to diversity will directly impact the level of participation families enjoy.

Parents' Personal Rights

Besides the legal rights outlined in the Individuals with Disabilities Education Act (IDEA), parents have the right to be parents and to approach the early intervention process differently than professionals do (Kilgo et al., 1999). To encourage families to develop self-advocacy and take control of their lives, professionals must acknowledge that parents have the following personal rights (Ferrell, 1985).

The Right to Feel Angry

Little in life prepares someone for parenting a child with special needs. The anger parents feel often comes from not being able to control, or change, the situation. Professionals can help parents manage their anger by getting them involved with the intervention/teaching process or by systematically directing the anger toward securing what they consider the best services for their child (Raver & Kilgo, 1991).

The Right to Seek Another Opinion

It is considered good practice to seek a second opinion with major medical decisions. Parents may choose to exercise that prerogative if they do not like a diagnosis or intervention plan. It is unwise for professionals to take this search for information personally. The process of searching for answers can afford parents a small sense of control over their lives, can allow them to learn more about their child's condition or needs, and may facilitate adaptation and empowerment in the long term.

The Right to Stop Trying

Parents must learn to protect their time and energy for the sake of their family. Even though from a professional's point of view, a suggested activity may take only ten minutes a day and be easily incorporated into the family's daily routines, for some exhausted parents, it may still be impossible some days. Professionals must respect parents' right to decide how time with their family will be used. Parents are attempting to balance their attention among all members of their family, not just their child with a disability/developmental delay. Fortunately, after some time off, many parents find new energy to return to the tasks that were postponed.

The Right to Be Annoyed with Their Child

No quality relationship is without its difficult times. The parents of a child with special needs may feel guilty for feeling disappointed or irritated with their child. To manage stress for long periods of time, parents need to be able to express their feelings and understand that their feelings toward their child will not always be all good, or all bad. Their child is a child first and a child with a disability/developmental delay second. All children can be annoying sometimes.

The Right to Be a Parent

It is unrealistic to expect parents to support their child's development *all* the time. Families need time to relax, to play without a goal, and to simply enjoy one another's company. Some activities that professionals suggest may not be natural for parents and may make them feel more like teachers than parents. Openly communicating to parents that having "up" and "down" days is all part of the adaptation process may help parents better understand the ebbs in their energy.

Early childhood special educators are treated with respect and dignity; parents deserve nothing less. Few say that parenting is easy, but most would agree that the majority of parents do the best job they can with the circumstances they face at any given moment. The efforts necessary to maintain family life can be overwhelming. Some parents become overstressed. A mother of a toddler with a disability had this to say:

Sometimes I feel I can't go on. [begins to cry softly] I am so tired and so sick of being pleasant and brave. Sometimes I just want to lock myself in my room and send everyone away—my husband, the kids, the therapists, and all those doctors we see every year, even when we don't want to. I want sympathy . . . and I get mad when I get it. I really want Stephanie to be normal. Who is going to do that for me?

BUILDING EFFECTIVE TEAMS

Young children and families often have needs that extend beyond the expertise of a single discipline. Teaming involves professionals from different disciplines working collaboratively to identify and implement services for children and families. Skills in group communication techniques, decision-making strategies, team conflict management, and team building are not commonly demanded of education professionals. Yet a lack of training in team processes may contribute to poorly functioning teams (Darling & Gallagher, 2003). The provisions of the IDEA require that a team assessment precede the development of an IFSP and an IEP (U.S. House of Representatives, 2004). The architects of the IDEA believe that team decisions provide safeguards against individual errors in judgment. Teams may include professionals from child development, counseling, general early childhood education, family life studies, health and recreation, nursing, nutrition, psychology, social work, ECSE, physical/occupational therapy, education of the deaf, education of the blind and visually impaired, and speech-language pathology.

Types of Teams

There are three approaches to teaming, which differ with respect to philosophy, organization, and implementation. Table 2.2 outlines the differences among the multidisciplinary, interdisciplinary, and transdisciplinary approaches to teaming.

Multidisciplinary teams obtain consultations from different disciplines, but evaluations are carried out independently with little opportunity for professional interaction, comparison, debate, or integrated planning. This approach lacks the benefits of group synthesis and, in some cases, may result in duplicative services for families.

Interdisciplinary teams involve professionals from different disciplines working together to assess and manage problems by actively participating in group decision making. Team members share information, but independently implement their sections of the IFSP or the IEP.

In contrast, **transdisciplinary teams** make every effort to work together as a team, rather than as isolated professionals. This approach not only involves the sharing of assessment, goal selection, and intervention, but also necessitates that team members function as a unit, sharing information and skills among the team (Bergen & Raver, 1994). This model was originally used by programs needing to provide comprehensive services with limited staff and facilities. Transdisciplinary teaming is a way of providing a child and family with the benefits of the whole team's expertise

through a single service provider. Team members support one another in developing a good "working knowledge" of each other's discipline so they can represent all team members in direct services to a child and family.

The rationale for the transdisciplinary team approach is that it (1) involves fewer people in working directly with the child and family; (2) improves continuity and integration of domains/subject areas in programming; (3) increases consistency in services offered in the home, center, or school system; and (4) improves integration of parent participation, particularly before children enter the primary grades. Team members conduct assessments together when feasible and advisable (such as arena assessments for infants-toddlers and preschoolers, which are discussed in Chapter 3), share assessment results, write integrated goals and objectives, and designate one professional (the primary service provider) who represents all members to provide direct services to the child and/or family. This results in integrated IFSPs and IEPs that promote specific skill mastery while supporting a child's general development. The reality is that some programs use different team approaches for different program functions. Some use transdisciplinary teaming for assessing and determining services and interdisciplinary teaming for implementing interventions.

Role of Transdisciplinary Team Members. It is the process of role sharing that separates transdisciplinary teaming from other team approaches. Members of a transdisciplinary team systematically cross discipline boundaries to develop an in-depth understanding of other disciplines so they are able to provide services to children and families who require skills outside their own discipline, when appropriate or necessary (Gable, Raver, & Sandler, 1991). The goal is to provide services to children and families that might not be available if strict disciplinary divisions were used. **Role sharing** involves a specialist systematically helping another team member acquire skills related to the specialist's area of expertise (Sandall et al., 2005). Being a member

TABLE 2.2 Differences in the multidisciplinary, interdisciplinary, and transdisciplinary team approaches

	Multidisciplinary	Interdisciplinary	Transdisciplinary
Assessment	Separate assessments by team members	Separate assessments by team members	Team members (when appropriate) and family conduct a comprehensive assessment together and separately.
Parent participation	Parents meet with individual team members	Parents meet with team or team representative	Parents meet with full team
IFSP/IEP development	Team members develop separate "pages" for their discipline	Team members share their separate "pages" with one another	Team members and parents develop an integrated plan based on family priorities
IFSP/IEP responsibility	Team members are responsible for implementing their section of the plan	Team members are responsible for sharing information with one another as well as for implementing their section of the plan	Team members are responsible and accountable for how the primary service provider implements the plan
IFSP/IEP implementation	Team members implement the part of the plan related to their discipline	Team members implement their section of the plan and incorporate other sections where possible	A primary service provider/teacher is assigned to implement the plan with the child and family with support from team members
Lines of communication	Informal lines	Periodic case-specific team meetings	Regular team meetings where information, knowledge, and skills are shared among team members
Guiding philosophy	Team members recognize the importance of contributions from other disciplines	Team members are willing and able to develop, share, and be responsible for providing services that are a part of the total plan	Team members make a commitment to teach, learn, and work together across discipline boundaries to implement an unified plan
Staff development	Independent (within own discipline)	Independent (within and outside own discipline)	Team development across disciplines and regular team building activities

From "Early Intervention Team Approaches: The Transdisciplinary Model" by G. Woodrufff & M.J. McGonigel in *Early Childhood Special Education: Birth to Three* (p. 166) edited by J.B. Jordan, J.J. Gallagher, P.L. Hutinger, & M.L. Kames. 1988, Reston, VA. The Council for Exceptional Children. Reprinted by permission.

of a transdisciplinary team does not mean giving up one's specific discipline; rather, it means using one's discipline in a different way. Although role sharing is a characteristic commonly associated with transdisciplinary teaming in infant-toddler programs, Lamorey and Ryan (1998) found that ECSE professionals report aspects of role sharing also occurring in interdisciplinary and multidisciplinary teams.

Team members who use role sharing are accountable for the quality of services provided. Each discipline has standards of professional responsibility that limit the sharing of some disciplinary roles. Each professional must clearly state when it is inadvisable to share skills, using his or her discipline's code of ethics or standards as a guide. Frequent consultations must be scheduled to discuss assessments, goal/objective setting, planning, strategies implementation, and intervention plan evaluation. Videotaping may help team members who can't "be there" understand the context of a situation so their feedback is more useful (Edelman, 2001).

This team model makes it difficult to view children as segregated areas of need. For example, a speech-language pathologist can no longer be concerned only with a child's communicative needs, but must assume a whole-child and whole-family approach (Benner, 1992). Naturally, the more severe or complex a child's special needs, and the more specialized the needed interventions, the less the chances of role sharing.

After surveying 199 respondents across 50 states, Lamorey and Ryan (1998) reported that there does not appear to be one commonly utilized team model in ECSE and that team members report similar positive characteristics of team effectiveness for each model. Whatever team model a program may use, effective teaming requires a good deal of planning.

Developing Effective Teams

Problems with teaming have been reported in all disciplines, not just education. It is unrealistic to expect team members to work well together immediately or to operate smoothly as a team indefinitely.

Avoiding Common Team Problems. The best teams are characterized as relaxed with direct communication (Beninghof & Singer, 1992). They cultivate a climate of open communication. Good teams must be created; they are not the natural outcome of placing professionals from different disciplines in the same room. Effective teams develop a mission statement, handle conflicts well, and have good communication.

First, to create more positive team operations, professionals must develop a mission statement. Problems arise when staff and administrators do not share similar perceptions and expectations. The mission statement lists the team's purpose, functions, and goals. This frequently involves developing an agenda or structure for meetings, including a time to celebrate successes. It is not uncommon for members from different disciplines to be trained in different missions, which may result in different goals, solutions, and outcomes. Teams must come to a consensus on the team's mission before they begin their work.

Second, teams need a plan for handling conflicts. Before conflicts are experienced, teams should devise a system for addressing disputes so conflicts are never handled in a haphazard manner. Team members must state the nature of the conflict as explicitly as possible, generate several means of resolving the conflict, and then conscientiously follow agreed-on solutions. Professionals who regularly practice this kind of problem solving often find that their own behavior is changeable and is the first place to look when routine practice is not successful (Ostrosky & Cheatham, 2005). For any conflict to lead to a positive outcome, it must be confronted immediately and managed by the team. Interestingly, some programs report that involving families as team members, as in the transdisciplinary team approach, lessens professional conflicts and discipline loyalties because the team is unified by the families' priorities.

Third, effective teams use team building to improve functioning and communication.

Team building refers to the process of team members engaging in continuous self-examination, gathering information about themselves as individuals and as a group, and learning and playing together (Garland & Linder, 1988). Informal team-building activities may involve observing other team members, rotating team responsibilities (e.g., bringing snacks, being timekeeper), sharing recreational activities with children and families, and structuring three minutes of "checking in" with each team member before team duties begin. More formal team-building activities may involve attending conferences together, assigning rotating times for team members to share discipline-specific information during meetings, and observing team members as they give discipline-specific assessments. All team functions work best when administrators create a climate supportive of change.

Successful teams acknowledge that rewarding teamwork is not a given, but is the result of good problem-solving, communication, and team-building skills (Beninghof & Singer, 1992). Usually, persons who are described as open, cooperative, and willing to share and listen are good team members. Team members must acknowledge that they need each other to accomplish their goals for children and their families.

The objective of teamwork is not to come to staff meetings to merely endorse what other professionals suggest from their area of expertise, nor is it to defend one's professional perspective. The objective is to use multiple perspectives to develop the best intervention plans and solutions for children. At times, disciplines may overlap in assessment and intervention areas, and this may strain team work. For example, a child psychiatrist, a social worker, an ECSE teacher, and a behaviorally trained pediatrician may all feel capable of managing an acting-out 4-year-old. However, each will have a slightly different view of what intervention with the child, and his or her family, should look like.

Professional differences and biases may never be eliminated completely, nor should they be. Input from a wide variety of professionals still offers the best potential for meeting the needs of children and families (Murray & Mandell, 2006).

Innovative approaches and solutions often result when a team of diverse professionals discusses and works toward solutions based on the expertise of each team member. Consequently, through teaming, team members learn to reach consensus by respecting diverse perspectives and to value *joint* ownership of a child's successes and failures.

CONCLUSION

Rachel's mother in the case study, like most parents, trusted professionals to bring hope and positive change to her child's life. Parents tend to expect teachers to be knowledgeable about their child's disability or developmental delay and use strategies that are appropriate for facilitating their child's development. Parents' emotional distress and anxiety, professionals' lack of cultural knowledge, and possible conflicts in values between professionals and families may, at times, mitigate against successful partnerships. Nonetheless, at the most basic level, the intervention process should help families recognize and develop their own abilities in parenting their children with special needs. Similarly, the quality of any team is no better than the quality of the disciplinary expertise, mutual respect, and group process skills of the participants. Differences and tension among team members must be avoided for the good of the child and the family (Mellin & Winton, 2003). Quality teamwork allows ECSE professionals to expand their individual knowledge base and better support parents as parents become more invested in their child's education.

SUMMARY

Building partnerships with families

- Members of the same family may experience a range of emotions and reactions to the diagnosis of a disability or developmental delay.
- The family-based approach is grounded in the understanding that involving and supporting families is a more powerful intervention than one that focuses exclusively on the child, that encouraging

family members to choose their level of involvement in their child's education benefits both the child and the family, and that when families identify their priorities for goals and services, intervention is more meaningful.

Communicating with parents and professionals

- Effective communication with parents and other professionals involves using nonverbal communication skills (e.g., controlling the physical surroundings and being a good listener) and verbal communication skills (e.g., using minimal encouragers, using reflecting content and emotions, using effective questioning, controlling the use of jargon, using reframing, using structuring, and using negotiation).

The family systems approach

- The family system approach acknowledges that a family's characteristics, interactions, and functions influence all members of a family and that professionals can use this knowledge to better support the child and his or her family.

Building effective teams

- The multidisciplinary, interdisciplinary, and transdisciplinary team models differ in philosophy, organization, and implementation which may impact the level of integration of services children and families receive.
- To avoid common team problems, teams must develop a mission statement, develop a system for handling conflicts, and participate in team-building activities.

DISCUSSION QUESTIONS/ACTIVITIES

1. Using Rachel's case study, discuss two characteristics of the family-based approach that professionals addressed.

2. Discuss differences and similarities in the three team approaches as they would be used in an infant-toddler program. Discuss assessment, family participation, IFSP development and implementation, and program philosophy.

3. Role-play a conference with a parent of a preschooler with communication delays. Assume the parent is unhappy with the level of services being offered and the fact that the child has not shown significant progress for the last seven months. Use some of the negotiation and communication strategies discussed in this chapter to bring this meeting to some mutually satisfying resolution.

REFERENCES

Al-Hassan, S., & Gardner, R. (2002). Involving immigrant parents of students with disabilities in the educational process. *TEACHING Exceptional Children, 34*, 52–58.

Arcia, E., & Gallagher, J. (1993). Who are the underserved by early interventionists? Can we tell? *Infant-Toddler Intervention, 3*, 93–100.

Bailey, D., Bruder, M. B., Hebbeler, K., Carta, J., Defosset, M., Greenwood, C., Kahn, L., Mallik, S., Markowitz, J., Spiker, D., Walker, D., & Barton, L. (2006). Recommended outcomes for families of young children with disabilities. *Journal of Early Intervention, 28*, 227–251.

Bailey, D., Buysse, V., Edmondson, R., & Smith, T. (1992). Creating family-centered services in early intervention: Perceptions of professionals in four states. *Exceptional Children, 58*, 298–309.

Banks, R., Santos, R., & Roof, V. (2003). Discovering family concerns, priorities, and resources: Sensitive family information gathering. *Young Exceptional Children, 6*(2), 11–19.

Beninghof, A., & Singer, A. (1992). Transdisciplinary teaming: An inservice training activity. *TEACHING Exceptional Children, 58*(3), 58–60.

Benner, S. (1992). *Assessing young children with special needs: An ecological perspective.* New York: Longman.

Bergen, D., & Raver, S. (1994). Implementing and evaluating transdisciplinary assessment. In D. Bergen, *Assessment methods for infants and toddlers: Transdisciplinary team approaches* (pp. 243–254). New York: Teachers College Press.

Brady, S., Peters, D., Gamel-McCormick, M., & Venuto, N. (2004). Types and patterns of professional-family talk in home-based early intervention. *Journal of Early Intervention, 26*(2), 146–159.

Brinker, D., Pretti-Frontczak, K., Johnson, J., & Straka, E. (2002). In D. Bricker (Ed.), Assessment, evaluation, and programming system for infants and children (AEPS): Vol. 1. Administration guide (2nd ed.). Baltimore: Paul H. Brookes Publishing.

Brotherson, M., & Goldstein, B. (1992). Time as a resource and constraint for parents of young children with disabilities: Implications for early intervention services. *Topics in Early Childhood Special Education, 12*, 508–527.

Cooper, C., & Allred, K. (1992). A comparison of mothers' versus fathers' need for support in caring for a young child with special needs. *Infant-Toddler Intervention, 2,* 205–221.

Correa, W., & Heward, W. (2003). Special education in a culturally diverse society. In W. Heward, *Exceptional children: An introduction to special education* (7th ed., pp. 86–119). Upper Saddle River, NJ: Merrill/Prentice Hall.

Corso, R., Santos, R., & Roof, V. (2002). Honoring diversity in early childhood education materials. *TEACHING Exceptional Children, 34*(3), 30–36.

Dardig, J. (2005). The McClurg monthly magazine and 14 more practical ways to involve parents. *TEACHING Exceptional Children, 38*(2), 46–51.

Darling, S., & Gallagher, P. (2003). Using self-assessments in early intervention training. *Journal of Early Intervention, 25*(3), 219–227.

Dinnebeil, L., Fox, C., & Rule, S. (1998). Influences on collaborative relationships: Exploring dimensions of effective communication and shared beliefs. *Infant-Toddler Intervention, 8*(3), 263–278.

Dunst, C. (2001). Participation of young children with disabilities in community learning activities. In M. Guralnick (Ed.), *Early childhood inclusion: Focus on change* (pp. 307–333). Baltimore, MD: Brookes.

Dunst, C., Herter, S., & Shields, H. (2000). *Interest-based natural learning opportunities* (YEC Monograph No. 3) (pp. 37–48). Longmont, CO: Sopris West.

Dyson, L., Edgar, E., & Crnic, K. (1989). Psychological predictors of adjustment by siblings of developmentally disabled children. *American Journal of Mental Retardation, 94,* 292–302.

Edelman, L. (2001). *Just being kids: Facilitator's guide.* Denver, CO: Western Media Products.

Ferrell, K. (1985). *Reach out and teach.* New York: American Foundation for the Blind.

Fletcher, L., & Deal, A. (1993). Parent-professional partnerships: Common misconceptions. *Family Enablement Project Messenger, 5*(1), 1–3.

Friend, M., & Cook, L. (2007). *Interactions: Collaboration skills for school professionals* (5th ed.). Boston: Pearson/Allyn & Bacon.

Gable, R., Raver, S., & Sandler, A. (1991). Assessing developmentally disabled children. In R. Gable (Ed.), *Annual advances in mental retardation and developmental disabilities* (Vol. IV, pp. 27–61). London: JAI Press.

Gallagher, P., Fialka, J., Rhodes, C., & Arceneaux, C. (2003). Working with families: Rethinking denial. *Young Exceptional Children, 5*(2), 11–17.

Garland, C. W., & Linder, T. W. (1988). Administrative challenges in early intervention. In J. B. Jordan, J. J. Gallagher, P. L. Hutinger, & M. B. Karnes (Eds.), *Early childhood special education: Birth to three* (pp. 5–28). Reston, VA: Council for Exceptional Children.

Glascoe, F. (1999). Communicating with parents. *Young Exceptional Children, 2*(4), 17–25.

Guralnick, M. (1997). *The effectiveness of early intervention.* Baltimore, MD: Brookes.

Hains, A., Rhymer, P., McLean, M., Barnekow, K., Johnson, V., & Kennedy, B. (2005). Interdisciplinary teams and diverse families: Practices in early intervention personnel preparation. *Young Exceptional Children, 8,* 2–10.

Healy, A., Keesee, P., & Smith, B. (1989). *Early services for children with special needs: Transactions for family support.* Baltimore, MD: Brookes.

Hooste, A., & Maes, B. (2003). Family factors in the early development of children with Down syndrome. *Journal of Early Intervention, 25*(4), 296–309.

Kilgo, J.L., & Raver, S.A. (1999). Collaborating with families. In S.A. Raver, *Intervention strategies for infants and toddlers with special needs: A team approach* (2nd ed.). (pp.332-361). Upper Saddle River, NJ: Merrill/Prentice Hall.

Johnson, B., McGonigel, M., & Kauffman, R. (1989). *Guidelines and recommended practices for the individualized family service plan.* Washington, DC: National Early Childhood Technical Assistance System and American Association for the Care of Children's Health.

Kazak, A., & Marvin, R. (1984). Differences, difficulties, and adaptations: Stress and social networks in families with a handicapped child. *Family Relations, 33,* 67–77.

Lamorey, S., & Ryan, S. (1998). From contention to implementation: A comparison of team practices and recommended practices across service delivery models. *Infant-Toddler Intervention, 8*(4), 309–331.

Linan-Thompson, S., & Jean, R. (1997). Completing the parent participation puzzle: Accepting diversity. *TEACHING Exceptional Children, 30*(2), 46–50.

Lynch, E., & Hanson, M. (Eds.). (2004). *Developing cross-cultural competence: A guide for working with young children and their families* (3rd ed.). Baltimore, MD: Brookes.

Matuszny, R., Banda, D., & Coleman, T. (2007). A progressive plan for building collaborative relationships with parents from diverse backgrounds. *TEACHING Exceptional Children, 39,* 24–31.

McWilliam, P., Tocci, L., & Harbin, G. (1998). Family-centered services: Service providers' discourse and behavior. *Topics in Early Childhood Special Education, 18,* 206–221.

McWilliam, R. A. (2000). It's only natural . . . to have early intervention in the environments where it's needed. In S. Sandall & M. Ostrosky (Eds.), *Natural environments and inclusion* (YEC Monograph No. 2) (pp. 17–26). Longmont, CO: Sopris West.

Mellin, A., & Winton, P. (2003). Interdisciplinary collaboration among early intervention faculty members. *Journal of Early Intervention, 25*(3), 173–188.

Moeller, M. P. (2000). Early intervention and language development in children who are deaf and hard of hearing, *Pediatrics, 106*(3), 43–52.

Montgomery, D. (2005). Communicating without harm: Strategies to enhance parent-teacher communication. *TEACHING Exceptional Children, 37,* 50–55.

Murray, M., & Mandell, C. (2006). On-the-job practices of early childhood special education providers trained in family-centered practices. *Journal of Early Intervention, 28*(2), 125–138.

Ostrosky, M., & Cheatham, G. (2005). Teaching the use of a problem-solving process to early childhood educators. *Young Exceptional Children, 9*(1), 12–19.

Ramey, C., & Ramey, S. (1992). Effective early intervention. *Mental Retardation, 30,* 337–345.

Raver, S. (1997). *Creating positive family-professional conferences.* Unpublished document, Old Dominion University, Norfolk, VA.

Raver, S. (1999). *Intervention strategies for infants and toddlers with special needs: A team approach.* Upper Saddle River, NJ: Merrill/Prentice Hall.

Raver, S. A. (2004). Teaching in natural environments in early intervention. In *Biwako Millennium 2002–2012: 17th National Conference on Mental Retardation* (pp. 48–52). Calcutta, India: National Institute for the Mentally Handicapped; Government of India.

Raver, S. A. (2005). Using family-based practices for young children with special needs in preschool programs. *Childhood Education, 82*(1), 9–13.

Raver, S., & Kilgo, J. (1991). Effective family-centered services: Supporting family choices and rights. *Infant-Toddler Intervention, 1*(3), 169–176.

Raver, S., & Lambert, K. (1995, September/October). Family-centered practices in early childhood special education: What are they and why use them? *Technical Assistance Center Network News,* 3.

Sandall, S., Hemmeter, M., Smith, B., & McLean, M. (2005). *DEC recommended practices: A comprehensive guide to practical application in early intervention/early childhood special education.* Longmont, CO: Sopris West.

Sandler, A., Warren, S., & Raver, S. (1995). Grandparents as a source of support for parents of children with disabilities. *Mental Retardation, 33,* 248–250.

Santos, R., & McCollum, J. (2007). Perspectives of parent-child interaction in Filipino mothers of very young children with and without disabilities. *Journal of Early Intervention, 29,* 243–261.

Skinner, D., Rodriquez, P., & Bailey, D. (1999). Qualitative analysis of Latino parents' religious interpretations of their child's disability. *Journal of Early Intervention, 22*(4), 271–285.

Smith, T., Gartin, B., Murdick, N., & Hilton, A. (2006). *Families and children with special needs: Professional and family partnerships.* Upper Saddle River, NJ: Merrill/Prentice Hall.

Stonestreet, R., Johnston, R., & Acton, S. (1991). Guidelines for real partnerships with parents. *Infant-Toddler Intervention, 1,* 37–46.

Summers, J., Hoffman, L., Marquis, J., Turnbull, A., Poston, D., & Nelson, L. (2005). Measuring the quality of family-professional partnerships in special education services. *Exceptional Children, 72*(1), 65–81.

Summers, M., Bridge, J., & Summers, C. (1991). Sibling support groups. *TEACHING Exceptional Children, 23*(4), 20–25.

Trivette, C., & Dunst, C. (2004). Evaluating family-focused practices: Parenting Experience Scale. *Young Exceptional Children, 7*(3), 12–19.

Trivette, C., & Dunst, C. (2005). DEC recommended practices: Family-based practices. In S. Sandall, M. Hemmeter, B. Smith, & M. McLean, *DEC recommended practices: A comprehensive guide to practical application in early intervention/early childhood special education* (pp. 107–120). Longmont, CO: Sopris West.

Turnbull, A., Summers, J., Turnbull, R., Brotherson, M., Winton, P., Roberts, R., Snyder, McWilliams, R., Chandler, L., Schrandt, S., Stowe, M., Bruder, M., DiVenere, N., Epley, P., Hornback, M., Huff, B., Miksch, P., Mitchell, L., Sharp, L., & Stroup-Rentier, V. 2007). Family supports and services in early intervention: A bold vision. *Journal of Early Intervention, 29,* 187–206.

Turnbull, A. P., & Turnbull, H. R. (Eds.). (2001). *Families, professionals, and exceptionality: Collaborating for empowerment.* Upper Saddle River, NJ: Merrill/Prentice Hall.

Turnbull, A., Turnbull, R., Erwin, E., & Soodak, L. (2006). *Families and exceptionality* (5th ed.). Upper Saddle River, NJ: Merrill/Prentice Hall.

U.S. House of Representatives (2004). *Education of Individuals with Disabilities Reauthorization of 2004.* Washington, DC: U.S. Congress.

Wehman, T., & Gilkerson, L. (1999). Parents of young children with special needs speak out: Perceptions of early intervention services. *Infant-Toddler Intervention, 9*(2), 137–167.

Whitbread, K., Bruder, M. B., Fleming, G., & Park, H. (2007). Collaboration in special education: Parent-professional training. *TEACHING Exceptional Children, 39,* 6–14.

Woods, J., & McCormick, K. (2002). Welcoming the family: A family-centered approach. *Young Exceptional Children, 5*(3), 2–11.

Zhang, C., & Bennett, T. (2001a). Multicultural views of disability: Implications for early intervention professionals. *Infant-Toddler Intervention, 11*(2), 143–154.

Zhang, C., & Bennett, T. (2001b). Beliefs about and implementation of family-centered practice: A study with Early Head Start staff in six states. *Infant-Toddler Intervention, 11*(3–4), 201–222.

Chapter
3

Assessment and Individualized Interventions

Sharon A. Raver

Overview

This chapter discusses assessment and programming for infants and toddlers, preschoolers, and primary-aged students, including

assessment

developing individualized programs

monitoring skill acquisition

CASE STUDY: Andre

Andre, the first child of Kathy and R. J. Weiss, was born at 30 weeks, with a birth weight of 2 pounds, 3 ounces. Andre's early life was punctuated by a series of medical crises. After release from the hospital, he was enrolled in an infant-toddler program where he received physical therapy and home visits once a week. Although the demands of Andre's care could be exhausting, the family had relatives who provided financial, emotional and childcare support.

By a corrected age of 36 months, Andre was assessed as functioning on age level in all areas except gross motor, where he manifested a seven- to nine-month delay. His family enrolled him in a daycare program for typically developing children. Andre's transition was difficult. He resisted interacting with the other children and usually refused to participate in climbing or running activities. With the help of a consultant early childhood special education teacher and a physical therapist, several intervention programs were implemented to encourage Andre to develop more appropriate peer interactions and better motor planning.

In kindergarten, Andre was slow to develop friendships and had difficulty with prewriting tasks and with alphabet discrimination. His gross motor skills had improved, but he still had problems with balance during some motor tasks, such as jumping.

In first grade, due to concerns about his social, reading, and writing skills, Andre was referred for a multidisciplinary assessment, which involved norm- and criterion-referenced instruments and direct observations. The results determined that Andre could benefit from services for a student with a learning disability. In second and third grade, he spent most of his day in a general education class and attended a resource room for reading instruction one hour a day. At the end of third grade, his mother reported that Andre still had difficulty "coming out of his shell," but was on grade level in all academic areas except reading. She mentioned that she had seen the most progress in his written language skills this year.

Although children progress at their own rates, it is generally understood that developmental sequences are essentially the same for all children (Roopnarine & Johnson, 2005). It is accepted that individual development is variable, marked by accelerations, regressions, and plateaus. Development proceeds in a hierarchical fashion in which rudimentary skills operate as prerequisites for more complex abilities. Skill acquisition moves from predominantly sensorimotor behaviors in infancy to verbally-mediated behaviors in childhood. Development also appears to be closely related to interactions between individual maturation and environmental stimulation.

A constant, stimulating environment seems to produce the most stable, predictable developmental outcomes in young children. Children who live in disruptive and disorganized environments tend to show more random performances across assessment intervals than children in predictable environments do (Bowe, 2004). In order to ensure that interventions are tailored to the specific needs of each child and that children with special needs are learning what they need to, early childhood special education (ECSE) professionals use assessment to begin the process of developing individualized programs for children.

ASSESSMENT

Assessment involves the systematic collection of information about a child. The specific instruments used to assess a child vary depending on state guidelines, the preferences of local regulatory agencies, the preferences of professionals, the purpose of the assessment, and the availability of tools (Andersson, 2004). Research has found that at times teachers' practices conflict with recommended assessment practices. For example, some teachers report using one assessment tool for multiple purposes and for purposes for which the instrument was not designed, as when they use a screening tool for program development (Grisham-Brown & Pretti-Frontczak, 2003).

Teachers must first determine the reason they need information about a child and then select the best strategy for this data-gathering process (Cook, 2004). ECSE professionals employ recommended assessment practices (Hemmeter, Smith, Sandall, & Askew, 2005) when they

❏ involve families in assessment by soliciting family concerns, the child's interests, the child's abilities, and child/family needs;

❏ select assessment tools and practices that are individualized and appropriate for each child and family;

❏ report assessment results in a manner that is both useful for planning program goals and objectives and understandable and useful for families;

❏ rely on materials that capture the child's authentic behaviors in routine circumstances; and

❏ meet legal and procedural requirements and guidelines.

The assessment process must be **multisource**, in that professionals must use multiple instruments (e.g., assessment tools, direct observation, parent surveys, checklists) and solicit information from multiple individuals (e.g., parents, therapists, general education teachers) to measure a child's status, functioning, and progress. Professionals also use a **multimethod** approach, in that they do not rely on a single procedure for gathering information, but choose many strategies in an attempt to accommodate each child's sensory, physical, and responsive differences (Taylor, 2006). Norm-referenced, criterion-referenced, play-based, and judgment-based measurements are common types of assessments used with young children.

Norm-Referenced Assessments

Norm-referenced tools are designed to compare a child's performance with that of other children of the same age. These tools require a standardized assessment protocol and specific materials so a comparison can be made to norms derived from a population of children. Norm-referenced tools provide a **basal age**, the age level at which all items are passed, and a **ceiling age**, the age level at which only one item can be passed. These instruments report **validity data**, the extent to which a tool is determined to perform the functions for which it was intended, and **reliability data**, the consistency of test performance over time. For these reasons, norm-referenced tools are commonly an integral part of the team assessment process for determining eligibility for special education services.

For infants, toddlers, and preschoolers, norm-referenced tests result in quantitative scores such as **developmental age scores**, the average age at which 50% of the normative sample achieved a particular raw score, and **percentile ranks**, the percentage of the population that performed at or below a given score. When a child has developmental needs, his or her developmental age will differ from his or her chronological age. For instance, it may be found that a 53-month-old child is functioning approximately at the level of a 29-month-old in fine motor and close to the level of a 32-month-old in the cognitive domain, rather than at his or her expected developmental age.

Norm-referenced tools used for primary-aged students (kindergarten through third grade) provide educators with grade-level equivalents, standard scores, and percentile ranks so a child can be compared to others the same age in reading, mathematics, social studies, science, and other subject areas.

Norm-referenced tools have certain advantages, in that they

❏ compare children to others the same age for eligibility and classification purposes,

❏ report reliability and validity information, and

❏ can usually be given in less than one hour.

Some of the disadvantages of norm-referenced tools are that they

❏ commonly compare children with disabilities to children without disabilities;

❏ may provide little information about *how* a child learns;

❏ are given in an "assessment setting," not a natural environment;

❏ may provide little help in identifying functional, appropriate objectives;

❏ may provide little information about *why* a child cannot complete an item satisfactorily; and

❏ may be biased against children with motor, emotional, sensory, or communication impairments/delays and children from culturally/linguistically diverse backgrounds.

Criterion-Referenced Assessments

Criterion-referenced and curriculum-based instruments compare a child to a designated standard. Usually, an approximate developmental age equivalent, by domain, is provided for children under age 6; for children over 6 years, a grade-level equivalent tends to be provided. This type of tool is used to determine a child's attainment of specific skills and objectives. It tends to provide information about "quality" of performance by having designations such as "pass," "no pass," and "emerging" for children under 6 years. Many criterion-referenced instruments combine assessment with a curriculum checklist so assessment and programming are directly linked.

Criterion-referenced/curriculum-based instruments like *The Carolina Curriculum for Infants and Toddlers with Special Needs* (Johnson-Martin, Attermeier, & Hacker, 2004) and *The Carolina Curriculum for Preschoolers with Special Needs* (Johnson-Martin, Hacker, & Attermeier, 2004) allow professionals to use available materials, to give subtests in the order that best suits a learner, and to include clinical judgment with results to more accurately describe a child's abilities. Additionally, criterion-referenced instruments often permit professionals to make adaptations, which can be helpful for developing intervention programs for children with more significant needs.

Some of the advantages of criterion-referenced instruments are that they

❏ encourage comparing a child to himself/ herself for monitoring purposes,

❏ usually offer a continuum of skills that are appropriate for programming,

❏ allow professionals to adapt or modify items/tasks to better reflect a child's competence as long as modifications and adaptations are reported,

❏ frequently are linked to curricula,

❏ usually may be administered individually or in small groups,

❏ may allow individual subtests to be given at different times, and

❏ may be given in natural environments.

Some of the disadvantages of criterion-referenced instruments are that they

❏ may be time-consuming to administer;

❏ may have some items that are not appropriate or functional for all children; and

❏ may be biased against children with motor, emotional, sensory, or communication impairments/delays and children from culturally/linguistically diverse backgrounds.

Play-Based Assessments

Play-based assessments involve semistructured play episodes arranged to elicit a child's "natural" or authentic behavior in the cognitive, social, emotional, motor, and communication areas (Linder, 2008). This form of assessment is commonly used with infants, toddlers, and preschoolers. Team members observe the same play/assessment session and discuss the results immediately afterward to develop a holistic assessment-programming process. Because all behaviors that need to be observed may not be presented in the initial assessment, other assessment times with the full team or with individual professionals may be required. Parents are usually involved as key partners in this type of assessment if they choose to be. Assessment may be conducted in a child's home using familiar toys, in a center-based program, or in an assessment center. Only checklists, direct observation, parental reports, and criterion-referenced assessments may be used for this type of assessment.

Some of the advantages of play-based assessments are that they

❏ render a "typical" sample of a child's behavior;

❏ render a sample of a child's interaction with an adult and materials, and occasionally with another child; and

❏ may produce a more comprehensive sample of behavior for children who are noncompliant or slow to establish rapport.

Some of the disadvantages of play-based assessments are that they

❏ may necessitate more than one testing session to gather sufficient information about a child's functioning and

❏ can be time-consuming.

Judgment-Based Assessments

The real challenge of any assessment is to observe each child's authentic behavior. Judgment-based assessments record a professional's perceptions and observations regarding the child's behavior and functioning (McLean, Wolery, & Bailey, 2004). Children with significant sensory impairments and/or neurological limitations are usually unsatisfactorily evaluated by conventional assessment instruments. Conventional tools may not have sufficient item density to capture small skill attainment, and most require communicative and/or motor responses to evaluate what a child knows.

Judgment-based assessments tend to be most useful for children who are difficult to assess, who have significant sensory deficits, and whose competence is not reflected by traditional assessment instruments and practices. After norm-referenced and criterion-referenced instruments have been used to determine whether a child is eligible for services, it becomes the responsibility of ECSE professionals to determine other, more accurate ways of determining what a child can and cannot do when significant delays or impairments are involved.

Judgment-based instruments rely on systematic observation to record both objective data (e.g., "Michael opened his mouth one inch when the food was brought toward his face.") and subjective data or impressions (e.g., "Michael smiled more when eating raspberry yogurt than the plain. He seems to prefer the sweeter taste."). Since judgment-based instruments utilize clinical judgment, they are prone to evaluator bias. Despite this, they can be useful when conventional assessments are not feasible or do not reflect subtle changes in a child's abilities.

Professionals attempt to gather the following information with judgment-based instruments: (1) if skills/behaviors are present; (2) if skills are being generalized; (3) how a child attempted a task; (4) why a child was unable to complete a task; (5) the level of support a child required in order to perform a task; (6) how a child responded when accommodations for sensory, physical, and temperamental differences were provided; and (7) the function of nontraditional responses to stimuli (e.g., eye widening when a particular toy is presented). The objective is to sufficiently quantify observed behaviors so skills that may not have been reflected in norm-referenced or criterion-referenced instruments may be identified, taught, and monitored.

Some of the advantages of judgment-based assessment tools are that they

❏ rely on professionals' clinical judgment and perceptions;

❏ may document areas of competence that are not evaluated by other assessments so families and professionals have a more complete picture of the child's abilities, including task persistence, ability to redirect, and adjustment to environmental changes;

❏ may help professionals and family members focus on strengths and the functionality of nontraditional responses to stimuli;

❏ may be used to document small skill and/or behavior changes that are not reported by other assessments; and

❏ may be useful in analyzing environmental factors that influence, enhance, or hinder a child's performance and behavior.

Some of the disadvantages of judgment-based assessments are that

❏ they rely on professionals' clinical judgment and perceptions and thus may be prone to evaluator bias,

❏ they are time-consuming, and

❏ different professionals may generate different results using the same tools.

The Purposes of Assessment

Assessments may be used for screening, eligibility, program planning, and monitoring purposes. Each purpose involves the use of different assessment tools and provides ECSE professionals with different kinds of information.

Screening. Screening is the first step in looking at how a child is functioning. If a screening tool determines that a child is not functioning typically, professionals are then informed that more comprehensive assessments must be given. Although screening instruments are useful in providing a first indication of potential problems, they should never be used as the only data source for assigning services for young children. Primary-aged children tend to be screened with curriculum-based instruments.

Eligibility. A team assessment is required to determine if infants, toddlers, preschoolers, and primary-aged students meet the eligibility guidelines for receiving special education services. Infants, toddlers, and preschoolers are given a battery of norm-referenced, criterion-referenced, and, when the child has complex needs, judgment-based instruments to determine if he or she meets the IDEA's definition of developmental delay or disability. Despite the fact that norm-referenced tools have historically been required for determining eligibility of services for infants and toddlers, many in the field have suggested using authentic assessments, such as curriculum-based tools, for this purpose (Bagnato, 2005; McLean, 2005). The research of Macy and colleagues (Macy, Bricker, & Squires, 2005) found that curriculum-based assessments were as effective in identifying infants and toddlers who needed services as traditional standardized, norm-referenced measurements were. Traditional, single-point-in-time measures of performance are often irrelevant to intervention planning and tend to be expensive to conduct (Vanderheyden, 2005).

For primary-aged students, a team will give the student multiple assessments to determine if he or she qualifies for an IDEA disability category such as mental retardation or behavior disorders. Primary-aged children are assessed with instruments that produce grade-level equivalents, standard scores, and percentile ranks.

Program Planning. Professionals tend to use criterion-referenced and/or curriculum-based instruments for program planning for infants, toddlers, and preschoolers. Preference is given to tools that have sufficient item density that they can detect small increments of progress and that allow professionals to report assessment information in a way that is immediately useful for making programmatic decisions.

Arena assessments are often used for children from birth to age 3, and occasionally for children who are 3 to 6 years old, for eligibility determination and program planning. Andre, discussed in the case study, received arena assessments regularly during his toddler and preschool years. **Arena assessments** involve several professionals assessing a child at one time. One professional, called a facilitator, interacts with a child while other team members, including the family (when appropriate), sit around the child in a large circle. The facilitator engages the child in play-oriented activities designed to demonstrate his or her strengths and needs. Figure 3.1 shows the physical arrangement of an arena assessment.

Before an arena assessment, team members meet with the facilitator to identify the skills and/or

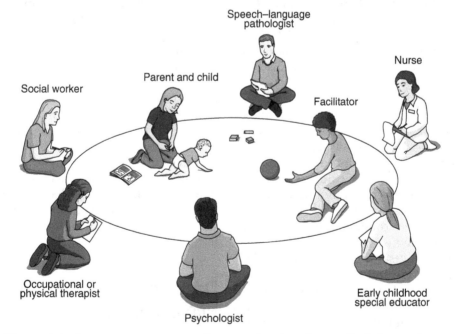

Figure 3.1 Arena assessments allow professionals to gain information about child's development based on the same observation of the child

Source: Adapted from a drawing by Adrienne Frank, Child Development Resources, Norge, VA.

behaviors that each team member would like to see from their discipline-specific, criterion-referenced assessment instrument. Following the assessment, if needed behaviors were not observed, another assessment time is arranged. Professionals who use arena assessments report that they save time and that, with training, professionals are able to see what they need to from their discipline evaluations while also observing the *whole* child.

After an arena assessment, team members meet to develop child and family outcomes/objectives, identify intervention strategies and procedures, and identify family/classroom routines in which goals may be most easily embedded without disrupting the activity or routine. Arena assessments foster integrated outcomes and interventions and promote team cohesion because educational programs are written by the group, not by individual professionals.

With primary-aged children, professionals use norm-referenced, criterion/curriculum-referenced tools, and informal and formal inventories for developing educational plans. Tools like *The Woodcock Reading Mastery Tests–Revised–Normative Update* (Woodcock, 1998) and *The KeyMath Revised: A Diagnostic Inventory of Essential Mathematics* (Connolly, 1998) evaluate a child's strengths and weaknesses in a subject area.

Monitoring. Gathering information about a child's progress toward specified outcomes, goals, and/or short-term objectives (also called benchmarks) is called **monitoring**. Monitoring tracks skill acquisition and permits professionals to determine if interventions are promoting a child's learning. When assessment of a child's functioning is approached as a continuous process, rather than a discrete activity with a prescribed beginning and end, changes in strategies and activities are more easily made. In fact, when asked, most ECSE professionals define good assessments as those that allow for observation of children during daily activities and play, permitting monitoring of progress over time (Grisham-Brown & Pretti-Frontczak, 2003). Observing a child perform a task in a real situation involves a process

known as **authentic assessment** (Losardo & Notari-Syverson, 2001), assessment through performance events, or **naturalistic assessment**.

Some teachers use **portfolio assessment**, the process of gathering a collection of a child's work that illustrates effort, progress, and achievements (Lynch & Struewing, 2001), to measure a child's authentic learning. This type of assessment involves gathering two types of information about a child: (1) observations (e.g., videotapes; audiotaped communication samples of infants, toddlers, and preschoolers; audiotapes of primary-aged children's oral reading) and (2) work samples (e.g., drawings that reflect cognitive changes for preschoolers; photographs of infants, toddlers, and preschoolers performing tasks they were unable to do previously; school work such as tests, projects, informal inventories, and checklists for primary-aged students) (Jarrett, Browne, & Wallin, 2006).

Monitoring requires systematic planning. When ECSE teachers have current data on a child's performance, communication among professionals, administrators, and family members is enhanced. Although collecting data is recognized as essential in special education, evidence suggests that regular data collection is neither widespread nor routine (Sandall, Schwartz, & Lacroix, 2004). The lack of systematic data collection is particularly evident in general early childhood settings that serve children with disabilities (Sandall et al., 2004). Strategies for improving data collection are discussed later in the chapter. Additionally, assessment instruments used for eligibility and program planning for specific domains are discussed in Chapters 5, 6, 7, and 8, while assessment instruments useful for children with specific disabilities are discussed in Chapters 9, 10, 11, and 12.

DEVELOPING INDIVIDUALIZED PROGRAMS

Professionals use information from assessments as one yardstick against which to measure young children's strengths and weaknesses. Observations

TABLE 3.1 Steps for making assessment-curriculum linkages for instructional targets for children from birth to 5 years

(A) Select assessment tools with relevance for programming.

(B) Determine child's developmental levels across domains.

(C) Identify item(s) from the assessment tool that a child needs to learn in each domain.

Example:

> *Tool: Learning Accomplishment Profile–Diagnostic* (1995)
> *Domain:* Cognitive: Counting
> *Child's Developmental Age:* 24 months
> *Selected assessment item:* "Identifies 'big' block on request"

(D) Align assessment item(s) and/or the child's developmental age to the curriculum's domain(s) and goals/objectives.

Example:

> *Selected curriculum: The Carolina Curriculum for Infants and Toddlers with*
>   *Special Needs* (2004)
> *Domain:* Cognition—Communication: Receptive Language
> *Developmental Age:* 21–24 months
> *Curriculum Item:* "Selects 'big' and 'little' when given a choice between two objects/pictures"
> *Domain:* Cognition—Visual Perception: Matching and Sorting
> *Developmental Age:* 24–30 months
> *Curriculum Item:* "Sorts by size (big and little)"

(E) Write measurable instructional objective combining information from both sources.

Example:

- When given different materials and experiences, Patel will sort by size ("big/little") and give "big/little" objects and pictures when requested by the teacher, 3/3 for 2 data days.

of how a disability or delay influences children's development, the expectations of learning environments in which children participate, the curricula used, and families' desires are also considered. Ideally, professionals select assessment tools that have a relevance to programming so that assessment and programming are linked. Table 3.1 shows how to move from an item on an assessment tool to developing a curriculum item, to gathering data for children under the age of 6 years. Discussion of how to develop educational plans follows.

Developing an Individualized Family Service Plan

The Individuals with Disabilities Education Act (IDEA, 2004) requires that an **Individualized Family Service Plan (IFSP)** be developed for any child from birth to age 3 who has been determined to need special education services to realize his or her potential. As stated earlier, the child and the family are considered cobeneficiaries of services in infant-toddler programs (Turnbull, Huerta, & Stowe, 2006). Programs serving infants and toddlers, and their families, tend to follow these basic principles (Sandall, Hemmeter, Smith, & McLean, 2005):

1) Programs acknowledge that infants and toddlers are dependent on their families, necessitating a family-based approach.

2) Programs define *family* in a way that reflects the diversity of each family's structure.

3) Programs acknowledge that each family has its own values, roles, beliefs, and coping styles; respect for racial, ethnic, cultural, and linguistic diversity is a cornerstone of practice.

4) Programs use strategies that foster supportive child-family interactions, offer flexible services for family-identified needs, and promote inclusion of the child and family into their community.

5) Programs recognize that no single agency or discipline can meet the diverse and complex needs of infants and toddlers and their families so a team approach is followed.

These principles shape the way IFSPs are written and implemented. Other guiding principles for developing IFSPs are listed in Figure 3.2.

States provide professionals with general guidelines for writing IFSPs to ensure that all necessary components of the plan are completed. The IDEA requires that an IFSP be developed promptly following assessment. With parental permission, however, services may begin before an IFSP is written. The plan must be reviewed with the family at least every six months. Each component of an IFSP has specific information for families and service providers so participants are clear about how the child and family will be supported. Figure 3.3 shows selected sections of an IFSP written for the Weiss family, the family profiled in the case study, when Andre was 20 months old. Each component of an IFSP will be discussed.

Statement of Developmental Levels. This section lists a team's assessment results and summarizes the findings regarding the child's developmental, health, and medical strengths and needs. The assessment is supposed to be comprehensive and involve families; however, there is still debate in the field regarding what constitutes comprehensiveness (Kovanen, 2001). The instruments used

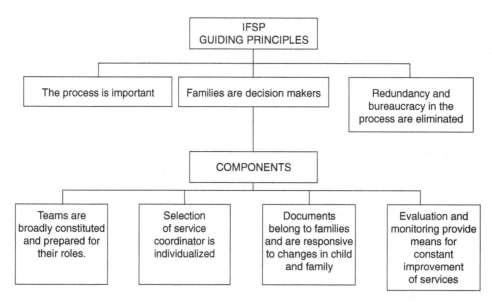

Figure 3.2 Guiding principles for the development of Individualized Family Service Plans

Figure 3.3 Excerpts from Andre Weiss' Individual Family Service Plan (IFSP) when Andre was 20 months old, receiving Infant-Toddler Services

Child and Family Typical Routines and Community Activities: The Weiss family enjoys watching movies at home, working in their yard, and riding bikes as a family. Mrs. Weiss reports that Andre loves the bike carrier. Andre's grandparents come for dinner every other Sunday evenings and the other weeks the Weiss family goes to the grandparents' home for dinner.

Family Identified Resources, Priorities and Concerns: Use Mr. and Mrs. Weiss report they enjoy support and help with child care from Mrs. Weiss' parents. Mr. Weiss' parents, and sister, live nearby and are also available when the family needs support. Mrs. Weiss takes Andre to physical therapy once a week at Alberti Hospital and follows up exercises and recommendations at home. Mrs. Weiss expressed concern about Andre's fine and gross motor progress and would like these areas to continue to be priorities for intervention. She reported that Andre continues to uncomfortable with unfamiliar people. She also reported that she is considering going back to work but has not made a decision yet, although she is looking for quality child care in her home.

Team Evaluation: The team evaluation was conducted over several home visits, and during the Family Picnic. Marci M., [physical therapist], Shanna L., the primary service provider [early childhood special educator], and Ken G [speech pathologist] conducted the re-evaluation. The following developmental scores were achieved:

Carolina Curriculum for Infants and Toddlers

Visual Pursuit and Object Permanence	18 months
Object Permanence: Motor and Visual	18 months
Auditory Localization and Object Permanence	21 months
Attention and Memory	21 months
Concept Development	21 months
Understanding Space	15–18 months
Functional use of Objects and Symbolic Play	18 months

Problem-Solving	21 months
Visual Perception	18 months
Prevocabulary/Vocabulary	18 months
Imitation: Sound and Gestures	18 months
Responses to Communication from Others	18–21 months
Conversation Skills	18 months
Self-Direction	18 months
Social Skills	18 months
Self-Help: Eating	21 months
Self-Help: Dressing	18 months
Self-Help: Grooming	21 months
Fine Motor: Tactile Integration	18 months
Fine Motor: Reaching, Grasping and Releasing	12–15 months
Fine Motor: Manipulation	15 months
Fine Motor: Bilateral Skills	12 months
Visual-Motor Skills: Pencil Control and Copying	18 months
Gross Motor Skills: Prone	12–15 months
Gross Motor Skills: Supine	N/A
Gross Motor Skills: Upright	9 months
Posture and Locomotion	N/A
Stairs	N/A
Jumping	N/A
Balance	N/A

Andre appears to be functioning close to age level in many developmental domains. Concept development, problem solving, self-help, and attention and memory are his strengths. He is able to walk around furniture, stoop and retrieve objects, while using one hand for support. He has not taken any independent steps. His self-help skills and balance have improved significantly since the last evaluation. He will benefit from intervention to help him move toward age-appropriate skills in the Fine Motor and Gross Motor domains.

Outcomes of Early Intervention:
Outcome I: Andre will improve his memory and fine motor skills by imitating actions he has observed performed with objects, immediately and later in the day or week, by April, XXXX.

Short-Term Objectives: When given a model and asked to imitate it, Andre will activate toys

(continued)

Figure 3.3 (continued)

by turning a handle and holding the toy with both hands, immediately and later in the day, by February, XXXX. (He will turn a crank/handle at least 2 turns on the jack-in-box, busy box and noise maker, 3/3 2 opportunities.)

When given a model and asked to imitate it, Andre will pull pop-beads apart (using both hands) and place each in a bucket, immediately and later in the day, by February, XXX. (He will pull apart at least 4 beads, 3/3 2 opportunities.)

When given a model and asked to imitate it, Andre will put at least 5 shapes in a shape ball, immediately and later in the day, by March, XXX. (He will put in the circle, square, triangle, polygon, hexagon, 3/3 2 opportunities).

Outcome 2: Mr. and Mrs. Weiss would like information about in-home child care in the area, by April, XXXX.

Short-Term Objective: Mrs. Weiss would like to have Alicia W.'s phone number so she can call her about child care since this family has recently found in-home care, by January, XXXX.

Learning Opportunities/Interventions/Family Activities: Outcome I will be arranged after breakfast since Andre is very alert then, when Mr. Weiss returns from work, and during bathtime. Andre's grandparents will purchase similar toys so they can play with them when Andre is in their home. Mrs. Weiss will bring one of his toys to the church nursery each week. Mrs. Weiss has agreed to rotate toys every 2 days and use hand-over-hand support as needed.

Comments on Progress: The service provider will check Andre's progress at least once a month during home visits and discuss progress with Mrs. Weiss as needed.

to evaluate a child's functioning are determined by characteristics of the child, diagnostic concerns, and the professional judgment of team members. Infants and toddlers are identified as having developmental delays, rather than being given a specific diagnostic label.

Statement of Family Resources and Needs. Information about the family's strengths and needs that relate to that family's ability to support the child's development is noted. This is premised on the belief that with the right kind of supports, every family can support the development of a child with special needs. "Needs" refer to such things as information about a child's condition, typical child development, respite care, job training, or perhaps childcare facilities (McLean et al., 2004). IFSPs consider the needs of the child as well as those of the child-family unit. For instance, if a child needs a specialized wheelchair, but a family is unable to afford it, an infant-toddler program might attempt to help the family obtain

the wheelchair as a way of supporting desired changes in the child, as well as the family.

It is important that interviews with parents not make them feel they are being judged or evaluated. Asking an open-ended question such as "What are your greatest challenges as a family at this time?" is less threatening than asking "What do you need help with?" Appropriate interviewing is critical because parents are more likely to be supportive of an IFSP if they are active participants in its development.

Expected Outcomes for Child and Family. IFSPs follow a family-based approach, so families' priorities for intervention and service preferences are followed as much as possible (Sandall et al., 2005). Most IFSPs combine child and family outcomes. **Child outcomes** are objectives that support the child's development and/or behavior. The best child outcomes are those that are easily integrated into daily home routines (Sandall et al., 2005). Outcomes must be measurable and are written differently among programs and across states. However, most are written similarly to this: "Before dinner most evenings, Sahara will walk the length of the sofa at least 3 times to get a toy, by the end of June."

Family outcomes focus on the needs of parents, siblings, and/or the family unit. Although challenging at times, family outcomes, too, must be stated in measurable terms so their efficacy can be evaluated (Bailey, McWilliam, Darkes, Hebbeler, Simeonsson, Spiker, & Wagner, 1998). For example, after receiving an unexpected medical diagnosis and a home heart monitor for his 13-month-old son, one father stated that his family's need at the time was to "get used to the equipment." As stated, this outcome is difficult to evaluate. The father's statement was later written as a measurable family outcome in this way: "The Jones family would like to learn how to operate, maintain, and appropriately respond to Simon's monitor, by the end of August." Teams must review each child and family outcome frequently to make certain necessary areas of support are covered, without introducing "service overkill" (Jung, 2005).

Criteria, Procedures, and Time Lines for Evaluation.

The goal of evaluation is to determine if services are meeting the stated needs of the child and his or her family. The specificity of criteria and procedures on an IFSP varies significantly among programs. Teams determine the type of data needed to evaluate whether a child or family outcome has been met. "Procedures" are the short-term objectives, or small steps, taken to achieve an outcome. Procedures may include strategies suggested to family members to assist a child's learning, such as a parent imitating an infant's play during floor time. Procedures may also involve therapy activities or statements about how the teaching of outcomes will be embedded into family designated routines. Since family outcomes are identified by parents, parents are the logical ones to evaluate whether or not family outcomes have been satisfied. The evaluation of IFSPs should be used as another structured means for constantly improving services (Sandall et al., 2005).

Although all states have requirements for aspects of child services, such as adult-child ratios and safety requirements, comparable requirements for quality of services, provision of recommended practices, and family support activities do not exist. The majority of programs continue to evaluate services based of documented improvement in child functioning, satisfaction with services (Bailey, 2001), and improved family quality of life, although this is difficult to measure (Dunst & Bruder, 2002).

Services Needed. This section lists specific services needed to meet the child's and the family's needs, including a statement of frequency and method of delivering services. Services may include home visits, therapies, services in center-based programs, and/or consultations in community programs, such as daycare centers or YWCA swimming lessons.

Dates for Services and Agencies Responsible. The specific dates when services will begin and end and when evaluations will be conducted are listed. A delineation of services, by agency, facilitates interagency communication and follow-through. Each state's lead agency is responsible for establishing formal agreements with other agencies. Some programs use Medicaid and other third-party payments to provide some support for early intervention services. Every service listed on an IFSP has costs attached, which may prompt stress in families when all costs cannot be covered (Shannon, Grinde, & Cox, 2003).

Name of Service Coordinator. The **service coordinator** tends to be the professional whose background is most immediately relevant to the needs of the child and his or her family. This professional serves as a single point of contact in helping parents obtain services. Families report high satisfaction when services are administered following a family-centered approach and low satisfaction when services do not adhere to this model (Romer & Umbreit, 1998). Coordinating services, coordinating the development of the IFSP, and making sure all necessary professionals are involved are tasks performed by service coordinators.

Procedures for Transition to Preschool Programs. This section lists steps for supporting a child's passage from Part C, infant-toddler programs, to Part B, preschool and school-age programs, of the IDEA (2004). When children are 3 years old, the state education agency assumes responsibility for their education. The transition from infant-toddler services to preschool services can be problematic as well as stressful for children and their families (Wischnowski, Fowler, & McCollum, 2000). The loss of a secure, and often intimate, relationship with professionals that families enjoy in infant-toddler programs can lead to an emotional crisis for some parents. To ease transitions, good communication between programs is critical. Additionally, programs need to identify a key person or guide for families to lessen the stress (Hanson et al., 2000).

Developing an Individualized Education Program

An **Individualized Education Program (IEP)** is required when a child is 36 months old and begins receiving preschool services. Although there are similarities between the IFSP and the IEP, there are also differences. Table 3.2 lists some of differences between the documents.

An IEP is a document that outlines a child's individualized instructional program, provides a basis for evaluation, and offers a regular opportunity for communication between among professionals involved in a child's education. Like the IFSP, the best IEP is person-centered and encourages collaborative relationships with families (Chambers & Childre, 2005). An IEP for a preschooler must contain information for the parents and describe how the child's disability affects the child's participation in appropriate activities (Turnbull et al., 2006). Table 3.3 shows annual goals and short-term objective/benchmark clusters from Andre Weiss's IEP when he was 3 years old. At the time this was written, Andre was classified as having a developmental delay and was being served in an inclusive daycare program.

Figure 3.4 shows a portion of Andre's IEP when he was in second grade, after he had been identified as having a learning disability. At that time, he received services from a special education resource teacher and a physical therapist and spent most of his day in a general education class. As indicated by this IEP, he was provided accommodations for state and district

---

TABLE 3.2 Comparisons between an Individualized Family Service Plan (IFSP) and an Individualized Education Program (IEP) for young children with special needs

Individualized Family Service Plan (IFSP)

- Defines the family and the child as the recipients of services
- Focuses on the natural environments in which the child and the family live and interact
- Encourages intervention within home and community routines
- Includes interventions, supports, and services from a variety of health and human service organizations as well as education

Individualized Education Plan (IEP)

- Defines the child as the recipient of services, although it may offer the family recommendations and suggestions
- Tends to focus on interventions in classroom/school settings
- Includes interventions, supports, and related services with primarily school-based personnel

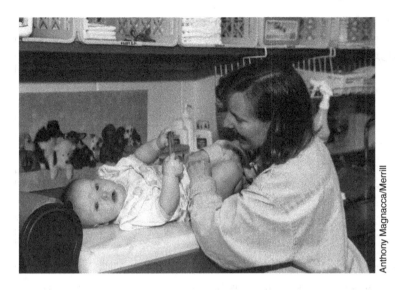

ECSE professionals collaborate with parents and caregivers to identify simple ways in which to embed development-enhancing activities into ongoing family activities.

assessments. Although he did not take alternative assessments, his school system elected to include both annual goals and short-term objectives/benchmarks in his IEP. Refer to Figure 3.4 as each component of an IEP is discussed.

Present Levels of Educational Performance. This section summarizes the child's strengths and weaknesses as identified by a team assessment. The IEP team includes professionals who are able to provide information about a child's needs in communication, motor areas, academics, and

---

TABLE 3.3 Annual goal and short-term objective/benchmark clusters from Andre Weiss's IEP when he was 37 months old, attending an inclusive daycare center

---

Annual Goal: Andre will improve his problem-solving skills/reasoning skills with objects by 6 months by June, XXXX.

Short-Term Objective/Benchmark 1: When given a variety of experiences, Andre will imitate an adult or peer in "solving" a problem involving materials, 3/3 opportunities for 2 days.
a. fits shovel in box when there are too many
b. completes shapebox when 3 pieces are missing and available in another shapebox
c. works with peer to construct an object from the story using at least 3 different materials and 1 "missing" material (he must ask for it)

Short-Term Objective/Benchmark 2: When given a variety of experiences and materials, Andre will imitate an adult or peer in creating patterns with blocks, 3/3 opportunities for 2 days.
a. block train
b. block building
c. block bridge with peer, taking turns

Short-Term Objective/Benchmark 3: When given a variety of puzzles, Andre will put together a 5-piece interconnecting puzzle with a peer, 3/3 opportunities for 3 days.

Figure 3.4 Excerpts from Andre Weiss' IEP when Andre was in second grade

INDIVIDUALIZED EDUCATION PROGRAM (IEP)

Student Name: Andre Weiss   Date: 7/5/XX
Student ID Number: 23XXX50   Grade: 2
DOB: 9/5/XX
Age: 8 yrs 2 months   Disability: Specific Learning Disability

PARTICIPANTS INVOLVED:

NAME OF PARTICIPANT	POSITION
Kathy and R. J. Weiss	Parents
Mr. Bill Sullivan	Asst. Principal
Peggy Histtery	Physical Therapist
Suzanne Sutner	Second Grade Teacher
Mariana Putney	Special Ed. Resource Teacher
Martha Weiss	Grandmother

PRESENT LEVEL OF PERFORMANCE:

Andre's is a second grade student whose disability inhibits his ability to read and write on grade level. He is able to perform on grade level in science and history when the material is read to him while no modifications are necessary for math, his preferred subject. He would benefit from intensive reading and written language instruction and the services of an occupational therapist to support his handwriting and balance needs. His parents report they would like to see him become more social with peers as well.

ASSESSMENT INFORMATION AND INSTRUCTIONAL NEEDS:

Andre passed the kindergarten literacy standards. Although he passed the first grade standard assessments in science, social studies, and mathematics (with scores of 170-200), he has not passed the first grade reading standards due to his difficulty with reading and reading. His sight reading vocabulary is at the I.8 grade level. Recent standardized testing revealed that he continues to perform below average in reading skills and he has particular difficulty with decoding, fluency and comprehension. His performance on these tests is consistent with the difficulties he experiences in class when independent reading is expected.

Additionally, Andre has difficulties with fine motor skills (particularly in handwriting), and dynamic and static balance. He benefits from taped readings of class material, computer-based books and programs for decoding and comprehension, repeated readings, and intensive reading instruction provided in the resource room. His teachers report he benefits from frequent reminders about what he should be doing. He prefers routines that allow him to track his own progress such as the computer reading program. He enjoys talking to adults over peers. He seems to appreciate when social interactions with peers are structured (e.g., group projects) and appears to require regular encouragement to join activities during physical education.

MEASURABLE ANNUAL GOALS

(1) ANNUAL GOAL: Andre will increase his reading fluency to the 2.5 grade level September, XXXX.

(2) ANNUAL GOAL: Andre will increase reading comprehension to the 3.0 grade level by September, XXXX.

How will progress toward this annual goal be measured? (check all that apply)

_X_ Classroom Participation	_X_ Observation	_X Criterion-referenced test: teacher–made
_X_ Checklist	____ Special Projects	_X Norm-referenced test: State Reading Assessment
_X_ Classwork	_X_ Tests and Quizzes	_X_Other: Fluency Evaluation
_X_ Homework	____ Written Reports	

SHORT TERM OBJECTIVES/BENCHMARKS

ANNUAL GOAL (1)

Objective/Benchmark #1: When given a story at the first grade level, Andre will read the story in 2 minutes with 40 or more words correct.

Objective/Benchmark #2: When given a story at the first grade level, Andre will read the story in 2 minutes with 50 or more words correct.

Objective/Benchmark #3: When given a story at the second grade level, Andre will read the story in 2 minutes with 55 or more words correct.

ANNUAL GOAL (2)

Objective/Benchmark #1: When given a story at the first grade level, Andre will read the story independently and answer 10 inferential questions with 80% accuracy.

Objective/Benchmark #2: When given a story at the second grade level, Andre will read the story independently and answer 10 factual questions with 90% accuracy.

Objective/Benchmark #3: When given reading in science, social studies, and language arts at the second grade level, Andre will read the material using the POSSE strategy (predict, organize, search, summarize and evaluate) at least 50% of the time.

SERVICES – LEAST RESTRICTIVE ENVIRONMENT – PLACEMENT:

Andre will receive more than 60% of his education in the general education classroom. It will be modified to support his below-grade level reading and written language skills.

Services will be provided in:
_X_ general education class(es)
_X_ resource room
___ special class(es)
___ special education day school
___ state special education program/school
___ residential facility
___ home-based
___ hospital
___ other (describe):

Service(s)	Frequency	Location	Duration m/d/y to m/d/y
Physical Therapy	30 min/every 2 wks	Liberty Elem.	8/30/XX-8/30/XX
Special Education Resource Class	1 hr/5 days wk	Rm. 108	8/30/XX-8/30/XX
Collaboration/consultation with 2nd grade team	M/W 3:15-4:15	Rm. 108	9/3/XX-9/3/XX

STATE AND DISTRICT-WIDE ASSESSMENTS:

Will the student be at an age or a grade level for which the student is eligible to participate in a state or district-wide assessment? ___No _X_Yes

ACCOMMODATIONS/MODIFICATIONS:

Accommodation(s)/Modification(s)	Frequency	Location	Duration
Classroom: • taped instructions before lesson • instructions re-read • assignments will be given ahead to family so they can help student prepare • additional time for in-class quizzes, tests (taken in resource room)	At least 3 X a week; when needed	Rm. 115	8/30/XX-8/30/XX

(continued)

Figure 3.4 (continued)

• ensure that appropriate books and assignments are in backpack • written assignments may be taken home to complete when unfinished at school • graphic organizers for science, social studies chapters • assistance in outlining chapters in resource room			
State /District Assessments: • instructions read to student • double time for all reading related sections • answers written directly in testing booklet • reading comprehension sections will be read to student	As needed	TBA	8/30/XX-8/30/XX

behavior. Like the similar section in the IFSP, this section should focus more on the child's strengths than weaknesses and should be written in positive language. Children with more significant learning needs may have their levels of performance described with alternative assessment procedures. Alternative assessments are discussed in Chapter 10.

Annual Goals. **Annual goals** are measurable statements describing long-term objectives for the child. They must be achievable in a year and identify ways to help the child be successful in either the general education curriculum or an adapted curriculum. They are written with observable terms, such as *write*, *verbally identify*, and *calculate*. Terms that cannot be easily measured, such as *know*, *appreciate*, and *understand*, are not used. Most states have established standards for reading, mathematics, social studies, and other subjects in the general curriculum for each grade level. For children participating in the general education curriculum, annual goals tend to be standards-driven, resulting in outcomes that can be measured by classroom, curriculum, district, or state assessments. Annual goals must identify (1) the learner, (2) the skill or behavior, (3) the criteria, and (4) the time when the skill will be achieved.

Short-Term Objectives/Benchmarks. **Short-term objectives** or **benchmarks** are the small steps that

will lead to completion of an annual goal. Objectives must be stated in ways that are observable, measurable, child-oriented, and positive (Polloway, Patton, & Serna, 2005). These intermediate steps permit professionals to determine if the child is making progress toward the annual goal. Short-term objectives/benchmarks include (1) the condition (the material or evaluation setting), (2) the child's name, (3) a clearly defined behavior, and (4) a performance criterion (Meisels & Atkins-Burnett, 2001). Many states use state- or districtwide assessments to determine if children have met the state or district standards required by the No Child Left Behind (NCLB) legislation (No Child Left Behind, 2002). Short-term objectives/benchmarks are required only for children who will receive alternative assessments (IDEA, 2004). These are usually children with moderate to severe disabilities who do not take the state- or districtwide assessments, but have their assessments aligned to alternative achievement standards (Brynes, 2004).

Statement of Special Education and Related Services and Supplementary Aids/Services. This section lists the types of special education services that will be provided (e.g., general education class with consultation, general education class and resource room), the professionals who will provide services, and the type of support services that will be delivered, such as transportation or speech-language therapy in the classroom or psychological services (Turnbull et al., 2006).

Statement of Program Modifications/Supports for School Personnel.
How the educational curriculum will be adapted (e.g., reading series at a different level than that used by others in the class) and what supports will be provided for school personnel (e.g., braille textbooks, a sign interpreter in the general education class, consultations with an occupational therapist to develop adapted writing materials for a child, etc.) are listed in this section.

Explanation of the Extent the Child Will Participate with Children Without Disabilities/Projected Dates of Services with Anticipated Frequency, Duration, and Location.
The least restrictive environment is the setting that is most appropriate for an individual child's needs. The IDEA (2004) states in Section 1412(a)(5):

To the maximum extent appropriate, students with disabilities [will be] educated with students who are not disabled, and special classes, separate schooling or other removal of students with disabilities from the regular educational environment [may occur] only when the nature or severity of the disability of a child is such that education in regular classes with the use of supplementary aids and services cannot be achieved satisfactorily for that student.

The percentage of time each week a child will participate in the general education curriculum is delineated in this section.

For some children, contact with children without disabilities might occur during lunch, during participation in nonacademic subjects such as music and art, and/or during participation in structured inclusion activities such as "Fun Fridays" with another class in the afternoon. Other children, particularly those with mild disabilities, may receive their education in the general education classroom, with special education services provided within that setting as needed. Still others may leave the general education classroom to go to a resource room where they receive individualized instruction from a special education teacher.

Statement of Individual Modifications in Administration of Statewide/Districtwide Assessments.
This section lists accommodations that will be provided for a child so he or she can participate in statewide and districtwide assessments. For example, because Andre Weiss's reading level was below grade level, portions of state and district assessments were read to him, his responses were recorded by a adult on the test booklet, and he was given additional time to take in-class, state, and district tests (see Figure 3.4).

Statement of How the Child's Progress Toward Annual Goals Will Be Measured and How Parents Will Be Informed of Progress.
The IEP lists when and how annual goals and objectives will be measured and when and how parents will be informed of progress. States that are examining the efficacy of three-year IEPs under the direction of the IDEA (2004) will evaluate IEPs at "natural transition points" that cannot be longer than three years. For young children with special needs, this will be the transition from preschool/kindergarten to school-age services.

The language used in IFSPs and IEPs must be family-sensitive. **Family-sensitive language** is positive and nonjudgmental. For instance, this judgmental statement was written on an IFSP for a 33-month-old child with cerebral palsy: "Kayla's parents do not seem to have realistic expectations for what Kayla can accomplish." This statement is unprofessional, offensive, and clearly insensitive to the family. To make the sentiment behind this statement family-sensitive, it could be rewritten this way: "Kayla's parents are optimistic about her potential and future."

Both the IFSP and the IEP require that information about a child be shared with the family as quickly as possible. However, professionals need to be sensitive to how much information any family member can absorb at one time. Further, results should be shared as many times as a family member may need. Difficulty with retention of information is a predictable reaction to stress. As the parent of an 8-year-old with moderate mental retardation related:

I probably asked the same two questions of every person I saw that first 6 months [of receiving services]. "What is wrong with my son?" "Will he ever be able to take care of himself?" I always felt [the professionals, doctors] knew more than they would tell me. . . . I couldn't remember what someone told me 5 minutes before. I wanted to see if they had the same answers. Of course, they didn't.

MONITORING SKILL ACQUISITION

Embedding learning opportunities into ongoing activities or routines is recommended practice for teaching infants, toddlers, and preschoolers and may be called **routine-based instruction** (Davis, Kilgo, & Gamel-McCormick, 1998; Raver, 2003) or **activity-based intervention** (Pretti-Frontczak & Bricker, 2004). This approach utilizes ongoing activities within family routines or within center-based programs to teach individualized objectives to children. Although embedding individual instruction into routines is a simple concept, research has shown that it can be challenging to implement (Pretti-Frontczak & Bricker, 2001). Professionals need a method for keeping track of objectives, or many teaching-learning opportunities may be overlooked (Horn, Lieiber, Sandall, & Schwartz, 2001).

An **individual activity-objective matrix (IAOM)** is a planning aid that can help professionals track the teaching and acquisition of objectives (Raver, 2004). This matrix lists a child's targeted objectives and identifies how a teacher will adjust *specific activities or routines* to teach that child needed skills or behaviors. Without this kind of planning, group instruction can easily unravel with young children. By using a matrix for each child, professionals are able to avoid on-the-spot decisions about how to engage a child or avoid the struggle to remember what a child should be learning. The matrix encourages teachers to distribute teaching of objectives throughout the day, within planned activities (e.g., circle time, snack time, table activity) as well as unplanned activities (e.g., arrival, walking to buses) (Macy & Bricker, 2006). It permits teachers to teach skills when they are related to children's play or a class activity. Figure 3.5 shows an IAOM for 4-year-old Li, who has cerebral palsy and significant communication delays.

Besides keeping track of what to teach, teachers need to track whether a child is learning targeted skills and behaviors and whether interventions are effective. To ensure that individualized teaching and monitoring are embedded into routines for toddlers and preschoolers in center-based programs, professionals follow three steps (Raver, 2003). Each step will be discussed using Li's matrix, which was written by Ms. Kelly, Li's teacher in her preschool class for children with developmental delays (see Figure 3.5).

STEP 1: Identify the skill(s) to be taught. Drawn from multidisciplinary assessments, criterion/curriculum-referenced assessments, checklists, direct observations, and interviews with the family, the skills the child needs to learn are listed by domain on the top row of the matrix. Often just the process of selecting and writing objectives on the matrix increases the chances that teachers will structure appropriate teaching episodes within scheduled activities (Horn et al., 2001).

Writing objectives in the exact way they appear in the curriculum or in assessment tools is never appropriate. ECSE professionals need to rewrite these objectives to make them more functional and more easily incorporated into routines. For example, the assessment item "finds toy under one of two containers after containers have been reversed" can be rewritten this way for a matrix: "systematically searches for objects seen hidden, then reversed." The way this statement is phrased increases the chances the teacher will teach a skill that will be generalized within and outside the classroom.

STEP 2: Teach identified objective(s)/outcomes during activities and routines. Teaching a skill within the context in which it will be used makes it more meaningful to a young child (McLean et al., 2004). Further, skills taught within routines may produce better generalization to different materials and people (Sandall et al., 2005). Naturally, there may be certain skills that are difficult to embed in a

Figure 3.5 Individual activity-objective matrix for the week of October 11–15 for 4-year old Li who attends a preschool class for children with developmental delays

Li	Shows organized search behaviors when containers reversed (Cognitive)	Moves with balance (Gross Motor)	Puts small objects in containers using both hands (Fine Motor)	Signs peers' names when requested (Exp. Language)	Points to picture when requested when 2 pics are presented (Recept. Language)
Opening Group	Uncovers friend's picture when hidden, reversed	Places and retrieves objects from high shelf [+]	Puts own picture in "girl box" slot, VA	Signs Josh/Daven when asked	Points to rain cloud/song symbols on calendar when req. [+]
Snack	Finds cup hidden under mat	Moves chair to table, I [−]	Puts spoon in narrow cup to stir chocolate milk	Signs Raylon/Sarah when requested, GMA	Points to grape & orange juice pic when requested
Art Center	Finds hidden then reversed supplies [+]	Gives material to friend at end of table using R-hand to stablize	Puts materials away in containers for clean up, GMA	Signs whose "product" teacher is holding [+]	Points to two parts of "product" when named [+]
Construction Center	Finds marbles hidden in block house	Climbs stairs to block shelf to put blocks away, GMA	Loads small sticks in truck bed, VA [−]	Signs name of friend who is playing next to her [+]	Points to block/stick when requested
Rest Time	Finds socks saw hidden under rest mat	Helps stack mats under table, GMA	Puts small books in small box after rest	Signs friend who is to her right	Points to shirt/pillow in pic when requested [−]
Story Time/ Closing Group	Uncovers picture from story	Does "Hokey Pokey" to closing song [−]	Puts activity symbol on template on calendar [−]	Signs/points to who made selected "product" that day when shown object	Points to two activity cards she participated in that day

routine. In this case, a teacher may need to arrange a situation to specifically teach that skill.

However, merely creating an opportunity for learning is not sufficient to ensure that learning will occur. That is by placing several pairs of socks and mittens in a center, a teacher is arranging an activity for teaching sorting. Yet, without direct instruction, most children with special needs may have difficulty learning the concepts of "same" and "different" from this activity as it is structured. Children with special needs require direct instruction to learn concepts. To accomplish this, teachers must structure short, intensive teaching episodes within activities and routines (Horn et al., 2001). Such a direct teaching episode is rarely longer than two to four minutes and focuses on what a particular child needs to learn from an activity. The matrix allows teachers to know what should be taught and to plan how they will teach it.

During opening circle, for instance, Ms. Kelly asked Li to get the witch hat for their song. The hat had been placed on the top shelf of the bookcase, so Li had to climb the two steps that had been placed in front of the bookcase to get the hat (gross motor objective). Before circle began, the paraprofessional was assigned to help Li navigate the steps by holding the railings and shifting her weight appropriately. This careful planning allowed Ms. Kelly to create a short, individualized teaching session for Li *within* circle time. She knew Li needed a lot of practice with this skill, so she structured several "embedded learning/teaching opportunities" throughout the day. The matrix focused Ms. Kelly's attention on what Li actually needed to learn within an activity, rather than on how well she painted witches in the art center. This kind of planning and individualized teaching was necessary to ensure that Li had sufficient practice to learn new skills.

STEP 3: Determine how and when monitoring will occur. Routines offer a good context for data collection. The data box located in the

lower right-hand corner of each objective box on an IAOM allows the teacher to take data on the child's responses to the teacher's probes within activities (see Figure 3.5). Although **naturalistic data**, data taken during activities, are not as precise as data from trial-by-trial probes or perhaps data taken in one-to-one teaching/assessment sessions, the process is nonthreatening and evaluates a child's functional use of a skill (Linder, 2008; Sandall et al., 2005). By monitoring child progress on targeted objectives during routines, the teacher is able to select materials that motivate the child as well as avoiding the trap of requiring the child to respond on command to traditional assessment tasks and materials. Teachers can also use instructional strategies that accommodate each child's sensory, physical, and communicative differences (Cook, 2004; Neisworth & Bagnato, 2005).

Procedures for collecting data should (1) be time efficient, (2) be tailored to the child's needs, (3) require minimal data-gathering skills, and (4) require minimal data-interpreting skills (Roach & Elliot, 2005). Data collection, like teaching, is most effective when it is dispersed throughout the day. Data can be taken any time during an activity or routine, even during "cleanup" or transitions (Werts, Wolery, Holcombe, Vassilaros, & Wolery, 2001). With naturalistic data collection, a teacher is not only tracking a child's progress on a skill, but also monitoring whether the child can demonstrate that skill when it is really needed (Puckett & Black, 2000).

It is common knowledge that data will be taken more frequently if the process is quick and does not disrupt the flow of an activity. To monitor the progress of children who learn more slowly or who need partial or full assistance, the level of support for a skill is also noted on the IOAM. With some of Li's gross motor tasks, for instance, "graduated manual assistance" (GMA) was needed. Table 3.4 shows the common levels of teacher assistance that may be coded on a matrix.

TABLE 3.4 Levels of assistance codes for an individual activity-objective matrix for children who require teacher support

VC = Verbal Command. Child responds to task when told to do it. Example: "Put the circle in, please."

VA = Verbal Assistance. Child responds to task when verbal guidance is given. Example: "Put the circle here, please."

M = Model. Child responds to task when given verbal direction while task is demonstrated. Example: "See, the circle goes here," while teacher places circle in the puzzle.

GMA = Graduated Manual Assistance. Child responds to task when told to do it while being given some level of physical assistance. Example: "The circle goes here, just like this," while gently guiding the child's hand toward the puzzle.

At the end of the day, data are transferred to individual domain graphs, such as Li's fine motor domain graph, shown in Figure 3.6. After the data are transferred to the appropriate domain graph, they are erased from the matrix, and the matrix is reused the following day. Data are recorded for each domain separately. As a child reaches the established criterion for mastery on an objective, that objective is deleted, and a new one is written in that space on the IAOM. Li's criterion for mastery for her current fine motor objective was 3/3 (100%) for two days. That is, although Ms. Kelly taught the skill throughout the day, she gave Li only three probes during the day. Objectives on the matrix were taught every day, although data may not have been taken every day on every objective.

Many teachers report that training paraprofessionals to take data on specific children is well worth the effort. In fact, involving paraprofessionals and other support staff in the development of an IAOM is a good way to help everyone see "the whole child." When this information is shared, related service providers, such as speech-language pathologists and physical therapists, are encouraged to use activities that support a child's objectives in all domains, not merely the objectives within the specialist's area.

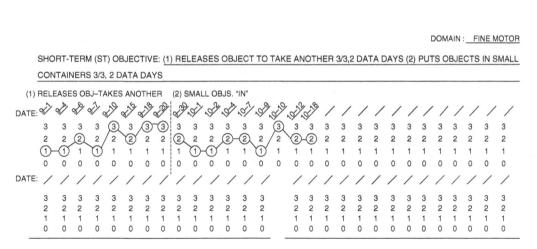

Figure 3.6 Fine motor data for Li from individual activity-objective matrix

Individualized Instruction for Primary-Aged Students

Special education for primary-aged children is defined by these instructional features: (1) individually planned programs for a particular setting; (2) specialized support services to meet the child's needs, such as speech-language pathology services; (3) intensive services; (4) goal-directed instruction with future environments in mind; (5) utilization of research-based methods; and (6) programs guided by the child's performance (Salend, 2005). Teachers can easily modify the IAOM system to monitor the daily progress of primary-aged children. Figure 3.7 shows an individual lesson-objective matrix for a second-grade student with learning disabilities in a general education class. Other monitoring procedures such as self-monitoring are discussed in Chapter 9. The bottom line is that ECSE teachers must take data on child progress regularly, whether in separate or inclusive classrooms, so they are able to make informed intervention decisions (Meisels & Atkins-Burnett, 2001).

Conclusion

Assessment is used for screening, making eligibility decisions, developing instructional programs, and monitoring children's progress. Norm-referenced, criterion-referenced, play-based, and/ or judgment-based instruments can be used for one or more of these purposes. Teams use information gained from team assessments to develop IFSPs and IEPs for young children. As was shown in Andre's case study and the documents developed for him and his family, professionals embed learning opportunities into home- and center-based routines when they are working with infants, toddlers, and preschoolers. Young children seem to learn best when they have multiple opportunities, distributed throughout routines, to learn new skills.

Additionally, professionals must have a system for individualizing instruction and monitoring the acquisition of skills that does not disrupt the flow of interaction and teaching. With appropriate planning, professionals are able to individualize what they teach children and make data collection an integral and reliable component of each day.

Summary

Assessment

- Assessment involves the systematic collection of information about a child and has these characteristics: (1) professionals involve families in assessment by soliciting the family's concerns, the child's interests, the child's abilities, and child/family needs; (2) assessment is individualized; (3) assessment provides useful information for intervention; (4) professionals share information in understandable ways; (5) professionals rely on materials that capture the child's authentic behaviors; and (6) professionals meet legal and procedural guidelines.

Developing individualized programs

- IFSPs have these components: (1) a statement of developmental levels; (2) a statement of family resources and needs; (3) the expected outcomes for the child and family; (4) the criteria, procedures, and timelines for evaluation; (5) the services needed; (6) the dates for services and agencies responsible; (7) the name of the service coordinator; and (8) procedures for transition to a preschool program.
- IEPs have these components: (1) present levels of educational performance; (2) annual goals; (3) short-term objectives/benchmarks (required only if a child is taking alternative assessments); (4) a statement of special education and related services and supplementary aids/services; (5) a statement of program modification/supports for school personnel; (6) an explanation of the extent the child will participate with children without disabilities and the projected dates of services; (7) a statement of individual modifications for statewide/districtwide assessments; and

Figure 3.7 Mathematics individual lesson-objective matrix for Minako, second grade student with a learning disability in a general education classroom

Week of: Feb 2–6

Minako Math	Objective: Follow written and oral directions	Objective: Identify operation by sign before beginning (+, −)	Objective: Regroup tens (addition)	Objective: Indentify operation in word problem	Objective: Verbally describe functions as she performs them	Objective: Addition Math facts (fluency)	Objective: Subtract. Math facts (fluency)
Full Math Group	Summarizes what was taught	States operation ✓	States the process of regrouping ✓		Verbally describes process ✓	1-7 facts −	1-5 facts
Small Math Group	Restates directions before beginning work	Circles operation sign	70% correct addition regrouping ✓ 73%	Writes operation(s) next to problem number	Verbally describes process to Ms. Betty	Computer game	Computer game ✓ − needed help
Math Indep. Work	Restates directions before beginning work in folder	States, circles operation ✓	70% correct on practice sheet ✓ 40%	Writes operation(s) next to problem number when approp. ✓	Uses self-talk to solve problems	Items added to practice sheet	Items added to practice sheet
Math Interest Center	Restates math objectives for dinosaur center		Calculates how many more T. Rex babies than mothers ✓ 100%	Writes operation before computation	Uses self-talk to solve problems	With partner calculates: how much water drank, food eaten	Computer game with dinosaurs

(8) a statement of how a child's progress will be measured and parents informed of progress.

Monitoring skill acquisition

- For infants, toddlers, and preschoolers in home- and center-based programs, the teaching and evaluation of individual objectives are embedded into ongoing activities and routines.
- Individualized instruction for primary-aged students involves individually planned programs for a particular setting, specialized support services to meet the child's needs, intensive services, goal-directed instruction, the use of research-based methods, and programs guided by the child's performance.

DISCUSSION QUESTIONS/ACTIVITIES

1. Describe two advantages and two disadvantages of using the following types of assessment instruments to plan individualized programs for infants, toddlers, and preschoolers and primary-aged students: (a) norm-referenced tools, (b) criterion/ curriculum-referenced tools, (c) play-based tools, and (d) judgment-based tools.

2. Identify one strategy for individualizing instruction for primary-aged students with mild special needs in a general education classroom.

3. Based on Andre's case study, write two additional outcomes for Andre using the assessment information from the IFSP that was developed when Andre was 20 months old (Figure 3.3).

REFERENCES

Andersson, L. (2004). Appropriate and inappropriate interpretation and use of test scores in early intervention. *Journal of Early Intervention, 27*(1), 55–68.

Bagnato, S. (2005). The authentic alternative for assessment in early intervention: An emerging evidence-based practice. *Journal of Early Intervention, 28*(1), 17–22.

Bailey, D. (2001). Evaluating parent involvement and family support in early intervention and preschool programs. *Journal of Early Intervention, 24*(1), 1–14.

Bailey, D., McWilliam, R., Darkes, L., Hebbeler, K., Simeonsson, R., Spiker, D., & Wagner, M. (1998). Family outcomes in early intervention: A framework for program evaluation and efficacy research. *Exceptional Children, 64*(3), 313–328.

Bowe, F. (2004). *Birth to eight: Early childhood special education* (3rd ed.). Sidney, Australia: Thomson/Delmar Learning.

Bricker, D., & Waddell, M. (2002). *Assessment, evaluation, and programming system for infants and children— Curriculum for three-to-six year olds* (2nd ed.). Baltimore, MD: Brookes.

Brynes, M. A. (2004). Alternative assessments FAQs (and answers). *TEACHING Exceptional Children, 36,* 58–63.

Chambers, C., & Childre, A. (2005). Fostering family-professional collaboration through person-centered IEP meetings. *Young Exceptional Children, 8*(3), 20–28.

Connolly, A. (1998). *KeyMath revised: A diagnostic inventory of essential mathematics.* Circle Pines, MN: American Guidance Services.

Cook, R. (2004). Embedding assessment of young children into routines in inclusive settings: A systematic approach. *Young Exceptional Children, 7*(3), 2–11.

Davis, M., Kilgo, J., & Gamel-McCormick, M. (1998). *Young children with special needs: A developmentally appropriate approach.* Boston: Allyn & Bacon.

Dunst, C., & Bruder, M. B. (2002). Valued outcomes of service coordination, early intervention, and natural environments. *Exceptional Children, 68*(3), 361–375.

Grisham-Brown, J., & Pretti-Frontczak, K. (2003). Using planning time to individualize instruction for preschoolers with special needs. *Journal of Early Intervention, 26*(1), 31–46.

Handicapped Children's Protection Act of 1986. 20 U.S. Congress Record 1401.

Hanson, M., Beckman, P., Horn, E., Marquart, J., Sandall, S., Greig, D., & Brennan, E. (2000). Entering preschool: Family and professional experiences in this transition process. *Journal of Early Intervention, 23*(4), 279–293.

Hemmeter, M., Smith, B., Sandall, S., & Askew, L. (2005). *DEC recommended practices workbook.* Missoula, MT: Division of Early Childhood of the Council for Exceptional Children.

Horn, E., Lieber, J., Sandall, S., & Schwartz, I. (2001). Embedded learning opportunities as an instructional strategy for supporting children's learning in inclusive programs. In M. Ostrosky & S. Sandall (Eds.), *Teaching strategies: What to do to support young children's development* (YEC Monograph No. 3) (pp. 59–70). Denver, CO: Sopris West.

Jarrett, M., Browne, B., & Wallin, C. (2006). Using portfolio assessment to document developmental progress of infants and toddlers. *Young Exceptional Children, 10,* 22–33.

Johnson-Martin, N., Attermeier, S., & Hacker, B. (2004). *The Carolina Curriculum for Infants and Toddlers with Special Needs* (3rd ed.). Baltimore, MD: Brookes.

Johnson-Martin, N., Hacker, B., & Attermeier, S. (2004). *The Carolina Curriculum for Preschoolers with Special Needs* (3rd ed.). Baltimore, MD: Brookes.

Jung, L. (2005). Can we all fit? Squeezing in better support with fewer people. *Young Exceptional Children, 8,* 19–27.

Kovanen, S. (2001). Comprehensiveness is a cliché: Professional practice in child assessment and planning. *Journal of Early Intervention, 23*(1), 25–34.

Linder, T. (Ed.) (2008) *Transdisciplinary play-based assessment & transdisciplinary play-based intervention (2nd ed.).* Baltimore: Brookes Publishing.

Losardo, A., & Notari-Syverson, A. (2001). *Alternative approaches to assessing young children.* Baltimore, MD: Brookes.

Lynch, E., & Struewing, N. (2001). Children in context: Portfolio assessment in the inclusive early childhood classroom. *Young Exceptional Children, 5*(1), 2–10.

Individuals with Disabilities Education Improvement Act of 2004, Pub. L. No. 108–446, (2004).

Macy, M., & Bricker, D. (2006). Practical applications for using curriculum-based assessment to create embedded learning opportunities for young children. *Young Exceptional Children, 9,* 12–21.

Macy, M., Bricker, D., & Squires, J. (2005). Validity and reliability of a curriculum-based assessment approach to determine eligibility for Part C services. *Journal of Early Intervention, 28*(1), 1–16.

McLean, M. (2005). Using curriculum-based assessment to determine eligibility: Time for a paradigm shift? *Journal of Early Intervention, 28*(1), 23–27.

McLean, M., Wolery, M., & Bailey, D. (2004). *Assessing infants and preschoolers with special needs* (3rd ed.). Upper Saddle River, NJ: Merrill/Prentice Hall.

Meisels, S., & Atkins-Burnett, S. (2001). The elements of early childhood assessment. In J. P. Shonkoff & S. J. Meisels (Eds.), *Handbook of early intervention* (2nd ed., pp. 231–257). Cambridge, England: Cambridge University Press.

Neisworth, J., & Bagnato, S. (2005). DEC recommended practices: Assessment. In S. Sandall, M. L. Hemmeter, B. Smith, & M. McLean (Eds.), *DEC recommended practices: A comprehensive guide to practical application in early intervention/early childhood special education* (pp. 45–69). Longmont, CO: Sopris West.

No Child Left Behind Act of 2001, Pub. L. No. 107–110, 115 Stat. 1425 (2002).

Polloway, E., Patton, J., & Serna, L. (2005*). Strategies for teaching learners with special needs* (8th ed.). Upper Saddle River, NJ: Merrill/Prentice Hall.

Pretti-Frontczak, K., & Bricker, D. (2001). Use of embedding strategy during daily activities by early childhood education and early childhood special education teachers. *Infant-Toddler Intervention, 11*(2), 111–128.

Pretti-Frontczak, K., & Bricker, D. (2004). *An activity-based approach to early intervention* (3rd ed.). Baltimore, MD: Brookes.

Puckett, M., & Black, J. (2000). *Authentic assessment of the young child.* Upper Saddle River, NJ: Merrill/Prentice Hall.

Raver, S. (2003). Keeping track: Routine-based instruction and monitoring. *Young Exceptional Children, 6*(3), 12–20.

Raver, S. A. (2004). Monitoring child progress in early childhood special education settings. *TEACHING Exceptional Children, 36*(6), 52–57.

Roach, A., & Elliot, S. (2005). Goal attainment scaling: An efficient and effective approach to monitoring student progress. *TEACHING Exceptional Children, 37,* 8–17.

Romer, E., & Umbreit, J. (1998). The effects of family-centered service coordination: A social validity study. *Journal of Early Intervention, 21*(2), 95–110.

Roopnarine, J., & Johnson, J. (2005). *Approaches to early childhood education* (4th ed.). Upper Saddle River, NJ: Merrill/Prentice Hall.

Salend, S. J. (2005). *Creating inclusive classrooms: Effective and reflective practices for all students* (5th ed.). Upper Saddle River, NJ: Merrill/Prentice Hall.

Sandall, S., Hemmeter, M. L., Smith, B., & McLean, M. (Eds.). (2005). *DEC recommended practices: A comprehensive guide to practical application in early intervention/early childhood special education.* Longmont, CO: Sopris West.

Sandall, S., Schwartz, I., & Lacroix, B. (2004). Interventionists' perspectives about data collecting in integrated early childhood classrooms. *Journal of Early Intervention, 26*(3), 161–174.

Shannon, P., Grinde, L., & Cox, A. (2003). Families' perceptions of the ability to pay for early intervention services. *Journal of Early Intervention, 25*(3), 164–172.

Taylor, R. (2006). *Assessment of exceptional students: Educational and psychological procedures* (7th ed.). Boston: Pearson.

Turnbull, R., Huerta, N., & Stowe, M. (2006). *The Individuals with Disabilities Education Act as amended in 2004.* Upper Saddle River, NJ: Merrill/Prentice Hall.

Vanderheyden, A. (2005). Intervention-driven assessment practices in early childhood/early intervention: Measuring what is possible rather than what is present. *Journal of Early Intervention, 28*(1), 28–33.

Werts, M., Wolery, M., Holcombe, M., Vassilaros, R., & Wolery, M. (2001). Embedding time delay procedures in classroom activities. In M. Ostrosky & S. Sandall (Eds.), *Teaching strategies: What to do to support young children's development* (YEC Monograph No. 3) (pp. 81–90). Denver, CO: Sopris West.

Wischnowski, M., Fowler, S., & McCollum, J. (2000). Supports and barriers to writing an interagency agreement on the preschool transition. *Journal of Early Intervention, 23*(4), 294–307.

Woodcock, R. W. (1998). *Woodcock Reading Mastery Tests–Revised–Normative Update*. Circle Pines, MN: American Guidance Service.

Chapter

4

Effective Instructional
and Accommodative
Practices

Sharon A. Raver

Overview

This chapter explores effective instructional practices in separate (self-contained) and inclusive settings, including

designing and managing the physical space

planning for instruction

instructional approaches

instructional strategies

increasing engagement in young children

inclusive and accommodative practices

CASE STUDY: Marina and Family

When Marina was adopted by Susan and Steve O'Daniel from an orphanage in Ukraine, she was 26 months old and showing a 4–5 month delay in expressive and receptive language, fine motor, and cognitive skills. Because of these delays and bonding concerns, the family received services from an infant-toddler program until Marina was 38 months old. By that time, Marina was a well-integrated member of the family of six.

At 3, Marina's parents indicated that they wanted her to attend a preschool for typically developing children. She received consultant services from an ECSE teacher for her continued mild delays in expressive language and social-emotional development. At 4½, Marina was diagnosed with attention deficit/hyperactivity disorder (AD/HD). The family began counseling, and a behavioral plan was introduced at home and in her preschool, which improved her sleep patterns and her compliance at home and school.

Since Marina tested at age level in school readiness, she attended a general education kindergarten, where she thrived on reading. Midyear, a Section 504 Accommodation Plan was developed at the request of the family and the kindergarten teacher to address Marina's verbal impulsivity and behavior during large-group instruction. Today, Marina has finished first grade, scoring at grade level in all subjects except reading, her scores for which place her on a mid-third-grade level. She is a motivated student who says she would like to be "a teacher or a star in a soap opera."

Programs for young children with disabilities are lively, dynamic places. Research has documented that young children with disabilities and delays learn best when they are actively engaged in activities and learning (Pretti-Frontczak & Bricker, 2004). Rather than leaving learning to chance, early childhood special education (ECSE) professionals carefully arrange environments to influence behavior, learning, and appropriate social interactions. To maximize positive developmental outcomes, both the physical and the instructional conditions of a setting must be manipulated to match the individual needs of children.

DESIGNING AND MANAGING THE PHYSICAL SPACE

An organized physical environment is the best place to begin when attempting to support a child's development and learning. Establishing order in the physical environment and following a schedule allow children, at home and in the classroom, to anticipate what will happen next and permit families and teachers to spend more quality time with children.

Teachers have learned that structuring the physical space can increase instructional time with children who require support with learning. Careful planning ensures that instruction is tailored to the individual needs of a child and that needed materials are available and developmentally appropriate. To increase the number of learning opportunities in classrooms serving children with diverse abilities, the duties of staff must be delineated, learning centers must be individualized, and materials and transitions must be well planned.

Using Staff Effectively

Staffing and supervision plans can influence the amount of learning that occurs in a classroom. A daily schedule that reflects both the learners' activities and staff responsibilities can increase teaching time and adult interactions (Santos, Lignugaris-Kraft, & Akers, 2000).

Infants, toddlers, and preschoolers in center-based programs benefit when schedules are designed so that one adult is preparing a zone or learning area while another adult is teaching. With this organizational pattern, called **zones**, children move from one adult to another without the adult collecting materials and children waiting for the next activity to begin. For example, as the teacher is conducting opening circle, the paraprofessional is setting up table activities and greeting late-arriving children. When the paraprofessional's tasks are completed, he or she joins the circle to support the teacher. Five minutes before circle is over, the paraprofessional moves again to the table area, and the children are directed to join him or her there. As the paraprofessional begins the table activity with the children, the teacher prepares the upcoming activity and then returns to coteach with the paraprofessional or supervise a different center. Zones require a daily schedule divided into activity-time blocks, with the specific tasks assigned to each adult outlined. Casey and McWilliam (2005) suggest that children with disabilities have higher levels of attention to tasks when zones are used for activities and transitions.

Scheduling staff time makes the day predictable, reduces downtime, improves children's behavior, decreases the time transitions take, and clarifies adults' tasks and responsibilities. Although zones are a common approach for children under the age of 5, they are not typically used in kindergarten through third-grade classrooms.

Organizing Learning Centers

Centers, designated regions of a classroom for teaching specific skills and/or activities, are a typical approach for teaching infants, toddlers, and preschoolers Usually, there is a "homemaking" center, a "block/ construction" center, a "reading/literacy" center, an "art" center, a "computer" center, and a center for "table activities," which may also double as the snack area and occasionally as the group-activities area. Generally, centers are separated by shelves, carpet, or room dividers and have pictures or signs identifying them (Phelps & Hanline, 1999).

The way materials are organized in centers can aid in teaching basic skills (Sandall, Hemmeter, Smith, & McLean, 2005). Block shelves should be arranged by shape, such as triangles together and squares together, and in descending size order from left to right to encourage early geometry concepts, classification, and **seriation** (the ordering of objects and pictures by a characteristic such as size or shade of color). When materials are color-coded or identified with a picture or label, children, paraprofessionals, and volunteers can easily find them and return them to the appropriate place (Morrison, 2004). Labels encourage symbolic representation and create a literacy-enhanced environment. Selecting materials for centers that require some adult assistance will increase teaching opportunities. Using a windup toy or an unopened bottle of glue is a way to create a dispersed natural teaching opportunity (FACETS, 2006).

Quiet activities, such as the "reading center" and the "computer center," should be placed together and away from avenues of traffic and louder activities. A center's purpose often changes as the day progresses. An area used as the "art center" in the morning may be later used as the "science center," with new materials and a new purpose introduced.

Centers need to be arranged so that they encourage appropriate peer interaction, peer conversation, and material sharing. If a play area is large and has several small crannies in which children can hide, it may allow children who are the least likely to interact to be in a play area without any positive social interaction. Ideally, centers are large enough to allow children to play on the floor and still permit adults to circulate among them to offer help; to provide brief, intensive teaching episodes for children to learn their individual objectives; and to guide play without interfering with the play of other children. Children with sensory impairments, such as those with hearing and visual impairments and sensory integration difficulties, particularly those under 3 years old, may

avoid areas with larger groups of children. These children may require additional teacher support to encourage participation in these conditions.

To ensure that appropriate skills are being learned, it is best to assign one adult to a center and control the number of children permitted to play there (Sadler, 2003). This is usually accomplished by limiting the number of "open" centers to only those that can be supervised by an adult so children with special needs receive needed direct instruction and are closely guided to development-enhancing materials and tasks.

Centers are not used as often with primary-aged students. However, when they are used, teachers have these purposes for them: (1) to review previously learned academic skills, (2) to apply learned skills in a new way, (3) to promote independent social interaction between small groups of students, (4) to encourage self-direction in learning (Polloway, Patton, & Serna, 2005), (5) to develop independent reading and research skills, (6) to encourage practice with basic skills such as addition and subtraction facts, and (7) to offer interest-based learning that focuses on individual or class topics. The goals for interest centers for students this age are to teach independent work skills and to promote generalization of skills. To create effective centers, ECSE professionals select materials carefully, plan transitions to and from centers, and manage materials' access.

Select Materials Carefully. Materials drive what happens in a center. For infants and toddlers, objects are more appealing than pictures; consequently, they should make up the majority of materials provided. Materials that are colorful and provide immediate feedback, such as sound, visual displays, and movement, are most motivating.

For preschoolers, centers and shelves should contain materials that promote communication, fine motor development, reasoning, and all types of play. Rotating toys and using the same toys for a number of different purposes can increase their interest (Sandall et al., 2005). Miniature people and animals are good for fostering play and communication. Having access to books and pictures representing people from different ethnic/cultural backgrounds, people with and without disabilities, and families with varying constellations encourages children to begin understanding human differences and to develop tolerance.

Provided materials should support curricular themes. Pictures of different buses, trucks, and cars can be taped to blocks in the block center when "transportation" is the theme. Props for themes, or units, should be selected thoughtfully because different materials will promote different kinds of interactions. For example, when the theme is "dinosaurs," teachers tend to add pictures and small replicas of dinosaurs to centers. However, when presented with these materials, children generally respond with aggressive play. But if a family of dinosaurs is provided, children's play tends to become more directed toward "family life" and is less aggressive (Phelps & Hanline, 1999). In some cases, it may be better to add props after children have participated in a center for a short period of time. In the block/construction center, for example, introducing theme-related materials after children have built their construction allows them to focus on construction skills first.

For primary-aged students, materials at centers should support a clearly stated objective, promote practice of the objective, and include all materials necessary to complete a designated task independently. For a science center, a teacher might provide two different plants and a microscope. Students would be instructed to use the microscope to examine and compare the plants, use the provided study guide to describe and draw the vein structure of each plant, and then graph comparisons. The organization of a center and the clarity of stated instructional purposes and tasks will directly influence the level of self-direction students are able to assume.

Plan Transitions. A **transition**, moving from one activity or routine to the next, can be challenging for young children. Transitions can trigger inappropriate or noncompliant behavior in some children, particularly children with pervasive developmental disorders (PDDs) and those with behavioral challenges (Chambers, 2006). Teachers must instruct the children who struggle with transitions how to move from one activity to the next by practicing a transition several times before real transitions are experienced. Students also need to practice how to appropriately gather and return materials used and to collect materials for a new activity or routine. **Corrective feedback**, teacher statements that precisely inform a child how to be accurate, can be an effective tool for improving some students' behavior, leading to smoother transitions (e.g., "That time you went to the snack table and came straight back. Nice thinking . . . you followed the rule"). Additionally, verbal reminders shortly before a transition occurs may help to emotionally prepare some students for change (e.g., "Hands down. Eyes on me. . . . In three minutes, we will move to the square table. Listen for the timer").

Primary-aged students, particularly those with conduct problems, may require frequent time reminders and may need to practice transitions many times, in isolation and then during scheduled times to learn how to transition appropriately. These students may also need to have transitions timed to help them learn to shorten them, thereby increasing instructional time.

Control Access to Materials. When teaching infants, toddlers, and preschoolers, ECSE teachers often cover shelves with curtains secured with Velcro so access to materials is controlled. This keeps a child from selecting a material or toy he or she has already mastered or one that is too difficult.

Teachers have a different purpose for materials when teaching primary-aged students. Instead of trying to control access to materials, teachers want to design an environment that fosters self-initiation, self-regulation, and increases personal responsibility. Therefore, teachers provide all materials necessary for completing tasks, such as paper, pencils, books, erasers, and workbooks, so the lack of materials is never a reason for noncompletion. Further, teachers encourage students to take more responsibility for their own learning by teaching them to recognize when environmental stimuli may be interfering with their participation. Generally, several study carrels, or study cubicles, are available in a classroom. A study carrel limits competing visual stimuli, provides a place for concentrated practice and study, and focuses a student's attention on necessary tasks. Encouraging students to determine when a study carrel will help them be more effective learners is one small step toward teaching them to assume more responsibility for their learning and to learn how to self-advocate.

PLANNING FOR INSTRUCTION

Once the physical space is adequately managed, professionals place attention on how instruction is prepared. Planning should be geared toward increasing children's *active participation* in learning. As Dr. Jim Ysseldyke (2001) stated: "If students do not have sufficient learning opportunities or are not actively engaged in responding to instruction, it is unlikely they will learn" (p. 305). In the classroom, ECSE teachers adopt a thematic or unit approach to teaching young children and stay alert to the stage of learning at which a child is performing. Readers are directed to the recommended practices listed in Appendices A, B, and D.

Using Thematic/Unit Curricular Organization

Thematic planning is the most common curricular structure for teaching infants, toddlers, and preschoolers. Themes integrate instruction in the different domains by teaching concepts and skills organized around a particular topic. In general, ECSE professionals rely on two curriculum sources. First, they select themes and identify developmentally appropriate activities from general early childhood curricula, such as *Daily Plans for Active Preschoolers* (Galloway, Ivey, & Valster, 1990). Common infant, toddler, and preschool themes are "My Family and I," "Zoo Animals," and "Summer Play" (Beaty, 1996). A weekly thematic plan for a separate ECSE class of 3- to 5-year-olds is shown in Figure 4.1. Some of the activities for

this plan are described in Box 4.1. Second, ECSE professionals use developmental checklists and curricula that list skills and behaviors children acquire at certain ages. This information is used to identify appropriate, individualized goals and objectives.

When thematic instruction is used with primary-aged students, it is called **unit teaching** because teachers integrate material from several subject areas into one unifying unit. This approach makes learning more concrete as well as promotes generalization. Most unit plans are project-oriented, involve a group of students, and may be more motivating to students who are difficult to engage in academic learning (Jenkins, 2005). Successful units have four characteristics: (1) Teachers pretest students' skills, (2) teachers have explicit instructional objectives, (3) teachers integrate multiple subject areas, and (4) teachers have clear evaluation criteria for learners' performances.

As standards-driven policies are forcing teachers to cover more content each year, unit plans allow teachers to use one activity to meet multiple cross-curricular objectives. For example, for the unit "Colonial Family Life," students might learn about farming of the period (social studies), write a story about making cheese (reading, writing), and divide into teams to make their own cheese, comparing the amounts of time different teams needed to make the cheese and graphing the data (mathematics). Teachers must have an understanding of where learners are in the learning process in order to offer effective differentiated instruction in self-contained and inclusive classrooms.

Understanding the Stages of Learning

All learners move through four stages of learning as they master new knowledge and skills, reflecting increasing competence (Polloway et al., 2005; Sandall et al., 2005). The first stage is called **acquisition**. When a child is at this stage, teachers demonstrate the skill and explain how the skill is performed. The second stage is called **proficiency**.

Figure 4.1 Thematic plan for a self-contained preschool classroom with the theme "The Ocean"

Target Vocabulary: shell, fish (verb/noun), crab, sand, swim, under, catch, octopus, starfish, sea

Time	Activity	Monday	Tuesday	Wednesday	Thursday	Friday
8:25–8:50	Opening Circle	Sing "Who came to school today"; weather chart; sing "I'm a little fishy"; discuss ocean (waves, sand, salty); select book for story	Sing "Who came to school today"; weather chart; sing "I'm a little fishy"; discuss ocean (octopus, fish, breathing); select book for story	Sing "Who came to school today"; weather chart; sing "I'm a little fishy"; discuss ocean (under, in, catch); select book for story	Sing "Who came to school today"; weather chart; sing "I'm a little fishy"; discuss ocean (starfish, fishing pole, sand castle); select book for story	Sing "Who came to school today"; weather chart; sing "I'm a little fishy"; discuss ocean (crab, pinch, cook); select book for story
8:55–9:40	Centers	Water table fishing	Shell sorting (big/little)	Fill buckets with objects pictured	Play-Doh (shells, octopus, starfish)	Ocean treasure chest naming
		Who caught the fish in the sea? (turn taking)	Feed the shark (throwing beanbags)	Matching shells (sorting by color, shape)	Counting shells in pails	Categories (in ocean—not in ocean)
9:45–10:00	Directed Play	Under the sea	Interactive aquarium dramatic play	Seafood café	Diving dramatic play	Submarine dramatic play
10:05–10:25	Art	Aquarium	Octopus	Crab	Starfish	Ocean in a bottle
10:30–11:00	Outside Play	Swim in my ocean	Dive under the ocean	Seafood limbo	The dolphin in the sea	Water play with swim suits
11:05–11:25	Snack & Cleanup	Blue Jell-O with Gummi Sea Creatures	Octopus hotdogs	Pretzel stick fishing poles, peanut butter & goldfish bait	Peanut butter and "jellyfish" sandwiches	Pasta shells with butter and parmesan cheese
11:30–11:55	Story Time	*Way Down Deep in the Deep Blue Sea* by J. Peck	*How to Hide an Octopus and Other Sea Creatures* by R. Heller	*What's It Like to Be a Fish?* by W. Pfeffer	*Over in the Ocean: In a Coral Reef* by M. Berkes	*What Lives in a Shell?* by K.W. Zoehfeld
12:00–12:30	Closing Circle	Review day; sing "What I learned"; swim to cubbies	Review day; sing "What I learned"; tiptoe in sand to cubbies	Review day; sing "What I learned"; follow shells to cubbies	Review day; sing "What I learned"; collect crabs/jellyfish to cubbies	Review day; sing "What I learned"; hop to cubbies wearing beach towels

Box 4.1 Selected Activity Descriptions for the Thematic Weekly Plan Shown in Figure 4.1

SONG LYRICS

"I'm a Little Fishy," sung to the tune of "I'm a Little Teapot."
I'm a little fishy, watch me swim.
Here is my tail, here is my fin.
When I want to have fun with my friends,
I wiggle my tail and dive right in!

CENTER ACTIVITY

Feed the Shark: Use a large cardboard box such as a computer box. Draw and paint a shark's head, as if swimming toward you, with mouth opened wide. Add paper teeth to the opening of the shark's mouth. Have children stand behind a line and tell them to use bean-bags to feed the shark! Make two sharks so children have less wait time.

DIRECTED PLAY ACTIVITY

Under the Sea: Have children cut out large pictures of different fish, color them with markers, and staple them to popsicle sticks. Hold up a bed sheet in front of an overhead projector.

Each child creates a shadow with his/her fish that dances in the "ocean."

ART ACTIVITY

Ocean in a Bottle: Cut plastic half-gallon milk bottles in half. Save the half with the spout for another project. Have the children add sand, shells, and sea creatures to the bottom. Cover the top with blue cellophane paper, overlap the cellophane on the sides by one inch, and tape the container closed.

OUTSIDE PLAY ACTIVITY

Swim in My Ocean: Set up a boundary with cones. The teacher stands in the middle and says, "Swim fishy, swim fishy, swim in my BLUE OCEAN." When the children hear the words "blue ocean," they run to the opposite side of the boundary. If they hear a different color, they do not run. As a variation, the teacher can tell children wearing clothing with the color named to run to the opposite side.

Direct instruction and guided practice continue during this stage, as teachers show a child how to perform the skill with **fluency** and assist the child in performing the skill with automaticity. The third stage is called **maintenance.** It involves helping learners retain skills over time, developing long-term retention. Professionals systematically fade direct instruction and reinforcement during this stage. The final stage of learning is called **generalization.** At this stage, learners are able to use new skills and knowledge with different materials, with different people, and in different settings or situations. Educators must stay alert to a child's stage of learning on a concept or topic to facilitate efficient learning. Teachers tend to use several instructional approaches when teaching young children.

INSTRUCTIONAL APPROACHES

Early childhood special educators need to know when, how, and how often to use an instructional approach with a child or group of children. To facilitate learning, parents and professionals use direct instruction, naturalistic instruction, and embedded learning opportunities. Each approach will be discussed.

Direct Instruction

Direct instruction, or **explicit instruction**, involves using precise instructions, structuring opportunities to practice skills with adult feedback, and arranging opportunities to apply skills and knowledge across time and situations. **Applied behavior analysis (ABA)** is type of direct/explicit instruction used to teach children (Essa, 1999). ABA involves systematically examining a behavior's antecedents (stimuli that occur before learning, such as materials or directions) and consequences (stimuli that follow learning, such as teacher praise), clearly defining instructional targets or objectives, and collecting data on teaching effectiveness and child learning. Typically developing children tend to be adept at learning through discovery, trial-and-error learning, and incidental learning, which involves learning through indirect exposure. Many children with disabilities and delays, however, may not learn as efficiently through casual interactions with their environment. For this reason, professionals may need to teach needed skills directly and systematically. Effective direct instruction involves using instructional time effectively, providing clear instruction, and structuring sufficient opportunities for practice. Table 4.1 lists some of the characteristics of effective classroom instruction and organization for young children with special needs.

Direct Instruction with Infants, Toddlers, and Preschoolers. Play is the best context for learning for very young children. However, some infants, toddlers, and preschoolers with special needs may not possess the necessary skills to learn in the same way their typically developing peers do. They may prefer to observe others' play rather than participating, may randomly move from one activity to another rather than becoming fully engaged in an activity, or may not have the skills to experiment or vary their interaction with materials.

When professionals have consciously "set the stage" for learning and the child does not learn what was intended, professionals must use direct instruction to teach the skill. To do this,

professionals first use assessment to determine what skill(s) the child needs to learn. Knowing precisely what the child should be learning allows professionals and parents to create and guide the child through a variety of learning opportunities.

For example, if children need to name and identify "circle," but are not learning it, teachers would provide direct instruction within an appropriate routine, which in this case might be the block center. To keep engagement high, teachers would use different techniques to teach the skill: (1) *Describe* a circle (e.g., "A circle has no corners."), (2) ask the children to *identify* other blocks with the same shape, and (3) have children *match* a teacher's construction with circles. After this teaching session, which is rarely longer than 5–10 minutes, children may be given time to use circles, and other shapes, to build what they choose. Before the children move on to the next routine, however, the teacher would ask them to *recall* the name of the shape they learned, describe it, and identify it to reinforce the proficiency and maintenance stages of learning. By providing short teaching episodes like this during routine activities, teachers are ensuring that learning occurs.

Direct Instruction with Primary-Aged Children. Direct instruction for students in kindergarten through third grade involves the following steps (Polloway et al., 2005):

❏ Explain the skill to be learned.

❏ Teach the skill by modeling the skill using several varied examples.

❏ Give the student opportunities to practice multiple examples of the skill.

❏ Give corrective feedback on the student's performance.

❏ Arrange for the student to use the skill in many ways so maintenance and generalization occur.

Direct instruction involves having clear expectations for learning and conduct as well as clear guidelines for how routines and procedures

TABLE 4.1 General characteristics of effective early childhood special education teaching and classroom organization

Rules and Procedures

– Rules are posted and discussed frequently.
– Behavior reminders and statements of desired behaviors are given *before* activities.
– Rule compliance is praised frequently.
– Adults continuously visually scan room.
– Adults reinforce appropriate behavior with precise praise and/or consequences.
– Adults use nonverbal signals to redirect/interrupt inappropriate behavior.

Instructional Time Management

– Instructional time is used productively.
– Noninstructional activities are minimized.
– Procedures for a clear beginning and end of activities are used.

Lesson/Activity Presentation

– Teacher states the objective(s) of the lesson.
– Teacher gains the students' attention.
– Teacher reviews prior learning relating to concept(s), when appropriate.
– Teacher models skills to be learned and requests imitation.
– Teacher requires rehearsal of skill(s) (e.g., uses varied, multiple examples).
– Teacher uses cues and prompts to increase rate of participation and correct responses.
– Teacher uses high rate of corrective feedback which is nonpunitive, immediate, and explicit.
– Teacher follows correct responses with specific praise.
– Teacher maintains a brisk pace.
– Teacher has students restate objective of activity/lesson at end of lesson as part of review.

Extended Practice and Evaluation

– Teacher provides daily, weekly, monthly skill(s) review.
– Teacher reteaches, as needed, based on students' performances.
– Teacher maintains continuous records of learning.

will be handled. Table 4.2 lists common classroom procedures teachers discuss with students in order to maximize instructional time with primary-aged students.

Naturalistic Instruction

Naturalistic instruction is the instructional approach most commonly used to teach infants, toddlers, and preschoolers with disabilities and delays. It is routinely taught to parents and family members for use in the home. Naturalistic instruction has four characteristics: (1) Instruction is embedded into an everyday routine; (2) interactions capitalize on the child's interests and follow the child's lead; (3) consequences for interactions tend to be natural consequences, such as getting what was requested, rather than artificial consequences like getting a sticker for requesting; and (4) the most natural contexts for teaching skills are selected (Rule, Losardo, Dinnebell, Kaiser, & Rowland, 1998). When planning for instruction within routines, it is important to

TABLE 4.2 Classroom procedures and expectations that must be discussed to maximize instructional time with primary-aged students with special needs

I. Room Use
- Teacher's desk and storage areas
- Students' desks and storage areas
- Storage for common materials
- Drinking fountains, materials, pencil sharpeners
- Restroom and restroom passes
- Centers, stations, or equipment areas
- Use of study carrels

II. Independent Work and Teacher-Directed Group Instruction
- Student attention during instruction
- Student participation
- Talking among students
- Appropriate ways to obtain help
- Out-of-seat procedures during independent work
- What to do when work has been completed
- Scheduled breaks

III. Transitions in and out of Classroom
- Beginning the school day
- Leaving the room
- Transitions between subjects/lessons
- Returning to the room
- Ending the day and preparing backpacks

IV. Procedures for Small-Group Instruction
- Getting the group ready
- Student movement
- Expected student behavior in small groups
- Expected behavior for students not in small group

V. General Procedures
- Attendance, lunch count and money
- Distributing materials
- Interruptions (PA announcements, visitors related support professionals, etc.)
- Library, computer lab, media room, office, therapy times
- Cafeteria
- Playground, recess, physical education, art, music
- Fire and disaster drills
- Classroom helpers
- Late assignments
- Homework
- Grading system
- Behavior plan and system
- Weekly home behavior and academic reports

remember that instruction should not interfere with the sequence and outcome of a routine. In other words, while a mother is folding clothes, she may be able to take a few minutes to teach the "same" colors to her preschooler, but she still has to finish the laundry.

Both direct and naturalistic approaches are used to teach young children. In truth, these approaches are not opposites, but rather form a continuum with many variations, as well as similarities, from which professionals and family members may choose. Both approaches create opportunities for children to communicate, initiate, and respond. Both initiate teaching with the level of physical or verbal assistance the child needs and then systematically decrease adult support as independent responding increases. For children 5 years of age and younger, direct instruction tends to be used when naturalistic instruction does not produce desired results. Direct instruction is the preferred approach for teaching primary-aged students. Direct and naturalistic instruction approaches are compared in Table 4.3.

Embedded Learning Opportunities/ Routine-Based Instruction

Everyday routines help children learn cultural roles, expectations, and desired behaviors (Dunst, Bruder, Trivette, Raab, & McLean, 2001). As stated in Chapter 3, embedding learning opportunities into regular routines and activities is a time-efficient and effective way to teach young children.

Embedded Learning Opportunities in the Home. Most opportunities for development in the home occur as part of daily living, child and family routines, and family and community traditions (Cripe & Venn, 1997). Many parents naturally embed teaching into play and care routines. Observant ECSE professionals capitalize on this occurrence and acknowledge its appropriateness for a child's development. Typically, multiple skills are taught within one routine. For instance, during dressing, Marina, discussed in the case study, was taught to raise her arms when requested (receptive language, gross motor development), sit with some support

---

TABLE 4.3 A comparison of direct and naturalistic instructional approaches

---

In direct instruction, adults usually

- initiate the focus or topic of what is taught;
- use direct comments or questions to guide learning;
- change focus or topic after the child responds;
- expect immediate responses;
- rely on directives (nonambiguous instructional statements such as "Tell me. Say: 'I want more,' " or "Put the red sock in the red box.")
- use extrinsic reinforcers such as adult praise, pats on the back, and smiles.

In naturalistic instruction, adults usually

- create opportunities for the child to initiate;
- use indirect commands (e.g., "I wonder where this shape should go?") or comments to maintain interactions;
- attempt to continue exchanges for multiple turns;
- pause periodically to provide time for the child to respond and/or initiate
- use naturally occurring consequences, such as getting to eat a cookie after requesting one, as well as adult attention and praise.

(gross motor development), and take turns hiding her face with a blanket (social, cognitive development). Dunst and colleagues (2001) identified four steps for supporting family members as they identify activities and routines during which they can comfortably provide their child development-enhancing experiences.

STEP 1. Identify the source of learning opportunities.
Parents often find this step helpful in identifying activities that already provide or could provide their child opportunities for learning. Families may be surprised at the richness of their lives and the number of learning opportunities they are already providing their child.

STEP 2. Identify natural learning opportunities.
Learning opportunities are best increased by promoting child participation in family and community activities. Any family routine, whether going to church or playing in the backyard, presents natural events in which a child may learn. The professional's role is to guide family members in selecting activities that will enhance the child's development and are mutually engaging (Dunst, Herter, Shields, & Bennis, 2001).

STEP 3. Focus on interest-based learning.
Involving children in activities that are interesting to them almost guarantees that they will benefit from the experiences. Professionals ask parents to identify routines that keep their child's attention and might be best for them to use when arranging development-enhancing opportunities. Strategies should evolve from this discussion between parents and professionals. To introduce a new intervention, procedure, or strategy, professionals demonstrate how to do it within a target routine and then observe careproviders as they practice it, offering feedback as needed. These supported demonstrations are important, since they help family members remember strategies and interventions after professionals leave the home (Raver, 1999).

STEP 4. Increase learning opportunities.
Children learn best when learning is distributed throughout the day. Some professionals find a simple reminder, such as a routine intervention plan, can help family members remember to engage their child in different kinds of learning; others find this is too formal for some families. If a plan is used, it should be kept simple and be used only as a source of positive communication between the family and the professional, not as a record of a family's compliance with a professional's recommendations. A home learning opportunities plan for Luisa is shown in Figure 4.2. Luisa has moderate-severe spastic cerebral palsy (discussed in Chapter 7), moderate cognitive delays, and a close relationship with her sister, Maria.

Embedded Learning Opportunities in Center-Based Programs. Center-based programs for children with developmental delays typically group eight toddlers or preschoolers by chronological age, developmental level, and/or needs. Rather than teaching children one-to-one, which tends to produce unreliable generalization, professionals embed individualized instruction into center-based activities in the following ways (Pretti-Frontczak & Bricker, 2004):

❑ Professionals engage in comprehensive observations of children across situations by responding to and directing children's actions within ongoing activities.

❑ Professionals modify planned activities in ways that yield desired outcomes by systematically adjusting antecedents and consequences.

❑ Professionals provide a sufficient number of opportunities for skills to be practiced and learned throughout a day.

❑ Professionals use nonintrusive strategies to evaluate the effectiveness of child and family outcomes.

Since many toddlers and preschoolers with special needs require repeated opportunities to

Figure 4.2 Home learning opportunities plan for the month of May for Luisa when she was 4 years, 4 months old

Luisa	Moves from sitting to standing with some support (Gross Motor)	Puts small objects in containers (Fine Motor)	Names objects/people in 1–2 word sentences (Expressive Language)	Points to objects/pictures when requested (Receptive Language)
Breakfast	Puts empty cup on table from sitting on floor	Puts picture of food eaten in "food box"	Names food eaten; names food eaten by others	Points to pictures of family/Biscuit in pictures when asked
Shopping	Reaches for objects placed on ground when standing next to stroller/chair/shopping cart, with little help	Puts keys in Mom's purse Puts coins in change purse	Names objects that Mom and sister show her	Shows pictures of what was purchased from choice of 3, when requested
Evening Family Walk (Mom/sister use parallel talk)	Stoops to find leaves and gives them to sister/Dad/Nana/Mom when requested	Puts small toys in tub for cleanup before walk	Names 3–5 things during the walk	Points to objects named by Mom/Dad/sister on walk
Playtime with Sister (Maria)	Moves from sitting in to standing next to furniture in 3–5 seconds, with balance	Completes puzzles, with some help Takes turn in games	Names who is playing with her (Georgia, Mimi, etc.)	Shows and finds toys named and described by sister

learn identified skills, professionals create short, intensive teaching sessions within ongoing activities and routines to teach needed skills (Bricker, Pretti-Frontczak, & McComas, 1998; Horn, Lieber, Sandall, & Schwartz, 2001). A number of instructional techniques are used to achieve this learning.

INSTRUCTIONAL STRATEGIES

ECSE professionals use a variety of strategies to "help children function more completely, competently, adaptively, or independently in their natural environment" (Sandall et al., 2005, p. 85). Besides selecting appropriate strategies, professionals must be able to demonstrate and explain different strategies and approaches to careproviders and support their efforts in using these strategies in home routines. Prompts, modeling, response-contingent feedback, the mand-model procedure, and choral responding are general strategies used

to develop skills and enhance communication in children through 8 years of age. Each will be discussed.

Prompting

A **prompt** is a signal, cue, or assistance an adult provides to generate a specific response (Roopnarine & Johnson, 2005). Prompts help the child respond correctly, allowing the child to receive positive reinforcement, which maintains his or her interest in attempting the skill again. As the child performs a skill more independently, prompts are systematically faded until he or she is able to perform the skill alone (Sandall et al., 2005).

Prompts can be verbal, gestural, pictorial, or physical. **Verbal prompts** are statements given to guide the child's response. For example, for infants, toddlers, and preschoolers, a verbal prompt might be "Hang your coat on the hook," or "Want juice?

Say, /j/." Giving the first sound of a correct answer would be an appropriate verbal prompt for primary-aged students, such as "The capital of Virginia is /r/. . . ." **Gestural prompts** involve physical movements intended to guide the child's response. Pointing to where the circle goes in a shapebox would be an example for toddlers and preschoolers. Pointing to the answer to a mathematics problem that is missing a dollar sign would be a gestural prompt for third-grade students. **Pictorial prompts** are picture cues that encourage a correct response. Showing a toddler a picture of his or her bed might help the child more willingly participate in the bedtime ritual. Pictorial prompts may also be used to help primary-aged students orally sequence story events. **Physical prompts**, also called **graduated manual assistance**, involve manipulating the child's hands or body to perform a task (Raver, 1999). This could be used to help preschoolers lace their shoes and first-grade students correctly write uppercase letters.

Prompting requires teachers to make moment-by-moment decisions about whether to provide or withdraw assistance. Using unnecessary prompts may create a dependence on adults and lead children to question their own abilities. To ensure this does not happen, ECSE professionals use hierarchical prompting. That is, adults use less-intrusive prompts (i.e., gestural prompts) and then move to more-intrusive support levels (i.e., verbal, pictorial and physical prompts) only when less-intrusive supports fail to impact behaviors (Bevill, Gast, Maguire, & Vail, 2001).

Modeling

When an adult asks a child to watch him or her demonstrate a task and then asks the child to perform it, the adult is using a process called **modeling**. Modeling is a powerful strategy for teaching young children, including children with limited receptive and expressive language (Biederman, Fairhall, Raven, & Davey, 1998). When teaching academics to primary-aged students, modeling is generally used during the acquisition stage of learning.

Response-Contingent Feedback

A teacher who gives a learner verbal feedback about his or her performance on a task is using **response-contingent feedback**. The teacher's statements should be rewarding and offer explicit instructional guidance. After a preschooler correctly linked four popbeads, for example, the child's teacher made this developmentally appropriate response-contingent statement: "Yes, you snapped four beads together in a row like mine." Global statements such as "Good for you" should be avoided, since they do not identify the specific skill teachers would like to see repeated. "You remembered to regroup your tens. Good thinking!" would be an appropriate response-contingent feedback statement to a primary-aged student learning to regroup in subtraction.

Mand-Model Procedure

This technique is known as a "question-pause-model" technique. An adult poses a question related to a child's interest and waits for a response; if the child does not respond or responds incorrectly, the adult verbally models the correct response for the child (Alpert & Kaiser, 1992). Although effective with all learners, this procedure is especially useful for children who tend to be low social and communicative initiators (Santos & Lignugaris-Kraft, 1997). For example, "How many pennies are in this set?" could be asked of a kindergartener who is learning to rote count to 10. If the child does not respond or responds incorrectly, the teacher would say: "Let's count them together. 1, 2, 3, 4, 5, 6. There are 6 pennies. Now, tell me how many pennies are in this set."

Active Student Responding

Effective ECSE teachers use a high rate of prompting and teacher-learner exchanges to structure frequent child responding when teaching toddlers, preschoolers, and school-aged students (Mathes, Clancy-Menchetti, & Torgensen, 2003; Mathes, Torgensen, Allen, & Howard-Allor, 2003;

Sobel & Taylor, 2006). A link has been found between primary-aged students' active participation with academic tasks and their ultimate achievement (Polloway et al., 2005). To guarantee that primary-aged students actively participate during the acquisition and proficiency stages of learning, teachers structure instruction so that students perform the following four actions, multiple times, with any concept or skill they are learning: (1) say, (2) write, (3) identify, and (4) manipulate.

The "say" action step means students say key concepts or skills aloud. The easiest way to increase student verbal responding is for teachers to frame questions in such a way that students have a good chance of answering them correctly, which encourages further participation. A teacher teaching punctuation might say: "The FIRST letter in every sentence is an uppercase letter. Michelle, please tell me which letter in each sentence is always uppercase." If Michelle could not answer the question, her teacher would prompt her, as many times and in as many ways as necessary, so she would eventually answer the question correctly. The objective is to ensure that each time a student is asked a question, the student is able to answer it correctly, allowing that student, and others, to rehearse the correct information and thereby increasing their interest in participating again. Another rationale for framing questions so that students can answer them is that it ensures students are given many opportunities "to be smart" and "feel smart" in front of their peers.

The "write" step involves writing key concepts. For example, a teacher may say: "As I write this new reading word on the board, you write it in your notebook at the same time." The "identify" step involves discriminating target skills from choices (e.g., "Everyone put your finger under the past tense verb in sentence 3"). The "manipulate" step involves performing some action with the key concepts, such as underlining, using a highlighter to mark, pointing to, circling, or putting a star next to critical information. A teacher may say: "The definition for *dissolve* is important in this chapter. Draw a happy face next

to that definition." Obviously, these actions, minus the "write" step, will also encourage active responding with toddlers and preschoolers. These structured actions assist children in acquiring new skills and knowledge while increasing their engagement in the learning process.

Increasing Engagement in Young Children

Engagement is defined as the amount of time children spend interacting appropriately with their environment (McWilliam & Bailey, 1992). The amount of engagement in a classroom has been determined to be a leading indicator of quality in ECSE programs (Ridley, McWilliam, & Oates, 2000; McCormick, Noonan, & Heck, 1998). Young children learn by looking, touching, tasting, telling, smelling—they must be *active* participants to learn. Although engagement is necessary for learning, engagement alone will not automatically result in learning. Yet engagement sets the stage for learning and is a critical deficit area for many children with special needs.

Engagement can be measured by recording (1) the amount of time the child is appropriately involved with learning materials, peers, and adults; (2) how long the child participates in a task, especially when the task is difficult; (3) the decision-making skills the child displays while involved in a task; and (4) the child's focused attention, which leads to in-depth learning (Blank & Hertzog, 2003). Although a child's disability does not predict his or her level of engagement, activity characteristics and teacher behaviors do significantly influence engagement (McCormick et al., 1998). That is, what teachers do and say when teaching shapes the level of engagement achieved (McWilliam & Bailey, 1995). Facilitation, direct assistance, positive affect, redirection, monitoring, and activity/lesson preparations are strategies teachers use to promote engagement in children before they enter first grade. These strategies are described in Table 4.4.

TABLE 4.4 Teacher behaviors that influence young children's engagement with adults, peers, and materials

Behavior	Definition
Facilitation	Assuming a participatory role in child/group activities, such as offering comments, questioning, elaborating on a child/group response, or joining in a child's activity.
Direct assistance	Helping a child/group participate in an activity by giving directions or prompts.
Positive affect	Indicating approval of a child through facial expression, tone of voice, verbal praise, or physical approval such as a pat on the head and/or providing comfort to a child that is upset.
Redirection	Suggesting/guiding to influence a child to take another course of action.
Monitoring	Walking around, observing engagement/nonengagement, and intervening when there is nonengagement.
Activity/lesson preparation	Providing a clear structure and purpose for activities/lessons, having materials close to activity/lesson, following a child's lead when appropriate, and scheduling the appropriate amount of time for activities/lessons.

As stated, the relationship between learning and academic engaged time is a strong one for primary-aged students. Low-achieving students tend to be engaged about 50% of the time compared to about 75% of the time with high-achieving students (Rock, 2004). The way teachers structure instruction will impact how much engagement is achieved. Providing adequate amounts of practice, using schedules, using scaffolding, and using computers for additional practice are ways to promote engagement in young children. Each will be discussed.

Providing Sufficient Skill Practice

Children acquire new skills through repetition. When infants pull to a stand and then purposely let go so they can pull up again, they are displaying the enjoyment of repetitive practice. Nonetheless, to maintain attention over several days, slight changes will need to be introduced into teaching sessions to keep children involved. For example, to keep an infant engaged in the peek-a-boo game that is teaching motor imitation, adults can add

blowing a kiss or saying "hi" every other time the child pulls the blanket off his or her face.

Primary-aged students also need slight changes to keep practice engaging, as they quickly learn to dread "drill and practice" sessions if these sessions are presented as "work" and always require seat-work. Varying how skills are practiced is essential for maintaining engagement. For instance, one day students can rehearse addition facts with a timed "2-minute test," while the next day they can drill the same facts in a *Jeopardy*-type game.

Using Activity Mini-Schedules

Teachers know what they will be doing during group activities, but children may not. An activity mini-schedule is a picture sequence of what will occur, in order, for a lesson, routine, or activity (Roybal & Wilson, 2006). Mini-schedules help children know what is coming next, which helps some children have better engagement. For instance, in Ms. Bellair's preschool class, the mini-schedule for opening group had three pictures representing the following: (1) greeting each

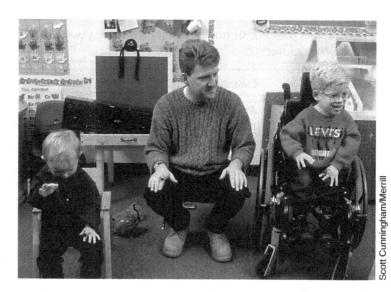

Professionals and parents use modeling, prompting, and active student responding to increase engagement in young children.

Scott Cunningham/Merrill

other and singing the name song, (2) completing the weather calendar, and (3) discussing what is in the "Surprise Can," which holds objects related to the theme for the week. As each task is completed, that picture is removed from the activity mini-schedule and placed in a "finished" box.

Using Scaffolding

Scaffolding involves adjusting the task, materials, group size, pace, presentation, and teacher support to promote learning (Torgesen, 2002). This means teaching in manageable steps to allow children to master each step of a task. For example, to increase engagement during play with toddlers and preschoolers, teachers can follow this scaffolding sequence:

1) Use indirect verbal commands to encourage further engagement. Indirect verbal commands are verbal suggestions that do not require the child to comply, such as "I wonder what you are going to do with that truck?"

2) Model a play action for the child. Sometimes just showing the child what he or she can do with a material may be sufficient to get the child engaged.

3) Model a play action for the child and give a direct verbal command. Direct verbal commands request the child to comply with the teacher's direction, such as "See my truck? Put your truck inside the garage like mine." Providing a model for play, called **correspondence training**, and using picture cues, pictures suggesting ways to play with a material, have been found to increase play engagement in some children. Bevill and colleagues (2001) found that preschoolers with moderate to severe disabilities required verbal reinforcement for imitation of play behaviors, as well as picture cues, to manifest change in their play initiations and play quality. Table 4.5 lists general techniques teachers use to modify activities for infants, toddlers, and preschoolers to foster engagement.

Using Computers to Support Learning

In the last decade, computer technologies have enabled young children with disabilities to play, learn, communicate, and interact with their environment to a greater degree than ever before. In some cases, computer applications have been an equalizer for children with disabilities, especially in inclusive programs. Yet, as with any

TABLE 4.5 Ideas for modifying activities to increase engagement when teaching infants, toddlers, and preschoolers with special needs

Adjust activities by
- changing what children do in them.
- adapting materials and their access.
- providing additional opportunities to respond.
- using shorter, more frequent activities to increase opportunities to respond.
- changing the social composition or rules for participation.
- training peers to engage in facilitative/peer tutoring.
- having a "tool box" of individually selected materials for children who can no longer attend to/participate in an activity as planned. These children work with their "tool box" materials while other children continue the original activity.

resource, the potential of computers is realized only when professionals integrate this technology into daily schedules (Judge, 2001). With the proliferation of software for young children, ECSE professionals may have difficulty choosing the most appropriate software for their needs. Different kinds of software provide vastly different educational outcomes. Haugland (1995) found that **open-ended software**, software that allows children to choose the pace and direction of their experience, made a more significant difference in children's developmental gains than did drill-and-practice software. **Drill-and-practice software** resembles electronic worksheets that reinforce memory and increase the rate of responding. This kind of software can be useful for developing skill proficiency and fluency with primary-aged children (Polloway et al., 2005).

A variety of peripherals can make a computer more accessible to children with a range of abilities. These may include a mouse, an alternate keyboard, a touch screen, or a range of switches. Placing two chairs at the computer encourages

children to help each other and to communicate about what they are learning.

If computer experiences are not successfully integrated into the curriculum, children will not benefit from having computers in the classroom. For example, when preschoolers are learning "small," "medium," and "large" in connection with the week's theme of "Bears," they may sort objects according to size in the homemaking center, and later, in the computer center, they can use *Millie's Math House* (Edmark Publishing) to further practice these concepts (Judge, 2001). Despite the fact that computers may make inclusion possible and, in some cases, lessen its time demands on teachers, having a computer in a classroom does not guarantee appropriate use.

INCLUSIVE AND ACCOMMODATIVE PRACTICES

Inclusion refers to the practice of placing children with special needs in the same programs as their typically developing peers and providing them with specially designed instruction and supports (Winter, 1999). About 75% of students with disabilities served are educated in general education classrooms (Prater, 2003). Inclusion opponents suggest that services for children with special needs may be diluted in general education and that general education is unprepared to meet the diverse needs of these students. Proponents of inclusion counter that expectations may be higher in general education and that students with special needs have access to more appropriate role models, which may improve their learning and social outcomes (Walther-Thomas, Korinek, McLaughlin, & Williams, 2000). Reactions to the inclusion movement have been varied, sometimes polarizing teachers, administrators, families, and advocacy groups (Rea, McLaughlin, & Walther-Thomas, 2002). Unfortunately, inclusion has progressed more by political agenda than data-driven decisions (Fuchs & Fuchs, 1995). Readers are referred to the DEC recommended practices for inclusion with young children listed in Appendix B.

The literature suggests that effective inclusion has the following three broad characteristics (Fuchs & Fuchs, 1995; Salend, 2005a):

❏ Team members have a commitment to inclusion.

❏ All principal parties have a shared philosophy and vision.

❏ There is adequate support from the school or central administration.

Appropriately trained personnel, at the classroom and leadership levels, are key to successful inclusion, despite the fact that this kind of training is not common in most teacher preparation programs (Lieber et al., 2000). Successful inclusion involves the provision of program and assessment accommodations, coplanning and collaboration, and consultation.

Program and Assessment Accommodations

Inclusive education requires differentiated instruction for *all* students in general education classes. This is achieved by modifying instruction and materials and by offering accommodations to students with learning and/or behavioral needs. An **accommodation** is any change to the delivery of instruction or assessment to access an individual's abilities, rather than his or her disabilities (National Center for Educational Outcomes, 2001). The purpose of accommodations is to allow students an equal opportunity to show what they know without the impediment of their disability (Washburn-Moses, 2003).

There are three levels of accommodation used in inclusive classrooms (Salend, 2005a). The first level is **access accommodations**, which are used for students who can participate at the same academic level as others and do not require adjustment in the structure or content of the general education curriculum. Examples are braille textbooks, sign language interpreters, and bilingual dictionaries. The second level is **low-impact accommodations**, which involve adjustments in teaching methods, but do not require significant changes in the structure or content of the general education curriculum. Examples of this level are spell-checkers, scheduling adjustments, note-taking support, graphic organizers, and study guides (the last two are discussed in Chapter 9). The third level is **high-impact accommodations**, which affect curricular expectations and are appropriate for students in inclusive settings who are not working on grade-level educational goals. Examples include content changes, alternative learning objectives, alternative materials, and alternative evaluation procedures (Shriner & Destefano, 2003).

In general, assessment or testing accommodations are more common than instructional accommodations (Destefano, Shriner, & Lloyd, 2001). Because of No Child Left Behind and the IDEA (2004), primary-aged students with learning and/or behavior problems must now be included in all state- and districtwide assessments, and schools are required to prepare these students for these assessments. Common testing accommodations include the following: (1) modifying the presentation of items and directions, such as repeating directions and answering questions about directions; (2) adjusting the timing of tests, such as offering more time to complete a test; (3) altering the schedule for tests, such as taking subtests over a period of days instead of taking the full test in one day; and (4) modifying the setting, such as taking tests in the special education class instead of the general education classroom (Elliott & Marquart, 2004; Fuchs et al., 2000).

Coplanning and Collaboration

Research has shown that **collaboration**, the process of professionals working together to make mutually acceptable decisions to support student learning, is essential for effective inclusion (Voltz, Brazel, & Ford, 2001; Wiggins & Damore, 2006). Unfortunately, for most professionals, collaboration continues to involve "on-the-job" training and is strongly linked to the personal strengths and commitment of the individuals involved (Buysse & Wesley, 2004; Vesay, 2004).

Issues relating to planning are frequently identified as an ongoing barrier to effective inclusion (Karge, McClure, & Patton, 1995). Because planning time will always be limited, professionals must use it as efficiently as possible. To do this, general and special education teachers should do the following during planning sessions: (1) Decide on the "big ideas," the major organizing principles of a unit or chapter that all students should learn; (2) analyze potential areas of difficulty for students with special needs; and (3) create strategies and supports that encourage learning in all students, including students with different abilities (Hawbaker, Balong, Buckwalter, & Runyon, 2001). Before a topic is introduced to a class, teachers must identify how different learning strategies, such as acronyms, rhymes, songs, keyword pictures, scaffolding, manipulatives, and additional prompts, will be used to teach the skill. Further, after adaptations and/or accommodations are provided, the impact on the performance of each student must be evaluated, and only those that are effective should be continued in the future (Weinfeld, Barnes-Robinson, Jeweler, & Shevitz, 2005). As Voltz and colleagues (Voltz, Sims, Nelson, & Bivens, 2005) state: "In diverse, inclusive classrooms, learners must understand that 'fair' does not mean that everybody gets exactly the same thing, but rather that everybody gets what they need" (p. 18).

Consultation

A common model of support in inclusive settings is consultation between general early childhood teachers and early childhood special educators. Consultation tends to focus on ways to prevent and address children's learning and behavioral issues that interfere with educating them. The truth is that procedures that are used successfully with children who are typically developing may need to be more systematic and structured to achieve the same outcomes with children with

disabilities (McDonnell, Brownell, & Wolery, 2001). Put simply, instruction for children with special needs has to be explicit and well planned, or it is less likely to be effective (Campbell, Milbourne, Silverman, & Feller, 2005). Similarly, consultations need to be explicit and well planned to change teachers' teaching procedures. In fact, Schepis and colleagues (Schepis, Reid, Ownbey, & Clary, 2003) found that only after general education preschool teachers had watched videotaped scenarios of examples of how to prompt and praise cooperative participation during free play, had received direct instruction regarding these strategies, and had been given on-the-job feedback were they able to produce more cooperative play between children with severe disabilities and those without disabilities in an inclusive program.

Inclusion of Infants, Toddlers, and Preschoolers

Inclusion of young children is based on the belief that the arrangement can be beneficial for children with and without disabilities (Bailey, McWilliams, Buysse, & Wesley, 1998). Research comparing the effectiveness of inclusive and self-contained programs for children with disabilities from birth to 5 years does not clearly find that one service model is more efficacious than the other for all children. Despite this, some studies report that preschoolers with mild disabilities appear to make as much progress in inclusive programs as children with similar characteristics enrolled in separate settings do (Buysse, Skinner, & Grant, 2001; Halahan & Costenbader, 2000; Guralnick, 2001; Rea et al., 2002). Although young children with disabilities and/or delays may benefit socially from inclusive placements by having playmates who are more socially competent, they are also at risk for peer rejection, and many may not develop appropriate social skills if they do not receive direct instruction in this area (Buysse et al., 2001). Not all inclusive programs, in truth, are willing or able to provide the intensive social and communicative training that is necessary for some children with special challenges. Further, the number of children with disabilities included in a classroom has recently been found to impact the learning outcomes of typical children. More problem behaviors and lower scores in print concepts were found in typical children when more than 20% of the children enrolled in a Head Start program had special needs (Gallagher & Lambert, 2006).

Children with Pervasive Developmental Disorders.

Pervasive developmental disorders (PDDs) include autism, Asperger's disorder, Rett's disorder, and childhood disintegrative disorder (Towbin, Mauk, & Batshaw, 2005). The primary features of these disorders are impairments in social skills and communication and a lack of varied interests (Fones & Rosemergy, 2005; Welton, Vakil, & Carasea, 2004). Because of weaknesses in social responsiveness and social learning, children with PDD may need intensive intervention in order to develop social interaction and communication skills. Generally, they do not learn from social modeling and incidental teaching alone, so they require direct instruction which involves breaking skills into small incremental steps and teaching these steps sequentially (McGee, 2000).

Learning should be supported by visual cue systems and manipulatives (Welton et al., 2004). Language comprehension may also be delayed, so pairing pictures with verbal concepts may improve a child's understanding (Frea, 1995). Visual schedules may decrease some inappropriate behaviors by making the environment more predictable and decreasing apprehension associated with events not easily understood or conceptualized. Picture or object schedules may aid transitions and increase predictability. Reading social stories (discussed in Chapter 6) prior to an activity or field trip also may help some children manage anxiety and improve behavior and may enhance their understanding of the perspective of others (Hagiwara & Myles, 1999).

Children with Cognitive Delays/Mental Retardation.

Children with cognitive delays may be delayed in all developmental domains. They may engage in more solitary play and manifest more nonplay behaviors, such as watching, than their typical peers do. Like the majority of children with special needs, these children cannot be expected to acquire social skills merely through casual social contact with age-peers (Guralnick, 2001). Differences in social and communication skills may be significant enough to discourage typically developing peers from choosing a child with cognitive delays as a play partner (Fujiki, Brinton, Isaacson, & Summers, 2001). For this reason, children with moderate to severe cognitive impairments require adult direction in how to use play materials appropriately and how to initiate and sustain social interactions with peers (Kim et al., 2003). Peer-mediated instruction is effective in teaching these skills and is discussed in Chapter 8.

The type of toys provided seems to affect children's cognitive level of play. For example, when children play with functional toys, they engage in significantly more functional play than constructive or dramatic play. Similarly, social toys (e.g., balls, free blocks, dress-up clothes) tend to encourage more positive social interactions than isolate toys (e.g., Play-Doh, puzzles, books) do.

Inclusion of Primary-Aged Students

Largely because of the complex array of factors influencing the effectiveness of inclusion, research evidence supporting inclusion for primary-aged students, like research with younger children, is equivocal. Hanson and colleagues (2001) studied 25 children and their families over the course of five years as the children moved from inclusive preschool placements to elementary schools. At the end of the five-year period, 60% of the children remained in some level of inclusive placement. In general, parents and others advocate inclusion until they, or their children, encounter obstacles (Hanson et al., 2001; Salend & Duhaney, 2002). Students themselves have identified attitudinal barriers as the most deleterious to their inclusive school experience (Pivik, McComas, & LaFlamme, 2002).

Infrastructure to Support Inclusion. Strong leaders who share a belief in and commitment to inclusive education clearly enhance its effectiveness. No program, however, can be successful unless adequate resources are in place. Too often, as with younger children, general and special educators of primary-aged students do not share a common goal. General educators may assume that ECSE teachers are in their classroom to teach the children with special needs, while ECSE teachers may assume their role is to provide support and guidance to the general educator and not to provide direct services to students. These kinds of misunderstandings will negatively impact students' outcomes.

Established times for team members to clarify "common goals," to identify roles and responsibilities, to observe one another, and to plan together have the potential of bridging some of these philosophical differences with time (Salend, 2005a). Marina's family, discussed in the case study, commented that a unified team allowed them to seek the best services for their child. However, the best way to develop collaborative relationships is through professional development programs in school systems that include ongoing staff development, technical assistance, supervision, clear administration guidance and support, frequent classroom evaluations, and incentives for continual improvement (Hanson et al., 2001).

Staff Communication. Good communication among team members is the backbone of quality inclusive classrooms (Rous, 2004). Unfortunately, teachers tend to communicate only when behavior problems are present or a crisis is pending. Yet more regular communication would produce better results, since it has the potential to interrupt *potential* behavioral and academic problems in children (Donegan, Ostrosky, & Fowler, 1996). Good communication involves clear delineation of the supports that will be offered to children. Figure 4.3 shows a checklist of common classroom-based instructional and testing accommodations that are commonly provided to primary-aged students.

Family Concerns. Family members, like students and their teachers, have different views of and experiences with inclusion (Soodak & Erwin, 2000). Parents have identified four barriers to inclusion at their children's schools: (1) the physical environment (e.g., lack of ramps, narrow doorways), (2) intentional attitudinal barriers (e.g., bullying, isolation), (3) unintentional attitudinal barriers (e.g., lack of awareness or understanding of disabilities), and (4) physical limitations (e.g., difficulty with dexterity that impacts completion of tasks) (Salend, 2004; Stuart, Flis, & Rinaldi, 2006).

Writing Section 504 Accommodation Plans

Students who do not qualify for special education services under the IDEA disability definitions, but who need some educational supports to participate in general education classes may be eligible for services under Section 504. This civil rights statute prohibits public or private schools that receive federal financial assistance from discriminating against children who have a mental or physical impairment that substantially limits a major life activity such as walking, seeing, speaking, or learning (deBettencourt, 2002). For identified students, schools must provide reasonable accommodations that give them access to the educational program equal to that given their typical peers. Many states provide a Section 504 Accommodation Plan to students with attention disorders, students with social maladjustments, students with communicable diseases (e.g., HIV) that substantially limit their learning, and students with long-term mental or physical impairments such as diabetes and Tourette's syndrome (Salend, 2005a).

There are no specific requirements concerning parental participation in or frequency of review of a Section 504 Accommodation Plan (deBettencourt, 2002). The majority of Section 504 Accommodation Plans list the general strengths of and general concerns about the

Figure 4.3 Sample classroom-based instructional and testing accommodations checklist

Classroom-Based Instructional Accommodations

- ❑ Word processor/spell-checker
- ❑ Note-taking assistance
- ❑ Use of technology (please specify)
- ❑ Learning strategies instruction
- ❑ Specialized seating arrangements
- ❑ Study skills instruction
- ❑ Memory aids and strategies
- ❑ Additional time to complete tasks
- ❑ Manipulatives
- ❑ Electronic textbooks
- ❑ Frequent comprehension checks
- ❑ Daily/weekly planner
- ❑ Redirection
- ❑ Tiered assignments
- ❑ Adapted directions
- ❑ Shorter assignments
- ❑ Shorter adaptations
- ❑ Frequent reinforcement
- ❑ Modeling
- ❑ Adapted textbooks
- ❑ Visuals to support instruction

- ❑ Adapted materials
- ❑ Adult assistance
- ❑ Peer-mediated instruction
- ❑ Verbal prompts
- ❑ Curriculum overlapping
- ❑ Self-correcting materials
- ❑ Cues to highlight information
- ❑ Adapted homework
- ❑ Calculators
- ❑ Graphic organizers
- ❑ Frequent communication with families
- ❑ Generalization strategies
- ❑ Listening/note-taking guides
- ❑ Frequent feedback
- ❑ Examples/models of correct response formats
- ❑ Prompting
- ❑ Concrete teaching aids
- ❑ Limited distractions
- ❑ Study guides

❑ Other (please specify) _____

Classroom-Based Testing Accommodations

- ❑ Items omitted
- ❑ Extended time
- ❑ Individual administration
- ❑ Directions/items read
- ❑ Adapted directions
- ❑ Word processor/spell-checker
- ❑ Adapted multiple-choice items
- ❑ Calculator
- ❑ Increased space in between items
- ❑ Fewer items
- ❑ Adapted matching items
- ❑ Adapted true-false items
- ❑ Adapted sentence completion items

- ❑ Proctor
- ❑ Scribe
- ❑ Separate location
- ❑ Breaks
- ❑ Alternate response mode
- ❑ Administrations over several sessions
- ❑ Cues to highlight information
- ❑ Oral test
- ❑ Cooperative group testing
- ❑ Extra-credit options
- ❑ Bonus points
- ❑ Writing mechanics waived
- ❑ Use of technology (please specify)

❑ Other (please specify) _____

Source: From *Creating Inclusive Classrooms*, by S. J. Salend, 2005 (5th ed., p. 525). Upper Saddle River, NJ: Merrill/Prentice Hall. Reprinted with permission of Pearson Education, Inc.

student, discuss the impact of the student's needs on classroom instruction, and list in-class accommodations as well as any accommodations necessary for state- and districtwide assessments. All pertinent parties are requested to sign the plan. In the case study, Marina was diagnosed with attention deficit/hyperactivity disorder (AD/HD) in preschool. Although she was on grade level in all subjects except reading, in which she was above grade level, Marina's parents and her first-grade general education teacher believed her attentional difficulties justified developing an accommodation plan for her. Marina's Section 504 Accommodation Plan is shown in Figure 4.4.

CONCLUSION

The way in which educators and parents control the physical space of a setting and select and utilize instructional strategies has a direct impact on children's engagement and learning. As shown in the case study of Marina and her family, professionals working with infants, toddlers, and preschoolers tend to use a combination of direct and naturalistic instruction to teach needed skills. Professionals teaching primary-aged students tend to offer a structured physical environment, employ direct instruction, and provide appropriate instructional and assessment accommodations for students in inclusive or self-contained

Figure 4.4 Section 504 Accommodation Plan for Marina, who is in a general education first grade

Name: Marina O'Daniel   School: Liberty Elementary
Age: 6.4 years   Grade: 1st grade
Date: October 10, XXXX
Follow-Up and Reevaluation: October 10, XXXX

General Strengths:
Marina O'Daniel, a happy, energetic 6-year-old girl, was diagnosed with Attention Deficit/Hyperactivity Disorder (AD/HD) by Dr. Skees, Psychotherapy Associates, when she was 4 years 4 months old. She enjoys art, computer games, and reading, particularly adventure stories. She is curious and shows good independent work habits when topics interest her.
    Presently, Marina receives psychotherapy services bimonthly. Mr. and Mrs. O'Daniel report they are in the process of having Marina's medication reevaluated. The present treatment plan with Dr. Skees seems to be improving Marina's attention and impulsivity.

General Concerns:
Marina has difficulty participating appropriately in large-group activities. She is eager to respond and, consequently, often interrupts the teacher during instruction or answers for other children. Her high energy level makes sitting at her desk for long periods of time difficult. In the afternoons, the accuracy of her independent work seems to decline. Additionally, she seems to have difficulty sharing with peers and waiting her turn with minimal verbal protesting.

Impact of Disability in the Classroom:
Marina's needs relate to her poor impulse control, high level of activity, and difficulty completing small group and large group assignments. Mr. and Mrs. O'Daniel report that they experience Marina's verbal interruptions at home, but to a lesser degree than was observed in school. They report they see improvements in Marina's ability to wait her turn since she began first grade. They also report that Marina has a strong bond with her sisters. All three girls enjoy reading to one another.

(continued)

Figure 4.4 (continued)

Goal	Accommodations	Person Responsible
1. Increase the rate of completion and the level of accuracy of Marina's work	A. After directions are given, Marina will be asked to repeat directions in her "own words." The teacher will attempt to check on her progress every 5–6 minutes when she is doing seatwork.	A. Ms. Brown, lst grade teacher
	B. Marina will be given a 1-minute break to stand next to her desk and stretch every 15 minutes when doing seatwork.	B. Ms. Matson, student teacher; Ms. Brown
	C. A "no-talking face" sign will be worn by teachers to remind Marina, and others, to raise their hands and wait to be called on before answering. If Marina talks out, she will be shown the sign, and the teacher will model hand raising while placing her finger over her lips.	C. Ms. Brown
	D. Marina will be given verbal praise and one token for every time she waits quietly, with her hand raised, to be called on. When she has 15 tokens, she will earn 5 minutes of computer time.	D. Ms. Matson
2. Increase the rate of appropriate interactions with peers during small-/large-group instruction	A. Marina will participate in structured social training activities that encourage turn taking and appropriate expression of feelings.	A. Ms. Brown, 1st grade teacher; Mrs. Fowlkes, counselor
	B. Marina will be given a leadership role in disseminating materials to foster peer sharing.	B. Ms. Brown; Ms. Matson, student teacher
	C. At the end of each day, Marina will discuss with Ms. Matson how well she believes she did that day in "being a good friend."	C. Ms. Matson

Participants:
Mr. and Mrs. Steve O'Daniel, Parents
Ms. Beatrice Brown, First Grade Teacher
Ms. Debbie Matson, Student Teacher
Mrs. Jean White, Principal
Mrs. Eileen Fowlkes, School Counselor

I agree with the Section 504 Accommodation Plan outlined above.

Parent(s)/Guardian _____ Date _____

Teacher _____ Date _____

Principal _____ Date _____

classrooms. Standards-based reforms have challenged general and special educators to redouble their efforts to create successful learning opportunities for *all* students in general education classrooms (Helwig & Tindal, 2003). The lack of needed resources, services, or staff preparation will deprive not only students with special needs, but the rest of the children in a class as well.

SUMMARY

Designing and managing the physical space

- Using staff effectively, carefully planning and teaching transitions, and conscientiously selecting materials are ways to structure environments to maximize learning for infants, toddlers, and preschoolers.
- Centers tend to be used for primary-aged students to review previously learned skills, apply learned skills in a new way, promote independent social interaction between small groups, encourage self-direction in learning, develop independent learning and research skills, encourage practice with basic skills, and offer interest-based learning.

Instructional approaches

- Children with disabilities and/or developmental delays benefit from direct instruction, explicit directions, clear models, and structured opportunities to practice skills with adult feedback.
- Embedded learning opportunities involve professionals directing children's actions within ongoing activities and routines, modifying planned activities in ways that yield desired outcomes, using natural antecedents and consequences, and providing sufficient opportunities for skill practice.

Instructional strategies

- Prompting, modeling, response-contingent feedback, the mand-model procedure, and active student responding are instructional strategies that support learning in young children with special needs.

Increasing engagement in young children

- Engagement is promoted by providing sufficient and varied skill practice, using activity mini-schedules, using scaffolding, and using computers to support learning.

Inclusion and accommodative practices

- Program accommodations provided in inclusive classes include access accommodations, low-impact accommodations, and high-impact accommodations.

DISCUSSION QUESTIONS/ACTIVITIES

1. Describe three ways professionals can increase engagement in toddlers and preschoolers with special needs in home- and center-based programs.

2. Discuss two barriers to improving collaboration in inclusive classrooms with primary-aged students with special needs.

3. Mrs. Brown, Marina's first-grade teacher, needs two new ideas for teaching Marina appropriate social skills (see the case study and Figure 4.4). Using information from Appendix C, identify three online references that may help Mrs. Brown develop activities for her class and Marina.

REFERENCES

Alpert, C., & Kaiser, A. (1992). Training parents as milieu language teachers. *Journal of Early Language Intervention, 16*(1), 29–39.

Bailey, D., McWilliams, R., Buysse, V., & Wesley, P. (1998). Inclusion in the context of competing values in early childhood special education. *Early Childhood Research Quarterly, 13*, 27–47.

Beaty, J. (1996). *Preschool appropriate practices* (2nd ed.). Fort Worth, TX: Harcourt Brace.

Bevill, A., Gast, D., Maguire, A., & Vail, C. (2001). Increasing engagement of preschoolers with disabilities through correspondence training and picture cues. *Journal of Early Intervention, 24*(2), 129–145.

Biederman, G., Fairhall, J., Raven, K., & Davey, V. (1998). Verbal prompting, hand-over-hand instruction, and passive observation in teaching children with developmental disabilities. *Exceptional Children, 64*(4), 503–511.

Billings, S. (1992). Efficiency of transition-based teaching with instructive feedback. *Education and Treatment of Children, 15*, 320–334.

Blank, J., & Hertzog, N. (2003). Strengthening task commitment in preschool children: Reflections from an early childhood program. *Young Exceptional Children, 7*(1), 11–20.

Bricker, D., Pretti-Frontczak, K., & McComas, N. (1998). *An activity-based approach to early intervention* (2nd ed.). Baltimore, MD: Brookes.

Buysse, V., Skinner, D., & Grant, S. (2001). Toward a definition of quality inclusion: Perspectives of parents and practitioners. *Journal of Early Intervention, 24*(2), 146–161.

Buysse, V., & Wesley, P. (2004). A framework for understanding and the consultation process: Stage-by-stage. *Young Exceptional Children, 7*(2), 2–9.

Campbell, P., Milbourne, S., Silverman, C., & Feller, N. (2005). Promoting inclusion by improving child care quality in inner-city programs. *Journal of Early Intervention, 28*(1), 65–79.

Casey, A., & McWilliam, R. (2005). Where is everybody? Organizing adults to promote child engagement. *Young Exceptional Children, 8*(2), 2–10.

Chambers, C. R. (2006). High-probability request strategies: Practical guidelines. *Young Exceptional Children, 9*(2), 20–28.

Cripe, J., & Venn, M. (1997). Family-guided routines for early intervention services. *Young Exceptional Children, 1*(1), 18–26.

deBettencourt, L. U. (2002). Understanding the differences between IDEA and Section 504. *TEACHING Exceptional Children, 34*(3), 16–23.

Destefano, L., Shriner, J., & Lloyd, C. (2001). Teacher decision making in participation of students with disabilities in large-scale assessment. *Exceptional Children, 68*(1), 7–22.

Donegan, M., Ostrosky, M., & Fowler, S. (1996). Children enrolled in multiple programs: Characteristics, supports, and barriers to teacher communication. *Journal of Early Intervention, 20*(2), 95–106.

Dunst, C., Bruder, M., Trivette, C., Raab, M., & McLean, M. (2001). Natural learning opportunities for infants, toddlers and preschoolers. *Young Exceptional Children, 4*(3), 18–26.

Dunst, C., Herter, S., Shields, H., & Bennis, L. (2001). Mapping community-based natural learning opportunities. *Young Exceptional Children, 4*(4), 16–25.

Edmark Publishing Company. *Millie's Math House.* San Francisco: Author.

Elliott, S., & Marquart, A. (2004). Extended time as a testing accommodation: Its effects and perceived consequences. *Exceptional Children, 70*(3), 349–367.

Essa, E. (1999). *A practical guide to solving preschool behavior problems* (4th ed.). Albany, NY: Delmar.

FACETS (Family-Guided Approaches to Collaborative Early Intervention Training and Services Training). Retrieved July 2006, from http://www.parsons.lsi.ukans.edu/facets/index.html

Fones, M., & Rosemergy, J. (2005). The autism puzzle. *Peabody Reflector, 74*, 22–24.

Frea, W. (1995). Social-communicative skills in higher-functioning children with autism. In R. L. Koegel & L. Koegel (Eds.), *Teaching children with autism: Strategies for initiating positive interactions and improving learning opportunities* (pp. 112–129). Baltimore, MD: Brookes.

Fuchs, D., & Fuchs, L. (1995). What's so "special" about special education? *Phi Delta Kappan, 76*(7), 552–530.

Fuchs, L., Fuchs, D., Eaton, S., Hamlett, C., Binkley, E., & Crouch, R. (2000). Using objective data sources to enhance teacher judgments about test accommodations. *Exceptional Children, 67*, 67–81.

Fujiki, M., Brinton, B., Isaacson, T., & Summers, C. (2001). Social behaviors of children with language impairment on the playground: A pilot study. *Language, Speech, and Hearing Services in Schools, 32*(2), 101–113.

Gallagher, P., & Lambert, R. (2006). Classroom quality, concentration of children with special needs, and child outcomes in Head Start. *Exceptional Children, 73*(1), 31–52.

Galloway, J., Ivey, L., & Valster, G. (1990). *Daily plans for active preschoolers: 80 ready-to-use daily activity plans for children 3–5.* West Nyack, NY: Center for Applied Research in Education.

Guralnick, M. (2001). Social competence with peers and early childhood inclusion: Need for alternative approaches. In M. J. Guralnick (Ed.), *Early childhood inclusion: Focus on change* (pp. 481–502). Baltimore, MD: Brookes.

Hagiwara, T., & Myles, B. (1999). A multimedia social story intervention: Teaching skills to children with autism. *Focus on Autism and Other Developmental Disabilities, 12*(4), 82–95.

Halahan, A., & Costenbader, V. (2000). A comparison of developmental gains for preschool children with disabilities in inclusive and self-contained classrooms. *Topics in Early Childhood Special Education, 20*(4), 224–235.

Hall, W., & Salmon, S. (2003). Chocolate chip cookies and rubrics: Helping students understand rubrics in inclusive settings. *TEACHING Exceptional Children, 35*(4), 8–11.

Hanson, M., Horn, E., Sandall, S., Beckman, P., Morgan, M., Marquart, J., Barnwell, D., & Chou, H. (2001). After preschool inclusion: Children's educational pathways over the early school years. *Exceptional Children, 68*(1), 65–83.

Haugland, S. (1995). Classroom activities provide important support to children's computer experiences. *Early Childhood Education Journal, 23*(2), 99–100.

Hawbaker, B., Balong, M., Buckwalter, S., & Runyon, S. (2001). Building a strong BASE of support for all students through coplanning. *TEACHING Exceptional Children, 33*(4), 24–30.

Helwig, R., & Tindal, G. (2003). An experimental analysis of accommodation decisions on large-scale mathematics tests. *Exceptional Children, 69*(2), 211–225.

Hemmeter, M., Smith, B., Sandall, S., & Askew, L. (2005). *DEC recommended practices workbook: Improving practices for young children with special needs and their families.* Missoula, MT: Division for Early Childhood of the Council for Exceptional Children.

Heward, W. L. (2006). *Exceptional children: An introduction to special education* (8th ed). Upper Saddle River, NJ: Merrill/Prentice Hall.

Horn, E., Lieber, J., Sandall, S., & Schwartz, I. (2001). Embedded learning opportunities as an instructional strategy for supporting children's learning in inclusive programs. In M. Ostrosky & S. Sandall (Eds.), *Teaching strategies: What to do to support young children's development* (YEC Monograph No. 3) (pp. 59–70). Denver, CO: Sopris West.

Individuals with Disabilities Education Improvement Act of 2004. Pub. L. No. 108–446.

Jenkins, R. (2005). Interdisciplinary instruction in the inclusion classroom. *TEACHING Exceptional Children, 37*(5), 42–48.

Judge, S. L. (2001). Integrating computer technology within early childhood classrooms. *Young Exceptional Children, 5*(1), 20–26.

Justice, L. (2004). Creating language-rich preschool classroom environments. *TEACHING Exceptional Children, 37*(2), 36–44.

Karge, B., McClure, M., & Patton, P. (1995). The success of collaboration resource programs for students with disabilities in grades 6 through 8. *Remedial and Special Education, 16*(2), 79–89.

Kim, A., Vaughn, S., Elbaum, B., Hughes, M., Sloan, C., & Sridhar, D. (2003). Effects of toys or group composition for children with disabilities: A synthesis. *Journal of Early Intervention, 25*(3), 189–205.

Lieber, J., Hanson, M., Beckman, P., Odom, S., Sandall, S., Schwartz, I., Horn, E., & Wolery, R. (2000). Key influences on the initiation and implementation of inclusive preschool programs. *Exceptional Children, 67*(1), 83–98.

Mathes, P., Clancy-Menchetti, J., & Torgensen, J. (2003). *K-PALS: Kindergarten peer-assisted literacy strategies.* Longmont, CO: Sopris West.

Mathes, P., Torgensen, J., Allen, S., & Howard-Allor, J. (2003). *First grade PALS: Peer-assisted literacy strategies.* Longmont, CO: Sopris West.

McCormick, L., Noonan, M., & Heck, R. (1998). Variables affecting engagement in inclusive preschool classrooms. *Journal of Early Intervention, 21*(2), 160–176.

McDonnell, A., Brownell, K., & Wolery, M. (2001). Teachers' views concerning individualized intervention and support roles within developmentally appropriate preschools. *Journal of Early Intervention, 24*(1), 67–83.

McGee, G. (2000). Social intervention yields positive response. *Advocate, 33,* 26–30.

McWilliam, R., & Bailey, D. (1992). Promoting engagement and mastery. In D. B. Bailey & M. Wolery (Eds.), *Teaching infants and preschoolers with disabilities* (pp. 229–255). New York: Macmillan.

McWilliam, R., & Bailey, D. (1995). Effects of classroom social structure and disability on engagement. *Topics in Early Childhood Special Education, 15*(2), 123–147.

Minishew, N., Meyer, J., & Dunn, M. (2003). Autism spectrum disorders. In S. Segalowitz & I. Rapin (Eds.), *Child neuropsychology Part II* (pp. 863–896). Amsterdam: Elsevier.

Morrison, G. (2004). *Early childhood education today* (9th ed.). Upper Saddle River, NJ: Merrill/Prentice Hall.

National Center for Educational Outcomes. (2001). *State participation and accommodation policies for students with disabilities.* Minneapolis: University of Minnesota.

O'Connor, K. (1995). Guidelines for grading that support learning and student success. *NASSP Bulletin, 79*(571), 91–101.

Phelps, P., & Hanline, M. (1999). Let's play blocks! Creating effective learning experiences for young children. *TEACHING Exceptional Children, 32*(2), 62–68.

Pivik, J., McComas, J., & LaFlamme, M. (2002). Barriers and facilitators to inclusive education. *Exceptional Children, 69*(1), 97–107.

Polloway, E., Patton, J., & Serna, L. (2005). *Strategies for teaching learners with special needs* (8th ed.). Upper Saddle River, NJ: Merrill/Prentice Hall.

Prater, M. A. (2003). She will succeed! Strategies for success in inclusive classrooms. *TEACHING Exceptional Children, 35*(5), 58–64.

Pretti-Frontczak, K., & Bricker, D. (2004). *An activity-based approach to early intervention* (3rd ed.). Baltimore: Brookes.

Rafferty, Y., Boettcher, C., & Griffin, K. (2001). Benefits and risks of reverse inclusion for preschoolers with and without disabilities: Parents' perspective. *Journal of Early Intervention, 24*(4), 266–286.

Rafferty, Y., Piscitelli, V., & Boettcher, C. (2003). The impact of inclusion on language development and social competence among preschoolers with disabilities. *Exceptional Children, 69,* 467–479.

Raver, S. (1999). *Intervention strategies for infants and toddlers with special needs: A team approach.* Upper Saddle River, NJ: Merrill/Prentice Hall.

Rea, P., McLaughlin, V., & Walther-Thomas, C. (2002). Outcomes for students with learning disabilities in inclusive and pullout programs. *Exceptional Children, 68*(2), 203–223.

Ridley, S., McWilliam, R., & Oates, C. (2000). Observed engagement as an indicator of child care program quality. *Early Education and Development, 11*, 133–146.

Risley, T. (1997). Family preservation for children with autism. *Journal of Early Intervention, 21*(1), 15–16.

Rock, M. (2004). Transfiguring it out: Converting disengaged learners to active participants. *TEACHING Exceptional Children, 36*(5), 64–72.

Roopnarine, J., & Johnson, J. (2005). *Approaches to early childhood education* (4th ed.). Upper Saddle River, NJ: Merrill/Prentice Hall.

Rous, B. (2004). Perspectives of teachers about instructional supervision and behaviors that influence preschool instruction. *Journal of Early Intervention, 26*(4), 266–283.

Roybal, R., & Wilson, K. (2006, March 29). *Here we are together: Strategies for successful large group activities.* Paper presented at the National Training Institute on Effective Practice, "Addressing Challenging Behavior— Supporting Young Children's Social/Emotional Development," Clearwater, FL.

Rule, S., Losardo, A., Dinnebell, L., Kaiser, A., & Rowland, C. (1998). Translating research on naturalistic instruction into practice. *Journal of Early Intervention, 21*(4), 283–293.

Sadler, F. H. (2003). The itinerant special education teacher in the early childhood classroom. *TEACHING Exceptional Children, 35*(3), 8–15.

Salend, S. (2001). *Creating inclusive classrooms: Effective and reflective practices* (4th ed.). Upper Saddle River, NJ: Merrill/Prentice Hall.

Salend, S. (2004). Fostering inclusive values in children: What families can do. *TEACHING Exceptional Children, 37*(1), 64–69.

Salend, S. (2005a). *Creating inclusive classrooms: Effective and reflective practices for all students* (5th ed.). Upper Saddle River, NJ: Merrill/Prentice Hall.

Salend, S. (2005b). Report card models that support communication and differentiation of instruction. *TEACHING Exceptional Children, 37*(4), 28–34.

Salend, S., & Duhaney, L. M. (2002). What do families have to say about inclusion? How to pay attention and get results. *TEACHING Exceptional Children, 35*(1), 62–66.

Sandall, S., Hemmeter, M. L., Smith, B., & McLean, M. (2005). *DEC recommended practices: A comprehensive guide for practical application in early intervention/early childhood special education.* Longmont, CO: Sopris West.

Santos, R., & Lignugaris-Kraft, B. (1997). Integrating research on effective instruction with instruction in the natural environment for young children with disabilities. *Exceptionality, 7*, 97–129.

Santos, R., Lignugaris-Kraft, B., & Akers, J. (2000). Tips for planning center time activities for preschool classrooms. *Young Exceptional Children, 2*(4), 9–16.

Schepis, M., Reid, D., Ownbey, J., & Clary, J. (2003). Training preschool staff to promote cooperative participation among young children with severe disabilities and their classmates. *Research and Practice for Persons with Severe Disabilities, 28*(1), 37–42.

Shriner, J., & Destefano, L. (2003). Participation and accommodation in state assessment: The role of Individualized Education Programs. *Exceptional Children, 69*(2), 147–161.

Smith, D. (2004). *Introduction to special education: Teaching in an age of opportunity* (5th ed.). Boston: Allyn & Bacon.

Sobel, D., & Taylor, S. (2006). Blueprint for the responsive classroom. *TEACHING Exceptional Children, 38*(5), 28–35.

Soodak, L., & Erwin, E. (2000). Valued member or tolerated participant: Parents? *Journal of the Association for Persons with Severe Handicaps, 25*(1), 29–41.

Stuart, S., Flis, L., & Rinaldi, C. (2006). Connecting with families: Parents speak up about preschool services for their children with autism spectrum disorder. *TEACHING Exceptional Children, 39*(1), 46–51.

Thurlow, M., & Johnson, D. (2000). High-stakes testing of student with disabilities. *Journal of Teacher Education, 51*(4), 305–314.

Torgesen, J. K. (2002). The prevention of reading difficulties. *Journal of School Psychology, 40*, 7–26.

Towbin, K., Mauk, J., & Batshaw, M. (2005). Pervasive developmental disorders. In M. L. Batshaw (Ed.), *Children with disabilities* (5th ed., pp. 365–388). Baltimore, MD: Brookes.

Vesay, J. (2004, February 21). *Linking perspectives and practice: Early childhood and early childhood special educators working together in the preschool inclusive classroom.* Paper presented to the Virginia Council for Exceptional Children Conference, Charlottesville, VA.

Voltz, D., Brazel, N., & Ford, A. (2001). What matters most in inclusive education: A practical guide for moving forward. *Intervention in School and Clinic, 37*, 23–30.

Voltz, D., Sims, M., Nelson, B., & Bivens, C. (2005). M2EECA: A framework for inclusion in the context of standards-based reform. *TEACHING Exceptional Children, 37*(5), 14–19.

Walther-Thomas, C., Korinek, L., McLaughlin, V., & Williams, B. (2000). *Collaboration for inclusive education.* Boston: Allyn & Bacon.

Washburn-Moses, L. (2003). What every special educator should know about high-stakes testing. *Exceptional Children, 35*(4), 12–15.

Weinfeld, R., Barnes-Robinson, L., Jeweler, S., & Shevitz, B. (2005). What we have learned: Experiences in providing adaptations and accommodations for gifted and talented students with learning disabilities. *TEACHING Exceptional Children, 38*(1), 48–54.

Welton, E., Vakil, S., & Carasea, C. (2004). Strategies for increasing positive social interactions in children with autism: A case study. *TEACHING Exceptional Children, 37*(1), 40–46.

Wiggins, K., & Damore, S. (2006). "Survivors" or "friends"? A framework for assessing effective collaboration. *TEACHING Exceptional Children, 38*(5), 49–56.

Winter, S. (1999). *The early childhood inclusion model: A program for all children.* Olney, MD: Association for Childhood Education International.

Wolfgang, C., & Wolfgang, M. (1995). *The three faces of discipline for early childhood: Empowering teachers and students.* (ERIC Document Reproduction Service No. ED410011).

Ysseldyke, J. (2001). Reflections on a research career: Generalization from 25 years of research on assessment and instructional decision making. *Exceptional Children, 67*(3), 295–309.

PART II

TECHNIQUES FOR PROMOTING DEVELOPMENT AND LEARNING

Chapter
5

Promoting Communication Development

Deena Bernstein

Liat Seiger-Gardner

Overview

This chapter discusses the development of communication and language in young children, including

overview of communication and language development

communication development in infants and toddlers

communication development in preschoolers

language characteristics of primary-aged students with language impairment

augmentative-alternative communication

CASE STUDY: **Paul and His Family**

Paul had just turned 2 when he was referred for evaluation. The speech-language pathologist's (SLP's) informal evaluation revealed Paul to be an engaging and communicative child. He exhibited eye contact, joint action, and joint attention. During free play, Paul displayed symbolic play by feeding the doll and putting her to bed. Turn-taking skills were revealed in play and vocalization, as were appropriate gestures for requesting. Informal assessment of Paul's language comprehension skills revealed that he was unable to identify familiar objects like cup and ball, but was able to follow simple verbal directions, such as "Give me the ball." Informal assessment of Paul's expressive language skills indicated that he was delayed in acquiring first words and had less than 50 words in his productive lexicon. The words he produced spontaneously were /shoe/, /baby/, and /tankyou/ (thank you). The only two-word combination he produced was /mommy shoe/ as a request for his mother to tie his shoe. He did not imitate any words modeled by the SLP. The Preschool Language Scale–4 (PLS–4) was administered and on the receptive language subtests, Paul scored within the normal limits, but on the expressive language subtests, he scored one standard deviation below the mean for his age. The team recommended that Paul receive two 45-minute speech and language therapy sessions each week to address these therapy goals: (1) learning to imitate gestures, familiar sounds, and words and (2) increasing expressive vocabulary through the use of modeling and other elicitation techniques.

Informal assessment of Paul at 4 years 6 months of age revealed reduced intelligibility in rapid connected speech due to the presence of two phonological processes: (1) final consonant deletion and (2) cluster reduction. A mean length of utterance (MLU) analysis of Paul's spontaneous language sample revealed an MLU of 3.68, which fell within the normal range for his age. However, some grammatical morphemes—for example, the present progressive form (-ing)—were used inconsistently. Paul's language sample was also characterized by a limited lexicon and word-finding difficulty. His pragmatic skills were typical for his age. Formal assessment, using the Clinical Evaluation of Language Fundamentals–Preschool (CELF–P), showed receptive skills within the normal range and expressive language skills one and a half standard deviations below the mean for his age. The team recommended that speech and language therapy be continued twice a week to increase Paul's intelligibility and expressive vocabulary, reduce his word retrieval difficulties, and improve his morphological skills. Paul's SLP provided direct therapy in a pullout program and offered guidance to his teachers in his general education preschool. At the end of kindergarten, based on test results and observations, Paul's early childhood special education team, and his family, suggested that Paul continue to receive speech and language services to support his emergent reading and writing skills.

While most children learn to communicate naturally and for the most part without formal instruction, there are children for whom learning to communicate is difficult. To overcome this challenge, these children require the assistance of various professionals, including speech-language pathologists (SLPs), early childhood special educators, and other related service professionals. Because communication and language are crucial to all educational and social functioning, parents tend to be concerned when their child experiences language-learning difficulties. They recognize that difficulties in communication will seriously hinder their child's educational and social experiences and opportunities. They also recognize that their child's communication skills have the best chance of improving when appropriate professional support is provided.

OVERVIEW OF COMMUNICATION AND LANGUAGE DEVELOPMENT

Communication disorders are among the most-prevalent disabilities in early childhood. According to the American Speech-Language-Hearing Association (ASHA) (1991) and the National Institute on Deafness and Other Communication Disorders (1991), the prevalence of communication disorders in the United States ranges from 10% to 15% of the general population. Communication disorders include disorders of fluency, articulation, voice, and language, with language challenges being the most prevalent in children of all ages.

While some types of language disorders are associated with conditions that can be identified at birth, some children with communication difficulties do not exhibit conditions that can easily distinguish them from their typically developing peers. This is because there is a tremendous amount of variability in the development of language in typically developing children. Some children speak their first words at 10 months and are using multiword combinations before they are 2 years of age, while others are slow to develop their language skills and may be close to age 3 before they are understood by their family and friends. The question is, How does one identify the child that might be at risk for later language and learning difficulties? In order to answer this question, professionals need to know the typical patterns of language development. It is this knowledge that helps determine if, and when, a child is deviating from the typical pattern or is moving in the right direction, albeit too slowly. The following sections trace communication development in infants, toddlers, preschoolers, and school-age children.

Communication, Speech, and Language

To the average person, the terms *communication*, *speech*, and *language* are synonymous and can be used interchangeably. However, these terms are very different and denote different aspects of development. **Communication** is the process by which individuals exchange information and ideas (Owens, 2005). It is an active process that includes a speaker, who formulates a message, and a receiver or a listener, who comprehends the message. Each partner must be alert to the needs of the other to ensure that messages are effectively transmitted and understood.

Speech is one of the modalities most commonly used for communication. It involves the oral-verbal mode of transmitting messages. Precise coordination of the oral musculature is necessary to produce speech sounds, words, and sentences. While individuals use primarily speech for the purpose of communication, it is not the only way to communicate. Writing, signing, text messaging, and even drawing are other modes of communication. The communication mode selected depends on the abilities of the speaker and the needs of the receiver.

For some children with disabilities, acquiring speech may not be a realistic goal. They may have limited physical control over their speech mechanisms, making it unlikely they will learn to produce intelligible speech, or they may have a severe hearing loss, which limits the amount and the quality of the speech input they receive, thus affecting their speech intelligibility. Other children may have developmental disabilities such as autism spectrum disorder or cognitive impairments that limit their ability to successfully communicate verbally. However, the majority of these children acquire the ability to communicate if they are given alternative means (Owens, 2002). A number of augmentative-alternative communication systems are available

to promote communication development in such children and are discussed later in this chapter and in Chapter 10.

Language is a socially shared code that represents ideas through the use of arbitrary symbols and rules that govern the combination of these symbols (Owens, 2005). It encompasses a finite set of rules that govern the combination of sounds, words, sentences, meaning, and use. Native speakers and listeners of any language learn the linguistic rule system of their language through everyday social-communicative interactions. This rule system can be divided into three components: form, content, and use. Included in the **form** of language are (1) rules that govern the sounds and their combinations, called **phonology**; (2) rules that govern the internal organization of words, called **morphology**, such as adding *ed* to form past tense or adding *s* to form plurals; and (3) rules that specify the structure of sentences and the order of the words within a sentence in order to produce a variety of grammatically correct sentence types, called **syntax**.

Content or **semantics** refers to the meaning of words and word combinations. It maps knowledge about objects, events, and people and the relationships among them (Owens, 2005). It allows language users to group similar words into categories based on their semantic features such as visual similarity or their similar functions such as nouns and verbs. It also refers to speakers' and listeners' mental dictionary or lexicon. **Use** or **pragmatics** refers to the rules that govern the use of language in social contexts. These rules govern the reasons for communicating as well as the socially appropriate use of language.

Although these components of language appear distinct, they are interrelated (Bloom & Lahey, 1978). The components of language, and their subsystems, are shown in Figure 5.1. They are essential in discussions of typical communication and language development and in the assessment of these abilities in children with language delays and disorders.

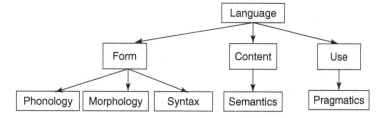

Figure 5.1 The components of language and their subsystems

Language Delay

A child is considered to have a **language delay** if he or she exhibits typical development in all areas except language. The development of language in a child with a language delay is believed to follow the same patterns seen in children with typical language development; however, the development of language is protracted, with the child reaching the same milestones at a slower rate. According to Leonard (1998), the term "delay" suggests a late start and the possibility of making up for lost time. This is discussed further in the subsequent "late bloomers" section. However, for many children with language impairment, an early delay in communication involves not only the late emergence of language, but also language difficulties that may continue until adolescence (Rescorla, 2005). Delayed language may open a gap that widens as children get older, making it difficult for them to "make up" the differences. Children from about 12 months to 5 years of age with delays in language tend to be labeled as having a language delay. In most states, if a child continues to display language delays and language differences after 5 years of age, the problem is viewed as a language impairment or language disorder.

Language Disorder

The American Speech-Language-Hearing Association (ASHA) (1982) defines language disorder as follows:

An impairment in the comprehension and use of spoken, written or other symbol system. The disorder may involve the form of language (morphology, phonology, and syntax), the content of language (semantic system), and/or the function of language for communication (pragmatic system) in any combination (pp. 949–950).

According to ASHA'S definition, a child with a language disorder may have difficulty in understanding language (language comprehension), in formulating language (language production), or in both. Deficits may be noted in listening and reading (**receptive language**) or in speaking and writing (**expressive language**). ASHA'S definition outlines the guidelines for considering language disorders and the components of language and the linguistic processes that might be impaired.

Additionally, childhood language disorders may be classified as primary or secondary. A **primary language disorder or impairment** is present when language differences cannot be accounted for by a peripheral sensory deficit such as a hearing loss, a motor deficit such as cerebral palsy, a cognitive deficit such as mental retardation, a social impairment such as autism spectrum disorder, or a harmful environmental condition such as lead poisoning or parental drug abuse. Primary language disorders are presumed to be the result of impaired development or dysfunction of the central nervous system (Leonard, 1998). A **secondary language disorder or impairment** is one that is associated with and presumed to be caused by factors such as sensory impairments (e.g., hearing loss) or cognitive impairments (e.g., mental retardation).

The sections that follow outline typical and atypical communication and language development from infancy through the primary grades.

This knowledge is vital for identifying and understanding children with communication, language, and learning difficulties.

Communication Development in Infants and Toddlers

Long before infants say their first words, they are acquiring communication skills that form the foundation of language. During their first months, infants demonstrate that they are social beings. They gaze into the eyes of their caregivers, and they are sensitive to the tones of the voices around them and to the facial expressions of those with whom they are interacting. They pay attention to the language spoken to them, and they take their turn in a conversation, even if it is just using **vocalizations** such as "cooing" sounds.

Infants are capable of producing intentional communication, and they are able to communicate specific desires and needs (Owens, 2005). In infancy, intentionality is signaled by the use of gestures, with or without vocalizations, coupled with eye contact and a persistent attempt to communicate a request. Infants cue their willingness to engage with their caregivers by providing nonverbal engagement cues (Bernstein & Levey, 2002). These include facial brightening, eye widening, smiling, head turning, and reaching for their caregiver. They also use disengagement cues that communicate the infant is "ready for a break" from an interaction. Disengagement cues include whimpering, frowning, and an increase in the rate of sucking (Brazelton, Koslowski, & Main, 1974).

Children's early vocal development is usually described in terms of stages. These stages include the following (Bernthal & Bankson, 2004):

1) **Reflexive and cry vocalizations stage,** which is observed during the first month of life.
2) **Cooing/gooing stage,** in which basic syllable shapes of a consonant followed by a vowel (CV) are observed, and rounded back vowels (/o/, /u/) and back consonants (/k/, /g/) are produced, usually between 2 and 3 months of age. At this stage, children can distinguish between their mother's voice and another voice and between utterances in a foreign language and those in their "mother" tongue.
3) **Expansion stage,** which is characterized by vocal play or the exploration of the vocal mechanism, as infants produce squealing sounds and growling.
4) **Reduplicated or canonical babbling stage,** in which the same consonant-vowel (CV) combinations are produced in repetitive strings, such as "*nanana.*" This pattern is observed at 6 months of age. Infants are able to follow their mother's gaze and pointing, while showing a preference for exaggerated intonation patterns, slower productions, and a high pitch voice.
5) **Varied or non-reduplicated babbling stage,** in which a variety of sounds and syllable strings that are not a reduplication of the same syllables increases. Infants at about 8 months of age begin to exhibit **jargon,** adultlike intonation patterns superimposed on rapidly produced multisyllabic strings of babble, which sounds like adult speech.
6) **Single words production stage,** in which infants produce their first words at about 12 months of age.

Semantic Development: The First Words

Once infants begin to communicate, the course of development appears to have some universal characteristics (Brown, 1973). Young children's early utterances are typically only one word in length and are simple in pronunciation and in meaning. First words refer to objects, events, and people in a child's daily life. English-speaking children's first words tend to be *nouns* such as "*car,*" *action words* such as "*push,*" modifiers such as "*mine,*" and personal- social words such as "*hi*" and "*no*" (Nelson, 1973). In addition to acquiring lexical or word knowledge that refers to objects or referents, a child uses his or her first words to code relationships among people, objects, and events. The

TABLE 5.1 Sample relational words for the one-word stage of language development

Category	Meaning	Example
Existence	The child notes an object.	Points and says, "that."
Nonexistence	The child notes an entity is absent.	Says, "no" or "gone."
Disappearance	The child notes an object or person has disappeared or is not there.	Says, "allgone."
Recurrence	The child requests the reappearance of an object or notes that an object has reappeared.	Says, "more."

Source: Adapted with permission from Owens, R. E. (2005). *Language Development: An Introduction* (6th ed., p. 248). Boston: Allyn & Bacon. (Copyright 2005 by Pearson Education.)

meanings that children convey at the one-word stage of development are presented in Table 5.1.

Pragmatic Development

During the prelinguistic stage of development, children combine gaze, gestures, and vocalizations to communicate their intention. By the time they use their first words, children understand that their "words" will produce a response from others. Table 5.2 lists the communicative functions of infants and toddlers at the single-word stage of language development. At this stage, children use gestures, like pointing, with words to communicate their intentions. This integration of nonverbal and verbal elements allows children to be active communicators.

TABLE 5.2 Communicative intentions of typically developing infants and toddlers at the one-word stage of language development

Child's Intention	Context	Example
Requesting an action	The child wants a toy she/he cannot reach.	Points to toy and says, *"uh, uh."*
Protesting	The mother wants the child to put on a coat.	Resists putting on coat, shakes head, cries, and says, *"no."*
Labeling	The child plays with a doll.	Touches doll's nose and says, *"nose."*
Answering	The parent and child are looking at a book.	Adult points to the picture of a car and asks child, "What's this?" Child responds, *"car."*
Greeting	The child is leaving grandmother's house.	Waves hand and says, *"Bye."*
Calling	The child is in his/her crib and the caregiver is in the kitchen.	Calls, *"Mama."*

Cognitive Correlates of Early Communication Development. Some cognitive abilities are highly correlated with the development of language. ECSE professionals often teach these cognitive correlates to children who do not develop them naturally in order to help the children develop a stronger foundation for later language development. The following five cognitive abilities are strongly linked to early communication development (Owens, 2005):

1) **Imitation.** In order for a child to imitate a behavior, the child needs to be able to participate in turn taking, attend to the behavior, and then reproduce it. Vocal and gestural forms of imitation are highly correlated with language development. The speech sounds and intonational patterns that typical infants produce during vocal play are imitations of the adult speech around them, and the gestures used by children in the prelinguistic stage are learned through imitation.

2) **Object Permanence.** Adults understand that if an object has been removed from view, it still exists and can reappear. This important skill is called **object permanence** and is developed within the first two years of life. An infant who lacks object permanence cries hysterically when unable to see his or her mother, even when the mother is present, but out of the infant's line of vision (Piaget, 1952). When a child acquires object permanence, he or she is able to name objects that are not physically present and eventually learns that one way to have an object reappear is by naming it.

3) **Causality.** When a child understands that he or she can cause things to happen, language becomes the means for causing changes. In the prelinguistic stage, infants use motor-based actions, such as pulling, pushing, and pointing, to produce changes in the environment. But as children mature linguistically, they come to understand that language is more efficient, allowing them to create changes by requesting, labeling, and protesting.

4) **Means-Ends.** When approaching a task, a child selects the best means available to reach his or her goal. As soon as the child develops language, language becomes the means to attain desired ends. When he or she wants the bottle that is placed on the kitchen table, the prelinguistic child will use motoric means to reach the desired end (the bottle), perhaps by either pulling the tablecloth that is under the bottle or requesting the bottle using gestures—for example, pointing or making a hand gesture that indicates requesting. The linguistic child will produce a word to request the bottle (e.g., "*baba*"), use a two-word combination (e.g., "*want baba*"), or as the child develops, use a simple sentence form to request the bottle (e.g., "*I want bottle, please*").

5) **Play.** Play skills are highly correlated with language at 10–13 months of age. Symbolic play, which begins to develop in the middle of the second year of life, is particularly important (Patterson & Westby, 1998). Symbolic play is the ability of a child to use one object to represent another, such as using a plate to represent a steering wheel or using a pot to represent a hat. Similarly, words in language are used to represent objects, people, and events.

The Role of Parents and Caregivers

The development of prelinguistic and linguistic communication does not occur in a vacuum. Caregiver–child social routines play an important role in communication development. During the first few months, infants take a responsive role in their interaction with caregivers. However, toward the end of the first year, they begin to develop intentional control and do more "initiating." Through daily routines, games, and interactions, infants have repeated opportunities to experience the effect of their actions on caregivers. Caregivers' ability to "tune in" to the child—to make adjustments in the timing, length, and the complexity of their language when they are interacting with a child—and their ability to introduce a variety of activities and experiences positively

Parents' interaction with their young children establish the foundation for social and communicative development.

contribute to the child's communication development and growth. Caregivers need to provide infants and young children multiple opportunities to practice and refine their vocal, gestural, and social-communicative behavior.

The Role of the Speech–Language Pathologist (SLP)

As part of the early intervention team, one of the roles of the SLP is to assess communication development. As has been noted in previous chapters, assessment, evaluation, and intervention require professionals to work as a team. Communication assessment and intervention are inseparable processes, especially with infants and toddlers due to their rapid rate of development during the first months of life. The two most commonly used models of communication assessment for very young children are the traditional and the dynamic approaches. An examination of the two models reveals that the traditional approach is more static, while the dynamic approach incorporates intervention into assessment. Regardless of the specific approach used, the importance of early identification of children at risk for communication disorders cannot be overstated (McCathern, Warren, &

Yoder, 1999; Oller, Eilers, Neal, & Schwartz, 1999; Robinson & Robb, 2002).

Traditional Assessment Approaches. The most commonly used traditional model of early communication assessment is the **developmental approach**. The traditional/developmental approach uses assessments that rely almost exclusively on age expectations and normative criteria. They include checklists of age-expected behaviors and represent a static form of assessment in which infants and toddlers are assessed and measured against a given set of age-referenced or milestone information that compares the child's communication ability to the abilities of age-peers. Table 5.3 lists commonly used traditional/developmental instruments used by SLPs for the communication assessment of infants and toddlers.

Dynamic Approach. Some researchers and practitioners believe that the traditional/developmental instruments available for very young children are too limited (Crais, 1999; Wetherby & Prizant, 1992). They advocate a more naturalistic approach to assessment in which specialists examine a child's communication skills within daily routines. Within the last few years, this has led to the **dynamic**

TABLE 5.3 Language and communication instruments for infants and toddlers that employ a traditional/developmental assessment approach

Infant-Toddler Language Scale (Rossetti, 1990)

Vineland Adaptive Behavior Scales (Sparrow, Balla, & Cicchetti, 1984)

Bayley Scales of Infant Development, Second Edition (Bayley, 1993)

Battelle Developmental Inventory-2 (Newborg, 2004)

TABLE 5.4 Play-based assessment instruments used to assess communicative development in infants, toddlers, and preschoolers

Communication and Symbolic Behavior Scales (Wetherby & Prizant, 1993)

Play Assessment (McCune-Nicholich & Carroll, 1981)

Carpenter's Play Scale (Carpenter, 1987)

Symbolic Play Scale (Westby, 1980, 1988)

Transdisciplinary Play-Based Assessment (TPBA) (Linder, 2008)

Knox Preschool Play Scale (Knox, 1974)

Play Checklist (Heidemann & Hewitt, 1992)

approach of communication assessment of infants, toddlers, and preschoolers.

This approach emphasizes the evaluation of the child's performance in natural contexts and determines the processes that could be used to foster better communication on the part of the child, incorporating intervention into assessment. The dynamic assessment approach involves (1) observing the child during routine activities, (2) observing the child while interacting with familiar people, (3) observing the child while manipulating objects, (4) observing the child during play, and (5) determining the strategies that may optimally stimulate the child to communicate at higher developmental levels.

Play-based assessment is particularly important in the dynamic approach. It allows professionals to collect information about the child's communication skills in play-oriented activities. Table 5.4 lists play-based tools used to assess communicative development in young children.

Whether professionals choose to utilize a traditional/developmental model or a dynamic model of assessment, best practice necessitates that family members be involved as an integral part of the assessment-intervention process and that assessment involve teamwork (Sandall, Hemmeter, Smith, & McLean, 2005). Because

there are fewer dynamic assessment tools, most SLPs tend to rely on traditional/developmental measurements. Paul, featured in the case study, was given both dynamic and traditional/developmental assessments. Table 5.5 lists tools that utilize a dynamic approach to the assessment of infants and toddlers.

TABLE 5.5 Language and communication instruments for infants and toddlers that employ a dynamic assessment approach

Assessing Prelinguistic and Linguistic Behavior (Olswang, Stoel-Gammon, Coggins, & Carpenter, 1987)

Communication and Symbolic Behavior Scales (Wetherby & Prizant, 1993)

MacArthur Communicative Development Inventories (Fensen, Dale, Reznick, Thal, Bates, Hartung, Pethick, & Reilly, 1993)

Trandisciplinary Play-Based Assessment (Linder, 2008)

General Principles of Communication Intervention with Young Children

Ramey and Ramey (1998) delineated a set of guiding principles for specialists involved in programming for young children with communication delays/disorders:

1) The earlier intervention begins and the longer it continues, the more beneficial it will be.
2) Program intensity matters. That is, the amount and degree of contact between specialists and other professionals and the child and his or her family influence the success of the program.
3) Programs that are designed only to train parents are not as effective as those that provide services to children *and* train parents.
4) Programs that address the needs of the child and his or her family in multiple ways are more likely to be successful than are programs that take a limited prospective.
5) Not all children will benefit equally from the services provided.
6) Unless there is an environmental support system that will help maintain the child's skills learned in intervention, gains may not be maintained over time.

General Approaches to Communication Intervention

SLPs may offer direct or indirect services to children and their families. **Direct services** involve the SLP providing services to the child; **indirect services** involve the SLP training others to provide services to the child and the child's family. Frequently, a combination of direct and indirect services is arranged. When implementing Individualized Family Service Plans (IFSPs) and Individualized Education Programs (IEPs), SLPs employ two basic approaches: naturalistic and direct.

Naturalistic Approaches to Communication Intervention. Naturalistic approaches to language and communication intervention are based on the assumptions that (1) young children learn to communicate using speech and language in a variety of routines and daily activities as they interact with their caregivers and others in their environment and (2) intervention is best conducted within the context of familiar situations. While program names differ, there are common elements that naturalistic programs possess:

❏ They follow the child's lead.
❏ They engage the child in relevant activities.
❏ They place attention on what the child is attending to (also called **joint attention**).
❏ They respond to any behavior that the child exhibits that might be construed as communication.
❏ They expand on the child's communication attempts and turn taking. (Sandall et al., 2005)

Embedding language and communication intervention within naturally occurring activities is apparent in a variety of teaching and intervention paradigms: transactional teaching (McLean & McLean, 1978), interactive modeling (Wilcox, Kouri, & Caswell, 1991), the ecological model (MacDonald & Carroll, 1992), and enhanced milieu teaching (Kaiser & Hester, 1994).

Direct Approaches to Communication Intervention. Direct intervention models are based on learning principles as defined in behavioral psychology. While direct intervention strategies are often incorporated into natural settings, the main difference between naturalistic and direct approaches lies in the amount of structure introduced into the setting. Using techniques such as modeling, reinforcement, chaining, and fading, the SLP begins direct intervention with a discrete skill such as mutual eye gaze, provides reinforcement to the child, and then moves to slightly more advanced skills as each skill is learned (Sandall et al., 2005). Most researchers believe that direct intervention approaches are not easily applied with infants, but may be effective in developing contingency awareness in infants and young children with severe disabilities.

By creating experiences in which there is joint attention, ECSE professionals are able to facilitate and expand a child's communication skills.

Milieu Teaching. The milieu teaching approach is a hybrid of the direct/behavioral approaches and the naturalistic approaches. In milieu teaching, adults deliberately arrange the environment in order to give the child a reason to communicate (Warren & Kaiser, 1986). Adults identify communication and language targets and apply teaching procedures to accomplish target objectives. Milieu teaching has the following basic features (Warren & Kaiser, 1986): (1) Parents and professionals talk about objects, events, and/or relationships that attract the child's attention; (2) parents and professionals model, imitate, and expand on the child's communication attempts; (3) parents and professionals repeat and clarify words and requests that the child does not seem to understand; and (4) parents and professionals use a higher pitched voice as well as "stress" to call the

child's attention to important information in utterances.

Milieu teaching, although grounded in a behavioral approach to communication intervention, does not use a rigid structure. The topic of each interaction and the reinforcement selected are child-centered (McCormick, Loeb, & Schiefelbusch, 1997). A typical intervention target for an infant might be increasing the frequency of communication behaviors, while an intervention target for a child at the one-word stage might be producing longer and/or more complex utterances or using more advanced forms to express familiar functions. Modeling, the mand-model procedure, time delay, and incidental teaching, discussed in Chapter 4, are used in milieu teaching (Alpert & Kaiser, 1992).

Facilitative Strategies for Promoting Communication in Young Children

Most researchers advocate that professionals and parents use those strategies commonly used by SLPs to promote communication in infants, toddlers, and preschoolers with communication difficulties. SLPs usually teach parents and ECSE professionals to employ the following facilitation techniques with children during their daily interactions.

Vocal Stimulation. Vocal stimulation encourages the child's use of sound in play. The adult imitates the child's vocal productions to encourage the child to use more and different vocalizations. The following example demonstrates the use of vocal stimulation for an infant who is sitting in a crib and randomly pushing a mobile.

> CHILD [PUSHES MOBILE]: *"ba . . . ba."*
>
> ADULT [IMITATES CHILD]: *"ba, ba."*

After a few turns imitating the child, the adult lengthens the "babbling" by saying *"baba."* Later the adult might produce CVs not in the child's repertoire—*"dada"* or *"papa"*—attempting to get the child to imitate.

Parallel Talk. With parallel talk, the child is not required to respond verbally. The adult describes the child's actions or his or her focus of attention. In the following example, a child is playing on the floor with several toys scattered around her.

[The child picks up a tractor and starts pushing it.]

ADULT: *"You are pushing the tractor."*

[The child turns the tractor over and turns the wheels.]

ADULT: *"You are looking at the wheels."*

Research has found that early childhood special educators use parallel talk more frequently than direct teaching strategies, particularly during play activities (Smith, Warren, Yoder, & Feurer, 2004).

Linguistic Mapping. Like parallel talk, linguistic mapping is usually used with children who are not verbal. With linguistic mapping, the adult provides a descriptive label after the child produces a *nonverbal* communicative act. In the following example, a child is walking past a bookshelf, pauses, and looks at the books.

CHILD: *"uh, uh."*

ADULT: *"Want book?"*

[The child puts her hand out.]

ADULT [GETTING THE BOOK AND PLACING IT IN THE CHILD'S HAND]: *"Book."*

The following facilitative techniques are described in the literature as beneficial in increasing the length and complexity of young children's language. They may be used with children who produce one-word utterances as well as with children who exhibit preschool-age language.

Expansion. When expansion is used, the adult fills in the necessary parts of the child's utterance while maintaining the child's meaning. Expansion provides a more mature form of the child's utterance while still retaining the child's word order. In the following example, a child is sitting next to a computer, holding a book in her lap.

[The child opens the book.]

CHILD: *"Book."*

ADULT: *"Book open."*

[The child turns several pages.]

[The child points to a picture of a dog.]

CHILD: *"Doggie 'ad."*

ADULT: *"Doggie is mad."*

Recasting. Recasting is a form of expansion, but involves a change in voice and mood. In the exchange that follows, a child is dumping books from a basket. Notice how the adult uses recasting and expansion together.

[The child slowly dumps books from a basket to the floor.]

CHILD [PICKING UP ONE BOOK AND OPENING IT]: *"My book."*

ADULT: *"Is the book open?"* (recasting)

CHILD [NODDING HER HEAD TO INDICATE YES]: *"Yeah. Open."*

ADULT: *"Yes, the book is open."* (expansion)

Expiation. Expiations are similar to expansions, but in expiation, the adult adds "something new," such as additional information. In the example that follows, this strategy has two functions. First, the adult wants to make the child attend to the initial phoneme in a word in order to produce a CV syllable structure. Second, the adult wants to add additional "meaning" to the child's utterance. The child is sitting on a paraprofessional's lap in a classroom and is attempting to get away. The SLP puts a book in the child's hands and begins to help the child turn the pages.

[The child looks at the book and then points to a picture of a bee.]

CHILD: *"ee."*

ADULT: *"The bee is buzzing."* (expiation, adding new information)

CHILD: *"ee."*

ADULT: *"The bee is eating."* (note the expansion "is eating")

CHILD: *"ee ee."* (the first *"ee"* marks the bee, and the second *"ee"* marks the eating)

Adult: *"The bee is eating."* (places stress on the initial /b/ in bee)

Child: *"Bee ee."*

In sum, this section has outlined the development of communication in infants, described early milestones of language acquisition, and discussed the need to provide early assessment and intervention to children who are at risk for language delays and impairments. The next section discusses the development of language and communication skills, assessment, and intervention with toddlers.

Communication Development in Toddlers

Most children with language impairment are not identified until about 2 years of age. In the absence of other significant disabilities such as motor or cognitive delays, the first evidence of a language delay is the late onset of the production of first words and a slow vocabulary growth (Leonard, 1998). Typical language-developing toddlers acquire their first words between 12 to 18 months of age and produce two-word combinations between 18 to 24 months of age, after they have at least 50 words (Nelson, 1973). Children who fail to meet these linguistic milestones are referred to as **late talkers** (Rescorla, 1989; Rescorla & Schwartz, 1990). This delay may be due to weak processing skills, weak articulatory skills, weak retrieval skills, weak conceptual skills, or weak rule-learning skills (Rescorla, 2002).

Delayed phonological development and delayed lexical or vocabulary development are the hallmarks of late talkers (Paul, 1991; Paul & Jennings, 1992; Rescorla & Ratner, 1996; Roberts, Rescorla, Giroux, & Stevens, 1998). Overall, late talkers are less vocal and verbal compared to their typically developing peers and less accurate in their consonantal or sound production. They tend to exhibit a more restricted and less complex array of syllable structures, using predominantly single vowels and CV syllables. The babbling period is extended and is less complex.

Further, there is a difference in the phonological processes of typically developing children and those of late talkers. Typically developing children use specific strategies to simplify the production of words called **phonological processes**. The most prevalent of these are (Ingram, 1981; Leonard, 1982; Schwartz, Leonard, Folger, & Wilcox, 1980):

1) **Consonant-cluster reduction:** reducing the cluster to one consonant—for example, /poon/ for /spoon/.

2) **Weak syllable deletion:** omitting the unstressed or weak syllable in multisyllabic words—for example, /nana/ for /banana/.

3) **Gliding:** substituting the glides (/w/ and /j/) for the liquids (/l/ and /r/)—for example, /twack/ for /truck/ and /wove/ for /love/.

4) **Final consonant deletion:** omitting the final consonant in words—for example, /ca/ for /car/.

These processes, used by typically developing children until their fourth birthday, usually disappear by their fifth birthday. This is not the case for late talkers; these processes persist over a longer period of time. That is, phonological development in late talkers follows a pattern similar to that of their typically developing peers; however, phonological development in late talkers is extended over a longer period of time (Paul & Jennings, 1992).

As previously noted, delays in lexical and phonological development are prevalent in late talkers at the age of 2.0. However, morphosyntactic delays are more prominent in late talkers at the age of 3.0 (Rescorla & Roberts, 1997). It is during this period (i.e., 2.0–3.0 years of age) that new morphological forms are evident in typically developing children: (1) Several grammatical morphemes (e.g., present progressive *ing*, prepositions, regular plural *-s*) appear, and (2) the basic sentence forms of subject-verb-object (e.g., *"She drinks milk"*) and subject-copula-complement (*"She is pretty"*) are produced (Brown, 1973). Table 5.6 shows the stages of morphosyntactical development in preschoolers' language.

TABLE 5.6 Stages of morphosyntactic development in young children's language

Stage	Age (months)	Morphosyntactic Characteristics	Examples
I	12–26	Single-word utterances and multiword combinations based on word-order/semantic-syntactic rules.	"Eat cookie" (action + object) "Daddy shoe" (possessor + possession) "Doggie bed" (entity + locative)
II	27–30	The appearance of grammatical morphemes.	"Mommy driving" (present progressive-ing) "I love dogs" (regular plural –s)
III	31–34	Simple sentence forms • Development of noun and verb phrases with the addition of grammatical morphemes, quantifiers, adjectives, and adverbs.	"Dave eats banana" (subject–verb–object) "Mommy's car" (possessive nouns) "Diana has *three* cats" (quantifiers) "She has a *blue* cap" (adjectives) "She runs *quickly*" (adverbs)
		• Development of different sentence types (declarative, interrogative, imperative, and negative).	"I'm eating ice cream" (declarative) "What are you eating?" (interrogative) "Throw me the ball, please" (imperative) "I don't want that" (negative)
IV	35–40	The appearance of embedded phrases and subordinate clauses within a sentence. Subordinate clauses are introduced by conjunction words (*after, although, before, until, while, when*) or relative pronouns (*who, which, whom, that*).	"The woman *in the blue dress* is my teacher" (embedded phrase) "The boy *we met last week* is in my class" (embedded clause)
V	41–46	The appearance of sentences conjoined with conjunction words (*and, if, because, when, but, after, before, so*).	"I play the violin *and* she plays the piano" "She cried *because* she fell down the stairs" "We went to school *after* we ate breakfast" "I like fruit *but* I don't like vegetables"

One of the measures most commonly used to assess the syntactic or grammatical development of a child's language is mean length of utterance (MLU), which is calculated from a child's language sample. MLU is considered a reliable predictor of language complexity in English-speaking children (Brown, 1973). Researchers have found that late talkers are delayed in syntactic complexity and morphological maturity based on their MLU scores (Paul, 1993; Paul & Alforde, 1993; Paul & Smith, 1993; Rescorla & Roberts, 1997). Late talkers have deficits in noun morphology, articles (*the, a*), pronouns (*she, his*), and verb morphemes such as contractible copulas (*She's a teacher*) and auxiliary verbs (*He is swimming*) (Paul & Alforde, 1993; Rescorla & Roberts, 2002).

Chronic morphosyntactic deficits at the sentence level are apparent in the narratives of

4-year-old late talkers (Paul & Smith, 1993). Narrating a story involves complex linguistic abilities, such as the ability to convey ideas and sequence events in a cohesive manner, the ability to use context-related vocabulary, and the ability to structure the story in a way that will aid the listener's understanding. Children's abilities or difficulties in content, form, and language use are evidenced in their narratives and are known to be a good predictor of later academic skills. Researchers have found that 4-year-olds who were identified as late talkers at age 2 performed significantly more poorly on all measures of narrative skills (e.g., cohesion, semantic content, lexical diversity, and syntax) compared to their typically developing peers (Paul & Smith, 1993). Their narratives reflected their difficulties in encoding, organizing, and linking schemes as well as in retrieving precise and diverse words from their lexicons.

Late Talkers Versus Late Bloomers

Many toddlers with slow expressive vocabulary growth "catch up" to their typically developing peers in expressive language skills by the time they are 3 or 4 years old (Paul, 1996; Rescorla & Lee, 1999; Rescorla, Mirak, & Singh, 2000; Whitehurst & Fischel, 1994). These children are referred to as "late bloomers" (Thal, Tobias, & Morrison, 1991; Thal & Tobias, 1992). **Late bloomers** make progress in vocabulary development after their second birthday and, by their third birthday, look very similar to their typically developing peers in terms of their expressive language skills (Rescorla, Mirak, & Singh, 2000). Nonetheless, other toddlers with expressive language delays never "catch up" and continue to show persistent language delays after 3 years of age.

SLPs must attempt to distinguish children with transient language difficulties such as late bloomers from those with persistent language impairments such as late talkers. Two factors have been identified as potential predictors of persisting language delays: (1) a delay in vocabulary comprehension (Thal, Reilly, Seibert,

Jeffries, & Fenson, 2004; Thal & Tobias, 1992) and (2) a delay in the use of conventional gestures, such as pointing and showing, and symbolic gestures, such as panting like a dog or sniffing to indicate a flower (Thal et al., 1991).

Children with typical language development use conventional and symbolic gestures to communicate (Caselli, 1990). The development of gestures for communication takes place at the same time first words emerge in toddlers, between 12 to 18 months of age. Late bloomers tend to use more communicative gestures, when compared to their typically developing peers, in order to compensate for their lack of words. In contrast, late talkers fail to show an increase in communicative gestures as a compensation for their verbal delay (Thal & Tobias, 1992). Consequently, the compensatory use of communicative gestures is a positive prognostic sign for later typical language development.

An important question asked by parents and professionals alike is, Do children who are considered late talkers "catch up"? Rescorla, Dahlsgaard, and Roberts (2000) reported that in longitudinal studies approximately 50% of late talkers identified between the ages of 2 years and 2 years 7 months exhibited MLU scores within the normal range by age 3. Of the 50% that were still delayed at age 3, half of these children exhibited MLUs in the normal range at 4 years (Rescorla et al., 2000). At age 5, about half of the late talkers still exhibited language delays; therefore, 75% to 85% of the late talkers identified at age 2 recovered and scored within the normal range by age 5 (Rescorla, 2002).

Assessment of Language Delays in Toddlers

Early assessment and identification of language delays are essential for generating optimal outcomes in children. To begin the process, a multidisciplinary assessment, in which each professional assesses the child individually, is arranged, and then all the evaluators come together to arrive at a diagnosis and develop an intervention plan, if one is needed. Professionals may use play-based assessments, communication-based assessments, parent questionnaires, comprehension assessments, or language sampling to assess the emerging language abilities of toddlers.

1) Play-Based Assessments. Play-based assessments provide information about a child's skills in meaningful activities, rather than sampling isolated skills in a formal testing situation. Observing children playing provides information about their

- knowledge and views of the world;
- ability to communicate with others (i.e., social skills);
- linguistic knowledge;
- speech production;
- cognitive abilities of tool use and symbolic play, two components highly correlated with language; and
- knowledge of social roles and event structures.

2) Communication-Based Assessments. Communication-based assessments examine a child's ability to use

- gestural and vocal means to express intentions;
- communicative functions, such as making requests for objects or actions, protesting, and answering;
- reciprocal strategies to initiate or respond to communicative attempts;
- social-emotional signaling, such as facial expressions and eye gaze, to communicate; and
- symbolic play, verbal expression, and language comprehension.

The developmental scales listed in Table 5.7 are used to identify a child's strengths and weaknesses in the areas of language. They provide the team information for determining intervention goals and objectives/benchmarks.

3) Parent Questionnaires. Direct testing of children with significant communication deficits or

TABLE 5.7 Communication-based assessment instruments used with infants, toddlers, and preschoolers

Communicative Evaluation Chart (Anderson, Miles, & Matheny, 1963)

Sequenced Inventory of Communicative Development (Hedrick, Prather, & Tobin, 1984)

Assessing Prelinguistic and Early Linguistic Behaviors in Developmentally Young Children (Olswang, Stoel-Gammon, Coggins, & Carpenter, 1987)

The Initial Communication Processes Scale (Schery & Wilcoxen, 1982)

Interaction Checklist for Augmentative Communication (Bolton & Dashiell, 1984)

ELM Scale: The Early Language Milestone Scale (Coplan, 1987)

children with other disabling conditions under the age of 3 may be expensive and time-consuming and may not produce representative samples of a child's linguistic abilities because of his or her unwillingness or inability to cooperate with the examiner. Consequently, SLPs often use parent questionnaires to gather information about a child's language abilities without testing the child directly. Since parents have experience with their child over a long period time and across many situations, parent questionnaires are less influenced by performance factors, such as fatigue or an unfamiliar environment or adult, and tend to be reliable.

4) Comprehension Assessments. Comprehension or receptive language is a predictor of later language development and is one of the characteristics that distinguishes late bloomers from late talkers. Comprehension may be assessed with standardized tests or informal procedures. Since there are few norm-referenced tools to assess the receptive language of children under the age of 3, most SLPs use informal measures for this purpose. Informal language comprehension instruments and procedures answer several questions:

a. Does the child understand single words without the support of nonlinguistic cues, such aspointing or looking at an object? For example, a collection of objects is placed in front of the child, and the clinician or educator asks the child for each object using a simple sentence form such as *"Give me _____ _____"* or *"Where is? _____ _____"* To test for the comprehension of verbs, the professional provides the child with an object and asks the child to manipulate it, as in *"Throw it"* or *"Kiss it."*

b. Does the child understand two-word combinations or semantic relations? To assess this ability, the clinician or ECSE professional uses word-order rules to evaluate the child's ability to produce multiword combinations, such as *"Eat apple."*

c. Does the child comprehend simple sentence forms by showing the ability to act out sentences or by identifying pictures that match a sentence?

5) Language Samples. Collecting a language sample is another strategy that can be used to assess toddlers' and older children's language abilities. **Spontaneous language sampling** is a commonly used tool that assesses the child's strengths and weaknesses in all language areas, from morphosyntax (e.g., the length and complexity of utterances and the use of grammatical morphemes) and phonology (e.g., consonant and vowel inventories, syllable structure complexity, and phonological processes) to semantics (e.g., vocabulary size) and pragmatics (e.g., communicative intents). Language samples are usually collected while the child is engaged in free play with others. These data are then transcribed and analyzed for the presence or absence of age-appropriate linguistic forms.

Children in the emerging language stage that present with slow language development are less talkative than their typically developing peers. Consequently, collecting a representative language sample may be difficult. There are two ways to overcome this obstacle:

a. *Parents' Diaries*. Professionals ask parents to keep a log of their child's spontaneous vocalizations during everyday activities. Parents are asked to note whether the vocalizations were spontaneous or imitation/repetition of adults' speech and whether vocalizations were directed to a particular person and related to a specific context (Miller, 1981).

b. *Audiotaping*. Parents or an ECSE teacher audiotapes the child during playtime/free time with peers/siblings or when the child is most vocal. The SLP analyzes the tape for sound productions (consonants and vowels), vocabulary (verbs, nouns, adjectives), and grammatical morpheme production.

Strategies for Promoting Communication in Toddlers with Language Delays

Early communication intervention appears to be effective in that it often provides a means for toddlers with language delays to "catch up" to their typical peers (Leonard, 1998). Since many children with delayed language appear to catch up to their typical peers eventually, some may question the value of providing ECSE services to all children exhibiting communication or language difficulties. However, the research suggests that delaying intervention produces adverse academic outcomes later in the child's life. Continuing difficulties in reading comprehension, verbal memory, grammar, and vocabulary have been reported in late bloomers during adolescence (Rescorla, 2005). Studies indicate that many late bloomers who seemed to have "recovered" at age 5 later revealed inferior performances on language tests when compared to their typically developing age-matched peers (Rescorla, 2002, 2005). Consequently, it is generally recommended that in cases where early services are not provided, parents expose late bloomers to games and activities that strengthen their abilities in word retrieval, verbal working memory, phonological processing and discrimination, and grammatical processing to support their later academic learning (Rescorla, 2002).

Depending on assessment results, intervention planning for toddlers may focus on enhancing functional and symbolic play skills, functional and symbolic gestures, the production of communicative intents such as initiating conversation, language comprehension, and/or the production of sounds, words, and word combinations (Paul, 1995). The following questions should guide intervention decisions for toddlers:

1) How often does the child initiate and respond to the communication attempts of others?

2) Does the child exhibit a variety of communication attempts such as requesting, protesting, calling, greeting, showing off, and commenting on objects and events in his or her environment?

3) Does the child use communicative gestures such as giving, showing, reaching, pointing, waving, and nodding?

4) Does the child babble, using sequences of consonants and vowels, in an attempt to communicate with others?

5) Does the child use eye contact and facial expressions to signal his or her intentions?

6) Does the child understand and produce words?

7) Is the child displaying symbolic play?

In addition to the facilitative strategies described earlier, script therapy and play-based therapy are frequently used by SLPs to promote communication skills in young children. **Script therapy** is a facilitative technique used to teach target communicative behaviors within the context of familiar routines, known as scripts (Olswang & Bain, 1991). Scripts are ordered sequences of events that describe familiar activities such as "taking a bath," "going to a birthday party," and "making dinner." These routines offer conventionalized, predictable contexts in which the clinicians can teach turn taking, conversational skills, and new linguistic forms. The child and the SLP and/or ECSE teacher reenact the script. The script serves as a context for introducing new target behaviors (e.g., gestures, communicative intents) and linguistic forms (e.g., words, grammatical morphemes).

Play-based therapy is also widely used as a context for language therapy with very young children. Virtually any aspect of language can be taught within this therapy approach. Professionals and parents use toys and play to teach skills needed by the child. The following section discusses communication development in, language and communication assessment for, and intervention with preschoolers.

COMMUNICATION DEVELOPMENT IN PRESCHOOLERS WITH SPECIFIC LANGUAGE IMPAIRMENT

It has been suggested that late talkers are a subset of specific language impairment (SLI) (Rescorla, 2000, 2002; Rescorla & Roberts, 2002). Preschoolers with SLI are identified by a process of exclusion. They typically have performance IQs within normal limits, normal hearing acuity, no behavioral or emotional disorders, and no gross neurological deficits, yet they present with significant deficits in language comprehension and production (Leonard, 1998). Children with language impairment that is secondary to another condition, such as autism, mental retardation, or hearing loss, are usually not diagnosed as either being late talkers or having SLI. As discussed, the term *late talker* is used to describe children who are delayed in acquiring language and who are between the ages of 2 and 4 years old. **Specific language impairment** is a term used for children exhibiting language impairment at the age of 4 years 0 months or older (Whitehurst & Fischel, 1994; Leonard, 1998). These children's difficulties can be manifested in one or all areas of language. Each will be discussed.

Limitations in Language Content: Semantics

Children with SLI exhibit a slower rate of vocabulary acquisition (Windfuhr, Faragher, & Conti-Ramsden, 2002) and have a less diverse and more restricted lexicon (Watkins, Kelly, Harbers, & Hollis, 1995). In the case study, Paul demonstrated difficulties with semantics. The semantic difficulties of preschoolers with SLI are apparent in their

1) speech errors that tend to be semantic in nature, such as saying dog for a horse, clown for a circus, and fish for a shark.

2) low performance on lexical comprehension tests (Lahey & Edwards, 1999; McGregor, 1997) and tasks focusing on multiple levels of noun hierarchy, such as superordinate nouns (e.g., *furniture)*, coordinate nouns (e.g., *chair*), and subordinate nouns (e.g., *rocking chair*) (McGregor & Waxman, 1998).

3) word-finding difficulties that involve difficulties in generating a specific word for any given situation (Rapin & Wilson, 1978). Difficulties are manifested in single-word naming tasks as well as in conversational discourse (German & Simon, 1991). The language of children with word-finding difficulty is characterized by repetitions, substitutions, reformulations, pauses, and the use of nonspecific words such as *stuff* and *thing* (Faust, Dimitrovsky, & Davidi, 1997; McGregor & Leonard, 1989).

The reduced lexical comprehension of children with SLI is apparent in their understanding and use of basic concepts that mark spatial relations (e.g., *on, in, above, behind*), temporal relations (e.g., *tomorrow, before, after*), kinship relations (e.g., *grandmother, sister, daughter*), causal relations (e.g., *because, why*), sequential relations (e.g., *first, next, finally*), and physical relations (e.g., *hard/soft, wide/narrow, shallow/deep*).

The difficulty preschoolers with SLI exhibit in semantics is not limited to concepts or nouns; verb learning also seems to pose a challenge for them. This appears to be the case because, in verb learning, a child needs to associate the verb with the physical action, which is transient. A smaller and less diverse verb lexicon and a heavy reliance on "all purpose" verbs such as *go, make, do,* and *look* have been reported to characterize preschoolers with SLI (Conti-Ramsden & Jones, 1997; Rice & Bode, 1993; Thordardottir & Weismer, 2001).

Limitations in Language Form: Phonology, Morphology, and Syntax

Children with SLI show many of the phonological characteristics seen in younger, typical language-developing children. They are late in acquiring their consonant inventory, but follow the same pattern of acquisition as typically developing children. Nonetheless, later acquired sounds such as /s/ and /v/ continue to be difficult for children with SLI even into the school-age years.

As shown in Table 5.8, typical language-developing children start to acquire grammatical morphemes as early as 27–30 months of age. Children with SLI display extraordinary difficulty in producing noun phrase morphology (e.g., noun plural -*s* inflection) and verb phrase morphology (e.g., third singular -*s*, regular past tense -*ed*, and copula *be* forms), with the latter being more challenging (Bedore & Leonard, 1998; Norbury, Bishop, & Briscoe, 2001; Rice, Wexler, & Cleave, 1995). When compared to age-matched peers, children with SLI produce verb and noun morphological markers less consistently and use them to a lesser extent in sentence completion tasks and in spontaneous speech (Leonard, Eyer, Bedore, & Grela, 1997; Rice & Wexler, 1996; Rice et al., 1995). Several studies suggest that children with SLI follow the same developmental path of morphological acquisition as their typically developing peers do, but their development is extended over a longer time period (Rice et al., 1995; Rice & Wexler, 1996). In fact, these researchers have

TABLE 5.8 The acquisition of grammatical morphemes in young children

Morpheme	Example	Age of Mastery (in months)
Present progressive -*ing* (no auxiliary verb)	*Mommy driving.*	19–28
In	*Ball in cup.*	27–30
On	*Doggie on sofa.*	27–30
Regular plural -*s*	*Kitties eat my ice cream.*	27–33
Irregular past	*came, fell, broke, sat, went*	25–46
Possessive '*s*	*Mommy's balloon broke.*	26–40
Uncontractible copula (verb *to be* as main verb)	*He is. (response to "Who's sick?")*	27–39
Articles	*I see a kitty.*	28–46
	I throw the ball to daddy.	
Regular past -*ed*	*Mommy pulled the wagon.*	26–48
Regular third person -*s*	*Kathy hits.*	26–46
Irregular third person	*Does, has*	28–50
Uncontractible auxiliary	*He is (response to "who's wearing your hat?")*	29–48
Contractible copula	*Man's big.*	29–49
	Man is big.	
Contractible auxiliary	*Daddy's drinking juice.*	30–50
	Daddy is drinking juice.	

Source: Adapted with permission from Owens, R. E. (2005). *Language Development: An Introduction* (6th ed., p. 243). Boston: Allyn & Bacon. (Copyright 2005 by Pearson Education.)

identified verb phrase morphology as a clinical marker for language impairment.

Morphology deficits of preschoolers with SLI are characterized by the following:

1) Their use of grammatical morphemes is limited.

2) They often omit morphemes, since they are likely to omit the *be* verb form (i.e., auxiliary) or the present progressive -*ing* form. Thus, they produce sentences such as *"I going to swim in the pool"* (omitting the auxiliary) and *"I'm play with the cars now"* (omitting the present progressive).

3) They make grammatical errors, since they are likely to misuse the *be* verb form. Thus, they produce sentences like *"She were going to the store"* (misuse of auxiliary *be* form) and *"The boy and the girl is not happy"* (misuse of copula *be* form).

They also misuse pronouns in discourse. For example, they might say, *"Him not nice," "Me play*

TABLE 5.9 The development of pronouns in young children

Age in Months	Pronouns
12–26	I, it
27–30	my, me, mine, you
31–34	your, she, he, yours, we
35–40	they, us, hers, his, them, her
41–60	its, our, him, myself, yourself, ours, their, theirs
47+	herself, himself, itself, ourselves, yourselves, themselves

Source: Printed with permission from Owens, R. (2005). *Language Development: An Introduction* (6th ed., p. 245). Boston: Allyn & Bacon. Copyright 2005 by Pearson Education.

with the doll," or *"This is not my book, it is her."* Again, Paul showed many of these morphological deficits at this age. Table 5.9 shows the typical developmental ages for the acquisition of pronouns in young children.

The limitations in syntactic structure of children with SLI are manifested in the reduced length and complexity of the syntactic forms they use. That is, they produce shorter sentences (Scott & Windsor, 2000), do not elaborate on the noun and verb phrases within sentences, and when attempting to produce complex sentences, often do so by adding simple conjunctions such as *and.* They fail to use prepositional phrases, as in *"The house on the beach is my parents',"* or verb-embedded phrases, as in *"She fought with courage"* or *"The girl in the blue dress is nice"* (Schuele & Tolbert, 2001; Schuele & Dykes, 2005).

Limitations in Language Use: Pragmatics

During the preschool years, children acquire many conversational skills. They gradually improve in responding to conversational partners, engaging in short dialogues of a few turns on a given topic, adjusting the language style to the listener, self-monitoring and self-correcting errors produced during conversation, providing clarifications, and introducing or changing the topic of a conversation. Yet children with SLI display difficulties in the following areas:

1) **The ability to engage in a conversation.** Difficulties initiating and sustaining conversation beyond a few exchanges and responding to other children's conversational initiations or interaction attempts characterize children with SLI (Hadley & Rice, 1991). They have difficulty asking for clarifications and providing clarifications in cases of communication breakdowns (Fujiki, Brinton, & Sonnenberg, 1990), and they exhibit difficulties resolving conflicts in a verbal manner, which may lead them to withdraw or become aggressive (Leonard, 1998).

2) **The ability to engage in peer interactions.** Children with SLI engage in fewer peer interactions than their typical peers do (Rice, Sell, & Hadley, 1991). Due to social-pragmatic difficulties, they are less likely to be picked by typically developing children as potential conversation partners.

3) **The ability to adjust their speech and language styles to the listener's age, social status, and language ability.** They show difficulty in adapting their speech and language to the listener (Leonard, 1998).

4) **The ability to listen and follow instructions.** Difficulties in auditory comprehension and short-term memory impede their ability to maintain the flow of conversation and follow through with directions.

5) **The ability to tell stories.** Difficulties in organizing sequentially, in understanding temporal and causal relations, and in formulating sentences affect their ability to coherently narrate stories.

The first step in identifying the individual strengths and difficulties of children with atypical language development is assessment.

Language and Communication Assessment of Preschoolers

One of the purposes of a language evaluation for preschoolers is to determine if a language disorder is primary, as in SLI, or secondary, resulting from other deficits. Information about the child's strengths and weaknesses and the family's concerns and priorities is also gathered. A child's language and communication skills can be evaluated using standardized/norm-referenced tests, criterion-referenced measures, and performance-based assessments. Table 5.10 lists standardized measures and Table 5.11 lists criterion-referenced measures that evaluate language and communication abilities in preschoolers.

Performance-Based Assessment Procedures. Performance-based assessments sample a preschooler's knowledge, abilities, and achievements in a naturalistic manner. Language sampling and the use of narratives are two common procedures used by SLPs. Language sampling in the preschool years tends to focus on syntactic structures and morphological markers, although it can be used to assess

TABLE 5.10 Standardized tests commonly used for preschool language evaluation

Clinical Evaluation of Language Fundamentals–Preschool (CELF-P) (Wiig, Secord, & Semel, 2004)

Preschool Language Scales (PLS) (Zimmerman, Steiner, & Pond, 2002)

Test of Language Development–Primary (TOLD:P) (Newcomer & Hammill, 1997a)

Test for Auditory Comprehension of Language (TACL) (Carrow-Woolfolk, 1999)

Peabody Picture Vocabulary Test (PPVT) (Dunn & Dunn, 1997)

Expressive One-Word Picture Vocabulary Test (EOWPVT) (Gardner, 2000)

TABLE 5.11 Criterion-referenced assessment tools for preschool language assessment

Assessment of Phonological Processes, Revised (Hodson, 1986)

Multilevel Informal Language Inventory (MILI) (Goldsworthy, 1982)

Preschool Language Assessment Instrument (Blank, Rose, & Berlin, 1978)

Sequenced Inventory of Communication Development (SICD) (Hedrick, Prather, & Tobin, 1984)

Wiig Criterion Referenced Inventory of Language (Wiig, 1990)

phonology (e.g., phonetic inventory, syllable structure complexity, and phonological processes), semantics (e.g., vocabulary size and lexical diversity), and pragmatics (e.g., conversational skills, the use of gestures, and maintenance of eye contact). As stated, language samples are collected while the child is engaged in play with familiar adults or peers or in more structured situations using therapy scripts.

Similarly, narratives are a common performance-based procedure used to evaluate the language abilities of preschool and school-age children with language impairments (Paul & Smith, 1993). Narratives have been found to differentiate between transient and persistent language impairments (Bishop & Edmundson, 1987). The analysis of narratives provides information about a child's (1) morphological and syntactic abilities (Scott & Windsor, 2000), (2) ability to use cohesive devices (e.g., *because, after, although, if*) to relate meanings across sentences (Hesketh, 2004; Liles, Duffy, Merritt, & Purcell, 1995; Paul & Smith, 1993; Purcell & Liles, 1992), and (3) ability to organize and sequence a story's content in a meaningful way (Liles et al., 1995; Paul & Smith, 1993; Ripich & Griffith, 1988; Scott & Windsor, 2000).

Since some preschoolers and school-aged children with language impairments have difficulty engaging in conversation, narratives can provide the structure needed to obtain a more representative sample of a child's abilities for the SLP and other professionals (Wagner, Nettelbladt, Sahlen, & Nilholm, 2000). Narratives can be elicited from children by having them use sequencing cards, use wordless books or by having them retell stories they have heard or describe routine events and personal experiences.

Strategies for Promoting Communication in Preschoolers

As discussed, preschoolers with SLI are at risk for developing academic problems due to their language difficulties (Catts, 1993; Catts, Fey, Tomblin, & Zhang, 2002; Schuele, 2004; Snowling, Bishop, & Stothard, 2000). School-age children with SLI most often have difficulty learning to read and write. Exposing preschoolers with language impairment to literacy activities early may help facilitate the development of their reading later. The following are early literacy activities that may be incorporated into home or classroom routines:

❏ *Phonological Awareness Activities.* These activities, which include sound play tasks, sound blending tasks, and sound manipulation tasks, are discussed more fully in Chapter 9.

❏ *Joint Story Reading.* When reading a book, parents/caregivers and teachers should do the following to best support a child's communication and literacy development (Fey, Catts, & Larrivee, 1995):

1) Stop periodically to ask the child inferential questions, such as those asking why, where, who, when, and what.

2) Expand the child's descriptions and introduce new grammatical forms and words as well as recasting the child's productions using grammatically correct forms.

3) Read the story multiple times, having the child take turns telling parts of the story.

The following section will examine the language characteristics of, assessment of, and intervention with children in kindergarten through the third grade.

LANGUAGE CHARACTERISTICS OF PRIMARY-AGED STUDENTS WITH LANGUAGE IMPAIRMENT

The term **language learning disability (LLD)**, like specific language impairment and late talker, refers to a language impairment that does not stem from a cognitive deficit, a sensory impairment, a social deficit, or a gross neurological deficit (Paul, 2001). It also refers to difficulties in both language and learning. In other words, primary-aged students who exhibit LLD experience difficulties in acquiring reading and writing.

As in children with SLI, the language impairment in children with LLD can be expressed in the following areas of expressive language:

1) **Speaking.** Students with LLD have difficulties in retelling stories or providing explanations, selecting and retrieving words, participating in classroom discussions and making relevant contributions to conversations, providing sufficient background information about a topic of conversation or indicating how ideas are related to the topic of conversation, and talking about events that occurred in the past.

2) **Writing.** Students with LLD have difficulties writing well-formed and grammatically correct sentences, mapping letter-sound correspondences, and spelling.

Difficulties in the following areas of receptive language are expressed:

1) **Listening.** Students with LLD have difficulties in following multistep directions, understanding others' explanations, and gaining information presented via the auditory route, that is, auditory processing difficulties.

2) Reading. Students with LLD have difficulties comprehending what they read, identifying and distinguishing between the most salient information in a story and the irrelevant information, connecting and sequencing ideas in stories, and using visual and contextual cues for understanding story lines.

Phonological Characteristics of Students with LLD

Children with LLD are usually intelligible. However, as preschoolers, they may have exhibited phonological deficits. These subtle, but lasting phonological deficits may underlie their reading difficulties during the early school years. School-age children with LLD have difficulties with tasks that require phonological awareness. This can be problematic, since phonological awareness is essential to achieving print literacy and also the best predictor of reading ability.

Syntactic Characteristics of Students with LLD

The language output of students with LLD may be characterized as simple and immature. Some of the syntactic characteristics follow:

1) **Use of simple sentence structures.** Students with LLD produce fewer complex sentence structures and fewer embedded clauses than their typically developing peers do (Marinellie, 2004).

2) **Limited elaboration on noun and verb phrases.** Students with LLD use fewer modifiers (e.g., *"Look at the big, red house."*), prepositional phrases (e.g., *"The house in the corner is mine."*), embedded clauses (e.g., *"The game I bought last year is now my brother's."*), and adverbs (e.g., *"She eats very quickly."*).

3) **Difficulty understanding passive sentences.** Students with LLD interpret passive structures based on the order of appearance of the subject and object in the sentence instead of

relying on the meaning of passive forms. For example, in the sentence *"The cat was chased by the dog,"* children with LLD will interpret it to mean *"The cat chased the dog,"* instead of the other way around.

4) **Difficulty with grammatical morphemes that are typically acquired later in development.** Comparatives (e.g., big–bigger) and superlatives (e.g., biggest) and advanced prefixes and suffixes (e.g., unrelated, rewrite, disinterested, accomplishment, madness) are a challenge for these children.

Semantic Characteristics of Students with LLD

The difficulties exhibited by children with LLD are apparent at the lexical as well as the sentence level. The following are some of the semantic characteristics of students with LLD:

1) small vocabulary size that is restricted to high-frequency or short words with low phonological complexity.

2) impoverished or not well elaborated semantic representations of words in the lexicon. Students' knowledge of word meanings is often restricted, revealing limited associations between words and poor categorization skills (Lahey & Edwards, 1999; McGregor, 1997; McGregor & Waxman, 1998; McGregor & Windsor, 1996).

3) difficulty understanding the meaning of abstract words, such as *wonder, thought,* and *anger* and the overuse of concrete words.

4) difficulty understanding and using words that mark temporal relations, such as *next week, yesterday,* and *tomorrow*; spatial relations, such as *behind* and *above*; quantity, such as *more* and *a lot*; order, such as *first* and *second*; and internal states, such as *wondering* and *expecting*.

5) difficulty with **word retrieval** or **word finding**, the momentary inability to retrieve already known words from the lexicon.

Word-finding difficulties are the most frequently observed lexical limitation of school-age children with language impairment (Faust et al., 1997; McGregor & Leonard, 1989). This difficulty is manifested in single-word naming tasks as well as in conversational discourse (German & Simon, 1991). The language of students with word-finding difficulty is characterized by repetitions, substitutions, pauses, and the use of nonspecific words such as *thing* (Faust et al., 1997).

6) difficulty understanding complex verbal directions and explanations. Children with LLD display difficulty integrating meaning across sentences and paragraphs, revealing their limited ability to process semantic information.

7) difficulty understanding and producing figurative language. These students interpret language literally. For example, a child with LLD may interpret a sentence like *"Break a leg"* as an insult, assuming that someone really wants him or her to get hurt instead of wishing him good luck (Seidenberg & Bernstein, 1986).

Pragmatic Characteristics of Students with LLD

The limitations children with LLD exhibit are manifested in their use of language to communicate, their social development, their peer relationships, and their classroom learning. Classroom conversations are different than the conversations children have with their peers or family members. In the classroom, the teacher decides on the topic of discussion, and students must follow that topic and cannot shift to their topic of interest. Turn-taking rules are also different in classroom conversations, since teachers decide on the order in which children will talk. Children with LLD have difficulty learning the rules of classroom conversation. They differ quantitatively from their typically developing peers by verbalizing much less during classroom conversations and by exhibiting difficulty clarifying miscommunications,

maintaining the topic of conversation, noticing a shift in the topic of conversation and adjusting accordingly, and contributing relevant information to conversations (Paul, 2001).

Furthermore, children with LLD have difficulty in narrative production. Compared to their typically developing peers, children with LLD reveal limitations in more than one aspect of discourse-narrative:

❑ They incorrectly use cohesive ties and often use fewer of them. Cohesive ties include pronouns and conjunctions (e.g., *after, because, while*) (Liles, 1985a, 1985b, 1987; Ripich & Griffith, 1988).

❑ They are less diverse in the vocabulary they use in narration (Paul & Smith, 1993).

❑ Their narratives are less informative, lack details, and are short with less overall organization (Scott & Windsor, 2000).

❑ They have poor understanding of temporal and causal relations and have difficulty answering inferential questions that assess the relationships between the story parts (Purcell & Liles, 1992; Merritt & Liles, 1987).

❑ They have difficulty with the complexity of sentences, the use of embedded clauses, and the elaboration of verb and noun phrases (Liles et al., 1995).

❑ They offer erroneous and irrelevant information when narrating a story. They often miss the key points or events in the story and focus on trivial details (Merritt & Liles, 1987).

While narration is difficult for children with LLD, expository texts or textbooks present an even greater challenge for them (Bernstein & Levey, 2002). Expository texts usually contain information that is new to the reader, thus making it difficult or impossible for the reader to use prior knowledge in order to comprehend the text. Compared to narratives, textbooks are very limited in the contextual support they provide, have no known structure (e.g., no settings, characters, main event, or consequences) to facilitate interpretation, and rely most heavily on children's ability to process linguistic information. Depending on the state or school system, many children diagnosed as having an LLD may be labeled as having a Learning Disability (LD) and are generally offered the support of an SLP and a special educator. This is discussed further in Chapter 9.

Communication and Language Assessment of Primary-Aged Students

Often primary-aged students are referred to an SLP for an evaluation based on an initial referral from parents or teachers. Teachers have the advantage of seeing a child perform multiple tasks and on multiple difficulty levels, work individually or in groups, and socialize and communicate with peers during class activities. Checklists that mark some of the characteristics of children with language difficulties can assist teachers in identifying children who are experiencing difficulties and following up with appropriate referrals. A sample teacher referral checklist is presented in Table 5.12.

SLPs also use norm-referenced measures to determine a child's eligibility for speech and language services. A score on a standardized test that is one to two standard deviations below the mean for the child's age is usually one of the criteria for eligibility. SLPs use test information to develop therapy goals as well as remediation and classroom support interventions. Common standardized tests used to determine the eligibility of primary-aged students for speech-language services are listed in Table 5.13.

Primary-aged students may also be assessed using curriculum-based language procedures that measure their ability to use language to learn classroom material (Paul, 1995) and systematic observations that measure their pragmatic skills and ability to adhere to classroom discourse rules and expectations. The SLP may act as a passive observer to assess the demands classroom activities place on the child and, in turn, the child's ability to handle and manage these demands. Additionally, the therapist may work directly with the classroom teacher to identify ways to facilitate the child's participation in the class and support his or her academic skills.

Strategies for Promoting Communication in School-Age Children with Language and Learning Impairments

Language intervention with school-age children is often provided by an SLP on an individual basis or in small groups outside the classroom. This is referred to as **pullout services**. In order to facilitate a child's participation in classroom activities, the clinician may also offer **"push-in" services**, where therapy is provided individually or in small groups in the classroom.

The following are some of the general strategies SLPs may suggest that ECSE teachers use in the classroom to facilitate language skills and learning for children with LLD:

1) Simplify questions using simple sentence structures when addressing the student.

2) Simplify directions by shortening them, using simpler syntactic forms, and using visual cues to facilitate auditory processing.

3) Require the student to repeat directions to ensure that directions are understood.

4) Provide extra time to process information and organize thoughts before expecting the student to answer a question.

5) Provide extra time to complete assignments, homework, and exams to compensate for processing difficulties.

6) Speak clearly and somewhat more slowly to allow the student to process the information.

7) Repeat and/or reformulate questions and directions before concluding that the student has failed to execute a direction. Redundancy is crucial and improves comprehension in children with LLD.

8) Provide cues to facilitate the retrieval of words when the student is experiencing word-finding difficulties. Cues can be phonological (for

TABLE 5.12 Teacher referral checklist for primary-aged students

Pragmatically Oriented Discourse Analysis

Student Name _____　Grade _____

Teacher _____　Date _____

To the teacher: Please circle the answer to each question that best describes your student's performance in class.

Does the student:

Give insufficient information when giving instructions or directions?	Yes	No
Use nonspecific vocabulary (thing, stuff, whatchamacallit)?	Yes	No
Perseverate or provide too much redundancy when talking?	Yes	No
Need a lot of repetition before even simple instructions are understood?	Yes	No
Give inaccurate messages; seem to talk when he or she "doesn't know what he or she is talking about"?	Yes	No
Make rapid and inappropriate changes in conversational topic without cues to the listener?	Yes	No
Seem to have an independent conversational agenda or give inappropriate and unpredictable responses?	Yes	No
Fail to ask relevant questions to clarify unclear messages, so that communication frequently breaks down?	Yes	No
Use language that is inappropriate for the social situation?	Yes	No
Produce long pauses or delays before responding?	Yes	No
Lack forethought and planning in telling stories and giving instructions?	Yes	No
Fail to attend to cues for conversational turns, interrupting frequently or failing to hold up his or her end of the conversation?		
Use inconsistent or inappropriate eye contact in conversation?	Yes	No
Use inappropriate intonation?	Yes	No

Please use the space below to describe any other concerns you have about this student's communication.

Source: Modified with permission from Paul, R. (1995). *Language Disorders from Infancy Through Adolescence: Assessment and Intervention* (p. 393). St. Louis, MO: Mosby-Yearbook (Copyright Elsevier).

example, providing the student with the initial sound(s) of words, such as *"It starts with the sound /z/"*) or semantic (for example, providing the student with the referent's category name, such as *"It is an animal,"* or with another referent from the same category, such as *"It is like a dog"*).

9) Provide additional instruction and an emphasis on phonological awareness. Activities in which students match words with the same initial sound(s), produce words with one sound left out, and reverse the sounds in words may help overcome phonological deficits that may underlie

TABLE 5.13 Standardized tests used for language and learning assessment of primary-aged students

Clinical Evaluation of Language Fundamentals (CELF) (Wiig, Secord, & Semel, 2004)

Test of Language Development–Intermediate (TOLD:I) (Newcomer & Hammill, 1997b)

Test of Word Finding (TWF) (German, 2000)

Test of Word Finding in Discourse (TWF–D) (German, 1991)

Woodcock Language Proficiency Battery (Woodcock, 1991)

Peabody Picture Vocabulary Test (PPVT) (Dunn & Dunn, 1997)

Expressive One-Word Picture Vocabulary Test (EOWPVT) (Gardner, 2000)

Test of Pragmatic Language (Phelps-Terasaki & Phelps-Gunn, 1992)

reading difficulties. Explicitly explain instructions. For example, state the topic of the lesson; outline the lesson; write important information on the board; and use pictures, diagrams, and charts to support the information provided auditorily.

10) Recast the student's statements, correcting ungrammatical elements and adding complexity.

11) Follow the student's statements with questions to allow the student to clarify and provide more information.

12) Explain the concepts being taught, especially abstract concepts, in greater detail, providing many examples from the student's life experience. Tie new information to familiar information to create an association in the student's memory that will facilitate future retrieval of the information.

13) Provide positive reinforcement for any verbal attempt at class discussion to encourage more participation.

14) Discuss explicitly classroom rules and expectations and how to ask for assistance or clarification.

15) Provide a preparatory description of all classroom activities to draw the student's attention to the task, allowing the student to "get ready."

16) Seat the child in the front of the class, close to the board, to facilitate attention and concentration.

17) Teach the child how to outline and mark key points in a story or in an expository text so the student is able to draw conclusions and inferences about what was read.

To summarize, students with LLD may display difficulties in speaking, writing, listening, and reading. These difficulties appear pronounced during the school years because they impact every aspect of academic achievement and peer relationships. This is discussed further in Chapter 9. SLPs play a critical role in detecting these difficulties and working with students' teams to identify strategies and accommodations that support students' learning.

AUGMENTATIVE–ALTERNATIVE COMMUNICATION

The preceding sections discussed ways to assess and facilitate the oral-verbal skills of young children. Yet, as noted earlier, there are some children for whom the competent use of an oral language system is not a realistic goal. For these children, professionals use augmentative-alternative communication (AAC) systems, which can help supplement a child's vocalizations and verbalizations and thus allow the child to become a better communicator (Beukelman & Miranda, 2005).

AAC systems include sign language, communication boards, FM systems (discussed in Chapter 11), voice output systems, and computer-assisted devices. In the past, AAC was recommended only when a child was able to comprehend more than he or she could intelligibly produce. This view is no longer held (Lloyd, Fuller, & Arvidson, 1997). Currently, the early use of AAC is recommended for infants and toddlers with severe developmental disabilities resulting from mental retardation, autism, and/or cerebral palsy. The purpose of using AAC during infancy and toddlerhood is to increase the child's activities in daily routines, expand his or her repertoire of communicative behaviors, and/or develop his or her intentional and symbolic communication abilities.

Contrary to common misconceptions, the use of AAC does not deter further development of speech and language. In fact, AAC actually facilitates symbol learning and increases verbalization, attention, intentional communication, and sociability (Owens, 2002). It also increases the range of meanings a child can communicate and the number of communication partners with whom a child can communicate. However, as noted by Shane, Lipschultz, and Shane (1982), it does not "solve all of the problems of the non-speaking individual" (p. 83).

Types of AAC Systems

There are two types of AAC systems: unaided and aided. **Unaided AAC systems** consist of manual communication, such as gestures, signs, and finger spelling. For infants whose disabling condition will affect their communication, such as children with Down syndrome, gestural communication may be an option. **Demonstrative gesturing** is used intentionally to convey meaning and involves behaviors such as pointing, reaching, showing, offering, giving objects, and touching objects. Some gestures, such as pointing and reaching, are used to convey a desire for an object or to direct attention. Others, such as touching, may communicate affection or encouragement. Finally, head movements, such as nodding, are used as a means of conveying "Yes" or "No" responses, and symbolic gestures, such as waving "Bye-bye," are taught to enhance a child's communication skills.

Aided AAC systems use a device such as a communication board or an electronic means of communication. Communication boards come in many different shapes and forms. They are easy to make and are adaptable and portable. The visual symbols used on communication boards may include pictures, models, drawings, specific symbols such as Bliss symbols, letters, or words. The less complex a symbol is, the easier it is for a child to acquire. For example, a large color photograph of a doll is easier than the word doll. With the growth of computer technology, AAC possibilities for nonverbal preschoolers and primary-aged children have expanded. New input systems can use graphics on a computer screen, and new output systems may include synthesized speech.

The use of computer-assisted communication systems has increased rapidly within the last decade. Because of inclusion, it has become even more important for a child with a language and communication disorder to have an effective means of communicating with peers who are disabled and not disabled (McCormick & Wegner, 2003). Of equal importance is the child's ability to access the curriculum, whether he or she is receiving a general education or a special education program. All AAC systems must be customized for each child's needs. For example, accessing a computer may be difficult for a child with severe motor challenges. In such a case, the interface switch between the child and the computer may have to be modified to suit the child's motor abilities.

CONCLUSION

Early identification of children with communication difficulties is essential, since language and communication skills are necessary for social development and school achievement. This chapter discussed the basic guidelines that SLPs follow when working in teams to evaluate and devise intervention plans to support communication in infants, toddlers, preschoolers, and school-age children. As was demonstrated in Paul's case study, the need for families and all professionals to work together in assessment and the delivery of services cannot be overstated. Although the characteristics, assessment, and intervention procedures discussed focus on primary language impairments, such as late talkers, children with SLI, and children with LLD, the strategies outlined are also effective with children with communication difficulties that are secondary to another condition, such as autism or mental retardation.

SUMMARY

Overview of communication and language development

- A child is considered to have a primary language disorder or impairment if the child exhibits typical development in all areas except language.

Communication development in infants and toddlers

- Late talker is a term used to describe children between the ages of 2.0 and 4.0 who exhibit delayed phonological development, delayed vocabulary comprehension, and delay in the use of conventional and symbolic gestures. These children are unlikely to "catch up" to age-peers without services and may experience continuing difficulties in reading comprehension, verbal memory, grammar, and vocabulary during the early school years.
- To facilitate communication and language, parents and professionals use vocal stimulation, parallel talk, linguistic mapping, expansion, recasting, expiation, script therapy, and play-based therapy with infant, toddlers and preschoolers.

Communication development in preschoolers with specific language impairment

- Specific language impairment (SLI) is a term used for children 4.0 years old or older who have IQs within normal limits, normal hearing acuity, no behavioral or emotional disorders, and no gross neurological deficits, and yet they experience significant deficits in language comprehension and production.
- Children with SLI may have difficulties in all or some aspects of receptive and expressive language.

Language characteristics of primary-aged students with language impairment

- Language learning disability (LLD) is a term used to refer to a language impairment that does not stem from a cognitive deficit, a sensory impairment, a social deficit, or a gross neurological deficit and that produces difficulties in all aspects of language and learning, particularly in the acquisition of reading and writing.
- Students with LLD may have a small vocabulary, poor categorization skills, and difficulty understanding abstract words and temporal-spatial markers, retrieving words, understanding complex verbal directions and explanations, understanding and producing figurative language, clarifying miscommunications, maintaining the topic of conversation, noticing a shift in the topic of conversation and adjusting accordingly, and contributing relevant information to conversations.

Augmentative-alternative communication

- The purpose of using augmentative-alternative communication (AAC) with a young child is to increase the child's participation in daily routines, expand the child's repertoire of communicative behaviors, and develop the child's intentional and symbolic communication abilities.
- Unaided AAC systems consist of manual communication, such as gestures, signs, and finger spelling. Aided AAC systems use a device such as a communication board or an electronic means of communication.

DISCUSSION QUESTIONS/ACTIVITIES

1. What are two linguistic characteristics of language form, content, and usage of children with SLI?

2. Explain three ways in which a language disorder might affect the preacademic achievement and social development of a preschooler.

3. Read a simple story to a second-grade student with LLD. Ask the child to retell the story to you. Answer the following questions: (a) How many details did the child provide? (b) What was missing from the child's organization in the retelling? (c) What was the complexity of the sentences the child used to describe each detail?

REFERENCES

Alpert, C. L., & Kaiser, A. P. (1992). Training parents as milieu language teachers. *Journal of Early Intervention, 16,* 31–52.

American Speech-Language-Hearing Association (1982). Committee on language, speech and hearing services in schools: Definitions of communicative disorders and variations. *ASHA, 24,* 949–950.

American Speech-Language-Hearing Association. (1991). Did you know? *Prospectives, 12,* 11.

Anderson, R. M., Miles, M., & Matheny, P. (1963). *Communicative evaluation chart from infancy to five years.* Cambridge, MA: Educators Publishing Service.

Bayley, N. (1993). *Bayley scales of infant development, Second Edition.* San Antonio, TX: Psychological Corp.

Bedore, L., & Leonard, L. (1998). Specific language impairment and grammatical morphology: A discriminant function analysis. *Journal of Speech, Language, and Hearing Research, 41,* 1185–1192.

Bernstein, D., & Levey, S. (2002). Language development: A review. In D. K. Bernstein & E. Tiegerman-Farber (Eds.), *Language and communication disorders in children* (5th ed., pp. 28–94). Boston: Allyn & Bacon.

Bernstein, D., & Tiegerman-Farber, E. (Eds.). (2002). *Language and communication disorders in children* (5th ed). Boston: Allyn & Bacon.

Bernthal, J., & Bankson, N. (2004). *Articulation and phonological disorders* (5th ed.). Boston: Allyn & Bacon.

Beukelman, D., & Miranda, P. (2005). *Augmentative and alternative communication: Supporting children and adults with complex communication needs* (3rd ed.). Baltimore, MD: Brookes.

Bishop, D., & Edmundson, A. (1987). Language impaired 4-year olds: Distinguishing transient from persistent impairment. *Journal of Speech and Hearing Disorders, 52,* 156–173.

Blank, M., Rose, S. A., & Berlin, L. J. (1978). *Preschool language assessment instrument.* Orlando, FL: Grune & Stratton.

Bloom, L., & Lahey, M. (1978). *Language development and language disorders.* New York: Wiley.

Bolton, S., & Dashiell, S. (1984). *Interaction checklist for augmentative communication.* Idyllwild, CA: Imaginart Communication Products.

Brazelton, T. B., Koslowski, B., & Main, M. (1974). The origin of reciprocity: The early mother-infant interaction. In M. Lewis & L. Rosenblum (Eds.), *The effect of the infant on its caretaker* (pp. 49–76). New York: Wiley.

Brinton, B., & Fujiki, M. (1982). A comparison of request response sequences in the discourse of normal and language disordered children. *Journal of Speech and Hearing Disorders, 47,* 57–62.

Brown, R. (1973). *A first language, the early stages.* Cambridge, MA: Harvard.

Carpenter, R. L. (1987). Play scale. In L. B. Olswang, C. Stoel-Gammon, T. E. Coggins, & R. L. Carpenter (Eds.), *Assessing prelinguistic and early linguistic behaviors in developmentally young children* (pp. 44–74). Seattle: University of Washington Press.

Carrow-Woolfolk, E. (1999). *Test for Auditory Comprehension of Language, Third Edition.* Austin, TX: Pro-Ed.

Caselli, M. (1990). Communicative gestures and first words. In V. Volterra & C. J. Erting (Eds.), *From gesture to language in hearing and deaf children* (pp. 56–67). New York: Springer-Verlag.

Catts, H. (1993). The relation between speech-language impairments and reading disabilities. *Journal of Speech and Hearing Research, 36,* 948–958.

Catts, H. W., Fey, M. E., Tomblin, J. B., & Zhang, X. (2002). A longitudinal investigation of reading outcomes in children with language impairments. *Journal of Speech, Language, and Hearing Research, 45,* 1142–1157.

Conti-Ramsden, G., & Jones, M. (1997). Verb use in specific language impairment. *Journal of Speech, Language, and Hearing Research, 40,* 1298–1313.

Coplan, J. (1987). *ELM scale: The early language milestone scale.* Austin, TX: Pro-Ed.

Crais, E. (1999). Detecting communication difficulties in infants and toddlers with feeding difficulties. In D. B. Kessler & P. Dawson (Eds.), *Failure to thrive in infants and children: A transdisciplinary approach to nutritional adequacy in childhood* (pp. 319–333). Baltimore, MD: Brookes.

Dunn, L., & Dunn, L. (1997). *Peabody Picture Vocabulary Test III.* Circle Pines, MN: American Guidance Service.

Faust, M., Dimitrovsky, L., & Davidi, S. (1997). Naming difficulties in language-disabled children: Preliminary findings with the application of the tip-of-the-tongue paradigm. *Journal of Speech, Language, and Hearing Research, 40,* 1037–1047.

Fensen, L., Dale, P. S., Reznick, J. S., Thal, D., Bates, E., Hartung, J., Pethick, S., & Reilly, J. S. (1993). *Guide and technical manual for the MacArthur Communicative Development Inventories.* San Diego, CA: Singular Press.

Fey, M., Catts, H., & Larrivee, L. (1995). Preparing preschoolers for the academic and social challenges of school. In M. Fey, J. Windsor, & S. Warren (Eds.), *Language intervention: Preschool through the elementary years* (pp. 3–37). Baltimore, MD: Brookes.

Fujiki, M., Brinton, B., & Sonnenberg, E. A. (1990). Repair of overlapping speech in the conversations of specifically language-impaired and normally developing children. *Applied Psycholinguistics, 11,* 201–215.

Furuno, S., O'Reilly, K. A., Hosaka, C. M., Inatsuka, T., Allman T., & Zeisloft, B. (1985). *Hawaii early learning profile (HELP) activity guide.* Palo Alto, CA: VORT.

Gardner, M. F. (2000). *Expressive one-word picture vocabulary test.* San Antonio, TX: Psychological Corp.

German, D. J. (1991). *Test of word finding in discourse (TWF–D)* Allen, TX: DLM Teaching Resources.

German, D. J. (2000). *Test of Word Finding (TWF).* Allen, TX: DLM Teaching Resources.

German, D. J., & Simon, E. (1991). Analysis of children's word-finding skills in discourse. *Journal of Speech and Hearing Research, 34,* 309–316.

Goldsworthy, C. (1982). *Multilevel Informal Language Inventory* (MILI). Columbus, OH: Merrill.

Hadley, P. A., & Rice, M. L. (1991). Conversational responsiveness of speech- and language-impaired preschoolers. *Journal of Speech and Hearing Research, 34,* 1308–1317.

Hedrick, D. L., Prather, E. M., & Tobin, A. R. (1984). *Sequenced Inventory of Communication Development.* Seattle: University of Washington Press.

Heidemann, S., & Hewitt, D. (1992). *Pathways to play.* St. Paul, MN: Redleaf Press.

Hesketh, A. (2004). Grammatical performance of children with language disorder on structured elicitation and narrative tasks. *Clinical Linguistics and Phonetics, 18,* 161–182.

Hodson, B. W. (1986). *The Assessment of Phonological Processes, Revised.* Austin, TX: Pro-Ed.

Ingram, D. (1981). *Procedures for the phonological analysis of children's language.* Baltimore, MD: University Park Press.

Kaiser, A. P., & Hester, P. P. (1994). Generalized effects of enhanced milieu teaching. *Journal of Speech and Hearing Research, 37,* 1320–1340.

Knox, S. (1974). A play scale. In M. Reilly (Ed.), *Play as exploratory learning* (pp. 247–266). Beverly Hills, CA: Sage.

Lahey, M., & Edwards, J. (1999). Naming errors of children with specific language impairment. *Journal of Speech, Language, and Hearing Research, 42,* 195–205.

Leonard, L. (1982). Phonological deficits in children with developmental language impairment. *Brain and Language, 16,* 73–86.

Leonard, L. (1998). *Children with specific language impairment.* Cambridge, MA: MIT Press.

Leonard, L., Eyer, J., Bedore, L., & Grela, B. (1997). Three accounts of the grammatical morpheme difficulties of English-speaking children with specific language impairment. *Journal of Speech, Language, and Hearing Research, 40,* 741–753.

Liles, B. Z. (1985a). Cohesion in the narratives of normal and language-disordered children. *Journal of Speech and Hearing Research, 28,* 123–133.

Liles, B. Z. (1985b). Production and comprehension of narrative discourse in normal and language disordered children. *Journal of Communication Disorders, 18,* 409–427.

Liles, B. Z. (1987). Episode organization and cohesive conjunctives in narratives of children with and without language disorders. *Journal of Speech and Hearing Research, 30,* 185–196.

Liles, B. Z., Duffy, R. J., Merritt, D. D., & Purcell, S. L. (1995). Measurement of narrative discourse ability in children with language disorders. *Journal of Speech and Hearing Research, 38,* 415–425.

Linder, T. (Ed.) (2008). *Transdisciplinary play-based assessment.* (2nd ed.). Baltimore, MD: Brookes.

Lloyd, L., Fuller, D., & Arvidson, H. (1997). *Augmentative and alternative communication: A handbook of principles and practices.* Boston: Allyn & Bacon.

MacDonald, J., & Carroll, J. (1992). Communication with young children: An ecological model for clinicians, parents, and collaborative professionals. *American Journal of Speech Language Pathology, 1,* 39–48.

Marinellie, S. A. (2004). Complex syntax used by school-age children with specific language impairment (SLI) in child-adult conversation. *Journal of Communication Disorders, 37,* 517–533.

McCathern, R. B., Warren, S. F., & Yoder, P. J. (1999). The relationships between prelinguistic vocalization and later expressive language impairment in young children with developmental delay. *Journal of Speech, Language, and Hearing Research, 42,* 915–924.

McCormick, L., Loeb, D. F., & Schiefelbusch, R. L. (1997). *Supporting children with communication difficulties in inclusive settings* (2nd ed.). Boston: Allyn & Bacon.

McCormick, L., & Wegner, J. (2003). Supporting augmentative and alternative communication. In L. McCormick, R. L. Schiefelbusch, & D. F. Loeb (Eds.), *Supporting children with communication difficulties in inclusive settings* (2nd ed.) (pp. 235–258). Boston: Allyn & Bacon.

McCune-Nicholich, L., & Carroll, S. (1981). Development of symbolic play: Implications for the language specialist. *Topics in Language Disorders, 2*, 1–15.

McGregor, K. K. (1997). The nature of word-finding errors of preschoolers with and without word finding deficits. *Journal of Speech and Hearing Research, 40*, 1232–1244.

McGregor, K. K., & Leonard, L. B. (1989). Facilitating word-finding skills of language-impaired children. *Journal of Speech and Hearing Disorders, 54*, 141–147.

McGregor, K. K., & Waxman, S. R. (1998). Object naming at multiple hierarchical levels: A comparison of preschoolers with and without word-finding deficits. *Journal of Child Language, 25*, 419–430.

McGregor, K. K., & Windsor, J. (1996). Effects of priming on the naming accuracy of preschoolers with word-finding deficits. *Journal of Speech and Hearing Research, 39*, 1048–1058.

McLean, J. E., & McLean, L. K. (1978). *A transactional approach to early language training.* Columbus, OH: Merrill.

Merritt, D. D., & Liles, B. Z. (1987). Story grammar ability in children with and without language disorder: Story generation, story retelling, and story comprehension. *Journal of Speech and Hearing Research, 30*, 539–552.

Miller, J. (1981). *Assessing language production in children: Experimental procedures.* Needham Heights, MA: Allyn & Bacon.

National Institute on Deafness and Other Communication Disorders Advisory Council. (1991). *Research in human communication, annual report* (NIH Publication No. 92–3317). Bethesda, MD: National Institutes of Health.

Nelson, N. (1973). Structure and strategy in learning to talk. *Monographs of the Society for Research in Child Development, 38*, 1–2.

Newborg, J. (2004). *The Battelle Developmental Inventory–2.* Chicago: Riverside.

Newcomer, P. L., & Hammill, D. D. (1997a). *Test of Language Development—Primary, Third Edition.* Austin, TX: Pro-Ed.

Newcomer, P. L., & Hammill, D. D. (1997b). *Test of Language Development—Intermediate, Third Edition.* Austin, TX: Pro-Ed.

Norbury, C. F., Bishop, D. V. M., & Briscoe, J. (2001). Production of English finite verb morphology: A comparison of SLI and mild–moderate hearing impairment. *Journal of Speech, Language, and Hearing Research, 44*, 165–178.

Oller, D. K., Eilers, R. E., Neal, A. R., & Schwartz, H. K. (1999). Precursors to speech in infancy: The prediction of speech and language disorders. *Journal of Communication Disorders, 32*(4), 223–246.

Olswang, L., & Bain, B. (1991). Intervention issues for toddlers with specific language impairments. *Topics in Language Disorders, 11*, 69–86.

Olswang, L., Stoel-Gammon, C., Coggins, T., & Carpenter, R. (1987). *Assessing prelinguistic and early linguistic behaviors in developmentally young children.* Seattle: University of Washington Press.

Owens, R. (2001). *Language development: An introduction* (5th ed.). Boston: Allyn & Bacon.

Owens, R. (2002). *Introduction to communication disorders: A life span perspective* (2nd ed.). Boston: Allyn & Bacon.

Owens, R. (2005). *Language development: An introduction* (6th ed.). Boston: Allyn & Bacon.

Patterson, J., & Westby, C. (1998). The development of play. In W. Haynes & B. Shulman (Eds.), *Communication development: Foundations, processes, and clinical applications* (pp. 135–162). Baltimore, MD: Williams & Wilkins.

Paul, R. (1991). Profiles of toddlers with slow expressive language growth. *Topics in Language Disorders, 11*, 1–13.

Paul, R. (1993). Patterns of development in late talkers: Preschool years. *Journal of Childhood Communication Disorders, 15*, 7–14.

Paul, R. (1995). *Language disorders from infancy through adolescence: Assessment and intervention.* St. Louis, MO: Mosby-Year Book.

Paul, R. (1996). Clinical implications of the natural history of slow expressive language development. *American Journal of Speech-Language Pathology, 5*, 5–21.

Paul, R. (2001). *Language disorders from infancy through adolescence: Assessment and intervention* (3rd ed.). St. Louis, MO: Mosby-Year Book.

Paul, R., & Alforde, S. (1993). Grammatical morpheme acquisition in 4-year-olds with normal, impaired, and late developing language. *Journal of Speech and Hearing Research, 36*, 1271–1275.

Paul, R., & Jennings, P. (1992). Phonological behavior in toddlers with slow expressive language development. *Journal of Speech and Hearing Research, 35*, 99–107.

Paul, R., & Smith, R. L. (1993). Narrative skills in 4-year-olds with normal, impaired, and late-developing language. *Journal of Speech and Hearing Research, 36*, 592–598.

Phelps-Terasaki, D., & Phelps-Gunn, T. (1992). *Test of Pragmatic Language*. San Antonio, TX: Psychological Corp.

Piaget, J. (1954). *The construction of reality in the child*. New York: Basic Books.

Piaget, J. (1952). *The origins of intelligence in children*. New York: International Universities Press.

Purcell, S., & Liles, B. Z. (1992). Cohesion repairs in the narratives of normal-language and language-disordered school-age children. *Journal of Speech and Hearing Research, 35*, 354–362.

Ramey, C. T., & Ramey, S. L. (1998). Early intervention and early experience. *American Psychologist, 53*, 109–120.

Rapin, I., & Wilson, B. (1978). Children with developmental language disability: Neurological aspects and assessment. In M. Wyke (Ed.), *Developmental dysphasia* (pp. 13–41). New York: Academic Press.

Rescorla, L. (1989). The Language Development Survey: A screening tool for delayed language in toddlers. *Journal of Speech and Hearing Disorders, 54*, 587–599.

Rescorla, L. (2000). Do late talkers turn out to have reading difficulties a decade later? *Annals of Dyslexia, 50*, 87–102.

Rescorla, L. (2002). Language and reading outcomes to age 9 in late-talking toddlers. *Journal of Speech, Language, and Hearing Research, 45*, 360–371.

Rescorla, L. (2005). Age 13 language and reading outcomes in late-talking toddlers. *Journal of Speech, Language, and Hearing Research, 45*, 459–472.

Rescorla, L., Dahlsgaard, K., & Roberts, J. (2000). Late-talking toddlers: MLU and IPSyn outcomes at 3;0 and 4;0. *Journal of Child Language, 27*, 643–664.

Rescorla, L., & Lee, E. C. (1999). Language impairments in young children. In T. Layton & L. Watson (Eds.), *Handbook of early language impairment in children: Vol. I.* (pp. 1–55). Albany, NY: Delmar.

Rescorla, L., Mirak, J., & Singh, L. (2000). Vocabulary growth in late talkers: Lexical development from 2;0 to 3;0. *Journal of Child Language, 27*, 293–311.

Rescorla, L., & Ratner, N. B. (1996). Phonetic profiles of typically developing and language-delayed toddlers. *Journal of Speech and Hearing Research, 39*, 153–165.

Rescorla, L., & Roberts, J. (1997). Late-talkers at 2: Outcomes at age 3. *Journal of Speech and Hearing Research, 40*, 556–566.

Rescorla, L., & Roberts, J. (2002). Nominal versus verbal morpheme use in late talkers at ages 3 and 4. *Journal of Speech, Language, and Hearing Research, 45*, 1219–1231.

Rescorla, L., & Schwartz, E. (1990). Outcome of toddlers with expressive language delay. *Applied Psycholinguistics, 11*, 393–407.

Rice, M. L., & Bode, J. V. (1993). Gaps in the verb lexicons of children with specific language impairment. *First Language, 13*, 113–131.

Rice, M. L., Sell, M. A., & Hadley, P. A. (1991). Social interactions of speech and language impaired children. *Journal of Speech and Hearing Research, 34*, 1299–1307.

Rice, M. L., & Wexler, K. (1996). Toward tense as a clinical marker of specific language impairment in English-speaking children. *Journal of Speech and Hearing Research, 39*, 1239–1257.

Rice, M. L., Wexler, K., & Cleave, P. L. (1995). Specific language impairment as a period of extended optional infinitive. *Journal of Speech and Hearing Research, 38*, 850–863.

Ripich, D. N., & Griffith, P. L. (1988). Narrative abilities of children with learning disabilities and nondisabled children: Story structure, cohesion, and propositions. *Journal of Learning Disabilities, 21*(3), 165–173.

Roberts, J., Rescorla, L., Giroux, J., & Stevens, L. (1998). Phonological skills of children with specific expressive language impairment (SLI–E): Outcome at age 3. *Journal of Speech, Language, and Hearing Research, 41*, 374–384.

Robinson, N., & Robb, M. (2002). Early communication and language assessment: A dynamic process. In D. Bernstein & E. Tiegerman-Farber (Eds.), *Language and communication disorders in children* (5th ed., pp. 126–180). Boston: Allyn & Bacon.

Rossetti, L. (1990). *The Rossetti Infant-Toddler Language Scale*. Moline, IL: Lingual System.

Sandall, S., Hemmeter, M. L., Smith, B., & McLean, M. (2005). *DEC recommended practices: A comprehensive guide for practical application in early intervention/early childhood special education*. Longmont, CO: Sopris West.

Schery, T., & Wilcoxen, A. (1982). *The Initial Communication Processes Scale*. Monterey, CA: CTB/McGraw-Hill.

Schuele, C. M. (2004). The impact of developmental speech and language impairments on the acquisition of literacy skills. *Mental Retardation and Developmental Disabilities Research Reviews, 10*, 176–183.

Schuele, C. M., & Dykes, J. (2005). A longitudinal study of complex syntax development in a child with specific language impairment. *Clinical Linguistics and Phonetics, 19*, 295–318.

Schuele, C. M., & Tolbert, L. (2001). Omissions of obligatory relative markers in children with specific language impairment. *Clinical Linguistics and Phonetics, 15,* 257–274.

Schwartz, R. G., Leonard, L. B., Folger, M. K., & Wilcox, M. J. (1980). Early phonological behavior in normal-speaking and language disordered children: Evidence for a synergistic view of linguistic disorders. *Journal of Speech and Hearing Disorders, 45,* 357–377.

Scott, C. M., & Windsor, J. (2000). General language performance measures in spoken and written narrative and expository discourse of school-age children with language learning disabilities. *Journal of Speech, Language, and Hearing Research, 43,* 324–339.

Seidenberg, P., & Bernstein, D. (1986). The comprehension of similes and metaphors by learning disabled and nonlearning disabled children. *Language, Speech, and Hearing Services in Schools, 17,* 219–229.

Shane, H., Lipschultz, R., & Shane, C. (1982). Facilitating the communicative interaction of nonspeaking persons in large residential settings. *Topics in Language Disorders, 2,* 73–84.

Smith, B., Warren, S., Yoder, P., & Feurer, I. (2004). Teachers' use of naturalistic communication intervention practices. *Journal of Early Intervention, 27*(1), 1–14.

Snowling, M., Bishop, D. V. M., & Stothard, S. E. (2000). Is preschool language impairment a risk factor for dyslexia in adolescence? *Journal of Child Psychology and Psychiatry, 41,* 587–600.

Sparrow, S., Balla, D., & Cicchetti, D. (1984). *Vineland Adaptive Behavior Scales.* St. Paul, MN: American Guidance Service.

Thal, D. J., Reilly, J., Seibert, L., Jeffries, R., & Fenson, J. (2004). Language development in children at risk for language impairment: Cross-population comparisons. *Brain and Language, 88,* 167–179.

Thal, D., & Tobias, S. (1992). Communicative gestures in children with delayed onset of oral expressive vocabulary. *Journal of Speech and Hearing Research, 35,* 1281–1289.

Thal, D., Tobias, S., & Morrison, D. (1991). Language and gesture in late talkers: A 1-year follow-up. *Journal of Speech and Hearing Research, 34,* 604–612.

Thordardottir, E. T., & Weismer, E. S. (2001). High frequency verbs and verb diversity in the spontaneous speech of school-age children with specific language impairment. *International Journal of Language and Communication Disorders, 36,* 221–244.

Wagner, C. R., Nettelbladt, U., Sahlen, B., & Nilholm, C. (2000). Conversation versus narration in pre-school children with language impairment. *International Journal of Language and Communication Disorders, 35,* 83–93.

Warren, S., & Kaiser, A. (1986). Incidental language teaching: A critical review. *Journal of Speech and Hearing Disorders, 51,* 291–298.

Watkins, R. V., Kelly, D. J., Harbers, H. M., & Hollis, W. (1995). Measuring children's lexical diversity: Differentiating typical and atypical learners. *Journal of Speech and Hearing Research, 39,* 1349–1355.

Westby, C. E. (1980). Assessment of cognitive and language abilities through play. *Language, Speech, and Hearing Services in Schools, 11,* 154–168.

Westby, C. E. (1988). Assessment of cognitive and language abilities through play. *Language, Speech, and Hearing Services in Schools, 11,* 154–168.

Wetherby, A., & Prizant, B. (1992). Profiling young children's communicative competence. In S. Warren & J. Reichle (Eds.), *Causes and effects in communication and language intervention* (pp. 217–253). Baltimore, MD: Brookes.

Wetherby, A. M. & Prizant, B. M. (1993). *Communication and Symbolic Behavior Scales.* Baltimore, MD: Brookes.

Whitehurst, G., & Fischel, J. (1994). Practitioner review: Early developmental language delay: What, if anything, should the clinician do about it? *Journal of Child Psychology and Psychiatry, 35,* 613–648.

Wiig, E. H. (1990). *Wiig Criterion Referenced Inventory of Language.* San Antonio, TX: Psychological Corp.

Wiig, E. H., Secord, W. A., & Semel, E. M. (2004). *Clinical Evaluation of Language Fundamentals–Preschool 2.* San Antonio, TX: Harcourt/Psychological Corp.

Wilcox, M. J., Kouri, T. A., & Caswell, S. B. (1991). Early language intervention: A comparison of classroom and individual treatment. *American Journal of Speech-Language Pathology, 1,* 49–62.

Windfuhr, K., Faragher, B., & Conti-Ramsden, G. (2002). Lexical learning skills in young children with specific language impairment (SLI). *International Journal of Language and Communication Disorders, 37,* 415–432.

Woodcock, R. W. (1991). *Woodcock Language Proficiency Battery–Revised.* Itasca, IL: Riverside.

Zimmerman, I. L., Steiner, V. G., & Pond, R. E. (2002). *Preschool Language Scale (PLS–4), English Edition.* San Antonio, TX: Harcourt Assessment.

Chapter
6

Promoting Cognitive and Literacy Development

Paige C. Pullen

Sharon A. Raver

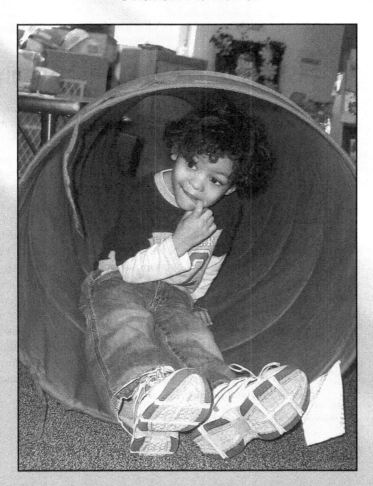

Overview

This chapter discusses intellectual development in infants, toddlers, preschoolers, and primary-aged students, including

theories of cognitive development and learning

the effects of early experience

cognitive milestones and intervention implications

assessment of cognitive development

promoting cognitive development and learning in infants, toddlers, and preschoolers

promoting cognitive development and academic learning in primary-aged students

CASE STUDY: The Lawrence Family

Mindy Lawrence was born premature (34 weeks gestation), weighing 3 pounds 10 ounces following a difficult birth. She was the third child of Melina and Frank Lawrence, business professionals. Following discharge, the family participated in biweekly home visits with an interventionist from an infant-toddler program. Since both parents worked, Nola, the family's babysitter, took Mindy to physical therapy appointments and was reliable in following activities suggested by the early intervention team.

At the age of 3, Mindy's evaluation revealed that she had four- to six-month delays in fine motor, communication, social, and cognitive development. Continuing twice-a-month physical therapy sessions, Mindy was enrolled in a full-day daycare/preschool program for typically developing children, with consultative support provided by an early childhood special education teacher. In first grade, with teacher and parent approval, the special education team determined that Mindy qualified for services for mild mental retardation. Now in third grade, she is on a second-grade level in both reading and mathematics. Mindy receives her education in a general education class with accommodations and attends a resource room two days a week. Her parents also pay for tutoring in reading two days a week. Mrs. Lawrence describes Mindy today as a "happy child who loves sports, music, and her dog."

Although the specifics of the process are still unclear, research has found evidence that development of the brain is not complete at birth, but changes rapidly during the first years of life (Zeanah, 2000). Many complex processes are involved as children develop the ability to think and reason. Learning appears to be a complex set of processes that vary according to the developmental level of the learner, the nature of the task, and the context in which the learning occurs.

Many theorists have developed working explanations for how learning and knowledge development occur. Their theories have influenced how early childhood special education (ECSE) professionals approach teaching in all domains.

THEORIES OF COGNITIVE DEVELOPMENT AND LEARNING

The effort to understand how individuals learn has led to the development of several theories. The behavioral theory, the information-processing theory, and the cognitive-development theory have influenced educational practices, each offering insight into how knowledge and learning occur as well as how adults can encourage learning in children. Each theory will be described briefly.

Behavioral Theory of Learning

This theory views learning as behavioral change. Educators attempt to identify environmental events and considerations responsible for such change, adjusting them to influence desired outcomes (Strain et al., 1992). Behavior, both adaptive and maladaptive, is viewed as learned. This learning occurs, or does not occur, as a result of the consequences of behavior. Simply stated, behavior that is followed by pleasant consequences tends to be repeated, and thus learned. Behavior that is followed by unpleasant consequences tends not to be repeated or learned. The behavioral theory does not deny the existence of physiological factors that may contribute to some behaviors, such as the effects of heredity or developmental stages (Ferster,

Culbertson, & Boren, 1975). The primary emphasis of this perspective is on manipulating the present environmental conditions maintaining behavior and on establishing and verifying functional relationships between such conditions and behavior (Alberto & Troutman, 2006).

Information-Processing Theory of Learning

This theory attempts to describe ways that individuals take information from the environment and then process, store, and later retrieve that information when needed. A learner's prior knowledge and the nature and organization of information to be learned are considered critical in how that information is stored and later remembered. **Encoding** is viewed as the process of preparing information for storage in short-term and long-term memory. This process can be achieved by recitation and elaborative rehearsal that links information to previous information to aid in its retrieval (Gredler, 2001).

Cognitive-Development Theory of Learning

This theory suggests that people pass through stages of intellectual development. Jean Piaget, a psychologist, proposed the most commonly known stage theory of development, which he believed described the cognitive and moral development of children. His views have impacted educators, particularly early childhood educators. Piaget believed that individuals use **assimilation**, the tendency to adapt the environment to enhance personal functioning, and **accommodation**, the tendency to change behavior to adapt to the environment, to progress cognitively. The process of maintaining a balance between these forces is called **equilibration**. Equilibration is seen as facilitating cognitive growth, as are maturation, experience, and social interaction (Piaget, 1952, 1957).

Each of these theories addresses issues pertinent to educating young children with developmental delays and disabilities. Although they make different assumptions about how learning and cognitive development occur, commonalities exist. The importance of attention and rehearsal for learning and the influence of the learners' environment on learning are acknowledged by each. Each also acknowledges that individuals outside the learner, as a part of the learner's environment, may significantly influence learning and the development of knowledge.

Today, **cognitive development** might be best described as a progressive change in internal mental processes, such as thinking, reasoning, and remembering, and in the ability to function adaptively in the world as a result of receiving information from the environment, understanding the meaning of this information, and using it to plan appropriate actions (Dunst, 1981). Cognition is expressed through the development of communication, social, and motor skills. Young children display attention, discrimination, and memory as they progress cognitively.

Attention involves the process of tuning in to relevant aspects of a task or situation and ignoring irrelevant stimuli. Some children with special needs may have to be taught how to focus on important aspects of materials or interactions in order to learn from them. For example, placing a toy on an infant's body or close to an infant's face may help the child screen out distracting visual and auditory stimuli that may interfere with attending.

Discrimination is the process of receiving and interpreting sensory information. When a child is able to distinguish between a picture of a dog and a picture of a cat, the child is demonstrating that he or she can identify likenesses and differences. This ability is essential for learning. Finally, **memory** involves the process of receiving information through attention and discrimination, storing it, and using it later. Some young children with special needs may use limited memory strategies. Consequently, they require repeated and varied experiences with the same information before it is stored or learned satisfactorily. A good deal of intervention with infants, toddlers, preschoolers, and primary-aged children is designed to help them develop and refine the cognitive processes of attention, discrimination, and memory through planned experiences.

THE EFFECTS OF EARLY EXPERIENCE

The past decades of child development research reveal that infants learn, respond, and interact from the moment they are born (Howe & Courage, 1997). The intellectual development of young children appears to occur as a result of the continuing interaction between inborn abilities and stimulation received from the environment (Bertenthal, 1996; Nelson & Bosquet, 2000; Raver, 1999). For this reason, the quality of early experiences is critical for optimal early cognitive changes. Early experiences may either facilitate or hinder a child's cognitive advancement. The impact of early experiences on infants and toddlers, preschoolers, and school-aged children are discussed.

Infants and Toddlers

Infancy and toddlerhood are remarkable times in a child's life in that he or she is nearly constantly creating new learning from everyday experiences. Studies of infant perception—the ability to learn or receive information by using the senses of sight, hearing, smell, and/or touch—indicate that the senses are the starting point for an infant's expanding understanding of the world (Lockman, 1983). Changes in memory, thinking, language, and concept development occur through a child's experiences and relationships with caring adults with whom there are ongoing interactions. Typically developing infants and toddlers actively seek information from their surroundings, act on this information, and enjoy influencing objects and people.

Some children with developmental delays or disabilities, however, may be more passive and have fewer exploratory skills, which may inadvertently reduce or alter their social contact with adults and their interaction with their environment. ECSE is founded on the understanding that parents, family members, and professionals can facilitate a child's learning by teaching and reinforcing skills through daily routines. Research has shown that when parents are guided in how to engage their child and shown how to provide experiences that match their child's current level of functioning, the cognitive development of children with mental retardation can be enhanced (Mahoney, Finger, & Powell, 1985).

The intensity of intervention, or early experiences, a child and family receives seems to be critical in supporting the cognitive development of infants and toddlers. **Intensity** relates to the nature and frequency of support and learning experiences provided. Parents who provide learning opportunities at home and do not rely solely on professionals to support their children's learning tend to have children with better developmental outcomes. When early intervention programs fail to show positive effects on intellectual or social performance in children living in poverty and those at risk for developmental problems, it is often the lack of intensity that seems to be identified as an important factor (Ramey, Ramey, Gaines, & Blair, 1995). Appropriate adult attention, affection, physical interaction, and guidance seem to be essential in fostering optimal cognitive development in infants and toddlers with special needs.

Preschoolers

How preschoolers spend their time with others seems to influence their cognitive functioning. The measured intelligence scores of preschoolers have been found to be associated with their families' ability to provide intellectually stimulating experiences (Bradley et al., 1994). Children from financially disadvantaged homes have been reported to be at risk for entering school with lower verbal and mathematics skills than their more financially advantaged classmates (Huston, 1994). Yet, when appropriate materials and experiences are provided for children with developmental delays or disabilities and for children living in poverty, cognitive development appears to be positively

impacted (Park, Turnbull, & Turnbull, 2002). In fact, a relationship has been found between maternal style of language facilitation at 3 years of age and later reading abilities of low-birth-weight children at 8 years of age (Fewell & Deutscher, 2004).

Dale and Cole (1988) found that programs that exposed preschoolers with nonspecific developmental delays to what was described as "developmentally-appropriate experiences" reported group gains in social, cognitive, and motor development, even when program treatment models differed. These researchers studied 80% of the original 205 subjects from their 1988 study in 2005 (when the subjects were adolescents). They found that early measures of language and cognitive ability continued to predict academic and cognitive outcomes (Dale, Jenkins, Mills, & Cole, 2005). That is, developmental disabilities and poor academic performance in the early years led to poor academic achievement at ages 12 and 16, especially when students displayed difficult temperament and/or behavior problems. This finding supports the findings of others who determined that many children with developmental delays as preschoolers continue to display primarily cognitive and learning disabilities that warrant special education placements when they are in elementary school (Keogh, Coots, & Bernheimer, 1995).

Although it is clear that intervention can produce positive changes in many preschoolers with disabilities and developmental delays (La Paro, Olsen, & Pianta, 2002), it is difficult to evaluate the relative efficacy of different intervention models. Short-term positive changes have been reported in all domains, including cognitive development, by programs using direct instruction curriculum models, mediated learning curriculum models, and activity-based curriculum models (Bricker et al., 1997; Dale & Cole, 1988; Pretti-Frontczak & Bricker, 2004; Losado & Bricker, 1994). Programs that use a direct instruction model tend to provide structured, step-by-step approaches with a strong reliance on teacher-directed strategies. Programs using a mediated learning model tend to use interactive, child-directed approaches. Programs using an activity-based model tend to embed learning opportunities into daily activities, using both teacher-directed and child-directed approaches.

Despite the fact that all three program models appear to produce positive developmental outcomes in many of the children studied, research suggests that programs that use the activity-based intervention model seem to produce better generalization of the skills taught. For example, when the vocabulary learning of children from a "pull-out direct instruction program" (i.e., one in which children were taken from the group and provided massed practice of individual skills in a one-to-one situation with an ECSE teacher) was compared with the vocabulary learning of children in an "activity-based instruction program" (i.e., one in which individual instruction was embedded into daily classroom activities by an ECSE teacher), Losardo and Bricker (1994) found that children with disabilities from 47 to 66 months of age acquired the vocabulary items more quickly in the "pull-out direct instruction" condition. However, generalization was significantly better for children who learned the vocabulary items in the "activity-based instruction" condition. In addition, subsequent maintenance of the gains was significantly greater for children in the "activity-based instruction" condition. These studies are significant in that they demonstrate that working with children in one-to-one learning situations may produce more rapid skill acquisition, but that meaningfully embedded learning opportunities produce better maintenance and generalization of learned skills. Since children with special needs must demonstrate what they know under "real" circumstances, teaching skills within home and school routines seems to produce the best long-term outcomes for these preschoolers.

COGNITIVE MILESTONES AND INTERVENTION IMPLICATIONS

Piaget's cognitive-development theory outlines four major cognitive stages, from birth to about 11 years of age, characterized by the sequential acquisition of more-complex cognitive skills

(Piaget, 1951, 1952). Because Piaget emphasized active child participation in the construction of knowledge, many professionals utilize his framework for planning ways to stimulate cognitive development in young children who are exhibiting delayed or atypical sensory and/or motor development. These stages will be discussed briefly.

Infants and Toddlers

Sensorimotor Period. Piaget called his first period of intellectual development, from birth to about 2 years of age, the **sensorimotor period.** In this stage, infants interact with their environment through reflexes. Patterns—or **schemas,** as Piaget called them—link with other behaviors and, if they produce certain results, are repeated. Infants develop and refine intellectual concepts through play by looking, listening, and manipulating to combine, modify, and invent new schemas. Trial and error characterize the beginning of this period, while by the time children are toddlers, they have developed symbolic thought, since they can quickly solve problems mentally without relying on sensory and motor actions (Piaget & Inhelder, 1969). Visual pursuit and object permanence, means–ends relationships, the construction of objects in space, and imitation are important concepts that develop simultaneously during the sensorimotor period (Piaget & Inhelder, 1969).

Visual Pursuit and Object Permanence. These two concepts involve the ability to attend to critical events in the environment and the development of systematic searching, organization, and memory skills. **Auditory localization**, turning the head toward a sound, and **visual pursuit**, visually following objects, are precursors to object permanence. **Object permanence** is the understanding that an object out of view still exists somewhere else (Langley, 1989). Instructional objectives for the development of object permanence might involve teaching a child how to search for an object in an organized way and increasing the number of events a child can retain in memory. An ECSE professional might teach a child to find a toy hidden first in a shirt pocket and then behind his or her mother's back to encourage the development of object permanence.

Means-End Relationships. This concept, often called problem solving, refers to the ability to use insight to solve problems (Piaget, 1952). Instructional objectives may include understanding tool use (i.e., how to use something to get something else) and using goal-directed behavior. The ECSE professional might show a child how to reach around a book to get an interesting object, how to play with toys and use them to interact with people, and how to push a rattle that is out of reach toward him or her using a bottle. These behaviors are viewed as the emergence of reasoning.

Construction of Objects in Space. This concept describes the ability to explore objects, perform several actions with them, and use them in appropriate ways. Professionals might advise parents to show their child how to release objects into containers and to imitate ways to use materials appropriately. Stacking rings, toddler play gyms, and blocks are good materials for facilitating these concepts.

Because these concept rely strongly on experimentation and persistence, some children with cognitive delays may experience difficulty with their development (Schwethelm & Mahoney, 1986). When this is the case, professionals teach family members how to use modeling to show a child how to perform a task within family routines in order to encourage the development of these skills.

Imitation. Imitation is the ability to reproduce behaviors observed (Piaget, 1951, 1952). Imitation is a major milestone that permits children to learn new skills efficiently. Imitation may be immediate, as when the child reproduces an action or sound after observing or hearing it, or it may be deferred. When a child reproduces an action or sound some time after observing or hearing it performed, it is called **deferred imitation**. Eventually, imitation leads to representational or imaginative play, as when a toddler plays the role of daddy by taking the keys to the front door and attempting to unlock the door.

Appropriate experiences with objects are necessary for infants to refine their exploration and imitation skills. Games such as Patty–Cake and Show Me Your (Eye/Tummy/Ear) and play with trucks and dolls can assist the development of motor imitation. Vocal imitation emerges after motor imitation. A child's thinking processes continue to be refined as the child moves into the next phase, the preoperational period.

Preschoolers

Preoperational Period. Piaget (1952) suggested that from about 2 to 7 years of age children experience another phase of cognitive development he called the **preoperational period**. He divided the preoperational period into the preconceptual stage (roughly 2 to 4 years of age) and the intuitive stage (roughly 4 to 7 years of age) (Ambron, 1975). The preconceptual stage is characterized by the first appearance of symbolic representation or imagination. At this stage, a child may not be able to solve problems when multiple attributes of a whole must be considered. That is, a toddler may have difficulty sorting the "big orange balls" from the "small green balls" when both are present in a center activity, but might be able to sort the orange balls from the green ones, since only the attribute of color has to be considered, not color *and* size.

Symbolic/Pretend Play. During the preconceptual stage, children learn to use language for things that occurred in the past and to use **symbolic play**, the ability to use one thing to represent something else. Teachers and family members can teach symbolic play by playing Let's Pretend. A mother can say, "Let's pretend this shoe is a phone. I am calling Auntie Lee [while holding the shoe to her ear]." Then she can hand the shoe to the child and say, "Auntie Lee wants Spencer."

Problem-Solving. Despite the fact that nearly any situation can be used to teach problem solving, professionals and parents may still need to structure situations to teach this important skill to children with developmental delays and/or disabilities. Adults create a situation that the child cannot solve independently so they can systematically guide the child toward a solution. For instance, a teacher may ask a child to put a toy on the top shelf, a shelf the child is unable to reach. When the child becomes aware of the "problem," the teacher can involve the class: "Jada has a problem. She needs to put her toy on the top shelf. What can she do? Let's think." When adults make situations functional and use appropriate guiding questions, children will learn how to generate, eliminate, and select reasonable "solutions" to everyday "problems."

Concept Vocabulary. Concept words are descriptive words such as *empty/full, light/heavy, large/larger/largest,* and *same/different.* Concept vocabulary must be taught through direct concept-related experiences (DeThorne & Watkins, 2001). Professionals must create learning opportunities in which target vocabulary/concepts are made concrete and taught directly (Justice & Pullen, 2003). Then children must be provided with multiple ways to practice discriminating and identifying the concept. During a cooking activity, for example, children can be encouraged to notice and comment on how foods change when combined, heated, or cooled. By systematically presenting new words (e.g., "The cookie batter is *lumpy* before it is mixed."), making relationships clear (e.g., "Remember last week—What was the waffle mix like before we used the mixer?"), asking open-ended questions to elicit reasoning (e.g., "I wonder what will happen when Gregory puts the molasses in?"), and providing multiple ways to discriminate and identify concepts, adults are increasing the chances that concepts will generalize to other materials, people, and settings (Beck, McKeown, & Kucan, 2002). Children master concepts and concept vocabulary at different ages. Table 6.1 shows the average age at which toddlers and preschoolers learn common concepts.

Classification. Matching is putting objects and pictures that are alike in a group. **Sorting** is separating objects and pictures by differences. **Classification** involves using matching and sorting to distinguish characteristics that form a group, such as families, animals, and foods.

Teaching the concept words *same/like* and *different/unalike* is critical in helping children understand any new concept. Adults may need to help children identify the most critical or relevant feature of an object or picture so it can be classified. **Attributes**, features or characteristics, help children make these discriminations. For example, when sorting pictures for "objects that would be found in a bedroom," a teacher or parent could point out that although toy cars might be found in a bedroom, real cars are usually kept outside the house, in garages. Consequently, only toy cars would be put in the "bedroom box."

To teach classification, teachers begin with simple, basic differences, such as asking children to put all the "red objects" (e.g., apple, red car, tomato) in a bucket. Then professionals move to more abstract concepts, such as "The *rule* for this bucket is all the red things that cannot be eaten." Consistently using the same vocabulary (in this case, *red*) helps children attend to the most relevant features of objects and pictures. Later changing the rules, but using the same pictures and objects, is a good way to help children improve reasoning by taking small steps.

Seriation. Seriation is ordering pictures or objects according to relative differences. This skill helps a child coordinate relationships related to differences in size and position. Nesting cups and some puzzles that picture objects in ascending or descending size require seriation. To teach this skill, teachers begin with objects that are very dissimilar, such as a newborn's shoe, an 8-year-old's shoe, and an adult's shoe. Gradually, finer differences are taught until a child can quickly place several shoes in order of size from smallest to largest. This concept is considered a prerequisite to understanding number concepts in the primary grades. Table 6.2 shows how household objects can be used to teach common concepts to preschoolers with special needs.

Social Stories. An ideal way to blend cognitive concepts, concept vocabulary, and social learning into a single activity is to write a social story about an activity or event a child, a class, or a family has shared. Social stories are short stories, usually only

TABLE 6.1 Sample concept vocabulary by age of acquisition

Age	Position	Number	Quantity	Quality
2.0–2.6	in off	one (2.4)		
2.6–3.0	on under out of together away from		big little tall all none	soft heavy
3.0–3.6	up top part toward		empty	hard fast same not same
3.6–4.0	around in front of high in back of next to	two three (3.8)	little full more less	pretty ugly noisy quiet different
4.0–4.6	beside bottom backward forward above over	four	short fat thin skinny long short wide narrow most least	rough smooth
4.6–5.0+	down low inside middle outside through near far center corner right left separate after in order first	five	many few whole half every each several almost as many equal a lot	light dark warm cool

Source: Peg Joseph contributed to this table. Developmental ages compiled from Nelson, K. G. (1988). *Planning individualized speech and language intervention programs: Objectives for infants, children and adolescents.* Tucson, AZ: Communication Skill Builders. Permission granted from PRO-ED.

TABLE 6.2 Common materials which can be used to facilitate the cognitive development of preschoolers

Material	Ideas for Teaching Different Cognitive Concepts and Skills
Plastic laundry basket	*Symbolic/pretend play:* (inside) use as boat, car, raft, fire truck; (on top) use as canoe with ruler as oars; go on a hike and use as mountain; pretend to be doing the laundry like Mom and Dad; make into house for doll; use as puppet theater; make into cage for zoo animals; make into dog house, pet carrier, or pet bed; make into giant bird's nest; use as a wagon to carry things.
	Problem solving: decide how to "lace" ribbon between holes; pass small balls through the holes into a box; decide how far away to stand to get beanbag inside with one toss; use as support for unsteady sitters; decide how to make it into a wagon, car, nest, dog bed, etc.; decide how to make different handles.
	Concept vocabulary: in/out; light/heavy; under/in/on/above/over; play Simon Says with clothing ("Put just one ____ in," "Put all the ____ in," etc.; blindfold child, drop objects into basket and child finds, labels an attribute such as size, shape, function.
	Matching: objects that are plastic, objects that are the same color, objects that are rectangles; with hole in center; put items of clothing in pairs and have blindfolded/not blindfolded child find ones that "match" or are the "same."
	Sorting: put paper cards that are the same color as basket in basket, those that are not the same, in another basket; sort clothing items in two laundry baskets—winter/summer, big/little, dirty/clean, colors, items that have numbers on them and ones that do not; put in sets of three and have child find the ones that are different.
	Classification: put pictures of things used in doing the laundry (detergent, clothes, etc.) in the basket, then pictures of clothes worn in the winter/spring/summer/fall; put boys' or girls' clothes in.
	Seriation: (on top) stack boxes from biggest to smallest; (inside) nest boxes from biggest to smallest; glue different-sized objects to top and put in order of size; glue many together and sequence by size/height; line up socks/shirts/mittens from smallest to biggest/biggest to smallest.
	Creativity: place paper on the outside and rub with crayons to create patterns; list all the things basket can be used for; make a backpack with straps; use as part of obstacle course; cover with blanket to make a tent; cover bottom with aluminum to make a "mirror"; use as drum in music band; make into the house for that week's character from the story.

Material	Ideas for Teaching Different Cognitive Concepts and Skills
	Imitation: wrap pipe cleaners around it with a pattern the child follows (red-blue- red); bang together to match beat; count them, teaching one-to-one correspondence; use to make patterns in Play-Doh; do something with the basket using a body part, and then have child do the same ("Put the basket on your knee like me.")—after imitating, the child gets to do something the adult imitates.
Plastic film containers	*Symbolic/pretend play:* create a tea set; use as a boat for small doll; use as finger puppets.
	Problem solving: stack with and without lids to make a tower; cut off bottom and drop small objects through or use as a tunnel; roll with and without lids down a wedge (ask child to predict which will roll faster); use as a nonstandard unit of measure; use as a Play-Doh/cookie cutter; display three small objects, place a container over one, ask child to identify hidden object.
	Concept vocabulary: in/out; light/heavy; under/in/on; above or over; play Simon Says with a Cheerio and the container using positional words; big/little; same/different; full/empty; full/half full; more/less; rote counting; one-to-one correspondence counting.
	Matching: match pattern of up-up-down; glue individual family pictures on each and create family units; assemble a set of containers with lids removed and have child match lids to containers; place shapes or colors on lids and containers and have child match.
	Sorting: fill with beans/rice/sand for sorting by sound/weight; cover with paper and sort by color or shape; fill with spices and sort by smell; put cotton balls soaked in various scents to sort by sweet/sour or nice/not nice smells; glue pictures of children on outside and sort who is "in school" that day and who is "not in school"; assemble a collection of objects that will and will not fit into the containers and then predict, test, and graph results.
	Classification: glue sandpaper, cotton, sponge, cloth, and silk on them and have child group by texture; hide objects under each and have child puts objects into groups such as foods.
	Seriation: assemble a collection of containers and sequence them from large to small; small, medium and large; small to large.
	Creativity: glue on paper to make toss game; make a mobile; spray different colors, thread string through the top of the container to make a necklace that can be used to carry a favorite treasure; make into finger puppets to re-create story; punch holes in top and use as a shaker for sand or glitter; make rhythm instruments.
	Imitation: fill, scoop, pour, use to make sand castles using damp sand; make circle prints by dipping into paint and stamping; play toss and catch; toss into/at a target; add face and legs to make holiday ornaments; cut small holes in top and lace with shoe lace.

Diane Postman contributed to this table.

one or two paragraphs, that tell a story from a child's perspective. They tend to describe how to respond to a situation appropriately or how to perform a skill appropriately (Gray, 2002).

Social stories can be written about literally any family or class experience, even something as apparently inconsequential as putting materials away when the timer goes off. The best social stories use pictures of real objects and children's names and pictures to make them more engaging and personal. For some children with significant developmental delays or pervasive developmental disorders (PDD), reading a social story before an activity and "pretending" to go through the experience before it actually occurs may improve attention and compliance during the actual activity. Figure 6.1 shows a favorite social story and recipe card a teacher prepared for a child with autistic spectrum disorder after the class made holiday ornaments.

Children at this stage of development may have difficulty arranging objects and pictures in sequence, so taking the events of a social story and making "sequence cards" may be helpful for teaching sequencing and aid in the development of memory strategies. As always, review of the steps used in any activity is critical for building sequencing skills (e.g., "First, we put the flour in the bowl, and then we . . .").

Representational thought in the preoperational period is considered to be faster and more flexible than it was in the sensorimotor period (Ambron, 1975). Children become better able to plan ahead and anticipate how actions or events may unfold, can learn from past experiences, and can communicate what they know.

Primary-Aged Students

Preoperational Thought/Intuitive Thinking Period.
Children between 5 and 7 years old were described by Piaget (1952) as beginning to understand conservation of amount, quantity, number, and weight. He concluded that at this age children can attend to more than one aspect of an object at a time, but may not always be able to justify or explain their conclusions verbally.

Concrete Operations Period.
Piaget described children from 7 to 11 years old as having the ability to organize their perceptions and use symbols. They are able to classify and categorize objects with multiple dimensions simultaneously. During problem-solving tasks, a child at this stage can describe verbally how the problem was solved, but still may have some difficulty with problems presented in a purely abstract way.

Assessment of Cognitive Development

Most cognitive assessment instruments attempt to assess the efficiency with which the child uses motor, communicative, and sensory skills to solve problems. Professionals may use formal and informal measurements to determine the level of a child's cognitive functioning.

Formal Cognitive Assessment

Infants, Toddlers and Preschoolers. Tools that measure cognitive development outline a sample of behaviors considered characteristic of a specific age range. Cognitive scales are based on the assumption that early reasoning abilities involve movement from lower to higher levels of functioning or thinking. Not all children can be successfully assessed using traditional cognitive assessment instruments, however. Most standardized assessments for children under the age of 3 years require specific motor responses to evaluate cognitive skills, and administration procedures usually do not accommodate for physical limitations. Many tools do not have a sufficient number of items to adequately assess children from 18 to 36 months of age (Guerette, Tefft, Furumasu, & Moy, 1999). Further, children with profound sensory, motor, social, or intellectual deficits may exhibit insufficient typical behavior to allow them to be measured by most traditional cognitive assessment tools.

Primary-Aged Students. When it is necessary to obtain a student's IQ for diagnostic purposes and determination of eligibility for special education

Figure 6.1 Mrs. Brownell's social story about making holiday ornaments and recipe card

WE MADE BAKER'S CLAY

We washed our hands with soap. We dried our hands with paper towels. We sat in our chairs with our backs touching the chair.

Jaedon put 4 cups of flour in a large bowl. Joseph put 1 cup of salt in the bowl. Angie put 1 and 1/2 cups of water in the bowl. Mrs. Brownell mixed the dough with a large, wooden spoon.

We sat in our chairs until our name was called. Then Mrs. Brownell gave me a small lump of dough to mix with my hands. I rolled it. I squeezed it between my fingers. I pounded it with my hand. I loved rolling the dough.

Mrs. Brownell made the dough flat with a rolling pin. I used cookie cutters to make circles ○, squares ■ and diamonds ◆. I put a hole in the top of each shape ◉. I put my shapes on a cookie ▭ tray.

Mrs. Brownell took the shapes home and cooked them in her oven. The next day, we put on a painting apron and sat in our chairs at the big table. I painted my shapes red, green and yellow. When they were dry, I put a blue ribbon through the hole. Mrs. Brownell helped me make a bow. We hung the ornaments next to the window. Mine will be a present for someone I love ♡. I am learning to cook. I am learning to wait my turn.

4 cups unsifted flour

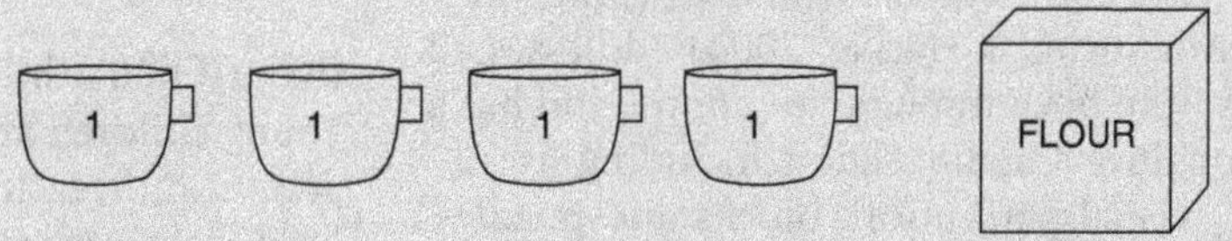

1 cup salt

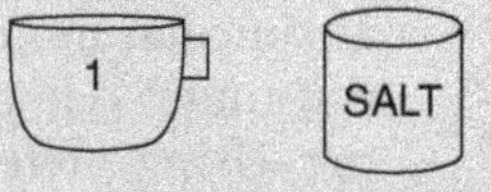

1½ cups water

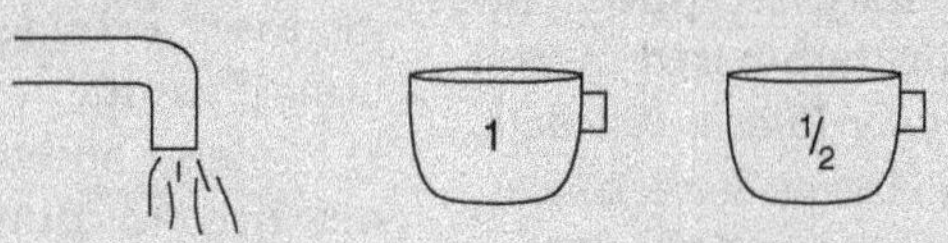

Mix thoroughly with hands

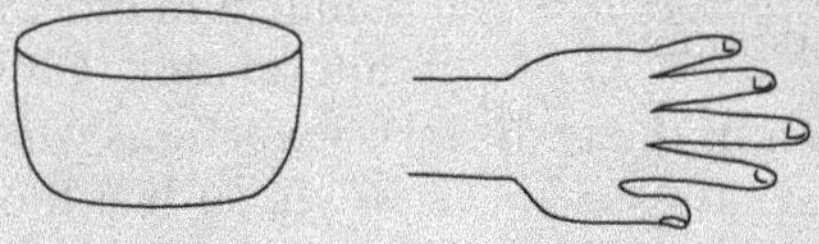

Knead for 4-6 minutes.

Bake in oven at 350 degrees until light brown.

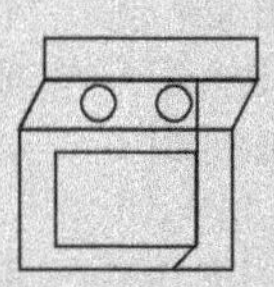

Create shapes or use a cookie cutter to make shapes. Baked and cooled pieces can be decorated with paints or magic markers.

services due to mental retardation or learning disabilities, the *Wechsler Intelligence Scale for Children, Fourth Edition* (WISC-IV) (Wechsler, 2003) may be used. The WISC-IV yields a full-scale IQ score from ten subtests in four different indices.

Informal Assessments

Infants, Toddlers, and Preschoolers. Global developmental curriculum-based scales such as the *Assessment, Evaluation, and Programming System (AEPS)* (Bricker, Cripe, & Slentz, 2002) and the *Hawaii Early Learning Profile, 0-3* (Furuno et al., 1979) allow educators to gain information about all developmental areas or to assess the cognitive domain separately. *The Carolina Curriculum for Infants and Toddlers with Special Needs* (Johnson—Martin, Attermeier, & Hacker, 2004) addresses all domains from birth through 36 months and has a strong cognitive domain section, including six subtests: (1) visual perception: blocks and puzzles, (2) visual perception: matching and sorting, (3) functional use of objects and symbolic play, (4) problem solving/reasoning, (5) number concepts, and (6) concept/vocabulary: receptive. The preschool version of this curriculum-based assessment, *The Carolina Curriculum for Preschoolers with Special Needs* (Johnson-Martin, Hacker, & Attermeier, 2004), covers all domains from 24 to 60 months. There are six subtests in the cognitive domain.

Primary-Aged Students. For children in the early primary grades, curriculum-based assessment (CBA) is conducted to provide information about a child's performance in the school curriculum. Typically, reading and mathematics programs adopted by school systems have their own set of assessments linked to the curriculum. Additionally, professionals may assess a student's academic skills by taking repeated rate samples of skills taught from the curriculum. For example, reading fluency rates and levels of accuracy in mathematics assignments may be tracked. CBA allows professionals to identify students who may need additional support, monitor a child's progress, and document progress for an Individualized Education Program (Mercer & Pullen, 2005).

Promoting Cognitive Development and Learning in Infants, Toddlers, and Preschoolers

Young children with special needs may follow typical patterns in some aspects of their cognitive development and atypical patterns in others. Consequently, cognitive goals should be selected because they enable children to increase practical interactions with their environment. Whether intervention is home- or center-based, there are several techniques that facilitate optimal cognitive development in infants, toddlers, and preschoolers with developmental needs. Four strategies are discussed.

Use a Child's Interests and Teach Through Play. Young children are more likely to stay in an interaction and learn when activities and materials hold their interest. Noting what interests a child at a particular moment and then using this interest constitutes one of the best ways to embed teaching. Using preferences in objects and activities increases a child's engagement and keeps interactions pleasurable for both the child and the adult.

Infants and toddlers who are slow to respond may need to continue an activity longer than other children in order to have sufficient time to process information. Children who are less able to learn from actions occurring at a distance from themselves, such as those with visual or hearing impairments and those who initiate interactions with low frequency, may require greater adult facilitation to maintain participation in interactions and play (Mahoney, 1988). Children with severe disabilities may require adults to pause 10 to 45 seconds to allow them an opportunity to react and initiate interactions, which may increase and extend their interactions (Halle, Alpert, & Anderson, 1984).

Once a child is engaged, however, it is important to follow the child's lead. By following a child's lead, an adult allows the child to dictate the direction of an interaction. For example, when Mindy, discussed in the case study, was 2 she banged her spoon on the tray instead of using it to eat her yogurt as her mother had intended. Her mother decided to follow Mindy's lead and banged her hand on the tray, too. They played the "banging game" for a few turns. Then Mrs. Lawrence gently guided her daughter's spoon into the yogurt, playfully getting her to bring the spoon to her mouth. By observing her child's interests and imitating her behavior, this mother used the opportunity to teach her daughter how to initiate play, imitate, and take turns.

To promote reasoning, professionals focus on creating opportunities for a child to exert control over objects, people, and events. Research has shown that infants and toddlers with special needs have more nonengaged time than peers without disabilities. This nonengagement tends to consist of passive behaviors, such as waiting or doing nothing, rather than active behaviors, such as crying or misbehaving (McWilliam & Bailey, 1995). Consequently, parents and professionals may need to be directive and explicit in showing children how to interact with, act on, and influence their environments.

Most routine care tasks can be playful as well as instructive for young children. Allowing a toddler to taste, smell, and touch food before it is cooked can change ordinary meals into fun learning experiences embedded with new vocabulary (e.g., *raw, cooked, stir*) and concepts (e.g., *cold/hot, slimy, hard/soft*). These types of learning opportunities are best distributed throughout the day so parents do not feel pressure to continue an interaction even though a child's attention has become strained and so children and parents are not overwhelmed.

Teach Turn Taking When Interacting with a Child.
Turn taking encourages the practice of skills while building on past experiences. As a child moves into the second year of life, it is important that parents and professionals begin to move toward developing more of a balance between adult-directed and child-initiated interactions. Adults can teach turn taking by following this sequence:

1) *Wait* for the child to take his or her turn.
2) If the child does not take a turn, *signal* the child to take a turn with a gestures first (e.g.,

pointing, looking expectantly, placing a hand on the toy); if this doesn't work, add words (e.g., "Mindy's turn").
3) If the child still doesn't respond, *prompt* (physically guide) the child to take his or her turn.

Introduce New Skills into Familiar Routines and Use New Routines for Generalization.
Predictable routines allow children to focus their attention on the specific requirements of a skill or task, rather than dividing their attention among the activity, the environment, and the skill. Since young children with special needs may have difficulty with **generalization** (the ability to transfer learning across situations, settings, materials, or people), it is usually necessary to teach generalization. That is, once a skill is reliably displayed in one routine, it is time to introduce other skills into the same routine. For instance, once a child can name two pictures in his book, his mother can work on getting him to identify (e.g., "Show me the turtle"—receptive language) and/or name (e.g., "What is this?"—expressive language) other pictures in the same book. Similarly, once a skill is displayed reliably in one routine, it is time to require that skill in a different routine or with different materials to train generalization. When a toddler can reliably request his shoes in the morning, for example, his mother can now have him request his shoes after nap to build generalization of the skill across situations.

Promote Literacy Awareness.
At first glance, it may seem that cognitive stimulation for very young children has little to do with subsequent school-age literacy. However, according to the National Research Council (1998), children learn academic skills along a developmental continuum that begins in infancy. The verbal ritual, This Little Piggy, begins the language-learning process that later will form the foundation of literacy expressed as reading and writing. To support emergent literacy in young children with disabilities, professionals and family members should do the following (Bingham & Pennington,

To support cognitive development, ECSE professionals teach turn-taking using a child's interests.

2007; Hanline, 2001; Roskos, Christie, & Richgels, 2003):

❑ Offer children abundant exposure to books and other printed materials, such as pointing out print in the environment (e.g., grocery lists, mail) and encouraging children to read along on parts of books they remember.

❑ Offer repeated interaction with writing materials and their use, such as dictating a child's message on grandmother's birthday card.

❑ Offer varied experiences that promote vocabulary development and oral language skills, such as focusing on important vocabulary and reviewing new words frequently when stories are read (e.g., "Remember that *huge* means very, very big!").

❑ Encourage development of the alphabetic principle by pointing out letter names and sounds.

Research has found that children with disabilities may have less stimulating literacy environments at home and in preschool than children without disabilities do (Marvin & Miranda, 1994). Professionals need to remind themselves and parents that today's developmental tasks,

such as filling a plastic bottle with dried beans, are preparing a child for the fine motor dexterity needed later for writing. *All* early developmental tasks support literacy skills children are expected to master once they enter school.

Preschoolers can learn the alphabet by being asked to pick out the letter on a recipe card that matches the first letter of their names (uppercase and lowercase), and with time, some may learn to read high-frequency words, such as *stir*, *spoon*, and *cup*.

Number and Number Sense. Preschoolers with delayed development require a good deal of experience to develop beginning skills in the concept of number. Frequent experiences involving comparison and counting in ways that are developmentally meaningful are required. For example, in preparing for snack, a teacher can require children to touch each napkin as they count them, teaching **one-to-one correspondence**. Rote counting can be taught by counting the number of milk containers going into the trash. Children can be offered turns for cleaning up based on who is "first," "second," and "third." The more actively children participate, the more meaningful their understanding of the preliteracy concept will be.

Story Time for Toddlers and Preschoolers. Story time offers an engaging context for teaching many cognitive and preacademic skills to toddlers and preschoolers. However, story time is a language-loaded activity that can be challenging to young children with cognitive and/or communication disabilities and/or delays. Teachers, and parents, may need to modify how they read stories to make them more developmentally appropriate for children with special needs. The following recommendations may help:

❑ *Unless children have the communicative and cognitive skills to benefit from it, avoid reading stories verbatim.* As children's attention begins to fade, try telling the story instead of reading it. This way a teacher can adjust the vocabulary and the length of the story to better match children's attention and abilities.

❑ *Give children a purpose for listening.* As stated before, children have to be actively involved in a task or activity to learn from it and to continue to pay attention. Listening alone may not be active enough for young children with special needs. Allow children to physically participate in stories by pretending to perform the actions of the characters. That is, when a character eats cereal in the book, ask the children to pretend they are eating cereal, too. When a story is about baby animals, ask the children to cry like a baby every time they hear the word *baby*.

❑ *Make stories more concrete by using props.* If the story is about a camel, glue pictures of a camel to popsicle sticks and give one to each child. Whenever the camel in the story does something, ask the children to make their camel do the same thing. Or have a plastic or stuffed camel that can be given to any child who is struggling to attend. These props are called holding materials. **Holding materials** give a child a reason to stay with the group without disrupting the story or the other children who are engaged in the story.

❑ *Re-read books to build vocabulary, to increase interest and to improve comprehension.* Children

with delayed communication can answer questions in more complex ways after they have read a story more than one time. Further, familiar stories tend to better hold the attention of children with delayed development. Making a copy of the story to send home for parents to read will also increase attention and build vocabulary when the story is read again at school.

❑ *Use a high rate of choral responding.* Choral responding requires children to give a verbal response (or approximation) in unison to a teacher's verbal model. This strategy is based on the premise that when presenting new material, teachers should "provide children with obligatory response situations within instructional arrangements that promote numerous response opportunities with clear reinforcement criteria" (Santos, Lignugaris-Kraft, & Akers, 1997, p. 15). In other words, while reading *Russ and the Almost Perfect Day* (Rickett, 2000), which follows Russ, who has Down syndrome, through his day at school, the teacher can pause periodically and say, "What kind of day was Russ having? [pause] Say, a very good day!" Often even children who are not verbal will attempt to vocally participate, since the required verbal response is modeled.

❑ *Structure a high rate of child-to-child verbal interaction.* Stop frequently to ask one child to tell another child something about the story. For instance, "Miquela, tell Becky what color Russ's shoes are in this picture. . . . Miquela, look at Becky when you speak to her, please."

The way professionals organize classroom activities can influence children's success (Bruns & Pierce, 2007). Instruction should begin just below a child's current developmental level to ensure success and then gradually move toward more complex skills. Activities should teach prerequisite skills first, followed by structured opportunities for learning target skills (International Reading Association, 2004). Tasks should begin with a review and then move from concrete to abstract, from rote learning to problem solving, and from the familiar to the unfamiliar. A good curriculum is an essential ingredient for any pre-school program. But it must be coupled with sound, empirically-based teaching strategies that promote each child's individual mastery of skills.

Promoting Cognitive Development and Academic Learning in Primary-Aged Students

The cognitive functioning of primary-aged students is reflected in their ability to learn academic subjects. Reading and mathematics tend to be most problematic for students with special needs in inclusive or separate/self-contained classrooms. Some of the ways to teach reading and mathematics to students experiencing mild learning challenges will be discussed.

Reading Instruction

To teach reading effectively, it is helpful to understand the general organization of how reading is learned, and the subskills involved in the process of reading. The National Reading Panel report entitled *Teaching Children to Read: An Evidence-Based Assessment of the Scientific Research Literature on Reading and Its Implications for Reading Instruction* (National Institute of Child Health and Human Development, 2000) synthesized research on methodologies of reading instruction and provided an overview of the most effective strategies teachers use. The importance of phonemic awareness, phonics, fluency, and comprehension was highlighted in the report. Each will be discussed briefly.

Phonemic Awareness. **Phonemic awareness** is the understanding that speech and words can be broken into smaller units of sound (Blachman, 2000; Lane & Pullen, 2004). One important phonemic awareness skill is blending sounds together. Given two parts of a word (*tea-cher*), a student blends those syllables together to read the word *teacher*.

Phonemic awareness is critical in learning to read and is required for children to learn to decode—that is, to "sound out" unfamiliar words (Bruns & Pierce, 2007; Snow, Burns, & Griffin, 1998). A lack of phonemic awareness typically results in difficulty acquiring reading skills. The National Reading Panel (National Institute of Child Health and Human Development, 2000) concluded that (1) phonemic awareness instruction helps children learn to read and spell and (2) phonemic awareness instruction is most effective when it focuses on only one or two types of phoneme (sound) manipulations, rather than on several types.

Phonics. One of the most common difficulties for children in learning to read is decoding unknown words in print. **Phonics instruction** involves systematically teaching letters and sounds—as well as how those letters and sounds go together to form words by blending, segmenting, and manipulating sounds—all of which are involved in teaching the alphabetic system. Knowing how to decode unknown words in print is necessary to gain meaning from what is read.

Fluency. **Reading fluency** involves three characteristics: (1) accurate recognition of words, (2) an appropriate rate or speed that facilitates understanding, and (3) prosody, or reading with expression and appropriate intonation (Hudson, Lane, & Pullen, 2005). To read fluently, a child must be able to read smoothly and to decode unknown words quickly. Reading fluency is highly correlated with reading comprehension and thus is necessary for a student's overall reading achievement. Fluency is an area of reading instruction that has been neglected in many primary classrooms. The National Reading Panel (National Institute of Child Health and Human Development, 2000) concluded the following: (1) Repeated and monitored oral reading improves reading fluency and overall reading achievement, and (2) no research evidence currently confirms that instructional time spent on silent, independent reading with minimal guidance and feedback improves reading fluency and overall reading achievement.

Reading and mathematics instruction with primary-aged students with learning and/or behavior needs must incorporate active student responding to enhance engagement and learning.

Comprehension. Reading comprehension is the ultimate goal of all reading instruction. Although much of the focus in the primary grades is on mastering the code, attention to comprehension should not be neglected and should be taught directly (Armbruster et al., 2001; National Institute of Child Health and Human Development, 2000). This is particularly important for students in the primary grades who are experiencing reading difficulties.

Models of Reading Instruction

Reading skills are typically taught in the primary grades using one of two approaches: a code-emphasis approach or a meaning-emphasis approach. As suggested by the names of the approaches, the code-emphasis approach emphasizes the importance of learning to decode effectively and efficiently. In the meaning-emphasis approach, comprehension is stressed, and word recognition is taught through whole-word methods and the use of context (Mercer & Pullen, 2005). These approaches differ in the skills they emphasize and when certain skills are introduced.

Code-Emphasis Programs. These programs begin by teaching letter sounds in a systematic way. For example, high-frequency letters are taught first, and the most common sound for each letter is taught before less common sounds for the same letter. First-grade students might first be taught the letter sound /s/, followed other high-frequency letter sounds, such as /a/ and then /m/. After learning those three letter sounds, students learn how to blend the sounds together to form words, such as *am* and *Sam*. Students practice reading passages that contain the letters and letter sounds they have been taught. The advantage to the code-emphasis approach is that it enables students to decode words that they have not yet encountered.

Meaning-Emphasis Programs. This approach teaches high-frequency sight words first. When students encounter an unknown word in text, they are encouraged to use multiple sources of information, such as the context and pictures, to determine what the word is. Decoding is not emphasized. In the prepared passages that students practice reading, words are not controlled by the letters and letter sounds students have learned. Letters and letter sounds are taught incidentally, rather than through direct instruction and systematically.

Research confirms that the code-emphasis programs are more effective in teaching students to decode (Bond & Dykstra, 1967; Chall, 1983; National Institute for Child Health and Human Development, 2000). Early systematic instruction in phonics results in earlier mastery of decoding skills than does less-systematic phonics instruction (National Institute for Child Health and Human Development, 2000). Without effective word-recognition and decoding skills, students are not able to comprehend what they read. Consequently, developing effective decoding skills is a necessary step in the acquisition of reading comprehension and other higher-level reading processes (Hammill, 2004; Mercer & Pullen, 2005).

Teaching Reading Skills to Primary-Aged Students.
In a comprehensive reading program, instruction is usually based on a core reading program. A core reading program, also called a basal program, provides teachers with an organized scope and sequence for teaching reading mastery that builds from one year to the next. These programs include objectives, strategies, lessons, and assessments, following a sequence developed by the reading program. Each lesson of a reading program tends to follow this sequence to develop mastery: (1) The teacher demonstrates a skill ("I do it" step), (2) the teacher and the child practice the skill together ("We do it" step), and (3) the child independently demonstrates the skill ("You do it" step) (Bruns & Pierce, 2007).

Although the core program is the basis for reading instruction in the primary grades, supplementary activities can also help create a rich literacy program. The following sections provide examples of motivating activities for teaching reading to students with special needs in general education or self-contained classrooms.

Teaching Phonemic Awareness. Activities to promote the development of phonemic awareness should be integrated into all activities throughout the school day. Activities that allow children to practice blending and segmenting phonemes are the most

valuable because children require those skills to learn how to decode words. In general, the more concrete a skill can be made, the more effectively students who are experiencing difficulties will be in learning the skill (Foorman, 2007). For example, using manipulative objects can help children learn sound/phoneme awareness. Elkonin (1963) suggested a strategy in which children put chips into boxes to count the sounds in words. Students may be shown a picture of a hat. Underneath the hat would be three connected boxes (see Figure 6.2). Students would then push one chip into each box for each sound they hear, /h/, /a/, /t/. After students become facile using chips to represent the sounds in the boxes, they can begin using letters to represent the sounds (Lane & Pullen, 2004). Once teachers add letters to a phonemic awareness activity, the activity becomes phonics.

Teaching Phonics. The use of manipulative letters can be a valuable supplemental activity to teach decoding skills to students who are slow in developing reading skills (Pullen, Lane, Lloyd, Nowak, & Ryals, 2005). To do this, ECSE professionals select target words from required reading material. Students begin the activity by spelling a target word with the manipulative letters (simple plastic magnetic letters work well). Then students are asked to change the word, one sound at a time. For example, if the target word is *play*, a teacher may ask the students to change *play* to *clay*. The activity continues as students manipulate the letters in the word to create new words, blending and segmenting each new word. This concrete practice with blending and segmenting words helps students gain the automaticity with decoding skills that is necessary for fluent reading.

Teaching Fluency. A proven strategy to improve fluency is **assisted repeated reading.** The teacher selects a short passage that is at the student's independent reading level (e.g., a passage a student can read with at least 95% accuracy). The teacher asks the student to read the passage aloud, providing feedback as needed, and documents the number of correct words the student could read

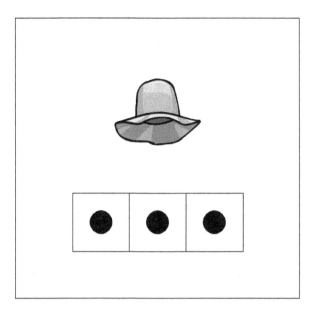

Figure 6.2 Phonemic activity card teaching the individual sounds of the word hat

per minute. The following day the student reads the same passage again. After each reading, the student's reading rate and accuracy are likely to increase. To monitor the student's progress, the student graphs his or her reading rate per minute each day so that improvement is visible, and concrete, for the student. Once a fluency rate goal is reached with a passage, the strategy is used with a new passage.

Monitoring Reading Progress

It is critical to monitor students' progress to determine whether or not they are benefiting from reading interventions. For example, aspects of early literacy development may be assessed using the *Comprehensive Test of Phonological Processing* (CTOPP) (Wagner, Torgesen, & Rashotte, 1999), which assesses phonological awareness and knowledge, phonological memory, and rapid naming. The *Monitoring Basic Skills Progress: Basic Reading* (MBSP) (Fuchs, Hamlett, & Fuchs, 1997) is a computerized assessment that provides teachers with class and individual reports with which

to monitor progress and plan instruction. Students with learning or reading disabilities require intensive, individualized, and specialized reading instruction to improve their skills (Nelson, Benner, & Gonzalez, 2003). These students have similar needs if they are experiencing difficulties with mathematics.

Teaching Mathematics

As in the teaching of reading, the effective teaching of mathematics requires an understanding of the knowledge children should obtain. Fortunately, recent documents have synthesized the research on effective teaching of mathematics to young learners. The National Research Council (NRC) report *Adding It Up: Helping Children Learn Mathematics* (2001) provides an overview of the mathematical knowledge children should acquire. According to the NRC report, mathematics proficiency includes (1) conceptual understanding, (2) procedural fluency, (3) strategic competence, (4) adaptive reasoning, and (5) productive disposition. Each strand is briefly described.

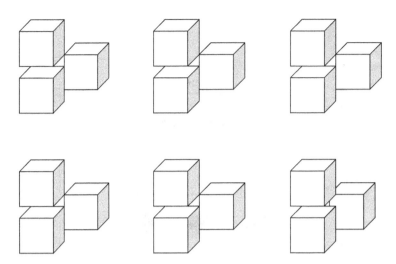

Figure 6.3 Pictorial representation of the multiplication problem 6 × 3 (6 groups of 3 cubes)

Conceptual Understanding. Conceptual understanding refers to the comprehension of mathematical concepts, operations, and relations. In other words, students' knowledge must be deeper than rote memorization of facts or of procedural algorithms. Although children in the primary grades may not be able to verbalize their understanding of a concept, their ability to represent problems in various ways demonstrates their understanding. For example, when learning multiplication, rather than simply stating the rote fact that 6 × 3 = 18, a child needs to demonstrate with manipulative materials what the problem represents (see Figure 6.3). Students may also create a story to describe the problem (e.g., "Each of six children received 3 pieces of candy. All together, they had 18 pieces of candy.").

Procedural Fluency. This refers to a student's understanding of the what, why, when, and how of mathematics procedures. Students must possess an understanding of procedures that allows for efficient and flexible use of procedures (National Research Council, 2001). Procedural fluency is aided by a student's conceptual knowledge. For instance, in order to perform basic computations, particularly multidigit computations efficiently, a solid understanding of place value is

required. Procedural fluency means that students do not need to rely on one particular algorithm, but rather possess multiple means of arriving at solutions quickly and accurately.

Strategic Competence. A student's skill in accurately representing and then solving a problem makes up strategic competence. Each day adults encounter situations in which they are required to use their mathematical knowledge to solve problems. In real-life situations, problems are not presented in a number sentence. Students who have strategic competence are able to solve real-world problems by representing a problem (often with a number sentence) and then solving it correctly (Kolb & Stuart, 2005).

Adaptive Reasoning. This is the ability to think logically about the relationships among concepts and situations (National Research Council, 2001). One way young children demonstrate their adaptive reasoning is by verbalizing how they solved a given problem. For example, in the strategy "Tell me how you know . . . ," students solve problems that have multiple paths to the correct answer. The child is provided paper, pencil, manipulative materials such as counting bears, and a calculator and can use any combination of materials to solve the problem. After the problem is solved, the child writes support for his or her answer in a journal. A child may also tell others how he or she solved the problem, using a strategy called "Think aloud" or verbal rehearsal, which aids memory (Hughes, 1996). This activity gives teachers an insight into children's adaptive reasoning and clarifies areas that need to be retaught when there are problems.

Productive Disposition. This involves a student's perception that mathematics is functional and valuable and that he or she can be successful at mathematics. Unfortunately, early failure with mathematics may lead students with special needs to develop a negative mathematics disposition. It is critical during the primary grades that children experience many successes to increase the chances they will develop a productive disposition.

Approaches to Teaching Mathematics

Like reading instruction, mathematics instruction should be based on empirical research and employ empirically supported practices. One approach common to mathematics instruction is the basal approach. In the basal approach, a core curriculum for primary mathematics instruction is adopted by the school system. Like a core reading program, the mathematics basal program provides an organized scope and sequence of skills to be taught, provides summative and formative assessments, presents a set of learning objectives, and offers activities and lessons to support students' learning of the objectives. An advantage of the basal approach is that it is organized systematically to ensure that new skills are built on previously learned skills and that the content for a specific grade level is addressed.

Some schools and districts do not rely on a basal approach, so teachers plan for instruction without a scope and sequence being provided to them. The content that is taught may be organized into units of study. Whether professionals are using a basal mathematics program or a teacher- or school system–developed program, each will teach the following skills from the major areas of mathematics: numeration and

number sense, operations of whole numbers, fractions and decimals, measurement, and geometry. Each area is discussed.

Numeration and Number Sense. This involves an understanding of our number system and place value. Instruction helps students learn skills such as counting, the representation of numbers in words or in symbols, and general place value concepts.

Operations of Whole Numbers. This involves algorithms for solving major operations of whole numbers, including addition, subtraction, multiplication, and division. Beyond the basic facts, children must gain computational fluency. That is, professionals must teach students how to perform mental mathematics and think flexibly about computation (Kolb & Stuart, 2005).

Fractions and Decimals. In this area of mathematics, students gain conceptual knowledge of part and whole relationships. The content taught includes fractions, mixed numbers, decimals, equivalent fractions, and problems that involve fractions or decimals.

Measurement. Measurement is a critical part of our everyday lives. To develop measurement skills, teachers present concepts relating to measuring length, volume, weight, time, and money. In addition to developing an understanding of these concepts, students need to be able to generalize their conceptual knowledge of whole numbers, decimals, and fractions and apply that knowledge to measurement techniques. Measurement of time and money tends to be challenging for students with learning and behavioral problems.

Geometry. This involves the study of geometric figures and spatial relations. Concepts such as symmetry are taught.

Reading problems, poorly developed logical reasoning skills, and instruction that focuses primarily on computation contribute to difficulty with mathematical problem solving (Ginsburg, 1997). Many students with learning and behavioral problems may also have difficulty sustaining attention and working carefully during mathematics instruction and may need additional help in learning problem-solving strategies. As with instruction in reading, when professionals teach specific skills using manipulatives to make the concepts less abstract, students with mathematics problems tend to learn more efficiently.

CONCLUSION

Research with typically developing children demonstrates that their perceptual and cognitive capabilities are well organized. Many consider reasoning and learning to be active processes that rely on appropriate environmental opportunities for their development. The Lawrence family, featured in the case study, found that the guidance they received from the ECSE staff helped them structure learning experiences for Mindy that improved her problem-solving, reasoning, pre-academic, and academic skills. For primary-aged students with learning and/or behavioral difficulties, intensive, individualized and specialized reading and mathematics instruction is necessary to allow these students to realize their potential.

SUMMARY

Theories of cognitive development and learning

- Attention, discrimination, and memory influence how children think, reason, and learn from their environment and experiences.

The effects of early experience

- Appropriate and stimulating early experiences and intervention can produce positive outcomes in children with developmental delays and/or disabilities.

Promoting cognitive development in infants, toddlers, and preschoolers

- To facilitate optimal cognitive development, professionals and parents may (1) use a child's interests and teach through play, (2) teach turn taking, (3) introduce new skills into familiar routines and use new routines for generalization, and (4) promote literacy awareness.

- To ensure that story time facilitates cognitive development in toddlers and preschoolers and is developmentally appropriate, parents and professionals must (1) when appropriate, avoid reading stories verbatim; (2) give children a purpose for listening; (3) provide props to make the story more concrete; (4) re-read books to build vocabulary and interest and to improve comprehension; (5) use choral responding; and (6) structure child-to-child verbal interactions.

Promoting cognitive development and academic learning in primary-aged students

- Professionals use manipulatives and varied practice to teach reading—including phonemic awareness, phonics, reading fluency, and comprehension—to students with learning challenges.
- Students with learning and behavior problems require the use of manipulatives and additional, intensive practice to develop skills in mathematics.

DISCUSSION QUESTIONS/ACTIVITIES

1) Explain how matching, sorting, classification, and seriation differ, and describe how you would arrange learning opportunities to teach these concepts to Mindy (see the case study) when she was 4–5 years old.

2) You have noticed that the general education teacher in a kindergarten class is having difficulty maintaining the attention of two children with delayed communicative and cognitive skills during story time. Discuss two suggestions you might offer this teacher to improve the developmental appropriateness of this activity for these children and increase their attention.

3) As an ECSE teacher, you have been assigned to coteach in a general education first-grade classroom for your first teaching experience. The class of 18 children has 5 children with special needs who have IEPs. Discuss how you will ensure that you provide a comprehensive preliteracy/literacy program to your students, not merely teach isolated reading or mathematic skills.

REFERENCES

Alberto, P., & Troutman, A. (2006). *Applied behavior analysis for teachers* (7th ed.). Upper Saddle River, NJ: Merrill/Prentice Hall.

Ambron, S. R. (1975). *Child development*. San Francisco: Rinehart Press.

Armbruster, B. B., Lehr, F., & Osborn, J. (2001). *Put reading first: The research building blocks for teaching children to read*. Washington, DC: National Institute of Child Health and Human Development and U.S. Department of Education.

Bandura, A. (1977). *Social learning theory*. Upper Saddle River, NJ: Prentice Hall.

Bandura, A. (1993). Perceived self-efficacy in cognitive development and functioning. *Educational Psychologist, 28*, 117–148.

Bayley, N. (1993). *Bayley scales of infant development, Second Edition*. San Antonio, TX: Psychological Corp.

Beck, I., McKeown, M. G., & Kucan, L. (2002). *Bringing words to life: Robust vocabulary development*. New York: Guilford Press.

Bertenthal, B. (1996). Origins and early development of perception, action, and representation. *Annual Review of Psychology, 47*, 332–354.

Bingham, A., & Pennington, J. (2007). As easy as ABC: Facilitating early literacy enrichment experiences. *Young Exceptional Child, 10*(2), 17–29.

Blachman, B. A. (2000). Phonological awareness. In M. Kamil, P. Mosenthal, P. Pearson, & R. Barr (Eds.), *Handbook of reading research* (Vol. 3, pp. 483–502). Mahwah, NJ: Erlbaum.

Bond, G. L., & Dykstra, R. (1967). The cooperative research program in first-grade reading instruction. *Reading Research Quarterly, 2*, 130–141.

Bradley, R., Whiteside, L., Mundfrom, D., Casey, P., Kelleher, K., & Pope, S. (1994). Early indications of resilience and their relation to experience in the home environments of low birthweight, premature children living in poverty. *Child Development, 65*(2), 346–360.

Bricker, D., Cripe, J., & Slentz, K. (2002). *AEPS curriculum for birth to three years*. Baltimore, MD: Brookes.

Bricker, D., McComas, N., Pretti-Frontczak, K., Leve, C., Stieber, S., Losardo, A., & Scanlon, J. (1997). *Activity-based collaboration project: A nondirected model demonstration program for children who are at-risk disabled and their families*. Unpublished report, University of Oregon, Center on Human Development, Early Intervention Program.

Bruns, D., & Pierce, C. (2007). Let's read together: Tools for early literacy development for all young children. *Young Exceptional Children, 19*(2), 2–10.

Chall, J. S. (1983). *Stages of reading development*. New York: McGraw-Hill.

Dale, P., & Cole, K. (1988). Academically based and cognitively based programs for young handicapped children: A comparative evaluation. *Exceptional Children, 54*, 439–447.

Dale, P., Jenkins, J., Mills, P., & Cole, K. (2005). Follow-up of children from academic and cognitive preschool curricula at 12 and 16. *Exceptional Children, 71*, 301–317.

DeThorne, L., & Watkins, R. (2001). Five tools for teaching vocabulary in the preschool classroom. In Ostrosky, M. & Sandall, S. *Teaching strategies: What to do to support young children's development (YEC Monograph No. 3)* (pp. 37–46). Longmont, CO: Sopris West.

Dunst, C. J. (1981). *Infant learning: A cognitive—linguistic intervention strategy*. Hingham, MA: Teaching Resources Corp.

Dunst, C. J. (2001). Participation of young children with disabilities in community learning activities. In M. J. Guralnick (Ed.), *Early childhood inclusion: Focus on change* (pp. 307–333). Baltimore: Brookes.

Elkonin, D. B. (1963). The psychology of mastering the elements of reading. In B. Simon & J. Simon (Eds.), *Educational psychology in the U.S.S.R.* (pp. 165–179). Stanford, CA: Stanford University Press.

Ferster, C., Culbertson, S., & Boren, M. (1975). *Behavior principles* (2nd ed.). Upper Saddle River, NJ: Prentice Hall.

Fewell, R. C., & Deutscher, B. (2004). Contributions of early language and maternal facilitation variables to later language and reading abilities. *Journal of Early Intervention, 26*(2), 132–145.

Foorman, B. (2007). Primary prevention in classroom reading instruction. *Teaching Exceptional Children, 39*(5), 24–31.

Fuchs, L. S., Hamlett, C. L., & Fuchs, D. (1997). *Monitoring basic skills progress: Basic reading, Second Edition*. Austin, TX: PRO-ED.

Furuno, S., O'Reilly, A., Hosaka, C., Inatsuka, T., Allman, T., & Zeisloft, B. (1979). *The Hawaii early learning profile and activity guide*. Palo Alto, CA: VORT.

Ginsburg, H. (1997). Mathematics learning disabilities: A view from developmental psychology. *Journal of Learning Disabilities, 30*(1), 20–33.

Gray, C. (2002). *My social stories*. London: Jessica Kingsley.

Gredler, M. (2001). *Learning and instruction: Theory into practice*. Upper Saddle River, NJ: Merrill/Prentice Hall.

Guerette, P., Tefft, D., Furumasu, J., & Moy, F. (1999). Development of a cognitive assessment battery for young children with physical impairments. *Infant-Toddler Intervention, 9*(2), 169–184.

Hack, M., Taylor, H., Drotar, D., Schluchter, M., Cartar, L., Wilson-Costello, D., Klein, N., Friedman, H., Mercuri-Minich, N., & Morrow, M. (2005). Poor predictive validity of the Bayley Scales of Infant Development for cognitive functioning of extremely low birthweight children at school age. *Pediatrics, 116*(2), 333–341.

Halle, J., Alpert, C., & Anderson, S. (1984). Natural environment language assessment and intervention with severely impaired preschoolers. *Topics in Early Childhood Special Education, 4,* 36–56.

Hammill, D. D. (2004). What we know about correlates of reading. *Exceptional Children, 70,* 453–468.

Hanline, M. (2001). Supporting emergent literacy in play-based activities. *Young Exceptional Children, 4*(4), 10–15.

Hanline, M., Milton, S., & Phelps, P. (2001). Young children's block construction activities: Findings from 3 years of observation. *Journal of Early Intervention, 24*(3), 224–237.

Harvey, S., & Goudvis, A. (2000). *Strategies that work: Teaching comprehension to enhance understanding.* Portland, ME: Stenhouse.

Howe, M. L., & Courage, M. L. (1997). Independent paths in the development of infant learning and forgetting. *Journal of Experimental Child Psychology, 67*(2), 131–163.

Hudson, R. F., Lane, H. B., & Pullen, P. C. (2005). Reading fluency: What, why, and how? *Reading Teacher, 54,* 702–714.

Hughes, C. (1996). Memory and test-taking strategies. In D. D. Deshler, E. Ellis, & B. Lenz (Eds.), *Teaching adolescents with learning disabilities: Strategies and methods* (2nd ed., pp. 209–266). Denver, CO: Love.

Huston, A. C. (1994). Children in poverty: Designing research to affect policy. *Society for Research in Child Development, 8*(2), 1–15.

International Reading Association. (2004). *Literacy development in the preschool years: A position statement of the International Reading Association.* Newark, NJ: Author.

Johnson—Martin, N., Attermeier, S., & Hacker, B. (2004). *The Carolina Curriculum for Infants and Toddlers with Special Needs* (3rd ed.). Baltimore: Brookes.

Johnson-Martin, N., Hacker, B., & Attermeier, S. (2004). *The Carolina curriculum for preschoolers with special needs* (2nd ed.). Baltimore: Brookes.

Justice, L. M., & Pullen, P. C. (2003). Promising interventions for promoting emergent literacy skills: Three evidence-based approaches. *Topics in Early Childhood Special Education, 23,* 99–113.

Keogh, B., Coots, J., & Bernheimer, L. (1995). School placement of children with nonspecific developmental delays. *Journal of Early Intervention, 20*(1), 65–97.

Kolb, S. M., & Stuart, S. (2005). Active problem solving: A model for empowerment. *Teaching Exceptional Children, 38*(2), 14–20.

Lane, H., & Pullen, P. (2004). *Phonological awareness assessment and instruction: A sound beginning.* Boston: Allyn & Bacon.

Langley, M. B. (1989). Assessing infant cognitive development. In D. Bailey & M. Wolery (Eds.), *Assessing infants and preschoolers with handicaps* (pp. 249–274). Upper Saddle River, NJ: Merrill/Prentice Hall.

La Paro, K., Olsen, K., & Pianta, R. (2002). Special education eligibility: Developmental precursors over the first three years of life. *Exceptional Children, 69*(1), 55–66.

Lockman, J. J. (1983). Infant perception and cognition. In S. G. Garwood & R. R. Fewell (Eds.), *Educating handicapped infants: Issues in development and intervention* (pp. 117–164). Rockville, MD: Aspen.

Losardo, A., & Bricker, D. (1994). Activity-based intervention and direction instruction: A comparison study. *American Journal on Mental Retardation, 98*(6), 744–765.

Mahoney, G. (1988). Communication patterns between mothers and mentally retarded infants. *First Language, 8*(23), 157–171.

Mahoney, G., Finger, I., & Powell, A. (1985). Relationship of maternal behavioral style to the development of organically impaired mentally retarded infants. *American Journal of Mental Deficiency, 90,* 296–302.

Marvin, C., & Miranda, P. (1994). Literacy practices in Head Start and early childhood special education classrooms. *Early Education and Development, 5*(2), 289–300.

Mayes, S. D. (1997). Potential scoring problems using the Bayley Scales of Infant Development–11 Mental Scale. *Journal of Early Intervention, 21*(1), 36–44.

McLean, M., Wolery, M., & Bailey, D. (2004). *Assessing infants and preschoolers with special needs* (3rd ed.). Upper Saddle River, NJ: Merrill/Prentice Hall.

McWilliam, R., & Bailey, D. (1995). Effects of classroom social structure and disability on engagement. *Topics in Early Childhood Special Education, 15*(2), 123–147.

Mercer, C. D., & Pullen, P. C. (2005). *Students with learning disabilities* (6th ed.). Upper Saddle River, NJ: Merrill/Prentice Hall.

Moran, D., & Whitman, T. (1985). The multiple effects of a play—oriented parent training program for mothers of developmentally delayed children. *Analysis and Intervention in Developmental Disabilities, 5*, 73–96.

National Institute of Child Health and Human Development. (2000). *Teaching children to read: An evidence-based assessment of the scientific research literature on reading and its implications for reading instruction: Reports of the subgroups* (Report of the National Reading Panel, NIH Publication No. 00-4754). Washington, DC: U.S. Government Printing Office.

National Research Council. (1998). *Preventing reading difficulties in young children.* Washington, DC: National Academy Press.

National Research Council. (2001). *Adding it up: Helping children learn mathematics.* Washington, DC: National Academy Press.

Nelson, C., & Bosquet, M. (2000). Neurobiology of fetal and infant development: Implications for infant mental health. In C. Zeanah (Ed.), *Handbook of infant mental health* (2nd ed., pp. 37–59). New York: Guilford Press.

Nelson, J., Benner, G., & Gonzalez, J. (2003). Learner characteristics that influence the treatment effectiveness of early literacy interventions: A metacognitive review. *Learning Disabilities Research and Practice, 18*, 255–267.

Nelson, N. (1988). *Planning individualized speech and language intervention programs: Objectives for infants, children and adolescents.* Tucson, AZ: Communication Skill Builders.

Newborg, J. (2004). *The Battelle Developmental Inventory–2.* Chicago: Riverside.

Park, J., Turnbull, A., & Turnbull, H. R. (2002). Impacts of poverty and quality of life on families of children with disabilities. *Exceptional Children, 68*(2), 151–170.

Piaget, J. (1951). *Play, dreams and imitation in childhood.* New York: Norton.

Piaget, J. (1952). *The origins of intelligence in children.* New York: International Universities Press.

Piaget, J. (1957). *Logic and psychology.* New York: Basic Books.

Piaget, J., & Inhelder, B. (1969). *The psychology of the child.* New York: Basic Books.

Pretti-Frontczak, K., & Bricker, D. (2004). *An activity-based approach to early intervention* (3rd ed.). Baltimore, MD: Brookes.

Pullen, P. C., Lane, H. B., Lloyd, J. W., Nowak, R., & Ryals, J. (2005). Effects of explicit instruction on decoding of struggling first grade students: A data-based case study. *Education and Treatment of Children, 28*, 63–76.

Ramey, C., Ramey, S., Gaines, K., & Blair, C. (1995). Two-generation early intervention programs: A child development perspective. In S. Smith (Ed.), *Advances in applied developmental psychology: Vol. 9. Two generation programs for families in poverty: A new intervention strategy.* Norwood, NJ: Ablex.

Raver, S. (1999). *Intervention strategies for infants and toddlers with special needs: A team approach* (2nd ed.). Upper Saddle River, NJ: Merrill/Prentice Hall.

Rickett, J. E. (2000). *Russ and the almost perfect day.* Bethesda, MD: Woodbine House.

Rogers, S., Donovan, C., D'Eugenio, D., Brown, S., Lynch, E., Moersch, M., & Schafer, S. (1981). *Early intervention development profile (revised).* Ann Arbor: University of Michigan Press.

Roskos, K., Christie, J., & Richgels, D. (2003). *The essentials of early literacy instruction.* Retrieved June 30, 2006, from http://naeyc.org/resources/journal

Santos, R., Lignugaris-Kraft, B., & Akers, J. (2000). Tips on planning center time activities for preschool classrooms. *Young Exceptional Children, 2*(4), 9–16.

Schwethelm, B., & Mahoney, G. (1986). Task persistence among organically impaired mentally retarded children. *American Journal of Mental Deficiency, 90*, 432–439.

Snow, C. E., Burns, S., & Griffin, P. (Eds.). (1998). *Preventing reading difficulties in young children.* Washington, DC: National Academy Press.

Snyder, P., Lawson, S., Thompson, B., Stricklin, S., & Sexton, D. (1993). Evaluating the psychometric integrity of instruments used in early intervention research: The Battelle Developmental Inventory. *Topics in Early Childhood Special Education, 13*(2), 216–232.

Strain, P., McConnell, S., Carta, J., Fowler, S., Neisworth, J., & Wolery, M. (1992). Behaviorism in early intervention. *Topics in Early Childhood Special Education, 12*(1), 121–141.

Torgesen, J. (2002). The prevention of reading difficulties. *Journal of School Psychology, 40*, 7–26.

Wagner, R. K., Torgesen, J. K., & Rashotte, C. A. (1999). *Comprehensive Test of Phonological Processing.* Austin, TX: PRO-ED.

Wechsler, D. (1989). *Wechsler Preschool and Primary Scale of Intelligence—Revised.* San Antonio, TX: Psychological Corp.

Wechsler, D. (2003). *Wechsler Intelligence Scale for Children, Fourth Edition.* San Antonio, TX: Psychological Corp.

Zeanah, C. (Ed). (2000). *Handbook of infant mental health* (2nd ed.). New York: Guilford Press.

Chapter
7

Promoting Fine and Gross Motor and Adaptive Skills Development

Toby M. Long

M. Janet Thomas

Jamie M. Hall

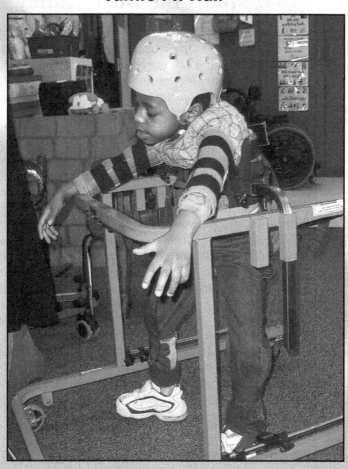

Overview

This chapter examines practices for supporting motor and adaptive development, including

theories of fine and gross motor development

treatment models

service delivery models

assessment practices

characteristics of children with physical disabilities

therapeutic intervention strategies

promoting adaptive skills development

assistive technology

CASE STUDY: The Bolle Family

Michael Bolle was born after a 25-week gestation period and weighed 920 grams (a little more than 2 pounds). He was the third child of a two-parent, professional family. Neonatal complications included respiratory distress syndrome and stage 1 retinopathy of prematurity (ROP) (see Chapter 12 for the definition). Michael was also intubated for several months. He was irritable and tolerated only minimal handling.

Michael was discharged at 6 months of age, requiring 24-hour nursing care and 24-hour oxygen therapy. He began receiving early intervention services as soon as he was home. Collaborating with the family, the infant-toddler program developed a flexible Individualized Family Service Plan, guided by Michael's changing health needs and his family's needs. Because of Michael's significant motor delays, the physical therapist served as the primary service provider and service coordinator. She helped the family discover efficient ways to comfort and console Michael, suggested oral feeding techniques, and encouraged play. She consulted regularly with the family, a community health nurse, and the family's part-time childcare provider.

At 16 months old, Michael was diagnosed with cerebral palsy. The physical therapist consulted with the team's occupational therapist and an assistive technology specialist to introduce switches to help Michael play independently for short periods. At 25 months old, the early intervention team began the transition process to a group daycare program.

By 3 years, Michael was attending a full-time childcare program. He was able to stand in a stander, move with a walker, pick up finger foods, and use a variety of switches to interact and play with other children. The intervention team helped the childcare staff embed therapeutic strategies into inside and outside play activities, art, and center activities and adapted a variety of materials with switches that all the children used.

When Michael transitioned to kindergarten, he was using a power-drive wheelchair and a simple computerized voice synthesizer communication device. Because the kindergarten staff were hesitant to include him due to his special devices and significant physical disabilities, his early childhood special education team consulted extensively with school staff prior to school and met regularly during the school year to support Michael's inclusion. A paraprofessional worked in the classroom to assist the teacher in adapting instruction for Michael. With continuous consultation between his teachers and therapists, Michael successfully completed first grade.

As academic demands increased, Michael's assistive technology was adapted, and his teachers were given close consultation so they felt comfortable providing the necessary technology in the general education classroom. Even with these additional adaptations and team support, it was clear that Michael needed more individualized support. In the middle of second grade, he began receiving services in a resource room for one hour a day, where he learned to organize his assignments and projects and received help with his ever-growing assistive technology. Michael's resource room teacher also had expertise in assistive technology, so he was able to adapt the general education curriculum to meet Michael's individual strengths and needs and worked daily with his general education teacher and paraprofessional. Although Michael is becoming increasingly independent, his physical disabilities will likely continue to present challenges for him. His team reports they are committed to providing Michael with the collaboration and accommodations necessary for him to continue to succeed in an inclusion program. With the unified support of his family and team, which is using a strength-based approach (see Chapter 10), Michael has become a valued part of his elementary school.

The development of efficient motor skills is an important prerequisite to cognitive, social, and communicative development in young children (Berenthal & Campos, 1987; Diamond, 2000). Environmental exploration, through controlled movement, provides the groundwork for later learning. Children with physical disabilities or motor development delays may have difficulty organizing their motor system for successful interaction with objects and people.

THEORIES OF FINE AND GROSS MOTOR DEVELOPMENT

How children develop and change has been attributed to a variety of theories. These theories try to account for the influence of factors such as genetics, experience, and culture on children's motor development changes. Three perspectives are considered the most influential and will be discussed.

Neuromaturational Theory

The neuromaturational perspective promotes the concept that as children grow and the central nervous system matures, skills will unfold in a predictable, hierarchical manner. Intervention based on this model promotes skills following a developmental sequence.

Motor Learning Theory

The motor learning-based model promotes the importance of practice for learning, retaining, and refining movements. Embedding therapy strategies into daily home and school routines ensures that skills are practiced within a meaningful context for a child (Hanft & Pilkington, 2000).

Sensorimotor Theory

The contribution of sensory processing to the development of body awareness, perception, and behavior is a foundation concept considered by therapists when promoting motor development. It is understood that information collected from the different sensory systems provides valuable input that allows children to learn more about their bodies and the environment. Providing everyday sensory experiences and opportunities helps promote foundations needed for motor planning and motor sequencing.

These three theories of development are generally incorporated into treatment choices to help young children learn to move efficiently and functionally.

TREATMENT MODELS

Although many treatment or therapeutic intervention programs are used, current practices promote the acquisition of functional movement and the importance of incorporating treatment into naturally occurring routines (Vanderhoff, 2004). Most physical therapists and occupational therapists use a combination of approaches, or a **holistic approach**. When working in a team, many therapists use an activity-based/routine-based intervention model. That is, therapeutic strategies and interventions are embedded into routines, rather than being offered only in individual therapy sessions.

Physical therapy and occupational therapy interventions have four objectives: (1) to promote active movement, (2) to promote functional skills, (3) to promote community integration, and (4) to prevent impairment. Therapists use a variety of strategies to achieve these objectives, including exercise, play, assistive technology, splinting, bracing, remediation, and the teaching of specific skills.

Approaches to Intervention

Therapists design intervention strategies to meet the specific needs of the child and the desired outcomes determined by the child's family and team. Depending on the child's needs, a therapist will often use a variety of approaches and expect to change approaches as the needs of the child change. There are four general approaches used by physical or occupational therapists.

The **remedial approach** is the most familiar to therapists, since many popular treatment strategies are based on this approach. The goal is to correct deficits that interfere with attaining typical motor skills. Therapists identify performance deficits and resolve them by promoting age-appropriate, sensorimotor abilities.

The goal of the **compensation approach** is to provide an alternative method of accomplishing a function when impairment prevents the skill or function from occurring. Assistive technology, adaptive equipment, or other devices are used to allow the child to perform a skill when the child is unable to perform it or has yet to master it. Compensation strategies help prevent further impairment or disability, such as tight muscles or scoliosis. Compensation strategies are also used to promote development. For example, providing a child who has little or no movement with a power-drive wheelchair encourages the child's independent exploration and supports the child's social and cognitive development.

In the **promotion approach**, therapists embed therapeutic interventions in natural activities and routines. The objective is to ensure that every activity the child participates in throughout the day is accomplished in a way that is beneficial, therapeutic, and functional for the child. This approach is rooted in developmentally appropriate practice (DAP) guidelines (Bredekamp & Copple, 1997), discussed in Chapter 1.

The purpose of the **prevention approach** is to avoid the development of secondary impairments or disabilities in children with known difficulties. For instance, proper positioning of a young child with cerebral palsy is used to help prevent scoliosis, joint contractures, or stiff joints, which may occur as the child grows older. All four approaches were found to benefit Michael, discussed in the case study.

Activity-Based/Routine-Based Intervention

Current practice supports embedding fine and gross motor therapeutic activities in daily routines to promote the generalization of skills in infants, toddlers, and young children. Team members, including the child's family, collaborate to develop integrated outcomes and goals, rather than establishing individual discipline- or domain-oriented goals (Bates, 2002). Physical therapists and occupational therapists work closely with families, and other professionals, to ensure that therapeutic activities are performed correctly and that regular follow-up with therapists is scheduled. Nonetheless, this orientation does not preclude a physical or an occupational professional from providing individual intervention when it is necessary and appropriate for a child.

Supports to Therapy

Because of the complexity of neuromotor dysfunctions, therapists use a variety of supports to help children move more efficiently or functionally. Assistive technology, such as a wheelchair; adaptive equipment, such as cushions and pencil grips; and orthotics (braces), such as ankle/foot orthoses and splints are frequently used. Children with spina bifida, for example, tend to be fitted with appropriate orthotics around 8 to 12 months of age when they are beginning to stand and attempting to walk. Children with significant neuromuscular disabilities such as cerebral palsy may undergo orthopedic surgeries to lengthen tendons or neurosurgery to reduce spasticity or rigidity. Today, due to expanding resources, many professionals and families are able to select a variety of services. Therapists play an important role in helping team members examine the effectiveness of available treatments.

SERVICE DELIVERY MODELS

Therapists decide on the most effective and efficient service delivery model for the child and his or her family, taking into consideration the outcomes identified by the team and the family, the strengths and needs of the child, the family's priorities, and the environment in which services will be delivered. Three models of service provision are usually offered: direct, monitoring, and consultation (Long & Sippel, 2000).

Direct Service Delivery

In the direct service delivery model, therapists provide one-to-one therapy, usually in a segregated setting such as a clinic, a specially designed room within a childcare or educational program, or a separate space within a classroom. Usually, the purpose of this model is to provide intensive, specialized remedial intervention to the child. Strategies are used to teach specific skills, introduce new behaviors or skills, change maladaptive behaviors, or increase the child's tolerance of sensorimotor experiences.

Recently, there has been a shift away from the provision of direct services for all children to integrated service delivery. **Integrated programming** is defined as individualized intervention designed to meet the unique strengths and needs of a child within an environment in which children with and without disabilities participate (Scott, McWilliam, & Mayhew, 1999). Research that has compared the benefits of integrated and direct service delivery has indicated little difference in the enhancement of skills in individual children (McWilliam, 1996).

Monitoring Service Delivery

Monitoring requires therapists to (1) design activities to be provided in a setting, (2) teach a service provider/professional (e.g., parent, childcare provider, general early childhood educator, ECSE teacher) specific methods for embedding therapeutic strategies in routines, (3) observe the service provider performing the activities and offer feedback and guidance, (4) adapt and update activities and strategies as necessary, (5) supervise the implementation of the therapeutic program, and (6) assume responsibility for documenting the child's performance.

Children and therapists benefit from the use of integrated therapy in three significant ways: (1) the amount of time a child is receiving the benefits of a therapeutic strategy is increased; (2) the strategy has an increased opportunity to promote generalization, as it is being performed within a naturally occurring activity and routine; and (3) the strategy is implemented over time, providing ongoing reinforcement of target behaviors. In the monitoring model, therapists are still highly involved in the care of a child, since they are responsible for ensuring that programming is implemented as designed and is adapted and modified as appropriate (Richardson & Schultz-Krohn, 2001).

Consultation Service Delivery

Collaborative consultation with therapists has three critical characteristics: (1) regular interaction among team members, (2) respect among team members for each other's expertise, and (3) the belief that the consultation will help reach the common goal of benefiting the child and family. As noted before, collaborative consultation recognizes that children with disabilities have complex needs that can be addressed only by creative use of all team members' expertise. Collaborative consultants are open to using various approaches to support children and families. Ideally, solutions to a child's specific challenges reflect a variety of approaches and service delivery options that may change as a child's need change.

ASSESSMENT PRACTICES

Assessment of children with atypical or delayed motor development, like that of typically developing children, may be conducted for screening, diagnosis, and/or program-planning purposes.

Screening

Screening is the first step in identifying infants, toddlers, and preschoolers who may require developmental support. Two popular screening tools are the *Denver Developmental Screening Test-II* (Frankenburg et al., 1992) and the *Ages and Stages Questionnaires* (ASQ) (Bricker & Squires, 2003). Both are considered reliable in identifying children at risk for motor delays, and they are easy to administer. The ASQ consists of a series of questions completed by family members and scored by a professional.

Diagnosis

Diagnostic tools compare a child to others the same age, permitting the team to determine a diagnosis and/or to determine eligibility for services based on set criteria. Most standardized, global diagnostic instruments provide information about whether a child has achieved motor milestones as well as milestones in other developmental domains. The *Peabody Developmental Motor Scales 2* (Folio & Fewell, 2000) is a norm-referenced standardized tool often used by physical therapists and occupational therapists. This tool assesses both fine and gross motor skills from birth to 6 years of age. Table 7.1 describes other commonly used tools for determining developmental status in the sensorimotor area of development.

Program Planning

As part of a team, physical therapists and occupational therapists are involved in developing Individualized Family Service Plans (IFSPs) and Individualized Education Programs (IEPs) and in implementing interventions. Generally, functional skills, rather than developmental milestones, are stressed in intervention plans. Most therapists use a "top-down approach" assessment process to develop programs. In this approach, desired outcomes guide the assessment process.

TABLE 7.1 Tools commonly used by physical therapists and occupational therapists for diagnostic purposes

Tool	Bayley Scales of Infant Development–III (Bayley, 2006)	Mullen Scales of Early Learning (Mullen, 1995)	Sensory Profile(s) (Dunn, 2002)
Purpose	Identify developmental delay Monitor developmental progress	Determine level of development Identify strengths and needs of child	Determine the effect of sensory processing and sensory modulation difficulties on behavior and social interactions Classify child's sensory profile
Age	1-42 months	Birth-68 months	Birth-adult
Areas Assessed	Gross Motor, Fine Motor, Expressive Language, Receptive Language, Cognition, Social-Emotional, Adaptive	Gross Motor, Fine Motor, Expressive Language, Receptive Language, Visual Perception	Auditory, Visual, Tactile, Vestibular, Oral Sensory, Multisensory
Time to Administer	25–60 minutes	15–60 minutes	15–20 minutes

Desired outcomes are statements that describe what the team would like to see the child do. Outcomes may be general ("I'd like to see Anna move around.") or specific ("Sasha needs to walk from the bus to the classroom in 6 minutes or less.") Top-down assessment procedures help to determine what factors are interfering with or promoting the child's accomplishment of the outcome (Campbell, 1991).

A **routine-based assessment** (McWilliam, 2003) determines the capabilities of the child within everyday activities. For example, a therapist would assess the child's climbing ability while the child ascends the stairs to go to his or her bedroom to take a nap or descends the stairs to go to the basement playroom to obtain a toy and would assess scooping with a spoon during snack time. Using routines to assess functional behaviors is helpful for program

planning for these reasons: (1) routines are meaningful to parents, caregivers, and teachers; (2) the use of routines promotes the development of goals that are functional and the identification of intervention strategies that are practical, take little time, and do not disrupt the ongoing activity; and (3) observing a child within a routine shows how the child solves problems.

Many new tools and strategies have a judgment-based assessment component. That is, information is gathered from individuals who see the child perform target skills on a regular basis, such as parents, teachers, and child care providers. Regardless of the tools used, the assessment process must provide a detailed description of the child's strengths and needs in order to develop appropriate therapeutic interventions (Long & Sippel, 2000).

CHARACTERISTICS OF CHILDREN WITH PHYSICAL DISABILITIES

Although interventions do not depend on a specific diagnosis, it is important that all team members have a basic understanding of common conditions typically referred for treatment to physical therapists and occupational therapists. Table 7.2 describes the etiology, or cause, and characteristics of common motor disabilities. Cerebral palsy, spina bifida and down syndrome will be discussed.

Cerebral Palsy

Cerebral palsy (CP) is a nonprogressive disorder of movement or posture caused by damage to the immature brain. Cerebral palsy may be associated with sensory impairments, visual impairments, seizure disorders, learning disabilities, communication disorders, intellectual disabilities, and behavior disorders. Although it is often difficult to accurately assess the cognitive status of children with more involved forms of cerebral palsy, mental retardation or learning disabilities have been reported in 50%–67% of children with cerebral palsy (Pellegrino, 2002).

The most widely accepted classification system for children with cerebral palsy was developed by the American Academy of Cerebral Palsy and Developmental Medicine (Minear, 1956) (see Table 7.3). Recently, the Gross Motor Function Classification System (Palisano et al., 1997) was developed to describe the functional level of individuals with cerebral palsy.

The incidence of cerebral palsy has held relatively constant during the last 50 years, remaining about 2 to 3 per 1,000 live births (Clark & Hankins, 2003). Of all cases of cerebral palsy, about 70% are acquired prenatally. Prenatal factors include those related to heredity, infections, Rh incompatibility, metabolic disorders,

TABLE 7.2 Motor characteristics of common disabilities

Condition	Etiology	Characteristics	Associated Conditions Seen in Some Children
Arthrogryposis multiplex congenta	Unknown, begins prenatally	Joint contractures, muscle atrophy, average cognition	Congenital heart defects, respiratory disorders
Cerebral palsy	Multiple prenatal, neonatal, and postnatal causes that lead to anoxia or brain hemorrhage	Disordered movement leading to atypical muscle tone, strength and joint limitations	Intellectual disabilities, speech disorders, visual deficits, hearing impairments, seizures, perceptual difficulties
Myelomeningocele (spina bifida)	Embryonic neural tube defect of genetic and environmental causes	Varying degrees of lower body paralysis due to protrusion of spinal cord through opening in the vertebrae	Hydrocephalus, bowel and bladder incontinence, loss of sensation, intellectual disabilities, visual-perceptual difficulties
Juvenile rheumatoid arthritis	Unknown, autoimmune	Painful, swollen joints and limited movement	Joint contractures and deformities

TABLE 7.3 Classification of cerebral palsy

Movement Disorder	Characteristics
Spasticity	Hypertonic, increased muscle tone, decreased voluntary muscle control
Athetosis	Slow, writhing movements of the arms and legs; the arms are often more involved and can involve muscles around the mouth
Ataxia	Decreased balance, lack of proximal muscle control, the legs are often more involved than the arms, very unstable gait

Type	Characteristics
Hemiplegia	One side of the body affected; the arms are often more involved than the legs
Diplegia	All extremities affected, but the legs are significantly more affected; spasticity often present in the legs
Quadriplegia	All extremities affected, but the arms are more involved than the legs; mental retardation common

fetal anoxia, and developmental deficits of the brain. Yet, in a large number of cases, the prenatal cause is unknown (Krigger, 2006). Perinatal factors are those that occur around the time of birth and include brain trauma or injury, asphyxia, and problems related to a premature delivery. Problems associated with prematurity account for approximately 40% of all cases of cerebral palsy (Himmelmann, Hagberg, Beckung, Hagberg, & Uvebrant, 2005), as was the case for Michael in the case study. Postnatal factors tend to include brain injury due to trauma, toxicity, anoxia, tumors, and brain infections, including bacterial and viral encephalopathy.

Spina Bifida

Myelomeningocele, meningocele, and spina bifida occulta are conditions caused by neural tube defects. With an incidence of 0.4 to 1.0 in every 1,000 live births, neural tube defects are among the most common birth defects (Detrait, George, Etchevers, Gilbert, Vekemans, & Speer, 2004). These defects are caused by abnormal fetal development, which results in a lack of bony closure around the spinal cord. Myelomeningocele involves a protrusion of the spinal cord. In meningocele, only the coverings of the spinal cord (meninges) are protruding. Spina bifida occulta is a bony defect in which there is failure of the posterior bones of the spinal column to form (Hinderer, Hinderer, & Shurtleff, 2000).

These spinal defects require immediate surgical repair, which damages the spinal cord. **Hydrocephalus** (a buildup of cerebrospinal fluid in the brain), lack of bowel and bladder control, learning disabilities, mental retardation, and bony abnormalities of the back and lower extremities are frequently associated with spinal defects.

The motor disability seen in children with myelomeningocele is characterized by flaccid paralysis in those muscles that receive innervation from the nerves at the level of the protrusion. Since meningocele and spina bifida occulta do not involve nerves, paralysis is not common (Liptak, 2005).

Down Syndrome

Down syndrome, the most common chromosomal abnormality, is caused when a child has extra chromosome material (Poe, 2005). A typically developing child has 46 chromosomes; the child with Down syndrome has 47. The most common type of Down syndrome is characterized by an extra chromosome on the 21st chromosome pair and is called **trisomy 21.**

Besides trisomy 21, there are two other forms of Down syndrome. The translocation type is caused by breakage of chromosome 21 during cell division. This broken piece of chromosomal material attaches to another chromosome, providing extra chromosome material. The third type is called mosaicism and accounts for 1%–2% of all cases. It is the result of some cells being affected, while others remain normal. The percentage of affected cells varies from child to child.

Congenital heart defects are present in about two-thirds of children with Down syndrome, and up to two-thirds have hearing loss (Roizen, 2002). **Hypotonia** (or low muscle tone), a flat nasal bridge, epicanthal folds, a small mouth, and low-set ears are common physical features. Additionally, a child with Down syndrome may have intestinal problems, respiratory infections, thyroid problems, and/or vertebral instability. The majority of individuals with Down syndrome have mild to moderate mental retardation (Bertoti, 1999). Hypotonia and joint hyperextensibility influence the child's ability to develop muscular stability, which, in turn, influences the development of motor milestones.

Other Conditions that Impact Neuromotor Development

Many developmental disabilities are difficult, if not impossible, to diagnose in the first two years of life. Generally, infants and toddlers who manifest atypical motor development or motor difficulties do not have an identified diagnosis. Parents or pediatricians may become concerned when a child is delayed in achieving motor milestones and/or has low or high muscle tone affecting their ability to develop motor skills. These children are usually eligible for infant-toddler services even if they do not have a formal medical diagnosis.

Autism. More and more children are being identified as having autism (Newschaffer, Falb, & Gurney, 2005). Children with autism may have delays in motor skill acquisition, **dyspraxia** (poor motor planning skills), low muscle tone, and sensory processing dysfunction, such as sensory defensiveness to sounds or touch (Yack, Sutton, & Aquilla, 2003).

Dyspraxia involves a child's ability to figure out how to accomplish a new motor task. Most individuals perform routine motor tasks such as brushing their teeth without much thought. However, when they encounter a novel motor task such as hitting a baseball, they have to think about the movement and plan for it. This ability is dependent on both cognitive and sensorimotor development. When motor planning difficulties interfere with daily routines, the disorder is referred to as dyspraxia. Children with dyspraxia often appear clumsy, may have difficulty climbing on the playground equipment, and may trip, fall, or bump into other children. Children with dyspraxia around the mouth may have difficulty learning to speak (Parham & Mailloux, 2001).

THERAPEUTIC INTERVENTION STRATEGIES

Therapists use a variety of strategies and approaches to remediate and maximize a child's motor development and functioning. Positioning and play will be discussed.

Positioning

Children with severe motor impairments often need to be positioned, and repositioned, to promote function and symmetrical body alignment, preventing further disability. Therapists show caregivers and other professionals how to position children in ways that promote social interactions with others and promote learning. For example, children should always sit at eye level with other children. Sometimes this means a chair must be adapted or modified. The creative use of blankets and rolled towels when a child is placed in a prone (stomach-lying), supine (back-lying), or side-lying position can help the child maintain that position while playing with toys or people.

Although a child may be placed in a position to help relax tight muscles, positioning is most often used to promote independent, functional skills. Infants, especially those born prematurely, may be positioned in ways to counteract some the atypical positions these children assume. Figure 7.1 shows

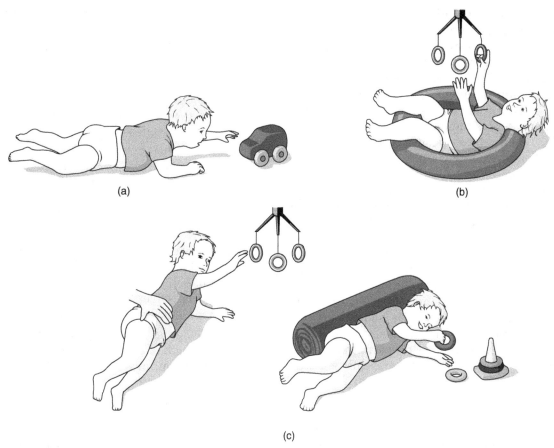

(a)

(b)

(c)

Figure 7.1 Activities for promoting symmetrical body alignment and functional skills in infants in prone, supine and side-lying positions: (a) To increase weight bearing on upper extremities; (b) To Promote flexion and reaching against gravity; (c) To promote reaching and grasping

Source: From *Tips for Tots: A Resource Guide for Your Infant and Toddler, Mighty Movements 1, 2* (pp. 1–2) by C. Baker and T. Long, 1989. Palo Alto, CA: VORT. Copyright © 1989 by Toby Long. Reprinted by permission.

how to position an infant appropriately in prone, supine, and side-lying positions.

Play with People and Objects

Social interactions and play between a child and a caregiver or professional offer the perfect context for therapeutic intervention. Children with atypical motor development need toys that can be manipulated and adapted easily. Basic adaptations can increase the appropriateness of play materials. For example, materials may need to be

stabilized, enlarged, or made more familiar. Changing the switch mechanism that controls the toy may allow the child to operate the toy independently. For example, a teacher can build up a toggle switch with masking tape so a child with limited dexterity can easily move it or change a toggle switch to a large button for a child who uses the full hand to hit the switch. Toys may need to be made less distracting by removing extraneous parts. Taping sections of the toy not being used or making the toy more inviting by adding sounds to its action may make a toy more engaging and appropriate for a child. Other toys may need to be more durable or safe.

Finally, toys may need to be made physically and mechanically accessible, a special concern for children with movement dysfunction. **Physical accessibility** entails changing the position of the toy in relationship to the child to allow the child better access to the material. Play gyms, which allow toys to be suspended, often increase the child's interaction and exploration with the materials. A child with significant motor impairments may need to be placed in a supported side-lying position to promote accessibility. **Mechanical adaptation** refers to making changes to the switches of mechanical toys to promote independent use. Switches are easy to change, and there is a large variety of switches available that increase a child's ability to use toys.

In addition to adapting toys or using toys as therapeutic equipment, play is ideal for movement exploration and motor improvement (Menear & Davis, 2007). Creative movement can be easily designed to meet therapeutic goals. In inclusive settings, creative movement and games can be arranged so that *all* children are involved in a way that is beneficial to everyone. Play-oriented activities increase the pleasure, engagement, and motivation of a child, the child's parents, and professionals.

Promoting Gross Motor Skills

The foundation for many games and sports-related activities for young children is the development of gross motor skills. Children who have difficulty executing gross motor skills smoothly and efficiently are often frustrated by motor games and may shy away from participation. However, professionals can structure activities that promote foundational motor skills, regardless of a child's abilities (Menear & Davis, 2007). The following fun activities can be conducted individually or within a group. Each game should be adjusted to the ability, motor needs, and age of individual children. Some can be easily incorporated into activities involving communication, cognitive

development, or preliteracy/literacy learning. Many of the following were adapted for Michael.

❏ *Snake:* An adult wriggles a rope on the floor like a snake. The child/children jump over it, trying not to touch the rope. If they touch it, they are "bitten by the snake."

❏ *Cart-Pull:* A child lies on his or her belly on a scooter while holding a rope with both hands. If the child cannot hold the rope with two hands, tie the rope around the child's torso. An adult pulls the child around by the rope. Encourage the child to hold his or her head up. If the child's head falls, stop pulling until the head is upright again.

❏ *Ping-Pong Blow:* A child/children get on all fours and blow a ping-pong ball down a specific path. A maze can be made using hula hoops. (This activity was adapted for Michael by having a hula hoop placed on a table.)

❏ *Rope-Walk/Balance Beam:* A child/children walk the length of a rope or small, elevated beam (about one inch higher than the floor). They are circus performers trying not to fall off while doing "tricks," such as hopping on the line, going sideways, crossing one foot over the other, and moving backward.

❏ *Animal Walk:* A child/children walk like different animals such as move like a snake or kick like a donkey. The other children try to guess what animal each child is pretending to be. No sounds are permitted!

❏ *Jolly Green Giant:* Tape a number of one-foot by one-foot cardboard shapes close together on the floor. A child/children attempt to step from one shape to the next without stepping off a shape.

❏ *River Cross:* A child/children jump, crawl, or belly crawl onto hula-hoop "rocks" in order to cross the "river" to avoid getting "wet."

❏ *Follow Doggie:* A child/children get on their hands and knees like a dog. Then a child "waves" different "paws" while remaining balanced on the other three "paws." Begin waving one one paw at a time; then slowly add additional waves.

Other common early childhood games that help promote gross motor skills include Tug of War, Tag, Duck Duck Goose, Crab Soccer (kicking large balls while moving on a scooter), Simon Says, and Hot Potato (Menear & Shapiro, 2004).

Promoting Fine Motor Development

The development of skilled hand use requires infants and young children to bear weight on their arms and to explore their environment by touching and manipulating a variety of materials with one and both hands. The following activities will promote foundational fine motor skills. They prepare infants, toddlers, and preschoolers for the more refined skills needed in school, such as tying shoes, cutting, and eventually writing.

❏ *Tummy Time:* Although babies should sleep on their back (American Academy of Pediatrics Task Force, 1992), when awake they should be placed on their tummy to encourage pushing up on their forearms, and eventually their hands. Placing a mirror or toy in front of a child will encourage the child to look up. This activity also provides important sensory feedback for building body awareness in the arms and hands (Chizawsky & Scott-Findlay, 2005).

❏ *Filling and Dumping:* Older infants, toddlers, and preschoolers enjoy filling containers and dumping them. They are learning and practicing grasping, releasing, and problem solving. Various everyday items, such as plastic lids to milk bottles, and other nonbreakable objects are good for filling plastic containers.

❏ *Two Together:* Creating opportunities for children to use both hands together is very important for functional hand use. Simple activities to encourage bilateral hand skills are opening and closing containers, holding and stabilizing paper while coloring, holding one toy while trying to retrieve another with the other hand, stringing beads, and building and taking apart interconnecting blocks and beads.

Appropriate fine motor development can be encouraged by planned play and learning experiences.

❏ *Moving Van:* To promote body awareness and to strengthen shoulders, have children push and pull large boxes and weighted containers around the floor or outside. Show children how, working together, they can push and pull heavier items than they are able to alone.

❏ *Edible Finger Painting:* Have children "paint" with whipped cream, pudding, or Jell-O to encourage tactile exploration. This may be beneficial for children who are reluctant to touch a variety of materials or textures. Refined finger dexterity requires tactile discrimination, which is enhanced by engaging in messy play.

❏ *Cutting:* To prepare preschoolers for cutting with scissors, have them use tongs to move small objects from one container to another to learn how to control the opening and closing necessary for scissor work. When introducing scissors, encourage the child to place the thumb in one loop, while the middle, ring, and baby fingers are positioned in the larger loop. The index finger is used to stabilize the blade of the scissors. Guide the child to approach the paper in a thumbs-up position, encouraging him or her to cut in a forward direction.

Handwriting. Handwriting requires a complex set of skills involving the whole child. To write efficiently and effectively, a child must possess adequate skills in attention, posture, balance, perception, memory, dexterity, strength, and coordination. The following activities develop prewriting skills in preschoolers and primary-aged children:

❑ *Lacing and Sewing:* Lacing macaroni on yarn and sewing with heavy thread and plastic "needles" are fun bilateral hand activities. Preschoolers can handle large macaroni, while primary-aged students can sew smaller noodles and work with thinner thread.

❑ *Finger Play:* To strengthen the small muscles of the hands needed for pencil skills, children can imitate finger movements, play with finger puppets, trace designs in sand, and duplicate forms with Play-Doh.

❑ *Tweezer Time:* Picking up small objects or small macaroni with a tweezer and placing them in a container will strengthen the finger and hand muscles necessary for later writing skills. Gradually reduce the size of the container opening.

❑ *Prewriting Activities.* To encourage appropriate finger control, break crayons and chalk into small pieces so the child has to hold the pieces with his or her fingertips. Encourage imitating writing shapes from a model. For some children, using an easel or other vertical surface is helpful in strengthening the whole arm and hand. For others, light weights may need to be added to the wrist to promote further strengthening. When the child is struggling with handwriting, an analysis of his or her approach to handwriting should be conducted by a therapist.

Learning to print or write in cursive can be frustrating for some children. It is important to begin with good writing habits, since it is easy for inefficient strategies to develop. Ideally, a child should be positioned comfortably in a chair, with feet flat on the floor and the trunk supported in an aligned, upright position. Paper should be positioned approximately 30° to the left for right-handed writers and 35°–40° to the right for left-handed writers. For some children, a pencil grip allows them to hold the pencil appropriately for writing. The proper grip promotes isolated thumb and finger control and can prevent fatigue in the hand.

The following suggestions can support a child who is finding writing challenging and can make handwriting fun.

❑ Place paper on a vertical surface like an easel to promote wrist extension and thumb and finger opposition. Raised lined paper provides a tactile cue to assist the child with alignment of the letters on the line.

❑ Use rainbow writing, tracing printed letters with different colored markers, focusing on correct letter formation. This activity is an engaging way to introduce new letter formation to the beginning writer.

❑ Practice writing on different surfaces that provide tactile feedback or in the air with eyes opened or closed.

❑ Have a child guess what letter another child is writing on his or her back.

Adapting Curricula

For children with sensorimotor or physical disabilities to benefit from early childhood curricula, therapists collaborate with other professionals on the team to adapt these curricula to better meet the individualized needs of each child. The following were used with Michael in the case study and are appropriate for adapting curricula for other children with severe motor dysfunction:

❑ Use proper handling prior to an activity to diminish detrimental effects of abnormal posturing and tone.

❑ Use positioning to help a child maintain an appropriate, functional posture.

❑ Arrange activities in a way that minimizes movements required by a child to accomplish the tasks.

❏ Give choices to the children to allow them to explore their interests.

❏ Allow children to work together, encouraging peer-to-peer support.

❏ Anticipate difficulties and plan to prevent atypical movements and promote functional, efficient skills.

❏ Modify activities as needed to adapt to a child's needs.

A few ECSE curricula have been developed specifically to promote motor skills. The most common are *Fit for Me: Activities for Building Motor Skills in Young Children* (Karnes, 1992), *The Carolina Curriculum for Infants and Toddlers with Special Needs* (Johnson-Martin, Attermeier, & Hacker, 2004), *The Carolina Curriculum for Preschoolers with Special Needs* (Johnson-Martin, Hacker, & Attermeier, 2004), and *Play and Learn: A Motor-Based Preschool Curriculum for Children of All Abilities* (Coleman & Krueger, 1999). Additionally, there are several books that describe motor activities appropriate for young children with motor delays and disabilities. For example, *Fine Motor Dysfunction: Therapeutic Strategies in the Classroom* (Levine, 1991), *PT Activities for Pediatric Groups* (Kane & Anderson, 1999), and *Hands at Work and Play: Developing Fine Motor Skills at School and Home* (Knight & Decker, 1994) are useful resources for ECSE teachers.

PROMOTING ADAPTIVE SKILLS DEVELOPMENT

In addition to promoting the acquisition of gross and fine motor skills, physical therapists and occupational therapists assist children in learning adaptive skills for daily living, such as feeding, dressing, and personal hygiene tasks. Children develop independence in self-care activities gradually. By the time a typically developing child enters kindergarten, basic self-care skills are established. Children with disabilities often have more difficulty developing these skills and may need assistance. Therapists may advise caregivers and professionals in ways to adapt or modify tasks to assist a child. Depending on the child's needs, modifications may need to be made to a task or to the child's environment.

Feeding

Infants and young children with central nervous system dysfunction frequently have oral-motor problems that lead to feeding difficulties. Atypical motor patterns controlling the lips, tongue, and facial musculature may also make feeding difficult. Feeding problems may be due to problems with the oral-motor processes, with the sensory processes, or with the feeding processes. Many children with neuromotor dysfunction have a combination of these problems.

To improve oral-motor functioning, team members must

❏ rule out any medical complications that could influence feeding functions;

❏ collaborate with the family, and other team members, to determine feeding needs and develop a plan; and

❏ provide intervention that considers all aspects of a child's physical needs.

Proper positioning is the first intervention to consider to diminish the effects of oral-motor difficulties. An infant should be positioned in a slightly reclined position, face to face with the caregiver, and with his or her head and trunk supported. Older children with significant motor dysfunction need to be supported with appropriate trunk alignment. They may need supports placed in the high chair, may need to use a feeder chair, or may need to use a wheelchair or other adapted seating system such as those shown in Figure 7.2.

Some children have specific problems with the muscles around the mouth. Therapists can instruct caregivers and parents in ways to hold such a child or support the mouth during feeding to counteract atypical oral-motor control.

Infants and young children who are hypersensitive to touch around or in the mouth should

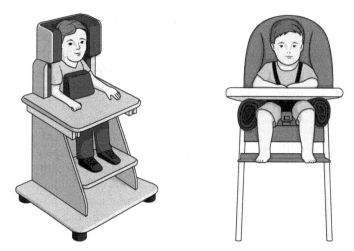

Figure 7.2 Ways to support trunk alignment in older children with significant motor dysfunction using supports in a feeder chair and a high chair (Illustrations by Rachel Brady, DPT, MS, PT, Research Associate, Georgetown University Center for Child and Human Development, Washington, DC)

be fed in a quiet environment with few distractions. Therapists can instruct caregivers in specific desensitization procedures such providing oral massage or placing food on the front half of the tongue, which may be less sensitive than the back of the tongue. To encourage chewing and tongue lateralization, it may be helpful to place food on the sides of the mouth for some children.

Older infants and toddlers should be encouraged to finger feed in preparation for self-feeding. Rolled towels placed in a child's high chair offer the trunk support needed for efficient arm use and self-feeding.

A child's wheelchair is usually designed for optimal support and comfort. Using it during mealtimes may offer the best positioning for feeding; however, all children need to eat at the same table as classmates or family. If a table cannot be adjusted to be at mid-chest level, a wheelchair tray may be used. Trays can be adjusted to meet the specific needs of the child. It is important that the tray or table surface be positioned at a level that encourages upright posture. Some children do not need a wheelchair, but armless chairs may not provide enough lateral support. Using a chair with

arms or placing an insert in a standard chair may provide the needed support. Some children who lack movement control or have very stiff movements may need hand-over-hand guidance to teach bringing a spoon to the mouth.

In addition to chairs, supports, and trays, there is a wide variety of utensils that are designed to increase independence in self-feeding. Utensils that have built-up handles are easier to grasp, spoons or forks that are bent are easier to scoop with, and straps can be used to maintain a child's wrist in the proper position. Bowls and plates are available with built-up sides or with detachable food guards, making it easier for a child to scoop food onto a spoon. Some bowls and plates have suction cups that adhere to the table or tray, stabilizing them.

Learning to self-feed is a complex process requiring a stable trunk position, efficient use of the extremities, and controlled oral-motor mechanisms. Consider the following in developing specific feeding programs: (1) the unique characteristics of the child (e.g., oral-motor strengths and weaknesses, food preferences), (2) the environment (e.g., distractions during feeding, time of day), (3) the caregiver/professional (e.g., level of anxiety, preparation), and (4) the feeding equipment (e.g., adapted bottle, chair).

Dressing

Another area of self-care that children must learn is dressing. Dressing includes putting on and taking off clothes and manipulating fasteners such as snaps, buttons, and zippers. Children may acquire dressing skills at different rates, depending on the family's routine and cultural views on the importance of these skills. In general, toddlers are able to remove loose clothing around 2 years of age. They can put on loose clothing around 3 years of age. Around the age of 5, a child is expected to dress alone except for difficult tasks such as tying shoes (Werner, 1999). Children who have difficulty using their muscles may find skills related to dressing challenging.

The following are general strategies to encourage the development of dressing skills in children:

❏ Be patient. Helping a child learn to dress himself or herself takes time. Resist the urge to simply do it for the child. Allow the child ample opportunities to put on and take off clothes.

❏ Use loose-fitting clothing without fasteners, such as those with elastic waistbands, which are easier for the child to put on independently.

❏ Encourage the use of clothes with fasteners that are easy to manipulate, such as snaps, large buttons, and Velcro. As the child gains proficiency with these easier fasteners, gradually introduce more difficult ones, such as small buttons, hooks, and zippers.

❏ If the child has a disability that affects one side of the body more than the other, put clothes on the affected side first.

❏ Children with poor balance may need to sit while dressing.

❏ If dressing is challenging or tiring for a child, especially during the early morning rush, professionals may suggest that parents require

their child to put on only one or two items and then have the parent finish the rest.

❏ Children with perceptual or spatial difficulties may find dressing particularly difficult. They may need additional help and creative cueing to differentiate back from front, left from right, or outside from inside. Color coding the backs and fronts of garments may help the child avoid putting clothes on backward.

❏ The use of shoes with Velcro fasteners, shoes with elasticized shoelaces, or slip-on shoes may be helpful for children who are unable to tie their shoes.

Parents and ECSE professionals need to remember to make dressing fun. Praise children for personal successes. Incorporating dress-up games and dressing and undressing dolls are other motivating ways to help children learn the skills necessary for dressing.

Personal Hygiene

Personal hygiene skills such as toileting, bathing, and oral care may require input from physical therapists and occupational therapists. Therapists commonly offer the team suggestions for compensating when the child lacks the skills to perform an activity or when the child has difficulty performing it because of muscular concerns such as muscle tightness or decreased flexibility.

Bath chairs and benches provide stability and increase safety for a child who is unable to sit independently or feel secure without support. Special commode seats are available to improve a child's ability to transfer onto the toilet and remain stable while seated. Seats with armrests and ones that raise the seat to ease transfer are also commercially available, as are safety straps. An upright sitting posture with feet placed firmly on the floor will assist the child with bowel movements. Simple clothing with few fasteners is also helpful, especially for children with fine motor dexterity concerns.

The bathroom's environment may also need to be changed to ease physical access to the tub, sink, and commode. Simple suggestions like providing a step stool so children can reach the sink may be helpful. Children who have poor balance or who feel insecure may need to have a step stool with arm supports.

As children get older, they will need to be able to open and close stall doors, including securing the lock. Children who are independent wheelchair users or users of walkers may need assistance or training in how to manage doorways and doors.

For children with weak grasps or wrist and forearm movement limitations, toothbrushes and hairbrushes with built-up handles may be easier to manage. A battery-operated toothbrush is more efficient for children with joint limitations, tight muscles, or weakness. There are many commercial devices designed to assist with grooming. Occupational therapists and physical therapists can assist parents, and professionals, with the selection of appropriate tools. However, most children learn which devices are helpful through trial and error.

ASSISTIVE TECHNOLOGY

The field of assistive technology (AT) has grown significantly over the last three decades. AT can assist children with disabilities to be more fully included in community activities (Long, 2005). AT encompasses both the devices and the services needed to ensure successful use of the devices. An **assistive technology device** is any item or piece of equipment, customized or commercially available, that will help a child increase, maintain, or improve function. Devices such as switches, computer access devices, augmentative communication systems, and mobility devices are examples. AT services include those that assist a child and his or her family with the selection, acquisition, or use of a device. Services include training the user and caregiver in the appropriate selection and use of the device, maintaining the device in working order, and performing any other activities that will ensure that the device continues to meet the needs of the child (Technology-Related Assistance for Individuals with Disabilities Act, 1988). Table 7.4 lists common low- and high-tech assistive devices.

TABLE 7.4 Examples of low- and high-tech assistive technology for children with atypical motor development

Low-Tech

- Velcro closures
- Suction cups
- Adapted utensils
- Picture communication boards
- Simple switches turning on toys, computers, electronic devices, and appliances

High-Tech

- Computerized communication devices
- Powered mobility
- Speech synthesizer
- Environmental control systems such as universal remote controls to open doors and turn on lights, electronic devices, and appliances
- Braille reader, which is a specially designed tool for individuals who are blind to transfer written words into braille

Both Part C (infant-toddler services) and Part B (preschool and school-age services) of the Individuals with Disabilities Education Improvement Act of 2004 stresses the importance of AT. Teams writing IFSPs and IEPs must discuss the need for AT in meeting the needs of a child, and this consideration must be documented. Many school systems have specific AT teams or AT specialists who assist teachers with the selection of appropriate technology and train professionals and students in appropriate AT use. As Michael's case study showed, once the team selects a device, it is imperative that training and support be offered to the child, the family, and all professionals serving the child. As the needs of the child change over time, reassessment of AT will always be necessary.

CONCLUSION

Today, more therapy services are integrated and embedded into a child's daily home life and the routines of his or her educational setting. Michael's case study demonstrates that more therapists are using a collaborative consultation model of service delivery in which they assume the responsibility of training family members, and professionals, in ways to manage and implement therapeutic activities with children with neuromotor deficits. Therapists are valued resources for assessment and intervention strategies for children with motor dysfunctions. Whatever model of teamwork or service delivery is used, physical therapists and occupational therapists continue to pursue their principal goal of promoting effective movement in children.

SUMMARY

Treatment models

- Intervention with fine and gross motor skills should promote active movement, promote functional skills, promote community integration, and prevent impairment.
- Depending on the child's needs and the constraints of his or her educational setting, physical therapists and occupational therapists use a remedial, compensation, promotion, or prevention approach, or a combination of these, to design intervention programs.

Service delivery models

- Direct, monitoring, and consultation service models are used by physical and occupational therapists to support the motor needs of young children.

Assessment practices

- Many therapists use a "top-down approach" to assessment for program planning, letting desired long-term outcomes guide the assessment process.

Characteristics of children with physical disabilities

- Cerebral palsy, spina bifida, Down syndrome, and autism are common conditions that manifest motor delays and/or motor dysfunctions.

- Children with dyspraxia have motor planning difficulties that interfere with daily routines.

Therapeutic intervention strategies

- Children with severe motor impairments may need to be positioned, and repositioned, to promote function and symmetrical body alignment and to prevent further disability.
- Physical accessibility entails changing the position of a toy or material in relationship to the child to allow the child better access to the material.
- Mechanical adaptation refers to making changes to switches of mechanical toys and materials to promote independent use.

Promoting adaptive skills development

- Depending on the individual child's needs, modifications may need to be made in the task or environment to assist him or her in learning adaptive skills for daily living, such feeding, dressing, and personal hygiene tasks.

Assistive technology

- An assistive technology device is any item or piece of equipment, customized or commercially available, that will help a child increase, maintain, or improve function, such as switches, computer access devices, augmentative communication systems, and mobility devices.

DISCUSSION QUESTIONS/ACTIVITIES

1. Since some therapists are uncomfortable with the collaborative consultation approach to service delivery, discuss the factors that account for these concerns and how they might be reconciled.

2. A 28-month-old child with cerebral palsy uses a baby walker to move around her home and child-care center. When she is in the walker, she is on her toes and is flexed over the top of it. The child's parents believe the walker is helping their daughter learn to walk. However, the physical therapist on the team believes that the child is not ready to walk, as her leg muscles continue to be very tight and she needs better weight bearing skills such as the ability to stand with her feet flat on the floor with proper alignment. Using a family-based approach, discuss how this conflict might be resolved.

3. Brian, a 7-year-old boy with a learning disability, attends a general education first-grade class. He is having great difficulty learning to write. He is scheduled to begin services with an occupational therapist soon. Discuss two adaptations and/or accommodations that the therapist could suggest to the child's general education teacher.

REFERENCES

American Academy of Pediatrics Task Force. (1992). Positioning and SIDS. *Pediatrics, 89 (6)*, 1120–1126.

Bates, J. (2002). Developing, implementing, and monitoring the IFSP/IEP. In B. Thompson (Ed.), *Preschool inclusion manual* (pp. 104–122). Lawrence: University of Kansas Circle of Inclusion Project.

Bayley, N. (2006). *Bayley scales of infant and toddler development* (3rd ed.). San Antonio, TX: Psychological Corporation.

Berenthal, B. I., & Campos, J. J. (1987). New directions in the study of early experience. *Child Development, 58*, 560–567.

Bertoti, D. B. (1999). Mental retardation: Focus on Down syndrome. In J. S. Teklin (Ed.), *Pediatric physical therapy* (3rd ed., pp. 283–313). Philadelphia: Lippincott Williams and Wilkins.

Bredekamp, S., & Copple, C. (Eds.). (1997). *Developmentally appropriate practice in early childhood programs* (rev. ed.). Washington, DC: NAEYC.

Bricker, D., & Squires, J. (2003). *Ages and Stages Questionnaires: A parent-completed, child-monitoring system* (2nd ed.). Baltimore, MD: Brookes.

Campbell, P. H. (1991). Evaluation and assessment in early intervention for infants and toddlers. *Journal of Early Intervention, 15*, 36–45.

Chizawksy, L. L. K., & Scott-Findlay, S. (2005). Tummy time! Preventing unwanted effects of the "Back to Sleep Campaign." *AWHONN Lifelines, 9*, 382–387.

Clark, S. L., & Hankins, G. D. V. (2003). Temporal and demographic trends in cerebral palsy—Fact and fiction. *American Journal of Obstetrics and Gynecology, 188*, 628–633.

Coleman, M. J. S., & Krueger, L. (1999). *Play and learn: A motor-based preschool curriculum for children of all abilities*. Minneapolis, MN: AbleNet.

Detrait, E. R., George, T. M., Etchevers, H. C., Gilbert, J. R., Vekemans, M., & Speer, M. C. (2004). Human neural tube defects: Developmental biology, epidemiology, and genetics. *Neurotoxicology and Teratology, 27*, 515–524.

Diamond, A. (2000). Close interrelation of motor development and cognitive development and of the cerebellum and prefrontal cortex. *Child Development, 71*, 44–56.

Dunn, W. (2002). *Infant/Toddler Sensory Profile*. San Antonio, TX: Harcourt Assessment.

Folio, M. R., & Fewell, R. R. (2000). *Peabody Developmental Motor Scales* (2nd ed.). Austin, TX: PRO-ED.

Frankenburg, W. K., Dodd, J., Archer, P., Bresnick, B., Maschka, P., Edelman, N., & Shapiro, H. (1992). *Denver II training manual*. Denver, CO: Denver Developmental Materials, Inc.

Hanft, B., & Pilkington, K. O. (2000). Therapy in natural environments: The means or end goal for early intervention? *Infants and Young Children, 12*, 1–13.

Hinderer, K. A., Hinderer, S. R., & Shurtleff, D. B. (2000). Myelodysplasia. In S. K. Campbell, D. W. Vanderlinden, & R. J. Palisano (Eds.), *Physical therapy for children* (pp. 621–670). Philadelphia: Saunders.

Individuals with Disabilities Education Improvement Act of 2004, Pub. L. No. 108–446.

Johnson-Martin, N., Attermeier, S., & Hacker, B. (2004). *The Carolina Curriculum for Infants and Toddlers with Special Needs* (3rd ed.). Baltimore, MD: Brookes.

Johnson-Martin, N., Hacker, B., & Attermeier, S. (2004). *The Carolina Curriculum for Preschoolers with Special Needs* (2nd ed.). Baltimore, MD: Brookes.

Kane, K. L., & Anderson, M. M. (1999). *PT activities for pediatric groups*. San Antonio, TX: Psychological Corp.

Karnes, M. B. (1992). *Fit for me: Activities for building motor skills in young children*. Circle Pines, MN: American Guidance Service.

Knight, J. M., & Decker, M. G. (1994). *Hands at work and play: Developing fine motor skills at school and home*. Tucson, AZ: Therapy Skill Builders.

Krigger, K. W. (2006). Cerebral palsy: An overview. *American Family Physician, 73*, 91–100.

Levine, K. J. (1991). *Fine motor dysfunction: Therapeutic strategies in the classroom*. Tucson, AZ: Therapy Skill Builders.

Liptak, G. S. (2005). Neural tube defects. In M. L. Batshaw (Ed.), *Children with disabilities* (5th ed.) (pp. 467–492). Baltimore: Brookes.

Long, T. (2005). Creating a system of care for children and youth with disabilities and special health care needs: The promise of technology. In *Proceedings: Building a system of care for children and youth with disabilities and special health care needs*. Washington, DC: The Consortium, Georgetown University Center for Child and Human Development.

Long, T., & Sippel, K. (2000). Screening, evaluating, and assessing children with sensorimotor concerns and linking findings to intervention planning: Strategies for pediatric occupational and physical therapists. In Interdisciplinary Council on Developmental and Learning Disorders (Eds.), *Clinical practice guidelines: Redefining the standards of care for infants, children, and families with special needs* (pp. 185–213). Bethesda, MD: ICDL Press.

McWilliam, R. A. (1996). A program of research on integrated versus isolated treatment in early intervention. In R. A. McWilliam (Ed.), *Rethinking pull-out services in early intervention: A professional resource* (pp. 71–102). Baltimore, MD: Brookes.

McWilliam, R. A. (2003). Giving families a chance to talk so they can plan. *AAHBEI News Exchange, 8,* 1–8.

Menear, K. S., & Davis, L. (2007). Adapting physical activities to promote overall health and development: Suggestions for interventionists and families. *Young Exceptional Children, 10,* 11–16.

Menear, K., & Shapiro, D. (2004). Let's get moving! Physical activity and students with physical disabilities. *Physical disabilities: Education and related services, 23*(1), 9–18.

Minear, W. L. (1956). A classification of cerebral palsy. *Pediatrics, 18,* 841.

Mullen, E. M. (1995). *Mullen Scales of Early Learning* (AGS ed.). Circle Pines, MN: AGS.

Newborg, J. (2004). *Battelle Developmental Inventory* (2nd ed.). Itasca, IL: Riverside.

Newschaffer, C. J., Falb, M. D., & Gurney, J. G. (2005). National autism prevalence trends from United States special education data. *Pediatrics, 115,* 277–282.

Palisano, R., Rosenbaum, P., Walter, S., Russell, D., Wood, E., & Galuppi, B. (1997). Development and reliability of a system to classify gross motor function in children with cerebral palsy. *Developmental Medicine and Child Neurology, 39,* 214–223.

Parham, L. D., & Mailloux, Z. (2001). Sensory integration. In J. Case-Smith (Ed.), *Occupational therapy for children* (4th ed., pp. 329–379). St. Louis, MO: Mosby.

Pellegrino, L. (2002). Cerebral palsy. In M. L. Batshaw (Ed.), Children with disabilities (5th ed.). Baltimore, MD: Brookes.

Poe, S. G. (2005). Family and disablement issues throughout childhood. In A. Cronin & M. B. Mandich (Eds.), *Human development and performance.* (pp. 246–262). Clifton Park, NY: Thomson Delmar Learning.

Richardson, P. K., & Schultz-Krohn, W. (2001). Planning and implementing services. In J. Case-Smith (Ed.), *Occupational therapy for children* (4th ed., pp. 246–264). St. Louis, MO: Mosby.

Roizen, N. J. (2002). Down syndrome. In M. Batshaw (Ed.), *Children with disabilities* (5th ed., pp. 307–320). Baltimore, MD: Brookes.

Scott, M., McWilliam, R., & Mayhew, L. (1999). Integrating therapies into the classroom. *Young Exceptional Children, 2,* 15–24.

Technology-Related Assistance for Individuals with Disabilities Act of 1988, Pub. L. No. 100-407.

Vanderhoff, M. (2004). Maximizing your role in early intervention. *PT: Magazine of Physical Therapy, 12,* 48–54.

Werner, D. (1999). *Disabled village children: A guide for community health workers, rehabilitation workers, and families* (2nd ed.). Berkeley, CA: Hesperian Foundation.

Yack, E., Sutton, S., & Aquilla, P. (2003). *Building bridges through sensory integration: Occupational therapy for children with autism and other pervasive developmental disorders* (2nd ed.). Las Vegas, NV: Sensory Resources.

Chapter
8

Promoting Social and Emotional Development

Tina L. Stanton-Chapman
Sharon A. Raver

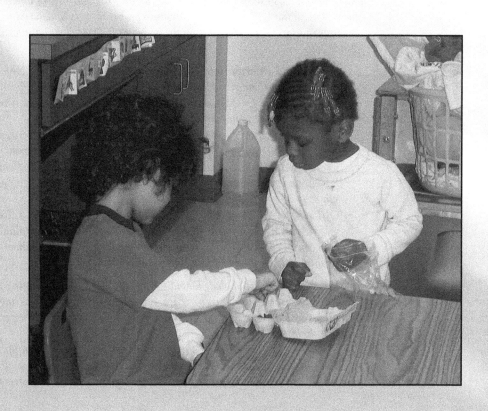

Overview

This chapter discusses the social-emotional development of infants, toddlers, preschoolers, and primary-aged children, including

social and emotional development in infants and toddlers

social and emotional development in preschoolers

social and emotional development in primary-aged students

managing challenging behavior

general strategies for promoting appropriate social and emotional skills

CASE STUDY: David

David is a third-grade student diagnosed as having a specific learning disability (SLD) due to reading difficulties. His general education teacher, Mrs. Williams, requested assistance from the school's Behavior Support Team (BST) because David's behaviors are impeding his learning and the learning of others in the class. Prior to the BST meeting, the team read his records to determine if there was information in his files that might be helpful. The following information was found:

- *Background Information: David had a normal delivery and typical early childhood development. He is currently in foster care and has been living with this family for eight months. He was placed in foster care when he was 5 years old because his birth mother could not care for him.*
- *Education History: The school team found David eligible for services for students with SLD due to difficulties in reading and reading comprehension in second grade. He has demonstrated academic progress on his Individualized Education Program goals each year and received "B" and "C" grades in all subjects.*
- *Office Referrals: David has received between 15 and 26 office discipline referrals each year from kindergarten to the present. The disciplinary actions have included talking to him, allowing him to continue his school work in a separate setting, and sending him home for the day.*

When the BST assembled, David's foster mother began by stating that David is one of five foster children in her care—of the other children, two have severe disabilities and two are infants. She admitted she has little time to spend with David individually.

Next Mrs. Williams shared classroom information with the group. She reported that David does well in mathematics, science, and social studies, but has great difficulty with reading, spelling, and language arts. He has several good friends in the class. Mrs. Williams also described the problem behaviors she observes during independent work: David often frowns, crumples his paper and/or throws it on the floor, throws pencils and books, and resists work that involves writing or independent reading.

Social-emotional development in young children involves the ability to regulate emotions and manage social relationships in ways that are acceptable to others (Squires, Bricker, & Twombly, 2004). The development of these skills is a dynamic process. **Social competence** is the ability to initiate and sustain interactions with others, to resolve conflicts, to develop and nurture friendships, and to accomplish interpersonal goals (Guralnick & Neville, 1997). Having at least a minimal level of social competence allows children to participate in social exchanges and play experiences in which more advanced skills are acquired.

Children become socially competent in the early childhood years through a process called socialization. **Socialization** is the means through which children become a functioning part of society and learn society's rules and values (Essa, 2003). Socialization is a lifelong process that begins at birth and later forms the foundation for adult values, attitudes, and behaviors. The socialization process and the acquisition of typical social and emotional skills follow a fairly predictable sequence in children under the age of 9.

SOCIAL AND EMOTIONAL DEVELOPMENT IN INFANTS AND TODDLERS

For this discussion, the period from birth to 36 months of age is considered the infant-toddler period. Since there is variation in the thinking as to when the infant stage ends and the toddler stage begins, all children in this section will be referred to as infants. The typical stages of social and emotional development of infants and toddlers are presented in Table 8.1. Attachment and social communication are essential skills developed during this period, and will be dsicussed.

Attachment

The socialization process begins with the parent-child or caregiver-child relationship. **Attachment** is formed when an emotional bonding occurs between an infant and a significant adult, such as a mother, father, or caregiver. The observable characteristics of attachment are mutual affection and the desire or need for proximity to each other. The earliest work in attachment of young children with disabilities was conducted by Skeels and Dye (1939). These researchers examined the effects of human interaction on orphaned, institutionalized children and found that intellectual functioning could be positively influenced by predictable caregiving relationships.

Infants typically form attachments during their first year of life. Ainsworth and her colleagues (Ainsworth, 1982; Ainsworth, Blehar, Waters, & Wall, 1978) described four phases that characterize the development of attachment. These attachment phases are summarized in Table 8.2. During stage three, infants develop separation and stranger anxiety, critical milestones in social and emotional development. **Separation anxiety** occurs when attachment between the mother or caregiver and the infant has grown quite strong. The infant experiences emotional difficulty leaving his or her mother or caregiver. This frequently occurs when a mother leaves her child at day care. For the daycare provider, the onset of separation anxiety means that the infant needs extra reassurance and well-established routines.

TABLE 8.1 Typical stages of social-emotional development in infants and toddlers (birth–3 years old)

Age	Social	Emotional
Birth to 6 months	Helpless; asocial; visually fixates at face; smiles at faces; recognizes mother; distinguishes between familiar person and stranger; expects feeding, dressing, & bathing	Generalized tension; delight; distress; smiles at face; enjoys being cuddled
6 to 12 months	Enjoys Peek-a-Boo; responsive to own name; waves "bye-bye"; plays Pat-a-Cake; understands "no"; gives and takes objects	Emotionally attached to mother; protests separation from mother; anger; affection; fear of strangers; curiosity
12 to 18 months	Obeys limited commands; repeats a few words; interested in his/her mirror image; feeds self	Dependent behavior; extremely upset when separated from mother; fear of bath
18 to 24 months	Does opposite of what he/she is told	Temper tantrums
2 to 3 years	Talks; uses "I," "you," and "me"; copies parents' actions; dependent; clingy; possessive about toys; enjoys playing alongside another child; resists parents' commands; gives orders; rigid insistence on sameness of routine	Fear of separation; violent emotions; anger; expresses anger, sorrow, and joy; sense of humor and enjoys playing tricks

Source: Adapted from (1) Ainsworth, M., Blehar, M. C., Waters, E., & Wall, S. (1978). *Patterns of attachment.* Hillsdale, NJ: Erlbaum. (2) Mowder, B. A. (1997). Family dynamics. In A. H. Widerstrom, B. A. Mowder, & S. R. Sandall (Eds.), *Infant development and risk* (2nd ed., pp. 125–153). Baltimore, MD: Brookes. (3) Lamb, M. E., Thompson, R. A., Gardner, W., & Charnov, E. L. (1985). *Infant-mother attachment: The origins and developmental significance of individual differences in strange situation behavior.* Hillsdale: NJ: Erlbaum.

Another behavior infants develop during stage three in Ainsworth's attachment theory is stranger anxiety. **Stranger anxiety** is the infant's display of fear and withdrawal when the infant is presented with an unfamiliar face (Widerstrom, Mowder, & Sandall, 1997). At this stage, an infant is able to distinguish the familiar face of his or her parent or caregiver from others and may show fear when introduced to an unfamiliar person. In general, infants require long periods of time to get accustomed to someone new. The security of familiar objects, such as a blanket or toy, and familiar people, such as a parent, daycare provider, or sibling, may help an infant become more comfortable with someone new.

Social Communication. The ability to communicate expressively and receptively has its roots in early parent-infant interactions. Research has revealed that spontaneous infant behavior is transformed into interactive behavior by a parent who responds to the infant (Hetherington, 1983). This interactive parent-infant behavior becomes socialized behavior in the context of the family (Mowder, 1997). Interactions characterized by parental attentiveness, responsivity, sensitivity, appropriate stimulation, and warmth promote infant social competence and communication (Belsky, Lerner, & Spanier, 1985; Bornstein, 1986).

Parent-infant interactions develop over time and are influenced by three major elements: (1) the personality characteristics of the parent, (2) situational influences on the parent, and (3) the infant's behavioral characteristics (Lamb, Thompson, Gardner, & Charnov, 1985). Ainsworth and colleagues (Ainsworth et al., 1978) identified sensitivity and a sense of self as a competent parent

TABLE 8.2 Stages of attachment

Phase Number and Age	Stage of Attachment
1: Birth to 8 weeks	Initial Preattachment
	In this phase, the baby shows orientation and signals without discrimination of figure. The infant behaves in a way that elicits the proximity of adults. These behaviors include crying, smiling, and cuddling. These behaviors tend to promote parent-infant contact.
2: 2 to 7 months	Attachment-in-the-Making
	The infant's behaviors toward others remain virtually the same except that they are oriented toward particular individuals—usually the mother and father.
3: 7 to 24 months	Clear-Cut Attachment
	The infant shows greater discrimination in his/her interactions with people and tends to have one person to whom attachment behaviors are directed. The child attempts to maintain proximity to this attachment figure by communication signals and locomotion (e.g., creeping, crawling, walking).
4: 24 months and up	Formation of a Goal-Directed Partnership
	The child is becoming more independent and is willing to explore the environment without needing the dominant authority figure nearby. He/she is also developing multiple attachments with other individuals.

Source: Adapted and printed with permission from Ainsworth, M., Blehar, M. C., Waters, E., & Wall, S. (1978). *Patterns of attachment.* Hillsdale, NJ: Lawrence Erlbaum Associates.

as major parental personality traits that contribute to the development of positive parent-child relationships. Situational influences involve parental factors such as parental stress and the presence of social support systems. Individual infant characteristics affecting the parental-child relationship include the child's soothability, irritability, and predictability (Mowder, 1997). Together, these factors interact and contribute to the infant's developing social and emotional competence.

Temperament and Emotions. Infant temperament is also an important issue in the social and emotional development of infants and toddlers (Halverson, Kohnstamm, & Martin, 1994; Kagan, Arcus, & Snidman, 1993; Rothbart, Ahadi, & Hershey, 1994). **Temperament** is defined as a tendency to exhibit frequently, consciously, and

voluntarily a pattern of behavior that is directed to a broad goal (Katz, 1993). Behavior is often a by-product of an infant's inborn temperamental disposition, and it is further shaped by how people react to the child.

Based on years of observational research, Thomas and colleagues (Thomas, Chess, & Birch, 1968) classified children into three general temperamental categories: (1) easy, (2) slow to warm up, and (3) difficult. Easy children follow a regular cycle in sleeping and eating, are easily distractible, have a reasonable attention span, display a moderate level of activity, are not overly sensitive to stimuli in their environment, and are generally described as happy. On the other hand, difficult children show opposite characteristics, such as irregularity, intensity in reactions, an inability to adapt, and a high activity level, and are generally described as unhappy. Slow-to-warm-up children fall in between the two extremes. Studies have shown significant stability correlations in children's temperament from infancy to school age (Chess & Thomas, 1996). Some children with significant delays or disabilities may be described as having difficult temperaments that may impact the parent-child relationship throughout their life.

SOCIAL AND EMOTIONAL DEVELOPMENT IN PRESCHOOLERS

When a child enters the preschool years, a number of critical social and emotional skills are mastered. Table 8.3 shows typical social-emotional achievements in 3- to 5-year-old children. Preschoolers are more cooperative than they were in the infant-toddler years and tend to use "we" more than the oppositional "I" (Landy, 2002).

Peer Interactions and Friendships

The preschool years are generally characterized by peer interactions and friendship. **Friendship** is defined as the close link between people typified by mutual concern, sharing, and companionship (Flaste, 1991). Usually by the age of 4, children can maintain friendships. Friendships serve four functions in the young child's social development (Hartup, 1992): (1) they provide a context for

skill learning, such as the ability to gain entry to play activities, to manage conflicts appropriately, and to exercise sensitivity and empathy; (2) they provide knowledge about selves, others, and the world; (3) they offer emotional and cognitive resources that children can access during their normal interactions and during times of stress; and (4) they provide models for subsequent relationships.

Coordinated interaction and positivity of social exchanges are seen as central dimensions of friendship interactions (Kerns, 2000). Coordinated interaction refers to the degree of continuation and complexity of play, whereas positivity of social exchanges refers to the degree of harmony and equality of interactions. In general, having friendships is related to positive social behaviors. Preschoolers with friends are more accepted, display more prosocial behaviors, and are less rejected than children without friends (Sebanc, 2003).

The Development of Play

Play serves both as a means of expression and as a means of interpretation for children (Lifter & Bloom, 1998). As a means of expression, play provides a way for children to embody their mental representations of the world. As a means of interpretation, play provides a way for children to demonstrate their knowledge of the complex

---

TABLE 8.3 Typical stages of social-emotional development in preschoolers (3–5 years old)

Age	Social	Emotional
3 to 4 years	Likes to share; uses "we"; cooperative play; imitates parents; practices sex-role activities; interested in playing with friend of same sex; imaginary friend	Affectionate toward parents; imaginary fears of dark, storms, and injury
4 to 5 years	Prefers to play with other children; starts showing an interest in competitive games and sports; prefers sex-appropriate activities	Feels responsibility and guilt; feels pride in accomplishment

Source: Adapted from (1) Ainsworth, M., Blehar, M. C., Waters, E., & Wall, S. (1978). *Patterns of attachment.* Hillsdale, NJ: Erlbaum. (2) Mowder, B. A. (1997). Family dynamics. In A. H. Widerstrom, B. A. Mowder, & S. R. Sandall (Eds.), *Infant development and risk* (2nd ed., pp. 125–153). Baltimore, MD: Brookes. (3) Lamb, M. E., Thompson, R. A., Gardner, W., & Charnov, E. L. (1985). *Infant-mother attachment: The origins and developmental significance of individual differences in strange situation behavior.* Hillsdale: NJ: Erlbaum.

spatial-temporal-causal interrelationships among objects, environments, persons, actions, and motives that make up the world of human action. Play essentially promotes mastery as children practice skills, it furthers cognitive development as thinking abilities are stretched, it encourages social interaction, it helps children work through emotions, its inventive nature makes it creative, and it is often a socializing event (Essa, 2003). For most children, the capacity for play develops in a predictable way and seems to be driven by intrinsic motivation (Landy, 2002). The typical stages of play are presented in Table 8.4.

Investigations of the play of young children with disabilities generally reveal that they exhibit the same developmental play sequences as typically developing children, but with some qualitative and quantitative differences (Field, Roseman,

De Stefano, & Koewler, 1982). Less-combinatorial play has been observed in children with mental retardation than would be expected based on their other abilities, and symbolic play appeared later (Guralnick & Neville, 1997). Atypically developing children are less likely to initiate play, they more frequently engage in isolated and toy-directed behaviors, and they display less social-interactive play (Buysse, Goldman, & Skinner, 2002). Further, children with special needs engage in more nonplay activities, have fewer group interactions, and, in general, have less cognitively sophisticated play than typically developing children do (Buysse et al., 2002). The ways in which early childhood special education (ECSE) teachers and parents can address these needs are discussed later in the general strategies section.

TABLE 8.4 Stages of play development

Age Range	Description and Examples
6–8 months	*Nonmeaningful manipulation of objects* (e.g., mouthing, banging, dropping).
8–12 months	*Purposeful exploration of objects.* Child shows knowledge of the appropriate use of objects (e.g., bangs toy drum; winds jack-in-the box).
12–18 months	*Self-related symbolic play.* Play mimics daily activities involving only the child and uses only real objects (e.g., child picks up an empty cup and pretends to drink).
18–24 months	*Other-related play.* Child's symbolic play behaviors begin to involve other recipients of actions, but the child still uses only real objects. At the end of this period, the child begins to combine action sequences by (1) performing a single action on a variety of different recipients (e.g., feeding a doll, then feeding mommy, and finally feeding self) and (2) performing a series of actions on a single recipient (e.g., feeding a doll, putting it to bed, and kissing it good night).
24–30 months	*Planned symbolic play.* Play behaviors are characterized by (1) the use of one object to represent another (e.g., a stick for a spoon); (2) evidence of planning prior to engaging in the play sequence (e.g., the child verbalizes or searches for props before initiating play); and (3) use of a doll or other object as the agent of the play action (e.g., the doll feeds the baby).
3–5 years	*Sociodramatic play.* Language begins to become an integral part of symbolic play. Pretend play sequences involve at least two or more children who (1) select a theme (e.g., going to the doctor); (2) assign roles (e.g., nurse, patient, doctor); and (3) use language appropriate to the different roles.

Source: Adapted with permission from Katz (2001). Playing at home: The talk of pretend play. In D. K. Dickinson & P. O. Tabors (Eds.), *Beginning literacy with language* (pp.53-73). Baltimore: Paul H. Brookes.

Symbolic Play. Play itself can be complex and take on many forms. **Symbolic play**, or pretend play, involves children taking the role of themselves and others in play and using objects for representations of other objects (Driscoll & Nagel, 2003). They pretend to wash their own hair, pretend to wash their mother's hair, and pretend to wash their doll's hair. Play becomes more complex when the child talks for the doll or her mom and when the child attributes feelings to the doll. The ultimate goal of symbolic play is to integrate previously learned ideas, information, and skills from all domains into social learning (Kostelnik, Soderman, & Whiren, 2004).

Development of Emotional Regulation

In order to deal with normal frustrations that occur every day, it is critical that children learn a number of coping strategies. **Emotional regulation** refers to the process by which children control internal reactions to emotions as well as their outward expressions. Optimal emotional regulation development appears to entail the acquisition of a flexible repertoire of coping strategies, such as active problem solving, recruitment of social support, and the capacity to tolerate the intensity of aversive emotion (Saarni, 1999).

For many young children, the development of emotional regulation follows a predictable pattern. Infants have limited or no ability to soothe themselves, and they can have intense emotions at times. By 4 years of age, typically developing preschoolers have more control of their emotions and have developed strategies to enable them to regulate their emotions themselves (Dowling, 2005).

During the preschool years, a full range of emotions is expressed, including guilt, shame, and embarrassment (Landy, 2002). New fears, such as fear of storms, death, or strangers, develop as the child becomes more aware of life's experiences. Consequently, the child becomes more capable of controlling his or her actions and feels guilt if he or she fails to do so. This ability to self-regulate is due to improved cognitive processing skills, which allow the child to better understand situations.

SOCIAL AND EMOTIONAL DEVELOPMENT IN PRIMARY-AGED STUDENTS

Children who are 5 through 8 years old are beginning to develop the capacity for long-term relationships. Many of the themes that began to

While primary-aged students are able to participate in games with rules, younger children have difficulty with this type of task.

emerge in the preschool years, such as peer friendships, continue to be refined in the primary grades. The typical stages of social and emotional development for kindergarteners through third graders are presented in Table 8.5.

Play in Kindergarten and the Primary Grades

Family life differences and socioeconomic and cultural backgrounds have a significant influence on children's play at this stage of development (Driscoll & Nagel, 2003). This is the time when children spend a large proportion of their day in school classrooms. School environments usually do not support play, but when they do, play tends to be presented as a learning activity.

Wing (1995) conducted a study that asked kindergartners, first graders, and second graders to discuss and categorize their classroom activities. Teachers of the children in the study described their programs as "hands-on, with lots of materials, children choosing what to do, free exploration" (Wing, 1995, p. 225). Learning in these classrooms involved children making choices about their learning activities and working in cooperative groups. The way in which the children categorized a classroom activity was related to whether they perceived it as obligatory or not. Children used "have to" to describe activities in mathematics, reading, writing, and calendar. When they talked about their play activities, they often used "get to" and "can" to describe the activities. When children were required to use materials that

TABLE 8.5 Typical stages of social-emotional development in primary-aged children (5–8 years old)

Age	Social	Emotional
5 to 6 years	Serious-minded; practical; enjoys cooperative and sociodramatic play; stronger desire to play with peers of same sex; stronger desire to participate in competitive sports and games with rules	Highly emotional; loves one minute and hates the next; wants to please and do the right thing; does not always tell the truth; not able to admit wrongdoing, as much as he/she tries; not able to tell the difference between mine and yours
6 to 7 years	Wants to be first and have the most possessions; may seem rude and aggressive when interacting with peers or adults; slow to follow directions	Usually relates strongly and warmly to parents; brief periods of being happy with themselves; easily excitable; impulsive and changeable
7 to 8 years	Procrastinates; polite and anxious to impress adults; forgets instructions; forms tighter friendships with a specific group of individuals	Quiet, rather negative emotions; maybe serious, self-absorbed, moody, worrisome, or suspicious; may feel disliked by others and says, "Nobody likes me"; jealous of siblings
8 to 9 years	Very demanding of parents, especially mother; sociable and outgoing; popularity and success are very important outside of family	Vigorous; dramatic; curious; impatient; wants affection and approval from others; easily disappointed if people don't behave as wished; can be quite critical of others; argumentative

Source: Adapted from (1) Ainsworth, M., Blehar, M. C., Waters, E., & Wall, S. (1978). *Patterns of attachment.* Hillsdale, NJ: Erlbaum. (2) Mowder, B. A. (1997). Family dynamics. In A. H. Widerstrom, B. A. Mowder, & S. R. Sandall (Eds.), *Infant development and risk* (2nd ed., pp. 125–153). Baltimore, MD: Brookes. (3) Lamb, M. E., Thompson, R. A., Gardner, W., & Charnov, E. L. (1985). *Infant-mother attachment: The origins and developmental significance of individual differences in strange situation behavior.* Hillsdale: NJ: Erlbaum.

they typically associated with play, such as blocks and teddy bears, in required learning activities, they quickly associated those materials and activities with "work."

Beginning about first grade, sociodramatic play decreases and games with rules become increasingly common in typically developing children. Sociodramatic play that continues to be displayed tends to be more imaginative or deal with fantasy. Children during this age period tend to do the following with their play (Driscoll & Nagel, 2003):

❏ They set the stage for their play or construct a play frame, such as "Let's pretend that we're going to a beauty salon."

❏ They transform objects and settings, such as "The sofa will be our house and this is the beauty salon [pointing to the area by the door]."

❏ They extend the play, such as "Now, pretend we are going to a wedding."

❏ They elaborate on character feelings or actions, such as "You are the flower girl at my sister's wedding."

❏ They change character roles, such as "Pretend that I paint nails now."

❏ They end the play or change the sequence, such as "Pretend that we are going to my grandma's house now."

Another common feature of play during this developmental period is problem solving in group pretend play. That is, children begin to include problems to be solved by the players in their play. For example, they may create a situation in which the lights go out during dinner or a baby becomes sick during a stroller walk. From their scenarios, they take a consistent series of steps to address or solve the problem they created. As children mature, these problem-solving scenarios become more complicated and extend into unfamiliar settings and plots (Kostelnik et al., 2004).

Games with Rules. Games with rules involve accepted, prearranged rules of play (Essa, 2003). Primary-aged children enjoy this type of play because they have a logical system of thinking and they desire order. Games with rules introduce competition into their play and are guided by a set of rules that are agreed to in advance by all players (Driscoll & Nagel, 2003). This is also the age when young children begin to compete in organized sports, such as baseball or soccer.

Peer Interactions and Friendships in the Primary Grades

Children in kindergarten and first, second, and third grades tend to interact with same-sex friends, and their peers are becoming a more significant influence in their lives. Children learn skills such as cooperation, how to be a good friend, and how to work and play in groups from these peer influences (Essa, 2003). In fact, by first or second grade, children develop a sense of groupness that means they are a part of a collective "we" identity. These groups are more stable and have stronger bonds than preschool friendships. Children who manifest atypical social and emotional development need to be guided in developing these skills. Suggestions for developing these skills are discussed later. Children at all ages also display a range of undesirable behaviors.

MANAGING CHALLENGING BEHAVIOR

There are many approaches to the management of unacceptable behavior that interferes with a child's learning, a child's peer relationships, a child's relationships with adults, and a child's personal happiness. Several will be discussed.

Principles of Behavior Management

The overall purpose of behavior management is to assist young children in displaying behaviors that are conducive to learning and to teach social behaviors that are appropriate for home and school settings. In effective adult-child interactions, the children's behavior is recognized, interpreted in context, and responded to contingently (Sandall, Hemmeter, Smith, & McLean, 2005).

According to Walker (1997), there are at least five principles of behavior management that professionals should follow:

1) **Negative consequences sometimes change behavior, but they do not change attitude.** Negative consequences, such as time-out, restriction of privileges, verbal correction, and physical punishment, will effect at least a temporary behavior change. However, unless used in combination with powerful positive reinforcement strategies, they will worsen the negative attitudes that underlie the misbehavior and increase the likelihood of subsequent misbehavior.

2) **Only positive reinforcement strategies produce long-term attitudinal change.** Children decide to behave appropriately because they are influenced by the consequences of their appropriate behavior (Sandall et al., 2005), not because they are forced into it. The consequences of children's behavior must be clearly structured so the complexity of their appropriate behavior is increased (Sandall et al., 2005).

3) **Negative consequences do not improve the behavior of impulsive children and frequently increase the frequency and intensity of their misbehavior.**

4) **Cognitive control of behavior can be learned through the use of appropriate positive reinforcement systems.**

5) **Positive reinforcement systems must be incremental in nature so that children can directly observe even small improvements in their behavior.** Well-designed positive reinforcement systems rely on incremental rewards where the range of reinforcement varies from no reinforcement to intense reinforcement so children can witness, in a tangible way, relative levels of progress.

Sound behavior management programs should be designed to prevent the occurrence of problem behavior, to deal directly with problem behavior when it occurs, and to assist families in dealing with problem behavior at home (Wolery & Fleming, 1992).

Schools have the responsibility to teach appropriate social behavior and behavior control as well as academic and independent living skills to young children with special needs.

Relationship Building with Young Children

Young children with impulsivity and high rates of inappropriate, noncompliant behavior can be challenging for families and professionals alike. One of the principal tasks of ECSE professionals is to provide children with instruction that will allow them to experience positive relationships with peers and adults while learning more appropriate ways to seek attention and interaction. Children who enter kindergarten without adequate social and emotional competence face a cascade of problems that often last into adulthood (Huffman, Mehlinger, & Kerivan, 2000). One essential component of any behavior management system is a commitment from the adults implementing it to build positive, reliable relationships with the young children who present the most behavior challenges. Doing this is the very foundation of good teaching (Joseph & Strain, 2004).

Carr and colleagues (Carr, McLaughlin, Giacobbe-Greico, & Smith, 2003) documented a powerful, positive correlation between poor rapport and the occurrence of problem behavior in dyads of caregivers and children. Their research showed that instruction in rapport building for caregivers resulted in reductions in problem behaviors. Taking the time to build positive relationships with children with problem behavior may save time that would be spent implementing more elaborate and time-consuming assessment and intervention strategies later. This is particularly important in light of research that shows teachers may avoid social and instructional opportunities with children who display chronic problem behaviors (Shores & Wehby, 1999). As Joseph and Strain (2004) state: "Whenever teachers and caregivers engage in strategies to build positive relationships [with children], it is as if they are 'making a deposit' in a child's relationship piggy bank" (p. 25). They recommend brief, focused interaction episodes and praise as keys to relationship building in young children.

Assessment of Undesirable Behavior

Since children communicate more through behavior than words, direct observational methods provide valuable information regarding a child's social, emotional, and behavioral functioning. In order to conduct observations in a manner that leads to useful information, target behaviors must be clearly identified and broken down into observable, measurable components that are operationally defined in each of the environments or settings of concern (Gimpel & Holland, 2003). Direct observations provide professionals the opportunity to determine the **antecedents**, what happens right before the behavior occurs, and **consequences**, what happens right after the behavior occurs, that may be maintaining the child's behaviors (Thompson, Felce, & Symons, 2000). The information gained from antecedent–consequence observations allows professionals to examine setting variables that may be influencing the behaviors of concern.

The following elements of the setting should be observed: (1) the adult's interactions with the child; (2) possible distractions or outside noises; (3) what antecedents and consequents occur when the child exhibits the problem behavior; and (4) the child's physical setting, including the amount of space available to the child, the child's proximity to other children, and the materials. Based on the information gained from these structured observations, professionals, and parents when appropriate, devise interventions to modify or disrupt the target behaviors or provide the child with alternative means to accomplish goals.

Intervention with Infants and Toddlers

Early intervention for infants and toddlers with challenging behavior is critical. Intervention approaches with this age group typically include teaching the parents interaction skills to assist the child in coping with difficult situations, regulating sensory input, understanding routines, and supporting the child's language and social development (Fox, 2006). These approaches are taught to parents in a way that supports the family and allows parents to learn to incorporate the strategies into their routines.

Research has shown that supporting parents in learning ways to manage their very young child's behavior may be accomplished by modeling, discussion and written materials, and rehearsal with feedback, which may use videotaped modeling (Reid, Webster-Stratton, & Baydar, 2004). Data show that modeling is more effective than written materials and that group training formats have advantages over individual training formats, especially in the areas of observational learning and cost effectiveness (Wolery & Fleming, 1992).

One intervention technique that has been found to be successful in parent-child relationship training is the Play and Learning Strategies Curriculum (PALS) (Baggett, 2006). PALS is a videotaped curriculum that teaches parents specific skills for interacting with their infants and toddlers. It utilizes videotaped examples of mothers and children to demonstrate each concept.

The topics covered include attending to infants' communicative signals, responding appropriately to their positive and negative signals, encouraging their cooperation, and responding to their misbehavior. The program is designed to be facilitated by a trained parent educator who presents each session to parents and coaches them in utilizing the specific techniques.

Intervention with Preschoolers

Use a Decision-Model Approach. To address challenging behaviors in preschoolers with social and emotional problems, professionals and parents follow a decision model. A **decision model** is a set of questions and guidelines that allow adults to make decisions about whether to intervene, which intervention(s) should be used, and whether the intervention(s) has been effective.

One decision model that has been found to be useful was developed by Wolery, Bailey, and Sugai (1988). The first step in this model is to identify the problem situation and state it in a goal format. In this step, the team determines whether a problem exists and, if so, the type of problem the child is manifesting. Problem behavior can take the format of a behavioral deficit (e.g., the behavior occurs too infrequently or does not last long enough) or inappropriate self-control (e.g., the behavior occurs in the wrong places or at the wrong times) (Wolery & Fleming, 1992). The team also determines whether the problem behavior is typical for children of that age or developmental level and writes an intervention goal.

For example, Mr. Browning reported that Simon, a 4-year-old with communication delays, was disrupting his opening circle time in his inclusive preschool classroom. A week of observations of Mr. Browning and Simon showed that Simon was reprimanded five to seven times during circle time and that children sitting next to Simon complained two to five times most sessions that Simon was touching, pushing, or talking to them. Based on these data, the team determined that a problem did exist.

The second step of this decision model is an assessment of the child and the environment. Here the team defines the problem behavior, identifies the function or the purpose of the problem behavior for the child (e.g., whether the behavior is done to obtain desirable events or is done to avoid or escape undesirable events), and determines whether some aspect of the environment could be changed to alter the problem behavior.

Using the same example, the first action Mr. Browning took was to define Simon's "disruptive behaviors" in opening circle as calling out without raising his hand; touching, pushing, and talking to children next to him; grabbing materials from the teacher to look at them; and continuing to sing after a song had stopped. Next Mr. Browning and the paraprofessional recorded the exact events that preceded these behaviors (antecedents) and those that followed these behaviors (consequences) for several days.

With these data, the team determined that Simon's behavior was a function of both a behavioral deficit and poor self-control. Simon's difficulty in comprehending and attending to the story and Mr. Browning's long passages of talking seemed to result in Simon grabbing materials from the teacher in an attempt to "see" them to aid his comprehension. Simon's delayed receptive language skills made the story component of the opening circle difficult for him. Since limited visual cues were used by Mr. Browning, Simon probably did not understand a good deal of what was being shared. This difficulty with comprehension also appeared to influence Simon's inappropriate touching, pushing, and talking to other children, since these behaviors tended to occur after the story was begun or during teacher discussion following the story. Simon's poor self-control appeared to be responsible for his calling out and singing a preferred song after it was completed.

Mr. Browning and the team hypothesized that Simon may have been using these behaviors to gain teacher attention and to avoid tasks that he did not like or tasks that were difficult for him. Further, it was noted that Mr. Browning usually gave Simon a turn when he called out or grabbed something. However, during nearly two weeks of observations, Simon received only two praise statements from Mr. Browning, and those did not address a specific behavior.

The team met to collaboratively develop an intervention plan. The plan for Simon consisted of seven components. First, Simon was given turns more frequently in circle time, when he was sitting quietly, to help him attend and wait. Second, small pillows were placed between Simon and the children next to him to discourage touching and pushing. Third, a picture activity schedule for opening circle was made. Simon was asked to take off the picture of each activity (e.g., calendar, name song) as it was completed and put it in his "all done" box during circle. This allowed Simon to be more appropriately active during group time and gave him visual cues regarding what had occurred and what was coming up. Fourth, Simon was given a duplicate copy of the book to "read" while Mr. Browning read the book to the class, and Simon was asked to show pictures to the class periodically as the story was read. Fifth, Mr. Browning ignored all talk-outs and modeled raising his hand with his other hand over his mouth when Simon called out. Only when Simon raised his hand and did not speak was he given a turn. Sixth, since Simon was developmentally about a year and a half behind the other children, it was determined that the length of the opening group was too long for his present ability. Consequently, after ten minutes, Simon was given a task to complete at a table near the group while the circle continued. As Simon's behavior improved, the time he spent at group was extended by two minutes each month. Finally, Simon was explicitly praised for all appropriate behaviors at least every two to three minutes (e.g., "You raised your hand without talking. Good thinking!") Since language comprehension was an issue, Mr. Browning made sure Simon saw his face when he praised him and he patted Simon's back.

The final step of the decision model is monitoring the child's progress and conducting ongoing assessment of the intervention plan. To determine if interventions are working, data are collected. The results of these frequent analyses allow data-driven decisions to be made regarding whether the plan should be continued, adjusted, or aborted.

Lentini, Vaughn, and Fox (2007) have developed a routine-based guide that is helpful in completing this decision-model process. (Their website, Creating teaching tools for young children with challenging behavior, is listed in Appendix C.) This guide provides professionals with options for responding to each decision step and is especially helpful in developing intervention plans. Another strategy that may be used to prevent, as well as to intervene with, problem behavior is the use of high-probability requests.

Use the High-Probability Request Strategy. High-probability requests are requests with which a child typically complies (Chambers, 2006), such as "Hands on your head." Low-probability requests are requests with which the child typically does not comply, such as "Help me pick up these puzzle pieces, please." The high-probability request strategy consists of giving a child three to five simple requests that the child typically follows. The requests are given consecutively and just prior to a request that has a history of low compliance. According to behavioral momentum theory (Nevin, Mandrell, & Atak, 1983), the child's compliance with a high-probability request sets the stage for compliance with the low-probability request. The behavioral momentum for complying influences the child to follow a request that typically results in noncompliance. The strategy has been found effective with children with autism, with severe emotional behavior disorder (Davis & Reichle, 1996), and with mental retardation (Ducharme & Worling, 1994).

Intervention with Primary-Aged Students

Longitudinal studies suggest that social, emotional, and behavioral competence in young children predicts academic success in the early elementary years (Raver, 2002; Zins, Bloodworth, Weissberg, & Wahlberg, 2004). The general belief is that children will have difficulty learning to read or doing other academic work if they have problems that distract them from educational activities, problems following directions, problems getting along with others, and problems controlling negative emotions (Smith, 2007). While most children learn positive social and emotional skills through their everyday interactions with adults and peers, many children do not.

Young children with special needs exhibit a wide range of social and behavioral difficulties. An intervention approach that is effective with one child may be less effective with another child. By understanding several approaches, the likelihood of success with all children can be increased. The real challenge for ECSE teachers is determining when to use an approach, with which child, and under which conditions. Several classroom behavior management strategies for decreasing undesirable behaviors will be discussed.

Positive Behavior Reinforcement. With this strategy, teachers use selective attention on a regular basis to reinforce their students for appropriate social and on-task behaviors (Gimpel & Holland, 2003). Whenever a teacher notices a child following a classroom rule and behaving appropriately, the teacher delivers a brief praise statement, such as "Keith, your eyes are on me and you are sitting in your seat—nice job." There are two fundamental rules for positive behavior reinforcement: (1) Feedback needs to be both specific and immediate, and (2) students need to be clear about what behaviors are desirable and undesirable (Stormont, Lewis, & Beckner, 2005).

For example, in one inclusive kindergarten class, the teacher had only one rule that she believed was important: "I will be kind." To make this rule effective, she broke it down into specific behaviors for each of the settings in which her students participated—the classroom, the playground, the bus, and the hallway. The teacher made a matrix showing what students should be doing when they were following the rule. For example, in the classroom, to be kind meant (1) sharing materials, (2) having quiet hands and feet, (3) using kind words with teachers and friends, and

(4) immediately following the teacher's directions. On the playground, the rule meant (1) taking turns, (2) using kind words with teachers and friends, and (3) immediately following the teacher's directions.

Although this strategy appears to be common sense, observations in special and general education teachers' classes indicate that most teachers use low levels of positive reinforcement (McIntosh, Vaughn, Schumm, Haager, & Lee, 1993). How teachers organize their classroom rules is critical for compliance with those rules.

Classroom Rules. Depending on students' ages and abilities, the class should participate in identifying the general categories of what constitutes appropriate and inappropriate behavior in a classroom, with teacher guidance. Effective classroom rules have these characteristics: (1) They are supported by positive consequences (e.g., "When I follow rule 1, I earn ten minutes of academic free time at the end of the day.") and negative consequences (e.g., "If I break rule l, I lose ten minutes of academic free time at the end of the day. I will begin my homework while children who followed this rule play academic games."), (2) they are stated simply and explicitly, (3) they are few in number (e.g., no more than five), (4) they are stated in observable terms, (5) they are posted and reviewed *each* day, and (6) they are written in positive terms (e.g., "I will keep my hands, objects, and feet to myself," rather than "I will not hit, push, or throw objects.").

To teach classroom rules, teachers should do the following (King, 2003):

❑ Verbally describe behaviors included in the rules and how they may change in various settings, such as when students are in the hallway or cafeteria.

❑ Provide explicit teaching of the rules.

❑ Have students model following and breaking the rules.

❑ Allow students to rehearse following the rules.

❑ Have students restate each rule with both positive and negatives consequences in their own words frequently.

Reinforcers. Positive reinforcement is a method teachers use to increase appropriate behavior in an individual child or a group of children. **Positive reinforcement** is the presentation of a stimulus following the target behavior (Bailey & Wolery, 1992). Reinforcers may be tangible, such as a reward certificate for good work; physical, such as a pat on the back; or verbal, such as "You followed rule 2 all morning. Great listening!" It is important to keep in mind that what is reinforcing for one child may not be reinforcing for another. Also, it is important to reevaluate the effectiveness of reinforcers as time passes. What may have been reinforcing for a child in September may no longer be reinforcing in February.

Token Reinforcement Systems. Token reinforcement systems increase the likelihood of appropriate behaviors in many students. When the teacher sees a child engaging in appropriate behavior, the teacher gives the student a token, which may be a star on a chart or a poker chip in a can, accompanied by a brief praise statement (Gimpel & Holland, 2003). When the child has earned a certain number of tokens by the end of the school day, the child is able to exchange them for a tangible reinforcer, such as stickers, school supplies, or a snack. The key to successful implementation of this technique is to determine what is reinforcing to children by asking them or observing their everyday preferences.

Decreasing Inappropriate Behavior. To improve the emotional and educational climate of a classroom, teachers attempt to change children's behavior. The following suggestions should guide teachers as they work to change students' inappropriate behavior (Morgan & Reinhart, 1991):

❏ Follow through consistently with the rules and consequences you and the class have selected.

❏ Do not establish consequences that are uncomfortable for you to implement.

❏ Listen and talk to students, but avoid disagreements or arguments.

❏ Focus on the most interfering problems first.

❏ Avoid comparing students' behaviors or abilities to one another.

Since unexpected changes in classroom routines can cause students who exhibit oppositional behavior to act out, following a consistent and predicable routine as well as structuring transitions is important. When students know what to expect in the classroom each day, they are more likely to believe that they are in control of their environment, which may reduce instances of defiance (Salend & Sylvestre, 2005).

Conducting Functional Behavior Assessments and Developing Interventions

Professionals use a functional analysis of behavior to assess the form and function of challenging behaviors (Baglin, Riley, & McCormick, 2004; Sandall et al., 2005). The steps discussed earlier in the decision model generate the same information that is gathered in a functional behavior assessment (FBA): (1) a description of the problem behavior, (2) the situations where the problem behavior is most and least likely to occur, and (3) the consequences that reward and maintain the problem behavior (Horner, Albin, Todd, & Sprague, 2006). Professionals gather information from several incidents and use direct observations, interviews, rating scales, and reviews of records to collect data for this assessment.

After the FBA process is completed, the next step is to develop, implement, and evaluate a positive behavior support plan. A **behavior improvement plan** (BIP) is an intervention plan developed to change the behavior of a child (Watson & Steege, 2003). Traditional behavior management methods worked to change the individual that was behaving inappropriately and focused on punishment. In contrast, a BIP focuses on changing the environment to avoid problem behavior and teaches the child new, or replacement, behaviors. This plan defines expected behaviors, offers the child instruction in how to execute the behaviors, and provides positive and negative consequences (Sandall et al., 2005).

GENERAL STRATEGIES FOR PROMOTING APPROPRIATE SOCIAL AND EMOTIONAL SKILLS

The general goals for skill development in the social domain are for children to gain emotional control, develop successful patterns of interaction with adults and peers, and acquire appropriate social skills. For children to progress toward these goals, they must have ample opportunities to attain positive interpersonal skills and learn to respond in an age-appropriate manner to behavioral expectations at home and in school.

Promoting Appropriate Social and Emotional Skills in Infants and Toddlers

Kostelnik, Whiren, Soderman, and Gregory (2006) identified several strategies parents and professionals may use to facilitate appropriate social and emotional development in infants and toddlers:

❏ *Respond to an infant's signals in a way that is appropriate for the developmental level of the child.* When an infant 6 months of age or younger cries, the child needs an adult to quickly attend to his or her needs. Older infants and toddlers have an increased ability to wait and will respond to speech and other signs of attention while waiting for care, but their patience is still limited. Responding promptly enables a child to learn that an adult will assist him or her in times of need, supporting the development of secure attachments and positive social interactions.

❏ *Comment during routine care about objects or actions that interest the infant.* Adults should maintain a face-to-face position, use simple sentences or phrases, use a good deal of expression, and allow time for the child to respond (Raver & Knitzer, 2002).

❏ *Use language to respond to an older infant's gestures.* Simple, short, direct statements tend to be the best response to gestures. For example, when a toddler points to a cup, say, "Want juice cup?"

❏ *Wait for a physical response to key phrases from a child who is not yet talking.* Before children begin to talk, they understand several words and phrases, even though they are not able to express them, such as "bye-bye" and "finished." However, they may take a little time to respond, despite understanding what was said. For this reason, it is important when asking a child if he or she has finished eating, to wait at least five seconds for the child's response. The child may respond by holding up his or her arms to be lifted out of the high chair or hand the adult his or her cup.

❏ *Tell the infant or toddler what you are going to do before you do it, and pause a second or two before starting.* Children need time to prepare for what is coming next. For example, say, "I'm going to change your diaper now."

❏ *Provide play materials and interaction experiences that encourage the child to explore the environment.* Provide toys that are at the child's present developmental age, but that still challenge his or her awakening interest in objects and people.

❏ *Praise each success.* Praising, cuddling, and cheering for a child who searches for a hidden toy or who is learning to sit encourage the child to continue learning and to enjoy it.

❏ *Encourage exploration by being physically available to the child during play.* Be available to the child to support, guide, acknowledge, and expand his or her play activities. In center-based programs for toddlers, organize playtime so that more than one adult is supervising floor time and interacting with the children.

❏ *Arrange social experiences between infants or toddlers when they are comfortable and alert.* Place small infants in seats so they can see each other. Toddlers need structured time to explore play areas together.

Use Positive Touch. For some children with delays and disabilities, positive touch has been used effectively to enhance caregiver-child interactions and increase the child's comfort (Pardew & Bunse, 2005). Positive touch involves massaging a young child with specific motions designed to relax and calm the child, often making him or her more open to interaction. Massage strokes include effleurage (e.g., long, slow stroking motions), pressure touch (e.g., gentle, firm pressure motions), kneading strokes (e.g., circular strokes), and milking strokes (e.g., moving back and forth with the hand in a "C" shape). The purpose of using positive touch is not to replace therapy or other types of interventions, but to offer parents a calming way to "connect" with their child. Research has shown that infant massage and positive touch are beneficial for bonding, stress reduction, and state regulation (Harrison, 2001) and for weight gain in preterm infants; they also can improve attentiveness and sleep problems in some children with autism (Escalona, Field, Singer-Strunck, Cullen, & Hartshorn, 2001).

Promoting Appropriate Social and Emotional Skills in Preschoolers

The success of peer-to-peer social interaction is influenced by children's ability to engage verbally. Verbal engagement provides a structure to support the exchange of ideas, thoughts, and experiences (Hadley & Schuele, 1995). To facilitate appropriate social skills in children with delays in this area, professionals use peer-mediated instruction and teach and reinforce the development of prosocial behaviors.

Peer-Mediated Instruction. One of the most persuasive arguments for inclusion is that children with atypical development have an opportunity to learn appropriate behaviors by watching typical peers and imitating them. However, placing children with special needs in an inclusive environment will not by itself ensure that appropriate social learning occurs (Buysse et al., 2002). Children who are delayed in their social and/or emotional skills have to be taught to model desired social behaviors used by more developmentally advanced peers or typically developing peers who are serving as peer models (Raver, 1980; Raver, Cooke, & Apolloni, 1978; Peck, Apolloni, Cooke, & Raver, 1978; Odom et al., 1999).

Peer-mediated teaching requires teachers to follow four basic steps. First, teachers train peer models to interact with the target child in predetermined ways. The purpose for the social training must be explained to the typical peer and his or her role as a peer model clearly outlined, including the need for the peer to give verbal reinforcement to the target child for the behaviors being taught (Simpson, Myles, Sasso, & Kamps, 1997). Second, play activities must be structured so typical and atypical children have many opportunities to interact. Third, professionals must use prompting and modeling with both typical and atypical children to increase selected social skills throughout the day (Hollingsworth, 2005). Finally, data are collected on the effectiveness of the interventions and adjustments made as needed.

Teaching children how to play with peers can be a challenging task. The following are strategies that adults may use to prompt or coach children to continue their play with peers (Kostelnik et al., 2006):

❏ *Suggest a related theme.* Extend the play theme that the children are currently using. For example, if the children are playing with dolls, suggest that they take the dolls on a picnic or a vacation.

❏ *Add a necessary prop to the children's play.* Children going on a vacation need a suitcase, whereas children going on a picnic need a picnic basket. Adding the necessary props will assist the children in following through with the theme.

❏ *Introduce new players from outside the play frame.* One way to introduce a new player is to indicate that the child would like to join the ongoing activity. Two types of prompts may be used. In the first one, the adult prompts the children who are currently playing to allow a new child to join by saying something such as "John has been watching you play and would like to play, too." Another strategy is to prompt the target child with the specific words to say to the children currently playing. For example, the adult may say to the target child, "Say, I want to play, too." Should the children playing not want the target child to participate, the adult must assist the target child in finding another place to play, providing several alternatives. ECSE teachers must keep in mind that small-group games and pretend play are more difficult to enter than art activities, for instance, because the children in pretend play already have established roles and relationships.

❏ *Teach children to use a clear signal when leaving the play frame.* It is important to teach typical and atypical children how to tell playmates when they do not want to take part in a specific type of play or when they want to leave the play. Target children can be prompted by a statement such as "Tell Jamal you don't want to play cars anymore" or "Katie doesn't know that you don't want to feed the baby anymore. Tell her."

Prosocial Behaviors. It is the ECSE professional's job to create an environment that fosters positive peer-peer and adult-child relationships (Sandall et al., 2005). Professionals deliberately target outcomes that build on a child's current skills and behavior and promote a sense of membership with a group (Sandall et al., 2005). Many studies have shown that adult prompting is effective in producing positive changes in social skills such as initiations, sharing, and play (Craig-Unkefer & Kaiser, 2002; Goldstein & Cisar, 1992). Unfortunately, the frequency of positive social behavior typically decreases when prompting is withdrawn. However, Stanton-Chapman and colleagues (Stanton-Chapman, Kaiser, & Wolery, 2006) found that prompting within social interactions may not be necessary if an intervention program provides extensive social skills training.

Shaping. Shaping involves using reinforcement to maintain or encourage a desired behavior a little bit at a time. Commonly, professionals use verbal prompts, physical assistance, and verbal reinforcement to encourage children to demonstrate components of target prosocial skills (Hollingsworth, 2005). A persistent problem in using shaping is the need to fade adult prompts and adult-mediated consequences. If these are not faded systematically, children may engage in high levels of the target behavior only when adult supports are provided.

Using positive words. Communication is key to teaching children how to engage in appropriate behavior. It is always best to tell a child what *to do* instead of what *not to do.* Often children with special needs have to be shown what is expected by modeling the behavior or using picture cues. Professionals need to remember that many children with developmental delays use inappropriate behavior because they do not yet understand social rules. Contractions such as "don't" can be difficult for young children to understand (Lentini et al., 2007). Instead of saying, "Stop throwing your toys," it is better to say, "Play with your toys on the floor." Similarly, statements like "Don't hit" need to be changed to "Hands down. Use your words/signs/pictures. Tell me what you want." Naturally, desired behaviors must be followed by enthusiastic encouragement and reinforcement.

Promoting Appropriate Social and Emotional Skills in Primary-Aged Students

Like younger children, school-age students with special needs often need systematic training in order to display appropriate social and emotional skills. To achieve this, professionals use class meetings and skill training to teach prosocial behaviors. These strategies proved successful for David, featured in the case study. David also needed to have language arts objectives adjusted to better match his present ability level which helped to increase his prosocial behaviors during these lessons.

Class Meetings. An efficient way to teach appropriate social and emotional skills is by having class meetings. There are three types of class meetings: open-ended, educational/diagnostic, and problem-solving (Gartrell, 2004). The open-ended class meeting discusses hypothetical problems, such as "What would you do if you wanted to play with a group of friends, but they said no?" The educational/diagnostic class meeting is used to discuss expected behaviors and consequences, such as rules for riding the bus on a field trip. The third type, the problem-solving meeting, discusses real conflicts occurring in the classroom. For example, a teacher might hold a class meeting when behavior in the hall had gotten out of control.

Class meetings provide a forum in which students can openly express their feelings without feeling threatened. Teachers are able to think out loud and guide students through the discussion (Morris, 2002). In addition, class meetings give students the foresight to anticipate troublesome or frustrating interactions and allow them to emerge from the meetings with a repertoire of alternative responses for situations. It is important that ECSE professionals use concrete language, keep the meeting topic focused, keep the meeting short, and have students review the outcomes or conclusions at the end of the meeting.

Planned Social Training Lessons. Planned social training activities are lessons given to the full class, small groups, or individual children to teach them how to respond to an array of situations, such as how to initiate contact, how to ask for help, how to negotiate conflict, or how to accept kindness. These lessons identify a needed skill and determine beforehand multiple ways the skill will be taught, such as through role-playing or structured cooperative games. Following the lesson, the teacher must track the effectiveness of the activity and must be vigilant about acknowledging children who demonstrate the targeted behaviors in the classroom after training (Kostelnik et al., 2006).

CONCLUSION

The acquisition of social competence begins at birth and continues throughout early childhood as a result of maturation and learning. Infants develop social-emotional competence in the context of their families, gradually coming to understand that others have goals of their own. As children progress through the preschool years, their social-emotional competence is further developed by interactions with peers. During the primary school years, adults support children's friendships and appropriate behavior through informal and formal coaching sessions. As David's case study illuminated, a critical role ECSE professionals play is facilitating positive interactions between children and adults by establishing environments that are conducive to learning and appropriate behavior and that are individualized.

SUMMARY

Social and emotional development in young children

- Social-emotional development involves the ability to regulate emotions and manage social relationships in ways that are acceptable to others.

Managing challenging behavior

- Intervention approaches with infants, toddlers, and preschoolers generally include teaching parents and caregivers to use management skills within routines through modeling, discussion, and rehearsal with feedback.
- Intervention approaches with primary-aged students generally include teaching compliance with rules and consequences, providing positive behavior reinforcement, and using token reinforcement systems.

General strategies for promoting appropriate social and emotional skills

- General strategies for infants and toddlers with special needs include responding to the child's signals in a responsive way, talking regularly to the child, and providing play materials and interactions that foster attachment and exploration.

- General strategies for preschoolers with special needs include having adults teach appropriate social interactions and play using modeling, peer-mediated learning, shaping, and guided play themes.
- General strategies for primary-aged students with special needs include using direct instruction to teach prosocial skills by conducting class meetings and teaching social skills lessons.

DISCUSSION QUESTIONS/ACTIVITIES

1. Using Table 8.2, describe the differences between the typical attachment noted in 2- to 7-month-olds and that noted in toddlers who are 24 to 36 months old.

2. Describe three characteristics of play in infancy, in preschool, and in the primary grades. (Table 8.4 will be helpful.)

3. Using David's case study, identify three actions that Mrs. Williams could take that might help David learn more appropriate behavior in the class and improve his learning.

REFERENCES

Ainsworth, M. D. S. (1982). Attachment: Retrospect and prospect. In C. K. Parke & J. Stevenson-Hide (Eds.), *The place of attachment in human behavior* (pp. 3–30). New York: Basic Books.

Ainsworth, M. D. S., Blehar, M. C., Waters, E., & Wall, S. (1978). *Patterns of attachment*. Hillsdale, NJ: Erlbaum.

Baggett, K. M. (2006, March 25). *Promoting infant social-emotional health: Parent-infant interaction coaching.* Presented at Addressing Challenging Behavior: The National Training Institute on Effective Practices Supporting Young Children's Social-Emotional Development Conference, Clearwater, FL.

Baglin, C. A., Riley, D., & McCormick, T. (2004). Functional assessments of problem behaviors. In C. A. Baglin, M. E. B. Lewis, & B. Williams (Eds.), *Recreation and leisure for persons with emotional problems and challenging behaviors* (pp.31-66). Baltimore, MD: Sagamore.

Bailey, D. B., & Wolery, M. (1992). *Teaching infants and preschoolers with disabilities* (2nd ed.). Upper Saddle River, NJ: Merrill/Prentice Hall.

Belsky, J., Lerner, R., & Spainer, G. (1985). *The child in the family*. Reading, MA: Addison-Wesley.

Bornstein, M. H. (1986). *The multivariate model of the interaction effects in human development: Categories of caretaking.* New York: New York University.

Buysse, V., Goldman, G., & Skinner, M. (2002). Setting effects on friendship formation among young children with and without disabilities. *Exceptional Children, 68*(4), 503–517.

Carr, E., McLaughlin, D., Giacobbe-Greico, T., & Smith, C. (2003). Using mood ratings and mood induction in assessment and intervention with severe problem behavior. *American Journal on Mental Retardation, 108*, 32–55.

Chambers, C. R. (2006). High-probability request strategy: Practical guidelines. *Young Exceptional Children, 9*(2), 20–29.

Chess, S., & Thomas, A. (1996). *Temperament: Theory and practice.* New York: Brunner/Mazel.

Craig-Unkefer, L. A., & Kaiser, A. (2002). Improving the social communication skills of at-risk preschool children in a play context. *Topics in Early Childhood Special Education, 22*, 3–13.

Davis, C., & Reichle, J. (1996). Variant and invariant high-probability requests: Increasing appropriate behaviors in children with emotional-behavioral disorders. *Journal of Applied Behavior Analysis, 29*, 471–482.

Dowling, M. (2005). *Young children's personal, social, and emotional development.* Thousand Oaks, CA: Paul Chapman.

Driscoll, A., & Nagel, N. G. (2003). *Early childhood education birth to 8: The world of children, families, and educators* (2nd ed.). Boston: Allyn & Bacon.

Ducharme, J., & Worling, D. (1994). Behavioral momentum and stimulus fading in the acquisition and maintenance of child compliance in the home. *Journal of Applied Behavioral Analysis, 27*, 639–647.

Escalona, A., Field, T., Singer-Strunck, R., Cullen, C., & Hartshorn, K. (2001). Brief report: Improvements in the behavior of children with autism following massage therapy. *Journal of Autism and Developmental Disorders, 31*(5), 513–516.

Essa, E. L. (2003). *Early childhood education* (4th ed.). Clifton Park, NY: Delmar Learning.

Field, T., Lasko, D., Munday, P., Henteleff, T., Kabat, S., & Talpins, S. (1997). Brief report: Autistic children's attentiveness and responsivity improve after touch therapy. *Journal of Autism and Developmental Disorders, 27*(3), 333–338.

Field, T., Roseman, S., De Stefano, L., & Koewler, J. (1982). The play of handicapped and nonhandicapped children in integrated and nonintegrated situations. *Topics in Early Childhood Special Education, 2*(3), 28–38.

Flaste, R. (1991, April 28). Sidelined by loneliness. *New York Times Magazine*, pp. 14–15, 23–24.

Fox, L. (2006). *Recommended practices: Supporting infants and toddlers with challenging behavior*. Retrieved April 27, 2006, from the Center for Evidenced Based Practice: Young Children with Challenging Behavior Web site: http://challengingbehavior.fmhi.usf.edu/ handouts/ SupportInfantsToddlers. pdf

Gartrell, D. (2004). *The power of guidance: Teaching social-emotional skills in early childhood classrooms*. Clifton Park, NY: Thomson Delmar Learning.

Gimpel, G. A., & Holland, M. L. (2003). *Emotional and behavioral problems of young children: Effective interventions in the preschool and kindergarten years*. New York: Guilford Press.

Goldstein, H., & Cisar, C. (1992). Promoting interaction during sociodramatic play: Teaching scripts to typical preschoolers and classmates with disabilities. *Journal of Applied Behavior Analysis, 25*, 265–280.

Guralnick, M., & Neville, B. (1997). Designing early intervention programs to promote children's social competence. In M. Guralnick (Ed.), *The effectiveness of early intervention* (pp. 579–610). Baltimore, MD: Brookes.

Hadley, P. A., & Schuele, C. M. (1995). Verbal interactions with peers in a preschool language intervention classroom. In M. L. Rice & K. A. Wilcox (Eds.), *Building a language-focused curriculum for the preschool classroom* (pp. 105–126). Baltimore, MD: Brookes.

Halverson, C. F., Jr., Kohnstamm, G. A., & Martin, R. P. (Eds.). (1994). *The developing structure of temperament and personality from infancy to adulthood*. Hillsdale, NJ: Erlbaum.

Harrison, L. L. (2001). The use of comforting touch and massage to reduce stress in preterm infants in the neonatal intensive care unit. *Newborn and Infant Nursing Reviews, l*, 235–241.

Hartup, W. W. (1992). Friendships and their developmental significance. In H. McGarle (Ed.), *Childhood social development: Contemporary perspectives* (pp. 175–205). Hillsdale, NJ: Erlbaum.

Hetherington, E. M. (1983). Socialization in the context of the family: Parent-child interaction. In P. H. Mussen (Ed.), *Handbook of child psychology: Vol. IV. Socialization, personality, and social development* (pp. 103–196). New York: Wiley.

Hollingsworth, H. L. (2005). Interventions to promote peer social interactions in preschool settings. *Young Exceptional Children, 9*(1), 2–11.

Horner, R. H., Albin, R. W., Todd, A. W., & Sprague, J. (2006). Positive behavior support for individuals with severe disabilities. In M. Snell & F. Brown (Eds.), *Instruction of students with severe disabilities* (6th ed., pp. 206–250). Upper Saddle River, NJ: Merrill/ Prentice Hall.

Huffman, L., Mehlinger, S., & Kerivan, A. (2000). Risk factors for academic and behavior problems at the beginning of school. In L. C. Huffman (Ed.), *Off to a good start: Research on the risk factors for early school problems and selected federal policies affecting children's social and emotional development and their readiness for school* (pp. 25–45). Chapel Hill: University of North Carolina, Frank Port Graham Child Development Center.

Joseph, G. E., & Strain, P. S. (2004). Building positive relationships with young children. *Young Exceptional Children, 7*(4), 21–28.

Kagan, J., Arcus, D., & Snidman, N. (1993). The idea of temperament: Where do we go from here? In R. Plomin & G. E. McClearn (Eds.), *Nature, nurture, & psychology* (pp. 197–210). Washington, DC: American Psychological Association.

Katz, L. (1993). Dispositions: Definitions and implications for early childhood practices. In *Perspectives from ERIC: EECE* (Monograph Series No. 4). Urbana, IL: ERIC Clearinghouse on Elementary and Early Childhood Education.

Kerns, K. A. (2000). Types of preschool friendships. *Personal Relationships, 7*, 311–324.

King, D. (2003). Tips to help new teachers with classroom management. *CEC Today, 10*(3), 12–14.

Kostelnik, M. J., Soderman, A. K., & Whiren, A. P. (2004). *Developmentally appropriate programs in early childhood education* (2nd ed.). Upper Saddle River, NJ: Merrill/Prentice Hall.

Kostelnik, M. J., Whiren, A. P., Soderman, A. K., & Gregory, K. (2006). *Guiding social development: Theory to practice* (5th ed.). Clifton Park, NY: Thomson Delmar Learning.

Lamb, M. E., Thompson, R. A., Gardner, W., & Charnov, E. L. (1985). *Infant-mother attachment: The origins and developmental significance of individual differences in strange situation behavior*. Hillsdale: NJ: Erlbaum.

Landy, S. (2002). *Pathways to competence: Encouraging healthy social and emotional development in young children*. Baltimore, MD: Brookes.

Lentini, R., Vaughn, B. J., & Fox, L. (2007). *Routine based support guide for young children with challenging behavior*.

Tampa: University of South Florida, Early Intervention Positive Behavior Support Project.

Lifter, K., & Bloom, L. (1998). Intentionality and the role of play in the transition to language. In A. Wetherby, S. Warren, & J. Reichle (Eds.), *Transitions in prelinguisitic communication: Preintentional to intentional and presymbolic to symbolic* (pp. 161–196). Baltimore, MD: Brookes.

McIntosh, R., Vaughn, S., Schumm, J. S., Haager, D., & Lee, O. (1993). Observations of students with learning disabilities in general education classrooms: You don't bother me and I won't bother you. *Exceptional Children, 60,* 249–261.

Morgan, S. R., & Reinhart, J. A. (1991). *Interventions for students with emotional disorders.* Austin, TX: PRO-ED.

Morris, S. (2002). Promoting social skills among students with nonverbal learning disabilities. *Teaching Exceptional Children, 34,* 66–70.

Mowder, B. A. (1997). Family dynamics. In A. H. Widerstrom, B. A. Mowder, & S. R. Sandall (Eds.), *Infant development and risk* (2nd ed., pp. 125–153). Baltimore, MD: Brookes.

Nevin, J., Mandrell, C., & Atak, J. (1983). The analysis of behavioral momentum. *Journal of Experimental Analysis of Behavior, 39,* 49–59.

Odom, S., McConnell, S., McEvoy, M., Peterson, C., Ostrosky, M., & Chandler, L. (1999). Relative effects of interventions supporting the social competence of young children with disabilities. *Topics in Early Childhood Special Education, 19,* 75–91.

Pardew, E. M., & Bunse, C. (2005). Enhancing interaction through positive touch. *Young Exceptional Children, 8*(2), 21–29.

Peck, C., Apolloni, T., Cooke, T., & Raver, S. A. (1978). Teaching retarded preschoolers to imitate the free-play behavior of nonretarded classmates: Trained and generalized effects. *Journal of Special Education, 12,* 195–207.

Raver, C. (2002). Emotions matter: Making the case for the role of young children's emotional development for early school readiness. *Social Policy Report for the Society for Research in Child Development, 16,* 1–20.

Raver, C., & Knitzer, J. (2002). *Ready to enter: What research tells policymakers about strategies to promote social and emotional school readiness among three- and four-year old children.* New York: National Center for Children in Poverty.

Raver, S. A. (1980). Ten rules for success in preschool mainstreaming. *Education Unlimited, 2,* 47–52.

Raver, S., Cooke, T., & Apolloni, T. (1978). Developing nonretarded toddlers as verbal models for retarded classmates. *Child Study Journal, 8,* 1–8.

Reid, M., Webster-Stratton, C., & Baydar, N. (2004). Halting the development of conduct problems in Head Start children: The effects of parent training. *Journal of Clinical Child and Adolescent Psychology, 33,* 279–291.

Rothbart, M., Ahadi, S., & Hershey, K. (1994). Temperament and social behavior in childhood. *Merrill-Palmer Quarterly, 40,* 21–30.

Saarni, C. (1999). *The development of emotional intelligence.* New York: Guilford Press.

Salend, S. J., & Sylvestre, S. (2005). Understanding and addressing oppositional and defiant classroom behaviors. *Teaching Exceptional Children, 37*(6), 32–39.

Sandall, S., Hemmeter, M. L., Smith, B., & McLean, M. (2005). *DEC recommended practices: A comprehensive guide for practical application in early intervention/early childhood special education.* Longmont, CO: Sopris West.

Sebanc, A. M. (2003). The friendship features of preschool children: Links with prosocial behavior and aggression. *Social Development, 12,* 249–268.

Shores, R., & Wehby, J. (1999). Analyzing the classroom social behavior of students with EBD. *Journal of Emotional and Behavioral Disorders, 7*(4), 194–199.

Simpson, R., Myles, B., Sasso, G., & Kamps, D. (1997). *Social skills for children with autism.* (ERIC Document Reproduction Service No. ED 414 697)

Skeels, H. M., & Dye, H. B. (1939). A study of the effects of differential stimulation on mentally retarded children. *Proceedings and Addresses of the American Association on Mental Deficiency, 44,* 114–136.

Smith, B. J. (2007). *Recommended practices: Linking social development and behavior to school readiness.* Retrieved April 27, 2007, from www.challengingbehavior.org

Squires, J., Bricker, D., & Twombly, E. (2004). Parent-completed screening for social emotional problems in young children: The effects of risk/disability status and gender performances. *Infant Mental Health Journal, 25*(1), 62–73.

Stanton-Chapman, T. L., Kaiser, A. P., & Wolery, M. (2006). Building social communication skills in Head Start children using storybooks: The effects of prompting on social interactions. *Journal of Early Intervention, 28,* 197–212.

Stormont, M., Lewis, T., & Beckner, R. (2005). Positive behavior support systems: Applying key features in preschool settings. *Teaching Exceptional Children, 37*(6), 42–49.

Thomas, A., Chess, S., & Birch, H. G. (1968). *Temperament and behavior disorders in children.* New York: University Press.

Thompson, T., Felce, D., & Symons, F. J. (2000). *Behavioral observation: Technology and applications in developmental disabilities.* Baltimore, MD: Brookes.

Walker, R. (1997, March). *Principles of behavior management.* Presented at the Tidewater Technical Assistance Early Intervention Conference, Virginia Beach, VA.

Watson, T. S., & Steege, M. W. (2003). *Conducting school-based functional behavioral assessments: A practitioner's guide.* New York: Guilford Press.

Widerstrom, A. H., Mowder, B. A., & Sandall, S. R. (1997). *Infant development and risk* (2nd ed.). Baltimore, MD: Brookes.

Wing, L. A. (1995). Play is not the work of the child: Young children's perceptions of work and play. *Early Childhood Research Quarterly, 10,* 223–247.

Wolery, M., Bailey, D. B., & Sugai, G. M. (1988). *Effective teaching principles and procedures of applied behavior analysis with exceptional students.* Boston: Allyn & Bacon.

Wolery, M., & Fleming, L. A. (1992). Preventing and responding to problem situations (pp. 363–406). In D. B. Bailey & M. Wolery (Eds.), *Teaching infants and preschoolers with disabilities* (2nd ed.). Upper Saddle River, NJ: Merrill/Prentice Hall.

Zins, J., Bloodworth, M., Weissberg, R., & Wahlberg, H. (2004). The scientific base linking social and emotional learning to school success. In J. Zins, R. Weissberg, M. Wang, & H. J. Wahlberg (Eds.), *Building academic success on social and emotional learning: What does the research say?* (pp. 1–22). New York: Teachers Press, Columbia University.

PART III

INTERVENTIONS WITH SPECIFIC POPULATIONS

Chapter
9

Techniques for Teaching Young Children with Mild Learning and Behavior Problems

Silvana M. R. Watson

Sharon A. Raver

Jonna Bobzien

Sabra Gear

Overview

This chapter discusses characteristics of and intervention practices with children with mild learning and behavior problems, including

the identification process

characteristics of young children with mild learning/behavior problems

individualizing instruction and tracking learning

strategies for promoting skill development

CASE STUDY: Shelly

Shelly, now 9 years old, was born by C-section four weeks early, weighing 5 pounds 6 ounces. She lives with her mother, a homemaker; father, an electrical engineer; and three sisters. The family's income is stable and provides enough for a comfortable home, good medical care, and an occasional family vacation.

Shelly did not attend preschool, but was active in gymnastics and dance classes with her sisters. In kindergarten, Shelly had good social skills and loved to color, paste, and cut, but had trouble attending to stories and answering questions about them. Her mother expressed concern because unlike her sisters, Shelly showed little interest in reading and writing. She could not rhyme words and had difficulty identifying letters and their sounds and matching simple words with corresponding pictures. Shelly's kindergarten teacher attributed Shelly's slow progress in these areas to the fact that she was a "young 5" when she started kindergarten and assured the family that she would "catch up." However, at the end of the year, it was recommended that Shelly repeat kindergarten because she was immature and not ready for first grade.

Despite repeating kindergarten, Shelly made slow progress in phonological skills in first grade. Her teacher offered special tutoring after school for Shelly and other children who were experiencing reading difficulties. The extra help seemed to make little difference in Shelly's reading skills. Eventually, Shelly was evaluated by a multidisciplinary team, which determined that she had average ability, but exhibited below-average skills in phonological awareness, reading decoding, and writing skills, qualifying her for services as a student with a learning disability— in her case, a reading disability. When Shelly was in second grade, she began to receive special education services in reading and writing, spending five hours a week in a resource room. All other instruction took place in her general education class. At present, Shelly's reading and spelling skills are monitored daily. She is making progress, even though she still lags behind in reading, writing, and spelling skills. Fortunately, Shelly has adequate comprehension when material is read to her, so she has been able to stay on grade level in other subjects with accommodations. Shelly is well liked by her peers and continues to love to read anything relating to horses.

States use the term *developmentally delayed* to describe infants, toddlers, and preschoolers who qualify for special education services. When children enter kindergarten or first grade, most states then use the Individuals with Disabilities Education Act (IDEA) disability categories to secure services for children who need additional supports. A few states have eliminated specific disability labels entirely for school-age students in favor of broader disability labels. Often the term *mild disabilities* is used instead of the IDEA designations. The specific disabilities served under the mild disabilities label vary among states, but usually students who are identified as having mild mental retardation, a learning disability, or a behavior disorder (or emotional disturbance) are considered to have mild disabilities. The process by which these children are identified for services will be discussed.

THE IDENTIFICATION PROCESS

Infants, Toddlers, and Preschoolers

During the first years of life, there are no reliable ways to distinguish between children whose problems will likely persist and those who will make adequate progress with time. Infants and toddlers with multiple and/or severe disabilities manifest delays of sufficient magnitude that they are identified early in life. In contrast, many infants and toddlers with mild disabilities may not display developmental differences severe enough to be identified until they are in kindergarten, first or second grade. When a child with mild needs is determined to be eligible for services, it is essential that all individuals working with the child on a regular basis, such as daycare

providers or general education teachers, be involved in the development and implementation of the child's program. This not only builds collaboration, but also gives the involved parties a feeling of shared responsibility that will benefit the child and his or her family.

Primary-Aged Students

Students with Mild Mental Retardation. Mental retardation is a lifelong, irreversible disability that manifests itself early in a child's life (Siperstein, Norins, Corbin, & Shriver, 2003). The IDEA implementing regulation defines mental retardation as

significantly subaverage general intellectual functioning, existing concurrently with deficits in adaptive behavior and manifested during the developmental period, that adversely affects a child's educational performance. (34 C.F.R. § 300.8(c)(6))

Mental retardation may be defined as mild, moderate, severe, or profound, depending on a child's IQ scores and functioning (American Psychiatric Association, 2000). The level of support a person requires in order to overcome limitations in adaptive skills can also be used to define mental retardation (Reynolds, 2006). In schools, intermittent or limited supports are commonly provided for students with mild mental retardation. Table 9.1 summarizes the IQ scores for the different levels of mental retardation and describes four levels of support that may be provided (American Association on Mental Retardation, 2002).

About 60% of the states utilize IQ criteria when defining mental retardation. The remaining states use a skills-based definition, an intensity-of-supports definition, or a combination of the

TABLE 9.1 Levels of mental retardation and range of supports required

Level of Mental Retardation	Range of IQ Test Scores and Levels of Necessary Support
Mild mental retardation	• IQ score: 50–55 to approximately 70–75 • <u>Intermittent supports</u> are provided on an as-needed basis. Students do not necessarily require continuous or daily support.
Moderate mental retardation	• IQ score: 35–40 to 50–55 • <u>Limited supports</u> are provided over a prescribed period of time. Intermittent and extensive supports may be necessary for some students as well.
Severe mental retardation	• IQ score: 20–25 to 35–40 • <u>Extensive supports</u> are provided, usually involving assistance on a daily basis in a number of settings.
Profound mental retardation	• IQ score: Below 20–25 • <u>Pervasive supports</u> are provided usually involving constant assistance across all environments, often of high intensity and may include life-sustaining measures.

two (Sabornie, Evans, & Cullinan, 2006). Currently, the largest segment of school-age children with mental retardation comprises those that are diagnosed as having mild mental retardation.

To determine if a student has mild mental retardation, a multidisciplinary team will give the student achievement tests, an IQ test, and adaptive skills assessments and use direct observation. Children scoring between 70–75 and 50–55 on an intelligence test are determined to have mild mental retardation. To measure adaptive behavior, professionals look at what a child can do in the social and self-help domains in comparison to other children the same age.

Students with Learning Disabilities. Appropriate early identification and services may diminish or eliminate problems that can affect a child's later academic and social performance in school (Catts, 1997; Deutscher & Fewell, 2005; Dowker, 2005; Stanton-Chapman, Chapman, Kaiser, & Hancock, 2004; Steele, 2004). However, when learning problems are mild, professionals and parents often wait until the child's problems are more severe before they seek services, which can

result in irreversible, long-term difficulties for some children (Siegel, 2003).

Risk Factors. There are several early indicators, or risk factors, that may signal potential school problems in kindergarteners and first graders (Deutscher & Fewell, 2005; Litt, Taylor, Klein, & Hack, 2005; Shaywitz & Shaywitz, 2004; Torgesen, 1997). The presence of one or more of these risk factors alone does not predict children who may eventually be identified as having a learning disability (Stanton-Chapman et al., 2004). However, they can alert the observant educator that a child may benefit from additional support. Table 9.2 presents a list of early indicators for learning disabilities compiled from multiple sources (e.g., Barkley, 2006; Coleman, Buysse, & Neitzel, 2006; Deutscher & Fewell, 2005; Gersten, Jordan, & Flojo, 2005; Lerner & Kline, 2006; Litt et al., 2005; Snow, Burns, & Griffin, 1998).

Like other mild disabilities, a learning disability is usually not identified until a child is in second grade. That is because it is difficult to accurately document "unexpected underachievement," the defining characteristic of a learning disability,

TABLE 9.2 Sample early risk indicators for learning disabilities

Biological and Environmental Risk Indicators:

- Family history of disabilities
- Prenatal substance exposure
- Late or no prenatal care
- Premature birth and/or low birth weight
- Exposure to environmental toxins or other harmful substances
- Abuse and neglect
- Hearing loss

Developmental Risk Indicators:

- Delay in gross and fine motor skills
- Auditory and visual perception problems (e.g., difficulties with auditory memory, phonological awareness, figure-ground discrimination, visual closure)
- Delay in speech and understanding and using language (e.g., limited vocabulary, difficulty understanding and following directions)
- Problems with attention (e.g., difficulty concentrating on a task, changing activities, or handling disruptions to routines; poor task persistence)

Emergent Literacy Risk Indicators:

- Poor phonological awareness skills (e.g., difficulty with rhyming, blending sounds to make words, letter-sound correspondence)
- Poor naming ability (e.g., slow response rate in naming objects, colors, letters, numbers)
- Poor number sense (e.g., difficulty understanding 5 is bigger than 4)
- Difficulty recognizing letters
- Inability to write own name

---

in young children who have not yet received formal academic instruction (Lyon et al., 2001; Steele, 2004; Synder, Bailey, & Auer, 1994). As a result, most students with learning disabilities are not identified until the ages of 9 through 14, after failing to perform well in one or more academic areas (U.S. Department of Education, 2002).

Defining Specific Learning Disabilities. The IDEA (2004) defines a specific learning disability as

a disorder in 1 or more of the basic psychological processes involved in understanding or in using language, spoken or written, which disorder may manifest itself in the imperfect ability to listen, think, speak, read, write, spell, or do mathematical calculations. (§ 602(30)(A))

This definition includes conditions such as perceptual disabilities, brain injury, minimal brain dysfunction, dyslexia, and developmental aphasia. It does not include learning problems that are primarily the result of visual, hearing, or motor disabilities; of mental retardation; of emotional disturbance; or of environmental, cultural, or economic disadvantage (IDEA, 2004). In the simplest terms, a student with a learning disability is intellectually typical and unexpectedly has difficulty learning one or more academic subjects.

One model for the identification of students with learning disabilities is the **discrepancy model**, in which professionals document intellectual-achievement discrepancies. Standardized achievement tests and intelligence tests are used to document an unexpected gap between a student's ability and his or her academic performance (Fletcher, Morris, & Lyon, 2003). For example, the presence of a below-average standard score on a reading achievement measure (e.g., a standard score of 80 on the *Woodcock Reading Mastery Test–Revised: Word Attack*) indicates "unexpected underachievement" when the child shows normal ability on an intellectual ability measure (e.g., a full-scale standard score of 105 on the *Wechsler Intelligence Scale for Children, Fourth Edition*). Another marker of a learning disability is the presence of uneven profiles of cognitive performance; that is, the child has strengths in many cognitive areas, but weaknesses in other areas that cause low achievement.

Recently, some researchers have characterized the discrepancy model for identifying a learning disability as essentially a "wait-and-fail model" (Fletcher et al., 2003; Fuchs, Mock, Morgan, & Young, 2003; Vellutino, Scallon, & Lyon, 2000). In contrast to the discrepancy model, the **response-to-intervention (RTI) model** noted in the IDEA (2004) stresses providing early prereferral prevention and intervention to students (Fuchs & Fuchs, 2007). In this model, students are offered increasingly more complex interventions based on data-based decisions, and outcomes are measured with repeated curriculum-based assessments (Fuchs & Fuchs, 2005b; Vaughn, Linan-Thompson, & Hickman, 2003). If a student consistently displays an "inadequate response to intervention," it may be inferred that the student has a learning disability and would profit from special education support. The RTI model is a multitier problem-solving process that requires close collaboration between general and special education teachers (Brown-Chidsey & Steege, 2005). Notwithstanding its intuitive appeal, the steps of RTI are not simple and have yet to be documented as empirically based. Additionally, there are a number of unanswered questions about the reliability, validity, and efficacy of RTI, especially when used with older students (Gerber, 2005; Mastropieri & Scruggs, 2005).

In the final analysis, a multimethod or "hybrid" model may be the most powerful approach to identifying students with learning disabilities (Fletcher et al., 2006). It includes (1) conducting repeated observations of the student; (2) employing RTI assessment and intervention; (3) administering formal and informal achievement assessments, such as neuropsychological measures of language and attention and tools evaluating phonological processing skills, working memory, executive function, and cognitive ability; and (4) administering oral and written comprehension assessments. Many believe the hybrid model has a better chance of supporting the development of appropriate interventions for students' Individualized Education Programs (IEPs).

Students with Attention Deficit/Hyperactivity Disorder. When students with attention deficit/hyperactivity disorder (AD/HD) receive special education services, they are usually considered to have a mild disability. The most recent diagnostic criteria for determining if a student displays AD/HD are outlined in the *Diagnostic and Statistical Manual of Mental Disorders* (DSM) (American Psychiatric Association, 2000). It separates AD/HD into three subtypes: (1) predominantly hyperactive-impulsive, (2) predominantly inattentive, and (3) combined. The DSM eligibility criteria that medical professionals use to identify a student with AD/HD are shown in Table 9.3.

The symptoms of AD/HD must be exhibited for at least six months, must develop by the age of 7, and must be present to a degree that is developmentally unusual (American Psychiatric Association, 2000). Six of the nine items listed for each type of AD/HD must be observed as deviant from the student's developmental level across two or more settings for a diagnosis to be made. Students with AD/HD can be included in the IDEA's disability category of "other health impairments" (OHI). However, special education services are provided only if the student's AD/HD adversely affects his or her educational performance.

There are several components in an evaluation of a child suspected of having AD/HD (Barkley & Edwards, 2006). The first component involves a clinical interview with parents, teachers,

TABLE 9.3 Diagnostic criteria for AD/HD

A. Either (1) or (2):

   1. Six (or more) of the following symptoms of *inattention* have persisted for at least 6 months to a degree that is maladaptive and inconsistent with developmental level:

   Inattention

      a. Often fails to give close attention to details or makes careless mistakes in schoolwork, work or other activities.

      b. Often has difficulty sustaining attention in tasks or play activities.

      c. Often does not seem to listen when spoken to directly.

      d. Often does not follow through on instructions and fails to finish schoolwork, chores, or duties in the workplace (not due to oppositional behavior or failure to understand instructions).

      e. Often has difficulty organizing tasks and activities.

      f. Often avoids, dislikes, or is reluctant to engage in tasks that require sustained mental effort (such as schoolwork or homework).

      g. Often loses things necessary for tasks or activities (e.g., toys, school assignments, pencils, books, or tools).

      h. Is often easily distracted by extraneous stimuli.

      i. Is often forgetful in daily activities.

   2. Six (or more) of the following symptoms of *hyperactivity-impulsivity* have persisted for at least 6 months to a degree that is maladaptive and inconsistent with developmental level:

   Hyperactivity

      a. Often fidgets with hands or feet or squirms in seat.

      b. Often leaves seat in classroom or in other situations in which remaining seated is expected.

      c. Often runs about or climbs excessively in situations in which it is inappropriate (in adolescents or adults, may be limited to subjective feelings of restlessness).

      d. Often has difficulty playing or engaging in leisure activities quietly.

      e. Is often "on the go" or often acts as if "driven by a motor."

      f. Often talks excessively.

   Impulsivity

      a. Often blurts out answers before questions have been completed.

      b. Often has difficulty awaiting turn.

      c. Often interrupts or intrudes on others (e.g., butts into conversations or games).

B. Some hyperactive-impulsive or inattentive symptoms that caused impairment were presented before age 7 years.

C. There must be clear evidence of clinically significant impairment in social, academic, or occupational functioning.

D. The symptoms do not occur exclusively during the course of pervasive developmental disorder, schizophrenia, or other psychotic disorder and are not better accounted for by another mental disorder (e.g., mood disorder, anxiety disorder, dissociative disorder, or a personality disorder).

Code based on type:

Attention-Deficit/Hyperactivity Disorder, Combined Type: if both Criteria A1 and A2 are met for the past 6 months.

Attention-Deficit/Hyperactivity Disorder, Predominantly Hyperactive-Impulsive Type: if Criterion A2 is met but Criterion A1 is not met for the past 6 months.

Coding note: For individuals (especially adolescents and adults) who currently have symptoms that no longer meet full criteria. "In Partial Remission" should be specified.

Source: Reprinted with permission from Diagnostic and statistical manual of mental disorders (pp. 92–93). Copyright 2000 American Psychiatric Association.

and the child by a medical professional such as a pediatrician or a psychologist. Second, an evaluation of the child is conducted, gathering information from multiple sources. For example, data may be obtained from standardized behavior scales such as the *Behavioral Assessment System for Children* (BASC–2) (Reynolds & Kamphaus, 2004) and the *Conners Rating Scales–Revised* (Conners, 2001). A medical examination, psychological testing, and surveys of major life activities involving family, peers, and school are also needed. To ensure appropriate assessment of and intervention with students with AD/HD, educators must consider the various characteristics and disorders these students exhibit and plan specific interventions to address them (Westby & Watson, 2004).

Students with Behavior Disorders/Emotional Disturbance.

In order for students in kindergarten through third grade to qualify for services based on their behavior or social-emotional needs, they must meet the IDEA definition for emotional disturbance (ED) (Cullinan, 2004). Many states also use the term *behavior disorders* for this population. The IDEA definition states that a student must exhibit at least one of the following five characteristics in an enduring and intensive way, such that

it adversely affects the child's educational performance (IDEA, 2004a): (1) an inability to learn that cannot be explained by intellectual, sensory, or health factors; (2) an inability to build or maintain satisfactory interpersonal relationships with peers and teachers; (3) inappropriate types of behavior or feelings under normal circumstances; (4) a general pervasive mood of unhappiness or depression; and/or (5) a tendency to develop physical symptoms or fears associated with personal or school problems. This definition has been criticized for being vague, contradictory, and ambiguous (Cullinan, 2004).

Either a student's parent or his or her teacher may request an initial evaluation to determine if the student meets the requirements for special education services. Fortunately, when intervention efforts are implemented during the primary years, educators are often able to focus on prevention, rather than remediation (Lane & Menzies, 2005). Prevention, or **prereferral intervention**, typically includes offering positive behavior supports, implementing behavior intervention programs to improve the student's behavior, and making curriculum modifications *before* a formal referral for evaluation for services is made (Lane & Menzies, 2005; Polsgrove, 2004). In some cases, a

Many children who will eventually qualify for special education services for students with mild disabilities when they are in the primary grades do not receive services during the preschool years.

formal evaluation may no longer be needed following prereferral interventions.

The team evaluation usually includes academic assessments and behavior ratings by parents, teachers, and the student as well as classroom-based observations (Polsgrove, 2004). The behavior assessment process involves both indirect and direct assessment procedures to identify conditions that trigger and maintain challenging behaviors (Fox & Gable, 2004). A copy of the evaluation report and eligibility determination is provided to the student's parents, who then decide whether to consent to services (IDEA, 2004b). When parental consent is received, the team develops an IEP with a behavioral plan that is intended to address behavior problems proactively, rather than allowing escalation to serious emotional and violent reactions (Kamps, Wendland, & Culpepper, 2006).

CHARACTERISTICS OF YOUNG CHILDREN WITH MILD LEARNING AND BEHAVIOR PROBLEMS

After the determination that a child will benefit from services, the team attempts to identify how much support the child will need to realize his or her potential at home, in school, and in the community. This process is based on the understanding that the child's needs can, and will, change. Children with mild disabilities display a range of communication, learning, social, preliteracy, and literacy characteristics.

Infants, Toddlers, and Preschoolers

Communication and Learning Characteristics. Some children with mild disabilities may learn and develop more slowly than a typical child in one or more domain areas. Some may express difficulties with memory and/or may have trouble solving problems verbally. A relationship between language and social development has been found in young children with mild special needs. Even children with minor communication delays seem to

gravitate to games and activities that demand little or no verbal language and spend significantly more time isolated from their peers than classmates with typical communication skills (Brinton, Fujiki, & McKee, 1998). It is not clear if children with language delays or impairments are excluded from play because they tend to be less adept at specific social skills that are important to participating in play activities, such as negotiation and cooperation, or if other skill limitations influence their participation. It is not surprising, therefore, that problem behaviors and delayed communication skills are frequently raised as concerns when preschoolers with mild disabilities participate in inclusive programs. A common characteristic of children with mild disabilities is that they often need more time than other children to learn the same skills. Most children benefit from individual instruction, and support.

Social Characteristics. Some infants and toddlers with mild needs may require guidance in learning how to sustain appropriate play and interaction with others (Conroy, Dunlap, Clarke, & Alter, 2005). As noted earlier, as children develop, early social behaviors and communication skills seem to run interrelated courses. Some research suggests that many of the social problems children with mild disabilities display may actually be related to difficulties with verbal comprehension and expression (Minishew, Meyer, & Dunn, 2003). Children with mild developmental needs tend to benefit from specific social training that shows them how to initiate play, how to take turns, and how to appropriately comment on play interactions.

Primary-Aged Students with Mild Mental Retardation

Communication. Many students with mild mental retardation are usually not diagnosed until they enter the primary grades. Before coming to kindergarten, their communication deficiencies may not be obvious. However, once they are faced with academic learning, their language problems become more problematic. A restricted vocabulary and memory difficulties tend to slow down their reading and writing achievement (Friend & Bursuck, 2002).

Social/Adaptive Behavior. Adaptive behavior is the ability to manage one's personal needs and live independently. Students with mild mental retardation usually learn to manage their basic daily needs about the same time as other children their age do. Occasionally, additional training is required to teach social or self-management skills, such as using appropriate manners, following the social rules of conversation, and getting along in a group. It is not uncommon for students with mild mental retardation to have a dual diagnosis of mild mental retardation and behavior disorders (Borthwick-Duffy & Eyman, 1990). In general, these students tend to live independently as adults. In fact, many may not even be considered to have cognitive limitations when they are adults (Beirne-Smith, Ittenbach, & Patton, 2002).

Learning Characteristics. The term retardation means to "slow down." Consequently, the lack of achievement in school is generally one of the first indicators of a cognitive impairment in young children (Sabornie et al., 2006). The learning problems noted in students with mild mental retardation tend to be related to the following difficulties: (1) difficulty focusing or maintaining attention, (2) an inclination to focus on irrelevant stimuli in the classroom instead of relevant features of the learning activity, (3) difficulty recalling and generalizing new skills and knowledge, and (4) difficulty with short-term memory, as, for example, when following directions (Bray, Fletcher, & Turner, 1997). Some students may resist learning or problem solving, in part due to the "learned helplessness" they have developed from experiencing frequent school failure.

Primary-Aged Students with Learning Disabilities

Students with learning disabilities are a heterogeneous group with varied disorders in several different academic and social domains (Cutting & Denckla, 2003; National Joint Committee on Learning Disabilities, 1988). Despite the differences in this population, all students with this disability display "unexpected underachievement" and an "inadequate response to instruction" in the general education classroom (Fletcher et al., 2006; Smith, 2004; Vaughn & Fuchs, 2003). Primary-aged students with learning disabilities have the following general communication, learning, and social/adaptive characteristics.

Communication Characteristics. The term **language learning disability** is often used to describe the large number of students with learning disabilities whose difficulties are related to language problems (McCormick, Loeb, & Schiefelbusch, 2003). As explained in Chapter 5, students with difficulties in one or more of the components of language will have problems sending and receiving messages. Such difficulties affect their ability to learn academic and social skills. For instance, problems with phonology will delay their acquisition of letter-sound correspondence and, consequently, impede their acquisition of reading and spelling.

Learning Characteristics. Academic difficulties are the most common characteristic of students with learning disabilities. Students with learning disabilities may have difficulty with basic reading skills, reading comprehension, written expression, and mathematical calculation and/or reasoning. However, reading problems are the most common concern observed in these students. Besides the deficits in language that directly affect academic performance and multiply across the school years, there are other learning issues that negatively impact the academic achievement of students with learning disabilities. Some of the areas are discussed below:

❏ *Slow naming speed.* Students with reading disabilities have been found to have deficits in *rapid naming* or *Rapid Automatized Naming (RAN)* of highly familiar visual symbols such as letters and colors (Bowers & Ishaik, 2003).

❏ *Memory problems.* Students may have problems encoding, processing, and retrieving learned information. Memory is directly linked to learning academic tasks (Swanson & Saez, 2003). **Working memory** has been described as the ability to hold information in short-term memory while processing other information (Siegel, 2003). Deficits in working memory have been specifically associated with reading, writing, and mathematics disabilities (Swanson & Sachse-Lee, 2001; Swanson & Saez, 2003; Wilson & Swanson, 2001).

❏ *Problems with attention and other self-regulatory behaviors.* Students may have difficulty determining which skills and strategies to use to perform a task and then have difficulty using those resources to complete the task. For example, attention and self-regulation deficits can affect reading comprehension. Students may be distracted by detail when reading or fail to understand the main ideas of the text (Berninger, Abbott, Vermeulen, & Fulton, 2006). When they recognize their lack of understanding, they may not have, or use, appropriate strategies to repair their comprehension failure (Westby & Watson, 2004).

❏ *Perceptual problems.* Students may have difficulty recognizing, discriminating, and interpreting shapes, letters, numbers, sounds, and other visual and auditory stimuli. Consequently, they may have difficulty processing the correct information, which, in turn, may depress their learning. A student, for instance, may have problems reading and spelling irregular words (e.g., *sight*), may confuse letters and words (e.g., *b–d or was–saw*), and may have problems blending sounds into words (Lerner & Kline, 2006; Smith, 2004; Fuchs & Fuchs, 2005a).

Social/Adaptive Characteristics. Social and emotional problems are often observed in students with learning disabilities and are cited as a characteristic in some definitions. The Interagency Committee on Learning Disabilities (1987) specifically lists social skills as one of the difficulties in students with learning disabilities. The definition of learning disability from the National Joint Committee on Learning Disabilities (1988) acknowledges that students with learning disabilities may have

"problems in self-regulatory behaviors, social perception, and social interaction" (p. 1). Some of the social-emotional needs of students with learning disabilities follow:

❏ *Self-concept.* A positive self-concept is often related to academic and social status. Some students with learning disabilities may display a pessimistic outlook or may have an inaccurate view of themselves. Others may exaggerate their social abilities despite being socially rejected by peers. Those who have an inaccurate view of their social abilities tend to have a deficit in social perception (Bryan, Burstein, & Ergul, 2004).

❏ *Social skills/social relationships.* Students with learning disabilities may be described as immature, inappropriate, and disruptive (Interagency Committee on Learning Disabilities, 1987). They may be ignored or judged negatively by their teachers and peers (Smith, 2004). Some social problems may be explained by their language deficits (e.g., they have difficulty taking turns in conversation and have problems describing how to play a game) and by their visual-perception weaknesses, which may negatively affect their ability to interpret others' facial expressions and gestures and to understand others' intentions and feelings.

Primary-Aged Students with Behavior Disorders/Emotional Disturbance

Social/Adaptive Behavior. The boundaries for social behaviors are often first crossed in social situations when a student's behavior does not meet acceptable norms. Students with behavior disorders may display a range of challenging externalizing and internalizing behaviors (Cullinan, 2002; Furlong, Morrison, & Jimerson, 2004; Gresham & Kern, 2004; Hallahan & Kauffman, 2006). Externalizing behaviors involve aggression, impulsivity, lying, stealing, and destroying property and are likely to result in negative consequences from school authorities. Conversely, while internalizing behaviors involve social withdrawal, fearfulness, anxiety, unhappiness, and depression and may not result in discipline problems, they may still significantly impede a student's academic achievement. Although externalizing and internalizing behaviors are not mutually exclusive, the most common type of problem for students with behavior disorders is externalizing behaviors (Hallahan & Kauffman, 2006). Boys are five times more likely than girls to display aggressive, acting-out, disruptive behavior, although antisocial behavior in girls is an increasing concern. Boys usually are identified earlier than girls. The conduct and compliance difficulties these students present highlight the importance of establishing a protective school environment with constructive involvement of parents and clear behavioral expectations and consequences (Trout, Epstein, Nelson, Reid, & Ohlund, 2006).

Learning Characteristics. Similar to students with mild mental retardation and those with learning disabilities, students with behavior problems are a diverse group (Trout et al., 2006). When compared to "typical" students, students with behavior disorders may display moderate to severe academic deficits in reading, mathematics, written expression, and/or science (Lane, 2004). According to Mattison and colleagues (Mattison, Hooper, & Carlson, 2006), neuropsychological deficits in language and attention are common. As these students progress through school, their academic deficits may remain stable or worsen (Lane, 2004; Montague, Enders, & Castro, 2005). Students with challenging behavior benefit from a structured learning environment (Kaiser, 2007). Effective instruction is the best line of defense in managing the noncompliant behavior these students evidence (Kauffman, 2005).

INDIVIDUALIZING INSTRUCTION AND TRACKING LEARNING

Children with mild disabilities may display some skills that are below their age level and others that are at their age level. Professionals first determine individual objectives for each child which

encourage the child to develop skills and behaviors he or she is lacking. To track whether infants, toddlers and preschoolers with mild learning and behavioral needs are learning these individual targets, teachers use the following: (1) observational data, (2) rating scales/checklists, and (3) permanent products (Ostrosky & Horn, 2002; Pretti-Frontczak & Bricker, 2004).

Observational data result from observing a child during specified periods of the day and recording his or her performance on predetermined individualized objectives. Data taken in this manner require staff to be familiar with each child's objectives as well as with how to embed teaching and monitoring in routines. A common problem for young children with delays and disabilities is transitions between scheduled activities in the classroom. Transitions, like learning, must be monitored. Figure 9.1 shows a completed transition assessment for Maria, a 4.6 year old child with moderate disabilities as a result of Down syndrome, who attends an inclusive preschool. This checklist helped Maria's general education teacher evaluate Maria's response to classroom rules, her approach to tasks, her level of self-control, her functional communication skills, and her transitions between activities.

Rating scales and checklists focus on whether or not a specified behavior occurred and, if so, the level of assistance the child needed to perform that behavior. For example, a teacher might record whether a child completed a puzzle and, if so, how much help he or she required. Some behaviors, such as social skills, may require the teacher to tabulate the number of times a behavior occurred. The teacher may count the number of times a child talked to another child, for instance, during a structured play routine. Rating scales and checklists are more helpful when they are placed in the area where data will be collected. That is, data sheets to monitor a child's toileting behaviors would be kept in the restroom, and data sheets for other domains might be kept at tables or near the circle area. When working with a child in an inclusive setting, it is important that ECSE teachers remember to gather information in a

Figure 9.1 Transition skills checklist for a preschool-aged child

TRANSITION SKILLS ASSESSMENT

Child's Name: Maria B.
School: St. Benedicts
Type of Classroom: Preschool

Date: January 13
Teacher: Ms. White

	No	Inconsistent	Yes	Comments
CLASSROOM RULES				
1. Moves through transitions smoothly		X		Needs considerable adult assistance—pictures and guidance.
2. Controls voice in classroom.		X		Cries during activities, screams, laughs.
3. Uses appropriate signal to get teacher's attention when necessary.		X		Infrequently needs attention, occasionally hits.
4. Waits appropriately for teacher to respond to signal.	X			Unaware she can revise attempts to signal.
5. Replace materials and "cleans up" own work space.		X		Needs considerable adult assistance.
6. Recognizes and stays within area boundaries in classroom.	X			Wanders in classroom if not redirected.
WORK SKILLS				
1. Refrains from disturbing or disrupting the activities of others		X		Rarely makes attempt to interact—grabs materials or grabs other kids.
2. Signals to get information about assigned tasks when did not understand.	X			Needs one on one—must be looking to attend to teacher.
3. Follows one direction related to task.		X		Needs many prompts—sign, gesture.
4. Occupies self with developmentally appropriate activity.	X			Solitary free play is inappropriate—perservative.
5. Recognizes materials needed for specific task	X			No attempt to prepare for task.
6. Selects and works on an activity independently	X			Little ability to attend with no adult.
7. Recognizes completion of activity and signals to adult that he/she is finished.	X			
8. Works on assigned tasks for 5 minutes.	X			2 minutes
9. Self-corrects errors.	X			
10. Recalls and completes task demonstrated previously.	X			
11. Uses crayons/scissors without being destructive.		X		With adult assistance is successful.

(continued)

Figure 9.1 (continued)

	No	Inconsistent	Yes	Comments
SELF MANAGEMENT				
1. Monitors appearance (wipes nose, uses napkin).	X			Needs 1–2 prompts.
2. Locates and uses a restroom with minimal assistance.	X			Toilet regulated and no request.
3. Will put on/take off outer clothing within a reasonable amount of time.		X		Needs adult assistance occasionally.
4. Eats lunch or snack with minimal assistance.		X		If she likes it, she is okay.
5. Seeks out adult for aid if hurt on the playground or cannot handle a social situation.	X			Cries and makes no attempt to seek comfort.
6. Stays with a group when outdoors according to school routine.	X			Often runs away and wanders alone.
7. Aware of obvious dangers and avoids them.		X		Some dangers she sees but others not.
COMMUNICATION				
1. Attends to adult when called.		X		Often does not look to sound source.
2. Listens to and follows directions given to a group.	X			Needs additional prompts one on one.
3. Communicates own needs and preferences (food, drink, bathroom).		X		Signs "more" "eat," uses communication board.
4. Stops activity when given a direction by an adult to "stop."		X		Occasionally will stop.
5. Attends to peer in large group.		X		Occasionally obsesses on one child.
6. Protests appropriately	X			Hits, pinches, scratches.
7. Requests assistance from adult or peer		X		Physical prompting.
8. Responds without excessive delay.		X		Take 5–7 seconds.
9. Uses functional communication system.		X		Small communication board, signs, some words.
SOCIAL BEHAVIORS				
1. Uses greetings.	X			Gives eye contact occasionally.
2. Complies with teacher commands.		X		
3. Takes direction from a variety of adults.	X			Difficult with a new person.
4. Makes a choice between preferred items or activities.			X	
5. Initiates interaction with peers and adults.		X		She is starting.
6. Plays cooperatively.		X		Needs assistance.
7. Responds positively to social reinforcement			X	

	No	Inconsistent	Yes	Comments
8. Interacts appropriately at snack and lunch		X		Occasionally throws others' food.
9. Expresses affection toward peers and adults in appropriate manner.	X			Grabs their head and squeezes.
10. Refrains from self-abusive behavior.			X	
11. Refrains from physically aggressive behavior toward others.		X		Initiates interaction by hitting occasionally.
12. Discriminates between edible and non-edible toys and objects.			X	
13. Uses play equipment in a developmentally appropriate manner during unstructured activities with limited adult supervision.	X			Needs adult assistance—climbing and running difficult.

Source: Adapted with permission from Circle of Inclusion, University of Kansas, Department of Special Education, Lawrence, KS.

manner that does not set the child apart from his or her peers.

The use of permanent products is another way to track a young child's progress. Permanent products may be videotapes, CDs, audiotapes, photographs, or samples of a child's work that document changes. Videotapes of a child's performance during opening group at the beginning of the year can be compared to tapes recorded later in the year to document improved compliance behavior. Photographs of a child's block structures taken throughout the year can show the progression from simple to more complex structures. An added bonus of photographs is that children, and their families, always love to see photographs of their work.

Primary-Aged Students

Teachers of primary-aged students with mild mental retardation, learning disabilities, and behavior disorders (e.g., mild disabilities) tend to use similar methods for individualizing and monitoring instruction and learning. Section 504 Accommodation Plans, the Universal Design for Learning, curriculum-based measures, functional

behavior assessments, and self-monitoring are used. Each will be discussed.

Section 504 Accommodation Plans. Some students with mild learning problems, such as students with AD/HD, may not meet the IDEA guidelines for receiving special education services, but are still protected under Section 504. To receive accommodations under Section 504, students must display a substantial limitation in a major life activity, such as learning. Most commonly, students who qualify for a Section 504 Accommodation Plan do not have a significant discrepancy between their ability and achievement scores (Smith, 2002), and yet they still need a little extra support to participate in the general education curriculum (Harlacher, Roberts, & Merrell, 2006). In general, the accommodations available under Section 504 are inexpensive and are provided in the general education classroom. They may include extended time on tests, special seating arrangements, modified tests, and adjusted class scheduling (deBettencourt, 2002). Chapter 4 provides a sample Section 504 Accommodation Plan for a first-grade student with AD/HD.

Universal Design for Learning. Since the majority of students with mild disabilities are educated in general education classrooms, particularly in the primary grades, all teachers have to know how to adapt their instruction to match each student's level of knowledge (Fore, Riser, & Boon, 2006). One strategy for doing this is the **Universal Design for Learning (UDL)** (Rose, 2000). UDL recommends that teachers make systematic adjustments in their teaching for all learner differences. UDL does not agree with the practice of using a single book or procedure, but encourages the development and use of diverse and varied curriculum materials and strategies (Rose, 2000). This practice is based on the belief that individualization is every student's right, not just the right of students with special needs. Teachers develop goals and objectives and select materials and methods of assessment that are tailored to individual student needs and strengths.

Curriculum-Based Measurement. The most common strategy for monitoring the progress of students with mild disabilities is curriculum-based measurement (CBM). CBM is a simple, yet reliable way to measure student progress in curricular domains across time (Sorrels, Reith, & Sindelar, 2004). It involves frequent assessment of student progress, which is then charted on easy-to-read graphs that students keep. Over time, this graph becomes a pictorial representation of a student's progress. Graphs are also used for determining skill areas in which a student requires reteaching or additional assistance (Deno, 2003).

Functional Behavior Assessment. Students with challenging behavior present a multitude of problem behaviors that impede their learning and test their teachers. To identify inappropriate behavior, the time at which the behavior generally occurs, triggers for the behavior, and classroom conditions that may influence or maintain the behavior, professionals conduct a functional behavior assessment (FBA). With the information from an FBA, a behavior intervention plan is developed. This behavior plan has multiple components: (1) the apparent function of the challenging behavior, (2) the instructional areas

and/or routines that will be adjusted or modified to alter the behavior, (3) a clear description of how adaptations/modifications will be implemented, (4) a list of consequences for making the behavioral changes, and (5) a list of positive behavior supports (e.g., positive consequences for *following* expected behaviors) (IDEA, 2004b). The behavior plan is designed to improve a student's behavior *and* learning, since these are related.

Kamps and colleagues (Kamps, Wendland, & Culpepper, 2006) found the process of developing and implementing an FBA was successful in reducing challenging behaviors in second-grade students with behavior disorders in a general education class. In this study, the students' general education teacher participated in the development of the FBA, using the information gathered to develop a plan for increasing students' on-task behaviors and decreasing their disruptive behaviors. For the intervention, the teacher gave the students additional attention when they manifested appropriate behaviors, modeled appropriate behaviors, and required the students to self-monitor. Self-monitoring consisted of the students recording their on-task behaviors during independent seatwork and the frequency of their replies during group choral responding.

Self-Monitoring. Challenging behavior may have a more adverse impact over time on the academic achievement of students with behavior disorders than other learning difficulties (Mattison, Spitznagel, & Felix, 1998). Consequently, developing and maintaining appropriate behavior and increasing compliance are essential components of any educational program. One technique that has been used successfully to increase appropriate behaviors is training students to self-monitor. Self-monitoring began as an assessment procedure (DiGangi, Maag, & Rutherford, 1991). However, because it helped students learn to self-regulate impulsive behaviors, it has become a therapeutic intervention (Blair, 2002). Self-monitoring involves self-observation of target behaviors and self-recording of frequency or duration of these behaviors (Patton, Jolivette, & Ramsey,

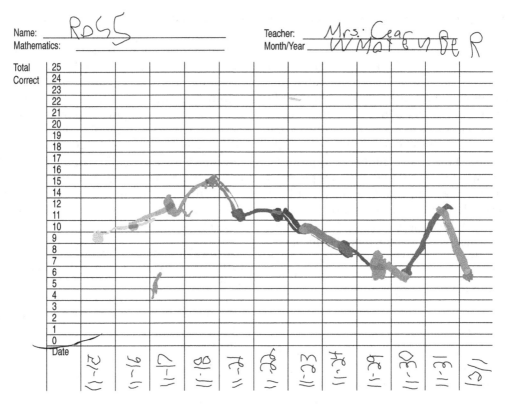

Self-Monitoring Mathematics Chart

Figure 9.2 Student's self-monitoring mathematics chart for total correct in a two-minute addition facts drill

2006). A student may learn to regulate talking-out-of-turn behavior by pressing a golf counter every time he or she raises his or her hand to answer a question during a 30-minute mathematics lesson. As the student's new behavior becomes routine, self-monitoring is gradually faded. Figure 9.2 shows a second-grade student's self-monitoring graph in mathematics.

STRATEGIES FOR PROMOTING SKILL DEVELOPMENT

Students with mild disabilities can face challenges in their home and school routines. Any of the strategies discussed in previous chapters and

many of the strategies that will be discussed in upcoming chapters would be appropriate to use when teaching children with mild disabilities. Additionally, task analysis, time delay, and instructional adaptation are also used to teach young children with mild developmental and learning needs. Each will be discussed briefly.

Task Analysis

Many skills are too complex or have too many steps to be acquired at one time by young children. When this is the case, teachers use **task analysis,** breaking the skill into small steps that are taught sequentially. A child's age, attention span, and cognitive abilities are considered when determining how many steps may be necessary for teaching a skill and how much support from the teacher or parent should be given. For example, to get a toddler to push the five buttons on an activity box, an adult would teach the skill to the child one button at a time. First, the adult would push the button to show the child that, when pushed, the button opens a door from which a dog pops out. Second, the adult would take the child's hand or arm, showing the child how to push the button. Slowly, the amount of assistance provided for the pushing action would be faded until the child was able to perform the action independently. Then a different button would be taught, using the same step-by-step method. Frequent corrective feedback and praise would be given. Task analysis is frequently used to teach preliteracy and literacy skills to primary-aged students.

Time Delay

Time delay is a strategy used to promote spontaneous interactions and enhance independent skill development in young children. The adult purposely withholds assistance until the child has had sufficient time to process an instruction or begin a task. For example, for a preschooler, an adult would give the child a response cue ("Put the red ones together.") and wait for the child to respond. If the child did not respond, the adult would give a prompt ("Use one hand. Red ones here.") and then wait 3–45 seconds, depending on the needs and age of the child, before giving additional assistance (Wolery, 2001). Time delay can be effective with toddlers, preschoolers, and primary-aged students who seem reluctant to begin tasks that they have already shown they are able to do or who have verbal processing problems. This technique works to reduce reliance on teacher-delivered support and reinforcement.

Instructional Adaptation

The following assumptions serve as the basis for adapting and modifying instruction in self-contained and inclusive settings: (1) All children do not need to be doing the same thing at the same time, (2) varying types and degrees of participation are appropriate, and (3) curriculum and school activities should be adjusted to accommodate each child's individual needs (Horn & Sandall, 2000). Because children with mild disabilities require deliberate instruction, professionals must determine the type of adaptations each child needs, ensure that all staff are familiar with each child's objectives, and plan how instruction will be delivered. Three general instructional adaptations may be provided for infants, toddlers, preschoolers, and primary-aged students:

1) Use the same activities and materials, but different objectives. The same materials and activities can always be used to teach multiple objectives at the same time. While one preschooler is working on classification by sorting objects according to size, another child can be labeling the same objects while releasing them into a bucket. In this way, the activity provides both children opportunities to work on their own different objectives. This adaptation was used frequently with Shelly, featured in the case study.

2) Use the same activity, materials, and objective, but adapt how the child responds. A child may understand a task, but have difficulty with the speech or motor component of the task. A child with a motor disability, for example, may be able to discriminate shapes, but cannot physically sort them. This child would have the same objective as everyone else, but would use eye gaze to indicate which shapes go into the designated boxes. All the children have the same learning objective, but some are given a different way of expressing what they know.

3) Use the same activity and the same or a different objective with adapted materials. Sometimes it is necessary to physically adapt play or instructional materials to facilitate children's participation. Such adaptations may increase stability, ease handling and accessibility, and/or increase attention to relevant stimuli. For example, Velcro, tape, or another nonslip material can be added to objects to avoid sliding, or critical information on a paper task can be made more visible by using a highlighter to identify the letter and sound the student is supposed to match on the page.

These general strategies are used by professionals to promote children's learning. Other techniques that facilitate communicative, social, preliteracy, and literacy development in children from birth through 8 years of age are discussed next.

Developing Communication Skills

Infants, Toddlers, and Preschoolers. Communication may be verbal or nonverbal, symbolic or nonsymbolic, and intentional or nonintentional. Communication gives children some level of independence and control over their environment. To foster communication development, professionals and parents must distribute communication training throughout the day, use functional communication training and employ the technique of sabotage. Each will be discussed.

Integrate Communication Facilitation Strategies Throughout the Child's Day. More communication that is functional may be achieved when adults intentionally manipulate interactions within daily routines. Interactions should focus on what motivates a child to communicate and ensure that the child participates *actively* in the interaction (Kaiser & Delaney, 2001). For instance, an anticipation box, a box that has objects that represent the day's activities in sequenced compartments, can trigger communication, since children can be stimulated to communicate about the experiences that have just occurred and discuss what will happen next.

However, it is important that professionals and parents not interpret embedded routine-based strategies to mean bombarding children with adult-dominated interactions. Children also need quiet time to practice skills, play, and learn to entertain themselves without adult guidance. To increase intentional communication in preconversational children, children who linguistically are below 3 years of age, professionals and parents should

❏ balance turns with waiting and with give and take,

❏ match the child's present communication level and blend this with communication that is just one step ahead of the child,

❏ respond to what holds the child's attention in the interaction, and

❏ reduce directiveness which can inhibit vocal and verbal communication, and instead use parallel talk (discussed in chapter 5) (McCathren & Watson, 2001)

Similarly, to increase spontaneous communication in conversational children, those who are linguistically 3 years of age and older, professionals and parents can

❏ be animated and rewarding,

❏ translate joint experiences into words and extend the child's vocabulary,

❏ talk about present and past experiences,

❏ avoid letting the child be a passive conversation or play partner,

❏ follow the child's conversational topic, and

❏ expand the child's play comments by adding information (Horn, Lieber, Sandall, & Schwartz, 2001).

Use Functional Communication Training. Functional communication training is a procedure used by professionals to determine the function of, or communicative intention underlying, challenging behavior and then identifying a functionally equivalent communicative behavior to serve as a replacement for the less desired behavior the child is using (Durand, 1990). The process of functional communication training teaches the child a more acceptable way of communicating. Replacement behaviors may be spoken words, phrases, gestures, signs, or pictures. This approach is based on the assumption that problem behaviors are meaningful and display communicative intent. Consequently, replacement communication behaviors should result in the same desired outcome for the child (e.g., getting attention, escaping an unpleasant task) and, therefore, reduce or eliminate the challenging behavior by making it redundant (Conroy et al., 2005).

Dunlap and colleagues (Dunlap, Ester, Langhans, & Fox, 2005) successfully taught mothers of toddlers to use functional communication training in their homes. The mothers were trained to model a communicative response to their child's needs in an attempt to reduce the child's challenging behavior. When the toddlers were taught to imitate simple phrases such as "play with me" and "help me," the frequency of challenging behaviors was reduced. This technique has been shown effective with toddler and preschoolers.

Employ Sabotage. One goal of intervention is to develop a child's communication abilities so that every conversational partner can serve as a potential communication facilitator. **Sabotage** is a naturalistic elicitation technique involving an intentional modification of or change to a routine, activity, or material such that it creates a structured communication training opportunity. There are three types of sabotage. Each will be described (Hepting & Goldstein, 1996; Raver, 1987).

1) Violating routine events. Intentional violation of routine events can be used to promote a protest and/or direct a child's attention to particular features of language. Purposely changing a scheduled routine (e.g., beginning the school day with "closing group"), changing the route to the lunchroom, or calling a child by another child's name prompts a child to tell the adult about the adult's "mistake."

2) Withholding objects or turns. Withholding objects or materials a child needs *creates* an opportunity for spontaneous communication. For example, giving milk to everyone except one child encourages the omitted child to communicate.

3) Violating object function. The ability to discriminate among specific characteristics of objects is a basic skill that toddlers and preschoolers must learn. Once children are aware of the specific function of an object, willful change of this functionality can initiate spontaneous protests and/or conversations in young children. For instance, using a toothbrush to comb your hair or attempting to paint with the wrong end of the paintbrush may urge even the most hesitant communicator to comment.

These techniques can be easily translated into enjoyable rituals within any activity at home or in school and offer a decisive undercurrent of purpose in promoting spontaneous language or communication in toddlers and preschoolers with language delays and/or disorders.

Primary-Aged Students. Students with mild disabilities may have problems with communication, especially pragmatics. Pragmatic difficulties are usually evidenced as difficulty in initiating, sustaining, and monitoring conversational dialogue and difficulty in adapting dialogue to fit various social situations. Pragmatics involves interpretation of both verbal and nonverbal cues from the listener. To improve pragmatics, students require opportunities throughout the day to talk and listen to communication that is used for various purposes, with different audiences, and in different settings (Schoenbrodt, Kumin, & Sloan, 1997). For example, a teacher can elicit pragmatics practice by providing topics for discussion that children have selected as interesting to them and having them discuss the topic for an audience of peers and then for an audience of adults so students learn to "switch" their conversation accordingly. During these sessions, it is important that the physical arrangement of the room allow students to see each other to encourage more appropriate reading of nonverbal and verbal cues.

Developing Social Skills

Infants and Toddlers. Parents of children with developmental delays may become frustrated and adopt a directive interaction style in an attempt to encourage their young child to achieve at higher levels (Mahoney & Robenalt, 1986). However, adult-directed activities may be of interest only to the adult and frequently are above a child's level of understanding. Infants with disabilities interacting with highly directive caregivers have been observed to assume a passive role in the interaction (Lussier, Crimmins, & Alberti, 1994). Family members may require assistance from professionals to learn how to match their child's style of learning and respond with a complementary style.

Preschoolers. Preschoolers with mild disabilities are more likely to be enrolled in inclusive classrooms than are children with more developmental needs. The following suggestions are useful in optimizing the social and emotional development of 3- to 5-year-old children with mild disabilities.

❏ *Be sure children understand classroom routines, rules, consequences, and expectations.* Besides reviewing rules, consequences, and expectations daily, teachers should make this information more concrete by using objects and/or pictures to represent each rule (Bruns & Gallagher, 2003). For instance, two small dolls hugging each other could represent the rule "I am gentle with my friends." Or teachers could use a picture of children from the class touching appropriately. The fundamental purpose of routines, rules, and consequences is to teach children a more appropriate way to manage conflicts and develop their self-control. This can occur only if all children understand the message.

❏ *Reward all positive peer-to-peer interactions.* Create opportunities for children to talk to each other about what they are doing and what they plan to do. If a child does not have the ability to do this spontaneously, give the child sequenced picture cards to use as visual prompts to "guide" the play. Use what a child knows to teach him or her something new (Santos, 2001). In other words, if a child knows how to blow bubbles, use this activity to teach the child to take turns with a friend.

Primary-Aged Students. A student's social and behavioral skills are critical in determining if the student will be educated successfully in a general education or a self-contained classroom (Snell & Janney, 2006; Sorrels et al., 2004). Students with

mild disabilities may have delays in the two major areas of social skills (Janney & Snell, 2006). First, prosocial skills are the skills one needs in order to get along with others. Second, self-management skills are the skills one needs in order to manage one's own emotions and behaviors. Social skills may need to be taught using direct instruction. Any social training program will follow these steps.

1) **Assess and plan.** A student's social skills must be evaluated using a checklist or assessment tool to identify his or her specific social needs. Based on this information and direct observation, a plan is developed to teach the skills. Often the student is involved in generating the plan so he or she has more personal investment in the process.

2) **Conduct small-group training sessions.** One effective way to develop social skills in young children is to structure formal training sessions. These short, structured lessons involve the following (Janney & Snell, 2006): (a) introducing the target skill, (b) identifying the skill steps for developing the new skill, (c) having the teacher model the skill steps, (d) structuring student role-plays to rehearse the skills, and (e) providing frequent feedback and reinforcement when skills are needed and used outside the training session.

3) **Support each student's generalization of the training.** Professionals must structure opportunities for students to integrate the new social skills and strategies into classroom routines. Once the behaviors are displayed at a high rate in the classroom, other environments such as the physical education class can be targeted for use of the new skills.

Skillstreaming in Early Childhood: Teaching Prosocial Skills to Preschoolers and Kindergarten Children (McGinnis & Goldstein, 1990) can be used with young children and *The Walker Social Skills Curriculum: The ACCEPTS Program* (Walker et al., 1983) can be used with primary-aged children who need to enhance their social skills. Each program offers assessment procedures, a sequence of skills organized by social skill area, descriptions of instructional procedures, and other teaching materials such as self-monitoring sheets.

Developing Preliteracy Skills

The need to have the skills required for successful school achievement arises early. However, increasingly large numbers of children enter school without the readiness skills they need to succeed (Fewell & Deutscher, 2004).

Some toddlers and preschoolers with mild disabilities have difficulty learning cognitive or preliteracy skills when they are compared to their typical peers. Yet there is little clear research that shows that preliteracy interventions are effective for preschoolers, that early preliteracy instruction positively affects later academic performance, or that preliteracy instruction is appropriate as a central focus during the preschool years (Lonigan, 2006; Missall, McConnell, & Cadigan, 2006). This issue has prompted lively debates among general ECE and ECSE professionals. The general guideline for ECSE teachers should be that only after a child with developmental delays and/or disabilities has mastered his or her foundation communication, social, fine motor, and cognitive skills, should it be considered developmentally appropriate to provide intensive preliteracy instruction. At times, unfortunately, preliteracy instruction is provided to preschoolers with delays or disabilities at the expense of other, more necessary basic skills training. The following general suggestions support the development of preliteracy skills in toddlers and preschoolers with mild disabilities.

❑ Provide opportunities for children to talk about what is read, focusing on the initial sounds and the meanings of words. Provide experiences that expand children's vocabulary by exposing them to new objects and concepts (International Reading Association & National Association for the Education of Young Children, 1998).

❑ Support task completion by using a picture sequence to represent work order or defining the length of an activity by the number of steps or materials a child must complete. In other words,

tell the child that his or her work is finished when he or she has stacked six blocks three times on different paper plates.

Numeracy. Despite a growing emphasis on early mathematical development, there remains a paucity of research in early mathematics performance with typical preschoolers. Teachers continue to be unclear about which skills to teach during the preschool years and which instructional methods to use to support optimal development (National Association for the Education of Young Children & National Council of Teachers of Mathematics, 2003). Even less is known about teaching numeracy to preschoolers with special needs. Most general early childhood and ECSE programs introduce number identification (0–15), number naming, object counting, and shape identification as core numeracy skills, when appropriate.

Developing Literacy Skills in Primary-Aged Students

Academic and behavioral intervention with children with mild disabilities has been described as "relentless, urgent instruction" characterized by attention to detail, structure, and distributed repeated practice (Polloway, Patton, & Serna, 2005). Children with mild disabilities in general education classrooms are expected to meet general education standards. Those in self-contained classrooms meet individual standards that use the general curriculum as a guidepost. In all cases, students with mild disabilities are expected, and are capable of, learning all academic subjects. Obviously, the techniques for teaching reading and mathematics discussed in Chapter 6 are also appropriate for teaching students with mild learning needs. The following section discusses the use of learning enhancement strategies and techniques teachers can use to improve reading comprehension and written language skills.

Learning Enhancement Strategies. To help young learners extract meaning from books, ECSE teachers use each child's background knowledge and graphic organizers.

Background Knowledge. Background knowledge is the prior knowledge students bring in their "backpack," the cumulative set of experiences that they use to make meaningful connections to new information (Coyne, Chard, Zipoli, & Ruby, 2007). One strategy that can help students activate and use their prior knowledge is KWL (Ogle, 1986). This strategy, which involves a three-column graphic organizer, can be used before, during, and after reading and can be used with both narratives and expository textbooks. The **K** represents "What I **K**now," the **W** represents "What I **W**ant to Know," and the **L** represents "What I Have **L**earned."

Graphic Organizers. Designed to facilitate learning, graphic organizers are visual and spatial displays of information. Examples of graphic organizers are story maps, Venn diagrams, semantic maps, and concept maps. Research has demonstrated that the reading comprehension of students with learning disabilities can be aided by the use of graphic organizers (Kim, Vaughn, Wanzek, & Wei, 2004).

Both of these strategies have been found effective in improving reading comprehension and learning in the core subjects in students with and without disabilities (Idol, 1987). Shelly's family (see the case study) reported that graphic organizers helped Shelly retain information she read which improved her writing skills as well as improved her grades.

Teaching Written Language Skills. Written language, the most sophisticated and intricate element of language, includes three areas: (1) written expression, (2) spelling, and (3) handwriting. Each one of these areas is a separate process, although they work together during writing (Abbott & Berninger, 1993). Many students with mild disabilities have problems acquiring written language skills because proficiency in written language requires integration of many cognitive processes, such as memory and reading abilities. One area of particular need for these students is spelling.

Students' spelling errors reflect their current developmental stage. That is, when students write *lrn* for *learn*, they are using beginning phonetic strategies and showing limited phonetic knowledge. However, when they write *biurifal* for *beautiful*, they are showing they understand and are following the rules for short and long vowels. Invented spelling allows children to communicate through written language without being overly concerned with the mechanics of writing. Invented spelling reveals children's phonological awareness of sounds, and when they use it, they tend to write more (Lerner & Kline, 2006).

Although invented spelling may be used for some written language assignments, instruction in spelling is still necessary for students—particularly students with mild disabilities. Teachers need to analyze the types of errors students make because instructional interventions need to be based on repeated errors (Berninger & Amtmann, 2003). For example, the spelling of *walkt* for *walked* indicates a morphological processing problem and should be addressed as such. However, the spelling of *stoped* for *stopped* and *kised* for *kissed* suggests the need to teach explicit spelling rules (Berninger & Amtmann, 2003).

Most primary-aged students with mild disabilities participate in the general education curriculum with individualized accommodations.

One effective approach to teaching spelling is the **word selection approach**, in which words are chosen by word pattern (e.g., *call, fall, tall*) or word frequency (i.e., selecting words based on how frequently they are encountered in print). Many words, particularly common rregular words, will have to be memorized.

Conclusion

Students with high-incidence disabilities represent the majority of students receiving special education services in the primary grades. Most students with learning disabilities, attention deficit disorders, mild mental retardation, or behavior disorders/emotional disturbance usually are not identified as having learning and/or behavioral problems until they are in the primary grades. To serve this group of children, specialized instruction in reading, mathematics and written language is generally required. Some students with mild learning and/or behavior problems may also benefit from specific instruction in communication and social/adaptive skills. Shelly's case study suggests that with appropriate team collaboration, general and ECSE teachers can create learning environments that appropriately address the varying abilities of children.

Summary

The identification process

- Children from birth to 5 years of age who are identified as having mild developmental needs receive services for developmental delays.
- Primary-aged students with mild disabilities are generally students who have been identified as having mild mental retardation, a learning disability, or a behavior disorder (or emotional disturbance).

Characteristics of young children with mild learning and behavior problems

- Many infants, toddlers, and preschoolers with mild developmental needs do not receive services until they enter kindergarten or first grade when they begin to experience difficulty with reading, mathematics, and/or written language.
- Primary-aged students with mild mental retardation may have a restricted vocabulary as well as memory and attention difficulties that may slow down their reading and writing achievement.
- Primary-aged students with learning disabilities may display slow word recognition, difficulties with working memory, problems with attention and other self-regulatory behaviors, and perceptual problems.
- Because primary-aged students with behavior disorders/emotional disturbance may display a range of challenging externalizing and internalizing behaviors that negatively impact their academic learning, they benefit from a structured learning environment.

Individualizing instruction and tracking learning

- To individualize and track the learning of infants, toddlers, and preschoolers, teachers use observational data and rating scales and/or checklists to identify individual objectives and use observational data, rating scales/checklists and permanent products to monitor each child's learning.
- Individualization and monitoring of the learning of primary-aged students with mild disabilities involve using Section 504 Accommodation Plans, Universal Design for Learning, curriculum-based measures, functional behavior assessments, and self-monitoring procedures.

Strategies for promoting skill development

- Task analysis, time delay, and instructional adaptation are strategies teachers use to teach young children with mild developmental/learning and behavioral needs.
- The communication and cognitive skills of children with mild disabilities are enhanced by (1) integrating communication facilitation techniques throughout the day, (2) providing functional communication training, and (3) using sabotage.
- The social and behavioral skills of children with mild disabilities are improved by directly and systematically teaching prosocial skills and self-management skills.
- Academic and behavioral intervention with primary-aged students with mild disabilities is intensive instruction characterized by attention to detail, structure, and distributed repeated practice.

- To improve the written language skills of primary-aged students with mild disabilities, teachers focus on explicit instruction on the mechanics of writing, including spelling.

DISCUSSION QUESTIONS/ACTIVITIES

1. Identify three skill areas that are challenging for students with mild disabilities. Discuss two general suggestions for improving skills in these areas for infants and toddlers, preschoolers, and primary-aged students.

2. Describe one difference in the communication, social, and academic skills of children with mild mental retardation, learning disabilities, or behavior disorders/emotional disturbance.

3. Using the information provided in the case study, describe how you would use Shelly's interest in horses to expand her reading comprehension and writing skills.

REFERENCES

Abbott, R., & Berninger, V. W. (1993). Structural equation modeling of relationships among developmental skills and writing skills in primary and intermediate grade writers. *Journal of Educational Psychology, 85*, 478–508.

American Association on Mental Retardation. (2002). *Mental retardation: Definition, classification and systems of supports* (10th ed.). Washington, DC: Author.

American Psychiatric Association (2000). *Diagnostic and statistical manual of mental disorders* (4th ed., text rev.). Washington, DC: Author.

Barkley, R. A. (2006). Etiologies. In R. A. Barkley (Ed.), *Attention-deficit hyperactivity disorder: A handbook for diagnosis and treatment* (3rd ed., pp. 219–247). New York: Guilford Press.

Barkley, R. A., & Edwards, G. (2006). Diagnostic interview, behavior rating scales, and the medical examination. In R. A. Barkley (Ed.), *Attention-deficit hyperactivity disorder: A handbook for diagnosis and treatment* (3rd ed., pp. 337–368). New York: Guilford Press.

Beirne-Smith, M., Ittenbach, R. F., & Patton, J. R. (2002). *Mental retardation* (6th ed.). Upper Saddle River, NJ: Merrill/Prentice Hall.

Berninger, V., Abbott, R., Vermeulen, K., & Fulton, C. (2006). Paths to reading comprehension in at-risk second-grade readers. *Journal of Learning Disabilities, 39*, 334–351.

Berninger, V. W., & Amtmann, D. (2003). Preventing written expression disabilities through early and continuing assessment and intervention for handwriting and/or spelling problems: Research to practice. In H. L. Swanson, K. R. Harris, & S. Graham (Eds.), *Handbook of learning disabilities* (pp. 345–363). New York: Guilford Press.

Blair, C. (2002). School readiness: Integrating cognition and emotion in a neurobiological conceptualization of children's functioning at school entry. *American Psychologist, 57*(2), 111–127.

Borthwick-Duffy, S. A., & Eyman, R. K. (1990). Who are the dually diagnosed? *American Journal on Mental Retardation, 94*, 586–595.

Bowers, P. G., & Ishaik, G. (2003). RAN's contribution to understanding reading disabilities. In H. L. Swanson, K. R. Harris, & S. Graham (Eds.), *Handbook of learning disabilities* (pp. 140–157). New York: Guilford Press.

Bray, N. W., Fletcher, K. L., & Turner, L. A. (1997). Cognitive competencies and strategy use in individuals with mental retardation. In W. W. MacLean, Jr. (Ed.), *Ellis' handbook of mental deficiency, psychological theory and research* (3rd ed., pp. 197–217). Mahwah, NJ: Erlbaum.

Brinton, B., Fujiki, M., & McKee, L. (1998). The negotiation skills of children with specific language impairment. *Journal of Speech, Language, & Hearing Impairments, 41*, 927–940.

Brown-Chidsey, R., & Steege, M. W. (2005). *Response to intervention: Principles and strategies for effective practice.* New York: Guilford Press.

Bruns, D., & Gallagher, E. (2003). Having their piece of the pie: Promoting communicative behaviors of young children with autism/PDD. *Young Exceptional Children, 6*(2), 20–27.

Bryan, T., Burstein, K., & Ergul, C. (2004). The socio-emotional side of learning disabilities: A science-based presentation of the state of the art. *Learning Disability Quarterly, 27*, 45–51.

Catts, H. W. (1997). The early identification of language based reading disabilities. *Language, Speech, and Hearing Services in Schools, 28*(1), 86–89.

Coleman, M. R., Buysse, V., & Neitzel, J. (2006). *Recognition and response: An early intervening system for young children at-risk for learning disabilities.* Chapel Hill: University of North Carolina, Frank Porter Graham Child Development Institute.

Conners, C. K. (2001). *Conners Rating Scales–Revised.* North Tonawanda, NY: Multi-Health Systems.

Conroy, M., Dunlap, G., Clarke, S., & Alter, P. (2005). A descriptive analysis of positive behavioral intervention research with young children with challenging behavior. *Topics in Early Childhood Special Education, 25,* 157–166.

Coyne, M. D., Chard, D. J., Zipoli, R. P., Jr., & Ruby, M. F. (2007). Effective strategies for teaching reading comprehension. In M. D. Coyne, E. J. Kame'enui, & D. W. Carnine, *Effective teaching strategies that accommodate diverse learners* (3rd ed., pp. 80–109). Upper Saddle River, NJ: Pearson Education.

Cullinan, D. (2002). *Students with emotional and behavior disorders: An introduction for teachers and other helping professionals.* Upper Saddle River, NJ: Merrill/Prentice Hall.

Cullinan, D. (2004). Classification and definition of emotional and behavior disorders. In R. B. Rutherford, M. M. Quinn, & S. R. Mathur (Eds.), *Handbook of research in emotional and behavioral disorders* (pp. 32–53). New York: Guilford Press.

Cutting, L. E., & Denckla, M. B. (2003). Attention: Relationships between attention-deficit hyperactivity disorder and learning disabilities. In H. L. Swanson, K. R. Harris, & S. Graham (Eds.), *Handbook of learning disabilities* (pp. 125–139). New York: Guilford Press.

deBettencourt, L. U. (2002). Understanding the differences between IDEA and Section 504. *Teaching Exceptional Children, 34,* 16–23.

Deno, S. (2003). Curriculum-based measures: Development and perspective. *Assessment for Effective Intervention, 28,* 3–12.

Deutscher, B., & Fewell, R. R. (2005). Early predictors of attention-deficit/hyperactivity disorder and school difficulties in low-birthweight, premature children. *Topics in Early Childhood Special Education, 25*(2), 71–79.

DiGangi, S. A., Maag, J. W., & Rutherford, R. B., Jr. (1991). Self-graphing of on-task behavior: Enhancing the reactive effects of self-monitoring on on-task behavior and academic performance. *Learning Disability Quarterly, 14*(3), 221–230.

Dowker, A. (2005). Early identification and intervention for students with mathematics difficulties. *Journal of Learning Disabilities, 38,* 324–332.

Dunlap, G., Ester, T., Langhans, S., & Fox, L. (2005). Functional communication training with toddlers in home environments. *Journal of Early Intervention, 28*(2), 81–96.

Durand, V. (1990). *Severe behavior problems: A functional communication training approach.* New York: Guilford Press.

Fewell, R., & Deutscher, B. (2004). Contributions of early language and maternal facilitation variables to later language and reading abilities. *Journal of Early Intervention, 26*(2), 132–145.

Fletcher, J. M., Francis, D. J., Boudousquie, A., Copeland, K., Young, V., Kalinowski, S., & Vaughn, S. (2006). Effects of accommodations on high-stakes testing for students with reading disabilities. *Exceptional Children, 72,* 136–150.

Fletcher, J. M., Morris, R. D., & Lyon, G. R. (2003). Classification and definition of learning disabilities: An integrative perspective. In H. L. Swanson, K. R. Harris, & S. Graham (Eds.), *Handbook of learning disabilities* (pp. 30–56). New York: Guilford Press.

Fore, C., Riser, S., & Boon, R. (2006). Implications of cooperative learning and educational reform for students with mild disabilities. *Reading Improvement, 43*(1), 3–12.

Fox, J. J., & Gable, R. A. (2004). Functional behavioral assessment. In R. B. Rutherford, M. M. Quinn, & S. R. Mathur (Eds.), *Handbook of research in emotional and behavioral disorders* (pp. 143–162). New York: Guilford Press.

Friend, M., & Bursuck, W. D. (2002). *Including students with special needs: A practical guide for classroom teachers* (3rd ed.). Boston: Allyn & Bacon.

Fuchs, D., & Fuchs, L. S. (2005a). Peer-assisted learning strategies: Promoting word recognition, fluency, and reading comprehension in young children. *Journal of Special Education, 39,* 34–44.

Fuchs, D., & Fuchs, L. S. (2005b). Responsiveness-to-intervention: A blueprint for practitioners, policymakers, and parents. *Teaching Exceptional Children, 38,* 57–63.

Fuchs, D., Mock, D., Morgan, P. L., & Young, C. L. (2003). Responsiveness-to-intervention: Definitions, evidence, and implications for the learning disabilities construct. *Learning Disabilities Research and Practice, 18,* 157–171.

Fuchs, L., & Fuchs, D. (2007). A model for implementing responsiveness to intervention. *Teaching Exceptional Children, 39*(5), 8–13.

Furlong, M. J., Morrison, G. M., & Jimerson, S. R. (2004). Externalizing behaviors of aggression and violence and the school context. In R. B. Rutherford, M. M. Quinn, & S. R. Mathur (Eds.), *Handbook of research in emotional and behavioral disorders* (pp. 243–261). New York: Guilford Press.

Gerber, M. M. (2005). Teachers are still the test: Limitations of response to instruction strategies for identifying children with learning disabilities. *Journal of Learning Disabilities, 38*, 516–524.

Gersten, R., Jordan, N. C., & Flojo, J. R. (2005). Early identification for students with mathematics difficulties. *Journal of Learning Disabilities, 38*, 293–304.

Gresham, F. M., & Kern, L. (2004). Internalizing behavior problems in children and adolescents. In R. B. Rutherford, M. M. Quinn, & S. R. Mathur (Eds.), *Handbook of research in emotional and behavioral disorders* (pp. 262–281). New York: Guilford Press.

Hallahan, D. P., & Kauffman, J. M. (2006). *Exceptional learners: An introduction to special education* (10th ed.). Boston: Allyn & Bacon.

Harlacher, J., Roberts, N., & Merrell, K. (2006). Classwide intervention with students with ADHD: A summary of teacher options beneficial for the whole class. *Teaching Exceptional Children, 39*(2), 6–13.

Hepting, N., & Goldstein, H. (1996). What's natural about naturalistic language intervention? *Journal of Early Intervention, 20*, 249–265.

Horn, E., Lieber, J., Sandall, S., & Schwartz, I. (2001). Embedded learning opportunities as an instructional strategy for supporting children's learning in inclusive programs. In M. Orlansky & S. Sandall, *Teaching strategies: What to do to support young children's development* (YEC Monograph No. 3) (pp. 59–70). Longmont, CO: Sopris West.

Horn, E., & Sandall, S. (2000). The visiting teacher: A model of inclusive ECSE service delivery. In S. Sandall & M. Ortrosky, *Natural environments and inclusion* (YEC Monograph No. 2) (pp. 49–58). Longmont, CO: Sopris West.

Idol, L. (1987). Group story mapping: A comprehension strategy for both skilled and unskilled readers. *Journal of Learning Disabilities, 20*, 196–205.

Individuals with Disabilities Education Act (IDEA) Amendments of 2004a, Pub. L. No. 108-446, Sec. 300.8(c) (4) (i).

Individuals with Disabilities Education Act (IDEA) Amendments of 2004b, Pub. L. No. 108-446, Sec. 300.530(d) (1) (ii).

Interagency Committee on Learning Disabilities. (1987). *Learning disabilities: A report to the U.S. Congress.* Bethesda, MD: National Institutes of Health.

International Reading Association & National Association for the Education of Young Children (NAEYC). (1998). *Learning to read and write: Developmentally appropriate practices for young children.* NAEYC: Washington, DC.

Janney, R., & Snell, M. E. (2006). *Teachers' guides to inclusive practices: Behavioral support.* Baltimore, MD: Brookes.

Kaiser, A. (2007). Addressing challenging behavior: Systematic problems, systematic solutions. *Journal of Early Intervention, 29*, 114–118.

Kaiser, A., & Delaney, E. (2001). Responsive conversations: Creating opportunities for naturalistic language teaching. In M. Orlansky & S. Sandall, *Teaching strategies: What to do to support young children's development* (YEC Monograph No. 3) (pp. 13–24). Longmont, CO: Sopris West.

Kamps, D., Wendland, M., & Culpepper, M. (2006). Active teacher participation in functional behavior assessment for students with emotional and behavioral disorders risks in general education classrooms. *Behavioral Disorders, 31*(2), 128–146.

Kauffman, J. M. (2005). *Characteristics of emotional and behavioral disorders of children and youth* (8th ed.). Upper Saddle River, NJ: Merrill/Prentice Hall.

Kim, A., Vaughn, S., Wanzek, J., & Wei, S. (2004). Graphic organizers and their effects on the reading comprehension of students with LD: A synthesis of the research. *Journal of Learning Disabilities, 37*, 105–118.

Lane, K. L. (2004). Academic instruction and tutoring interventions for students with emotional and behavioral disorders: 1990 to the present. In R. B. Rutherford, M. M. Quinn, & S. R. Mathur (Eds.), *Handbook of research in emotional and behavioral disorders* (pp. 462-486). New York: Guilford Press.

Lane, K. L., & Menzies, H. M. (2005). Teacher-identified students with and without academic and behavioral concerns: Characteristics and responsiveness. *Behavioral Disorders, 31*(1), 65–83.

Lerner, J., & Kline, F. (2006). *Learning disabilities and related disorders: Characteristics and teaching strategies* (10th ed.). Boston: Houghton Mifflin.

Litt, J., Taylor, H. G., Klein, N., & Hack, M. (2005). Learning disabilities in children with very low birthweight: Prevalence, neuropsychological correlates, and educational interventions. *Journal of Learning Disabilities, 38*, 130–141.

Lonigan, D. (2006). Conceptualizing phonological processing skills in prereaders. In S. B. Neuman & D. Dickinson (Eds.), *Handbook of early literacy research* (2nd ed., pp. 77–89). New York: Guilford Press.

Lussier, B., Crimmins, D., & Alberti, D. (1994). Effect of three adult interaction styles on infant engagement. *Journal of Early Intervention, 18*, 12–24.

Lyon, G. R., Fletcher, J. M., Shaywitz, S. E., Shaywitz, B, A., Torgesen, J. K., Wood, F. B., Schultz, A., & Olson, R. (2001). Rethinking learning disabilities. In C. E. Finn, Jr., R. A. J. Rotherham, & C. R. Hokanson, Jr. (Eds.), *Rethinking special education for a new century* (pp. 259-287). Washington, DC: Thomas B. Fordham Foundation and Progressive Policy Institute.

Mahoney, G., & Robenalt, K. (1986). A comparison of conversational patterns between mothers and their Down syndrome and normal infants. *Journal of the Division for Early Childhood, 10,* 172-180.

Mastropieri, M. A., & Scruggs, T. E. (2005). Feasibility and consequences of response to intervention: Examination of issues and scientific evidence as a model for the identification of individuals with learning disabilities. *Journal of Learning Disabilities, 38,* 525-531.

Mattison, R. E., Hooper, S. R., & Carlson, G. A. (2006). Neuropsychological characteristics of special education students with serious emotional/behavioral disorders. *Behavioral Disorders, 31*(2), 176-188.

Mattison, R. E., Spitznagel, E. L., & Felix, B. C. (1998). Enrollment predictors of the special education outcome for students with SED. *Behavioral Disorders, 23,* 243-256.

McCathren, R., & Watson, A. (2001). Facilitating the development of intentional communication. In M. Orlansky & S. Sandall, *Teaching strategies: What to do to support young children's development* (YEC Monograph No. 3) (pp. 25-36). Longmont, CO: Sopris West.

McCormick, L., Loeb, D. F., & Schiefelbusch, R. L. (2003). *Supporting children with communication difficulties in inclusive settings: School-based language intervention* (2nd ed.). Boston: Allyn & Bacon.

McGinnis, E., & Goldstein, A. P. (1990). *Skillstreaming in early childhood: Teaching presocial skills to preschool and kindergarten children.* Champaign, IL: Research Press.

Minishew, N., Meyer, J., & Dunn, M. (2003). Autism spectrum disorders. In S. Segalowitz & I. Rapin (Eds.), *Child neuropsychology, Part II* (pp. 863-896). Amsterdam: Elsevier.

Missall, K., McConnell, S., & Cadigan, K. (2006). Early literacy development: Skill growth and relations between classroom variables for preschool children. *Journal of Early Intervention, 29,* 1-21.

Montague, M., Enders, C., & Castro, M. (2005). Academic and behavioral outcomes for students at risk for emotional and behavioral disorders. *Behavioral Disorders, 31*(1), 84-94.

National Association for the Education of Young Children & National Council of Teachers of Mathematics. (2003). *Learning paths and teaching strategies in early mathematics, 58*(1), 41-43.

National Joint Committee on Learning Disabilities. (1988). *Letter to NJCLD member organizations.* Retrieved November 27, 2007 from http://education.gsu.edu/dcdd/information/nationaljcld/1.htm

O'Connor, R. E., Fulmer, D., Harty, K. R., & Bell, K. (2005). Layers of reading intervention in kindergarten though third grade: Changes in teaching and student outcomes. *Journal of Learning Disabilities, 38,* 440-455.

Ogle, D. M. (1986). A teaching model that develops active reading of expository text. *Reading Teacher, 39,* 564-570.

Ostrosky, M., & Horn, E. (Eds.). (2002). *Assessment: Gathering meaningful information* (YEC Monograph No. 4). Longmont, CO: Sopris West.

Patton, B., Jolivette, K., & Ramsey, M. (2006). Students with emotional and behavioral disorders can manage their own behavior. *Teaching Exceptional Children, 39*(2), 14-21.

Polloway, E., Patton, J., & Serna, L. (2005*). Strategies for teaching learners with special needs* (8th ed.). Upper Saddle River, NJ: Merrill/Prentice Hall.

Polsgrove, L. (2004). Assessment and evaluation: Introduction. In R. B. Rutherford, M. M. Quinn, & S. R. Mathur (Eds.), *Handbook of research in emotional and behavioral disorders* (pp. 117-121). New York: Guilford Press.

Pretti-Frontczak, K., & Bricker, D. (2004). *An activity-based approach to early intervention* (3rd ed.). Baltimore, MD: Brookes.

Raver, S. A. (1987). Practical procedures for increasing spontaneous language in language-delayed preschoolers. *Journal of the Division of Early Childhood, 11,* 226-232.

Reynolds, C. (2006). Childhood disorders. In E. Fletcher-Janzen & C. R. Reynolds (Eds.), *The special education almanac* (pp. 203-204). Hoboken, NJ: Wiley.

Reynolds, C., & Kamphaus, R. (2004). *Behavioral assessment system for children* (2nd ed.). Circle Pines, MN: American Guidance Service.

Rose, D. (2000). Universal Design for Learning. *Journal of Special Education Technology, 15*(2), 56-60.

Sabornie, E. J., Evans, C., & Cullinan, D. (2006). Comparing characteristics of high-incidence disability groups: A descriptive review. *Remedial and Special Education, 27*(2), 95-104.

Santos, R. (2001). Using what children know to teach them something new: Applying high-probability procedures in the classroom and at home. In M. Orlansky & S. Sandall, *Teaching strategies: What to do to support young children's development* (YEC Monograph No. 3) (pp. 71–80). Longmont, CO: Sopris West.

Schoenbrodt, L., Kumin, L., & Sloan, J. M. (1997). Learning disabilities existing concomitantly with communication disorder. *Journal of Learning Disability, 30,* 264–281.

Shaywitz, S. E., & Shaywitz, B. (2004). Reading disability and the brain. *Educational Leadership, 61,* 6–11.

Siegel, L. S. (2003). IQ discrepancy definitions and the diagnosis of learning disabilities. *Journal of Learning Disabilities, 36,* 2–67.

Siperstein, G., Norins, J., Corbin, S., & Shriver, T. (2003, June). *Multinational study of attitudes toward individuals with intellectual disabilities (general findings and calls to action).* Boston: Special Olympics.

Smith, C. R. (2004). *Learning disabilities: The interaction of students and their environments* (5th ed.). Boston: Pearson Education.

Smith, T. (2002). Section 504: What teachers need to know. *Intervention in School and Clinic, 37,* 259–266.

Snell, M. E., & Janney, R. (2006). *Teachers' guides to inclusion practices: Social relationships and peer support.* Baltimore, MD: Brookes.

Snow, C., Burns, M., & Griffin, P. (1998). *Preventing reading difficulties in young children: The report of the National Research Committee.* Washington, DC: National Academy Press.

Sorrells, A. M., Reith, H. J., & Sindelar, P. T. (2004). *Critical issues in special education: Access, diversity, and accountability.* Boston: Pearson.

Stanton-Chapman, T. L., Chapman, D. A., Kaiser, A. P., & Hancock, T. B. (2004). Cumulative risk and low-income children's language development. *Topics in Early Childhood Special Education, 24,* 227–237.

Steele, M. M. (2004). Making the case for early identification and intervention for young children at risk for learning disabilities. *Early Childhood Educational Journal, 32,* 75–79.

Swanson, H. L., & Sachse-Lee, C. (2001). Mathematical problem solving and working memory in children with learning disabilities: Both executive and phonological processes are important. *Journal of Experimental Child Psychology, 79,* 294–321.

Swanson, H. L., & Saez, L. (2003). Memory difficulties in children and adults with learning disabilities. In H. L. Swanson, K. R. Harris, & S. Graham (Eds.), *Handbook of learning disabilities* (pp. 182–198). New York: Guilford Press.

Synder, P., Bailey, D., & Auer, C. (1994). Preschool eligibility determination for children with known or suspected learning disabilities under IDEA. *Journal of Early Intervention, 18,* 380–390.

Torgesen, J. K. (1997). The prevention and remediation of reading difficulties: Evaluating what we know from research. *Journal of Academic Language Therapy, 1,* 11–47.

Trout, A. L., Epstein, M. H., Nelson, J. R., Reid, R., & Ohlund, B. (2006). Profiles of young children teacher-identified as at risk for emotional disturbance: A pilot study. *Behavioral Disorders, 31*(2), 162–175.

U.S. Department of Education. (2002). Twenty-fourth annual report to Congress on the implementation of the Individuals with Disabilities Education Act. Washington, DC: Author.

Vaughn, S., & Fuchs, L. S. (2003). Redefining learning disabilities as inadequate response to instruction: The promise and potential problems. *Learning Disabilities Research and Practice, 18,* 137–146.

Vaughn, S., Linan-Thompson, S., & Hickman, P. (2003). Response to instruction as a means for identifying students with reading/learning disabilities. *Exceptional Children, 69,* 391–409.

Vellutino, F. R., Scallon, D. M., & Lyon, G. R. (2000). Differentiating between difficult-to-remediate and readily remediated poor readers: More evidence against the IQ–achievement discrepancy definition of reading disability. *Journal of Learning Disabilities, 33,* 223–238.

Walker, H. M., McConnell, S. R., Holmes, D., Todis, B., Walker, J., & Golden, N. (1983). *The Walker social skills curriculum: The ACCEPTS program.* Austin, TX: PRO-ED.

Westby, C. E., & Watson, S. (2004). Perspectives on attention deficit hyperactivity disorder: Executive functions, working memory, and language disabilities. *Seminars in Speech and Language, 25,* 241–254.

Wilson, K., & Swanson, H. L. (2001). Are mathematics disabilities due to a domain-general or domain-specific working memory deficit? *Journal of Learning Disabilities, 34,* 237–248.

Wolery, M. (2001). Embedding time delay procedures in classroom activities. In M. Orlansky & S. Sandall, *Teaching strategies: What to do to support young children's development* (YEC Monograph No. 3) (pp. 81–90). Longmont, CO: Sopris West.

Chapter
10

Techniques for Teaching Young Children with Moderate/Severe or Multiple Disabilities

Eva Horn

Cynthia R. Chambers

Yumiko Saito

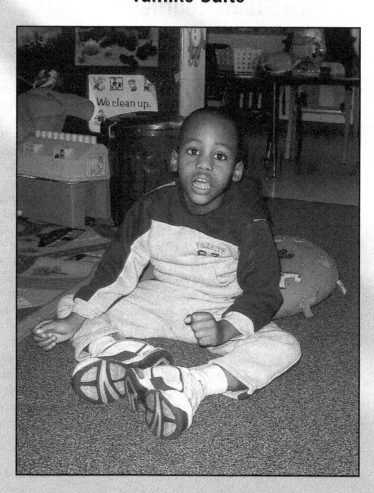

Overview

This chapter discusses the development in infants, toddlers, preschoolers, and primary-aged children with significant disabilities, including

definitions of moderate/severe and multiple disabilities

general characteristics of children with severe and multiple disabilities

using a needs-based approach to intervention

forming educational teams for children with severe and multiple disabilities

assessment considerations

curriculum development for children with severe and multiple disabilities

CASE STUDY: Lourdes

Lourdes was 2 years old when she and her family were referred to an infant-toddler program. She lived in a rural community with her grandmother, Manuela. Lourdes' family physician communicated to the family that Lourdes probably wouldn't survive, given her multiple disabilities: mental retardation, cerebral palsy, visual impairment, and serious health impairments. Transportation was a problem because of Manuela's poor health and the family's limited resources. The family's rural community did not have a preschool or a childcare program. The local school district housed all early childhood special education programs 35 miles away in a larger town. Manuela commented that she did not feel comfortable with a program that was not close by in case of an emergency.

Lourdes' team provided home-based services and began planning for her transition to a Head Start program with special education and related services provided when Lourdes turned 3. Lourdes' Individualized Family Services Plan outcomes at this time included establishing a communication system for expressing basic requests and improving her movement and ability to hold positions. All team members (infant-toddler as well as preschool) helped raise money for the equipment that Lourdes needed and assisted her grandmother with expenses. These events helped Lourdes' team begin to know each other as people, not just as teachers, physical therapists, and nurses.

At three and a half, Lourdes began to attend Head Start one afternoon a week. Her time at the center was slowly increased, but she was frequently absent due to illness. She was alert to the children around her, and they looked forward to her arrival. As time passed, the staff grew more comfortable with her needs and learned to use her equipment to make her a part of the group, not just an observer. Lourdes' Individualized Education Program goals continued to focus on increasing her expressive communication through the use of augmentative communication—in this case, a picture communication system for requesting and rejecting—and moving her upper extremities for reaching and grasping. Related service providers and the early childhood special education teacher visited at home and at Head Start to assure that modifications were made to allow Lourdes to participate as fully as possible. At age 5, Lourdes moved to the local kindergarten program. The fact that many of her Head Start peers moved with her made her transition much smoother. Her early childhood special education teacher followed Lourdes into the program to support her inclusion.

Despite Lourdes' many challenges—the severity of her disabilities, her family's limited resources, her poor prognosis, the community's limited resources, and the remoteness of her home—she is defying the odds by living. Her inclusion has not been easy, but many professionals have made Lourdes' inclusion possible by offering direct and indirect services. Her team has had to overcome personal and agency barriers; however, the team reports that it has been worth it. Now, in the second grade, Lourdes goes to her elementary school like everyone else.

Source: Adapted from the *Circle of Inclusion* website, http://circleofinclusion.org.

Young children with severe and multiple disabilities have unique needs and challenges. Often the magnitude of the delays of this group of children is significant enough to result in relatively easy identification (Martin & Baker, 2001). Further, the intensity of their needs means that delays are likely to have a pervasive impact on each child's development and are likely to continue to impact the family and the child well beyond the early childhood years (Chen, 1997). While all the strategies and approaches for enhancing development discussed in other chapters are useful, children with severe and multiple disabilities can present some unique challenges. To support the learning of young learners with complex needs, ECSE professionals follow these principles:

❑ All young children, regardless of the extent of their disabilities, have a right to actively participate in meaningful ways in the natural environment.

❑ The support and learning needs of these young children are multiplied by the number and magnitude of their disabilities, and these needs must be responded to both individually and collectively.

❑ All young children must be viewed as a whole, rather than focusing on the individual areas of disability and need.

❑ All young children have value and the potential to learn, grow, and develop (Roberts, 2004).

Thus, to best serve young children with moderate, severe and multiple disabilities and their families, early childhood education must offer specialized supports and services within the context of high-quality early education environments.

DEFINITIONS OF MODERATE/SEVERE AND MULTIPLE DISABILITIES

There is no single definition for severe and multiple disabilities. In group-based settings such as preschools and elementary schools, severe and multiple disabilities tend to be coupled as a single disability area. Traditionally, children have been labeled as having severe or profound disabilities when they display profound intellectual limitations. However, not all children with severe and multiple disabilities have cognitive impairments. Children with severe and multiple disabilities may experience a variety of disabilities that may singly or concomitantly present the need for extensive supports.

The regulations implementing the Individuals with Disabilities Education Improvement Act (IDEA) of 2004 provide the following definition for 3- to 21-year-olds, but this definition is also used for younger children:

The term "severe disability" refers to children with disabilities who, because of the intensity of their physical, mental, or emotional problems, need highly specialized education, social, psychological, and medical services in order to maximize their full potential for useful and meaningful participation in society and for self-fulfillment. (34 C.F.R. § 315.4(d))

These regulations also provide the following definition for multiple disabilities:

"Multiple disabilities" means concomitant impairments (such as mental retardation–blindness or mental retardation–orthopedic impairment), the combination of which causes such severe educational needs that they cannot be accommodated in special education programs solely for one of the impairments. (34 C.F.R. § 300.8 (b)(6))

Children with severe disabilities constitute roughly the lowest intellectually functioning 1% of the population (Leonard & Wen, 2002). In the 2002 Census, approximately 12% of individuals with a disability were categorized as having a severe disability. However, prevalence figures can vary from one report to another because of the social construct of disability (Molloy & Vassal, 2002). That is, what constitutes a severe disability is determined by how a particular society or group of people interprets the concept. Therefore, what constitutes having a severe disability varies from one person to another. In truth, prevalence estimates of children with severe and multiple needs are fairly broad guesses, usually lacking precise criteria.

General Characteristics of Children with Moderate/Severe and Multiple Disabilities

Describing the characteristics of children with severe and multiple disabilities has challenges similar to those in defining severe disabilities. Heller and colleagues (Heller, Alberto, Forney, & Schwartzman, 1996) provide six major categories, based on medical characteristics and educational implications, that provide a foundation for describing the characteristics of children with moderate/severe and multiple disabilities: (1) neuromotor impairments, (2) degenerative diseases, (3) infectious diseases, (4) orthopedic and musculoskeletal disorders, (5) sensory impairments, and (6) major health impairments. Using this framework and adding a category for neurodevelopmental disorders, the following section will provide a description of the basic characteristics of children with severe and multiple disabilities.

Neuromotor Impairments

Neuromotor impairments include disorders that involve the central nervous system and affect both the nerves and the muscles. These disorders include cerebral palsy, spinal cord disorders and injuries, seizure disorders, and traumatic brain injuries. Neuromotor impairments such as cerebral palsy and spinal cord disorders (e.g., spina bifida and spinal cord injuries) can impair a child's movement and posture, inhibiting or preventing the child from freely maneuvering through his or her environment. Although neuromotor impairments vary in their severity, such limited movements, whether minor or severe, can affect a child's quality of life if appropriate supports are not in place.

Seizure disorders have many attributes, but one key similarity is that seizures are the result of involuntary behavior. Seizures may present themselves in the form of a blank stare, a stiffening or shaking of the body, or a loss of consciousness (Heller et al., 1996). While some children may be significantly affected by their seizure disorder, for others this disorder may be a mild inconvenience. In many cases, seizure activity can be controlled by medication. However, the medication can have adverse side effects that negatively impact children's learning and behavioral functioning.

Traumatic brain injuries are injuries acquired as a result of an external physical force such as an impact to or a shaking of the head. These injuries differ in their onset, severity, and permanence (Savage, Depompei, Tyler, & Lash, 2005). As a result of a brain injury, children may experience impairments in cognition, communication, physical ability, sensory input, and behavior. Given that children with traumatic brain injuries undergo a period of healing, their prognosis is different than that of children with other disabilities. Professionals and families must work together to develop educational plans that address the potentially shifting needs of these children.

Degenerative Diseases

Degenerative diseases cause the function or structure of tissues or organs in affected body areas to deteriorate progressively (Heller et al., 1996). Some examples of degenerative diseases include **muscular dystrophy**, which involves degeneration of muscles and muscle weakness; **spinal muscular atrophy**, which entails degeneration of motor neurons surrounding the spinal cord and brain stem; and cancer. As these diseases progress, children experience a loss of functioning. As professionals and families collaborate to educate children with degenerative diseases, they should address issues related to adaptation of the environment and curricula. They also need to consider each child's perceptions of death and how these perceptions affect the child's functioning.

Infectious Diseases

Infectious diseases are those diseases that arise when an individual takes in a biological agent such as a virus, bacterium, or parasite. These diseases can be placed into two categories: congenital infections and acquired infections. **Congenital infections** are diseases that are passed on from the mother to the fetus. **Acquired infections** are acquired after birth. Infectious diseases include the human immunodeficiency virus (HIV), which in its later stage is referred to as acquired immune deficiency syndrome (AIDS); lower respiratory infections; meningitis; tuberculosis (TB); syphilis; and hepatitis B. These diseases can limit a child's strength, vitality, and alertness, ultimately affecting a child's functioning across all developmental domains. The exact educational implications can be determined through collaboration between professionals and families.

Orthopedic and Musculoskeletal Disorders

Many children with severe or multiple disabilities can develop orthopedic or musculoskeletal disorders that are secondary to their primary diagnosis (Orelove & Sobsey, 1996). Orthopedic or musculoskeletal disorders may also be a child's only diagnosis. Such disorders may include **scoliosis**, which involves the curvature of the spine, as well as other back or spinal disorders; hip conditions, which may result in dislocation; **contractures**, which involve the shortening of muscles or tendons; juvenile rheumatoid arthritis; and disorders of the foot or ankle. Such disorders may cause the child pain or discomfort as well as hinder the child's ability to move and increase the child's need for instructional modifications.

Sensory Impairments

Sensory impairments include impairments such as visual and hearing impairments that influence children's input from sensory modes. The sensory information received by children experiencing sensory impairments may be limited or unavailable, which may affect these children's functioning. These limitations require unique adaptations in the presentation of information and concepts to enable children to optimize successful educational performances.

Major Health Impairments

Major health impairments include blood disorders (e.g., hemophilia and sickle cell disease), congenital heart defects, chronic renal failure (i.e., chronic kidney failure or disease), and Type 1 diabetes (i.e., insulin-dependent diabetes mellitus or juvenile diabetes). For some children, the symptoms of these impairments can be controlled by medication, and the children experience little impact on their development and learning. However, for others, medication may be ineffective or may not allow a child to experience typical development. A possible result of uncontrolled symptoms can be death, making crucial the collaboration between professionals and families to identify signs and symptoms, appropriate modifications, and appropriate procedures to handle medical emergencies.

Neurodevelopmental Disorders

The final category of impairments is neurodevelopmental disorders. These disorders are caused by differences or irregularities in brain development as a result of genetic and environmental factors. Some examples of neurodevelopmental disorders include fragile X syndrome, fetal alcohol syndrome, and autism spectrum disorder. **Fragile X syndrome**, the most common hereditary cause of mental retardation, is a genetic disorder resulting from mutation of a gene on the X chromosome. Aside from intellectual disability, behavioral characterisics may include stereotypic movements such as hand flapping and atypical social development, particularly shyness and limited eye contact. Some individuals with fragile X syndrome also meet the diagnostic criteria for autism. While full-mutation males tend to present with severe intellectual disability, the symptomology of full-mutation females runs the gamut from minimally affected to severe intellectual disability.

Fetal alcohol syndrome (FAS), the result of prenatal exposure to alcohol, is a preventable cause of physical and mental disabilities. A child with FAS may have difficulties with learning, memory, attention span, or a variety of other issues that may impact the child's educational experience.

Autism spectrum disorders (ASDs) range from a severe form, called autistic disorder, to a milder form, **Asperger syndrome**. If a child has symptoms of either of these disorders, but does not meet the specific criteria for either, the diagnosis is **pervasive developmental disorder not otherwise specified (PDD–NOS)**. Other rare, very severe ASDs are Rett syndrome and childhood disintegrative disorder. All children with ASDs demonstrate the following: (1) deficits in social interaction, (2) deficits in verbal and nonverbal communication, and (3) repetitive behaviors or interests. In addition, they will often have unusual responses to sensory experiences, such as certain sounds or the way objects look. Each of these symptoms may be displayed as a mild to a severe limitation.

As noted above, these disorders are associated with atypical behaviors such as stereotypic movements and atypical social interaction and communication. Children can experience these disorders singly or with other disorders, and the effects of the disorders are long-term. These children's needs demand that professionals and families work collaboratively to obtain an appropriate education, one that focuses on improving functioning, especially their interactions with others.

USING A NEEDS-BASED APPROACH TO INTERVENTION

Understanding the characteristics of children with moderate/severe and multiple disabilities is crucial, but even more essential is developing an understanding of the needs and supports required by children with these disabilities. These children may share some attributes, but they possess their own uniqueness as well. As professionals and families develop programs for children with severe and multiple disabilities, the special needs and necessary supports of *each* child must drive the process. This section provides an overview of the four areas of need—medical, physical, educational,

TABLE 10.1 The components of a needs-based approach to intervention with young children with moderate/severe and multiple disabilities

Medical needs	Given that children with moderate/severe and multiple disabilities tend to be less healthy than other children, it is crucial that professionals and families work together to design and monitor procedures concerning children's medical needs.
Physical needs	Children with moderate/severe and multiple disabilities often exhibit delays in motor development, which can result in difficulties with mobility, sitting, and standing.
Educational needs	Children with moderate/severe and multiple disabilities need supports in place that enable them to achieve educational outcomes that are desired for all children.
Social-emotional needs	Given that children with moderate/severe and multiple disabilities may need assistance in accessing opportunities to engage in interactions with others and other individuals may need assistance in understanding the communicative acts of children with these disabilities, professionals and families systematically support and facilitate social opportunities.

and social-emotional needs—that should be addressed when developing interventions for young children. Table 10.1 provides a brief summary of these four need areas.

Medical Needs

The presence of specific medical or health care needs may require accommodations so that children can more successfully participate in typical home and school settings. These needs may be intense and require substantial effort by adults. Despite this, these needs alone do not condone placing children with moderate/severe and multiple disabilities in more restrictive settings. Yet the needs of these children do place greater responsibility in the hands of professionals and families to work together to enable effective inclusion. In some cases, professionals and families may find themselves implementing procedures that have in the past been considered the responsibilities of medical professionals (Turnbull, Turnbull, Shank, Smith, & Leal, 2001). These responsibilities include cleaning or inserting catheters, feeding by tube, managing respiratory ventilation systems, and administering medications. Under the IDEA, young children with moderate/severe or multiple disabilities who have

medical needs may be entitled to medical services as a related service to enable them to attend school.

Given that children with severe and multiple disabilities tend to be less healthy than other children (Thompson & Guess, 1989), it is crucial that professionals work with families to design and monitor procedures concerning these children's medical needs. Attention and consideration must be given to their behaviors or patterns, which may be the result of medication or other medical issues, diet, and physical activity. Focus on these aspects of each child's life can help improve the quality of his or her experiences and ultimately result in more learning opportunities in school.

Physical Needs

Children with moderate/severe and multiple disabilities often exhibit delays in motor development, which can result in difficulties with mobility, sitting, and standing. Motor difficulties may range from those that affect the whole body to those that affect only part of the body. Although some children may never be able to develop basic mobility, sitting, or standing skills without support, other children with severe and multiple disabilities may develop these skills at a later period than may be seen in typically developing children. These physical issues can interfere with a child's ability to function in home routines and activities, such as bath time, play, meals, and family recreation. With appropriate adaptations and services, most children with moderate/severe and multiple disabilities can more fully participate in daily activities.

Educational Needs

The desired educational outcomes of children with moderate/severe and multiple disabilities do not differ significantly from those of their typical peers. These outcomes include the development of skills, membership, and relationships (Snell & Brown, 2000). However, although the outcomes do not differ, the educational needs of children with severe and multiple disabilities tend to be greater. These children need supports in place that enable them to achieve the educational outcomes that are desired for all individuals.

Although strategies for including children with severe and multiple disabilities in typical and natural environments will be discussed more thoroughly later in this chapter, several points warrant multiple iterations. First, in order for children with moderate/severe and multiple disabilities to be able to access learning activities and peers, they must be positioned in such a way that they have an opportunity to see, to hear, and to manipulate learning materials. Proper positioning allows children to engage and interact with those around them, whether they are family members, professionals, or classmates.

Second, children with severe and multiple disabilities often communicate in ways other than the traditional method of speech. Although their forms of communication may differ, children with moderate/severe and multiple disabilities adopt forms of communication that can relay their wants and needs. Communicative acts may consist of an eye blink, a turn of the head, sign language, or assisted forms of communication such as communication boards and electronic communication systems. Some of these communication

methods will come natural to the child, and other methods will need to be systematically taught.

Third, a driving goal in the education of children with moderate/severe and multiple disabilities is to assist them in becoming self-determined. One component of being self-determined is being able to make choices for one's self. Often, for children with significant needs, choices are made for them. However, if choices are provided and children are encouraged to make their own choices, they are learning to acquire aspects of self-determination. By learning how to make choices, children are moving away from dependency and moving toward having more control over their lives. This is clearly demonstrated by Lourdes' program, discussed in the case study.

Social-Emotional Needs

Although the obvious goal of education is to improve children's skills, an equally important goal is facilitating children's social development and engagement. Social development encompasses many skills, but the most significant can be described as those relating to relationships and membership in community (Staub, Spaulding, Peck, Gallucci, & Schwartz, 1996). Given that children with severe and multiple disabilities may need assistance in engaging in interactions with others and other individuals may need assistance in understanding the communicative behaviors of these children, professionals and families must create social opportunities. If all members of a child's team do not view social interactions and opportunities as important, the child's social and emotional needs may not be met. Having relationships and feeling like a member of a group are crucial to everyone's well-being. Educational programs should reflect this value, and teams are key players in ensuring that children have that opportunity.

When professionals use a needs-based approach to supporting the learning of children with moderate/severe and multiple disabilities, it is possible to identify the individual supports each child needs to have greater access and engagement across environments. Children with significant disabilities require the support of a number of professionals who form a team to ensure that their medical, physical, educational, and social-emotional needs are met daily.

FORMING EDUCATIONAL TEAMS FOR CHILDREN WITH MODERATE/SEVERE AND MULTIPLE DISABILITIES

Given the variety of combinations of physical, medical, educational, and social-emotional challenges that young children with significant disabilities bring to each learning environment, which may be a home, school, or community setting, a diverse set of individuals and disciplines is needed to provide support. Since the early 1950s, those in the field of special education have recognized that one or two individuals and/or disciplines cannot appropriately meet the diverse and often extensive needs of children with severe and multiple disabilities (Snell & Janney, 2000). Although current recommended practices in ECSE (Sandall, Hemmeter, Smith, & McLean, 2005) call for team members to work collaboratively, professionals and family members also have specific training backgrounds, philosophical approaches, experiences, and specialized skills. A team's success is dependent on the competence of the individual team members and on the mutual understanding and respect each has for the skills and knowledge of the other team members (McWilliams, 2005).

Roles and Responsibilities of Team Members

As noted in Chapter 2, all team members have some roles and responsibilities that are generic and shared across members, some that are implemented in smaller subteams, and some that are unique to the individual discipline. Giangreco and colleagues (Giangreco, Edelman, & Broer, 2003) identified four important functions for team members serving children with severe and multiple disabilities: (1) designing modifications to allow for active participation or to prevent negative outcomes such as regression, pain, or deformity; (2) translating discipline-specific knowledge for and sharing it with other team members; (3) acting in the role of a resource, support, or both to the child's family; and (4) implementing discipline-specific techniques to promote child learning, to prevent negative outcomes, or both.

Different individuals from the same discipline may not necessarily have the same expertise due to differences in training and experiences. Teams should be configured differently for each student, depending on the array of services needed to provide the appropriate support to implement a child's Individualized Family Services Plan (IFSP) or Individualized Educational Program (IEP). Consequently, when determining who is on the child's team, child and family priorities and needs must be matched with the potential team members who can contribute the necessary knowledge, regardless of their title.

Teams for young children may include one or more of the following: parent or legal guardian, early interventionist/early childhood special educator, general early childhood educator, physical therapist, occupational therapist, speech-language pathologist, educational psychologist, assistive technology specialist, educator for the visually impaired/orientation and mobility specialist, audiologist, and other specialists as needed. Given that the team for a child with moderate/severe and multiple disabilities may include specialists that are less frequently a part of a team for children with less extensive needs, the specific roles of some team members will be discussed as they relate to supporting a child with significant disabilities.

Early Interventionist/Early Childhood Special Education Professional

The ECSE teachers's role on the IFSP/IEP team is complex and includes a broad range of responsibilities and skills. This professional sees that a child with moderate/severe and multiple disabilities learns, through direct instruction and through the sharing of expertise and skills with family members, the general early educator, paraeducators, related service providers, bus drivers, cafeteria workers, and other adults who regularly interact with the child. The EI/ECSE professional also works with a child's typical peers or siblings in the home, childcare settings, and classrooms within the child's school to enhance their skills in engaging and communicating with the child. They often function as a service coordinator. For example, frequently the ECSE teacher serves as a liaison between the family and other school personnel (Turnbull & Turnbull, 2006) by supervising paraprofessionals (Giangreco et al., 2003), serving as a member/coordinator of the child's team, and advocating for the child.

General Early Childhood Educator

The IDEA (2004) clearly states that no less than one general education teacher of the child (if the child is, or may be, participating in a regular education environment) must be included on the child's team. For infants, toddlers, and preschoolers, it may not always be immediately obvious what the "regular education environment" is or which person is the "regular education teacher." For example, a toddler may be receiving the bulk of his or her early intervention services in the "natural learning environment" of the family's home. However, twice a week the toddler attends a "mother's day out" program in the community. The teacher(s)/caregiver(s) of this program should become part of the child's team.

Members of the child's team determine all environments in which the child participates on a regular basis. As noted in earlier chapters, the concept of natural learning environment is typically reserved for infant and toddler intervention; however, the concept actually is very useful across all the early education years. In the Division of Early Childhood (DEC) recommended practices, natural learning environments have been defined as "settings in which children without disabilities spend time" (Sandall et al., 2005, p. 304). Thus,

teams should consider including adults from all the environments where the child and the family regularly spend time, such as the home, childcare programs, family daycare homes, children's hour at the library, and gymnastics classes.

The general early educator's role on the team is to provide expertise regarding the general education curriculum; the activity plans for each session, session schedules, and routines; program rules and expectations; and generally the culture of the general education program. This educator also shares responsibility for ensuring that the child with moderate/severe and multiple disabilities is provided with opportunities to *actively participate* in daily activities and learn from the general education curriculum (Horn, Thompson, Palmer, Jensen, & Turbiville, 2004). Finally, the general early childhood educator should share the responsibility, with other team members, of designing, delivering, and evaluating a child's progress in his or her individualized program.

Physical Therapist

The primary responsibility of the physical therapist (PT) is providing essential information to team members regarding optimal physical functioning in age-appropriate and developmentally appropriate activities. Additionally, the PT consults with other team members, providing training to these individuals and giving suggestions, and constructs adaptive devices or equipment to support needed environmental modifications. The pediatric PT brings specialized knowledge regarding physical development, including how structural development needs to be integrated with functional movement to improve physical competence (Campbell, Palisano, & Vander Linden, 2006). The PT brings important medical knowledge to the team concerning terminology, etiology, postsurgical interventions and precautions, and medical and health conditions. This knowledge allows the PT to act as a liaison with physicians for the team as needed.

Occupational Therapist

The roles and responsibilities of the occupational therapist (OT) on the team share some similarities with those of the physical therapist. The pediatric OT brings expertise in typical and atypical motor development with particular emphasis on fine motor, visual-motor, and self-care; understands the integration of sensory information and its effect on motor performance, balance and coordination, and automatic movement; knows how to prevent acquired deformities; supports oral-motor development; and uses adaptive equipment and materials particularly related to self-care activities. Information on the development and maintenance of a young child's functional skills for active participation in the general curriculum and daily activities—including the use of the upper extremities, fine motor skills, sensory perception, range of motion, muscle tone, sensorimotor skills, posture, and oral-motor skills—is brought to the team by the OT. Like the PT, the OT brings medical expertise and acts as a liaison with the medical community.

Speech-Language Pathologist

The role of the speech-language pathologist (SLP) on the team is to bring specialized information about all aspects of communication interventions—receptive and expressive domains, modes, and intent; articulation and fluency; and voice quality and respiration—and to consult with audiologists in cases of children with hearing impairments or deafness (Prelock, 2000). Some, but not all, SLPs have experience and training in alternative augmentative communication and/or oral-motor and feeding skills. When this is the case, this knowledge can be critical support to the team in appropriately serving the child.

Assistive Technology Specialist

The primary responsibilities of the assistive technology specialist focus on the child's use of high- and low-technology devices to promote active and independent engagement (Copely & Ziviani, 2004). Assistive technology devices are designed and selected to remove barriers to participation in communication, environment management, social interactions, mobility, and recreational activities.

Educator for Students with Visual Impairments and Orientation and Mobility Specialist

As will be explained further in Chapter 12, the role of the teacher for students with visual impairments is to provide information to the team to address the unique needs presented by a young child with visual impairments. This specialist may provide (1) functional vision assessments; (2) direct instruction in the use of residual vision, specialized materials such as tactile communication, optical devices, and low vision aids; and (3) adaptations to curriculum materials and activities to ensure that the child has access and is actively engaged.

The orientation and mobility (O&M) specialist provides support to the child as he or she learns to maneuver safely and efficiently in the environment and may also provide additional support as the child transitions to a new environment, such as a new classroom or even a new home. Finally, both disciplines work closely with other team members to provide advice and assistance on environmental modifications and enhancements that address the unique challenges presented by the child with visual impairments or blindness and other disabilities.

Audiologist

The audiologist brings specialized knowledge in assessment of hearing impairments. Once a child is assessed, the audiologist provides guidelines to the team on adaptive equipment, such as hearing aids, as well as environmental adaptations that help the child compensate for his or her hearing impairment (McCormick-Richburg & Goldberg, 2005). Today, as more young children receive cochlear implants, the audiologist, together with the SLP, provides support to the team to allow the child to learn to use the new audio input.

Other Specialists

Educational teams and families are likely to need other specialists from time to time to address specific needs. These individuals may include dentists, optometrists, respiratory therapists, rehabilitation engineers, nutritionists, nurses, and physicians. These individuals will function as occasional or temporary members, providing services that are typically time-limited to address specific concerns.

ASSESSMENT CONSIDERATIONS

Many in the field have questioned the value of including children with more significant disabilities in large assessment systems (Kleinert, Kearns, & Kennedy, 1997). However, if one considers that the heart of the current educational reform efforts is the belief that educational assessment (i.e., measuring what children have learned) and accountability (i.e., ensuring that these outcomes are used to improve intervention) are fundamentally important, one can see the value of including these students in the assessment process. In fact, the development of alternative assessments to monitor the development of individual children and assess the impact of their programs reflects core values held by those in the ECSE field.

Alternative Assessments for Young Children with Moderate/Severe and Multiple Disabilities

The first step in planning and implementing the assessment process is to determine what kinds of learning should be measured. That is, should a professional measure the child's learning with respect to his or her IFSP outcomes or IEP goals, or should assessment be more broadly based on the child's development and learning gains as noted in the general curriculum, or should assessment be a

combination of both (Kleinert & Kearns, 1999)? If a commitment to the concept that every child has a right to access and make progress in the general education curriculum is fundamental to ECSE programs, then the third option is the preferred approach. In other words, access to the general curriculum provides the point of focus for designing learning opportunities that allow a young child with moderate/severe and multiple disabilities to do the following: (1) practice functional skills from the child's IFSP or IEP, (2) actively engage in activities within the child's learning environment, and (3) develop foundational developmental and academic skills in environments like those of their typical peers (Horn et al., 2004).

The connection between program planning and outcomes assessment is established by the focus on the general curriculum and the child's learning environment. This tie should be continuous such that the outcome assessment results provide the basis for the next set of child goals and program plans. In this fashion, an assessment system that truly links what to target for teaching (i.e., curriculum), delivery of intervention, assessment of outcomes, modification of intervention, and establishment of new targets forms a continuous quality-improvement loop. Since young children with significant disabilities tend to have a slower rate of learning and may have atypical ways of showing what they have learned, the connection between assessment and programming decisions is particularly important. Table 10.2 outlines the steps professionals follow when linking assessment to programming for young children with significant learning needs.

The process of designing a linked assessment system requires several tasks of a child's team, including identifying the standards or expected learning outcomes, determining the alternative assessment format to be used, delivering and monitoring the intervention plan, and using the assessment results in planning modifications and the next learning targets. The same process would be followed for infants, toddlers, preschoolers, or primary-aged children. Each of these steps will be discussed briefly.

TABLE 10.2 Steps for designing a linked assessment system for young children with moderate/severe and multiple disabilities

---

1. Identify the standards or expected learning outcomes.
2. Determine the alternative assessment format to be used.
3. Deliver and monitor the intervention plan.
4. Use the assessment/monitoring results to plan modifications and the next learning targets.

Identify Standards or Expected Learning Outcomes

First, the team must determine the curriculum and the specific performance expectations for each child and ensure that they are linked to the early learning standards delineated in the state (Gronlund, 2006). These two components, the curriculum expectations and the early learning standards, provide a map for the team members as they develop appropriate IFSP outcomes and IEP goals for children with significant disabilities.

Determine the Assessment Format

Second, consideration must be given to the assessment strategies that are appropriate for measuring and monitoring each child's progress. Ysseldyke and Olsen (1999) suggested a range of formats that alternate assessments can take, including observations of student performance; structured interviews and checklists; performance records such as instructional data, graphs, and anecdotal records; and performance tests on specific tasks. Portfolios and performance events are two of the more commonly used alternative assessment formats for learners with significant disabilities. These were discussed in Chapter 3.

Using Continuous Monitoring and Data Collection

Finally, a plan must be put in place that lists specific strategies for continually, effectively, and efficiently monitoring and documenting a child's progress toward identified outcomes. This plan must include clearly articulated schedules for collecting data and identify the techniques to be used to compile and summarize the data collected. The team must then plan for regular opportunities to share and discuss the data. First of all, the team needs to confirm through discussion that all team members agree that the data reflect their perceptions of the child's progress and that all critical areas are being assessed. Then, the team needs to discuss any modifications to instruction or to the specific learning targets being assessed. A new assessment plan is then put in place with any needed modifications to the assessment process and the intervention plan. Finally, the cycle of deliver, assess, and plan for young children with moderate/severe and multiple disabilities begins again.

CURRICULUM DEVELOPMENT FOR CHILDREN WITH MODERATE/SEVERE AND MULTIPLE DISABILTIES

A curriculum can be described in brief terms as the "course of study" for a given group of learners. The curriculum provides a blueprint for children's learning that the ECSE teacher and team follow as they develop daily learning activities and intervention plans (NAEYC & NAECS/SDE, 2003). Just as a contractor building a house for a family follows a blueprint to ensure that the house meets the family's expectations in terms of quality and design, professionals follow a curriculum that helps them meet community, family, and child expectations as well as the child's unique learning needs. Several challenges come to mind when discussing curriculum as a part of planning interventions for children with moderate/severe and multiple disabilities.

First, given that learning standards have only recently become available and are not yet comprehensively available for children from birth to 5 years of age, early educators are still at a significant disadvantage in having the supports in place for developing and implementing a high-quality comprehensive curriculum (Scott-Little, Kagan, & Stebbins Frelow, 2003). Second, there is rarely an established curriculum that will meet the needs of all learners with severe and multiple disabilities (Browder, Wakeman, & Flowers, 2006). Even when ECSE teachers plan for access to the general curriculum or use a specially developed functional curriculum, it is seldom clear how to determine what to teach learners with complex learning needs. Because of the multiple needs presented by young children with severe and multiple disabilities, educators need tools for designing personalized curricula (Knowlton, 1998).

Given the importance of these two issues for children with severe and multiple disabilities, a discussion of curriculum development strategies follows. The discussion begins with a brief overview of the desired life outcomes for individuals with severe disabilities. This overview is followed by discussion of the process by which these life outcomes may be achieved using the general curriculum within inclusive and self-contained educational settings.

Desired Life Outcomes

Hughes and her colleagues (Hughes, Hwang, Kin, Eisenman, & Killian, 1995), through a review of the literature on indicators of quality of life, identified the following as potentially important outcomes for learners with severe and multiple disabilities. That is, the individual should be able to (1) have meaningful social relationships, (2) be employed, (3) have a sense of personal satisfaction, (4) have a home, (5) participate in recreation and leisure activities, (6) be socially accepted and

have status, (7) have material well-being, (8) have a sense of civic responsibility, (9) have a sense of normalization about his or her daily life and routines, and (10) be self-determined.

One of the most important of these indicators, and certainly one that impacts the ability to achieve and maintain the other outcomes, is self-determination (Wehmeyer, Garner, Yeager, & Lawrence, 2006). The individual who is self-determined can define for himself or herself what constitutes a good life and then pursue it. **Self-determination** is a complex, multidimensional construct that generally describes the extent to which individuals gain control over their lives. The essential components are internal motivation, the acquisition of specific skills, and a supportive and responsive environment (Brown & Cohen, 1996). The interaction of these three components creates the context for the display of self-determined behavior by an individual. The concept of self-determination has emerged as a guiding principle in the development of curriculum and the prioritization of outcomes for children and adults with severe and multiple disabilities (Algozzine, Browder, Karvonen, Test, & Wood, 2001). In short, autonomy or mastery of self-determination should be considered a primary outcome of education.

Autonomy in the early childhood years takes the form of basic skill development, such as learning independent mobility or independent personal care (Brown & Cohen, 1996). These early successes produce feelings of pride and begin to develop a foundation on which later successes are built. For very young children with disabilities, successes are often harder to come by because the nature of the disabilities experienced makes the acquisition of the "building block" tasks (e.g., independent mobility) a more challenging and, therefore, a slower process. Slower acquisition, paired with well-intentioned, but overly intrusive instructional strategies, such as too frequent verbal and physical prompts, may limit opportunities for the young child with significant disabilities to have autonomous experiences. As the child grows older, opportunities for critical thinking may also be limited. Family members and caregivers may fear the outcomes of poor decisions and thus guide the child's safe passage through developmental stages to adulthood by making many, if not all, decisions for the individual.

A lack of successful autonomous experiences may actually lead to a pattern of dependency sometimes referred to as learned helplessness. Poor self-perceptions emerging from learned helplessness and limited opportunities for autonomous experiences may diminish the individual's internal motivation to act in a self-determined manner (Palmer & Wehmeyer, 2003). Therefore, when designing a curriculum for young children with significant disabilities, ECSE professionals must remember that learning to have control over critical aspects of life is essential. And, just as the typically developing child strives for control by demanding preferred foods, toys, or favorite activities, and often by rejecting decisions made by their parents or teachers, so may a child with multiple disabilities. Learning how to make choices, learning how to make those choices known to others, and having choices honored constitute critical milestones for young children with significant disabilities who are attempting to achieve the valued life outcome of self-determination.

Supporting Access to the General Curriculum

When addressing the process for supporting the learning of autonomy or self-determination through access and participation in the general curriculum, professionals assume different expectations for children based on their age and needs. To understand strategies that may be suitable for infants, toddlers, preschoolers, and primary-aged children, the following discussion embeds examples using Lourdes and her family from the case study provided at the beginning of the chapter.

Infants, Toddlers, and Preschoolers. A high-quality classroom is a necessary foundation for serving young children with moderate/severe and multiple disabilities (Wolery & Bredekamp, 1994). However, placement in a quality inclusive or

self-contained classroom alone will not provide a level of instruction sufficient to address the individual needs of children with significant disabilities. To individualize what occurs in educational settings, each child's team develops goals and objectives that (1) meet the unique needs of the child, (2) are meaningful for the child, and (3) are functional in a variety of contexts. Nonetheless, these goals and objectives must not become the child's curriculum. Developing appropriate goals and supporting the individual needs of young children with severe and multiple disabilities require ECSE teachers to build their educational programs with the expectations of the general education curriculum as a foundation. Meeting the mandate of access to and progress in the general curriculum requires educators not only to help each child access and participate in activities, but also to provide opportunities for that child to learn the important content reflected in the curriculum offered to all children in the regular early childhood education program (Nolet & McLaughlin, 2000). The general curriculum should be viewed as the cornerstone to which all instruction is anchored.

Identifying the General Curriculum. The first step is to identify the general curriculum. A curriculum is not simply the array of activities that occur within the infant or preschool program. Rather, a curriculum is an interrelated set of plans and activities that are intended to result in identifiable outcomes that pertain to student learning (Marsh & Willis, 1995). Sometimes ECSE teachers will find that these outcomes are stated directly, as is the case in the early learning standards established in many states. At other times, curricular outcomes are simply implied by the program's choice of activities and materials. Curriculum is the "what" of early education; it is the content that educators provide and that which children learn (Nolet & McLaughlin, 2000). It is separate from the strategies or procedures used to teach children the content, although the line between curriculum and instruction often is difficult to separate in day-to-day practice.

Because ECSE professionals working with young children with severe and multiple disabilities will find themselves working in a range of settings, identification of the early childhood general curriculum is not always a simple task. For example, the ECSE teacher working with Lourdes (see the case study) when she was 3 years old found at least four curricula across the programs in which children on her caseload were participating. The Head Start program used the *Creative Curriculum for Early Childhood* (Trister-Dodge & Colker, 1992), one program implemented a Montessori curriculum, another used developmentally appropriate practices (DAP), and yet another used a behavior analytic approach. Each of these curriculum approaches represented different levels of specificity in the scope and sequence of the content that was to be taught. Further, these curricula represented different levels of specificity for the teaching strategies to be used. Ultimately, all high-quality early childhood education programs have at the heart of their curriculum the objective that children will make progress in the domains of communication, social competence, fine and gross motor skills, cognitive abilities, and adaptive behaviors. The method used and the emphasis placed on each developmental domain may vary greatly.

The primary task in identifying the curriculum for young children with severe and multiple disabilities actually becomes identifying the most critical knowledge across developmental domains that all children will be expected to learn as a result of participating in the program and the approximate time frame in which the children will need to acquire the knowledge and skills. This list does not need to be exhaustive, but it should represent the most critical knowledge all the children need to acquire. This "knowledge" then becomes the top priority in developing the individualized child outcomes and in planning access to and progress within the general curriculum. For Lourdes and her classmates in her Head Start program, some of these "top priority" outcomes were (1) use of communication skills to satisfy basic needs and to have access to and

control of their environment, (2) use of social competence within groups with peers and adults, (3) use of physical skills that allow for active participation with the various aspects of the environment and independent mobility that allows for safe and free movement around the environment, and (4) use of problem-solving skills to address dilemmas that arise within everyday activities. Each of these priority outcomes was seen as necessary for a child to be successful in kindergarten.

Modifying the Curriculum. Children with moderate/severe and multiple disabilities must have opportunities to participate as fully as typically developing children do in all activities. Educators must ensure these children's access to the preschool curriculum by making appropriate adaptations and modifications. Early education teachers also must know how to embed individualized instruction into ongoing activities and routines.

As noted in Chapter 4, **curriculum modification or adaptation** is a change in a classroom activity or material that allows a child to participate (Sandall et al., 2002). Increased participation creates more opportunities for children to learn and progress developmentally. Teachers should use a curriculum modification strategy when a child is interested in the ongoing activities, but is not able to fully participate, or when a child may not stay with the activity long enough (Cavallaro & Haney, 1999; Thompson et al., 2002). The key is to help the child participate. Researchers from the Early Childhood Research Institute on Inclusion (ECRII) identified and described eight types of modifications and adaptations: environmental support, material adaptations, special equipment, use of children's preferences, simplification of the activity, adult support, peer support, and invisible support (Lieber, Schwartz, Sandall, Horn, & Wolery, 1999; Sandall et al., 2002). Table 10.3 provides a brief description of each category. We will examine each of these and see how Lourdes' team utilized them to facilitate her participation in Head Start.

Three of these modification strategies address changing or adding materials or events. *Environmental support* refers to altering the physical,

TABLE 10.3 Ways to modify curricula for young children with moderate/severe and multiple disabilities

Environmental support	Alter the physical, social, and temporal environment to promote participation, engagement, and learning
Material adaptations	Modify materials so that the child can participate as independently as possible
Special equipment	Use teacher-made and commercially available therapeutic equipment to promote independence and learning
Use of children's preferences	Identify child preferences and integrate them into activities/lessons to make them more motivating
Simplification of the activity	Break complicated activities into smaller parts or change or reduce the steps involved
Adult support	Adults use modeling of an appropriate behavior, join the child in play, praise the child, and/or provide encouragement
Peer support	Adults provide peers with support and training so they can help children reach learning objectives
Invisible support	Adults rearrange aspects of naturally occurring activities behind the scenes to support the child's participation

social, and temporal environment to promote participation, engagement, and learning. For example, Lourdes' Head Start teacher changed the layout of the classroom slightly to allow Lourdes' wheelchair to move easily from one area of the classroom to another, even when one of her peers with less experience and skill was "driving."

*Material adaptation*s occur when teachers modify materials so that a child can participate as independently as possible. Examples of material adaptations for Lourdes included stabilizing materials by taping the paper for painting to the table, using Velcro straps to hold the paint brush in Lourdes' hand to compensate for her weak grasp, using nonskid backing under the paint cup, and using contact paper as backing for collages because gluing was too difficult for her.

Special equipment was another modification that was frequently used for Lourdes. This included homemade equipment as well as commercially available therapeutic equipment. For example, Lourdes had a special switch positioned on the tray of her adapted wheelchair that she

could press to "ask" for assistance. A beanbag chair was added to the circle areas to provide Lourdes with supportive positioning during group activities when everyone sat on the floor.

Two of the modification strategies—the *use of children's preferences* and *simplification of the activity*—focus on matching activities with the child's abilities and preferences. If a child is not taking advantage of an activity or a learning opportunity, the adults must identify the child's preferences and integrate them into the activity to make the activity more motivating. Lourdes' physical therapist indicated that Lourdes needed to actively participate in moving her limbs, particularly her legs. Her Head Start teachers noted how well she attended during the group circle time, particularly during finger play songs. Consequently, they added new songs that required "peddling" and stepping movements of the children's legs. Her team was pleased that Lourdes moved her legs "like" her friends during the songs.

Simplifying a complicated activity by breaking it into smaller parts or by changing or reducing the steps involved is the second strategy in this group. When Lourdes was completing puzzles with the other children, for example, she was provided with a puzzle in which only two, and later three, pieces were taken out of place. The other pieces were taped down so they could not be removed. Lourdes was able to use a sliding movement to push the pieces into their correct "slots."

The final set of three modification strategies focuses on providing *adult, peer, or invisible support* to the child. In adult support, an adult may model an appropriate behavior, join the child in play, praise the child, and/or provide encouragement. Lourdes with her paintbrush in hand and everything set up to paint was just watching the other children as they painted. One of the teachers came over and commented that Lourdes seemed to be really enjoying seeing what the other children were painting. She then turned to Lourdes and said, "Let's see what you can paint." She then assisted Lourdes in getting paint on her brush and praised her brush strokes on the paper, noting that she had the same color as another child.

Peers also can help children with severe disabilities achieve their learning objectives. For example, Lourdes' preschool teacher had her peers provide her with picture choices of the next

center she would like to participate in and then "drive" her chair to the area after she had indicated her choice.

Finally, invisible supports occur when adults rearrange aspects of naturally occurring activities to support a child's success in participating. Lourdes' classmates, for instance, made a card with a heart shape created by red paint fingerprints of each child as a farewell gift for a volunteer. The adults made sure that Lourdes was the first to place her finger print since her accuracy of hitting a "target" was limited. Because of this "invisible" support, Lourdes did not place her finger print on top of another child's, and she was a successful and integral part of the project.

Embedded Learning Opportunities. Curriculum modifications, used well, can help achieve one goal of inclusion: active participation of young children with severe disabilities and typically developing children in the same setting. However, modifications alone may not be sufficient to ensure that a child has sufficient learning opportunities to meet individually defined needs involving the top priority outcomes of the general curriculum. To address this, ECSE professionals embed instruction in existing routines (Bricker & Cripe, 1992; Horn, Lieber,

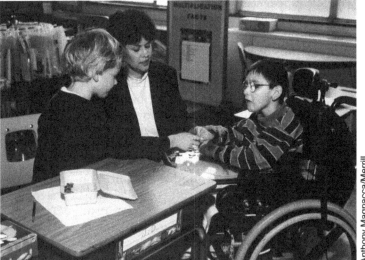

With appropriate training, peers may be helpful in assisting classmates with significant disabilities in learning individual priority outcomes related to the general education curriculum.

Anthony Magnacca/Merrill

Sandall, Schwartz, & Li, 2000). As noted in other chapters, embedding is based on the premise that in order for many children to achieve their learning objectives, merely providing access to the general early childhood curriculum is inadequate. Educators need to provide instruction through modeling, verbal prompting, and physical guidance in order for children with moderate/severe and multiple disabilities to learn new or more complex skills.

Primary-Aged Students. The primary school years provide a range of experiences that affect the young child's physical, social, emotional, and intellectual development. Classroom routines anchor the daily work of teachers and provide the context in which IEP goals and objectives/benchmarks can be embedded. To understand how to create responsive classroom supports, it is first important to understand the elementary general education curriculum.

Although schools vary in their curricular and instructional practices, there are common factors that affect the delivery of instruction for all learners (Salisbury, Evans, & Palombaro, 1997). These factors are correlated with effective instruction and tend to be prominent in schools that are building a capacity to think and act inclusively: (1) assignment to age-appropriate, grade-level classrooms; (2) adequate time for planning; and (3) instruction embedded in classroom routines and activities.

Assignment to Age-Appropriate, Grade-Level Classrooms. Inclusive elementary schools assign children with disabilities, including those with significant needs, to the grade-level classroom they would attend if they did not have a disability. For Lourdes, this meant that when she was 5, she entered kindergarten along with her neighborhood and Head Start peers. Each year Lourdes has moved to the next grade level like her peers.

Adequate Time for Planning. In order to appropriately support all children's participation and learning, elementary schools must provide ample time, on an ongoing basis, for the educational team to plan for the instructional and support needs of all the

children they serve. Jorgensen and colleagues (Jorgensen, Fisher, Sax, & Skoglund, 1997) have identified several strategies that successful inclusive schools have used to create time for planning, preparing, teaching, and conferencing:

❏ changing staffing patterns—that is, bringing in regular substitute teachers; using other adults to create release time; creating a hobby period for all elementary students to participate in once a week, staffed with parents and community volunteers; having older students working with minimal supervision with younger students; grouping two smaller classes together for periods of time under the supervision of one teacher, thereby releasing the second;

❏ using block scheduling, which creates fewer classes and more opportunities to meet;

❏ restructuring or rescheduling time—that is, having teachers teach more minutes four days per week, releasing time on the fifth day for planning time; staggering schedules; creating a common lunch and/or planning period for teachers, followed by a planning period or lunch period, respectively; and

❏ adding time to the school day or year, thus shortening classroom time each day, but adding more days to the school year; extending the school day; moving to a year-round schedule; adding dedicated meeting days to the school year.

In addition to ongoing planning, transition planning must be conducted as children move from one grade level to the next or from one school to the next. Transition planning provides the opportunities for family members and other members of the educational team (current and future) to share information, coordinate support plans, and orient the children to their new classroom, teachers, and peers.

Extensive transition planning occurred for Lourdes as she moved from the first to the second grade. Adults who attended her transition planning session included the sending and receiving general and special education teachers, her mother, the SLP, the vision specialist, and the occupational therapist. The transition planning team emphasized the importance of maintaining Lourdes' time in general education to maximize her exposure to verbal peers and discussed the importance of implementing class activities and routines to ensure Lourdes' safety.

The educational team that was *sending* Lourdes recommended the following: (1) instructional practices that provided opportunities for Lourdes to learn self-help skills and maximize her residual vision; (2) use of appropriate reinforcers, such as music, manipulatives, choice of activities, and peers (particularly her girlfriends); and (3) specific strategies for promoting her inclusion in everyday school activities. Lourdes' *receiving teachers* requested the following: (1) training in lifting and positioning, (2) assistance with developing a hygiene and germ control plan and supporting her complex health care needs, and (3) specific information about the ways Lourdes learns best. The transition team recommended that a paraeducator be provided in Lourdes' new class to act as extra hands in the classroom. Sharing information and including key adults in the transition process helped ensure that Lourdes' transition was as smooth as it could be and that she would be successful and welcomed in the next grade.

Instruction Embedded in Classroom Routines and Activities. Elementary classroom routines, like those in infant-toddler and preschool programs, provide natural opportunities for teaching children with severe and multiple disabilities important knowledge and skills. In the primary grades, children learn procedural skills that help them regulate their own behavior. For example, children learn to keep work materials organized, manage free time, make decisions about how to spend their time, respond to time requirements, and work within groups.

Each day Lourdes' teacher updated an interactive bulletin board that served as an organizer and assisted all the students in the class in developing

important skills and habits. The board included "Activities for Today," brief descriptions of the assignments, and important due dates and folders for children to use to submit their completed work. Obviously, Lourdes required additional support to understand and organize her day. Each day her SLP and teachers created a picture schedule for Lourdes to follow. The staff created opportunities for Lourdes to be independent, identify her preferences, and work on her individualized objectives within regular group activities with her peers.

For Lourdes, the general education classroom and related special classes (e.g., art, library, physical education) provided her with many opportunities in which IEP and other important priority skills could be taught. Lourdes' teachers and therapists used an "IEP at a Glance" matrix, which identified where Lourdes' goals and objectives could be best met during the school day. For example, her physical therapists decided to teach posturing supported by a head strap during lunchtime. Lourdes' general and special education teachers determined that the "reading club" provided opportunities for Lourdes to select preferences using eye gaze and/or to request objects with movement cues. Her teachers also identified cooperative learning games as opportunities for Lourdes to use her switch to indicate changes in activities. Finally, her teachers created opportunities for Lourdes to select peers to assist her during class transitions through the use of eye gaze at enlarged photographs of her peers.

As we review Lourdes' progress from her early intervention services, preschool education within the Head Start program, and kindergarten to the primary grades, we see that the common thread is the integration of the general education curriculum and learning standards with desired life outcomes. Lourdes was given access to the general education curriculum while she simultaneously made progress toward her individualized goals and objectives. The process required a number of team planning and implementation activities. For Lourdes and other children with significant disabilities, these activities included the following:

- ❏ identifying and reviewing the general curriculum and learning standards,
- ❏ establishing individual child learning priorities through comprehensive assessment and team collaboration,
- ❏ analyzing the general education environment to determine modifications and adaptations that need to be put into place to support participation and learning, and
- ❏ identifying those outcomes that are not being addressed directly or with sufficient intensity through the general education curriculum and designing embedded learning opportunities to address them.

CONCLUSION

Ensuring that very young children with moderate/severe and multiple disabilities are active participants in all aspects of their lives and that they make meaningful progress toward valued life outcomes can be a daunting endeavor for parents and educators. Given the myriad of educational, health, social, and emotional needs of these children, a successful outcome requires collaboration and planning among large numbers of individuals. Providing individualized instruction within high-quality programs is the way ECSE professionals ensure that infants, toddlers, preschoolers, and primary-aged children learn and develop to their optimal level. Individualization—or put another way, steps to ensure a match between what is offered and what is needed—is a critical component of a quality program. Through collaborative family and team partnerships, young children with severe and multiple disabilities like Lourdes are now educated in a variety of settings, including inclusive classrooms. Educators have come to the understanding that although these children may present substantial educational challenges, they deserve the right to grow, learn, and prosper like everyone else.

SUMMARY

Definitions of moderate/severe and multiple disabilities

- Severe disability refers to children who, because of the intensity of their physical, mental, or emotional problems, need highly specialized education, social, psychological, and medical services to maximize their full potential.
- Multiple disabilities refers to children with concomitant impairments that cannot be accommodated in special education programs solely for one of the impairments.

General characteristics of children with moderate/severe and multiple disabilities

- Children with moderate/severe and multiple disabilities may have neuromotor impairments, degenerative diseases, infectious diseases, orthopedic and musculoskeletal disorders, sensory impairments, major health impairments, or neurodevelopmental disorders that significantly impact their mobility, learning, and access to people and objects around them.

Using a needs-based approach to intervention

- Given the multiple needs of children with moderate/severe and multiple disabilities, successful outcomes require collaboration and planning among large numbers of individuals who as a group are knowledgeable of the unique needs and abilities these children present.

Assessment considerations

- Appropriate assessment should lead to designing learning opportunities for young children with significant disabilities that allow them to: (1) practice functional skills, (2) actively engage in activities within their learning environment, and (3) develop foundational developmental and academic skills in environments similar to those of their typical peers.
- A comprehensive system of service delivery begins and ends with a linked assessment system involving what needs to be taught (curriculum), delivery of intervention, assessment of outcomes, modification of intervention, and establishment of new targets based on collected data.

Curriculum development for children with moderate/severe and multiple disabilities

- Children with complex educational needs require teachers to design personalized curricula with these characteristics: (1) The are grounded in desired life outcomes, (2) they support access to and participation in the general education curriculum, (3) they promote the development of self-determination, and (4) they support learning based on individualized needs. Each curriculum should be delivered with appropriate modifications and adaptations and with the teaching of goals/objectives embedded in daily learning opportunities.

DISCUSSION QUESTIONS/ACTIVITIES

1. James is a 4-year old preschooler with multiple disabilities. He can eat, drink, and swallow, but has not learned how to use utensils. He gazes at his peers, but rarely initiates any form of communication. He is working on goals that will increase his social participation during mealtimes and improve his fine motor functioning, which is limited by cerebral palsy. Discuss two strategies the educational team, including his family, can introduce to support James in meeting his goals during snack time at his preschool and during dinner at home.

2. Mr. Garrison is a school physical therapist who has children on his caseload from five elementary schools. Currently, he spends one day a week at each school. Maggie, a first grader with severe disabilities that affect her ability to move from one location to the next and sit for extended periods of time, presents Mr. Garrison with a dilemma. Discuss three ways in which Maggie might receive needed supports in her classroom even when Mr. Garrison is not available.

3. Discuss two ways in which the ECSE team, including the family, can work together to align functional goals and objectives with meaningful engagement in the general education curriculum for preschoolers and primary-aged children with significant educational needs.

REFERENCES

Algozzine, B., Browder, D., Karvonen, M., Test, D., & Wood, W. (2001). Effects of interventions to promote self-determination for individuals with disabilities. *Review of Educational Research, 71*, 219–277.

Bricker, D., & Cripe, J. J. (1992). *An activity-based approach to early intervention.* Baltimore, MD: Brookes.

Browder, D. M., Wakeman, S., & Flowers, C. P. (2006). Assessment of progress in the general curriculum for students with disabilities. *Theory into Practice, 45*(3), 249–259.

Brown, F., & Cohen, S. (1996). Self-determination and young children. *Journal of the Association for Persons with Severe Handicaps, 21*(1), 22–30.

Campbell, S. K., Palisano, R. J., & Vander Linden, D. W. (2006). *Physical therapy for children* (3rd ed.). London: Elsevier–Mosby/Saunders.

Cavallaro, C., & Haney, M. (1999). *Preschool inclusion.* Baltimore, MD: Brookes.

Chen, D. (1997). *Effective practices in early intervention: Infants whose multiple disabilities include both vision and hearing loss* (Report for OSEP Grant No. H025D30002). Northridge: California State University. (ERIC Document Reproduction Service No. ED406795)

Circle of Inclusion. (1999). *Circle of inclusion preschool project*, University of Kansas. Retrieved January 10, 2007, from http://circleofinclusion.org

Copely, J., & Ziviani, J. (2004). Barriers to the use of assistive technology for children with multiple disabilities. *Occupational Therapy International, 11*(4), 229–243.

Giangreco, M. F., Edelman, S. W., & Broer, S. M., (2003). Schoolwide planning to improve paraeducator supports. *Exceptional Children, 70*(1), 63–79.

Gronlund, G. (2006). *Making early learning standards come alive: Connecting your practice and curriculum to state guidelines.* St. Paul, MN: Redleaf Press.

Heller, K. W., Alberto, P. A., Forney, P. E., & Schwartzman, M. N. (1996). *Understanding physical, sensory, and health impairment.* Pacific Grove, CA: Brooks/Cole.

Horn, E., Lieber, J., Sandall, S., Schwartz, I., & Li, S. (2000). Supporting young children's IEP goals in inclusive settings through embedded learning opportunities. *Topics in Early Childhood Special Education, 20*, 208–223.

Horn, E., Thompson, B., Palmer, S., Jensen, R., & Turbiville, V. (2004). Preschool. In C. H. Kennedy & E. M. Horn (Eds.), *Inclusion of students with severe disabilities* (pp. 207–221). Boston: Allyn & Bacon.

Hughes, C., Hwang, B., Kim, J., Eisenman, L. T., & Killian, D. J. (1995). Quality of life in applied research: A review and analysis of empirical measures. *American Journal on Mental Retardation, 99*(6), 623–641.

Individuals with Disabilities Education Improvement Act (IDEA) of 2004, Pub. L. No. 108-446, Sec. 315.4 (d).

Jorgensen, C. M., Fisher, D., Sax, C., & Skoglund, K. L. (1997). Curriculum and its impact on inclusion and the achievement of students with disabilities. *CISP Issue Brief, 2*(2), 1–21.

Kleinert, H., & Kearns, J. (1999). A validation study of the performance indicators and learner outcomes of Kentucky's alternative assessment for students with significant disabilities. *Journal of the Association for Persons with Severe Handicaps, 24*(2), 100–110.

Kleinert, H., Kearns, J., & Kennedy, S. (1997). Accountability for all students: Kentucky's alternative portfolio assessment for students with moderate and severe cognitive disabilities. *Journal of the Association for Persons with Severe Handicaps, 22*(2), 88–101.

Knowlton, E. (1998). Considerations in the design of personalized curricular support for students with developmental disabilities. *Education and Training in Mental Retardation and Developmental Disabilities, 33,* 95–107.

Leonard, H., & Wen, X. (2002). The epidemiology of mental retardation: Challenges and opportunities in the new millennium. *Mental Retardation and Developmental Disabilities Research Reviews, 8,* 117–134.

Lieber, J., Schwartz, I., Sandall, S., Horn, E., & Wolery, R. (1999). Curricular considerations for young children in inclusive settings. In C. Seefeldt (Ed.), *The early childhood curriculum: Current findings in theory and practice* (3rd ed., pp. 243–265). New York: Teachers College Press.

Losardo, A., & Bricker, D. (1994). Activity-based and direct instruction: A comparison study. *American Journal of Mental Retardation, 98,* 744–765.

Marsh, C., & Willis, G. (1995). *Curriculum: Alternative approaches, ongoing issues.* Englewood Cliffs, NJ: Merrill/Prentice Hall.

Martin, S., & Baker, D. C. (2001, June). *Families and children with severe disabilities: Daily lives, systems and concerns.* Paper presented at the annual meeting of the American Association of Behavioral and Social Sciences, Las Vegas, NV. (ERIC Document Reproduction Service No. ED462811)

McCormick-Richburg, C., & Goldberg, L. R. (2005). Teachers' perceptions about minimal hearing loss: A role for educational audiologists. *Communication Disorders Quarterly, 27*(1), 4–19.

McWilliams, R. A. (2005). Interdisciplinary models. In S. Sandall, M. L. Hemmeter, B. J. Smith, & M. E. McLean (Eds.), *DEC recommended practices: A comprehensive guide for practical application in early intervention/early childhood special education* (pp. 127–146). Longmont, CO: Sopris West.

Molloy, H., & Vassal, L. (2002). The social construction of Asperger syndrome: The pathologising of difference? *Disability and Society, 17,* 659–669.

NAEYC (National Association for the Education of Young Children) & NAECS/SDE (National Association of Early Childhood Specialists in State Departments of Education). (2003). *Early childhood curriculum, assessment, and program evaluation: A joint position statement.* Washington, DC: NAEYC. Retrieved January 10, 2007, from http://www.naeyc.org/about/positions/cape.asp

Nolet, V., & McLaughlin, M. J. (2000). *Accessing the general curriculum: Including students with disabilities in standards-based reform.* (ERIC Document Reproduction Service No. ED448546)

Orelove, F. P., & Sobsey, D. (Eds.). (1996). *Educating children with multiple disabilities: A transdisciplinary approach* (3rd ed.). Baltimore, MD: Brookes.

Palmer, S., & Wehmeyer, M. (2003). Promoting self-determination in early elementary school: Teaching self-regulation, problem-solving and goal setting skills. *Remedial and Special Education, 24,* 115–126.

Prelock, P. A. (2000). Multiple perspectives for determining the roles of speech-language pathologists in inclusionary classrooms. *Language, Speech, and Hearing Services in Schools, 31,* 213–218.

Roberts, S. (2004). Sensory and motoric needs. In C. H. Kennedy & E. M. Horn (Eds.), *Inclusion of students with severe disabilities* (pp. 164–184). Boston: Allyn & Bacon.

Salisbury, C., Evans, I., & Palombaro, M. (1997). Collaborative problem-solving to promote the inclusion of young children with significant disabilities in primary grades. *Exceptional Children, 63,* 195–209.

Sandall, S., Hemmeter, M. L., Smith, B. J., & McLean, M. E. (2005). *DEC recommended practices: A comprehensive guide for practical application in early intervention/early childhood special education.* Longmont, CO: Sopris West.

Sandall, S., Schwartz, I., Joseph, G., Chou, H., Horn, E., Lieber, J., Odom, S., & Wolery, R. (2002). *Building blocks for successful early childhood programs: Strategies for including all children.* Baltimore, MD: Brookes.

Savage, R. C., Depompei, R., Tyler, J., & Lash, M. (2005). Paediatric traumatic brain injury: A review of pertinent issues. *Pediatric Rehabilitation, 8*(2), 92–103.

Scott-Little, C., Kagan, S., & Stebbins Frelow, V. (2003). Creating the conditions for success with early learning standards: Results from a national study of state-level standards for children's learning prior to kindergarten. *Early Childhood Research and Practice, 5*(2). Retrieved January 10, 2007, from http://ecrp.uiuc.edu/v5n2/little.html

Snell, M. E., & Brown, F. (2000). Development and implementation of educational programs. In M. E. Snell & F. Brown (Eds.), *Instruction of students with severe disabilities* (5th ed., pp. 115–172). Upper Saddle River, NJ: Merrill/Prentice Hall.

Snell, M. E., & Janney, R. E. (2000). Teachers' problem-solving about children with moderate and severe disabilities in elementary classrooms. *Exceptional Children, 66*(4), 472–490.

Staub, D., Spaulding, M., Peck, C. A., Gallucci, C., & Schwartz, I. S. (1996). Using nondisabled peers to support the inclusion of students with disabilities at the junior high school level. *Journal of the Association for Persons with Severe Handicaps, 21*(4), 194–205.

Thompson, B., & Guess, D. (1989). Students who experience the most profound disabilities: Teacher perspectives. In F. Brown & D. H. Lehr (Eds.), *Persons with profound disabilities: Issues and practices* (pp. 3–41). Baltimore, MD: Brookes.

Thompson, B., Wickham, D., Wegner, J., Mulligan Ault, M., Shanks, P., & Reinertson, B. (2002). *Handbook for the inclusion of young children with severe disabilities.* Lawrence, KS: Learner Managed Designs.

Trister-Dodge, D., & Colker, L. J. (1992). *Creative Curriculum for Early Childhood.* Washington, DC: Teaching Strategies.

Turnbull, A., & Turnbull, R. (2006). *Families, professionals, and exceptionality: Positive outcomes through partnerships and trust* (5th ed.). Upper Saddle River, NJ: Merrill/Prentice Hall.

Turnbull, R., Turnbull, A., Shank, M., Smith, S., & Leal, D. (2001). Severe and multiple disabilities. In R. Turnbull, A. Turnbull, M. Shank, S. Smith, & D. Leal (Eds.), *Exceptional lives: Special education in today's schools* (3rd ed., pp. 300–334). Upper Saddle River, NJ: Merrill/Prentice Hall.

Wehmeyer, M. L., Garner, N., Yeager, D., & Lawrence, M. (2006). Infusing self-determination into 18–21 services for students with intellectual or developmental disabilities: A multi-stage, multiple component model. *Education and Training in Developmental Disabilities, 41*(1), 3–13.

Wolery, M., & Bredekamp, S. (1994). Developmentally appropriate practice and young children with disabilities: Contextual issues in the discussion. *Journal of Early Intervention, 18,* 331–341.

Ysseldyke, J., & Olsen, K. (1999). Putting alternative assessments into practice: What to measure and possible sources of data. *Exceptional Children, 65*(2), 175–186.

Chapter

11

Techniques for Teaching Young Children with Hearing Loss

Jan Christian Hafer

Overview

This chapter discusses the social and learning needs of infants, toddlers, preschoolers, and primary-aged children with hearing loss, including

definitions, causes and types of hearing loss

taking a visual perspective

impact of hearing loss on development and learning

communication approaches

technologies that supplement and support sound

involving families

strategies for promoting auditory development

strategies for promoting visual communication

strategies for promoting preliteracy and literacy development

effective inclusion approaches

CASE STUDY: Anna and Her Family

Anna was identified at 5 months with a profound hearing loss. Her hearing parents, Susan and Jim, immediately enrolled her in an infant-toddler program in which the family received weekly home visits with an early intervention teacher and services from a center-based speech therapist and audiologist. Her parents spoke to Anna and used one- and two-word sign combinations that the speech therapist taught them.

When Anna turned 1 year old, her mother met a deaf mother, Kara, and her deaf toddler, Kiki, at a toddler group for children with hearing loss. Susan observed the ease with which Kara communicated with Kiki and noticed Kiki's well-developed communication skills. Soon after, Susan and Jim enrolled in a sign class. Anna's language skills developed rapidly as her parents increased the quality and quantity of their signed conversations with her. Anna also developed awareness of loud sounds and began using her voice to gain her parent's attention.

When Anna was 24 months old, Susan and Jim decided to have her receive a cochlear implant. At the same time, they enrolled Anna in a bilingual charter school for the deaf. They stated that they believed that communicating in American Sign Language (ASL) and optimizing Anna's auditory and speech skills with a cochlear implant would provide her with the best opportunity to develop all her skills.

At age 3, Anna was functioning at age level in her language skills and had developed speech that was intelligible to her family and teachers. Her preschool conducted all instruction in ASL and provided auditory and spoken language support for families who requested it. When Anna turned 5, her parents requested a half day of kindergarten in an ASL class and a half day in a general education class (spoken English class). Beginning reading instruction was initiated in Anna's ASL class and then reinforced in her general education class.

Now in third grade, Anna attends her local elementary school. She receives the services of an interpreter/tutor who sign-interprets when Anna requests it for classroom situations that are difficult for her, such as during rapid discussions. Anna is reading on grade level and is bilingual in both ASL and spoken English. She continues to maintain friendships with children who are both hearing and deaf/hard of hearing.

Families with children who are deaf or hard of hearing typically do not expect to have a deaf child and have no experience with people who are deaf. The birth of a child with hearing loss presents special challenges not only for the child and the child's parents, but also for all members of the family (Calderon & Greenberg, 1993). Traditionally, a medical model that emphasizes the habilitation of a child's deficits has been utilized to educate young children with hearing impairment. More recently, a multidimensional, sociocultural model that emphasizes a child's strengths, particularly vision, is guiding intervention programs serving young children who are deaf or hard of hearing. This chapter discusses some of the information early childhood special educators must have to serve effectively on educational teams supporting the development and learning of children with hearing loss. To begin the discussion, professionals need the same vocabulary in order to craft truly individualized approaches for children who are deaf and hard of hearing and for their families.

DEFINITIONS

To serve families and children appropriately, professionals must share a common language. The field of deaf education, like all specialized fields, has its own terminology. Professionals who work with children who are deaf or hard of hearing should be comfortable with the following terminology:

sociocultural model: Deaf people regard themselves as members of a cultural and linguistic minority that are bound together by the use of sign language. In this view, the condition of deafness is not considered a limitation or a disability, but rather requires an adaptation to a "visual" way of life.

medical-disability model: In this model, deafness is viewed as a condition that must be fixed (Tucker, 1993). The standard for a successful life is determined by how well a person with a hearing loss "blends in" with hearing people. "Normalization" is considered best achieved by auditory and speech therapy.

Deaf: When capitalized, the word implies a person with a hearing loss who uses American Sign Language as his or her primary language and shares common values, rules of behavior, and traditions that encompass a sociocultural view of being deaf—rather than a medical-disability view. Many Deaf people have a unique "Deaf Perspective," often referred to as the "Deaf Way," that defines their way of life (Andrews, Leigh, & Weiner, 2004).

deaf: When spelled with a lowercase *d*, this term refers to the actual condition of hearing loss.

Deaf Culture: This term refers to the traditions, language use, and shared experiences of people who are Deaf (Padden & Humphries, 2005). Deaf Culture has its own stories, jokes, and visual arts—all centered on the act of seeing and hence the use of American Sign Language.

American Sign Language (ASL): This is the language used by the majority of deaf people in the United States. It has its own structure and grammatical rules, which are visual-gestural in nature, rather than auditory-oral as is the case with spoken English.

sign language: This all-inclusive term indicates some form of visual communication such as Signed English, in which signs are put in English word order and some elements of the English language are given an invented sign. Sign language may be used with or without voice (speaking the words at the same time).

hard of hearing: This term refers to a child who has enough hearing that he or she is able to learn language primarily through the auditory-verbal channels without intensive special instruction.

hearing impaired: This term is used to indicate a person with a hearing loss. However, in this chapter, the terms *deaf* and *hard of hearing* will be used because most people who are deaf or hard of hearing refer to themselves this way and not as hearing impaired.

cochlear implant: This is a surgically implanted electronic device that may allow a person who is deaf to hear the auditory signal at near normal levels.

In addition to this terminology, professionals need a basic understanding of the causes and types of hearing losses that impact the development of very young children.

Causes and Types of Hearing Loss

Deafness or hearing loss does not cause delays in cognitive, social-emotional, visual, or motor development, but the inability to hear may have a profound impact on communication, the acquisition of language, academic achievement, and family relationships. The cause, type, degree, severity, and time of onset of a hearing loss will influence development in different ways. To understand how hearing loss affects children, it is important to consider the causes and types of hearing losses.

Causes of Hearing Loss

Hearing loss falls into two causal categories: nongenetic and genetic (Andrews et al., 2004). The most common nongenetic causes are infections such as rubella, cytomegalovirus, meningitis, Rh incompatibility, ototoxic drugs, prematurity, and noise-induced hearing loss, although noise-induced hearing losses are rarely found in children. A **prelingual hearing loss** occurs before a child has developed speech and language; a **postlingual hearing loss** occurs after that time. Table 11.1 lists some of the characteristics of common nongenetic causes of hearing loss.

About one-third of the cases of childhood deafness involve genetic causes that include syndromes that present deafness with other medical or physical differences (Andrews et al., 2004). Parents may want to receive genetic counseling if it is determined there is a genetic cause for their child's deafness. Table 11.2 lists some of the more common genetic causes of hearing loss and how they may be manifested in a young child.

It is helpful for parents and professionals to know the cause of a child's deafness so they have more information about how the child's development may be affected and what special needs the child may display. For example, if the cause of deafness is an ototoxic drug such as alcohol or cocaine, the child will need to be monitored for developmental delays. However, it is essential for professionals working with young children who are deaf or hard of hearing to acknowledge that knowing the cause of deafness is often of little value to many Deaf people, who tend to view themselves holistically (Andrews et al., 2004).

Types of Hearing Loss

Hearing loss may be described as sensorineural, conductive, or mixed. A **sensorineural loss** is caused by a problem in the inner ear, cochlea, or

TABLE 11.1 Nongenetic causes of hearing loss

Etiology	Insult	Possible Outcomes
Rubella	Eye, ear, brain, heart	Deaf-blindness, learning disabilities, idiosyncratic effect on residual hearing, impulsivity, distractibility
Meningitis	Ear, brain	Severe hearing loss, possible aphasia, distractibility, possible effect on vestibular system
Congenital toxoplasmosis	Eye, ear, brain	Eye scarring, microcephaly, seizures, stable or progressive hearing loss, motor and cognitive delays
Erythroblastosis fetalis	Ear, brain	Hearing loss, seizures, cerebral palsy, possible language problems
Ototoxic drugs	Ear, brain	Fetal alcohol syndrome; conductive or sensorineural hearing loss; mental retardation; learning, behavioral, and emotional difficulties
Prematurity	Eye, ear, brain	Vision impairments, hearing loss, cognitive and motor delays
Cytomegalovirus	Ear, eye brain	Hearing loss, hyperactivity, learning disabilities, motor difficulties, mental retardation, cerebral palsy, emotional problems
HIV	Ear, brain	Hearing loss, developmental delays

TABLE 11.2 Genetic syndromes and hearing impairment

Syndrome	Inheritance Pattern	Outcomes
Waardenburg	Dominantly inherited, wide-set eyes (may be bright blue), white forelock of hair, vestibular dysfunction, normal intelligence	Possible hearing loss
Usher	Progressive loss of vision, present with hearing loss	Requires ongoing readjustment to manage further loss of vision
Branchial-Oto-Renal (BOR)	Autosomal dominant syndrome, malformed external ears, tiny holes in ear and neck, kidney problems, hearing loss	Requires identification and treatment of kidney problems
Jervell and Lange-Nielsen	Autosomal recessive trait, profound hearing loss with congenital heart problems (fainting)	Possible sudden death unless treated
Treacher-Collins	Dominant inheritance, conductive hearing loss, malformed outer ears, flat cheekbones, downward sloping eyes	Conductive loss treated with surgery

auditory nerve. This kind of hearing loss is characterized by a decreased sensitivity to sound and a decreased clarity of sound. Hearing technologies, such as hearing aids, may amplify sound, but may not always provide clear access to spoken language.

A **conductive loss** occurs in the outer or middle ear and may be corrected with medications (antibiotics for **otitis media**, or ear infections, for example) or a surgery called myingotomy. If treatment for conductive hearing loss is delayed, a permanent hearing loss may result. A conductive loss in a young child can cause delays in speech and language in a short period of time, so parents and educators need to be vigilant in providing appropriate services.

A **mixed loss** has both sensorineural and conductive components. A child with a mixed hearing loss may experience difficulties with both loudness and clarity of sound. In early childhood, ear infections are a frequent occurrence. For a child who has a sensorineural loss, the addition of a temporary conductive loss caused by ear infections can complicate activities such as auditory training and can greatly reduce a child's functional use of hearing.

Severity of Hearing Loss

Hearing loss can also be described by the severity of the loss, or how loud a sound must be at different pitches before a child can hear it. Hearing loss is usually described by the terms *slight, mild, moderate, severe,* and *profound,* depending on the child's average hearing level, in decibels, throughout the frequencies most important for understanding speech. To determine the nature of a child's hearing loss, an audiologist assesses responses to different sounds and plots the results on an audiogram. Figure 11.1 shows an audiogram with the relative loudness and pitch of common environmental and speech sounds. Pitch, or frequency of sound, is measured in hertz (Hz) and is plotted along the horizontal axis of an audiogram, while the loudness or intensity of sound is measured in decibels (dB) and is plotted along the vertical axis. The point where the two converge is a child's level of hearing for a particular sound. During a hearing test different sounds are presented, ranging from low to high (Hz) and

from the softest to the loudest (dB) intensity. This information is then plotted on an audiogram.

The sounds used to develop an audiogram are pure, or single-frequency tones, although sounds in everyday life are multifrequency, consisting of both high- and low-frequency elements. The rumbling of thunder is a low-frequency sound. The chirping of a bird is a high-frequency sound. Speech sounds are in the 500–4,000 Hz range (Nober, 1996). A child with a mild hearing loss may still have some difficulty in fully developing speech and language abilities even though he or she hears speech without a hearing aid. A child with a profound hearing loss will not hear speech, even with amplification, and will need a visual form of communication. Note that most speech sounds fall near the middle of the audiogram in Figure 11.1.

TAKING A VISUAL PERSPECTIVE

A child who is deaf or hard of hearing is a *visual* person. Deaf people were described by George Veditz, a deaf educator who was also deaf, in 1912 as "first, last, and for all time, the people of the eye" (Veditz, 1912, p. 30). Despite recent advances in hearing technologies, the primacy of the visual sense for individuals who are deaf is just as true today. Ninety percent of parents of young children who are deaf or hard of hearing are hearing (Sass-Lehrer, 1999). For this reason, one of the greatest challenges parents and professionals face is learning to see the world through the eyes of a child with a hearing loss. This involves learning to modify *all* interactions with the child to encompass visual and auditory means of learning.

Today, American Sign Language (ASL) is widely used in the United States. The general population has come to view ASL as an authentic language. High schools and colleges offer ASL to fulfill their foreign language requirements. Signing to hearing infants and toddlers is the latest craze for parents who want to enhance their children's language and learning abilities in the early years.

Compared to a decade ago, children with hearing loss, and their families, have vastly increased opportunities to learn sign language and to interact

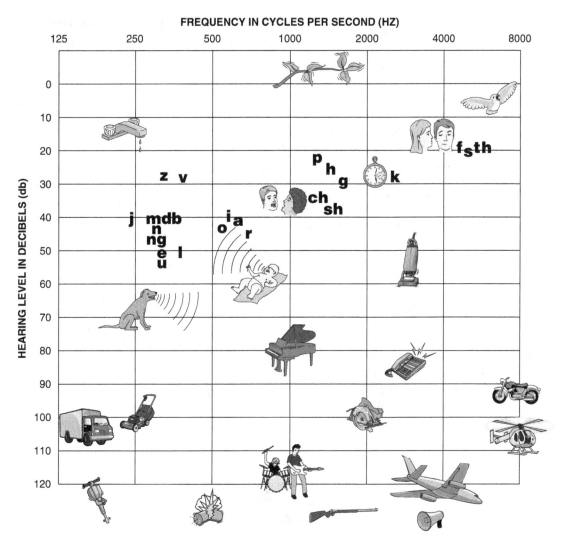

Figure 11.1 An audiogram showing where common sounds are located

with Deaf adults to explore what it means to be deaf. Early exposure to the Deaf Culture can reduce social isolation during the teen years for children with hearing loss (Christiansen & Leigh, 2002). Psycholinguists and educators today recognize the importance of both the auditory and the visual channels for language acquisition and learning in children with hearing loss (Hafer & Stredler-Brown, 2003). Children who are deaf or hard of hearing today can indeed "have it all."

A Life-Span Developmental Framework for Intervention

When one works with the family of a young child who is deaf or hard of hearing, there is an immediate need to live and respond "in the moment" to the child's and family's specific needs. Of course, as time passes, these needs will change. The most effective professionals employ a "whole child–whole family" approach that keeps the child's and the family's resources and needs in mind, attending to the most pressing needs at any given time (Meadow, 1980).

Professionals must serve as guides to parents so they can see the "big picture" of what it means to be deaf (Traci & Koester, 2003). This often involves an understanding and appreciation of the Deaf Culture. Children with hearing loss and their families need professionals who employ a life-span developmental framework, who communicate the importance of Deaf role models, and who respond to parents' interests and questions as well as broaching topics that parents may be unaware of in order to provide complete and accurate information (Arehart & Yoshinaga-Itano, 1999). Equally important, professionals must assure parents that they do not have to choose between sign and speech for their child (Hafer & Stredler-Brown, 2003). In fact, as demonstrated by Anna's family in the case study, parents are increasingly demanding that their child receive the full array of communication tools and opportunities available, including cochlear implants with auditory and speech therapy as well as classroom teachers (deaf and hearing) who are fluent in ASL (Hafer, Rooke, & Charlifue-Smith, 2008b).

IMPACT OF HEARING LOSS ON DEVELOPMENT AND LEARNING

One can never predict exactly how deafness will affect an individual. Outcomes depend on many factors, such as the age of onset, the age at which intervention was begun, the use of hearing aids, the quality of sign language a child experiences, the presence of other disabling conditions, and the family's socioeconomic status (Sebald & Luckner, 2007). The most pervasive impact of a hearing loss on a child is on the child's language development and social-emotional health. If a child does not have complete access to a free exchange of communication, language proficiency as well as social-emotional health may be affected.

Young children with a hearing loss have many characteristics. They are as heterogeneous as hearing children. According to the *Annual Survey of Deaf and Hard of Hearing Children and Youth of 2004–05* conducted by the Gallaudet University Research Institute, there are approximately 37,500 students who are deaf and hard of hearing in the United States in pre-K through 12th-grade programs, or 1.5 per 1,000 (Mitchell,

Research has shown that families who receive early services for their children with hearing loss experience less stress and are better able to adapt their language and communication styles to the needs of their child.

2004). Approximately 60% of these students are categorized as hard of hearing, while the remaining 40% are considered to have a severe to profound hearing loss (Mitchell, 2004).

One-third of the parents surveyed by Meadow-Orlans, Mertens, and Sass-Lehrer (2003) reported that their children had special needs in addition to having a hearing loss. This indicates the need for early and frequent assessment to identify learning challenges and for comprehensive planning to provide appropriate activities and services. The value of early services for children with hearing loss cannot be overstated. Children who are identified by 6 months of age and receive appropriate early intervention services are 2.6 times more likely to have language skills at or near the typical range than children who receive services later (Yoshinaga-Itano, Sedey, Coulter, & Thomson, 2000). Further, young children with hearing loss that are enrolled in effective early education programs have better social development and emotional-behavioral adjustment, regardless of gender, ethnicity, socioeconomic status, communication choice, degree of hearing loss, or the presence of multiple disabilities (Moeller, 2000). One of the principal objectives of early education is to support families as they explore communication options for their children.

COMMUNICATION APPROACHES

Parents of young children who are deaf or hard of hearing face an array of communication choices for their children that range from a pure aural-oral approach to a bilingual-bicultural approach. Nothing in the field of education of the deaf creates more controversy than the discussion of communication and language approaches for children. In reality, no one approach is best for every child with a hearing loss. The vast majority of professionals acknowledge that sign language and other forms of visually-based communication do not negatively impact the development of speech, but rather appear to boost the development of language (Crittenden, Ritterman,

& Wilcox, 1986; McNally, Rose, & Quigley, 1994; Yoshinaga-Itano, 2006). Although most Deaf people use sign language, they also to varying degrees use speech, **speechreading** (lipreading) and hearing aids. An individual's success in communicating through speech, speechreading, and audition varies widely. The age of onset of the hearing loss, the degree of the loss, the integrity of the central nervous system, the quality of education received, and the degree of family support all impact how successful a child will be with speech. Parents and professionals need to determine how much emphasis to place on the development of speech and auditory skills for a child, based on that child's capabilities and the family's preference.

Most Deaf parents overwhelmingly choose to communicate in ASL; however, many use a combination of speech and signs, and a very few choose only to speak to their children who are deaf. Like hearing parents, Deaf parents have individual preferences. In general, the less **residual hearing** (remaining hearing) a child has, the more likely it is that some form of visual communication will be utilized.

For young children with significant hearing loss, the debate is beginning to shift from the "manual versus oral" debate to that of which communication system or language is best suited for *that* child and family and will also afford that child the best opportunity for developing literacy. The communication approach selected must be one family members believe they can use consistently. If parents find that their child's communication needs change or that their child's language abilities are not progressing at a satisfactory rate, they should be encouraged to be open-minded and work closely with professionals to explore other communication and language options. The challenge for early childhood professionals is to provide sufficient information to support parents' decision-making process. There are four communication approaches available to parents and their children who are deaf or hard of hearing: monolingual, language-mixing, cued speech, and bilingual. Each will be discussed.

Monolingual Approaches

Auditory-verbal (A–V) and auditory-oral (AO) are two approaches to communication that emphasize the speech and auditory pathways, also known as the oral approach (Estabrooks, 2000). In this approach, 100% of the time is devoted to developing speech and auditory skills. All interactions and instruction are conducted through the spoken word only. The A–V approach concentrates on developing the auditory channel through listening only. It involves speechreading, a visual pathway, to strengthen auditory and speech skills. Both of these methods require hearing in the speech frequencies (aided or with a cochlear implant) in order to be effective.

Language-Mixing Approaches

The goal of language-mixing approaches is to develop English language proficiency and to support speech. In these approaches, speech is considered to be the primary means of communication, with signs providing the visual support. English and auditory training, while addressed to varying individual degrees, are not seen as the primary pathway to language. Language-mixing approaches make use of manually coded English (MCE). There are many forms of MCE, and all have the goal of making a child's home language (that is, English) visually accessible (Andrews et al., 2004). MCE sign systems take the vocabulary of ASL and sign it in English word order. To further illustrate English on the hands, these sign systems add invented signs for English morphemes, such as /ing/ and /ed/. Some of the more well known MCE systems are *Signed English* (Bornstein, 1974), *Signing Exact English (SEE–2)* (Gustason, Pfetzing, & Zawolkow, 1980), and *Conceptually Accurate Signed English (CASE)* (Centers for Disease Control and Prevention, 2007). The presence of sign language does not necessarily imply the absence of speech. Most programs for children who are deaf adhere to a philosophy of total communication, which involves the use of both speech and sign (Nowell & Marshak, 1994).

Cued Speech Approach

This approach relies on handshapes made near the mouth in conjunction with the lip movements of speech in order to provide a visual form of the spoken language, whether it is English, French, or Farsi (Cornett, 1967). The cues help to clarify speech sounds, such as the sound /k/, that are not visible on the lips. Proponents of this approach believe it is a viable path to English (or other spoken language), though it is not completely effective as a form of expressive communication. Cueing assists children with hearing loss in accessing the phonological information in spoken language and, therefore, is considered a bridge to literacy. Cued speech is also considered by some to be easier for hearing family members to learn (LaSasso & Metzger, 1998).

Bilingual Approaches

Bilingual-bicultural programs use the language of the Deaf community, ASL, as the language of instruction and teach English through reading and writing. Deaf individuals who are bilingual-bicultural have competency in both ASL and English and function in both the Deaf community and the larger culture (Baker & Baker, 2000). Bilingual-bicultural programs advocate for ASL as the first language of children who are deaf. Proponents of this approach believe that deaf children are visual learners, so early ASL acquisition is emphasized in order to provide the basis for English language development. Speech development and auditory training are treated as a separate set of skills to be developed if parents choose to do so.

Along with these communication approaches, parents have technologies choices that may be used to augment their children's ability to make meaning from sound.

TECHNOLOGIES THAT SUPPLEMENT AND SUPPORT SOUND

An important part of working with parents of children who are deaf or hard of hearing is guiding them to receive appropriate support for determining the best technology for their children. Teachers trained specifically in teaching children with hearing impairments and audiologists generally assume this responsibility. Today, advancements in the technology that enhances hearing and the range of services and perspectives in deaf education may complicate the decision-making process for parents and educators alike. Decisions about personal hearing aids, group FM systems, and, more frequently, cochlear implants need to be made so a child's ability to utilize the auditory pathway is improved.

Hearing Aids and Group FM Systems

A hearing aid is the most common technology used to support sound. A **hearing aid** is an amplification device that makes sound louder. Hearing aids can differentially amplify certain frequencies and are tailored to each child's individual pattern of hearing loss (House, 1999). Group assistive listening devices, such as a **FM device**, control problems caused by distance and noise in the classroom (Crandell & Smaldino, 2001). The teacher wears a small microphone transmitter, and the child wears a receiver that doubles as a personal hearing aid.

Many factors influence the "success" of enhancing residual hearing, including the hearing status of the child. In general, the greater the hearing loss is, the more tenuous the benefit of amplification becomes. Children with mild or unilateral losses need close monitoring, but will develop speech and auditory skills commensurate with those of their hearing peers. There is a danger, however, that some of these children may miss the subtleties of language and may be accused of "not paying attention" when the teacher is unaware that the child's ear is turned toward the sound source. Most children with moderate losses can benefit from amplification and are expected to develop speech with therapy. Children with severe hearing losses can benefit from visual support in some form, such as sign language or cued speech, to support their language development. These children require intensive speech therapy. Children

with profound hearing losses have a much more difficult time developing language and speech through audition or hearing alone (Yoshinaga-Itano, 2003). For these children, vision is the primary pathway to language, with speech and auditory skills seen as supplemental skill areas. These children increasingly are receiving cochlear implants to provide them the opportunity to acquire spoken language skills (Geers, 2006).

Cochlear Implants

Perhaps the most exciting technological advancement for children with profound hearing loss has been the development of the cochlear implant. As of 2005, over 70,000 people worldwide had received cochlear implants, with half of these being children (Clerc Center, 2007). Not all people with profound hearing loss can be helped by cochlear implants, but those who are tend to hear a wider range of sounds more clearly than with hearing aids. Cochlear implants work by bypassing damaged hair cells in the cochlea and stimulating remaining neural tissue with an electrode implanted in the cochlea (Beiter & Shallop, 1998). All cochlear implants consist of an external component and an internal or implanted component.

As noted above, not everyone is a good candidate for a cochlear implant (Li, Bain, & Steinberg, 2004). Candidacy requirements change as the technology advances; however, the current criteria to be considered for a cochlear implant are as follows: (1) profound bilateral sensorineural hearing loss (increasingly candidates with severe hearing loss are being considered), (2) negligible benefit from hearing aids (if an infant has not been provided amplification, then a team decision is made as to the probable benefits of amplification for the child), (3) intact auditory nerve, (4) no medical contraindications for surgery, and (5) family and educational environments that support the use of cochlear implants (Li et al., 2004). The age at which a cochlear implant is provided is decreasing each year. At present, the Food and Drug Administration is recommending implants for children 12 months of age and older, although this is not a legal requirement.

The superiority of cochlear implants over hearing aids for speech reception and production is evident with children in both oral and signed environments across studies conducted from 1994 to the present (Geers, 2006). As very young children who are deaf receive implants and their families participate in infant-toddler and preschool programs, increasing numbers of children are being placed in general education kindergarten settings with age-appropriate language skills (Moog, 2002).

Involving Families

Families of children who are deaf or hard of hearing face a variety of challenges and bring a wide range of strengths to parenthood. Parental reactions to the discovery that their child has a hearing impairment could be plotted on a continuum from profound grief and shock to elation. While it may be understandable to some that a parent could be saddened by the diagnosis of a hearing loss in their child, it may be surprising that Deaf parents, more often than not, are happy with the news that a new member of the next Deaf generation is born. A shared language and life experience, a strong and supportive community, and a healthy "nonpathological" view of being deaf are elements that influence, in a positive way, Deaf parents' reaction to the diagnosis of a hearing loss. Hearing parents, on the other hand, are often overwhelmed by their absolute lack of understanding of what it means to be deaf. Some families adapt quickly, while others spend years trying to cope with the concerns they experience (Hintermair, 2000).

Regardless of the challenges for families, the benefits of early intervention services and the benefits of family involvement in positively impacting the development of children with hearing loss are well documented. Moeller (2000), for example, found that the age of enrollment in early intervention services was one of the significant factors in language outcomes in children with hearing loss when they were 5 years old. Regardless of the degree of hearing loss, in this study children who were enrolled earliest (e.g., at 11 months of age) demonstrated significantly better vocabulary and verbal reasoning skills at age 5 than did later-enrolled children with hearing loss. Further, the most successful children in this study were those with a high level of family involvement. It has been shown that families who receive early services may have less stress and are better able to adapt their language and communication styles to the needs of their child (Sebald & Luckner, 2007). Ideally, families receive services from professionals who have training and experience in the field of deaf education (Arehart & Yoshinaga-Itano, 1999). Contact with other parents of children who are deaf or hard of hearing and with adults who are Deaf or hard of hearing is essential to obtaining the kind of information that can be of immediate help to families—particularly with decisions regarding communication strategies (Hintermair, 2000; Meadow-Orlans, Mertens, Sass-Lehrer, & Scott-Olson, 1997; Sass-Lehrer, 1999).

As professionals have come to understand, collaborating with families is much more than a series of activities; it is a pervasive attitude (Esler, Godber, & Christenson, 2002). To build partnerships with families, professionals need to arrange the following activities:

❏ Provide new parents with opportunities to meet other parents of children with hearing loss, particularly parents of older children, for support and guidance.

❏ Provide opportunities for hearing parents to meet Deaf adults and adults who are hard of hearing. Direct experience with adult role models helps parents develop realistic and positive expectations for their child's potential.

❏ Provide sign language classes designed specifically for families so *all* family members learn to communicate with the child with a hearing loss.

❏ Provide opportunities for parents and other family members to participate in activities in the Deaf community, such as sporting events, worship, Deaf clubs, silent suppers, and school events.

❏ Use videotape to document a child's communication behaviors, and then use this record to help parents develop responsive communicative behaviors with their child.

❏ Educate parents regarding the care and maintenance and the importance of *consistent* use of their child's hearing aid.

❏ Communicate with families frequently, based on families' needs, allowing parents to be proactive, rather than reactive (Sebald & Luckner, 2007).

The sensory aid that parents select for their child may affect the family's perception of their involvement in their child's education. DesJardin (2005) studied two groups of mothers with young children with prelingual deafness: 24 mothers of children with hearing aids and 30 mothers of children with a cochlear implant. This researcher found that mothers of the children with a cochlear implant rated their early intervention program lower than did the other mothers, but the mothers of the children with cochlear implants perceived themselves as more efficacious in the care and maintenance of their child's sensory device and in their involvement in developing their child's speech-language skills.

STRATEGIES FOR PROMOTING AUDITORY DEVELOPMENT

Auditory development, the ability to hear and make sense of sounds, requires training a child to *listen*. Most children with hearing loss have some residual hearing that can be enhanced through technology or auditory training, although the trained use of residual hearing may or may not result in functional hearing. Regardless of the communication approach used, children with hearing loss need to increase their attention to, and ability to discriminate, speech and environmental

sounds. Most children with hearing loss use their vision to enhance their understanding of what they hear. Attention to the enhancement of auditory and speech skills does not exclude the use of a visual-manual language and, in fact it tends to increase the chance of successful use of auditory-oral skills (Clerc Center, 2007).

To enhance auditory skills, a child should always wear his or her hearing aid, and the hearing aid should be in good working order. The aid or implant should be checked several times during a day to make sure it is working properly. If a child does not respond to sounds in the usual way, ECSE professionals need to check the hearing aid and then, if it is working, be alert for signs that the child may be getting an ear infection, which will depress the child's ability to hear.

Children need to learn to listen to what is being said, to imitate sounds and words, to follow directions, and to comply with requests. Children should be expected to meet these expectations whether they are learning a visual-manual language or using speech. The following are general strategies that parents and professionals may employ during daily routines to improve listening and watching in infants, toddlers, and preschoolers (Hafer, Rooke & Charlifue-Smith, 2008b). Some of these strategies involve a combination of auditory and visual techniques with the primary objective of supporting auditory development. Depending on an individual child's auditory capabilities and the setting, teachers and/or parents will determine the degree to which auditory and visual signals are emphasized.

1) Speak near the child's ear. This helps the child discriminate speech from background noises. Speak in a normal, clear tone.

2) Draw attention to sounds. Children with a hearing loss need support to pay attention to sounds. Adults should point out noises by saying "Listen, I hear the phone ringing" and then pointing to their ears and to the phone.

3) Gain the child's attention before speaking. Parents and professionals need to learn that visual attention is sequential and that they must wait until the child looks at them *before* communicating. Adults can ensure visual attention to their face before speaking by tapping the child's shoulder or by moving a toy from the child's line of vision up to the adult's face. Once the child is looking at the speaker, the speaker should maintain direct face-to-face contact. This enables the child to see the way sounds are formed, read facial expressions, attend to signs/speech, and focus on the content of the message.

4) Speak at a regular volume. Speaking normally will minimize distortion of the auditory signal and will encourage listening. Use simple sentences and speak at a normal rate.

5) Use the pitch that is easiest for the child to hear. Some children hear better at a certain pitch. Infants normally tune in to higher pitches, so adults naturally use a higher pitch when they address an infant. Once the child's hearing is evaluated, adults will have an idea of the types of sounds the child will be better able to hear. Use toys that produce sounds that the child can hear as well as those that challenge the child to listen.

6) Use acoustic highlighting techniques. Use sentences that are rich in intonation, melody, and expression. Children are better able to pick up sounds when there is variation in intonation and a rhythmic cadence. Varying the typical sentence pattern to include more of a singsong rhythm can make children want to listen. Occasionally, use whispering to encourage listening and to emphasize important aspects of words or phrases.

7) Pair sounds with meaning. Children like to know what sounds they are hearing. Help a child understand what is making sounds by demonstrating (e.g., animal sounds), pointing out environmental sounds (e.g., the flushing toilet), and having the child produce the sound (e.g., pushing the "on" button on the dryer). After repeated exposure to such pairings, the child will begin to attach meaning to the sounds he or she hears.

8) Play listening games. Help children learn to listen for and discriminate sounds by playing games involving sounds. After the child has seen an object and sound paired several times (see above), try having the child identify the sound without the visual referent. For example, play the sound of a drum, a horn, or a guitar (on tape or on the instrument while the child is blindfolded or turned away). The child can point to the picture of what was heard or gesture, sign or say the word for the sound. This is the "I Hear a _____ Game". Let the child choose sounds for the adult to guess as well to make it more fun.

Environmental Modifications for Improving Auditory Communication and Learning

The design of the environment can play a critical role in enhancing a child's auditory skills. The following environmental adaptations and modifications may be used for infants, preschoolers, and primary-aged children who are deaf or hard of hearing (Lewis & Doolag, 1999). All of these strategies were used within daily routines by Anna's parents and teachers (see the case study) to support her communication.

1) Sit on the side of the child's better-hearing ear. If the child has a cochlear implant or is wearing a hearing aid, move closer to the child.

2) Provide a visual link to the source of sound. Children will be better able to understand what they hear if they *see* the facial expressions and lip movements of the speaker or *see* the sound source, such as watching a bell ring. In a classroom or center, arrange seats in a semicircle so the child with a hearing loss can see all classmates talking or signing (Hafer, Spragins, & Hardy-Braz, 1996).

3) Reduce background noise. Turn off the television, radio, or stereo and reduce other background sounds, such as fans, so the child can focus on spoken language. Shut windows or doors to reduce street noise and sounds from other rooms (Williams & Finnegan, 2003). Speech must be at least 30–40 dB louder than background sounds for a child to be able to attend to it. Draperies, carpeting, upholstery, and acoustical tile can all help absorb background noise. It is a good idea to check with the child's audiologist or a specialist in the education of children with hearing impairment for further tips to reduce noise in the home or classroom for individual children.

4) Make listening games a part of everyday life. Have a child identify sounds in the house, in the classroom, and outdoors. For example, at home, try to identify the sounds of the paper being delivered, the door bell ringing, or the dishwasher running. In the the classroom, identify the electric pencil sharpener turning, the bookcase door being closed, and another class passing in the hall. Outdoors try to identify the sounds of birds, a river, or busses passing by.

5) Conduct frequent hearing aid checks. Hearing aid checks ensure that children are hearing what is happening around them. The hearing specialist or audiologist should instruct parents and teachers on basic troubleshooting strategies.

6) Teach peers how to gain the attention of a child with a hearing loss. Hearing children should be taught how to alert their classmate who is deaf or hard of hearing to direct his or her attention if needed, such as by tapping the child's shoulder.

Sound Localization Skills

Being able to locate sounds in the environment is a significant part of a child's auditory skill development. **Sound localization** is the child's ability to identify the source or origin of a sound. The ability to localize sound may be negatively influenced by hearing loss in one or both ears or by physical abnormalities that affect a child's ability to filter sound. Hearing aids improve hearing, but not sound localization. Some children may be able to hear an approaching car, but may not know the direction from which it is coming.

To help infants, toddlers, and preschoolers locate the source of a sound, parents and professionals may do the following in their daily interactions with a child:

1) Pair visual regard of a sound-making toy or object with a sound from that object. For example, if a child hears the sound of a musical toy and looks in the direction of the toy, repeat the sound of the toy and comment, "Yes. It makes music!"

2) Play "find the sound" games. Use noisemaking objects and make a game out of searching for the sound. Start with sounds that are close and fairly loud, such as the sound made by shaking a tin of beans under a table. Say, "Do you hear that? Where is it?" Once the child starts to understand the "listen and search" sequence, try making noises with different loudness and timbre, such as those made by a whirling birthday noisemaker and a sack of rice. When the child can easily localize closely placed sounds, record various sounds on a tape recorder and hide the tape recorder in different spots around a room.

3) Provide cues to sounds. Whenever an unexpected noise is made in the environment, say, "Listen, I hear a _____" and look toward the sound. Have the child watch the adult approach the sound, such as a timer that is ringing, or show the child the cause of the sound whenever possible, such as the neighbor mowing his lawn. This practice will encourage the child to look for the cause of unexpected sounds.

Environmental Modifications for Supporting Sound Localization. The following suggestions and strategies will aid infants, toddlers, preschoolers, and some primary-aged children in improving their ability to identify the source of sounds:

1) Noises are easier to locate when they are on the side of the better-hearing ear. When playing listening games, make noises or place sound-making objects first on the child's "better listening" side.

2) Sounds are easier to locate when they are closer, rather than farther away. Start sound identification games in close proximity to the child and gradually move the sound-making objects to more distant locations.

3) Help children follow a conversation. When a conversation is taking place between other people, point to the person who is talking to help the child follow the verbal interchange between speakers.

4) Work collaboratively with the child's audiologist and educational hearing specialist/teacher of the deaf and hard of hearing. This will enable parents and early childhood special educators to design auditory activities that are attainable and functional for each child.

Responding to Sounds

Children not only need to hear sounds, but also need to attach meaning to those sounds so that they can respond appropriately. Children who are hard of hearing and have auditory processing problems or attentional problems may find it difficult to associate meaning with the sounds they hear. Accurate understanding is always demonstrated by an appropriate response to the sounds heard. Children who do not respond appropriately may ignore the sounds (e.g., keep doing what they were doing before the communication or sound); have an approximate, but incorrect response (e.g., the adult says, "Give me your hand," and the child gives the adult his hat); or give a totally incorrect response (e.g., the child hears a timer go off and goes to answer the door). These activities will help parents and professionals develop a child's ability to respond appropriately to sounds:

1) Read the child's cues related to sounds. Look for facial expressions following a sound, such as a curious look or a vocalization that rises in intonation, indicating a question; a look of surprise, shown by the raising of eyebrows; or a look of distress, demonstrated by a furrowed brow. Then be concrete in explaining the meaning of the sound and demonstrate how to respond to it.

2) Reword to help the child understand. When sounds, words, or complicated sentences are used, some children need to have the message restated to help them understand. For example, a teacher may substitute a different word, use a simile or definition of the word, reword the sentence, or restate the word, phrase or sentence. The adult needs to determine which of these is most likely to help the child appropriately interpret and respond.

3) Provide wait time. Many children need time to process what they have heard and translate the sounds into meaningful information. Some children who are hard of hearing or have auditory processing difficulties may need at least ten seconds to understand the message.

4) Encourage exploration and experimentation. Children who have difficulty hearing need to have opportunities to discover and learn by *doing*. They need to explore their environment and discover through tactile and movement experiences the differences among various types of vibrations, movements, and sounds. They need to learn the associated meanings of things, such as "hard" and "soft," through experiential learning. For instance, "soft" can mean a light pressure or a quiet noise. Language and conceptual understanding will grow as a child's ability to compare and categorize experiences improves through his or her direct experience.

Environmental Modifications to Aid Appropriate Responses to Sound. There are specific adaptations to the environment that parents and teachers can make that will support children's ability to respond appropriately to sound. The following are ideas for providing a more supportive listening environment for infants, toddlers, preschoolers, and primary-aged students who are hard of hearing:

1) Use picture cues. Picture cues that relate to routines such as dressing, eating, or participating in classroom assignments, activities, or centers can support the development of gestures, verbalizations, or sign language. A picture schedule can explain the sequence of events in an activity and help a child better understand verbal directions. A list of classroom rules with pictures associated with the words can be used along with language when a child breaks a rule. Using pictures of family members and classmates will ensure a child identifies the person who is being discussed.

2) Provide correct lighting. It is important that lighting be on the face of the speaker and not in the eyes of the child. Avoid having a speaker stand in front of a window, as that will throw shadows on his or her face, making lip movements, facial expressions, or signs more difficult to see. Be aware of special situations such as watching a movie. If the lights are out and the teacher speaks, he or she must have lighting on his or her face so the child with a hearing loss can see.

3) Pair a sound with a visual cue. A visual cue, such as blinking the lights, may tell the child who is hard of hearing that it is time to clean up. When the light is paired with the sound of the cleanup bell, over time the child may be able to respond to the bell alone.

4) Make directions specific, rather than general statements. For example, say, "Put all the dolls in this box," rather than "These will go in there."

5) Give instructions one or two steps at a time, rather than all at once. This will allow the child to comprehend and respond accurately to each step. Parents can practice simplifying instructions for routines that have many steps by giving directions for each part of the routine individually, such as "Go put on your pajamas. It is time for bed," so a child is not overwhelmed. Teachers might say, "We will do centers first. Then we will go on the field trip to the zoo."

6) Restate important information in more than one way. Adults need to use phrases such as "That means . . ." or "Another way to say that is . . . ." A teacher might say, "Another way to think of a veterinarian is an animal doctor."

7) Repeat the comments and questions of other students. A child who does not hear or understand the other children will most likely not indicate this. Instead, the child may stare vacantly at the other children or be distracted by another activity when he or she did not hear.

Imitation of Sounds

Once a child can localize sounds and responds appropriately to sounds, the child needs to learn to imitate sounds. To teach this, parents and professionals must make sure the mouth of the speaker is clearly visible while talking. First, adults imitate the infant's or toddler's own vocalizations and actions. Children will imitate sounds in their own repertoire *before* they will imitate novel sounds modeled by an adult. Even infants who are profoundly deaf will make noises and babble until they are about 6 months old. Parents and professionals can take advantage of this time to encourage the production of sounds. Use tactile and visual cues to reinforce vocalizations, such as tapping on the child's arm as he or she vocalizes.

1) Wait for the child. Adults must wait for the child to look at them. Once the child looks at the adult, the adult can make a sound or comment on what is happening. Many children need time to think about how to make a sound or words. "Wait time" is needed again, before repeating the sound or word. If the child does not look, the adult can use a gentle tap on the arm or leg to attract his or her attention. The adult may then tap an object or point to an object and name it. This association between the word and the object is critical so the child is learning to listen to the meaning of the sound, not just imitating random sounds and syllables.

2) Provide many opportunities for repetition in context. Hearing children need to use a word over 200 times in context for it to become part of their language repertoire. Children with hearing loss may need additional practice. Just having the child imitate sounds is not motivating and will, in all likelihood, lead to resistance. Rather, it is better for parents and professionals to use sounds and words the adults want a child to learn in meaningful situations. The first consonant sounds a child learns, for example, are sounds using the lips together, as in /b/, /m/, and /p/. Adults should explore the child's environment (e.g., home, daycare center, preschool) to find common words that start with these sounds, such as *baby*, *bottle*, *mama*, *monkey*, *puppy*, and *papa*. The adult holds up an object, repeats the object name several times, and then waits before the next repetition.

3) Prioritize key words for the child's routines, favorite objects, and activities. When working on imitation, it is important not only to choose words that have sounds a child is developmentally ready to make, but also to select words that are important to the child to ensure the child's motivation. Start with low- and mid-frequency vowel sounds such as /a/ or /oo/. Play games that entice the child to use the words. For example, the adult can show the child something the child likes and then hides it under a blanket. When the child looks at the adult to see what happened, the adult can say the object name slowly and clearly. At first, any sound the child makes should bring the toy out. Slowly, the adult needs to increase the demands so that a closer and closer approximation of the object name is necessary before the child gets the toy. Along the same line, the child should be given many opportunities to initiate "reading" to adults by pointing to pictures and vocalizing. Research has found that it is best to find a quiet spot for talking, reading, and playing vocal (sounds) or verbal (words) imitation games. A quiet environment with few visual and auditory distractions will enable the child to be more focused on speech sounds (Hafer Rooke & Charlifue-Smith, 2008a).

Promote Spoken Language Within Home Routines

Homelife offers the perfect situation for promoting and reinforcing language. During snack or meal times, it is natural for parents to pass an item of food across a child's field of vision. This is a cue that brings the child's attention to the topic of conversation. As the child visually follows the bowl, the parent can hold the bowl beside his or her mouth. Once the child is attending, the adult can make an exaggerated expression and label the item, "Peas!" To encourage the child to repeat the word, the parent can say, "I want _____," letting the child fill in the blank. Any approximation is praised, and the correct word is restated (e.g., Child: "Peh." Adult: "Yes. PEAS!"). It is best to use short phrases and make sure the child is attending to the person talking. Family members must be reminded to use a gesture to show when they are talking.

Diapering or toileting is another time for rhythmic activities and face-to-face communication. This is a good time to introduce words related to body parts, location (e.g., on, top, in), and action words. While the child is lying quietly on the changing table and is a captive audience, parents should point out sounds in the environment. For example, during diapering, Mom picks up Alex's feet and sings a song, rocking his feet back and forth to the music while she sings. He laughs and moves his feet. She takes his hands and claps them to the rhythm of the song as she sings. She then puts his diaper on while labeling each action: "Legs up." "Diaper on." "Snap pants." "All done!" Mom can then hold Alex up so he can see and say, "Listen, Alex." She steps on the diaper pail pedal and imitates the sound it makes: "Clunk! All gone!"

As the child becomes more independent and begins toilet training, the adult can have the child listen to the sounds in the bathroom, such as the toilet flushing and the toilet lid closing. Attention to these sounds is important so the child remembers to flush and knows when the water is turned off. The adult can also use this routine to expand the child's vocabulary to include labels for the action steps, such as *push*, *open*, *close*, and *turn*.

Dressing is another routine that offers multiple embedded language and communication training opportunities. As with toileting, dressing provides a chance to build vocabulary through imitation of words in a functional context. For instance, while dressing Dustin, Dad taps him on the shoulder. Dustin looks at his father. "Foot," Dad says. Dustin lifts his foot and says, "oot." Then Dad helps him get his foot in the hole of his shorts. Dad taps Dustin's shoulder again. Dustin looks at his father. "Arm." Dustin stands looking at his father without moving. Dad points to Dustin's arm and says, "Arm." Dustin then lifts his arm and says, "Am." Dad repeats, "Yes . . . arm," while he puts on the shirt. Dad gives Dustin a big hug, waits for Dustin to look at him, and says, "All done, Dustin." It is important to notice in this scenario how the dad used wait time, modeling, gestural cueing, and reinforcement of verbalizations.

Doing errands involves going out into the community where there is a lot of background noise. It is important for children with a hearing loss to learn to distinguish various noises, especially what is a background noise compared to a sound that should be the focus of attention. Doing activities in the community is the right time to point out various sounds in the environment so the child recognizes what they are. For example, Mom holds Justin's hand as they walk out to the car. She stops, sits on the front steps with him, and points to her ear. "Listen, Justin. What do you hear?" Justin turns his head both ways and then shakes his head. Mom points up in the air. Justin looks up. He points to the white trail of an airplane and says, "Ayplane." Mom points to her ear again. Justin tips his head so his ear points toward the sky. He smiles and says, "Ayplane."

STRATEGIES FOR PROMOTING VISUAL COMMUNICATION

When a child is exposed to a visual-manual language such as ASL from a very early age, the child develops language through this visual-manual mode naturally and effortlessly. If a hearing child is born to Deaf parents who sign, the child's first language will be ASL.

Children learn a language when it is presented to them in a clear, fully developed form and they have extensive opportunities to interact with other users of that language. Just as hearing children value and learn to use their hearing abilities to develop language and speech, children who are deaf or hard of hearing use their visual skills to monitor their environment and to communicate. When a child who is deaf or hard of hearing sees the door light flash, he or she goes to the door or alerts his or her parents that someone is at the door. When a baby cries and the baby cry light flashes, the deaf older sibling responds appropriately and alerts his parents, in the same way a child with typical hearing would when he or she heard the crying.

Hearing infants babble with their voices, and deaf infants, in addition to babbling, manually babble, or "mabble," with their tiny hands. Handshapes, in combination with movements and position in space, when consistently associated with their referents, will be learned as words (signs), and signs modified by movement and facial expressions and combined with other signs form a complete language. Anything one can say in spoken English can be "signed" in any visual language, such as ASL or SEE–2. Deaf adults use the elements of facial expressions (including lip formations and movements), gestures, body movements, and handshapes to create the visual equivalent of sounds and speech. Demonstrating and modeling accurate, articulate signing for children is essential to their complete language development. Deaf adults, and other fluent signers, use visual communication techniques such as getting down at the child's eye level, signing in closer proximity to the child, and providing an opportunity for the child to copy the sign to aid in "articulation" (Erting, Prezioso & Hynes, 1990). Imitating things in the environment that move, such as animals, machines, and people, is fun for children and helps them refine their visual-motor expression, which is an important element of communicating in a visual language. ASL storytellers are masters at this skill and can help parents and teachers develop it.

In ASL, a person changes the rate (speed) or size and intensity of signing to indicate differences in meaning. For example, if a person wanted to say "He walked slowly," he could sign the word for "walk" in a slow manner. If a person wanted to say "I live in a small house," she could sign the word for "house" in a smaller space. The signer can also indicate intensity by signing more loosely or firmly. If the signer really wants someone to "STOP," then it would be signed firmly. Adults must encourage children to play with their language and modify their expression accordingly. As always, fluent sign models for children are essential. Figure 11.2 shows several ASL signs that would be useful for very young children.

Infants, Toddlers, and Preschoolers

Infants and toddlers with hearing loss tend to be alert, active, and curious (Sass-Lehrer, 1999). They rely on vision and physical interactions with the environment to learn about their surroundings. Many experience the same rate and sequence of development that normally hearing children do. Mohay (2000) outlined several strategies to support very young children in attaining **visual attention**, which is the foundation of fluency in visual languages. These strategies are well known in the Deaf community and are used by Deaf parents as they communicate with their children.

❏ Use nonverbal communication, such as smiling, facial expressions, and gestures, to support the development of looking. Attracting visual attention is essential to communicating with a visual language.

❏ Use touch to gain visual attention. Touching, patting, or stroking is an effective strategy used by deaf parents to attract their child's attention. Deaf parents also use touch to provide positive feedback and reassurance when they are out of their child's visual field.

❏ Gain visual attention with movement by waving a hand, moving an object into the child's line of vision, or swaying back and forth to train the child to attend to the adult's face.

❏ Use pointing to direct attention while still permitting language input. Visual attention is sequential, not simultaneous. That is, deaf parents gain the child's attention, tell the child what he or she will see, and then direct the child's attention to the topic. They also place their signs near the object under discussion so the child can see both the object and the sign.

❏ Reduce the frequency of communication so that communication is recognized as important. Children who are deaf or hard of hearing must switch their attention between activities and the person with whom they are communicating. Deaf parents typically communicate less often and wait for their child to look at them in order to ensure that their child will see the parents' communications as important.

❏ Use short utterances that minimize disruptions in a child's activities and demand less memory as the child shifts visual attention from one focus to another.

❏ Position one's body and objects in the child's visual field. Deaf parents conserve the child's energy by placing themselves behind or next to their child, curving their body around so the child can see both them and the object of interest.

❏ Use bracketing. Deaf parents name an object, then point to the object, and then sign the name for the object again, thereby clarifying the meaning of their language.

❏ Modify signs. Deaf parents modify signs by repeating, enlarging, and prolonging them and by placing them close to the object of attention. This promotes understanding by allowing the child a longer period of time to internalize the language.

Like children with typical hearing, children who are deaf or hard of hearing need continual immersion to learn their visual language.

Figure 11.2 Common signs for young children with hearing loss

Source: Reproduced from "Come Sign With Us: Sign Language Activities for Children" by Jan Hafer (Washington, DC: Clerc Books, Gallaudet University Press, 1996). Reprinted by permission of the publisher. Copyright 1996 by Gallaudet University.

To maintain a child's visual attention, use **child-directed signing**, which uses exaggerated facial expressions, exaggerated sign size, expanded sign space, rhythmic movement, and redundancy to capture a child's attention and promote comprehension (Bailes, 2001). Signs may need to be repeated to provide emphasis or to ensure that the sign was seen. Adults may also need to frequently mold a child's hand into the correct sign shape. When adults slowly sign the target word so the handshape, movement, and placement are clear, it is easier for the child to learn the sign.

Of course, as with speech, sign approximations are accepted, since some signs are motorically complex and, therefore, may be more difficult for a child to make. As noted earlier, babies who sign from birth manually babble, or "mabble." Parents and professionals should imitate mabbles in the same way adults imitate a hearing child's babbling. All of these activities train a child's eyes to see his or her visual language.

Strategies for Teaching Visual Communication to Infants, Toddlers, and Preschoolers. The best way to learn a visual language is in the context in which the language is needed to make "things happen." The following are suggestions for teaching young children how to use and comprehend a visual language (McLaughlin, Small, Spink-Mitchell, & Cripps, 2004):

1) Hold the child and move about the room, gently moving the child's body by rocking and swinging, while smiling and signing the names of objects.

2) Share simple ASL stories using repeated words of two to three signs. For example, sign EYES, EYES, BLUE, BLUE, BLUE. Sign simple ASL poetry using one handshape while varying the movement to show a phrase such as LEAVES FALLING, FALLING, DOWN. Deaf adults can offer more ideas.

3) Play visual imitation games, such as Clap-Clap-Clap, or tap on the child's head three times. Wait for the child to respond or imitate.

4) Play the LIGHTS ON/OFF game. Hold an infant or toddler with one arm and turn the light switch on and off. Point to the light, sign LIGHT ON, and then point to the light. Turn the light off and sign LIGHT OFF. Repeat. Make sure the adult gives the child time to look at the light and back at the adult before the game is continued.

5) Sign one handshape or ASL word. For example, sign the "I LOVE YOU" handshape; then have it "take off," fly around as an airplane

does, and "land" on the child's tummy or head.

6) Be sure to always tell the infant or young child where an adult is going when he or she leaves a room.

7) The adult can hold the child on his or her lap, facing out. The adult then can sign on the child's body and use pointing to direct attention to the object signed.

8) Position a mirror in the child's room so the child can see the parent enter and leave or place the crib or bed facing the door.

9) Be sure to inform a child about the things that happen outside his or her visual range. For example, a parent needs to tell a child when he or she sees Daddy walking outside, or a teacher can tell a child when someone at the next table has finished his or her puzzle.

10) Play handshape games with the child. For example, pretend to think of and then sign as many signs as you can that use the "5" handshape, such as MOTHER, FATHER, and TREE.

These practical suggestions will help a child develop language through the visual-motor channel and may be used by parents and professionals during any activity or in any setting. These skills lay the foundation for preliteracy learning.

Promoting Preliteracy Development

Establishing an environment that supports visual learning is important for preschoolers or kindergarteners who are deaf or hard of hearing, whether they are in a self-contained or an inclusion classroom. All children benefit when a classroom is organized around the needs of visual learners. Table 11.3 lists some of the common accommodations teachers use to support preliteracy skills in preschoolers with hearing loss. Interestingly, many of these adjustments are also appropriate and beneficial for children

---

TABLE 11.3 Basic classroom accommodations for developing preliteracy skills in preschoolers who are deaf or hard of hearing

---

- Ensure that the teacher is in the direct line of sight of the child with a hearing loss.
- Place children in a circle or semicircle for clear sight lines for group discussion and instruction.
- Reduce visual distractions in the classroom that may block sight lines for communication, such as objects hung from the ceiling that may block sight lines.
- Utilize visual alerting devices in the classroom, such as visual fire alarms, visual door alerts, and visual message boards, and teach the entire class their purpose.
- Use technology to enhance visual learning. Multimedia CD–ROMs that contain material such as movies and graphics (in ASL/English), digital video cameras, and still cameras are effective tools for supporting the learning of concepts.
- Utilize role-playing to increase comprehension of stories. Acting out the story is fun and is an effective means of reinforcing vocabulary.
- Show ASL story videotapes available at the local library. Have fun practicing signing as the class watches the videotapes together.
- Use puppets, flannel board characters, and props during stories to illustrate characters and their actions to enhance comprehension and vocabulary development.

---

with communication delays, such as children with autism.

Storytime Activities

Book reading must be an interactive process for children with hearing loss so the adult can monitor what the child sees and hears and is able to teach turn-taking skills. If the adult just reads the book, he or she has no idea what the child may be comprehending. To increase comprehension, adults should place the child on his or her lap, with the adult's mouth close to the child's better-hearing ear, and should talk slowly. The adult should read the book slowly, pausing to point to each picture and label it and waiting for the child to imitate or respond in some way (Hafer, Rooke & Charlifue-Smith, 2008b).

Research has shown, in fact, that when mothers are trained how to share reading and joint writing about the story with their kindergarteners with hearing loss, the children make more gains in vocabulary, reading, and writing skills (Aram, Most, & Mayafit, 2006). This kind of parental involvement in preliteracy and literacy development has been

found to be a predictor of higher functioning in language, early reading, and social-emotional development in children who are deaf (Calderon, 2000).

When reading to an individual child or a group, the child with a hearing loss who is learning sign language can benefit from books with the signs included with the words. This supports listening and emerging literacy understanding in both children who can hear and children who are using an auditory-oral or a manually coded communication approach. Research has revealed that signing target vocabulary functions as a multisensory aid that helps both hearing children and children with hearing loss learn to read sight words (Daniels, 2001; Hafer, 1984; Hafer & Wilson, 1986).

Visual supports for words can be provided in a variety of ways. Professionals can use **sandwiching** to teach new words and common vocabulary by following this sequence: (1) The teacher signs the word, (2) the teacher fingerspells the word (when appropriate), (3) the teacher points to the object or picture of the object when available, and (4) the teacher points to the word in print. Techniques such as these help preschoolers and kindergarteners enter elementary school with a stronger preacademic foundation.

PROMOTING LITERACY DEVELOPMENT

Many primary-aged children with hearing loss have difficulty with academic learning, particularly reading and mathematics. Studies have found that children with hearing loss lag behind their hearing peers and that the gap widens as the children get older (American Speech-Language-Hearing Association, 2001; Traxler, 2000). Deaf children learn to read without hearing the sounds of language, although the ability to utilize phonics may enhance their reading abilities. In programs where ASL is the primary language of discourse, a bilingual approach to achieving English literacy in reading and writing is employed (Bailes, 2001). Primary-aged students who are visual language users learn English as a second language. If their first language is ASL, they learn to think in both languages and learn the differences between signs and printed English, utilizing fingerspelling as an effective "bridge" between the languages. **Fingerspelling** is the use of a manual alphabet to spell out proper nouns for which no sign exists.

Another important "lesson" for children in the bilingual classroom is learning what it means *to be Deaf* from culturally Deaf teachers. Morgan (2004) and Singleton and Morgan (2004) videotaped three Deaf teachers in a bilingual preschool during everyday interactions. These teachers expressed through their daily narratives what it meant to be Deaf as well as demonstrating how to interact with hearing people.

Strategies for Teaching Literacy in a Bilingual Environment

Teachers of the deaf and hard of hearing in bilingual classrooms use many techniques to help young children learn academics and expand their language and communication. The following activities and strategies are used to develop literacy skills in primary-aged students (Bailes, 2001):

1) When reading, the teacher deliberately silently reads the text first, perhaps skimming the text with a finger to give a visual cue to the children that he or she is reading. The book is then put down and translated into ASL.

2) The teacher keeps ASL and English "visible." The teacher positions the book so the

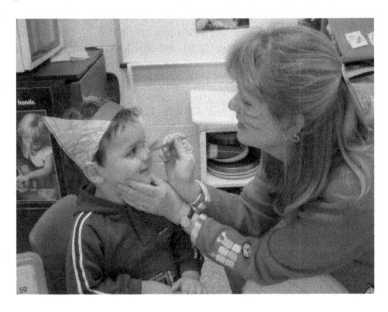

Rewording a phrase or sentence may help children with hearing loss better interpret and respond to auditory messages.

children can see the print as he or she signs. The book should be propped next to the teacher so he or she can refer to the pictures and text as it is translated into ASL.

3) The teacher uses miniature signs (signing near the book or on a picture so the children can look at the signs and/or the pictures at the same time).

4) The teacher introduces vocabulary words with fingerspelling first and then connects them to printed English.

5) When working on specific language skills, the teacher has the children wear "ASL" hats when they have a skill-building activity on expressive ASL and "English" hats when they are working on a written English activity or lesson.

6) Teachers use eye gaze effectively to encourage class participation. For example, when encouraging the group, they use explicit G-gaze (group gaze) behaviors; when eliciting an individual response, they use explicit I-gaze (individual gaze) behaviors.

7) Teachers elaborate on the text and/or information to ensure comprehension. They are not initially concerned about students knowing each word in the text, but aim for the conceptual "big picture." When retelling information, they move progressively toward less elaboration and more direct translation of the text.

Teaching Phonics in a Bilingual Environment.

Bilingual classroom programs teach phonics and phonemic awareness for reading to children who are deaf and hard of hearing by using an approach called Visual Phonics. Visual Phonics can be used with any communication approach. This program uses 46 handshapes and written symbols to represent phonemes. The system was developed in 1982 by a mother of three deaf children and is produced by the International Communication Language Institute (2007). The goal of phonic instruction is to clarify the sound-symbol relationship between spoken English and print (Waddy-Smith & Wilson, 2003). At the Clerc Center in Galluadet University, Visual Phonics is introduced to infants who are deaf or hard of hearing as a natural part of the communicative spectrum that includes ASL, speech, speechreading, and audition. With primary-aged students, the system is used to develop a sound–symbol connection for reading and to support developing speechreading skills.

Teaching Literacy in a Language-Mixing Communication Environment

A language-mixing approach—or total communication, as it is also called—has become the most widely used method of instruction in public schools for students with hearing loss (Andrews et al., 2004). As stated earlier, programs with this emphasis advocate the use of a variety of forms of communication to teach English literacy to students. Practitioners of a language-mixing approach maintain that the simultaneous presentation of the English language by speech and manual communication (signing and fingerspelling) makes it possible for children to use either one or both types of communication (Hawkins & Brawner, 1997). Teachers who practice this approach speak as they sign and make a special effort to follow the form and structure of spoken English. Several English-based sign systems such as *Signing Exact English (SEE–2))* (Gustason et al., 1980) have been designed with the intention of facilitating the development of reading, writing, and other language skills. These sign systems borrow many signs and features of ASL, but attempt to follow correct English usage and word order. Most commonly, a teacher who specializes in the education of the deaf will teach children who are deaf to read and write. Most students who are hard of hearing and have hearing losses of less than 90dB are included in general education settings with varying support from a hearing specialist or teacher of the deaf for supplemental reading instruction if needed, although some may not need additional support.

Wurst, Jones, and Luckner (2005) found that coteaching arrangements for third- and fourth-grade students helped students who were deaf and hard of hearing and their peers make significant gains in reading and writing. All students were taught by two teachers—a general education teacher and a teacher of students who are deaf or hard of hearing—who planned, taught, and shared equal responsibility for the entire class each day. Hearing students were encouraged, but not forced, to develop signing skills. All students learned to use the following techniques to boost reading comprehension: mental imagery, story mapping, prediction, cause and effect, summary, KWL charts (discussed in chapter 9), outlining, comparison and contrast, and blending the writing and reading processes. To aid comprehension, activities were made concrete. For example, to begin the compare-and-contrast activities, the students compared and contrasted their two teachers. Additionally, students used sticky notes to flag unknown words, to identify questions, and to provide examples to show comprehension. The students with hearing loss seemed to respond well to these strategies as well as the dramatic demonstrations, the posting of summarized lessons on classroom walls, and small-group and individual reading conferences.

When students who are deaf or hard of hearing are included in general education classrooms, teachers must provide accommodations that emphasize the visual aspects of communication. Such accommodations are advantageous for all students, irrespective of their hearing ability. Some of the most common adaptations and accommodations follow (Williams & Finnegan, 2003).

❏ Face the class when delivering instructions. Teachers are frequently unaware of how often they speak while writing on the board or removing materials from cabinets.

❏ Make sure one's mouth is fully visible while speaking. Teachers may unwittingly put a pen in their mouth or stand with a part of their face obscured by the overhead projector arm.

❏ Position one's body in front of the student with a hearing loss when offering individual assistance, instead of sitting or kneeling beside the student.

❏ Address the student directly. For example, don't ask the interpreter, "What is *his* favorite book?" Rather, face the child and say, "What is *your* favorite book?"

❏ Identify students by name when conducting large-group discussions. Doing so allows the student who is hard of hearing to identify and turn toward the classmate who is speaking.

❏ Write key information such as new vocabulary, instructions, and homework assignments on the board.

❏ Maximize visual and tactile access to information. Engage in copious use of real objects, charts, illustrations, graphic organizers (discussed in chapter 9), demonstrations, and models when introducing, explaining, and reinforcing information and concepts.

❏ Use advance organizers such as outlines of key information to introduce lessons.

❏ Increase wait time during lessons to allow the interpreter to complete the presentation of information. This pace will allow hearing classmates time to assimilate information as well.

❏ Use captioned versions of films, videos, and TV programs. Captioned Media Program (CMP) at www.cfv.org is an excellent source of captioned films.

❏ Provide the interpreter with a preview of the content to be taught. A key dimension of sign language interpreting is conceptual accuracy. Being able to review key concepts in advance will allow the interpreter to present the information in the most efficient and accurate way.

❏ Meet regularly with the interpreter to assess the delivery of communication services.

❏ Learn signs for vocabulary frequently used in your classroom. An online sign dictionary can be found at http://handspeak.com.

❏ Have hearing classmates learn some basic signs.

❏ Provide students with typical hearing with information about deafness and ways they can better interact with their classmate who has a hearing loss.

❏ Maintain the same level of expectation for the student who is hard of hearing as for other students in the class.

EFFECTIVE INCLUSION PRACTICES

The decision to place children who are deaf or hard of hearing in settings designed for children who can hear should always be made with communication access as the top priority. The most effective environments for children who are deaf or hard of hearing have the following five characteristics (Sass-Lehrer & Bodner-Johnson, 2003; National Association of State Directors of Special Education, 2006): (1) The child with a hearing loss has full access to language; including direct communication with the teacher and peers in the child's preferred language; (2) the program attempts to include Deaf role models and peers for language and positive self-image development; (3) the classroom is a visually rich environment with many avenues for accessing information; (4) personnel who are responsible for implementing the child's educational program are knowledgeable about children who are deaf and their needs, including the needs of their families; and (5) appropriate accommodations are made in the classroom to maximize the child's auditory skills, such as acoustic tiles, carpet, and drapes, and assistive technology is made available on an individualized basis. Naturally, all educational placement decisions should be individualized and support a family's preferences.

CONCLUSION

This chapter briefly described the challenges, choices, and educational options for supporting the development and learning of young children with a hearing loss. As shown in Anna's case study, it is important that parents and ECSE professionals maintain a visual perspective as they plan appropriate interventions for children and their families. The presence of Deaf adults and peers in the lives of children with hearing loss and their families is essential for coming to understand what it means to be Deaf in America today. Advances in technology have increased the opportunities for children who experience hearing loss, allowing many to develop speaking and listening skills. Enhancing auditory and speech skills as shown in Anna's story, does not exclude the use of a visual-manual language and, in fact, increases the chance of successful use of auditory-oral skills in young children (Yoshinaga-Itano, 2003).

SUMMARY

Causes and types of hearing Loss

- Hearing loss may occur due to nongenetic and genetic causes and may be described as sensorineural, conductive, or mixed.

Communication approaches

- Parents of children with hearing loss may choose among four communication approaches: monolingual, language-mixing, cued speech, and bilingual.

Strategies for promoting auditory development

- Auditory development involves training in sound attending, sound recognition, and employing appropriate responses to sound.

Strategies for promoting visual communication

- Just as hearing children learn to use their hearing abilities to develop language and speech, children who are deaf or hard of hearing learn to use their visual-manual skills to interact with their environment and to communicate.

Promoting preliteracy development

- Parents and professionals use sandwiching to teach new vocabulary: (1) Sign the word/phrase, (2) fingerspell new words (when appropriate), (3) point to the object or picture of the object or action when available, and (4) point to the word in print.

Promoting literacy development

- To teach reading and reading comprehension to students with hearing loss, teachers should use mental imagery, story mapping, prediction, cause and effect, summary, KWL charts, outlining, comparison and contrast, dramatic demonstrations, summarized lesson posting, and small-group and individual reading conferences.

DISCUSSION QUESTIONS/ACTIVITIES

1. Describe three topics that might be of interest to parents of an infant who was recently identified as deaf. Discuss how the ECSE professional and the teacher of students who are deaf and hard of hearing might organize information for a discussion with this family.

2. Discuss what it means to be visually oriented from the perspective of a child who is deaf or hard of hearing.

3. Develop a one-page summary of communication options for parents of children with hearing loss. Share this with a parent of a primary-aged child who is deaf or hard of hearing. As you share the information with the parent, note questions or comments he or she makes about the different communication options. Incorporate this parent's comments and questions into your final summary sheet.

REFERENCES

American Speech-Language-Hearing Association. (2001). *Effects of hearing loss*. Retrieved October 15, 2007 from www.asha.org

Andrews, J., Leigh, I., & Weiner, T. (2004). *Deaf people: Evolving perspectives from psychology, education and sociology*. Boston: Pearson Education.

Aram, D., Most, T., & Mayafit, H. (2006). Contributions of mother-child storybook telling and joint writing to literacy development in kindergarteners with hearing loss. *Language, Speech & Hearing Services in the Schools, 37*(3), 209–223.

Arehart, K., & Yoshinaga-Itano, C. (1999). The role of educators of the deaf in the early identification of hearing loss. *American Annals of the Deaf, 144*, 19–23.

Bailes, C. (2001). Integrative ASL-English language arts: Bridging paths to literacy. *Sign Language Studies, 1*(2), 147–174.

Baker, S., & Baker, K. (2000). *Educating children who are deaf or hard of hearing: Bilingual-bicultural education*. ERIC Digest Document No. ED553.

Beiter, A. L., & Shallop, J. K. (1998). Cochlear implants: Past, present, future. In W. Estabrooks (Ed.), *Cochlear implants for kids* (pp. 3—29). Washington, DC: Alexander Graham Bell Association of the Deaf.

Bornstein, H. (1974). Signed English: A manual approach to English language development. *Journal of Speech and Hearing Disorders, 3*, 330–343.

Calderon, R. (2000). Parent involvement in deaf children's programs as a predictor of child's language, early reading, and social-emotional development. *Journal of Deaf Studies and Deaf Education, 5*, 140–155.

Calderon, R. & Greenberg, M. T. (1993). Considerations in the adaptations of families in school-aged Deaf children. In M. Marschark & M. D. Clark (Eds.) *Psychological perspectives on deafness* (pp. 27-47). Hillsdale, NJ: Erlbaum Associates.

Centers for Disease Control and Prevention. Cochlear implants. Retrieved March 25, 2007, from www.cdc.gov

Christiansen, J. B., & Leigh, I. W. (2002). *Cochlear implants in children: Ethics and choices*. Washington, DC: Gallaudet University Press.

Clerc Center. (2007). *Visual phonics*. Gallaudet University. Retrieved March 25, 2007, from www.ClercCenter.com

Cornett, O. (1967). Cued speech. *American* Annals *of the Deaf, 112*, 3–13.

Crandell, C., & Smaldino, J. (2001). Improving classroom acoustics: Utilizing hearing-assistive technology and communication strategies in the educational setting. *Volta Review, 101*(5), 47–64.

Crittenden, J. B., Ritterman, S. I., & Wilcox, E. W. (1986). Communication mode as a factor in performance of hearing-impaired children on a standardized receptive vocabulary test. *American Annals of the Deaf, 131*, 356–360.

Daniels, M. (2001). *Dancing with words: Signing for hearing children's literacy*. Westport, CT: Bergin & Garvey.

DesJardin, J. L. (2005). Maternal perceptions of self-efficacy and involvement in the auditory development of young children with prelingual deafness. *Journal of Early Intervention, 27*, 193–209.

Estabrooks, W. (2000). Auditory-verbal practice. In S. Waltzman & N. Cohen (Eds.), *Cochlear implants* (pp. 225-246). New York: Theime.

Erting, C. J., Prezioso, C., & Hynes, M. (1990). The interactional content of deaf mother-infant communication. In V. Volterra & C. Erting (Eds.), *From gesture to language in hearing and deaf children* (pp. 97–106). New York: Springer-Verlag.

Esler, A., Godber, Y., & Christenson, S. (2002). Best practices in supporting home-school collaboration. In A. Thomas & J. Grimes (Eds.), *Best practices in school psychology: Vol. 1* (pp. 389–411). Bethesda, MD: National Association of School Psychologists.

Geers, A. (2006). Spoken language in children with cochlear implants. In P. Spencer & M. Marschark (Eds.), *Advances in spoken language development in deaf and hard of hearing children* (pp. 244–270). New York: Oxford University Press.

Gustason, G., Pfetzing, D., & Zawolkow, E. (1980). *Signing Exact English (SEE-2).* Los Alamitos, CA: Modern Signs.

Hafer, J. C. (1984). *The effects of signing as a multisensory technique to teach sight vocabulary to learning disabled students.* Unpublished doctoral dissertation, university of Maryland, College Park.

Hafer, J.C., Rooke, C.C., & Charlifue-Smith, R. (2008a). Hearing screening and modification of TPBA for children who are deaf or hard of hearing. In T. Linder (Ed.), *Transdisciplinary play-based assessment,* 2nd ed. (TPBA2) (pp. 265–298). Baltimore: Paul H. Brookes Publishing Co.

Hafer, J. C., Rooke, C. C. & Charlifue-Smith, R. (2008b). Facilitating communication development: Strategies for improving hearing and communication. In T. Linder (Ed.), *Transdisciplinary play-based intervention,* 2nd ed. (TPBI2) *(pp. 453–482).* Baltimore, MD: Paul H. Brookes.

Hafer, J., Spragins, A., & Hardy-Braz, S. (1996). Developmental assessment for the young set: The play's the thing. *Perspectives in Education and Deafness, 14,* 8–10.

Hafer, J., & Stredler-Brown, A. (2003). Family-centered early education. In B. Bodner-Johnson & M. Sass-Lehrer (Eds.), *The young deaf or hard of hearing child: A family-centered approach* (pp. 127–149). Baltimore, MD: Brookes.

Hafer, J. C., & Wilson, R. (1986). *Signing for reading success.* Washington, DC: Gallaudet University Press.

Hawkins, L., & Brawner, J. (1997). *Educating children who are deaf/hard of hearing: Total communication.* ERIC Document Reproduction Service No. ED414677

Hintermair, M. (2000). Hearing impairment, social networks, and coping: The need for families with hearing-impaired children to relate to their parents and to hearing-impaired adults . *American Annals of the Deaf, 145,* 41–51.

House, J. (1999). Hearing loss in adults. *Volta Review, 99*(5), 161–166.

International Communication Language Institute. *Visual phonics.* Retrieved March 25, 2007, from www.icli.org

LaSasso, C., & Metzger, M. (1998). An alternative route for preparing deaf children for BiBi programs in the home language as L1 and cued speech for conveying traditionally spoken languages. *Journal of Deaf Studies and Deaf Education, 3*(4), 265–289.

Lewis, R., & Doolag, D. (1999). *Teaching special students in general education classrooms.* Upper Saddle River, NJ: Merrill/Prentice Hall.

Li, Y., Bain, L., & Steinberg, A. (2004). Parental decision-making in considering cochlear implant technology for a deaf child. *International Journal of Pediatric Otorhinolaryngology, 68,* 1027–1038.

McLaughlin, L., Small, S., Spink-Mitchell, V., & Cripps, J. (2004). *A parent guidebook: ASL and early literacy.* Mississauga, Ontario, Canada: Ontario Society for the Deaf.

McNally, P., Rose, S., & Quigley, S. (1994). *Language learning practices in deaf children.* Austin, TX: Pro-Ed.

Meadow, K. (1980). *Deafness and child development.* Berkeley: University of California Press.

Meadow-Orlans, K., Mertens, D., & Sass-Lehrer, M. (2003). *Parents and their deaf children: The early years.* Washington, DC: Gallaudet University Press.

Meadow-Orlans, K., Mertens, D., Sass-Lehrer, M., & Scott-Olson, K. (1997). Support services for parents and their children who are deaf or hard of hearing: A national survey. *American Annals of the Deaf, 142*(4), 278–293.

Mitchell, R. (2004). National profile of deaf and hard of hearing students in special education from weighted survey results. *American Annals of the Deaf, 149*(4), 336–348.

Moeller, M. P. (2000). Early intervention and language development in children who are deaf and hard of hearing. *Pediatrics, 106,* 43–44.

Mohay, H. (2000). Language in sight: Mothers' strategies for making language visually accessible to deaf children. In P. Spencer, C. Erting, & M. Marschark (Eds.), *The deaf child in the family and at school* (pp. 151–166). Mahwah, NJ: Erlbaum.

Moog, A. (2002). Changing expectations for children with cochlear implants. *Annals of Otology, Rhinology, and Laryngology, 111,* 138–142.

Morgan, D. D. (2004). *Deaf teachers' practices: Supporting and enabling preschool deaf children's development of a participative identity.* Unpublished doctoral dissertation, University of Illinois at Urbana-Champaign.

National Association of State Directors of Special Education. (2006). *Meeting the needs of students who are deaf or hard of hearing: Educational services guideline.* Alexandria, VA: Author.

Nober, E. H. (1996). Audiology and education. In G. E. Sanford (Ed.), *The handbook of pediatric audiology* (pp. 314–342). Washington, DC: Gallaudet University Press.

Nowell, R., & Marshak, L. (1994). An orientation for professionals working with deaf clients. In R. C. Nowell & L. E. Marshak (Eds.), *Understanding deafness and the rehabilitation process* (pp. 1–12). Boston: Allyn & Bacon.

Padden, C., & Humphries, T. (2005). *Inside Deaf culture.* Cambridge, MA: Harvard University Press.

Sass-Lehrer, M. (1999). Techniques for infants and toddlers with hearing loss. In S. A. Raver, *Interventions and strategies for infants and toddlers with special needs: A team approach* (pp. 259–297). Upper Saddle River, NJ: Merrill/Prentice Hall.

Sass-Lehrer, M., & Bodner-Johnson, B. (2003). Early intervention: Current approaches to family-centered programming. In M. Marschark & P. E. Spencer (Eds.), *Deaf studies, language and education* (pp. 65–81). New York: Oxford University Press.

Schlesinger, H. S. (2002). A developmental model applied to problems of deafness. *Journal of Deaf Studies and Deaf Education, 5*(4), 349–361.

Schlesinger, H., & Meadow, K. (1972). *Sound and sign: Childhood deafness and mental health.* Berkeley: University of California Press.

Sebald, A., & Luckner, J. (2007). Successful partnerships with families of children who are deaf . *Teaching Exceptional Children, 39,* 54–60.

Singleton, J. L., & Morgan, D. D. (2004, April). *Becoming Deaf: Deaf teachers' engagement practices supporting deaf children's identity development.* Paper presented at the annual meeting of the American Educational Research Association, San Diego, CA.

Traci, M., & Koester, L. S. (2003). Parent-infant interactions: A transactional approach to understanding the development of deaf infants. In M. Marschark & P. E. Spencer (Eds.), *Deaf studies, language and education* (pp. 65–81). New York: Oxford University Press.

Traxler, C. B. (2000). The Stanford Achievement Test (9th ed.): National norming and performance standards for deaf and hard of hearing students. *Journal of Deaf Studies and Deaf Education, 5*(4), 337–348.

Tucker, B. (1993). Deafness: The dilemma. *The Volta Review, 95,* 105-108.

Veditz, G. (1912). *Proceedings of the Ninth Convention of the National Association of the Deaf and the Third World Congress of the Deaf, 1910.* Philadelphia: Philocophus Press.

Waddy-Smith, B., & Wilson, V. (2003). See that sound: Visual phonics for deaf children. *Odyssey, 5,* 1.

Williams, C. B., & Finnegan, M. (2003). From myth to reality: Sound information for teachers about students who are deaf. *Teaching Exceptional Children, 35*(3), 40–45.

Wurst, D., Jones, D., & Luckner, J. (2005). Promoting literacy development with students who are deaf, hard of hearing and hearing. *Teaching Exceptional Children, 37*(5), 56–62.

Yoshinaga-Itano, C. (2003). From screening to early identification and intervention: Discovering predictors to successful outcomes for children with significant hearing loss. *Journal of Deaf Studies and Deaf Education, 8*(1), 11–30.

Yoshinaga-Itano, C. (2006). Early identification, communication modality, and the development of speech and spoken language skills: Patterns and considerations. In P. E. Spencer & M. Marschark (Eds.), *Advances in the spoken language development of deaf and hard-of-hearing children* (pp. 298–327). New York: Oxford University Press.

Yoshinaga-Itano, C., Sedey, A. L., Coulter, D. K., & Thomson, V. (2000). Infant hearing impairment and universal hearing screening. *Journal of Perinatology, 20,* 132-137.

Chapter
12

Techniques for Teaching Young Children with Low Vision and Blindness

Tanni L. Anthony

Overview

This chapter discusses characteristics and intervention practices with children with vision problems and visual impairment, including

definitions of vision problems and visual impairment

prevalence of visual impairment

specialized related-services professionals

types and causes of vision problems and visual impairment

impact of vision loss on development

assessment

specialized areas of instruction

CASE STUDY: Maddie

Maddie is a 4-year-old who loves her floppy-eared stuffed dog, Sam, and playing "school." She has vision only in one quadrant of one eye due to a congenital retinal disorder. She is primarily a tactile and an auditory learner.

Maddie attends a school district inclusive preschool program that is Montessori in design. Rita, who is both a certified teacher of the visually impaired (TVI) and an orientation and mobility (O&M) specialist, has worked with Maddie for two years. Sara, Maddie's general education teacher, has found that Maddie benefits from the same things that other preschoolers do: structure, organization, consistency, child-led experiences, social opportunities and guidance, and, most importantly, hands-on learning. Sara has also learned how the materials in her classroom could be adapted for Maddie. Tactile markers and braille labels were added to cubbies, centers, books, and toys.

During the first few months of Maddie's preschool experience, Rita stayed in the classroom to facilitate activities and groups and to provide adults and children with strategies for working and interacting with a child with a visual impairment. The time Rita spent in consultation and planning with Sara diminished as Sara's familiarity with how to nurture Maddie's experiences expanded.

The current areas of focus have been Maddie's social experiences with peers, learning to read and write using braille, and orientation and mobility skills. Rita has worked with Sara to embed braille in the activities and routines of the classroom. Maddie has learned about braille in the same way her sighted peers have learned about print. Her hands seek out braille in storybooks and other materials that are labeled in print and braille in the classroom. She has a braillewriter in her classroom and at home, which she uses to "scribble" and pretend write. Storybooks have accompanying objects and tactile components to reinforce the stories' concepts, since Maddie does not have visual access to the book's pictures. Maddie has peel-off braille labels of her name that she uses to label her artwork. Her mom has learned braille and supports early literacy activities at home. Maddie is surrounded by people who know her strengths and see her as a typical child who happens to have a visual impairment.

Special thanks to Maddie's mom, Paula, and her TVI/O&M specialist, Rita, for their contributions to this case study.

Imagine walking into a busy early childhood special education preschool classroom. Canvassing the room, a few children may stand out as having a vision problem. One boy playing alone at the sand table has an eye that has a tendency to cross. A pretty little girl with Down syndrome is looking at a book with her friend, holding the book about five inches from her face. Another child, a surviving twin of a premature birth, looks up as you walk by, and you notice that her eyes are moving quickly back and forth. Will any of these children have a vision concern that will significantly affect their development?

While some vision concerns are more obvious than others, it has been estimated that 1 in 20 young children exhibits some type of a visual challenge (Schor, 1990). Menacker and Batshaw (1997) report that disabilities involving genetic syndromes, neurological damage, and/or prenatal infections are likely to have an associated vision concern.

It is important for all early childhood professionals to be aware of populations that are at high risk for vision concerns, to know warning signs of a vision problem, and to know which professionals should be on the intervention team when a child has an identified visual impairment. This chapter will provide an overview of some of the needs of young children with visual impairment and offer general ideas for supporting their development. Many definitions are used to describe children who do not see or who do not see well.

DEFINITIONS OF VISION PROBLEMS AND VISUAL IMPAIRMENT

It is helpful to sort out the differences between a vision problem and a visual impairment. A **vision problem** typically involves a concern with visual performance that can be treated with a medical procedure or prescription lenses, whereas a **visual impairment** involves vision loss that cannot be corrected to within normal ranges. The little boy playing in the sand table does have an eye that occasionally crosses. The intervention team noticed that the crossing was more pronounced when he was tired. Under the guidance of a **pediatric ophthalmologist,** a medical doctor specializing in the eye care and eye surgery of children, this child was prescribed a patch to wear over the eye that did not cross for a certain part of each day. Over a three-month period, the child's eye crossed less. The child's mother shared that the family will continue to see the eye doctor, since her son may be a candidate for corrective surgery if the crossing persists.

The girl holding the book close to her face has a vision problem called refractive error, which will be explained in the section on common causes of vision problems. She is very nearsighted and benefits from glasses prescribed by an **optometrist**, a person trained and licensed to examine eyes, diagnose vision problems and visual impairments, and prescribe glasses. After wearing glasses for only a month, the staff of her preschool program reported that she now pays more attention during "looking" activities and, for the first time, comments on the details in pictures.

The majority of pediatric vision problems will not result in permanent visual impairment. Certain vision problems, if detected in infancy and the preschool years, respond favorably to medical treatment, like those of the first two children described. The earlier a vision problem is detected, the better the outcome is from possible treatment (Whetsell, 1996).

However, not all vision concerns identified in the early years are correctable. The rapid eye movement exhibited by the child who was born prematurely is called **sensory nystagmus**. Nystagmus, in this situation, is poor vision due to damage to both eyes in the first year of life. In this child's case, the visual impairment was the result of an eye condition called retinopathy of prematurity (ROP), which will be explained in the section on causes. Despite two retinal surgeries, this child has a permanent visual impairment. The child will be a good candidate for a **low-vision evaluation**. An eye doctor, usually an optometrist, who specializes in low vision will determine the child's prescriptive needs for near and/or distance magnification devices that may be used at home, in the classroom, and within her community.

In order to be classified as having a visual impairment under the IDEA (2004), a child must have an eye examination to determine the health and optimal functioning of the child's eyes with or without prescriptive correction. Infants, toddlers, preschoolers, and children from 6 to 9 years of age can be evaluated successfully by a pediatric ophthalmologist or optometrist. Early intervention and ECSE professionals can observe visual functioning, but cannot diagnose a vision problem or determine whether a child's vision would benefit from medical or prescriptive treatment. These responsibilities are managed by an eye-care specialist during a thorough visual examination.

In the event that a visual issue cannot be treated and the child's vision remains permanently altered, a variety of terms may be used to describe the visual impairment. **Visual impairment** is an umbrella term used to describe uncorrectable and permanent vision loss that impacts day-to-day visual functioning. A person who is considered visually impaired may be totally blind or may have varying degrees of compromised visual functioning.

The two areas most often addressed in defining visual impairment are visual acuity and visual field. **Visual acuity** describes the clarity of the visual image, with 20/20 being the standard notation for normal vision. The bottom number of the visual-acuity equation increases (e.g., 20/40, 20/200, 20/400) as a person's visual acuity worsens. To better understand a visual-acuity notation, envision a room that is 200 feet long. At one end of the room on the wall is a large clock. A person with 20/20 visual acuity can stand at the other end of the room, 200 feet away from the clock, and tell the time. A person with 20/200 visual acuity will need to stand 20 feet away from the same clock to determine the time. A person with 20/400 acuity will need to be 20 feet away from the item that the person with 20/20 vision can see at 400 feet. These are examples of distance-vision acuity. In addition, a child's near-vision acuity should be evaluated to determine visual performance for close-viewing tasks.

Visual acuity is determined typically through the use of optotype charts where numbers, letters, shapes, or pictures give precise clinical measurements that relate to the Snellen equivalents of 20/20, 20/40, and so on, depending on the size of the optotype and its distance of presentation. Infants and young children who are not able to verbally identify or point to identical optotypes (this requires the ability to match) can still be examined for the presence of refractive error (need for prescriptive lenses) with an instrument called a retinoscope while the eyes are dilated during an eye examination. Another procedure used with young children or children with additional disabilities is called the **forced-choice preferential looking procedure,** which involves special grating cards with black and white lines with different cycles of frequencies (Daw, 1995). A child is visually presented with two targets, one a uniform gray stimulus and one a certain level of grating. Gradually, the examiner introduces grating cards that are less visually distinct than the prior ones until the child is no longer able to demonstrate a visual preference between the two cards. The examiner then notes the level of distinction or grating that the child can distinguish.

Visual field is defined as "the extent in which objects are visible to a stationary eye" (Leat, Shute, & Westall, 1999, p. 245). A normal visual field extends about 180 degrees from one side of the head to the other side when one is looking straight ahead. The top of the visual field is slightly above one's head (50 degrees), and the bottom field parameter is below the chin (70 degrees). Visual-field loss can manifest in a number of ways, such as (1) **tunnel vision** (visualize looking through a tube where **peripheral vision,** or side vision, is unavailable); (2) absent or compromised **central vision** (the "straight-ahead" best viewing vision); (3) missing quadrants or spots of vision (**scotomas** or blind spots); (4) the opposite, where there are just spots of vision ("Swiss cheese" vision); and/or (5) **hemanopsia** (loss of half the vision field in each eye).

An individual can have reduced visual acuity, reduced visual field, or both. Other complications, though usually not noted in regulatory definitions of vision loss, include compromised color vision, eye-teaming abilities, and interpretation of the visual image.

Within the spectrum of the term *visual impairment*, a number of other definitions are used to describe specified levels of visual functioning. One such term is **legal blindness**. This is a term most often used for federal or state program entitlement purposes (Ferrell, Raver, & Stewart, 1999) and involves central visual acuity of 20/200 or less in the best eye after correction or a visual-field loss where the peripheral field is no greater than 20 degrees in the better eye (Koestler, 1976).

According to the IDEA (2004) eligibility criteria, special education services must be provided when the nature of a child's vision loss requires such services (Pugh & Erin, 1999). Most state eligibility definitions include acuity- and field-loss

criteria as well as other considerations, such as whether there is a progressive vision loss. Most ECSE and school-age programs for children with visual impairment have an entrance visual acuity of 20/70. The term **low vision** describes corrected and useable vision in the better eye starting at 20/70 distance-vision acuity (Corn & Koenig, 1996). Some states have expanded the definition of blindness/visual impairment to include learners identified with cortical visual impairment (Colorado Department of Education, 2000). **Cortical or cerebral visual impairment** is typically measured not in terms of visual acuity and/or field loss, but by neurological evidence of damage to the visual pathways and/or visual cortex with subsequent loss of visual functioning. More information about this condition is included in upcoming sections.

Visual impairment can be **congenital**, occurring at birth, as in the case of children who are born with **congenital cataracts**, an opacity of the internal lens of the eye. Another example of congenital visual impairment is **albinism**, a genetic condition affecting the pigment of the eyes and sometimes the skin and hair. Visual impairment may also be **adventitious**, or acquired after birth. Children and adults may lose their sight, for example, due to **optic atrophy**, a condition affecting the health of the optic nerve. There are also eye conditions that affect the macular health of young children, thus impacting their central vision.

Visual impairments are static or progressive. A **static visual impairment** should not worsen over time. For example, the child with albinism will not show a decrease of visual function as he or she ages unless there is an unexpected complication from another eye condition. **Progressive visual impairments** include **retinitis pigmentosa**, where the retina loses function over time and the vision loss typically progresses over many years from poor night vision and limited peripheral vision to possible total blindness.

While a medical diagnosis is necessary to determine if a child's vision is corrected at its optimal level, a clinical examination in an eye doctor's office may not yield significant functional information.

Two children with the same diagnoses, such as **aniridia,** a condition affecting the eyes' iris, may have visual acuities at 20/200 in each eye and yet may present completely different visual performances. **Functional vision** is a term that describes how a person uses his or her vision in everyday living environments despite diminished acuity, field, color vision, eye teaming, and/or interpretation of the visual image. Many internal and external factors influence a child's functional vision. Internal factors include postural stability, fatigue, illness, stress, motivation, and the possible effects of medication (Anthony, 2000). External factors include lighting, glare, contrast, colors, familiarity, size, visual clutter, background complexity of a visual array, and ambient noise (Anthony, 2000).

Children with visual impairment are highly diverse in their level of visual functioning and the presence of additional disabilities. Evidence of accompanying disabilities, including hearing loss, seizure disorder, and/or physical disabilities, is well documented in children with visual impairments (Bishop, 1991; Deitz & Ferrell, 1993; Hatton, Bailey, Burchinal, & Ferrell, 1997; Dote-Kwan, Chen, & Hughes 2001). About 50%–70% of children with visual impairment have additional disabilities, including deaf-blindness. These learners have the same needs for specialized vision assessment and instruction as children with visual impairment and no other disabilities do.

Some children may enter an early childhood or ECSE program based on an identified disability or an at-risk condition not directly understood to be associated with a vision problem (Allen & Fraser, 1983). Children with mild visual impairment might not be identified until there are developmental and/or academic achievement consequences from their visual impairment (Hatton, 2001).

PREVALENCE OF VISUAL IMPAIRMENT

A relatively small percentage of persons with visual impairment in the United States are children. It has been estimated that 1 in 3,000 children has a severe visual disability (Foster, 1988) and that the prevalence of visual impairment in

American children under 5 years of age is 0.42 to 0.86 per 1,000 (Kirchner, 1989).

One data collection challenge specific to the incidence of visual impairment is the federally mandated December 1 Count, an annual count of special education students in public schools. Children with Individualized Education Programs (IEPs) are reported in one primary-disability category. There are fewer than 2 in 1,000 school-aged children counted as having a *primary* disability of visual impairment receiving special education in the United States (U.S. Office of Special Education, 2004). However, this procedure results in serious underreporting, as it excludes learners with visual impairments who are counted in other primary-disability categories, such as multiple disabilities (Kirchner, 1989; Vaughn & Scholl, 1980), and typically does not include infants and toddlers. The American Printing House for the Blind (APH) Registry, which also completes a national count, indicated that, in 2005, there were 54,637 children, from birth through 21 years of age, with legal blindness across the country (APH, 2005). Included in this number were 5,401 infants and toddlers (for those states submitting data on this age group) and 5,691 preschoolers.

SPECIALIZED RELATED-SERVICES PROFESSIONALS

There are two educational professionals specifically trained to address the unique learning needs of children with visual impairment. A certified **teacher of students with visual impairments (TVI)** has a university degree in the education of children and youth who are blind/visually impaired, including those who have additional disabilities and/or deaf-blindness. A TVI performs the following essential functions on infant, toddler, preschool, and school-age teams: (1) provides information about common challenges associated in each developmental domain due to early onset of visual impairment; (2) interprets eye reports; (3) recommends and procures specialized technology; (4) provides specialized instruction, such as teaching braille codes or training the child to use prescribed low-vision devices; (5) works with families and with general and ECSE teachers to modify home routines or classroom instruction and assignments; (6) offers specific suggestions for accommodations that support learning and participation; and (7) completes and/or consults in educational assessments.

The second professional who has specialized training to support the learning of children with visual impairment is an **orientation and mobility (O&M) specialist**. An O&M specialist is a related-service provider who has specific training in supporting the travel needs of individuals of all ages with visual impairment. An O&M specialist provides the following supports to children and the team: (1) helps team members identify a child's motor and movement skills and needs, (2) determines the need for adapted mobility devices and/or a long cane, and (3) teaches children specific strategies for travel within familiar and unfamiliar environments. Like the TVI, this specialist should be consulted when assessing and developing intervention plans for young children

with visual impairment. An individual may be dually certified as a TVI and an O&M specialist.

TYPES AND CAUSES OF VISION PROBLEMS AND VISUAL IMPAIRMENT

Children may experience poor visual functioning for a variety of reasons. The four most common vision problems in young children are amblyopia, strabismus, refractive errors, and, to a lesser extent, color vision deficiency (American Academy of Ophthalmology, 1997; Gerali, Flom, & Raab, 1990). The prevalence and characteristics of each of these conditions are summarized in Table 12.1.

The little boy at the sand table with the occasional eye crossing was found to have strabismus and was treated by the family's eye doctor. Infants as young as 6 months that show signs of poor eye alignment should be referred to an eye-care specialist (Schor, 1990). If the eye is not treated, the result may be suppression of vision in the affected eye, leading to amblyopia.

Children born prematurely or with deafness, cerebral palsy, or a syndrome, such as the little

TABLE 12.1 Four common vision problems found in young children

Vision Problem	Description	Prevalence
Amblyopia	Also called *lazy eye*. Involves suppression of a weaker eye.	2%–5% of children (Daw, 1995; Menacker & Batshaw, 1997; Simons, 1996; von Noorden, 1996).
Strabismus	A misalignment of the eyes, which causes one or both of the eyes to deviate (American Academy of Ophthalmology, 1997).	3%–4% of the general pediatric population, 15% of premature infants, and 40% of children diagnosed with cerebral palsy (Menacker & Batshaw, 1997).
Refractive error	Blurred vision due to nearsightedness, farsightedness, and/or astigmatism (imperfect curvature of the cornea).	Close to 5% of the school-age population (American Academy of Ophthalmology, 1997).
Color deficiency	Can range from a slight color deficiency (red-green color confusion) to total color blindness.	Red-green color blindness in 8% of Caucasian males and 0.5%–1% of Caucasian females (Goble, 1984).

girl at the beginning of the chapter with Down syndrome, often have an increased incidence of refractive error. Most refractive errors can be corrected with prescriptive lenses, such as glasses or contact lenses.

Color vision problems present a challenge to the young child, as preschool and elementary instruction involves color identification, matching, and sorting. One parent noted that her two sons, both of whom have color vision deficiencies, experienced problems finding the dyed eggs during Easter egg hunts, matching their clothes, and reading bar graphs in mathematics (Barbara Graydon, personal communication, December 2005). Other education-related problems experienced by children with color vision challenges include teasing by peers because of choosing unusual colors for artwork (such as green people), a reluctance to read out loud stemming from a text passage written in blue on a purple background, and frustration with detecting the boundary lines of a gym game because they were drawn with orange chalk on the green grass (Agape Optometry Center, 2006).

Causes of Visual Impairment

There are many reasons why a young child may have a visual impairment. Early-onset visual impairment may be the result of an inherited condition, a disruption of the development of the eye in utero due to prenatal toxins or other factors, an anoxic (i.e., without oxygen) episode, a physical trauma to the eye and/or brain, and/or a postnatal infection (Ferrell, Raver, & Stewart, 1999). The three leading causes of pediatric visual impairment in the United States are cortical visual impairment, retinopathy of prematurity, and optic nerve hypoplasia (Ferrell, 1998; Steinkuller et al., 1999; Hatton, 2001; World Health Organization, 1992). All these conditions result in varying levels of functional vision. Each will be briefly discussed, identifying cause, characteristics, and prevalence.

Cortical Visual Impairment. Cortical visual impairment or **cerebral visual impairment (CVI)** occurs when there is congenital or acquired damage to the posterior visual pathways, to the visual cortex, or to both areas of the brain (Jan & Groenveld, 1993). Simply put, it is visual impairment due to brain damage. Typical causes of CVI are oxygen deprivation, head trauma, and/or infections of the central nervous system (Good et al., 1994). Deficiencies associated with CVI include variability of vision, poor visual attention, field loss, and light sensitivity (Jan & Groenveld, 1993; Jan, Groenveld, Sykanda, & Hoyt, 1987).

Cortical visual impairment can be a self-standing diagnosis, or it can be accompanied by ocular visual impairment, vision loss resulting from damage to the eye (Jan & Groenveld, 1993). Ferrell (1998) found that 91% of children with a diagnosis of CVI had one or more additional disabilities. The most common secondary disabilities with CVI are cerebral palsy and seizure disorder. Cortical or cerebral visual impairment is a leading cause of pediatric visual impairment in the developed world (Brodskey, Baker, & Hamed, 1996). Its prevalence has been estimated as high as 72 per 100,000 children (Flanagan, Jackson, & Hill, 2003).

Retinopathy of Prematurity. Premature infants, especially those with low birth weights, are at significant risk for a host of vision concerns, including blindness (van Hof–van Duin & Pott, 1996). Common vision problems associated with premature birth include strabismus and mild to severe refractive error (Menacker & Batshaw, 1997). Close to two-thirds of infants weighing less than three pounds will develop some degree of **retinopathy of prematurity (ROP)** (Keith & Doyle, 1995), which affects the retina of the eye. At its most serious level, ROP can involve total retinal detachment, which results in blindness in one or both of the affected eyes.

The prevalence of ROP has increased in the past two decades due to the survival of very-low-birth-weight infants (Phelps, 1993). Premature infants with a birth weight less than 1.65 pounds or 750 grams are 50% more likely to have a severe visual impairment due to ROP.

Optic Nerve Hypoplasia. The third leading cause of visual impairment in young children in the United States is **optic nerve hypoplasia (ONH)**, or underdeveloped optic nerves in one or both eyes. The condition occurs in utero while the optic nerves are developing.

The range of vision loss in children with ONH is vast. Visual acuity may range from normal levels to light perception only. Field loss and astigmatism are common. ONH is often associated with other central nervous system problems, such as endocrine problems or midline neurological anomalies (Blind Babies Foundation, 1998). Children with ONH should also be evaluated by an endocrinologist for a possible related growth hormone deficiency (Erin, Fazzi, Gordon, Isenberg, & Paysse, 2002).

There are many other visual impairment diagnoses besides the three reviewed. A TVI is trained to help families and ECSE teachers interpret eye reports, including the details of a particular eye condition and its unique functional vision implications. Visual impairment affects every aspect of a child's development in some way.

THE IMPACT OF VISION LOSS ON DEVELOPMENT

Vision is unique for its role in organizing other sensory information and its provision of simultaneous information from near and distant locations (Teplin, 1982, 1995). A mild-to-severe visual impairment can alter all facets of a child's development. The more significant the visual impairment is, the more potential impact there may be on a child's development (Hatton et al., 1997).

If developmental concerns and educational needs are not addressed proactively, developmental hurdles may lead to lifelong problems that can affect adult independence and employment. Providing appropriate literacy and career-linking experiences during the formative years will improve employment outcomes later in life (Wolffe, 1999).

Characteristics of Children with Vision Loss

Research on young children with visual impairment has often had significant methodological limitations. Sample size is frequently low because of the relatively small numbers of children who are totally blind or who have comparable vision functioning and the small number of children with visual impairment who do not have additional disabilities. Further, the research has often been comparative in nature, which Warren (2006) asserts may be a flawed methodology, since it focuses almost exclusively on the effects of visual impairment without examining the possible benefits. Researchers frequently have failed to examine the outcome of educating children in environments in which there are high expectations and in which equal access is provided. Simply put, these studies may not have taken into account why certain children of the same age and visual functioning may have a wide range of performance, including age-appropriate and even precocious development. Warren (2006) stresses the value of case studies with children with visual impairment, as this design offers rich insight into the individuality of children by examining family support and environmental support factors that appear to facilitate the child's experiences.

While there are numerous research studies involving young children with visual impairment, only a handful have had an impressive sample size and were longitudinal. Two studies that have these characteristics are the Visually Impaired Infants Research Consortium (VIIRC) and Project PRISM. The first study examined the developmental patterns of 314 children with visual impairments from birth through 5 years of age (Ferrell & Mamer, 1992). The second study was a five-year longitudinal study that involved 203 children with visual impairment between the ages of birth and 5 years (Ferrell, 1998). Both studies have provided important information about the developmental sequence and challenges of young children with visual impairment, including those with additional disabilities.

These studies have found evidence of on-time milestone attainment in many domains as well as verification of specific developmental challenges in other domains. In general, visual impairment should be considered a "disability of access." Without the same information that sighted peers receive, the child who is visually impaired is at risk for fragmented information and/or missed learning opportunities. Professionals working with children with early-onset vision loss must assume the responsibility of creating equal access to developmentally appropriate learning opportunities in the home and in school. Professionals must promote high expectations, while attempting to diminish possible overprotectiveness manifested by some family members and professionals. As a rule, what is expected of the sighted child should also be expected of the child who is blind or visually impaired (Ryles, 2004). With high expectations in mind, it is helpful to understand some the developmental challenges that vision loss may impose on young children. Cognitive, communication, fine and gross motor, and social-emotional development will be discussed, as will characteristics of preliteracy and literacy development.

Cognitive Development

Infants, Toddlers, Preschoolers, and Primary-Aged Students. Early-onset visual impairment will affect the quantity and quality of information available to a child for understanding his or her world. The child who is blind is faced with constructing reality without the benefit of vision, which is the most critical sense for the acquisition of knowledge (Bigelow, 1986).

One might conclude that hearing is an immediate "fill-in" for a very young child who is blind or visually impaired. However, sound is *not* a substitute for sight in the first year of life (Fraiberg, 1968). Auditory information is not tangible, and without sight to confirm the sound source, listening and holding are two separate events. Bigelow (1986) summarized this reality in this way: "The

sensory information available to blind children, particularly auditory information, may not provide them with adequate cues for the construction of external reality[, that is,] to hear something may not initially cue blind children to the existence of something and/or its location in space" (p. 355).

Hearing, unlike seeing, usually does not provide continuous feedback. Unlike the sighted child who has steady access to a visual situation, the child who is blind does not have a constant supply of auditory information, and what is provided may or may not have meaning to the child. Most sounds are intermittent and even random throughout the child's day. Without vision to confirm the presence of a sound source, these noises will not have much meaning to the young child until there is *direct personal experience* to associate what is happening with the sounds. Making this association concrete and meaningful for a child is one of the jobs professionals assume. They guide parents, and others, in specific ways to help a child connect sounds with objects, people, actions, and events.

Even school-age children are at risk for misinterpreting sounds due to a lack of personal experience. One child with blindness interpreted the sounds of cupboards and drawers opening and closing and pots and dishes rattling with actual cooking. Without having any explanation or being shown what was happening, the child did not understand that food was being taken from the pantry, mixed in bowls, and heated on the stove before it magically appeared in front of her (Sally Mangold, personal communication, October 1996).

Object Permanence. Hearing and vision play an important role in the acquisition of **object permanence,** the understanding that objects exist even when they are out of sight. The infant with sight is lured by visual interest to reach out for nearby objects, whereas the child with significant visual impairment must wait for the acquisition of true object permanence in order to conceptualize a world beyond immediate touch. Research has indicated that children who are blind acquire object permanence over a wide age-range, including evidence of on-schedule acquisition based on sighted norms (Fraiberg, Siegel, & Gibson, 1966; Rogers & Puchalski, 1988).

The varied age-range of object permanence acquisition should be regarded not as a delay, but perhaps as a fair consequence of blindness. Bigelow (1986) suggests that both sighted and blind children seem to acquire object permanence through comparable cognitive processes. Infants with sight will reach for an object in view by 24–28 weeks of development, but there is no equivalent achievement for infants with visual impairment until 10 months or later, when true object permanence is demonstrated (Fraiberg et al., 1966). Children with sight have the advantage of having access to the world beyond their body because the objects are visually "there." The child with vision loss will have fewer experiences with reaching out to touch and explore objects because the objects are not "there" for them. Parents and early interventionists need to work together to create situations in which the smallest movement will put the child with visual impairment in contact with objects so that exploration and reaching are learned as close to typical attainment times as possible.

Learning about objects and the world is reinforced by consistent and frequent play opportunities. All children benefit from repeated practice with object manipulation and social interaction. If an object is dropped, the sighted child and often the child with low vision can visually locate the object and, if it is within easy reach, can retrieve the object for continued play. When a child is significantly visually impaired, the object may be thought to be lost, and play is disrupted or discontinued. It is important that adults create numerous opportunities for repeated object exploration and play throughout the day as well as teach the child with visual impairment how to search for dropped objects.

Imitation. Imitation is largely motivated by vision. As children observe others doing tasks, they repeat what they have seen. It may be as simple as mimicking certain facial expressions, stacking blocks into a tower like a playmate, making a sandwich like the one big brother made yesterday, or copying the homework assignment off the board. Most children with visual impairment will not benefit from visual imitation. At times, it will be helpful for parents and teachers to physically guide the child through certain actions and/or to use language to describe the movements needed. When physically guiding a child, it is best to work from behind the child so the action is modeled as it naturally occurs from the child's perspective.

Incidental Learning. Children with vision benefit from incidental learning all the time. **Incidental learning** involves gathering information simply by observing people and objects. Incidental learning begins in infancy and continues throughout a person's life.

An infant with sight sees the mobile over her crib rotate and hears its music as her mother winds it up each night. This repeated observation leads to an eventual understanding of early cause and effect (i.e., an action causes a result). A preschooler with sight notices the teacher walking toward the cupboard and knows that soon the teacher will say it is time for afternoon snack. This child observes further that the crackers are stored in the cupboard by the microwave, while the cheese and juice come from the refrigerator. This observation not only confirms the location of objects, building spatial relationships, but also instills the notions that there are different places to store food (i.e., classification) and that food from the refrigerator is cold (i.e., the concept of temperature). A student with sight in first grade examines the large alphabet letters on the classroom wall and notices the ones that are in her name as well as the fact that the letter *B* is next to a picture of a bat, ball, and balloon.

These same situations are different for children with significant vision loss. The infant with visual impairment learns that the music of the mobile is preceded by a light breeze to her face. The preschooler learns that the sounds of cupboards and the refrigerator opening and closing signal the preparation of snack. The first grader learns that her name is comprised of individual letters and that a letter can represent the first sound in certain words as she masters the braille code, but she is unaware of the alphabet strip on her classroom wall. In the absence of visually based incidental learning, the child with significant vision loss learns through touch, sounds, and smells *only*. If the child has low vision, learning will also come from opportunities for closer viewing.

Children with visual impairment learn concepts or understandings about people, objects, events, and symbols through *deliberate exposure* and *direct teaching*. To build concepts, parents and professionals must ensure that children with vision loss have experiences similar to the visually based incidental learning experiences that their sighted peers have every day.

Interestingly, reduced opportunities for incidental learning may impact career development even for very young children (Wolffe, 1999). Unless a child with visual impairment is exposed methodically to the milieu of everyday employment, there are missed opportunities to observe and learn about the work of others, such as the mailperson delivering mail and the bank teller handling a deposit. Without these observations and the information gained from them, children with vision loss have fewer notions about the wide variety of jobs that they might aspire to pursue unless someone consciously makes this information available.

Concept Development. To develop a complete and comprehensive understanding of concepts, children require repeated and frequent interactions with people and objects. Concept development can never be taken for granted with children with vision loss who learn about the world from a part-to-whole perspective. Children with sight see the whole object and then focus on a particular detail. The child who is blind moves from a "part" of an object to the "whole" and requires time to learn about the features of objects firsthand. If a child's only experience with a spoon is to have the bowl of the spoon dipped into her mouth while being fed, the child will have a limited understanding of *spoon*. To expand the concept of spoon, the child

needs to hold it, throw it, mouth it, explore it from its handle to its bowl, and bang it so its physical properties and function are more completely understood.

Later, when the child is a preschooler, large plastic spoons can be used in the sandbox for transferring sand into containers, and different-sized metal spoons can be experienced during snack, with smaller ones used for eating soup, larger ones used for serving food, and slotted ones used for capturing solids and letting liquid fall through. These varied opportunities with the concept of spoon fuel the child's ability to generalize that there are many types of the same item and that there is more than one function for most items. Children must experience these differences *firsthand*, since they do not have visual access to all the varieties any object may present. Maddie's preschool teacher, discussed in the case study, found that providing more examples of concepts for Maddie aided the concept learning of all the children in her class.

Some visually based concepts, such as colors, mirror images, shadows, and outer space are complicated for a young child with visual impairment to understand. It is important to put such concepts into the perspective of a child's current developmental level. The preschooler can be exposed to trees of varying heights, starting with a small sampling that can be explored from top to bottom. As the tree's height increases, there can be discussion about how the top of the tree or even branches cannot be reached unless the child is lifted higher and then they cannot be reached even when sitting on Dad's shoulders. This makes the concepts of high/higher and tall/taller more concrete. This experience can be used to build a framework for understanding the extreme heights of buildings, clouds, and outer space. Later, after the primary-aged student is exposed to and understands topographical maps, vertical space will be better conceptualized.

Fazzi and Klein (2002) recommend linking visually based concepts to those that can be represented through auditory or tactile means. This may not provide a true understanding of the

Maddie, discussed in the case study, participates in a messy, two-handed art activity designed to help her develop the tactile skills she will need to be an effective braille reader and writer later in the primary grades.

visual concept, but may result in an improved conceptual framework for the child. For example, shades of colors may be equated to different volumes of sound, growing louder as the color becomes bolder. A pink color may be a soft sound, while red is a loud bang. While these examples do not teach the true quality of colors for preschoolers and primary-aged students, they provide a basis for understanding how colors can be different in their prominence of hue. Teachers certified in the area of visual impairments will work with parents and teachers of preschoolers and primary-aged students to ensure that children with vision loss have a steady diet of appropriate, concrete opportunities for concept development.

Social-Emotional Development

Infants and Toddlers. Early communication and caregiver-child connection are accomplished through facial expressions, body movements, cries, and vocalizations. Eye contact is a typical way adults "connect" with an infant. When an infant is significantly visually impaired and eye contact is not an avenue of connection, professionals must guide parents in finding other ways to connect with their child. For example, the caregiver might find that the infant responds positively to nuzzling the side of

his head or gently patting his chest and/or to the soothing croon of a familiar voice. These actions tell the child "I am here for you."

Without sight to announce one's arrival, a young child with significant visual impairment may startle if picked up without auditory and/or tactile cueing. This startle may be concerning to parents or caregivers, who may not understand that the child did not have preparation for being picked up suddenly. Voice and touch cues, such as first talking to the child ("I am going to pick you up") and then patting him or her before moving one's hands underneath the child's body to pick the child up, give the child a signal that something is about to happen and who will be doing it.

There is evidence that mothers of infants with vision loss make positive adaptations to compensate for their child's lack of vision (Preisler, 1991). In her study of ten infants with blindness, Fraiberg (1977) found that the infants with blindness manifested social smiling at about the same time as infants with sight. The smiles were initiated first through tactile stimulation such as tickling, bouncing, nuzzling, and then voice stimulation. In this study, smiling during the first year appeared to be more a response to another person's social contact than a means to initiate social contact. This finding was supported by Rogers and Puchalski (1986), who commented further that the blind infants' smiles in response to their parents' social behavior served to continue the interaction.

Preschoolers and Primary-Aged Children. A child develops emotional security and learns social rules as he or she matures, both of which are reinforced by those around the child. A toddler with sight looks across the room, receiving reassurance that her mother is still there. A preschooler with sight receives a nod of approval for appropriate behavior or an admonishing look for unsafe or inappropriate behavior from her teacher. These are examples of nonverbal communications that are not available to the child with no or limited distance vision. The inability to benefit from nonverbal information may affect the ability of a child with a visual impairment to interpret and generalize from the actions of others (Ferrell, Raver, & Stewart, 1999). Consequently, the adults in a child's life must provide direct verbal information to replace any nonverbal communication a child may be missing in order to expand a child's knowledge base. For example, a parent might say, "Andrew saw you when he came into the playground and is running over to say hi."

Further, children with visual impairment may be at risk for social behavior differences that may impede their peer and adult relationships. Without the benefit of visually mediated peer interaction, for example, some young children with vision loss may focus only on their own interests and activities, may abruptly change conversational topics, and/or may be less responsive to their conversational partner's comments or topics (Anderson, Dunlea, & Kekelis, 1984a; Chernus-Mansfield, Hayashi, Horn, & Kekelis, 1985; Zell Sacks, Kekelis, & Gaylord-Ross, 1999). Some children may have fewer self-initiated social interactions and may spend more instructional time alone, waiting to be approached by their peers (Hoben & Lindstrom, 1980). For these reasons, specific social-skill training that teaches how to initiate and participate in conversations and social interactions, how to make transitions from one activity to the next, and what is socially

appropriate behavior is vital for children with visual impairment.

Children who are visually impaired benefit from interactions with both peers and adults who are visually impaired. Many states have summer enrichment opportunities or other social experiences for children. These programs give children a chance to talk about life as a person with a visual impairment. Interaction with adult role models is helpful, since many parents may not have personal experience with adults who are blind or who have low vision.

Language Development

There are differing opinions on the impact of early visual impairment on communication and language development. Some have reported that young children with vision loss may miss or misinterpret early communication signals (Mills, 1988), may have a heightened use of "labeling" versus "requesting" language (Dunlea, 1989), and may have increased use and duration of echolalia, repeating what is said (Dunlea, 1989; Erin, 1993; Pring, Dewart, & Borckbank, 1996). Since they cannot maintain a visual connection with others, children with visual impairment may pay more attention to language than do sighted peers of the same age (Perez-Pereira & Castro, 1997).

As discussed previously, vision plays a critical role in early nonverbal communications. An infant with sight indicates interest by directing eye gaze or by reaching toward an object or person of interest. The infant with sight will gaze at his or her mother's shiny necklace. If the mother wants her child to touch the necklace, she might say, "That's mommy's necklace. It's shiny." The child's visual regard *initiated* this conversation with her mother. The lack of directed gaze and reaching actions in a child with blindness may complicate a parent's interpretation of communicative intentions in young children (Mills, 1988). Early intervention professionals will need to help family members learn how to support communicative dialogues that are not dependent on eye gaze or visually directed reaching. For instance, the same conversation may be initiated with a child with visual impairment when the child's hand brushes the necklace or when the mother deliberately touches her child's hand to the necklace.

Parents and ECSE professionals need to learn how a child's body posturing indicates listening or attentive behavior. Rather than turning his or her face toward a voice, the child with significant vision loss may turn his or her head away or at an angle. This is called **ear pointing**, and the child is posturing to actually listen better. The child may also become very quiet, as opposed to showing the expected increase in body activity when he or she hears something new. Or the child's face may become very still. Any of these behaviors may signal listening and attentiveness in a young child.

Rowland (1983) noted in her study that the three infants with blindness produced fewer vocalizations during or after an adult's vocalizations when they were compared to infants with sight. Rowland offered the following interpretation for this behavior: "Listening may be so critical to the interpretation of the distal environment that it would be maladaptive for the blind infant to clutter the auditory environment with her own vocalizations" (p. 127). In other words, adults must be careful to provide a balance of language input during play so there is no interference with a child's listening and active engagement.

Vocabulary Development. Some researchers have reported a delay in the onset of first words in children with visual impairment (McConachie & Moore, 1994). Others who have examined vocabulary development have found comparable vocabularies in sighted children and children with blindness (Mills, 1988). Fraiberg and colleagues (Fraiberg et al., 1966) found that in their study once the children with blindness gained locomotion, which allowed for increased object interaction experiences, the vocabulary gap with sighted peers decreased.

Although there have been reports of acquisition delays in the pronoun "I" (Fraiberg & Adelson, 1973; Mulford, 1988) and of delay in and confusion of other pronouns (Anderson, Dunlea, &

Kekelis, 1984b; Dunlea, 1989) in children who are visually impaired, a recent study by Perez-Pereira and Conti-Ramsden (1999) did not find evidence of delays in personal reference words. Rather, these results suggest that pronoun reversals (e.g., *he* for *she* or *you* for *me*), which occur with some children with significant visual impairment, should not be considered typical of all children with blindness.

Research has provided insight into how adults model language to young children with visual impairments. Parents of children with visual impairments have been reported to use more verbal directives instead of describing what is around or happening to the child (Anderson, Dunlea, & Kekelis, 1993; Moore & McConachie, 1994). Other studies have shown that while mothers of children with blindness may provide more directive input to their children than do mothers of children with low vision or typical vision, many of the directives contained descriptive language that might be helpful in establishing joint attention and conversational participation (Perez-Pereira & Conti-Ramsden, 2001; Kekelis & Prinz, 1996).

Maternal directiveness may be facilitative if its purpose is to provide information to the child and guide play interaction (Campbell, 2003). However, too much directiveness may hamper communicative and play interactions. Working together professionals and families can find ways to embed communication facilitation into routines so that play and social interactions are appropriately supported.

Erin (1986) found that children with blindness between 4 and 10 years of age used a question-asking format within their conversations at a higher frequency than did their sighted peers of the same age. Younger children with visual impairments tend to ask more questions during conversations than do older children with visual impairments, and children with blindness of all ages tend to ask more questions than do their peers with low vision. Erin concluded that both age and degree of vision loss contributed to question asking as a tool to engage and promote conversations as well as to obtain information that the children could not obtain visually. McGinnis (1981) reached the same conclusion, noting that question asking was used as a means to change the topic in preschoolers who were 3 to 5 years old.

If a child has both visual impairment and additional disabilities that affect communication and language development, a communication system involving a display of objects, tactile symbols, pictures, and/or visual symbols (for the child with low vision) will have to be designed for the student's expressive and receptive communication use. The TVI on a child's team plays an important role when determining the size, spacing, complexity, and visual arrangement of this kind of communication board (Anthony, 2002). If a tactile array is utilized, the TVI can assist the educational team in determining the most appropriate tactile symbols for the learner.

Fine and Gross Motor Development

Vision stimulates and verifies a child's interactions with the environment (Rosen, 1999). Early-onset visual impairment may affect the acquisition of fine and gross motor milestones and their quality of execution. Researchers have found the following motor differences in young children who are blind or visually impaired:

❏ evidence of differences in the rate and sequence of some fine and gross motor milestones (Fraiberg, 1977; Hart, 1983; Henderson, 1960; Sonksen, Levitt, & Kitsinger, 1984);

❏ evidence of general delays in all mobility milestones, particularly cruising around furniture, walking independently, and walking up and down stairs (Celeste, 2002; Whinnery & Barnes, 2002), with children with the least vision tending to display the poorest motor outcomes;

❏ evidence of lower postural tone (Jan, Robinson, Scott, & Kinnis, 1975; Sonksen et al., 1984; Brown & Bour, 1987); and

❏ evidence of some reduced quality of movement skills (Brown & Bour, 1987; Stone, 1995).

The severity of a child's visual impairment will contribute significantly to the child's achievement in motor development.

The Development of Reaching. Reaching out in space is a critical step for a child with visual impairment. Bigelow (1986) described reaching as "one of the first self-initiated contacts that blind children make with the external world" (p. 355). The sequence of reaching behavior by infants with blindness highlights the power of touch over sound (Bigelow, 1986; Fraiberg, 1968, 1977). The first evidence of reaching occurs just after an object that makes sound, that is held at midline, is taken from the child's hands. The reaching action is in response to the tactile confirmation of the object before it is removed from the child's hands. Next the child is able to reach at midline for a continuous sounding object that has not touched the child's hands. Touch first, then sound, serves as a cue to an object's existence and location.

The quality, accuracy, and endurance of reaching will further be affected by a child's base of trunk support, postural tone, and upper extremity strength. Placing an infant in the prone position, that is, on their tummy, is essential for strengthening his or her upper body since the infant works against gravity to lift the head and bear weight on the forearms (Brown & Bour, 1987). The development of muscles in the upper body is tied to later fine and gross motor tasks such as reaching upward, crawling, carrying heavier objects, using an adaptive mobility device or long cane, and/or pressing the braillewriter keys (Anthony, Bleier, Fazzi, Kish, & Pogrund, 2002).

Infants who are blind have been reported to dislike being placed in the prone position (Rosen, 1999). The influence of reduced visual incentive to lift one's head in the prone position (Schneekloth, 1989) and the effects of low postural tone are challenges for infants with visual impairment. Without intervention to create specific situations to learn and reinforce these skills, infants with visual impairment may be at risk for not fully developing appropriate neck, shoulder, forearm, stomach, and back muscles (Brown, Anthony, Shier Lowry, & Hatton, 2004). The early interventionist working with Maddie and her family (see the case study) found that brushing Maddie's hand with a windup radio while she lay on her tummy and then holding the radio just above her head encouraged Maddie to reach up and search for the sound source with her hand and to raise her head, strengthening her upper back and neck and teaching her searching behavior.

Gross Motor Development and Movement. Some of the delays in mobility milestones and the poor quality of movement in infants with significant visual impairment are related to the presence of low postural trunk tone (Jan et al., 1975). **Postural tone** describes the tension in the body's muscles and provides "motoric readiness for movement" (Rosen, 1999, p. 175). **Hypertonicity** (too much postural tone) affects the ability to control and grade movement, while **hypotonicity** (too little postural tone) affects postural stability. Postural tone provides the support base that infants, toddlers, and preschoolers need for independent sitting and for mobility skills such as rolling, crawling, and walking (Anthony et al., 2002).

The presence of low-normal postural tone in children with visual impairment without a motor-related diagnosis such as cerebral palsy seems to be the result of a lack of visual tutoring of the vestibular and proprioceptive senses. A 2001 study of 14 infants born blind noted that the first sign of motor delay was observed at 3 months of age when head lift in the prone position was limited or absent (Prechtl, Cioni, Einspieler, Bos, & Ferrari, 2001). These researchers concluded that the limited head control and righting seen throughout the end of the first year of life suggested a delay in vestibular function from the lack of visual calibration. That is, without visual feedback of body movements, there is less opportunity for these infants to deliberately move their bodies. The lack of visual feedback to motor skills may inhibit a child's development of postural tone, which plays a significant role in balance and posture (Rosen, 1999).

Low postural tone has an impact on the age of motor milestone acquisition (Jan et al., 1975; Brown & Bour, 1987). A study of 91 children with visual impairment found that 80% percent of the children without hypotonia achieved sitting, crawling, and walking milestones within typical age ranges, compared to 30%–40% of those children with hypotonia (Jan et al., 1975). Children with hypotonia also evidenced decreased endurance in motor activity, poor abdominal strength, and out-toeing.

Optical righting, righting one's head in alignment with the visual horizon, involves more mature head righting and equilibrium reactions and will also be affected by a significant vision loss (Brown & Bour, 1987). Without optical righting, there is reduced incentive to turn the head as the body is moved in different positions from midline. Poor optical righting reduces the infant's ability to acquire head control, which, in turn, affects the development of neck and trunk muscles.

Quality of movement, the level of refined execution of a motor skill, is further affected by low postural tone. The child may need to use atypical postural adjustments or "fixing" to support movement or sustain a posture (Rosen, 1999). The postural fixing may provide temporary stability, but may also limit mobility and the development of true postural stability in the future (Brown & Bour, 1987). For example, the child with low trunk tone may keep his legs far apart, sit with a rounded back, and/or keep his hands on the floor in order to maintain an upright sitting posture. These compensations are needed to do what the trunk cannot do, which is to maintain an upright sitting position without the benefit of furniture support. This type of self-positioning, however, compromises the child's movement independence, as any challenge to gravity such as turning or reaching up to find a toy will release the posture needed to stay upright. Compensatory movements often seen with walking include positioning the legs farther apart than usual, shuffling or taking very small steps to maintain as much contact as possible with the floor, and/or locking the knees. Nonetheless, physical therapy and direct instruction can improve postural tone and movement and may eliminate many other atypical motor patterns observed in young children with vision loss.

Infants, toddlers, and preschoolers with significant visual impairment appear to rely more on their conceptual understanding of objects and space to initiate locomotion than do their peers with sight (Bigelow, 1992). For instance, Fraiberg (1977), who followed ten infants who were totally blind over a ten-year period, reported that although the children had the physical ability to move in space, as evidenced by their raising themselves to sit, crawl, and walk, they were delayed in mobility skills due to the absence of visual incentives or to compromised knowledge of space beyond their bodies. However, static motor milestones such as sitting and standing were accomplished generally at the same time that sighted peers did these skills. These results were replicated in 1994 when ten children with light perception only were followed for three years (Troster, Heckler, & Brambring, 1994). When there is an absence of visual enticement, there is less reinforcement to engage in motor activities such as changing positions or initiating locomotion. Consequently, parents and professionals must create situations that encourage a child to reach into space, move freely, and alter his or her position frequently (including crossing the body at midline) within home and school routines.

Movement Transition Skills. With visual impairment, **movement transitions skills**—moving from one position to another, such as moving from a sitting to a kneeling position—may be influenced. This is probably because children have low postural tone and poor trunk rotation and have fewer or no opportunities to observe others making these transitions (Adelson & Fraiberg, 1974; Brown et al., 2004; Troster & Brambring, 1993). In addition, there are reports of school-age children with visual impairments, including those with low vision, with balance challenges and gross motor skills that are less developed than their fine motor skills (Bouchard & Tetreault, 2000).

In some cases, fine and gross motor differences may be the result of a lack of opportunity and training as much as they are a response to limited or absent vision (Raver, 1990). Related service providers will guide teams, and families, in appropriate ways to approach a child's motor challenges. A physical and/or an occupational therapist can help address the impact of low postural tone and offer exercises that increase upper extremity and hand strength. An O&M specialist can work with the early intervention/preschool team and later with the school education team to determine if the child will benefit from adapted mobility devices or a long cane to encourage safe self-initiated movement. Adapted mobility devices and long canes can be used very successfully with young children, but there are a variety of factors that must be discussed with an O&M specialist to ensure success. With primary-aged students, the O&M specialist will teach new travel routes, the use of travel tools such as tactile maps, street crossing safety, and bus travel.

Children with visual impairment, particularly primary-aged students, should have the same access to physical education as their peers. Families, TVIs, O&M specialists, and special and general educators must ensure that appropriate adapted physical activities are provided daily.

Preliteracy and Literacy Development

Children who are visually impaired should have the same preliteracy and literacy expectations and opportunities as their classmates with sight. However, often these children have fewer daily literacy-related observations, primarily due to reduced incidental learning (Day, McDonnell, & Heathfield, 2005). The case study of Maddie at the beginning of the chapter demonstrates how family and team involvement can modify any environment so appropriate preliteracy and liteacy stimuli and experiences are provided. Rex and colleagues (Rex, Koenig, Wormsely, & Baker, 1995) found that children between birth and 8 years of age who were classified as prospective or actual braille readers had significantly fewer literacy experiences than did children who were classified as print or print-braille readers, primarily due to environments that were less enriched with braille materials. The young child who is visually impaired may be unable to watch people across the room or even a few feet away read and write during their daily activities. The computer in the family room may be viewed only as a sound source, not as a place where brother keyboards a homework assignment and surfs the Web. The grocery list on the refrigerator may be missed as well as mother reading the mail and writing checks to pay bills. Yet these experiences create the link between literacy tools and literacy actions, providing a reason for reading and writing for children.

Developing Reading and Writing Skills. All children benefit from real-life experiences with objects and their labels in order to develop an understanding of the information presented in books. Koenig and Farrenkopf (1997) analyzed 254 first-through third-grade stories from three basal reading series to identify experiences necessary to bring meaning to the stories included in the series. They identified 20 general themes, involving experiences generally gained through daily life activities, such as doing and making things, friendships, community and home experiences,

and traveling. These researchers concluded that children who have had the experiences portrayed in the stories are more likely to take meaning from the books. Thus, they state: "Gaining hands-on, multisensory experiences is not a 'frill' in the education of children with visual impairments; *it is a necessity*" (p. 23). The need for *immediate* and *direct* experiential ties to literacy cannot be overstated for young children with vision loss.

Visual impairment will restrict a child's exposure to print and braille symbols unless there is continuous effort to ensure that these literacy materials are accessible in a child's home and school environments (Koenig & Holbrook, 2002). Prospective braille readers may not have a literacy footing equal to that of their sighted peers due to the lack of early exposure to braille (Craig, 1996). Just as the sighted child has exposure to print in storybooks, so should the child with visual impairment have constant braille exposure for appropriate literacy development. This commitment was clearly made by the professionals who served Maddie.

Specialized Materials. Access to appropriate materials in the early years is a key factor in a child's development of literacy. Craig (1996) found that only 51% of the children between birth and

Katelyn Metzger/Merrill

For well developed reading and writing skills, students with visual impairments need access to specialized equipment such as braillewriters at home as well as at school.

8 years of age who were classified as potential braille readers had access to a braillewriter in the home. A **braillewriter** is a tool designed to manually produce braille by pushing down a combination of six keys to produce individual braille cells. In Craig's study, only 20% had a **slate and stylus**, the slate being a pocket-sized, hinged device and the stylus being a push tool used with the stylus to write braille; the latter is considered the "braille pencil" due to its portability.

Other equipment needs may include **screen-reading programs** that provide auditory access to computer and Internet information, screen enlargement programs to enlarge text on the computer screen, braille notetakers, and **closed circuit televisions** that enlarge print, pictures, and even objects for improved viewing. These are just a few examples of the technology that may be appropriate in primary classrooms to level the playing field. In addition to technology directly used by a student, technology is needed to produce braille and tactile materials for the student, such as software programs to convert text into braille, braille embossers, and tactile graphic kits.

Additionally, low expectations for early literacy skills may plague the child with visual impairment (Koenig & Holbrook, 2002). Untrained personnel may be daunted at the prospect of a young child learning braille or mastering print with magnification. Professionals should work with parents to ensure high literacy expectations at home (Craig, 1996).

Misperceptions about braille as an important and viable literacy mode may further complicate matters. The decision to teach braille to a child with visual impairment can often be made when the child is very young. The IDEA (2004) mandates that an IEP team determine the needs for braille instruction. The assessment data from the TVI will be an important factor in determining a child's learning media.

Access to appropriate developmental and educational services must include an assurance that instructional materials will be made available to students in the appropriate media and at the same time as comparable materials are made available to their sighted peers, according to goal seven of *The National Agenda for the Education of Children and Youths with Visual Impairments, Including Those with Multiple Disabilities* (Huebner, Merk-Adam, Stryker, & Wolffe, 2004). Daily instruction-related print materials may be produced in braille by the TVI or, more often, by a school district **braillist**, who has specific knowledge of the braille code and is skilled in braille production. To ensure that materials are provided in a timely fashion, it is imperative that the student's teacher(s) work closely with the TVI to provide instructional materials in advance so materials can be brailled for the student by the time they are presented in class (Swenson, 1999).

Many states have Instructional Resource Centers (IRCs) that work directly with school district TVIs to process orders for braille books. If a book has not been brailled before, it must be brailled by a certified Library of Congress braille transcriber in order to be added to national and state collections. The costs of producing a book in braille may vary, but the average cost of a literary book without many tactile graphics is $3,000 to $5,000 per book. One helpful solution to the problem of textbook production and availability is on the horizon: To be eligible for certain funding, states are required by the IDEA (2004) to adopt the **National Instructional Materials Accessibility Standard (NIMAS)** and to contract with textbook publishers to provide their instructional materials directly to purchasers in specialized formats or to provide electronic files of these materials to the National Instructional Materials Access Center for the purpose of translation into large-print, braille, audio, and digital formats.

ASSESSMENT

Some assessment considerations for children with visual impairment and blindness will be discussed. Further, elimination of visual bias from state- and districtwide assessments will be addressed.

Vision Screening

All children should be screened on a regular basis for possible vision problems. Vision screening should occur *prior* to the completion of developmental or academic assessment to allow for any needed assessment adaptations and to obtain an optimal result (Anthony, 2002).

Functional Vision Assessment

A teacher certified in visual impairment has the expertise and responsibility to conduct a **functional vision assessment** (FVA) with a child who has a diagnosed visual impairment. The purpose of an FVA is to assess how a child uses their vision in daily activities and to identify what helps or hinders the child's visual performance (Anthony, 2000). If a child has a low-vision device such as a magnifier, the FVA should include specific information about how the child functions with the device in home, school, and community settings. The TVI will work with other team members, including the child and his or her parents, to gather and interpret the child's medical records, conduct observations of the child in a variety of settings, and interview key people who have knowledge of the child's visual functioning for this assessment.

Based on the FVA findings, a TVI will assist teachers in making environmental accommodations and adjustments. Table 12.2 shows some of the most common types of visual accommodations made for young children with visual impairment.

Learning Media Assessment

A complementary assessment to the FVA is the **learning media assessment (LMA)**, which allows the educational team, under the guidance of a TVI, to systemically select learning and literacy media such as braille for a student with visual impairment (Koenig & Holbrook, 1995). The purpose is to determine the child's efficiency in using sensory information (visual, auditory, and tactile) and the types of sensory materials that will be needed for communication, learning, and literacy activities.

Developmental and Academic Assessment

Developmental assessment practices followed for young children with visual impairment are in most ways the same as those followed for children with typical sight, with the addition of two vital considerations (Anthony, 2002). One consideration is selecting an appropriate assessment tool. Standardized tools cannot predict a developmental sequence that is valid for children with visual impairment, since many children with severe visual impairment do not appear to follow the exact sequence and rate of development that their sighted peers do. The second consideration is the need for the examiners to have an understanding of the effects of visual impairment on learning and of the child's needs for test accommodations (Pugh & Erin, 1999; Anthony, 2002).

TABLE 12.2 Examples of visually-based accommodations for young children with visual impairment

Lighting:	type, intensity of illumination, positioning
Contrast:	level of intensity, color combination choices
Glare control:	covering reflective surfaces, no lamination
Visual array:	more white space, fewer items, less detail
Enlargement:	font/symbol enlargement, magnification use

State- and DistrictWide Assessments for Primary-Aged Students

As children with visual impairments enter the primary grades and participate in mandatory state- and districtwide assessments, these tests should be provided, as appropriate, in braille or large-print formats. Further, visually-based questions may have to be altered or eliminated to eradicate unnecessary bias. All instructional and testing accommodations must be clearly delineated in these children's IEPs.

SPECIALIZED AREAS OF INSTRUCTION

Students with visual impairments have instructional needs beyond the scope of the general curriculum content. The expanded core curriculum for children with blindness and visually impairment addresses nine additional learning areas: (1) compensatory academic skills, including communication modes (e.g., skills in organization, listening, braille, low-vision devices, and augmentative or alternative communication systems); (2) social interaction skills; (3) recreation and leisure skills; (4) use of assistive technology; (5) orientation and mobility; (6) independent living skills; (7) career education; (8) visual efficiency skills; and (9) self-determination (Hatlen, 1996; American Foundation for the Blind, 2007). Some components of this specialized curriculum increase access to the general education curriculum, while others are unique to the learning needs of children with visual impairment.

Continuum of Placement and Inclusionary Practices

As with any child receiving special education services, children with visual impairments may receive their educational services in a variety or combination of settings with the support of a TVI and an O&M specialist. Children may receive services through specialized programs unique to children with visual impairments as well as educational programs open to all children. Several states have specialized early intervention programs only for infants, toddlers, and preschoolers with visual impairments.

CONCLUSION

Children with visual impairment are a highly heterogeneous group with varying ages of onset of vision problems, varying degrees of vision loss, and present with varying functional implications of their vision loss. Some have additional disabilities, and some do not. Research has provided a framework for identification of potential hurdles that may result from visual impairment and has also suggested paths for successful intervention to modify or eliminate these challenges. An individualized approach is recommended to ensure the optimal developmental path for each child who is visually impaired. Further, as revealed in Maddie's case study, the services of a certified teacher of students with visual impairments and an orientation and mobility specialist are vital to the child, and the child's educational team, beginning in infancy and continuing throughout the child's school years.

SUMMARY

Definitions of vision problems and visual impairment

- Visual impairment is an umbrella term used to describe uncorrectable and permanent vision loss that impacts day-to-day visual functioning.

Specialized related-services professionals

- A certified teacher of students with visual impairments (TVI) has a university degree in the education of children and youth who are blind/visually impaired, including those who have additional disabilities and/or deaf-blindness.
- An orientation and mobility specialist (O&M) has specific training in supporting the travel needs of individuals of all ages with visual impairment.

Types and causes of vision problems and visual impairment

- The four most common vision problems in young children are amblyopia, strabismus, refractive errors, and color vision deficiency.

- The three leading causes of pediatric visual impairment in the United States are cortical visual impairment, retinopathy of prematurity, and optic nerve hypoplasia.

Impact of vision loss on development

- Children with vision loss may not benefit from incidental learning, so information should be made accessible through concrete, firsthand experience as much as possible.
- Children with visual impairment will benefit from social skills training on how to initiate and participate in conversations and social interactions and how to make transitions from one activity to the next.
- Young children with limited or absent vision tend to have language that is similar to that of their age-peers, although some may have difficulty interpreting nonverbal communication, may have more "labeling" than "requesting" language, and may have increased use of echolalia.
- Young children who are blind or visually impaired may acquire some fine and gross motor milestones at different ages and follow a different sequence than their peers with sight.
- Children with visual impairment require continuous exposure to preliteracy and literacy experiences, braille (as appropriate), and use of specialized equipment to develop strong literacy skills.

Assessment and specialized instruction

- Assessment of young children with visual impairment should include a functional vision assessment and a learning media assessment.
- Young children with visual impairment require instruction in preacademic/academic skills, social interaction skills, recreation and leisure skills, use of assistive technology, orientation and mobility, independent living skills, career education, visual efficiency skills, and self-determination.

Discussion Questions/Activities

1. Discuss three developmental domains in which a young child who has a visual impairment may be at risk. Identify one strategy you could use in each area to assist the child in achieving his or her full potential.

2. Using Maddie's case study, identify three ways Sara, Maddie's general education teacher, benefited from having a TVI and an O&M specialist on the team.

3. Describe three materials and/or pieces of equipment that may be helpful for a child who is blind to use in his or her home and educational settings.

References

Adelson, E., & Fraiberg, S. (1974). Gross motor development in infants blind from birth. *Child Development, 45*(1), 114–126.

Agape Optometry Center. (2006). *Color vision.* Retrieved October 29, 2006, from http://www.agape1.com/color%20vision.htm

Allen, J., & Fraser, K. (1983, Fall). Evaluation of visual capacity in visually impaired and multi-handicapped children. *Rehabilitative Optometry, 1*(3), 5–8.

American Academy of Ophthalmology. (1997). *Preferred practice pattern: Pediatric eye evaluations.* San Francisco: Author.

American Foundation for the Blind. (2007). *Braille Bug Reading Club.* Retrieved July 15, 2007, from http://www.afb.org

American Printing House for the Blind. (1997). *Annual report.* Louisville, KY: Author.

American Printing House for the Blind. (2005). *Distribution of federal quota.* Retrieved December 15, 2007, from http://www.aph.org

Anderson, E. S., Dunlea, A., & Kekelis, L. (1984a, May). *The role of visual perception in conversational interaction.* Paper presented at the International Communication Association Conference, San Francisco.

Anderson, E. S., Dunlea, A., & Kekelis, L. (1984b). Blind children's language: Resolving some differences. *Journal of Child Language, 11*, 645–664.

Anderson, E. S., Dunlea, A., & Kekelis, L. (1993). The impact of input: Language acquisition in the visually impaired. *First Language, 13*, 23–49.

Anthony, T. L. (2000). Performing a functional low vision assessment. In F. M. D'Andrea & C. Farrenkopf (Eds.), *Looking to learning: Promoting literacy for students with low vision* (pp. 32–83). New York: American Foundation for the Blind Press.

Anthony, T. L. (2002). The inclusion of vision development guidelines in the transdisciplinary play-based assessment: A study of reliability and validity (Doctoral dissertation, University of Denver). *Dissertation Abstracts International, 63*(12), A4271 (Pro Quest Information No. 30-74361).

Anthony, T. L., Bleier, H., Fazzi, D. L., Kish, D., & Pogrund, R. L. (2002). Mobility focus: Developing early skills for orientation and mobility. In R. L. Pogrund & D. L. Fazzi (Eds.), *Early focus: Working with young children who are blind or visually impaired and their families* (2nd ed., pp. 326–404). New York: American Foundation for the Blind Press.

Bigelow, A. (1986). The development of reaching in blind children. *British Journal of Developmental Psychology, 4,* 355–366.

Bigelow, A. (1992). Locomotion and search behavior in blind infants. *Infant Behavior and Development, 15,* 179–189.

Bishop, V. E. (1991). Preschool visually impaired children: A demographic study. *Journal of Visual Impairment and Blindness, 85*(2), 69–74.

Blind Babies Foundation. (1998). *Pediatric visual diagnosis fact sheet: Optic nerve hypoplasia.* San Francisco: Author.

Bouchard, D., & Tetreault, S. (2000). The motor development of sighted children and children with moderate low vision aged 8–13. *Journal of Visual Impairment and Blindness, 94*(9), 564–573.

Brodskey, M. C. (1996). The apparently blind infant. In M. C. Brodskey, R. S. Baker, & L. M. Hamed (Eds.), *Pediatric neuro-ophthalmology* (pp. 11–41). New York: Springer-Verlag.

Brodskey, M. C., Baker, R. S, & Hamed, L. M. (Eds.) (1996). *Pediatric neuro-ophthalmology.* New York: Springer-Verlag.

Brown, C. J., Anthony, T. L., Shier Lowry, S., & Hatton, D. D. (2004). Motor development and movement. In T. L. Anthony, S. S. Lowry, C. J. Brown, & D. D. Hatton (Eds.), *Developmentally appropriate orientation and mobility.* Chapel Hill: FPG Children Development Institute, University of North Carolina.

Brown, C., & Bour, B. (1987). *Volume V–K: Movement analysis and curriculum for visually impaired preschoolers.* Tallahassee: Bureau of Education for Exceptional Students, Florida Department of Education.

Campbell, J. (2003). Maternal directives to young children who are blind. *Journal of Visual Impairment and Blindness, 9*(6), 355–365.

Celeste, M. (2002). A survey of motor development for infants and young children with visual impairments. *Journal of Visual Impairments and Blindness, 96*(3), 169–174.

Chernus-Mansfield, N., Hayashi, D., Horn, M., & Kekelis, L. S. (1985). *Heart to heart: Parents of blind children talk about their feelings.* Los Angeles: Blind Children's Center.

Colorado Department of Education. (2000). *ECEA rules: Rules for the administration of the Exceptional Children's Education Act.* Denver: Author.

Corn, A. L., & Koenig, A. J. (1996). Perspectives on low vision. In A. J. Corn & A. J. Koenig (Eds.), *Foundations of low vision: Clinical and functional perspectives* (pp. 3–25). New York: American Foundation for the Blind Press.

Craig, C. J. (1996). Family support of the emergent literacy of children with visual impairments. *Journal of Visual Impairments and Blindness, 90,* 194–200.

Daw, N. W. (1995). *Visual development.* New York: Plenum Press.

Day, J., McDonnell, A., & Heathfield, L. (2005). Enhancing emergent literacy skills in inclusive preschools for young children with visual impairments. *Young Exceptional Children, 9,* 20–28.

Deitz, S., & Ferrell, K. A. (1993). Early services for young children with visual impairment: From diagnosis to comprehensive service. *Infants and Young Children, 6*(1), 68–76.

Dunlea, A. (1989). *Vision and the emergence of meaning.* New York: Cambridge University Press.

Dote-Kwan, J., Chen, D., & Hughes, M., (2001). A national survey of service providers who work with young children with visual impairments. *Journal of Visual Impairment and Blindness, 95*(6), 325–337.

Erin, J. N. (1986). Frequencies and types of questions in the language of visually impaired children. *Journal of Visual Impairment and Blindness, 80,* 670–674.

Erin, J. (1993). Language samples from visually impaired four and five year olds. *Journal of Childhood Communication Disorders, 13,* 181–191.

Erin, J. N., Fazzi, D. L., Gordon, R. L., Isenberg, S. J., & Paysse, E. A. (2002). Vision focus: Understanding the medical and functional implications of vision loss. In R. L. Pogrund & D. L. Fazzi (Eds.), *Early focus: Working with young children who are blind or visually impaired and their families* (2nd ed., pp. 52–107). New York: American Foundation for the Blind Press.

Fazzi, D. L., & Klein, M. D. (2002). Developing cognition, concepts, and language. In R. L. Pogrund & D. L. Fazzi (Eds.), *Early focus: Working with young children who are blind or visually impaired and their families* (2nd ed., pp. 107–153). New York: American Foundation for the Blind Press.

Ferrell, K. A. (1998). *Project PRISM: A longitudinal study of the developmental patterns of children who are visually impaired: Executive summary: CFDA 84.0203C:*

field-initiated research HO23C10188. Greeley: University of Northern Colorado.

Ferrell, K. A., & Mamer, L. (1992). *The Visually Impaired Infants Research Consortium (VIIRC) pilot study results.* Unpublished manuscript, University of Northern Colorado at Greeley.

Ferrell, K. A., Raver, S. A., & Stewart, K. A. (1999). Techniques for infants and toddlers with visual impairment. In S. A. Raver, *Intervention strategies for infants and toddlers with special needs: A team approach* (2nd ed., pp. 298–330). Upper Saddle River, NJ: Merrill/Prentice Hall.

Flanagan, N. M., Jackson, A. J., & Hill, A. E. (2003). Visual impairment in childhood: Insights from a community-based survey. *Child Care, Health & Development, 29,* 493–499.

Foster, A. (1988). Childhood blindness. *Eye, 2,* 27–36.

Fraiberg, S. (1968). Parallel and divergent patterns in blind and sighted infants. *Psychoanalytic Study of the Child, 23,* 264–301.

Fraiberg, S. (1977). *Insights from the blind: Comparative studies of blind and sighted infants.* New York: Basic Books.

Fraiberg, S., & Adelson, E. (1973). Self representation in language and play: Observations of blind children. *Psychoanalytical Quarterly, 42,* 539-562.

Fraiberg, S., Siegel, B., & Gibson, R. (1966). The role of sound in the search behavior of a blind infant. *Psychoanalytical Study of the Child, 21,* 327–357.

Gerali, P. S., Flom, M. C., & Raab, E. L. (1990). *Report of children's vision screening task force.* Schaumburg, IL: National Society to Prevent Blindness.

Goble, J. L. (1984). *Visual disorders in the handicapped child.* New York: Dekker.

Good, W. V., Jan, J. E., DeSa, L., Barkovich, A. J., Groenveld, M., & Hoyt, C. S. (1994). Cortical visual impairment in children. *Survey of Ophthalmology, 38*(4), 351–364.

Hart, V. (1983). Motor development in blind children. In M. E. Mulholland & M. V. Wurster (Eds.), *Help me become everything I can be* (pp. 74–79). New York: American Foundation for the Blind Press.

Hatlen, P. (1996). The core curriculum for blind and visually impaired students, including those with additional disabilities. *RE:View, 28*(1), 25–32.

Hatton, D. D. (2001). Model registry of early childhood visual impairment: First-year results. *Journal of Visual Impairment and Blindness, 95*(7), 418–433.

Hatton, D. D., Bailey, D. B., Burchinal, M. R., & Ferrell, K. A. (1997). Developmental growth curves of preschool children with visual impairments. *Child Development, 68*(5), 788–806.

Henderson, F. (1960). Little bumps that say something. *Exceptional Children, 26,* 261–266.

Hoben, M., & Lindstom, V. (1980). Evidence of isolation in the mainstream. *Journal of Visual Impairment and Blindness, 74,* 289–292.

Huebner, K. M., Merk-Adams, B., Stryker, D., & Wolffe, K. (2004). *The National Agenda for the Education of Children and Youths with Visual Impairments, Including Those with Multiple Disabilities* (Rev. ed.) New York: AFB Press.

Hyvärinen, L. (1995). Effect of impaired vision on general development. In L. Hyvärinen (Ed.), *Vision testing manual 1995–1996* (pp. 1–7). Villa Park, IL: Precision Vision.

Individuals with Disabilities Education Improvement Act (IDEA) of 2004, Pub. L. No. 108-446, Sec. 1400 (c).

Jan, J. E., & Groenveld, M. (1993). Visual behaviors and adaptations associated with cortical and ocular impairment in children. *Journal of Visual Impairment and Blindness, 87*(4), 101–105.

Jan, J. E., Groenveld, M., Sykanda, A. M., & Hoyt, C. S. (1987). Behavioral characteristics of children with permanent cortical visual impairment. *Developmental Medicine Child Neurology, 29,* 571–576.

Jan, J., Robinson, G., Scott, E., and Kinnis, C. (1975). Hypotonia in the blind child. *Developmental Medicine and Child Neurology, 17,* 35-40.

Keith, C. G., & Doyle, L. W. (1995). Retinopathy of prematurity in extremely low birth weight infants. *Pediatrics, 95,* 42–45.

Kekelis, L. S. (1999). A field study of a blind preschooler. In S. Zell Sacks, L. S. Kekelis, & R. J. Gaylord-Ross (Eds.), *The development of social skills by blind and visually impaired students: Exploratory studies and strategies* (pp. 39–58). New York: AFB Press.

Kekelis, L. S., & Prinz, P. M. (1996). Blind and sighted children with their mothers: The development of discourse skills. *Journal of Visual Impairments and Blindness, 90,* 423–434.

Kirchner, C. (1989). National estimates of prevalence and demographics of children with visual impairments. In M. C. Wang, M. C. Reynolds, & H. J. Walberg (Eds.), *Handbook of special education research and Practice: Vol. 3. Low incidence conditions* (pp. 135–153). Oxford, England: Pergamon.

Koenig, A. J., & Farrenkopf, C. (1997). Essential experiences for the early development of literacy. *Journal of Visual Impairment and Blindness, 91,* 14–24.

Koenig, A. J., & Holbrook, M. C. (1995). *Learning media assessment of students with visual impairments: A resource guide.* Austin: Texas School for the Blind and Visually Impaired.

Koenig, A. J., & Holbrook, M. C. (2002). Literacy focus: Developing skills and motivation for reading and writing. In R. L. Pogrund & D. L. Fazzi (Eds.), *Early focus: Working with young children who are blind or visually impaired and their families* (2nd ed., pp. 154–187). New York: American Foundation for the Blind Press.

Koestler, F. A. (1976). *The unseen minority: A social history of blindness in the United States.* New York: McKay.

Langley, M. B. (1998). Alignment and ocular mobility. In M. B. Langley (Ed.), *Individualized systematic assessment of visual efficiency for the developmentally young and individuals with multihandicapping conditions* (Vol. 1, pp. 1–33). Louisville, KY: American Printing House for the Blind.

Leat, S. J., Shute, R. H., & Westall, C. A. (1999). *Assessing children's vision: A handbook.* Oxford, England: Butterworth-Heinemann.

McConachie, H. R., & Moore, V. R. (1994). Early expressive language of severely visually impaired children. *Developmental Medicine and Child Neurology, 36,* 230–240.

McGinnis, A. R. (1981). Functional linguistic strategies of blind children. *Journal of Visual Impairment and Blindness, 4,* 210–214.

Menacker, S. J., & Batshaw, M. L. (1997). Vision: Our windows to the world. In M. L. Batshaw (Ed.), *Children with disabilities* (4th ed., pp. 211–239). Baltimore, MD: Brookes.

Mills, A. (1988). Visual handicap. In D. Bishop & K. Mogford (Eds.), *Language development in exceptional circumstances* (pp. 150–164). Edinburgh, Scotland: Churchill Livingston.

Moore, V., & McConachie, H. (1994). Communication between blind and severely visually impaired children and their parents. *British Journal of Developmental Psychology, 12,* 491–502.

Mulford, R. (1988). First words of the blind child: The child's development of a linguistic vocabulary. In M. D. Smith & J. L. Locke (Eds.), *The emergent lexicon* (pp. 293–338). London: Academic Press.

Perez-Pereira, M., & Castro, J. (1997). Language acquisition and the compensation of visual deficit: New comparative data on a controversial topic. *British Journal of Developmental Psychology, 15,* 439–459.

Perez-Pereira, M., & Conti-Ramsden, G. (1999). *Language development and social interaction in blind children.* Hove, England: Psychology.

Perez-Pereira, M., & Conti-Ramsden, G. (2001). The use of directives in verbal interactions between blind children and their mothers. *Journal of Blindness & Visual Impairment, 95*(3), pp 133–149.

Phelps, D. L. (1993). Retinopathy of prematurity. *Pediatric Clinics of North America, 40,* 705–714.

Prechtl, H.F., Cioni, G., Einspieler, C., Bos, A.F., & Ferrari, F. (2001). Role of vision on early motor development: Lessons from the blind. *Developmental Medicine and Child Neurology, 43,* 198–201.

Preisler, G. M. (1991). Early patterns of interaction between blind infants and their mothers. *Child Care, Health, and Development, 17,* 65-90.

Pring, L., Dewart, H., & Borchbank M. (1996). Social cognition in children with visual impairment. *Journal of Blindness & Visual Impairment, 92,* 754–768.

Pugh, G. S., & Erin, J. (Eds.). (1999). *Blind and visually impaired students: Educational guidelines.* Watertown, MA: Perkins School for the Blind.

Raver, S. A. (1990). Effect of gaze direction on evaluation of visually impaired children by informed respondents. *Journal of Visual Impairment and Blindness, 84,* 67–70.

Rex, E. J., Koenig, A. J., Wormsely, D. P., & Baker, R. L. (1995). *Foundation of braille literacy.* New York: American Foundation for the Blind.

Rogers, S., & Puchalski, C. (1986). Social smiles of visually impaired infants. *Journal of Visual Impairment and Blindness, 80,* 863–865.

Rogers, S., & Puchalski, C. (1988). Development of object permanence in visually impaired infants. *Journal of Visual Impairment and Blindness, 82,* 137–142.

Rosen, S. (1999). Kinesiology and sensorimotor function. In B. B. Blasch, W. R. Weiner, & R. L. Welsh (Eds.), *Foundations of orientation and mobility* (2nd ed., pp. 170–199). New York: AFB Press.

Rowland, C. (1983). Patterns of interaction between three blind infants and their mothers. In A. E. Mills (Ed.), *Language acquisition in the blind child: Normal and deficient* (pp. 114–132). Kent, England: Croom Helm.

Ryles, R. (2004). Is your child age-appropriate? *Future Reflections, 23*(2), 25–34.

Schneekloth, L. (1989). Play environments for visually impaired children. *Journal of Visual Impairment and Blindness, 83*(4), 196–211.

Schor, D. P. (1990). Visual impairment. In J. A. Blackman (Ed.), *Medical aspects of developmental disabilities in children birth to three* (2nd ed., pp. 269–274). Rockville, MD: Aspen.

Shaw, D. E., Fielder, A. R., Minshull, C., & Rosenthal, A. R. (1985). Amblyopia—Factors influencing age of presentation. *Lancet, 1,* 207–209.

Simons, K. (1996). Preschool vision screening: Rationale, methodology, and outcome. *Survey Ophthalmology, 41,* 3–30.

Sonksen, P. M., Levitt, S., & Kitsinger, M. (1984). Identification of constraints acting on motor development in young visually disabled children and principles of remediation. *Child Care, Health, and Development, 10,* 273–286.

Steinkuller, P. G., Du, L., Gilbert, C., Foster, A., Collins, M. L., & Coats, D. K. (1999). Childhood blindness. *Journal of AAPOS, 3,* 2–32.

Stone, J. (1995). *Mobility for special needs.* London: Cassell Wellington House.

Swenson, A. W. (1999). *Beginning with Braille: first experiences with a balanced approach to literacy.* New York, NY: AFB Press.

Teplin, S. (1982). Assessment of visual acuity in infancy and early childhood. *Acta Ophthalmologica Supplement, 157,* 18–26.

Teplin, S. (1995). Visual impairment in infants and young children. *Infants and Young Children, 8*(1), 18–51.

Trief, E., Duckman, R., Morse, A. R., & Silberman, R. K. (1989). Retinopathy of prematurity. *Journal of Visual Impairment and Blindness, 83*(10), 500–504.

Troster, H., & Brambring, M. (1993). Early motor development in blind infants. *Journal of Applied Developmental Psychology, 14*(1), 83–106.

Troster, H., Heckler, W., & Brambring, M. (1994). Longitudinal study of gross-motor development in blind infants and preschoolers. *Early Childhood Development and Care, 104,* 61–78.

U.S. Office of Special Education. (2004). *Individuals with Disabilities Education Act (IDEA) Data.* Washington, DC: Author. Retrieved June 15, 2007 from http://www.ideadata.org/

van Hof-van Duin, J., & Pott, J. W. R. (1996). The Rotterdam C-chart: Visual acuity and intraocular acuity differences in very low birth weight and/or very prematurely born children at age of 5 years. In F. Vital-Durand, J. Atkinson, & O. J. Braddick (Eds.), *Infant vision* (pp. 171–183). New York: Oxford University Press.

Vaughn, M., & Scholl, G. (1980). Where have all the children gone? *DVH Newsletter, 25*(2), 6–7.

von Noorden, G. K. (1996). Examination of patient: III. Sensory signs, symptoms, and adaptations in strabismus. In G. K. von Noorden (Ed.), *Binocular vision and ocular motility* (5th ed., pp. 206–296). St. Louis, MO: Mosby.

Warren, D. H. (2006, September). *An individual differences approach.* Presentation at the Research in the Rockies Conference, Vail, CO.

Whetsell, W. O. (1996). Brain development and early stimulation. *Kennedy Center News, 34,* 1–2.

Whinnery, K., & Barnes, S. (2002). Mobility training using the MOVE curriculum: A parent's view. *Teaching Exceptional Children, 34*(3), 44–50.

Wolffe, K. E. (1999). The importance of career education. In K. E. Wolffe (Ed.), *Skills for success: A career education handbook for children and adolescents with visual impairments* (pp. 12–26). New York: American Foundation for the Blind Press.

World Health Organization (1992). *International statistical classification of diseases and related health problems* (10th ed.). Geneva, Switzerland: Author.

Zell Sacks, S., Kekelis, L. S., & Gaylord-Ross, R. J. (1999). *The development of social skills by blind and visually impaired students: Exploratory studies and strategies.* New York: American Foundation for the Blind Press.

Appendix

A

DEC Recommended Practices Strand: Child-Focused Competencies

1. Physical space and materials are structured and adapted to promote engagement, play, interaction, and learning by attending to children's preferences and interests, using novelty, using responsive toys, providing adequate amounts of materials, and using defined spaces.

2. The social dimension of the environments is structured and adapted to promote engagement, interaction, communication, and learning by proving peer models, peer proximity, responsive adults, and imitative adults; and by expanding children's play and behavior.

3. Routines and transitions are structured to promote interaction, communication, and learning by being responsive to child behavior and using naturalistic time delay, interrupted chain procedure, transition-based teaching, and visual cue systems.

4. Play routines are structured to promote interaction, communication, and learning by defining roles for dramatic play, prompting engagement, prompting group friendship activities, and using specialized props.

5. Environments are designed and activities are conducted so that children learn or are exposed to multiple cultures and languages by, among other practices, allowing children and families to share their cultures and languages with others, to the extent that they desire.

6. Learning environments meet accepted standards of quality, including curriculum, child-staff ratios, group size, and physical design of classroom.

7. Interventionists ensure the physical and emotional safety and security of children while children are in their care.

8. A variety of appropriate settings and naturally occurring activities are used to facilitate children's learning and development.

9. Services are provided in natural learning environments as appropriate. These include places in which typical children participate, such as the home or community settings.

10. Interventionists facilitate children's engagement with their environment to encourage child-initiated learning that is not dependent on the adult's presence.

11. Environments are provided that foster positive relationships, including peer-peer, parent/caregiver-child, and parent-caregiver relationships.

12. Practices are individualized for each child based on: (a) the child's current behavior and abilities across relevant domains instead of the child's diagnostic classification; (b) the family's view of what the child needs to learn; (c) interventionists' and specialists' view of what the child needs to learn; (d) the demands, expectations, and requirements of the child's current environments. The practices as well as goals are individualized.

13. Practices target meaningful outcomes for the child that build upon the child's current skills and behavior and promote membership with others.

14. Data-based decisions are used to make modifications in the practices. Child performance is monitored and data are collected to determine the impact of the practices on the child's progress, and monitoring must be feasible and useful within the child's environments and is used to make modifications of intervention if needed.

15. Recommended practices are used to teach/promote whatever skills are necessary for children to function more completely, competently, adaptively, and independently in the child's natural environment. These skills should include teaching those that maximize participation and membership in home, school and community environments—including those that are typical or similar to other persons' in that environment. Attention should be given to the breadth and sophistication of the child's skills.

16. Children's behavior is recognized, interpreted in context, and responded to contingently, and opportunities are provided for expansion or elaboration of child behavior by imitating the behavior, waiting for the child's responses, modeling, and prompting.

17. Interventionists are agents of change to promote and accelerate learning, and learning should be viewed in different phases that require different types of practices. Phases are: acquisition—learning how to do the skill, fluency—learning to do the skill smoothly and at natural rates, maintenance—learning to do the skill after instruction has stopped, and generalization—learning to apply the skill whenever and wherever it is needed.

18. Practices are used systematically, frequently, and consistently within and across environments and across people.

19. Planning occurs prior to implementation, and that planning considers the situation to which the interventions will be applied.

20. Practices are used that are validated, normalized, useful across environments, respectful, and not stigmatizing of the child and family and that are sensitive to cultural and linguistic issues.

21. Consequences for children's behavior are structured to increase the complexity and duration of children's play, engagement, appropriate behavior, and learning by using differential reinforcement, response shaping, high probability procedures, and correspondence training.

22. Systematic naturalistic teaching procedures such as models, expansions, incidental teaching, mand-model procedure, and naturalistic time delay are used to promote acquisition and use of communication and social skills.

23. Peer-mediated strategies are used to promote social and communicative behavior.

24. Prompting and prompt fading procedures are used to ensure acquisition and use of communicative, self-care, cognitive, and social skills.

25. Specialized procedures are embedded and distributed within and across activities.

26. Recommended instructional strategies are used with sufficient fidelity, consistency, frequency, and intensity to ensure high levels of behavior occurring frequently.

27. For problem behaviors, interventionists assess the behavior in context to identify its function, and then devise interventions that are comprehensive in that they make the behavior irrelevant (child's environment is modified so that problem behavior is unnecessary or precluded), inefficient (a more efficient replacement behavior is taught), and ineffective (reinforcement and other consequent events are used).

Source: Reprinted with permission from Hemmeter, M. L., Smith, B., Sandall, S., & Askew, L. (2005). *DEC recommended practices workbook: Improving practices for young children with special needs and their families* (pp. 10–14). Missoula, MT: Division of Early Childhood/Council for Exceptional Children.

Appendix

B

DEC Recommended Practices Strand: Inclusion Competencies

—·—·—·—·—·—·—·—·—·—·—·—·—·—·—·—·—·—

> **Practices taken from these areas:**
>
> I = Interdisciplinary Model Practices
> C = Child-Focused Practices Practices
> PS = Policies, Procedures, and Systems Change Practices
> PP = Personal Preparation Practices

I9. Team members focus on the individual child's functioning in the contexts in which he or she lives, not the service.

I15. Team members use the most natural and least intrusive intervention strategies available that result in desired function.

I17. Team members plan to provide services and conduct interventions in natural learning environments.

C8. A variety of appropriate settings and naturally occurring activities are used to facilitate children's learning and development.

C9. Services are provided in natural learning environments as appropriate. These include places in which typical children participate, such as the home or community settings.

C10. Interventionists facilitate children's engagement with their environment to encourage child-initiated learning that is not dependent on the adult's presence.

C11. Environments are provided that foster positive relationships, including peer-peer, parent/caregiver-child, and parent-caregiver relationships.

C18. Practices are used systematically, frequently, and consistently within and across environments and across people.

C19. Planning occurs prior to implementation, and that planning considers the situation to which the interventions will be applied.

PS7. Public policies provide for sufficient, alternative, flexible fiscal and administrative requirements that facilitate: (a) the effective use of natural and inclusive settings, (b) interagency coordination at the "systems" level, and (c) interdisciplinary collaboration at the "direct-service" level (Medicaid waivers, child care subsidies, blended funding, itinerant services, etc.).

PS21. Program policies support the provision of services in inclusive or natural learning environments. Strategies are used to overcome challenges to inclusion.

PP13. Students/staff learn to apply instructional strategies in natural environments.

PP31. Field experiences occur in a variety of community-based settings in which children with and without disabilities and their families receive Early Intervention/Early Childhood Special Education services, including natural environments and inclusive programs.

PP63. Teachers and staff from early education programs and community child care centers are provided with knowledge and skills relative to the inclusion of young children with disabilities.

Source: Reprinted with permission from Hemmeter, M. L., Smith, B., Sandall, S., & Askew, L. (2005). *DEC recommended practices workbook: Improving practices for young children with special needs and their families* (pp. 61–63). Missoula, MT: Division of Early Childhood/Council for Exceptional Children.

Appendix
C

Websites for Professionals and Families

- -

Children with Disabilities

General Resources

East Tennessee Children's Hospital: Developmental Milestones

http://www.etch.com/healthdevms.cfm
Presents a brief overview of typical developmental milestones from birth to 15 months and possible problems at each age, with links to information about feeding, swallowing, physical therapy and occupational therapy, and language development.

National Information Center for Children and Youth with Disabilities (NICHCY)

http://www.nichcy.org
Offers information for families so they can make informed decisions about their child's education and offers information relevant for service providers and administrators regarding FAQs about disabilities. (English, Spanish)

Zero to Three

http://www.zerotothree.org
A national nonprofit organization whose mission is to promote the healthy development of infants and toddlers by supporting and strengthening families, communities; Website includes policies, research reports, and technical assistance for parents and professionals. (English, Spanish)

Our-Kids: Devoted to Raising Special Kids with Special Needs

http://www.our-kids.org
International, family-friendly Website that offers discussion groups, family stories, advice, defeats, and accomplishments for parents and family members.

Autism Spectrum Disorder

AutismInfo.com

http//www.autisminfo.com
Provides information about autism, including current research efforts and resources about treatment options with links for information about applied behavior analysis (ABA), medical and dietary interventions, and professional organizations. (English, Chinese, Spanish, French, Portuguese, German, Japanese, Italian, Korean)

Autism and Pervasive Developmental Disorders

http://autism.about.com
Gives an overview of autism, FAQs, common characteristics, current research issues, and links to treatment options; readers can sign up for a free newsletter.

Autism Speaks

http://www.autismspeaks.org
Helps families find answers by funding research and education efforts and by spearheading the development of a national registry of individuals with autism.

National Center on Birth Defects and Developmental Disabilities: Autism Information Center

http://www.cdc.gov/ncbddd/dd/ddautism.htm
Website maintained by a division of the Centers for Disease Control and Prevention that provides information about diagnosis, causes, prevalence, and treatments of autism spectrum disorders; offers a link to the Autism Spectrum Disorders Kids' Quest, a series of Websites provided to educate children about developmental disabilities.

Cerebral Palsy

Cerebral Palsy: Hope Through Research

http://www.ninds.nih.gov/disorders/cerebral_palsy/detail_cerebral_palsy.htm
Discusses diagnostic questions related to cerebral palsy, including questions relating to causes and treatments; provides information about research projects being conducted.
(English, Spanish)

Cerebral Palsy–Neurology Channel

http://www.neurologychannel.com/cerebralpalsy
Provides information about cerebral palsy, including types, causes, treatments, risk factors, complications, prognosis, and information about orthopedic and neurological surgeries for cerebral palsy.

CP Resource Center

http://www.twinenterprises.com/cp
Gives general information about cerebral palsy, contains a dictionary to help parents understand medical terms, and discusses periventricular leukomalacia (PVL) and its relation to cerebral palsy and hippotherapy.

Kids Health for Kids: Cerebral Palsy

http://kidshealth.org/kid/health_problems/brain/cerebral_palsy.html
Website for children to learn about cerebral palsy; could be used to explain cerebral palsy to an older sibling of a child recently diagnosed or to help a child with cerebral palsy understand his/her condition at an older age.

Down Syndrome

Down Syndrome: Health Issues

http://www.ds-health.com
Provides parents and professionals articles regarding specific health issues related to Down syndrome, such as gastroesophageal reflux, blood disorders, and thyroid function.

Down Syndrome: Understanding the Gift of Life

http://www.nas.com/downsyn
Website created for and by families with members who have Down syndrome that includes lists of organizations, support groups, conferences, inclusion/educational resources, family essays, FAQs, medical articles, and a toy store.

Early Childhood Mental Health

The Federation of Families for Children's Mental Health

http://www.ffcmh.org
Family-run organization dedicated to helping children with mental health needs and their families achieve a better quality of life by providing leadership to develop and sustain a nationwide network of family-run organizations that focus on changing how systems respond to children with mental health needs and their families.

Hard of Hearing/Deafness

Collaborative Early Intervention National Training e-Resource

http://center.uncg.edu/index.asp
Website targeted toward professionals who serve families with infants and toddlers who are deaf or hard of hearing that includes communication options, Web-based training for service providers, and an extensive list of resources.

Early Intervention Bibliography

http://www.tr.wou.edu/dblink/lib/resources.htm
Website from the National Informational Clearinghouse on Children Who Are Deaf-Blind that links to information about deaf-blindness, disability, educational and technical assistance, and medical issues.

Laurent Clerc National Deaf Education Center

http://clerccenter.gallaudet.edu/infotogo
Website from the Laurent Clerc Center at Gallaudet University that provides information about assistive devices, hearing aids, sign language and speechreading, and that discusses classroom issues.

Learning Disabilities

LD Online

http://www.ldonline.org
Provides comprehensive information about learning disabilities for professionals, parents, kids, and teachers, including a monthly newsletter and an online store.

Learning Disabilities Association of America

http://www.ldanatl.org
Website produced by an organization dedicated to supporting people with learning disabilities that offers information about learning disabilities for parents, teachers, professionals, and other adults as well as legislative updates.

A Parent's Guide to Helping Kids with Learning Difficulties

http://www.schwablearning.org
Website for parents of children with learning difficulties that includes articles with tips about how to help children succeed, how to identify and manage learning difficulties, and how to connect to other parents.
(English, Spanish)

Mental Retardation

American Association on Mental Retardation

http://www.aamr.org
Provides a comprehensive overview of issues related to mental retardation and sponsors many policy initiatives that affect people with mental retardation.

The Arc of the United States

http://www.thearc.org
Organization that advocates for the inclusion of people with intellectual and other developmental disabilities; this Website includes information on public policy and position statements on guardianship, housing, and behavioral supports.

Kids Health for Kids: Mental Retardation

http://kidshealth.org/kid/health_problems/
birth_defect/mental_retardation.html
Website created to help children understand mental retardation.

Prematurity

March of Dimes

http://www.marchofdimes.com
Official Website for the organization that addresses issues relating to newborns, prematurity, birth defects, and children with low birth weight; targeted to parents, professionals, and researchers.

Medline Plus: Premature Babies

http://www.nlm.nih.gov/medlineplus/
prematurebabies.html
Resource for healthcare professionals with sections on drug information, an encyclopedia, a dictionary, news pages, links to clinical trials; information on coping, diagnosis/symptoms, nutrition, research, specific conditions/aspects, treatment, directories, organizations, and statistics.

Premature-infant.com

http://premature-infant.com
Family-friendly Website that has touching stories and supportive information for parents and medical personnel regarding GERD, infant massage, kangaroo care, positioning, pain, RSV, and feeding issues.

Visual Impairment/Blindness

American Foundation for the Blind

http://www.afb.org
Organization that provides a variety of services, including policy development, publications, and services for people of all ages with visual impairments.

American Printing House for the Blind

http://www.aph.org
Source of publications and adapted educational equipment for children and youth who are visually impaired.

National Association of Parents of Children with Visual Impairments

http://www.NAPVI.org
Nonprofit organization for parents of children with visual impairment that provides publications and other resources.

National Federation of the Blind

http://www.nfb.org
Website for an organization for the blind in the United States that provides publications for parents and professionals and a national parent organization.

Interaction with Families

The Father's Network

http://www.fathersnetwork.org
Provides news, resources, and articles by fathers, developed to celebrate and support fathers and

families raising children with special health care needs and developmental disabilities. (English, Spanish)

Disability Is Natural

http://www.disabilityisnatural.com
Contains thought-provoking articles, products, books, and videos to promote new ways of thinking about inclusion and disability.

MUMS: National Parent-to-Parent Network

http://www.netnet.net/mums/index.htm
Features a parent-to-parent matching service to connect parents to parent support groups to promote emotional support and information regarding their child's care.

National Center for Cultural Competence

http://www.gucchd.georgetown.edu/nccc
Organization whose mission is to increase the capacity of health and mental health programs to design, implement, and evaluate culturally and linguistically competent service delivery systems. (English, Spanish)

Speech and Language Development in Young Children

http://members.tripod.com/Caroline_Bowen/devel1.htm
Presents information about the acquisition of language in early childhood, the role of parents in facilitating these skills, and language and communication milestones.

Tools for Coping with Life's Stressors

http://www.coping.org
Contains many links to help parents in coping with issues related to raising a child with special health care needs, such as Tools for Communication and Tools for a Balanced Lifestyle.

Individualized Family Service Plan (IFSP)

Individualized Family Service Plans

http://www.head-start.lane.or.us/education/special-needs/IFSPs.html
Presents parent-friendly information about the process of creating an IFSP, including legal timelines, parental rights, participants, and transportation.

Individualized Education Program (IEP)

Special Education Individual Education Plan

http://www.teach-nology.com/teachers/special_ed/iep
Offers information for special education teachers about developing IEPs and what to do when services are not implemented as planned.

Individualized Education Plan Guide for Parents

http://www.altonweb.com/cs/downsyndrome/index.htm?page=iepguide.html
Written by parents of children with special needs; presents detailed information about what to do before, during, and after the IEP meeting to ensure optimal services for a child.

Rehabilitation Act of 1973, Section 504

Overview of ADA, IDEA, and Section 504

http://www.ericdigests.org/1996-3/ada.htm
Provides an overview of these major laws, including the purpose of the law, whom the law protects, funding requirements, educational responsibilities, procedural safeguards, due process, and evaluation.

Program Implementation

Coaching in Natural Environments

http//www.coachinginearlychildhood.org
Website designed for professionals to share information and resources about providing services for infants and toddlers, and their families, in natural settings.

Creating Teaching Tools for Young Children with Challenging Behavior

http://challengingbehavior.fmhi.usf.edu/tools.html
Provides practical intervention information and forms developed for providing positive behavior support for young children within routines.

Division for Early Childhood (DEC)

http://www.dec-sped.org/
Nonprofit organization that advocates for professionals who work with children with special needs, and their families, from birth to 9 years of age; Website includes links to publications, journals, position statements, conferences, projects, and professional training opportunities.

Early Intervention Research Institute

http://www.eiri.usu.edu

Targets professionals who serve infants and toddlers; presents information on research, training, and technical support, including service coordination, support systems, and family quality-of-life issues.

FACETS: Family-Guided Approaches to Collaborative Early-Intervention Training and Services

http://www.parsons.lsi.ku.edu/facets

Provides a description of a federally funded program that offers practical information and resources for training professionals in family-guided activity-based interventions.

Assistive Technology

Simplified Technology for Children with Disabilities

http://www.lburkhart.com/main.htm

Discusses the use of assistive technology and augmentative communication to increase functioning in young children with disabilities, including directions for making simplified technology from common items.

Family Guide to AT

http://www.pluk.org/AT1.html

Family-friendly Website that provides a detailed overview of assistive technology, giving a case scenario with ideas about how to use assistive technology to help solve particular problems.

Learning Disabilities Online: AT and LD

http://www.ldonline.org/ld_indepth/technology/bowzer_reed.html

Family-friendly Website that provides information about the use of assistive technology for children with learning disorders.

Least Restrictive Environment/Inclusion

Circle of Inclusion

http://www.circleofinclusion.org

Website for early childhood professionals and families that offers demonstrations of effective practices in inclusion for children from birth through 8 years of age.

The National Head Start Disabilities Services Training Center

http://www.edc.org/CCF/ntc

Offers a series of downloadable training guides to strengthen the capacity of early childhood programs to reach and serve children with disabilities and their families.

Individuals with Disabilities Education Act (IDEA)

Council for Exceptional Children (CEC)

http://www.ideapractices.org

Website of the CEC, an international professional organization dedicated to improving educational outcomes for individuals with exceptionalities; includes current governmental policies and professional standards for teachers, administrators, paraprofessionals, and related support service providers, publications, and conference information.

Part B—Preschool Services

IDEA Partnership

http://www.ideapartnership.org

Up-to-date IDEA information source for anyone working with individuals with disabilities, including features for the IDEA (2004) and the No Child Left Behind Act and information about partnerships on state and national levels.

Part C—Infant-Toddler Services

Indiana First Steps Early Intervention

http://www.eikids.com

Targets therapists, parents, service coordinators, and other professionals working with children with disabilities from birth to age 3 by focusing on therapists' issues and equipment exchange.

Transition to Part B Services

Planning Transitions to Preschool

http://www.dblink.org/lib/topics/chenminor.htm

Presents an overview of the process of transition and related issues, including developing a planning team, setting goals and identifying challenges, defining roles, and developing a written transition plan.

Source: Compiled by J. M. Hall, M. J. Thomas, T. M. Long, and S. Raver.

Name Index

Subject Index